What We Have Done

What We Have Done

*An Oral History
of the
Disability Rights Movement*

Fred Pelka

University of Massachusetts Press

AMHERST AND BOSTON

LC 2011050377
ISBN 978-1-55849-919-5 (paper); 918-8 (library cloth)

Designed by Sally Nichols
Set in Minion Pro
Printed and bound by Thomson-Shore, Inc.

Library of Congress Cataloging-in-Publication Data

Pelka, Fred, 1954–
 What we have done : an oral history of the disability rights
movement / fred pelka.
   p. cm.
 Includes bibliographical references and index.
 ISBN 978-1-55849-919-5 (pbk. : alk. paper) — ISBN 978-1-55849-918-8
(library cloth : alk. paper) 1. People with disabilities—Civil rights—
United States—History. 2. People with disabilities—Legal status,
laws, etc—United States—History. 3. United States. Americans with
Disabilities Act of 1990. I. Title.
 KF480.P45 2012
 346.7301'3—dc23

                                                        2011050377

British Library Cataloguing in Publication data are available.

Cover photo: Wheels of Justice march on the US Capitol, March 12, 1990.
Courtesy of Tom Olin.

First row, left to right: George Roberts (holding the "We Shall Overcome" sign);
Stephanie Thomas (in her chair); Janine Bertram Kemp; Frank Lozano and his dog
Frazier; Jennifer Keelan (in her chair) and her sister Kailee (walking beside her).

Second row, left to right: Isaiah Thomas; Evan Kemp Jr.; Justin Dart Jr. being pushed
by Jay Rochlin; Michael Winter; Edie Olin (pushing Jennifer's chair).

*For my parents, and for all those
who struggle for human rights*

Contents

Preface   ix

List of Acronyms   xv

Introduction   1

1. Childhood   30

2. Institutions, Part 1   48

3. Discrimination, Part 1   61

4. Institutions, Part 2   77

5. The University of Illinois   94

6. Discrimination, Part 2, and Early Advocacy   113

7. The Parents' Movement   131

8. Activists and Organizers, Part 1   151

9. Institutions, Part 3   174

10. Activists and Organizers, Part 2   183

11. Independent Living   197

12. The Disability Press   227

13. The American Coalition of Citizens with Disabilities   246

14. The HEW Demonstrations   261

15. Psychiatric Survivors   283

16. Working the System   303

17. Institutions, Part 4   312

18. Self-Advocates   324

19. DREDF and the 504 Trainings   339

20. Activists and Organizers, Part 3   355

21. ADAPT   376

22. Deaf President Now!   397

23. The Americans with Disabilities Act—"The Machinery of Change"   413

24. Drafting the Bill, Part 1   429

25. Insiders, Part 1   444

26. Drafting the Bill, Part 2   460

27. Lobbying and Gathering Support   470

28. Mobilizing the Community   481

29. Experts   489

30. Insiders, Part 2   503

31. Wheels of Justice and the Chapman Amendment   514

32. Lobbyists   527

33. Senators   535

34. Victory   542

35. Aftermath   548

Notes   557

Interview Sources   599

Index   603

Illustrations follow page 260

Preface

"Nothing about us, without us" is one of the most compelling slogans to come out of the disability rights movement. The phrase succinctly conveys one of the movement's central themes, reflecting the fact that people with disabilities, down through the ages, have generally been seen as objects of scorn or pity, "cases" to be cured or "managed," problems to be confronted or ignored.[1] The most basic decisions about their lives—decisions about where they should live, if and how they should be educated, if and where they should work, and whether they could or should marry and raise families—have most often been made entirely without their input. Advocates have had to raise their voices, often in frustration and anger, sometimes in desperation, to a society that assumes they have no voice at all.

My purpose in this book is to recount the political struggle for disability rights in the United States, focusing on the decades immediately preceding the passage of the Americans with Disabilities Act of 1990. I do this by using the first-person accounts—the voices—of people with disabilities.[2] Occasionally I feature the account of an ally—a parent or non-disabled advocate whose work was crucial to the success of the movement or who was a witness to seminal events. The vast majority of the narratives featured here, however, are told by those who had most at stake in the success or failure of the movement: people who are themselves disabled.

I have organized the narratives thematically in several broad categories, collected in chapters ordered more or less chronologically. Even so, someone reading the book from beginning to end will notice that there are shifts backward and forward in time. Such shifts are inevitable, since the various facets of the disability rights movement generally operated independently of one another before joining the broad, cross-disability coalition that advocated for the passage of the ADA. One could even say, as Paul Longmore does in his oral history, that "there is no single, homogenous disability rights movement [at all]. There really are at least a half dozen movements . . . and each one reflects the interests and issues and needs and concerns of a particular disability constituency. . . . In the last generation or so, since the mid-1970s, they've allied with one another politically. . . . That's how the ADA got passed."[3]

I have dedicated several chapters to particular events or campaigns that I regard as crucial milestones on the road to the ADA: the campaign in 1977 to force HEW secretary Joseph Califano to sign regulations implementing Section 504 of the Rehabilitation Act of 1973, for example, and the Deaf President Now! campaign at Gallaudet University in spring 1988. There are also chapters devoted to pivotal organizations, including Disabled in Action (DIA) and American Disabled for Accessible Public Transit (ADAPT). When we get to the struggle to pass the ADA itself, I have divided the narrative into segments on drafting the bill, those inside and outside Washington who advocated for its passage, and crucial events that culminated in the bill's being signed into law.

The interviews I use are taken primarily from three sources. The first is the collection of oral histories compiled under the auspices of the Regional Oral History Office of the Bancroft Library at the University of California at Berkeley, as part of its project on the Disability Rights and Independent Living Movements (DRILM). The project officially began in 1996, when Susan O'Hara and Mary Lou Breslin approached the university with the idea of recording the histories of those individuals who spearheaded the founding, first, of the Physically Disabled Students' Program at UC Berkeley and, second, the Center for Independent Living, also in Berkeley. The scope of the project was expanded in 2000 to encompass accounts of disability activists across the country, when I was invited to join the effort.

The second source are interviews recorded by the Disability Rights Education and Defense Fund (DREDF) in association with Access Video, and under the auspices of the University of San Francisco, with funding provided by the National Institute on Disability and Rehabilitation Research. These videotaped "leadership interviews" were conducted in 1999–2000 to mark the tenth anniversary of the passage of the ADA and are also archived at the Bancroft Library.

Third are interviews I conducted myself, unconnected with the DRILM. Some of these, for instance, my interviews with Justin Dart Jr., were done before I approached the University of Massachusetts Press with the idea for this book. The bulk, however, were conducted during the past five years, as I sought to fill the gaps in both the Bancroft and DREDF collections. Among these are interviews with leaders in the psychiatric survivor and self-advocates movements and with leaders in the campaign for a Deaf President Now.

In addition, I have drawn on other collections to educate myself about various issues. Included in this category are the oral histories archived at The Eugene and Inez Petersen Collection of Life Stories of Deaf People housed at the Rochester Institute of Technology, Rochester, New York; the accounts of institution residents as recorded in *Lest We Forget*, a documentary film produced by Jeff Moyer and distributed through Partners for Community Living in Dayton, Ohio; and the MindFreedom Personal Story Project online oral histories of the psychiatric survivor movement. My thanks and appreciation go to the curators and sponsors of all these collections.

In editing the interviews I have used as light a hand as possible, to retain the original character of each individual voice. In some instances I compressed particular accounts (signaled with ellipses and bracketed interpolations); in others I asked interviewees during follow-up sessions to elaborate on a story already told, and then wove the additional material into the original account. Whenever possible I checked with the interviewees to ensure that my editing in no way altered the tone or content of their story.

I was, of course, able to use only a small portion of each interview, some of which lasted eight or more hours and involved hundreds of pages of transcript. In most cases, depending on the wishes of the interviewee, the original recordings have been deposited at the Bancroft Library.

Sadly, many of the people who could have illuminated aspects of the early part of this history—for example, Paul Strachan, cofounder of the American Federation of the Physically Handicapped in the 1940s, and Elizabeth Boggs, a cofounder of the Arc in 1950—have died, as have many younger advocates before I or others were able to record their stories. Eunice Fiorito is one such loss, Frank Bowe, another. Connie Panzarino, who played a crucial role as a bridge between the disability and the lesbian communities, died only weeks before our first scheduled session. Ed Roberts and Justin Dart Jr. both died after they were interviewed, before I could follow up with questions. Other individuals for various reasons chose not to be interviewed or not to share their stories with the public, at least not at this time.

In a specialized history such as this there are bound to be events, individuals, and concepts mentioned which are unfamiliar to the general public, and I have provided identifying information in notes.. I hope that these notes, together with the index, will enable those entirely new to the movement to read the book without difficulty.

A final note about terminology. In writing about Deaf culture and politics I have followed the practice of Deaf community scholars Carol Padden and Tom Humphries (among others) of using "Deaf" with an uppercase "D" to denote those people who use American Sign Language as their primary language and consider themselves to be part of a linguistic minority, in contrast to lowercase "deaf," people who are deaf or hard-of-hearing not necessarily involved in Deaf culture. Thus, in references to a Deaf activist such as Gary Olsen or Bridgetta Bourne-Firl, I use a capital D, but in describing how Title IV of the Americans with Disabilities Act mandates the provision of telephone-relay services for people who are deaf, hard-of-hearing, or have a speech disability, I use the lowercase.[4]

Projects such as this one are possible only through the generous support and gracious cooperation of very many people. First and foremost are those individuals, from Michael Auberger to Hale Zukas, who agreed to sit for interviews, either with me or with others. Then there are the people who provided advice and encouragement through the years. Chief among them are Mary Lou Breslin, senior policy analyst at DREDF, who was always willing to talk and point me in the right direction and who, along with Paul Longmore, reviewed early drafts of the book and provided much needed correction and clarification; Fred Fay, whose knowledge of the movement was comprehensive and invaluable; and Ann Lage, director of the DRILM, for guidance on whom to interview and what to ask.

I also want to extend my appreciation to Ann Lage, Susan O'Hara, and all the others at the DRILM for inviting me to be a part of their work. Chief among the interviewers whose work I drew on are Sharon Bonney, Susan T. Brown, Kathy Cowan, David Landes, Esther Erlich, and Denise Sherer Jacobson.

Involved in the DREDF Leadership Interviews were Phyllis Ward, who produced the videotapes and conducted the interviews along with Mary Lou Breslin, and Patrisha Wright and Arlene Mayerson, who consulted on whom to interview and what to ask. Thanks also to David Nold, who converted the DREDF interviews from VHS to DVD.

My thanks also go to Gayle Bluebird, the curators at Gallaudet University, Cyndi Jones and William G. Stothers at MAINSTREAM online, and (once again) Mary Lou Breslin, for helping me to locate and allowing me to use photographs they have collected over the years. Special thanks go to Ken Stein for his photographs documenting the early days of the Center for Independent Living in Berkeley and his help identifying the people in the group portrait taken by

Ken Okuno; to Dr. William Bronston for his photographs of the Willowbrook State School in Staten Island, New York; and to Tom Olin for sharing his remarkable image archive of the disability rights movement, which includes thousands of photographs of demonstrations and other events that he took over several decades, many of which first appeared in *Mouth* magazine. Thanks also to Catherine Engstrom at DREDF for tracking down the releases for the DREDF interviews; to Katherine O'Kane, Eve Baker, Micah Schneider, and Amy Hasbrouck for their gracious (and unpaid) help with transcribing; to Christian G. Appy at the University of Massachusetts Amherst for his invaluable advice on all things oral history; to my editor at the University of Massachusetts Press, Clark Dougan, whose enthusiasm for the project kept me from getting too very discouraged as I missed deadline after deadline; and to Carol Betsch, managing editor at the press, and her colleague Mary Bellino, for their thoughtful questions and meticulous editing.

I also thank the John Simon Guggenheim Memorial Foundation for its generous support, without which this project would not have been possible.

Finally, I want to express again my heartfelt thanks to my friend, partner, and advocate of many years, Denise Karuth. Not only did she help with the transcribing, suggest the title, and read and offer many useful comments on the various drafts, but, as always, her steady love saw me through those times when I thought I might never see an end to this project.

Acronyms

ACB	American Council of the Blind
ACCD	American Coalition of Citizens with Disabilities
ADA	Americans with Disabilities Act
ADAPT	From 1983 to 1990 American Disabled for Accessible Public Transit; post-1990 American Disabled for Attendant Programs Today
AFPH	American Federation of the Physically Handicapped
ARC	See NARC
CAPH	California Association of the Physically Handicapped
CCD	Consortium for Citizens with Disabilities
CIL	Center for Independent Living, or alternately ILC, Independent Living Center
CRRA	Civil Rights Restoration Act
DAV	Disabled American Veterans
DIA	Disabled in Action
DPN	Deaf President Now
DRC	Disability Rights Center
DREDF	Disability Rights Education and Defense Fund
EPVA	Eastern Paralyzed Veterans of America
HEW	The federal Department of Health, Education, and Welfare (now split into the Department of Education and the Department of Health and Human Services)
IDEA	Individuals with Disabilities Education Act, originally the Education for All Handicapped Children Act
ILC	Independent Living Center

LPA   Little People of America

MPLF   Mental Patients' Liberation Front

MPLP   Mental Patients' Liberation Project

NAD   National Association of the Deaf

NARC   Originally the National Association for Retarded Children, then the
             National Association for Retarded Citizens, then the Association for
             Retarded Citizens of the United States (ARC), now simply "the Arc."
             (The acronyms ARC and NARC are often used interchangeably.)

NCD/NCH   National Council on Disability, formerly the National Council on the
             Handicapped

NCIL   National Council on Independent Living (pronounced "nickel")

NFB   National Federation of the Blind

PARC   Pennsylvania Association for Retarded Children

PDSP   Physically Disabled Students' Program (at the University of
             California, Berkeley)

PVA   Paralyzed Veterans of America

SSDI   Social Security Disability Insurance

SSI   Supplemental Security Income

UCP   United Cerebral Palsy Associations, Inc.

What We Have Done

Introduction

May it please the Court, I think if the appellants' construction of the Fourteenth Amendment should prevail here, there is no doubt in my mind that it would catch the Indian within its grasp just as much as the Negro. If it should prevail, I am unable to see why a state would have any further right to segregate its pupils on the ground of sex or on the ground of age or on the ground of mental capacity. If it may classify it for one purpose on the basis of admitted facts, it may, according to my contention, classify it for other.[1]

WITH THESE WORDS ATTORNEY JOHN W. DAVIS, ARGUING BEFORE THE US Supreme Court in defense of racial segregation in *Brown v. Board of Education,* unwittingly drew what was to become the defining analogy of the American disability rights movement of the second half of the twentieth century.

"I remember vividly the delight between Gunnar [Dybwad] and myself when we discovered this," says Thomas K. Gilhool. Gilhool had been retained in 1969 by the Pennsylvania Association for Retarded Children (PARC) as the lead attorney in its landmark right-to-education case, *PARC v. Pennsylvania.* Gunnar Dybwad, as the former executive director of the national Association for Retarded Children and an activist for the rights of children with disabilities, had for years been urging parents to use the federal courts to force admission of their children to the public schools. Both of them saw the PARC case as the opening salvo in their fight to close down the massive state institutions in which tens of thousands of disabled children were confined. In this effort, they were relying on the same Fourteenth Amendment rights to due process and equal protection under the law that were at issue in *Brown*, and so finding that the analogy had already been drawn in argument before the Supreme Court was understandably

gratifying.[2] At the time, the Fourteenth Amendment was their only recourse in making the case that children with disabilities had the right to a public school education—since federal disability rights law, as we know it today, did not exist.

What Davis had been trying to do, of course, was frighten the Court with the prospect that once segregation on the basis of race was found to be unconstitutional, segregation on the basis of gender and even disability—mental or otherwise—would likewise be called into question. Given the context (Davis made his argument in 1952), it was perhaps not such a bad strategy. If anyone ranked lower in American social status than southern "Negroes," it would be those people labeled "mentally retarded." Indeed, the "scientific" or "diagnostic" terms still in use at the time to differentiate alleged levels of mental disability included "moron," "imbecile," and "idiot." Give people with black skin the right to an integrated, public school education, Davis was, in effect, saying, and you might as well bestow the same right on "idiots," "morons," and "imbeciles."[3]

There was, in fact, legal precedent for denying civil rights to people with disabilities—particularly mental disabilities. In 1927, the Court, in *Buck v. Bell,* had ruled that the forced sterilization of people with disabilities was not a violation of their constitutional rights. "It is better for all the world," wrote Justice Oliver Wendell Holmes Jr. on behalf of the majority, "if instead of waiting to execute degenerate offspring for crime, or to let them starve for their imbecility, society can prevent those who are manifestly unfit from continuing their kind. . . . Three generations of imbeciles are enough."[4] As a result of this ruling, Carrie Buck, not yet twenty years old, was forcibly sterilized.[5]

Justice Holmes, in linking mental disability with crime and defining the alleged disability/criminality nexus as an inherited trait was echoing the beliefs of the eugenics movement, which had provided much of the "scientific" evidence presented in the case. In fact, Carrie Buck was not a criminal, indeed she may not even have had a mental disability. Her principal offense, aside from becoming pregnant after being raped in foster care, was to belong, as the author of the Virginia sterilization law, Harry L. Laughlin, put it, "to the shiftless, ignorant, and worthless class of anti-social whites in the South."[6] The Court's decision in *Buck v. Bell* unleashed a torrent of forced sterilizations of people labeled mentally retarded and diagnosed as epileptic or mentally ill, and is generally considered a nadir in American disability history.[7]

In one of the more interesting juxtapositions that occurred during this history, Thurgood Marshall, special counsel for the NAACP, wrote a letter in late

1953 to Jacobus tenBroek, asking for a meeting while Marshall was traveling through California. TenBroek was a noted constitutional scholar and author of *The Anti-Slavery Origins of the Fourteenth Amendment*. "As you know," Marshall wrote, "we are trying to get together as much material as possible for our rearguments of the school segregation cases in the Supreme Court this fall." Marshall noted how he and his colleagues had "taken full advantage of your book . . . and many of our research people have been using it."[8]

Apparently the meeting never happened, which is unfortunate, given the nature of tenBroek's other work. As well as being a professor of speech and political science at UC Berkeley and coauthor of a major book on the imprisonment of Japanese Americans during World War II (*Prejudice, War, and the Constitution*), tenBroek was also a cofounder in 1940 of the National Federation of the Blind. Blinded by an accident at age seven, tenBroek had had his own bitter experiences with discrimination as a member of a particular "class."[9]

Marshall nevertheless was prepared for Davis's sally. During his turn before the Court, he addressed the question of whether a ruling in favor of black public school students would necessarily expand the constitutional rights of girls or of children with disabilities. "Insofar as the argument about the states having a right to classify students on the basis of sex, learning ability, et cetera, I do not know whether they do or not, but I do believe . . . that any of the actions . . . that affect any classification must be tested by the regular rules set up by this Court." And furthermore: "I think we must once again emphasize that under our form of government, these individual rights of minority people are not to be left to even the most mature judgment of the majority of the people, and that the only testing ground as to whether or not individual rights are concerned is in this Court."[10]

Little more than two decades later, these very questions of "individual rights of minority people" as they related to citizens with disabilities would come to be tested before the Court, with Gilhool and others arguing on their behalf. Thurgood Marshall would also be there, this time as one of the nine justices charged with determining the outcome.

That people with disabilities are an oppressed minority with protected rights is a relatively new idea and is an American innovation. Robert Funk, one of the earliest disability rights attorneys and cofounder and first executive director of the Disability Rights Education and Defense Fund (DREDF), has recounted the history of what he calls "the humanization of disabled people" in America as the journey of individuals with disabilities from "objects of pity and fear . . . who are incapable and neither expected nor willing to participate in or contribute to society" to a "disability rights movement" which maintains that "disabled people have the constitutional and human right to equal citizenship, that is, the right to be treated as a person worthy of dignity and respect."[11]

This transition from "pity and fear" to "equal citizenship" has been little short of revolutionary. Indeed, the very notion that people with disabilities are entitled to define their own identity rather than having it imposed on them by outside authorities is itself unprecedented. The historical record shows that disability has been defined cross culturally by the non-disabled majority and that the treatment of people with disabilities has been inextricably linked to prevailing social attitudes about physical and psychological difference. Furthermore, definitions of disability are fluid, changing over time, depending on social circumstances. In some cases a particular condition, impairment, or illness might be perceived as a significant disability where in other circumstances the same particulars of individual difference are barely noticed, if at all. Such was the case in the preindustrial North American colonies. As the sociologists and policy analysts Sharon Barnartt and Richard Scotch note, "Many types of impairments were not severe enough to prevent a person from working on a farm or in small-scale production. For example, deafness might not prevent a person from working in the fields, although loss of arm mobility might."[12]

Moreover—and this is a critical point for disability rights advocates—in societies where "accommodations" are made as a matter of course, the role of disability or impairment in determining social or economic status can be much less prominent. One of the clearest examples of such a situation is the early nineteenth-century island community of Martha's Vineyard, where "the deaf and hearing citizens were so integrated that deaf people did not form a community apart from their hearing fellows [as they did, for example, in Paris in the 1770s]. Both the hearing and the deaf persons used sign language, and deaf individuals usually chose hearing persons for spouses."[13] Integration was so complete that historian Nora Groce, writing about the community 150 years later, was unable to find distinctions between deaf and hearing people in such areas as marital status, income, and property ownership. Since, as she notes in her title, "everyone here spoke sign language," hereditary deafness on Martha's Vineyard, for all intents and purposes, ceased to be a disability.[14]

Martha's Vineyard, however, is notable for being a rare exception to the

rule. More usually, the majority culture has been unwilling, even when able, to accommodate those living with disabilities. And so, however they are defined, Americans with disabilities have generally found themselves, as the activist Justin Dart Jr. put it, the nation's "poorest, most oppressed group."[15] The reason for this is bound up with how disability itself has been explained and perceived, and how non-disabled authorities have defined what it means to be a person with a disability.

The Religious or Moral Model: Unholy, Unclean, "Special"

Probably the most ancient and most consistently applied framing of disability has been in religious or moral terms: the presence of a disability is perceived as a reflection, sometimes good, often bad, on the character of the disabled individual and as a form of divine judgment on that person's family and community. As social policy analysts Aliki Coudroglou and Dennis L. Poole put it: "Through the ages, the disabled have been seen as both demon-possessed and protected by the gods, embraced by attitudes of both reverence and revulsion, and cloaked in such diverse roles as the great prophet Tiresias or the brutal Caliban."[16]

"The persistent thread within the Christian tradition," writes theologian and sociologist Nancy Eiesland, "has been that disability denotes an unusual relationship with God and that the person with disabilities is either divinely blessed or damned: the defiled evildoer or the spiritual superhero."[17] Christians are not alone in this notion. In Zimbabwe, Malaysia, and Indonesia people with disabilities report that religious tradition regards disability as a form of "divine punishment" for alleged sinfulness.[18] "Persons with disabilities may be seen as threats to others, capable of 'infecting,' or unable to practice self-care and therefore 'dirty'" in a ritual or religious sense.[19]

Further, if the presence of a disability is seen as tainting the person, it follows that the ability to cure or remove illness or disability is perceived as a sign of holiness or spiritual power—from the miracle cures performed by Jesus to the present-day "healing services" conducted by mainstream Christian denominations and the "faith healings" extolled by televangelists. "There are many in the Church," writes Episcopal priest Rev. Nancy J. Lane, "who have an obsession with wanting disabled bodies to be 'healed,' meaning fixed, turned into something society defines as 'normal.' Disability is seen as a basic flaw rather than a human variation."[20]

The stigmatizing of people with disabilities often occurs in the context of a "just world theory" of life, described by philosopher Melvin Lerner and elucidated in relation to disability by women's studies scholar and cultural critic Rosemarie Garland-Thomson: "According to Lerner, the human need for order and predictability gives rise to the belief that people get what they deserve or that the way things are is the way they should be. . . . if something 'bad'—like having a disability—happens to someone, then there must be some 'good' reason—like divine or moral justice, for its occurrence." The danger inherent in this explanation for disability is obvious: "Although this doctrine provides a psychological safeguard against the intolerable randomness of experience, it results in victim-blaming and scapegoating of those who are different. . . . The belief that disabled people are simply the losers in some grand competitive scheme or the once-accepted conviction that masturbation caused blindness attest to the prevalence of just-world assumptions about disability. Perhaps the most unfortunate current just-world assumption is that AIDS is a moral judgment on homosexuals and intravenous drug users."[21] Indeed, as late as the summer of 1990 this particular application of just-world thinking would have an almost catastrophic impact on the campaign for passage of the Americans with Disabilities Act, as is recounted in chapter 31.

Even when disability isn't taken as a sign of individual culpability, it is nevertheless a state of being that renders a person "other" in the community. The French historian Henri-Jacques Stiker notes that, although "disability was an everyday reality" for the ancient Hebrews—, "legal uncleanness was attached to the disabled, who could, of course, participate in cultic observances but never as priests who made sacrifices. The sanctuary could not be profaned. The disabled had the status of prostitutes or of women whom menstruation made unclean. One had to be without defect in order to approach God's place of residence."[22] This concept that disability renders an individual unfit to function as intermediary between God and community survived well into the twentieth century—if not beyond. And so Tony Coelho, one of the original congressional sponsors of the Americans with Disabilities Act, entered politics only after being refused admission to seminary by the Roman Catholic church solely because of his disability.[23]

According to Stiker, the religious systems of Graeco-Roman antiquity were even less tolerant of perceived physical or mental difference than Hebrew scriptures. In both ancient Athens and Sparta infants with disabilities were "exposed," taken "outside to an unknown location and [left to] . . . expire in a hole in the ground or drown in a course of water."[24] The birth of disabled infants was believed to "signal the possibility of misfortunes and are explained by the anger of the gods. Deformed infants are exposed because they are harmful, maleficent. They implicate the group."[25]

"The majority of the disabled" of this era, writes professor of classics Robert Garland, "even when they were lucky enough to be essentially self-reliant, must have led lives of extreme isolation, hardship, and privation. That was due to the restrictions which in many cases their disabilities imposed upon their freedom of movement, the limited opportunities they had for gainful employment, and the disdain in which they were generally held both by their families and by society at large. It follows that we are investigating the condition of a class of people who for the most part were not merely marginalized, but outcast in the fullest sense of the word." Furthermore, "just as disdain for the disabled appears to have been a widespread phenomenon, so the disabled themselves were encouraged to feel a certain shame for their own physical condition."[26] Disability rights activists today would call this "internalized oppression"—the absorption by oppressed people of the judgments and assumptions of the majority culture.

Given the influence of both the Hebrew scriptures and the Graeco-Roman worldview in shaping Western thought, it is no surprise that many of these prejudicial ideas about disability would have been part of the cultural heritage of European colonists in the New World. In Puritan New England, the presence of a disability in a newborn was often interpreted as a form of divine judgment, particularly if one or both parents had in any way earned the enmity of the colony's religious/political elite. And so, when a "malformed, stillborn infant" was born to colonist Mary Dyer, the religious authorities of seventeenth-century Massachusetts were quick to draw a connection to the "heretical" religious views of Dyer, her midwife Jane Hawkins, and their mentor Anne Hutchinson.[27]

That these notions persist can be seen in the way people with disabilities have been depicted in literature and popular culture. Whether in children's books (Captain Hook in *Peter Pan*) or adult literature (Shakespeare's Richard III and Melville's Captain Ahab), a disability is often used to embody monstrous evil or diabolic obsession. The obverse of this is what literary scholar Leonard Kriegel calls "the Charity Cripple," of whom Dickens's Tiny Tim is probably the best-known example. Kriegel notes that writers "like to think of themselves as rebels, but the rebellions they are interested in usually reinforce society's conception of what is and is not desirable. And most writers look at the cripple and the wounds he bears with the same suspicion and distaste that are found in other 'normals.'

. . . The world of the crippled and disabled is strange and dark, and it is held up to judgment by those who live in fear of it."[28]

Popular films and television, especially before the 1980s, similarly use disability to denote the strange and the evil. From the handless Dr. No to the wheelchair-using Dr. Strangelove to the burn-mutilated child molester Freddy Krueger, disability (and especially a prosthesis) seems an easy way for filmmakers to inform the audience, "This character is a villain." And as if popular stereotypes aren't enough, sometimes the characters themselves make the connection for us. "Tell me," James Bond asks Dr. No, "does the toppling of American missiles really compensate for having no hands?"[29]

"Many of the ancient myths and stereotypes of people with disabilities still exist," according to human relations scholar George Henderson and psychologist Willie V. Bryan. "Although few persons currently subscribe to abandoning or killing people with disabilities, many do associate disabilities with sin and the Devil. They either consciously or subconsciously think that *disability* is a synonym of *bad*. More often than not, *able-bodied* is associated with *good*, i.e., Christ and the angels, cleanliness, and virtue. None of the great artists ever created images of angels with disabilities. Conversely, persons with disabilities have been associated through the ages with all that is bad."[30]

The Medical Model

While purely religious interpretations of disability have persisted, the modern era has given rise to the medical model, by which disability is defined not as a spiritual or moral failing but in terms of illness and pathology.

"The medical model," writes disability rights activist and attorney Deborah Kaplan, "came about as 'modern' medicine began to develop in the 19th century, along with the enhanced role of the physician in society. Since many disabilities have medical origins, people with disabilities were expected to benefit from coming under the direction of the medical profession."[31] Here too, however, the ideal was that the person with the disability be cured and again "made whole." In this model a failure to cure was not attributed to the spiritual or moral state of the disabled person (at least not overtly) but rather to a failure of medical science. Even so, the continued emphasis on cure vs. pathology, according to Richard Scotch, "assumes an idealized notion of 'normality' against which disabled people are constantly being compared. 'Able-bodiedness' is seen as the acceptable criterion of normality."[32] Furthermore, as Kaplan notes, "under this model, the problems that are associated with disability are deemed to reside within the individual. In other words, if the individual is 'cured' then these problems will not exist. Society has no underlying responsibility to make a 'place' for persons with disabilities, since they live in an outsider role waiting to be cured."[33]

Those who could not be cured were expected to be cared for by their families. In the early days of the republic, the responsibility for housing and feeding people with disabilities whose families could not or would not do so was often "bid out" to those willing to provide such care at least cost to the state. "This system of societal indifference," Funk notes, "was so subject to abuse that public sentiment compelled reforms, which resulted in state-funded institutions to house indigent disabled citizens. A further specialization occurred in time, with the establishment of institutions for specific categories of disabled persons such as deaf and blind children, the mentally ill, feeble-minded and retarded." Funk labels this as a movement "from the attic to the warehouse."[34]

The best-known of these early reformers were Samuel Gridley Howe and Dorothea Dix, active during the middle decades of the nineteenth century. Their original goal in establishing state-funded schools and philanthropic institutions—for example, Howe's School for the Blind in eastern Massachusetts—was to educate people with disabilities, particularly children, to be self-sufficient so they could become integrated as adults into general society. With few exceptions, however, this goal was eventually abandoned, as reformers came to realize that education alone wasn't sufficient.[35] As one early educator of the blind would report, "The old prejudices and aversions of employers and the general public remained intact; the newly trained graduates of the schools were given little or no chance to prove their abilities, but instead found all doors closed against them."[36]

Eugenics: The Disabled Person as Threat to Society

One measure of how virulent "the old prejudices and aversions" remained can be seen in the rise of the eugenics movement during the late nineteenth and early twentieth centuries and the relative ease with which the proponents of a pseudo-scientific craze were able to shape American social and education policy, especially in regard to people with cognitive and developmental disabilities. Tim Cook, a disability rights attorney, describes how, "fueled by the rising tide of Social Darwinism, the 'science' of eugenics, and the extreme xenophobia of those years, leading medical authorities and others began to portray the 'feeble-minded' as a 'menace to society and civilization . . . responsible in large degree for many if not all of our social problems.'"[37]

Cook's reference to xenophobia points to another aspect of the eugenics movement that is crucial in understanding how social definitions of disability evolve over time and serve a variety of interests and purposes. Disability, as historian Douglas Baynton explains, "has functioned historically to justify inequality for disabled people themselves, but has also done so for women and minority groups. That is, not only has it been considered justifiable to treat disabled people unequally, but the concept of disability has been used to justify discrimination against other groups by attributing disability to them."[38] For example, the charge of "moral imbecility" was often leveled against poor white southerners (especially women), immigrants, and African Americans. Cook observes that "the Jim Crow system established after *Plessy* [*v. Ferguson*] and the government-supported, systematic segregation of persons with disabilities during precisely the same time period were no mere coincidences of historical events. The historical record abounds with evidence that disability discrimination emanated from the same attitudes and prejudices fomenting at the turn of the century regarding race. Public officials felt that a solution regarding disability, equal to the severity and the magnitude of the 'problem' of racial intermixing, was imperative."[39]

Indeed, Baynton describes how disability, "was a significant factor in the three great citizenship debates of the nineteenth and early twentieth centuries: women's suffrage, African American freedom and civil rights, and the restriction of immigration. . . . Opponents of political and social equality for women cited their supposed physical, intellectual, and psychological flaws, deficits, and deviations from the male norm. . . . Arguments for racial inequality and immigration restrictions invoked supposed tendencies to feeble-mindedness, mental illness, deafness, blindness, and other disabilities in particular races and ethnic groups." Conversely, arguments in favor of women's rights, racial justice, and a non-xenophobic immigration policy "took the form of vigorous denials that the groups in question actually had these disabilities; they were not disabled, the argument went, and therefore were not proper subjects for discrimination. Rarely have oppressed groups denied that disability is an adequate justification for social and political inequality."[40]

But while stereotypes and pejorative attitudes regarding disability were pressed into service to justify racial, gender, and class oppression, it was people with disabilities themselves (and those perceived as having disabilities) who were the most explicit targets of the eugenics movement. Across the country eugenicists went to state legislatures and to the federal courts to argue that people with disabilities needed to be segregated in all aspects of life, not only "for their own good"— the argument often used to justify their exclusion in the past—but to safeguard the very existence of the nation.

Tim Cook describes how, during the early decades of the twentieth century, "in virtually every state, in inexorable fashion, people with disabilities—especially children and youth—were declared by state lawmaking bodies to be 'unfitted for companionship with other children,' a 'blight on mankind,' whose very presence in the community was 'detrimental to normal' children, and whose 'mingling . . . with society' was 'a most baneful evil.' Persons with severe disabilities were considered to be 'anti-social beings' as well as a 'defect . . . [that] wounds our citizenry a thousand times more than any plague.'" In conclusion, then, "persons with disabilities were believed to simply not have the 'rights and liberties of normal people.'"[41]

As a result, hundreds of thousands of people with disabilities, many of them children, were incarcerated in the state "school and hospital" system that was massively expanded in this period. Furthermore, by 1930, some thirty states had passed legislation authorizing the forced sterilization of people with disabilities, those perceived as having disabilities, or other undesirables such as sex offenders.[42] It was in this context that the Supreme Court rendered its decision in *Buck v. Bell,* so that by the 1970s some 63,000 Americans were reported to have been sterilized without their consent. This figure, however, is little more than an estimate, and "is probably not even close to the actual number of coerced sterilizations because so many went unreported, occurred in states that had no legal oversight of coerced sterilization, or were wrongly reported as voluntary when in fact the patient or inmate was coerced by prison authorities or health officials."[43]

Eugenics was largely discredited by the 1940s, to some degree because of its association with Nazi Germany, which adopted eugenicist arguments and rhetoric to justify its policies of extermination, most especially of people with intellectual disabilities through its "T-4" program of the early 1940s.[44] Even so, coercive sterilization laws remained on the books in many states until well into the 1970s, and the effects of the eugenics movement would be felt for decades following their repeal, not least by those Americans with disabilities who were institutionalized, and in many cases mutilated, by its adherents.[45]

The Deserving Handicapped:
Disability as the Inability to Work

Not everyone with a disability could be cast as a "moral imbecile" or as "the progeny" of genetically inferior "foreign hordes." Neither were all Americans with disabilities "feeble-minded." What about workers disabled on the job or soldiers disabled in their country's service?

Whereas previously most Americans had grown up and worked on family farms, by the 1900s the majority of working Americans lived in an urban environment and earned wages outside the home. And so, a family member with a disability who in earlier times might have been an economic asset—helping with the crops or doing craft work at home—was now much more likely to be a liability. In addition, industrialization brought with it a much higher likelihood of disability through industrial or work-related accidents.

To cope with these new realities, reformers advocated a state system of workers' compensation insurance to provide an income for those no longer able to continue in the workplace. The first states to adopt such programs were Wisconsin and New Jersey in 1911. "Designed to aid workers who had been injured on the job, it removed control over the money, medical care, and other services given to injured workers from the hands of employers, the courts, and the community. It transferred that control to state governments."[46]

These programs would have important implications for all disabled Americans, whether or not their disability was work related. To qualify for workers' compensation, a person had first to prove that he or she indeed had a disability. The arbiters of this process were doctors, whose judgment was in most cases final. This led to a distinction between "the deserving" disabled and those who were "shirkers" or "malingerers." These categories were carried into all subsequent disability-related programs, including later federal "income maintenance" programs such as Social Security Disability Insurance (SSDI, established in 1956 for workers whose disability was not work related) and Supplemental Security Income (SSI, established in 1972 for people with limited income and assets disabled at birth or before they were old enough to hold a job).[47] These "income maintenance" programs, besides linking disability to an inability to work, also required that the recipient of any aid remain nearly destitute in order to qualify for benefits, thus locking them into a state of perpetual poverty.

The historian and disability studies scholar Paul K. Longmore describes how "the designers of disability-related early-modern poor relief and modern social-service programs believed that many non-disabled or only partially disabled workers would make false claims in order to win exemption from work. Given that expectation, the policy makers identified prevention of fraud as the central problem in welfare administration. . . . Application of medical definitions would supposedly catch fraud, thereby ensuring that only those with legitimate claims to societal aid would get it." The problem, Longmore goes on to define, is that "this ideological framework for disability welfare policies seriously misconstrues the causes and character of disability. Disability is not an entity that a clinical examination can correlate with the numbers on a schedule of impairments. It is not located in pathological individual bodies. It is not simply caused by impairments or by physiological features that depart from the typical. Instead, disability is produced through the dynamic interplay of a complicated constellation of factors that includes, not only stigmatized physical and mental limitations and physiological differences, but also physical and architectural environments, social arrangements and cultural values, and the impact of public policies themselves."[48] Longmore's critique of "this ideological framework for disability welfare policies" is also a succinct expression of a core insight of the disability rights movement: that disability "is not a fixed thing. It is an elastic and dynamic social category."[49]

The failure to recognize this simple but important reality was at the heart of the second ramification of adopting a medical definition of "disability." As Scotch and Barnartt explain, in an urbanized, industrialized society "in which economic success was primarily based upon working at paid jobs, disability came to be defined in economic terms as the inability to work."[50] And if disability is defined as the inability to work, it follows then that anyone working a steady job was by definition not "disabled"—no matter what his or her physical or mental attributes or impairments.

At the time this seemed perhaps a not unreasonable assumption. However, as rehabilitation came to augment cure as a response to disability, more and more people found themselves in the position of having a significant impairment and yet being able and quite willing to work. This in itself wasn't entirely new (many people with disabilities down the ages have worked—including those consigned to state institutions, where residents with disabilities did much of the labor involved in maintaining the very facilities in which they were confined). What was new, coming into the second half of the twentieth century, was the explosive increase in the expense of medical care and the establishment of private health insurance (as opposed to the national health systems established in Europe) to pay for that care.[51] Under this new system, private for-profit insurers generally refused to offer insurance to people with "pre-existing" conditions. With the creation of the Medicare and Medicaid programs in the 1960s, and the linking of eligibility for those programs to federal programs such as SSDI and SSI, people dependent on these programs for their health insurance would find themselves redefined as "not disabled" as soon as they started a paying job.[52]

In his essay Longmore offers himself as a prime example of what happened when a person living with the reality of disability confronted "the ideological framework" on which American disability policy of the twentieth century was based. Born in 1946, Longmore contracted polio in 1953, which left him with "no use of my arms, limited use of my right hand, and, because of a severe spinal curvature I use a ventilator [to assist with breathing] a good deal of the time. As a result, I employ aides in my home to do the housekeeping and to assist me with tasks like showering, shaving, dressing, and eating. As of October 1988 . . . the wages paid to my personal assistants, plus the rental of my ventilators, exceeded $20,000 a year. (By the turn of the century, those [annual] costs topped $45,000). Disability-related living and work expenses have posed the fundamental problem of my adult life. The plain fact is, I am unlikely ever to earn enough . . . to cover such costs."[53]

Despite these obstacles, Longmore earned his PhD in history, and in 1988 finished his first book, a scholarly examination of the life of George Washington.[54] But despite his accomplishments, Longmore's dream of becoming a college professor seemed forever out of reach. The lack of a national health program and the unwillingness of the private sector to cover his medical and disability-related expenses forced Longmore to remain on the federal disability rolls, and "to maintain eligibility for government aid, I had to refrain from work."[55] And so, instead of joining the work force, paying taxes, and thus defraying at least some of the expense of his care, Longmore was consigned by the "work disincentives" built into the "all or nothing" definition of disability to be unemployed his entire life.[56] The final insult came as Longmore's first book was about to be published. Any royalties he earned from sales, he was told, would compromise his eligibility for assistance. It would, according to the rules governing such assistance, count as "unearned income."

In response, Longmore organized a public burning of his own book in October 1988. "Everyone in the crowd looked on quietly, soberly. Several wept. . . . I asked my friend Carol Gill, a disabled psychologist who participated in the protest, why she thought so many people had reacted so strongly. She said that she believed that those friends and colleagues were partly expressing their love for me. At the same time, she said, the entire protest . . . gave tangible form to the pain they felt about their lives. They too felt thwarted by a government that stymies their efforts to work and make a life. They too felt dehumanized by a society that devalues them."[57]

Vocational Rehabilitation and the "Whole Man" Model

The entry of the United States into World War I, and the return from that conflict of thousands of severely disabled troops, prompted a new approach to the problem of how best to deal with disability. The concept of "rehabilitation"—of combining advances in medicine with Howe's idea of vocational education to train or retrain disabled people to assume a place in the working world—was applied first to returning soldiers (under the Smith-Sears Veterans Vocational Rehabilitation Act of 1918) and then to disabled civilians (under the Smith-Fess Civilian Rehabilitation Act of 1920).

As noted earlier, social reformers such as Samuel Gridley Howe in the mid-nineteenth century had fostered the creation of publicly supported schools to educate children with disabilities so that they might be integrated into mainstream society. But by the turn of the twentieth century those state schools and institutions had been co-opted, under the influence of the eugenics movement, to become instruments of segregation, isolation, and state-sanctioned repression.

Yet, even when lifelong institutionalization wasn't imposed, and the overt hostility of the eugenics movement was rejected, the rehabilitation model presented its own pitfalls for people with disabilities. The "whole man" theory of disability and rehabilitation, as defined by Dr. Howard Rusk and other advocates of "vocational rehabilitation," came to the fore after World War II. According to this seemingly more sophisticated approach, taken by (almost always non-disabled) professionals, it was necessary not only to deal with the functional difficulties inherent in a specific impairment or illness but also to take into account "the deeper strata of personality in terms of unconscious motivation."[58]

And there lay the problem. Under this model, people with disabilities who needed aids such as wheelchairs and prosthetics or help obtaining an education were to present themselves to a team of rehabilitation experts, who "would put together a diagnosis . . . grounded in one assumption—that most people with physical or mental ailments were 'maladjusted.'" Political scientist Ruth O'Brien explains how "borrowing loosely from an American version of Sigmund Freud's ideas about the personality problems of people with disabilities, rehabilitation experts believed that their problems came from a conviction that they should be exempt from the normal customs and laws that govern society. It was this attitude that gave disabled people license to 'wreck havoc' upon the rest of society. The supposed hostility that they manifested, as well as other similar personality disorders, could be attributed to their frustration with their physical or mental impairments. Disabled people were unemployable, the argument went, because of their 'twisted and maladjusted personalities.'"[59]

Under this "counselor knows best" model, a person with a disability had less insight into his or her own situation, including his or her own potential for employment and life in the community, than rehabilitation experts equipped with the latest tests for measuring personality, motivation, and intelligence.[60] Furthermore, any complaint about access, any anger a person with a disability might feel about instances of overt discrimination, would be seen not as an understandable, even necessary response to oppression, but rather as evidence of a deep-rooted personality flaw that could only be addressed by a non-disabled rehabilitation professional. As O'Brien succinctly puts it, "This policy provided that disabled people accommodate society rather than have society accommodate them."[61]

Of course, not all rehab counselors were hostile or even unsympathetic toward their clients; and significant progress was made for many people with disabilities, even during the heyday of "counselor knows best" in the 1950s and 1960s. Mary Switzer, the director of the federal Office of Vocational Rehabilitation during this period, was instrumental in spearheading (with Boyce Robert Williams) such important innovations as the National Theatre of the Deaf and the Helen Keller Center for Deaf-Blind Youth and Adults.[62] Under her management, vocational rehabilitation programs provided assistance to tens of thousands of people with a wide variety of disabilities, including many who would later become activists in the movement, and federal funding for the program increased fortyfold.[63] Switzer, along with Howard Rusk, Henry Viscardi, and other rehabilitation professionals, forcefully advocated for the involvement of people with disabilities in the mainstream of American life.

But the spirit of paternalism and the refusal to understand disability as a political issue (beyond the politics of advocating for increased funding and authority as a federal/state bureaucracy) put severe limits on what progress could be made. Even worse, as O'Brien remarks, rehabilitation professionals at times actively opposed legislation that might have offered some measure of workplace security or protection against discrimination. Their ideological position was based, again, in the "whole man" theory of rehabilitation, which "focused on barriers in the minds of disabled people." Any civil rights approach would do nothing to address this perspective but would instead act to undermine the authority of rehabilitation counselors, doctors, and other "experts" as they sought to help their clients.[64]

This system of rehabilitation had other problems as well. Because the focus was on training people for work, rehab counselors tended to "cherry pick" their clients, using state and federal funds to provide services to people with less severe disabilities, who were more likely to have a positive outcome and thus produce a higher success rate for the office. People with the most severe disabilities, and who presumably were most in need of rehabilitation, were precisely the people whom the rehab bureaucracies, as they developed in the 1940s, '50s, and '60s, were least interested in assisting.

"Isolated, Institutionalized, and Ignored"

By the mid-twentieth century, then, Americans with disabilities lived under a system of virtual apartheid, in which those with discernable disabilities were most often hidden away in institutions, special schools, or in family basements and attics, or, at best, isolated in their homes, while those who could "pass" as non-disabled—people with epilepsy, for instance, or emotional or cognitive disabilities—tried their best to conceal and deny their identity. This isolation was reinforced by the physical infrastructure—streets without curb cuts, buildings without ramps, public transit systems that were virtually impossible for people with mobility or perceptual disabilities to use—so that it was rare even to see a person with such a disability out in public. In this way society's judgment of disability was literally carved in stone.[65]

Other barriers to the public square were less visible but just as difficult to breach. The nation's communication system, for example, was predicated on the assumption that every individual who might need to use a telephone could hear and speak. Popular entertainment, public education, court room proceedings, government hearings, even law enforcement and medical care, all were conducted or delivered with the assumption that deaf and hard of hearing people and people with speech disabilities simply did not exist.[66]

"Perhaps the word that best describes the historical treatment of persons with disabilities is *separation*," notes political scientist Jacqueline Vaughan Switzer. "Although in some cultures the family takes responsibility for the care of disabled persons, for the most part this has been the exception rather than the rule in the United States. More commonly, disabled persons have been isolated, institutionalized, and ignored."[67] This very isolation—not to mention the poverty and social deprivation it engendered—made it difficult for anything like a national disability rights movement to coalesce.

The power of "ableism"—as disability rights advocates term the mix of social attitudes that have constrained people with disabilities from achieving their full civil and human rights—can be measured by the fact that the most successful American politician of the twentieth century was forced to take extraordinary measures to conceal his disability. Although it was widely known that Franklin Delano Roosevelt was a polio survivor, the extent of his disability was a secret carefully guarded not only by the president and his inner circle but also by the press. As a part of this "splendid deception"—as historian and disability rights activist Hugh Gregory Gallagher labeled it—journalists were prohibited from taking photographs of Roosevelt in his wheelchair or of the ramps built to accommodate him at the White House. FDR himself, a man who led the nation through economic depression and world war, evidently believed that he would not be elected or reelected president if the true extent of his disability became known.[68] The traditional models of disability, then, were hardly of much use to people with disabilities. Whatever protection the religious model might have provided through injunctions to take pity on them was far outweighed by the demoralization engendered by such pity, exacerbated by the notion that disability was a form of divine punishment or even demonic possession. The breakthroughs in preventing, ameliorating, and even curing various disabling conditions which the medical model brought—and these were substantial—had to be seen in context with the concomitant loss of autonomy and dehumanization of treating people as sets of symptoms.[69] Whatever gains the rehabilitation model may have achieved for some disabled individuals, and whatever advantage accrued to others through the legal definitions that entitled them to benefits under state and federal programs, did little or nothing to integrate them into mainstream society or to provide any hope of real empowerment as individuals or as citizens. And none of these models did anything to change society itself to become more accommodating to people with disabilities. Frank Bowe, a disability activist and scholar, summed up the result in his 1978 manifesto, *Handicapping America:*

> We smile at the poster child and hope for her, but when she wants to go to school we do not let her attend ours and when she grows up we do not want to know her. When disabled adults apply for jobs for which they are qualified we look for ways to deny them employment. When they seek housing we suggest that they look somewhere else. And we are very persuasive, because our homes, buildings, and communities are often inaccessible to wheelchairs, feature communications systems deaf people cannot use, and have safety warnings blind people cannot read. Yet we do more: almost each new day brings to light cases of disabled people being vandalized, discriminated against, raped, denied permission to marry, fired, institutionalized, deprived of their children, sent to out-of-the-way "special" programs, robbed, and even killed.[70]

Other forms of oppression are more subtle. Often language itself devalues and objectifies people with disabilities. The message that disabled people are "defective" has been implicit in everything from the Jerry Lewis Labor Day telethons for the Muscular Dystrophy Association ("I'd like to play basketball like normal, healthy, vital and energetic people. . . . When I sit back and think more rationally, I realize my life is half . . . I just have to learn to try to be good at being half a person") to the passing remark by a family member or a complete stranger, "If I were you, I'd kill myself."[71] Indeed, such public devaluation and shaming is among the most common experiences recounted by people with disabilities, especially those who came of age before the 1980s. In "Traveling," the poet Katherine Simpson describes the impact of one such incident.

> I avoid the East Bay Terminal
> in San Francisco,
> Since that Thanksgiving twenty years ago,
> When taking the bus to family in Berkeley,
> I was accosted. *If you need a job,*
> *join the circus. I saw a boy just like you*
> *Back home in Mexico. He made a living,*
> *Painting with his feet.*[72]

The Emergence of Disability Rights

Americans with disabilities have not been passive through this long and bitter history. As far back as the 1850s, Deaf Americans had organized themselves into clubs and associations, and the National Association of the Deaf was founded as an explicitly political organization in 1880.[73] In the 1930s, the League of the Physically Handicapped, based in New York City, protested discrimination by the federal Works Progress Administration against workers with disabilities.[74] and the National Federation of the Blind (NFB) and the American Federation of the Physically Handicapped (AFPH), both founded in 1940 (although the AFPH wasn't formally incorporated until 1942), urged an end to employment discrimination in the private sector.[75] The labor movement provided the conceptual model for these early activists, so that, according to this often unarticulated analysis, people with disabilities were analogous to exploited workers, who could best win their rights through organizing, while the primary goal remained entering or reentering the workforce and then winning better conditions from employers.

"'The right to organize" was particularly important to the NFB, which in the 1940s was predominantly concerned "with the bedrock issues of economic and social security."[76] The idea of an organization founded and run explicitly by blind people themselves was a shock, even a threat, to what Jacobus tenBroek termed "the blindness system"—that network of government and philanthropic organizations, invariably run by sighted people, charged with educating and rehabilitating blind Americans. NFB organizers were targeted by those in the system who had the power to deny them government services or access to the sheltered workshops and government-building vending stands that employed the plurality of blind people working for wages in the 1940s and '50s. In 1957, Senator John F. Kennedy (D-MA) introduced legislation to redress this grievance, declaring, "It is important that our blind citizens be protected against any exercise of this kind of influence or authority to interfere with their freedom of self-expression through organizations of the blind." The bill failed to pass, but the attention it garnered helped the NFB in efforts to pass similar legislation on the state level.[77]

The AFPH also focused largely on employment. Its founder, Paul A. Strachan, was a former union organizer who as an adult had lived with a variety of disabilities. His early activism included pushing for enactment of the Smith-Fess Act or Federal Vocational Training Act of 1920, which established the nation's first federal civilian rehabilitation program. In 1940, Strachan was further disabled when he was injured in an automobile accident in which he broke his spine and was made deaf.

"While recovering from this accident, Strachan decided to devote the remainder of his life to fighting discrimination against people with disabilities. Strachan told the *Washington Post* that his decision 'was born of personal experience,'" describing how, because of his disabilities, he had been "cast upon the human scrap pile, despite a fierce desire to live, to work, and to achieve." Strachan initially approached the National Association of the Deaf (NAD) with the idea of forming a cross-disability political organization, but its leaders "feared that signed language and the cultural autonomy of the deaf community would be threatened in such a coalition."[78] Similarly, the NFB would later express reservations about entering cross-disability organizations such as the American Coalition of Citizens with Disabilities, fearing that issues peculiar to blind people would receive less attention in such a context.

As president of the AFPH, Strachan, according to Nora Groce, "almost single-handedly shepherded a campaign through many sessions of Congress, urging the establishment of what he called 'National Employ the Physically Handicapped Week.'"[79] In 1945, Congress passed legislation endorsing Strachan's "Week," and President Truman asked Major General Graves B. Erskine to plan the 1946 observance for the first week of October. Truman then "encouraged Secretary of Labor Lewis Schwellenbach to take the lead in organizing the program. Schwellenbach quickly worked to launch the President's Committee on National Employ the Physically Handicapped Week, calling the first meeting of the organization in September, 1947."[80] Congress authorized an annual appropriation for the committee in 1949. "Very early on, committee members recognized the need for a year-round effort to promote the employment of people with disabilities, and in 1952 the committee changed its name to the President's Committee on Employment of the Physically Handicapped."[81] "In 1955, President Eisenhower issued Executive Order No. 10640, which established the committee as a permanent organization."[82] The committee would play a pivotal role in the nascent disability rights movement, providing an opportunity (and funding) for prominent activists to meet one another at its annual meetings in Washington.[83] The committee also provided a forum for individuals such as Harold Russell, a disabled veteran who became the public face of the "Hire the Handicapped" campaigns.

The US entry into World War II and the induction into the military of millions of working men and women had created a "manpower" shortage that led to the employment of thousands of previously "unemployable" Americans with disabilities.[84] With the end of the war these gains were quickly erased, but the tens of thousands of men (and some women) permanently disabled during the conflict expected assistance and acceptance from the nation they had served. Medical advances, particularly the development of antibiotics, meant that people with even the severest of disabilities, for example, spinal cord–injured para- and quadriplegics, could now expect to survive years, even decades, after their initial injuries. Taking advantage of the newly passed GI Bill of Rights, many disabled veterans hoped to attend college, obtain their degrees, and seek employment side by side with their non-disabled peers.

They also organized, forming groups such as the Blinded Veterans Association in 1945 and the Paralyzed Veterans of America (PVA) in 1947,[85] while civilian groups, such as Just One Break (JOB) founded by Henry Viscardi, focused less on political advocacy than on remedial training of people with disabilities hoping to enter the workforce.[86] During the late 1940s, then, a variety of groups and individuals were working, more or less independently of one another, to improve the lives of people with disabilities. In addition to the NFB and the AFPH—both of which continued to be active—and the newly formed PVA, individuals such as Tim Nugent, Elizabeth Boggs, and Gini Laurie all took on different aspects of the work.

Nugent, whose oral history is included in this book, founded the disabled students' program at the University of Illinois, first at Galesburg, then at Urbana-Champaign. This program not only provided the opportunity for a college education to people who would otherwise have been excluded (in the process educating future activists including Fred Fay, Mary Lou Breslin, and Kitty Cone), it also became the testing ground for such innovations as lift-equipped buses, curb cuts, and wheelchair ramps. By the end of the 1950s, Nugent was working with the American National Standards Institute (ANSI) to formulate guidelines for these and other features of architectural and transit access.[87]

Elizabeth Boggs earned her doctorate in theoretical chemistry from Cambridge University in 1941, and during World War II was part of the Manhattan Project developing the atomic bomb. Her son Jonathan, born in 1945, suffered a high fever in infancy which left him severely brain damaged. By this time the Boggs family had moved to New Jersey, and as Jonathan grew older he and his family began to experience the discrimination against children with disabilities and their families so prevalent at the time. Boggs, after taking Jonathan to a variety of "experts," soon concluded that the advice they gave was based less on science than on myth and stereotype. Boggs returned to school to study special education and social work, and in 1950 was among the principal founders of the National Association of Parents and Friends of Mentally Retarded Children, which in 1953 became the National Association for Retarded Children (NARC). The NARC, together with other parents' organizations such as United Cerebral Palsy, Inc. (UCP), founded in 1949, grew to play a major role in the disability rights movement of the 1970s and beyond, particularly in fighting for the right to education for children with disabilities.[88]

Gini Laurie, born in 1913, had originally planned to become a physician but was stymied by the sexism of the time. After marrying and moving to Cleveland, she became a volunteer at the Toomey Pavilion rehabilitation center during the polio epidemic of 1949. Polio survivors in the 1940s generally spent many months if not years in rehab and hospital settings, during which many formed intense personal relationships with their peers and the staff. In an effort to keep former patients and staff in touch with each other after discharge, Laurie founded the *Toomeyville Gazette*. By the end of the 1950s. what had started as a mimeographed newsletter had turned into the *Toomey j. Gazette,* with Laurie its (still unpaid) editor. By this time the *Gazette* had a national readership of polio survivors. In addition to offering useful "how to" features on everything from turning newspaper pages with a mouth-stick to designs for cheek-operated telephones and an "over-bed typewriter mount," the *Gazette* also began running articles of a more political nature, providing a forum for discussions on the independent living movement, legislation, and movement politics in general. By 1970, when its name changed one last time, Gini Laurie and her *Rehabilitation Gazette* were important voices in the growing disability rights movement.[89]

Despite these and other efforts, however, the situation for Americans with disabilities was hardly improved. By the 1960s, children with disabilities were still routinely segregated into "special" classes or institutions, and adults with visible disabilities rarely were able to enter the workplace. Those few organizations with any semblance of a disability rights agenda had lost much of the momentum they had generated since 1940. The AFPH foundered in the late 1950s, riven by internal disputes and perhaps plagued by the burnout chronic in social change organizations.[90] The NFB continued into the sixties and beyond (and is still prominent), but it, too, was torn by internal conflicts, with a dissident faction breaking away to found the American Council of the Blind (ACB) in 1961.[91] And within all these groups there existed the divisions that plagued and continue to plague American society in general—divisions of race and class, of gender and sexual identity.[92]

It was the successes of the African American civil rights movement, more than any other single factor, that sparked the resurgence of disability rights activism in the late 1960s and early 1970s. As the ramifications of *Brown v. Board of Education* began to be felt across America, advocates such as Gunnar Dybwad came to see civil rights litigation and legislation as useful tools for advancing a disability rights agenda. The movement's sit-ins and demonstrations also offered a model for disability activists such as Judy Heumann and Fred Fay. In fact, activists such as Rev. Wade Blank and Mary Jane Owen did their first political work not in disability rights but in the civil rights and antiwar movements. As the more militant factions of the civil rights movement began to speak of "black pride" and "black power," disability activists began to examine their own internalized oppression and to question the assumption that disability was a flaw or defect rather than an intrinsic part of the human condition.[93]

It was in this context that polio survivor Ed Roberts began attending classes at the University of California, Berkeley, in 1962, living at the Cowell Hospital, the on-campus health facility, because it provided the only accessible dorm space and was the only campus residence able to accommodate the "iron lung" respirator he used at night to breathe. The publicity generated by Roberts's presence drew others with physical disabilities to the university, and these students became the core group around which the Physically Disabled Students' Program was established in 1970. Some of these same students also formed the more loosely organized Rolling Quads in 1969 (renamed the Disabled Students Union in 1973), an activist group demanding better access on campus.[94] Meanwhile, the parents' movement continued to grow, largely as a peer support and social service network but also becoming more "political" until, in 1969, two ARC chapters filed the first federal right-to-education cases on behalf of students with disabilities. Together, *Mills v. Board* and *PARC v. Pennsylvania* can be seen as the *Brown v. Board* of the disability rights movement, with *PARC* in particular bringing the idea of disability as a civil rights issue to national attention.[95]

In 1972, the Berkeley student activists, together with people with disabilities in the San Francisco Bay area, set up the Center for Independent Living, Inc., the first of what would be hundreds of independent living centers (ILCs) around the country, founded to provide severely disabled people the services they needed in order to leave or stay out of nursing homes and other chronic care facilities. Though focused around service delivery—for example, wheelchair repair and the finding and training of personal care assistants for help with such everyday tasks as getting into and out of bed, toileting, and cooking—the ILCs also had a political edge, often lobbying not only to sustain and enlarge these services but also to push for architectural and transportation access in their host communities. The late 1960s and early '70s also saw the appearance of more explicitly political groups: the California Association of the Physically Handicapped (CAPH) on the West Coast, and Disabled in Action (DIA) in New York and Philadelphia. Local activist organizations also formed in Texas, St. Louis, and Denver, often coalescing around ILCs or student groups.[96]

Separate from these groups, but similar in outlook, methods, and goals, were the first overtly political organizations of the "psychiatric survivor" movement—the Insane Liberation Front in Portland, Oregon, founded in 1970, and the Mental Patients' Liberation Front in Boston and the Mental Patients' Liberation Project in New York City, both founded in 1971.[97] All of these groups had moved beyond the old labor model for organizing, turning instead to the civil rights movement and then later to the women's movement for theory, tactics, and inspiration.

Evidence of this new disability consciousness can be seen in the title of an article published in 1969: "Uncle Tom and Tiny Tim: Some Reflections on the Cripple as Negro." The author, Leonard Kriegel, himself a polio survivor since age twelve, noted how

> the cripple . . . is a social fugitive, a prisoner of expectations molded by a society that he makes uncomfortable by his very presence. For this reason, the most functional analogy for the life he leads is to be found in the Negro. For the black man, now engaged in wresting an identity from a white society apparently intent on mangling its own, has become in America a synonym for that which insists on the capacity of its own being. . . . For the cripple, the black man is a model because he is on intimate terms with a terror that does not recognize his existence and is yet distinctly personal. . . .
>
> Stereotypes persist long after reality fades away; for us, Uncle Tom still prays on bent knees while Tiny Tim hobbles through the world on huge gushes of sentiment and love. But let us see the world as it is, for the world itself has perfected the ability to see what it wishes to see and only what it wishes to see.[98]

It is not, of course, a perfect analogy; there are substantial differences between racism and ableism, between the struggles of the civil rights and the disability rights movements.[99] People with disabilities belong to what is sometimes called "an open minority"—meaning anyone can at any time become disabled, no matter what his or her community of origin. On the one hand, this can be seen as an additional problem for those trying to organize a disability rights movement. As Kriegel observed in 1969, and others have noted since, people with disabilities aren't born into a distinct disability culture with its own native language, customs, and traditions.[100] (The major exception being the Deaf community, which has long considered itself a minority culture within the hearing world—with many Deaf people eschewing any connection to disability).[101] In fact, Americans with disabilities are divided from one another not only by race and gender and sexual orientation—as are Americans in general—but also by disability itself, so that polio survivors, for example, may see themselves as having little in common with blind Americans, and vice versa.

There are, however, also advantages to being "an open minority," which disability activists have put to good use. For one thing, the experience of disability is so common (even if generally unacknowledged) that most every extended American family has at least one or more members with a significant disability.[102] This reality cuts across all the other divides of American society. And so, while Americans with disabilities in general may have lower incomes and less education than the median, it is also true that some individuals have access to resources usually unavailable to other minority activists. Justin Dart Jr., for example, disabled by polio as a teenager, could dedicate to the cause not only a portion of his family fortune but, more important, his family's connections to the highest echelons of the Republican Party, then in power at the White House. Indeed, disability cuts across partisan political divisions as well, so that the late Edward M. Kennedy, the liberal Democratic senator, and George H. W. Bush, the conservative Republican president, shared intimate experiences with disability that made them receptive, when the time came, to the notion of disability rights.[103]

But whatever the differences, the civil rights analogy caught on, and by the mid-1970s activists were using the language, the strategies, and even the tactics of the civil rights movement. In 1971 the federal court accepted a consent decree coming out of the *PARC* litigation, in which for the first time it found that children with disabilities had an inherent right to access to a free public education. The decree caught the attention of activists all across the country, leading to a flurry of right-to-education litigation that culminated in the passage of the Education for All Handicapped Children Act of 1975.

During this same period, the Rehabilitation Act of 1973, particularly its Section 504, prohibiting discrimination on the basis of disability by any public or private entity receiving federal funds, provided a new and potent tool for activists.[104] Section 504, as Paul Longmore observed, "had been drafted by Senate staffers with little or no experience of disability issues, who nonetheless recognized that prejudice was a problem for disabled Americans." When President Richard M. Nixon pocket-vetoed the first two versions of the act, DIA in New York and the more "radical" activists on the President's Committee on Employment of the Handicapped in Washington demonstrated in protest.[105]

Through 1976 and early 1977 a national, cross-disability movement, loosely organized within the framework of the American Coalition of Citizens with Disabilities (ACCD) under the direction of Frank Bowe, identified 504 as its principal legal tool. When the newly elected Carter administration delayed issuing the first set of regulations implementing the law, ACCD called for a day of "national action" to dramatize the issue and put pressure on the administration. On April 5, 1977, demonstrations across the nation brought together unprecedented numbers of disabled persons, including some, in Washington and San Francisco, who occupied the offices of HEW. These actions lasted at most a day or two, except in San Francisco, where more than a hundred activists occupied a floor of the regional federal office building until April 30—to this day the longest nonviolent occupation of a federal facility in American history.[106]

How and why activists were able to sustain such a campaign in San Francisco, and the role the California action had in forcing the promulgation of the regulations, are dealt with in detail in chapter 14, "The HEW Demonstrations." Suffice it to say here that the action and example of the demonstrators in San Francisco galvanized the movement as nothing had before, and—with the exception of the Deaf President Now campaign of 1988—nothing has since. As Longmore notes, "The activists successfully got most of the news media to present their cause as a civil-rights issue, a struggle between ordinary disabled people and federal bureaucrats and politicians who were 'trying to steal our civil rights.'"[107] Seemingly overnight, people with disabilities went from being virtually invisible in American politics to being an active and vocal constituency dedicated to the proposition that disability would no longer be framed exclusively in terms of religion and charity, medicine and rehabilitation, welfare and income maintenance.

The White House Conference on Handicapped Individuals, held May 23–27, 1977, which had been years in the planning, coincidentally occurred in the immediate aftermath of the HEW triumph. Although some participants would later dismiss the conference as mostly talk, it did enable three thousand people with disabilities and their allies to gather and compare notes and to form friendships and alliances, many of which would last for decades.[108] It also produced some 142 resolutions, among them one that called for the Civil Rights Act of 1964 and the Voting Rights Act of 1965 to be amended to include people with disabilities.[109] Nothing, however, was done to follow through on such an ambitious legislative agenda.

Instead, Section 504 itself led to a host of concepts original to disability rights law. In its entirety 504 amounted to only one sentence:

> No otherwise qualified handicapped individual in the United States,
> as defined in section 7(6), shall, solely by reason of his handicap, be
> excluded from participation in, be denied the benefits of, or be sub-
> jected to discrimination under any program or activity receiving
> Federal financial assistance.

But its enforcement required the courts and the community to answer a number of questions that spoke to the heart of the disability experience. Who, under this law, was an "otherwise qualified handicapped individual"? What precisely was "discrimination" as it applied to people with disabilities, and what did an employer, a state agency, a school, or a business have to do not to fall under legal sanction? The answers, generated in a series of landmark federal and Supreme Court decisions, fostered new concepts that would over time become the bedrock principles of disability rights law, as phrases such as "reasonable accommodation" and "undue burden" entered the legal lexicon.[110]

The momentum, however, was suddenly threatened with the inauguration of President Ronald Reagan in January 1981. The Reagan administration took as its central premise the idea that "government isn't the solution to our problems, government *is* the problem" and was thus skeptical, if not downright hostile, toward any use of the federal government to advance or enforce civil rights.[111] Activists were catapulted into defending the gains made in the 1970s from efforts to weaken the Section 504 regulations, while federal funding for the nascent independent living movement, provided under the Rehabilitation Act of 1978, was drastically curtailed. In such an environment, the prospect of expanding the scope and power of federal disability rights protections seemed unlikely, at best.

Nevertheless, that is precisely what happened. The characteristics that made the disability community unique, different from all other civil rights constituencies—most especially its inclusion of people across all political, social, and economic spectrums—enabled the movement to prod a series of conservative administrations to work in conjunction with liberal legislators to pass, over the opposition of conservative legislators and lobbyists representing the business community, the single most sweeping expansion of federal civil rights protections since 1964. Indeed, the period from 1980 to 1990—what lobbyist Patrisha Wright has dubbed "the golden age of disability rights legislation"[112]—saw a remarkable succession of legislative milestones, beginning with the Civil Rights of Institutionalized Persons Act of 1980 (signed by President Carter), moving through the Voting Accessibility for the Elderly and Handicapped Act of 1984, the Air Carrier Access Act of 1986, the Fair Housing Amendments Act of 1988, and the Civil Rights Restoration Act of 1988 (passed over President Reagan's veto), and culminating in the passage of the Americans with Disabilities Act of 1990.[113]

The last three bills are of particular significance in that here, for the first time, the idea of disability rights was incorporated into the agenda of organizations representing the broad spectrum of civil rights constituencies, most notably the Leadership Conference on Civil Rights. Although disability rights activists may have been among the least influential of these in the campaigns to win passage of the Fair Housing Amendments and Civil Rights Restoration acts, the ADA was clearly passed virtually entirely through the efforts of Americans with disabilities and their allies. Quite simply, the Americans with Disabilities Act of 1990 marks the political arrival, and at this writing the high point, of the national disability rights movement.

The world has changed since Davis argued for racial segregation in 1952 and Kriegel wrote his article in 1969. The election of Barack Obama as the nation's president in November 2008 is one measure of that change. Others are as evident as the nearest curb cut or elevator with braille signage, the availability of closed captioning on TV and sign language interpreters in court rooms and hospitals, the use of terms such as "reasonable accommodation" in our law and "wheelchair accessible" in our daily lives.

The disability rights movement, then, has made enormous progress in allowing all of us to perceive "the world as it is." It has in many instances not only changed the physical infrastructure but also provided us all with new ways of understanding our shared humanity. No longer a scourge of God, an individual pathology, or a "spoiled identity,"[114] disability for the first time in history is coming to be recognized as an integral and valued part of the human experience.

How all this happened, how Americans with disabilities went from being "social fugitives," outcasts and the "prisoners of expectations" to building a movement for radical change is the story this book tells, in the words of those who drew up that agenda, engaged that environment, and forever transformed our society.

It is my great privilege to share their words and stories in these pages.

1
Childhood

THE IDEA THAT DISABILITY IS A TAINT, A STATEMENT ABOUT THE inherent worth or character of the person with the disability, works itself out most painfully on children with disabilities who absorb, often without knowing, this prevalent but generally unspoken judgment. It can be manifest in everything from schools with names such as "The Industrial School for Crippled and Deformed Children"[1] to run-ins on the street with complete strangers wanting to know "what's wrong with you?" to a popular culture that routinely uses disability to denote wickedness (think of Captain Hook, Doctor Strangelove, and every malevolent fictional character sporting an eye patch, prosthetic, or facial scars).[2] This harsh social environment is then used to justify segregated education and even institutionalization, as when parents are told that their child needs to be "protected" from society, and will be "better off with her own kind."

Disability has in fact often been considered so shameful, so deviant, that even to talk about it has been perceived as distasteful or demeaning. In interview after interview many of the major figures in the disability rights movement of the 1970s and '80s describe how their parents "never talked about" their disability. Neil Jacobson's parents went a step further. Jacobson spent hours a day doing physical therapy in a vain effort to get him to walk. "I never had a wheelchair until I was in high school. . . . My father built a dog house for the wheelchair, because he didn't want the wheelchair in the house. To him, the wheelchair was a symbol of disability. A symbol of pity."[3]

Add to this the fact that many of these children needed (or were told they needed) surgeries or other treatment, sometimes painful, often requiring hospitalization or extended separation from parents and home. The result was that some children came to see themselves as essentially powerless, flawed, even unworthy of the love that "normal" children generally take for granted.

Of course, every child's experience is different, and this isn't to say that every person with a disability who grew up prior to 1970 lived a life of abject misery. (Nor does it mean that the advent of the disability rights movement has set everything right). But any understanding of the disability rights movement—why it was necessary, what it has meant, and why it took so long to happen—has to incorporate an understanding of how destructive these all-pervading social messages have been. Almost every activist with a congenital disability, or one acquired early in childhood, recalls both the insidious effect of this cultural environment, and the epiphany that came with understanding, finally, that the problem was *out there*—in society—and not *in here,* in his or her own character. For some, this realization would not come until they were well into adulthood. For many, it wouldn't come at all until participation in some action—for instance the Section 504 demonstrations of 1977, or an ADAPT blockade of the late-1980s.

One response to this realization has been the development of "disability pride"—even what some describe as "disability chic." Another response has been a sense of anger that has empowered many movement activists through much of their political lives.

"People talk about how some of us are very angry," Ed Roberts told film maker Billy Golfus in 1997. "Of course we're angry. We've been through the worst kind of atrocities, attitudes toward us that see us as vegetables, that see us as sick and unable and having no future. I mean that's *got* to piss you off. And to me, anger is one of the best things we've got going in this movement. Because when you're angry, that gives you a tremendous amount of energy."[4]

Lee Kitchens
"The only little people that you saw anything about besides in the movies were circus performers."

———

Lee Kitchens was a brilliant engineer who developed the first hand-held calculator for Texas Instruments in the early 1970s. He was also a little person—someone the general public back then would commonly call a "midget"—a label which is seen by little people themselves as a term of derision.

Born in 1930, Kitchens joined Little People of America (LPA) soon after its founding in 1957, and in the 1970s was a founding member of the Texas Coalition of Citizens with Disabilities. Kitchens died in May 2003.

In the thirties, short stature was a rare situation—as it is today—and you didn't find many people of short stature out in public. Other people, other kids, adults, whatever, would make fun of you, make remarks, things of that sort. However, in 1930, when I was born, the treasurer of the state of Texas was a little person and my mother had a newspaper clipping about him. He was her role model, if you will. She never met him, didn't know any other people of short stature, or any other parents that had a child of short stature. I never saw another little person until I was about sixteen.

Society pretty much had the idea that people of short stature could only make a living in some form of show business or the circus, and were essentially second class citizens. That was the perception and perception was reality. Many little people had been denied proper education and there-fore were either unemployed or unemployable.

In my immediate family they had a much broader outlook. My grandmother had a college education, so did one of my aunts and one of my uncles, and my mother had a year and a half of college. They understood that education was the key to the future, and so academic excellence was a requirement and you did what you had to do. You made "A's" and anything less than an "A" was goofing off. You could get by with a few "B's," but a "C" was like an "F" and you just made sure that that never happened. I had an uncle that was injured in World War I, and he had to be supported by the family because he was unable to work in a physical way and did not have the education. So there was a good example of what happens if you're not prepared to compete with your head.

My life in school wasn't all that great. There was a lot of teasing, but I had a good friend who interceded for me whenever it was necessary. I guess the kids finally got used to you and unless you became a real worrywart or something, they would tolerate you. Things were a little better in college because there you had a better segment of the population, which were more likely to accept you for what you did, as opposed to what they saw. Then in the workplace you were measured by what you produced. They didn't care whether you had three heads as long as you could do what's needed. The younger years are the toughest and the teenage years are the hardest. That's true for any kid.

I didn't date until I was twenty-one and first started meeting other little people. A couple of times I attempted to and got turned down, and so you don't put yourself in that position to be rejected, you just avoid it. I didn't participate in the senior prom or anything of that sort. That's not true today. In our little people's organization some families would import another little person to be able to accompany a person to the senior prom. And of course at our national conference at least for one week out of the year you're on parity with everyone else. An average sized person can feel very out of place at one of our meetings. That's their problem, not ours.

People talk about self-image. I never gave it a lot of thought. I was always interested in *things,* you know, model airplanes, and wasn't necessarily a people person. I guess that's what led me into engineering. I knew I was different and there wasn't anything I was going to be able to do about it. I just learned to live with it.

There was a guy about my age playing in the band in another high school, who was the first little person I met. But I didn't meet him until I was eighteen. It was a cold reception because that guy—who I got to know later on—was the macho type in that he did his own thing in spite of his size. Initially I don't guess he was very comfortable with me. Maybe it was like what it was like for a lot of little people, seeing yourself in the mirror for the first time. Later on I got to know him and we got the little people's organization going and he married one of the little people. But still, I don't think he really ever had his act together and later on he committed suicide. So I don't think he ever really was able to accept himself for what he was.

There was some poor advice from the medical profession, ideas about putting me in casts for whatever reason. But you have to under-stand the medical profession didn't have much exposure to short stature. They couldn't even distinguish between one type or another, even though I was seen at the Mayo Clinic as an infant for a cleft palate, for which I had two surgeries. Still, the best advice from the family doctor was, "Take him home and treat him like you would any other child." My parents did the best they could in that regard but still I didn't get to do things at the same age as my sister did. I never drove a car until I was twenty-one because my dad assumed it couldn't be done, and I had to force the issue, when I was in a position to equip a car and drive it whether they liked it or not. But that was at age twenty-one.

The only little people that you saw anything about besides in the movies were circus performers. When I went to college I did some research on the term "midget," which was the only term I'd ever heard. The term "dwarf" came up, but there was painfully little information in the literature.

It's funny when you hear in public, "Hey Momma, look at the little—!" and that's all you hear because they've clamped their hands over the child's mouth. But that goes on all the time. It's human nature. I'll never forget my son staring at a person in a wheelchair [who] just had one leg. I felt, "Golly, he's been around so many little people!" But he hadn't been around any people in a wheelchair with one leg. So it's human nature and one of the things little people have to learn is that, Hey, people are naturally curious. Some are rude about it but some are just naturally curious. Some are discreet, some are not.

Corbett O'Toole
"The neck-up thing."

Corbett O'Toole was raised in a large, working class, Roman Catholic family in Boston, Massachusetts, and experienced what she describes as the "separate realities" often experienced by children with disabilities. On the one hand she was viscerally aware of what polio had done to her body, and of the day-to-day realities of living with a disability. But she was also aware of what she called "a gentleman's agreement" at home and at school to pretend that her disability didn't exist. Of course, this "agreement" didn't change anything about her body, nor the way the world at large responded to her as a girl who was "different" and "crippled."

After finishing college she decided to move to California for the climate, a fairly common consideration for anyone who has had to manage crutches or a wheelchair in the snow and ice of a northeastern winter. She arrived in Berkeley in 1973, and soon became involved in "women's stuff"—feminist consciousness raising and activism—and the nascent independent living movement.

Corbett O'Toole continues to live in California, where she remains active in the Disabled Women's Alliance and the Society for Disability Studies.

———

I was born in August of '51 and by September of 1952 I had polio. I was paralyzed from my neck down. They put me in a full body cast that had slits on the side and my mother would take me out twice a day and exercise my muscles and then put me back in it. So I laid flat on my back or flat on my stomach from my neck to my toes in a cast from the age of one to the age of two and a half.

When I was two and a half they sent me away to a rehab center for six months. And what they did was to limit family visits to thirty minutes once a week. My parents could come to visit on Sunday afternoons. Otherwise they couldn't come.

But it was where I learned to walk, where I got my first braces. I had two full steel leg braces and I got the trunk support with a corset. Then when I was three-ish, I was walking well enough that I could come home. I came home with crutches, braces, a corset, and night casts. By then my brother had been born and my mother was pregnant with my sister Patricia. So that's the background of how it was growing up with my family—with some of the physical context.

My parents—my mother, particularly—really thought a lot about the options that I was going to have as a disabled kid. There were two different public elementary schools within walking distance. In Boston, another option was to send me to a school called the Industrial School for Crippled Children—that was the official name of it. It was across town. They bused kids in from the larger Boston metropolitan area. Basically it was a warehouse for kids that the local schools were refusing to accommodate. It wasn't a public school in the sense that it didn't have a quality education, it didn't have science labs. It was a quasi-institutional environment. My mother decided that she was going to send me to public school. She called the local public school and they told her in the spring to come register for the fall. So she registered. She called them and said, "My daughter has polio, she walks with crutches."

At that time the kindergarten classroom was in the basement with [the] mentally retarded classrooms. The other classrooms were upstairs. The kindergarten teacher freaked out about having a handicapped child in a regular classroom. She went off to Tufts University, which was a local educational institution, and took a class over the summer called "A

Handicapped Child in a Regular Classroom"—probably in those days it was called in a "normal" classroom—to prepare for my arrival. So, I show up quite unknown to all of this stuff—doing okay. My mother had really worked hard with me on independence and I was totally taking care of myself—could go to the bathroom by myself, take a bath by myself, put my clothes on and off—you know, the kind of stuff that you need to know in order to survive. So I went to school and I was functioning pretty independently.

When the kindergarten year was ending, the principal went to my mother and said that I was not going to be allowed to continue in public school because there were stairs. You had to go upstairs to the first floor to get to the first and second grades. They had decided it was too dangerous for me to do that, and that it was inappropriate for me to be in public school anyway. They felt they didn't have to accommodate a disabled kid, and that there was the Industrial School for Crippled Children if my mother really thought that having an education was important.

So my mother went home and reviewed her options. We were members of the local Catholic church and they had a school, there was a group of nuns that lived there and were the teachers. So my mother called up and found out what their schedule was and showed up—she had learned a lesson: she did not tell them I was disabled, did not warn them I was coming. They told her, whatever—August 15—you come and register your kid for first grade and school starts on, whatever—September 10.

So August 15 she dragged me in, my siblings in tow, and said, "Here she is." And they mumbled in shock, and she said, "I'm a Catholic. I belong to this church. You take children who belong to this church. She is my daughter, this is a school, she's ready for first grade."

Then when I was seven, nine, eleven, sixteen, I had surgeries, which for me as a kid felt like somebody's signing off your rights to protect your body. They say, "Here, cut her, make her hurt." And I'm being told to shut up because, "it's for your own good." I'm not saying that, in the long run, I wouldn't have made the same decisions, but as a kid you don't have any choice.

There's a lot of stuff for me about image of disability and my disability. I felt very split in my life and certainly in my body. I had this one life where I was at school and in a family, doing regular stuff and just a member of the community. And because both in my family and in my school people had known me for a long time, the issue of disability didn't really come up in a very direct way. I had gotten them used to what I could do and they knew not to ask me to do other kinds of things. So we had, if you will, this gentleman's agreement where my disability just didn't get talked about either at home or at school.

But then I had this public life where it was me walking down the street, whether I was going to school or in the store, or whatever. I lived in a very ethnically strong neighborhood. Almost everybody's grandparents were from either southern Italy or from Ireland, so there were people for whom "village" was a very alive concept. And on almost a daily basis between my house and wherever I was going, a neighborhood person would stop me because I was walking with crutches.

They would say to me, "What's wrong with you?"

I would answer, "I have polio."

And they would ask, "How did you get polio? Didn't you take this vaccine?" It was after '56 or '57, which is when I would be out walking by myself. I would explain that I got it before the vaccine was available.

And then they would start telling a story that had one of two or three themes. One theme was, "That's really awful and can't they do anything for you?" Another theme was, "You should follow my aunt/ cousin/ sister/ brother/ father's advice because they did 'X.'" Now in those days it wasn't "New Age" remedies, in those days it was a surgery or a therapy—whatever.

My mother modeled the way I had to handle these conversations. If they happened with her, she made me stand there and talk to the people and answer them politely. And they would always end with, "I'll pray for you," or "I'm really sorry for you," or something along that line. I hated those conversations. I once wrote about this. and it was Jennifer [Bregante] who said to me, she thought it was something that had only happened once, that I had just told the story a thousand times. But it happened pretty much every day. When Jennifer finally went back to Boston with me and we walked to the local bus stop and it happened in front of her, she was really dumbstruck by the pervasiveness of this experience.

Anyway, what I learned pretty early on was that I, as a person in public, made people uncomfortable. How they interpreted their discomfort was to make me miserable, to say bad things to me, to hurt my feelings, to shame me, to basically single me out as an oddity that was unacceptable and needed to be modified, fixed, or whatever.

The hospital was another environment. It was me with the doctors, being in an environment where my legs were examined by strange men discussing what parts to cut and what parts not to cut. Where I was asked to be compliant, not only with their treatment and their discussions with me, but with their follow-up care. They'd say, "Go home and do these exercises—stretch your foot this way, wear your cast like this, wear your braces every day."

So I learned at a pretty early age to have what I call the "neck up thing," where from the neck up I existed as a person, but pretty much from the neck down, I didn't exist. The whole experience of my body was something that other people touched, other people manipulated, other people could hurt. Adults would sign off and allow other adults to do things to me that I didn't want and that were painful. It was a cause of shame and it was like a public stigmata—a mark. It gave people who didn't know me at all the right to make decisions and interfere in my life, either in a casual way, such as the strangers on the street would, or in a direct way, like the doctors. And I couldn't get rid of it! I couldn't hide it, or get away from it, or make it invisible.

What the polio had taught me was that I could get through anything. I had had a full body cast for a year and a half, I had been sent away to an institution for six months—and the thing I think was hardest for me about both of those was everybody saying that there's nothing going on, it's no big deal. Everything's fine. And I was freaking out, but there was no space to express it.

Fred Weiner
"It wasn't until I went to Gallaudet that I felt that I fit in somewhere."

———

Born in 1963 of Deaf parents, Fred Weiner has been active in Deaf politics for several decades, and was instrumental in advocating for passage of Title IV of the Americans with Disabilities Act, (which covers telecom-munications services for "hearing-impaired and speech-impaired individuals"), among other achievements. His work on telecommunications access is of particular importance, forcing Congress first to provide telephone access to the federal government (including Congress itself), and then making the entire telecommunications grid more accessible to people with hearing and speech disabilities through the use of interpreter relay services.[5] To Weiner and other advocates of Title IV, telephone (and later internet) access for people who are Deaf or have speech disabilities is not a social service, but a civil right.

Fred Weiner, as of this writing, is executive director of program development at Gallaudet University.

I am culturally Deaf. Technically, I'm actually "hard of hearing." My hearing loss was progressive. When I was born, I had a lot of hearing, and when I started school at about the age of five, my decibel loss in my better ear was 25 dB. And now it's about 75/95. Seventy-five in one ear, 95 in the other ear, in terms of decibel loss.

My parents definitely had it harder. I mean, they were in a different era and so the view of deaf people during their time was much more negative compared to my era and when I started working. Also, my parents were profoundly deaf, and they grew up in hearing families so they didn't have access to communication within the family. So the sense of self-empowerment that I had wasn't there.

I know that my parents were both very bright people. And I think they were definitely underemployed. My dad, for example, a printer, was a valued employee, however he was frustrated. He told me one day that his boss asked him if he wanted to become the foreman. And my father said, "I would need someone who would help me with the phones." And the boss said, "Well, forget it, then." You know, "If you can't handle the phones, then you can't be the foreman."

And that's when he got laid off, during the recession in '73. As a deaf man in his forties with no other skills other than the printing profession, it was hard for him to find employment. So, he did different odd jobs to survive. He worked at a gas station pumping gas, and he sold things at flea markets. He even did electrical repair for people's homes—no license, mind you. Same with my mom. My mom was probably the brightest one in the family, but she was a woman, a deaf woman, so there wasn't a lot of opportunity for her. But when my dad was laid off she did go back to work and she was a key punch worker, and did some other office work.

Because of the stigma of being deaf, my parents during the '60s impressed upon me that they wanted me to go to a public school. They didn't want me to go to a school for the deaf like they did. They would tell their friends, "Our son Fred can hear. He can use the phone, sometimes." So, I hung around with hearing kids from school, and I hung around with CoDAs [hearing Children of Deaf Adults]. And I hung around with Deaf kids. So, really I had a pretty good mix of com-munication styles, differ-ent cultures, different ex-pectations of me.

With hearing friends or in situations with hearing people, I wanted to fit in, I wanted to be part of the group. But then I would switch to the Deaf group and, of course, I would be signing with everybody. And I would always look forward to the weekends, to be honest with you, because I knew I was getting together with people who signed. That was my element. My father was very involved with the local Deaf Club.[6] He was an athletic director, for softball, basketball. We went to a lot of Deaf events that were related to sports, and were definitely social on the week-ends. And my parents always took great pains to tell me what's happen-ing in the world, talking about what's going on in the newspaper, what they read, what's going on in the Deaf community, with their friends. So we had a very vibrant discussion at the dinner table.

I started elementary school in New York at PS 238, and then I went to James Madison High School, in Brooklyn, as well. And at that time there were no support services, no interpreters, nothing like that.

High school is where the problems really started. My hearing started to go down hill, and most of my close friends went to a different high school after middle school. So that's why, after my sophomore year, be-cause my brother went to Gallaudet and I come from a Deaf family, I was able to get into Gallaudet under special consideration. I applied for admission into the model high school there, but the people at the high school said I should go straight to Gallaudet. So I did, entering college at age sixteen.

I also was a camper at Youth Leadership Camp, the YLC, that the Na-tional Association for the Deaf sponsored for young Deaf individuals.[7] A lot of Deaf leaders came out of that camp. Frank Turk was the founder of that, and he was one person who really had a big impact on me. There were other individuals, like Frank Sullivan and Mac Norwood.[8] Later on I was a fraternity president, so I got to hang around with a lot of older alumni. Mac was considered the father of modern captioning. I got to talk with him and socialize with him.

But up to that point, I guess I was confused as an individual. I mean, was I Deaf? Was I hearing? Where did I fit in? Where did I belong? It wasn't until I came to Gallaudet that I felt that I finally fit in somewhere.

Diane Coleman
"It felt like they cleared the corridors so nobody could see us."

Diane Coleman, at the time of this writing, is the director of advocacy at the Center for Disability Rights, Inc., in Rochester, New York. Prior to this she was executive director of the Progress Center for Independent Living in Oak Park, Illinois, the client assistance program coordinator for Tennessee's Protection and Advocacy Agency, and an attorney with the California Attorney General's Commission on Disability, among other things.

Born in 1953, her options didn't always seem so open. In fact, as a child with a disability, one of her first experiences of "special education" was being taught to weave baskets and make potholders, which, she says, was "really sad."

I was adopted at ten days old, roughly. My parents adopted me because they thought they could not have any other children. I think they waited a number of years, and then when they were five years married, they adopted me. Then they promptly began to have children, four of them after that, so I have four siblings. My father was, at that time, working for Ingersoll-Rand, drafting schematics for boats. My mother was a homemaker, and we lived in post–World War II housing: little box houses in the suburbs in Michigan.

When I was about six months old, they discovered that I had a dislocated hip. So we went through a series of operations and full body casting 'til that issue was corrected. By the age of two, I was out of the cast. I was slow to learn to walk, but they thought it was because of my hip. By the time I was six, I was having enough trouble climbing steps and things like that, they figured that there must be something else going on.

They decided that I had muscular dystrophy, which was incorrect. I found out later [that the doctors] told my parents that I would die by the age of twelve, which was not true either, obviously. It took a few more years for them to decide, when I was nine, to send me to one of the clinics in Chicago, to have a fuller diagnosis. They determined then that I had spinal muscular atrophy.[9]

I remember those years as very happy years, with friends around. The thing that was hard was not always being able to keep up. For example, in kindergarten, I didn't play in the playground. If I tried to play the kinds of things the other kids were doing, I would fall down and get hurt. I felt left out in that regard, but otherwise I had friends at home, and we played in the sandbox, and I had a good time.

After mainstream kindergarten, the result of the diagnosis was to put me in segregated special ed., for grades one through six. It was called Upjohn School, named after the Upjohn Company, which was based in Battlecreek, Michigan. Upjohn School was attached by a corridor to another school—a regular kids' school. I remember every Thursday they would have "handicapped kids" go to the library, and it felt like they cleared the corridors so that nobody would see us. We would go to the library, get our books, and come back to our segregated school.

I was on the lower floor, and each classroom had I'd estimate about twenty, twenty-five kids [with] physical disabilities, and some developmental. They had the kids who were deaf or blind upstairs; we didn't generally mix. I didn't understand it really, other than the idea that they were doing some different set of teaching methods or accommodations. We were all brought to school in buses that were just for us, so it was a very segregated situation.

Now, this was in the fifties and early sixties. Disability was bad—that's how I was raised. That part of you was bad. What's good about you is these other things, but what you need to do is [to] accomplish in spite of your disability, which is a bad thing. Now, I'm not saying that was emphasized—it was just understood.

I started using a [wheel]chair at age eleven, during sixth grade. I think that they handled it very well, actually. It was harder and harder for me to walk safely. I had braces on my feet, by then, to keep my ankles from collapsing, but I was unstable. They gave me a manual wheelchair to push, because it gave me some stability and I could move along—kind of like a walker in its effect. But guess what? Whenever I felt too tired, I would just go sit in it. In other words: they enabled me to choose for myself, at the pace I wanted to do it. Then they got me a motorized chair.

All of the equipment issues, and many of the clinic issues were handled through the Muscular Dystrophy Association. One reaction of my family, particularly my mother, was to get involved with the Jerry Lewis Labor Day telethon stuff.[10] I knew that they were paying for things that otherwise we could not afford, and that the school was not providing. This was pre-education law requirements also.[11] The diagnostic work that was done, similarly, would not have been done without them. Obviously, [today] I think the health care system should provide all of this, then we wouldn't need any of that [charity].

Once in a while, they would have a local program—TV or whatever, and they might interview me and my mom, and I'd get to say one word, or something. I'd be the cute little kid. I was never a "poster child"—I wasn't *that* cute. But, they found it somewhat interesting to have me on a number of times.

My family certainly supported me to concentrate on school. My father was a big factor in that. His belief was that I would need to concentrate on getting a good education, and excelling in school to the greatest extent I could, because otherwise I would not be able to earn a living. He often thought that what that ought to be was writing. In fact, throughout my education, including all the way to graduation from graduate school, he believed that I would not be able to make it in what he termed, "the real world." But when I graduated with a MBA and a juris doctor from UCLA, he thought I should become a computer programmer for a law firm. I wasn't involved in computer programming, but he thought I could sell myself that way. He did not think I was going to sell myself as a lawyer, in spite of my education.

To some extent, they enabled me to do other things, socially, but it was hard. Transportation was difficult—anywhere I wanted to go, I'd have my parents with me. I didn't get to do after school things, the same way other kids did. So, I used my time in the late afternoon and evening to study. The other thing my father did, which was devastating to me, was that he conveyed to me that one of the reasons I had to be financially sufficient was because, "Let's face it, you're never going to get married." He said this to me when I was about thirteen.

By the time I was in my early teens, by the time I was in a wheelchair, I needed help to get up and down from a seated position, even though I could still bear weight. That meant my mother had to assist me with every transfer. I was put in a Milwaukee brace, throughout my teenage years. [This] is a brace that goes from hips to chin, and holds your back from becoming severely curved—more severely curved than it was. But the management of that brace and the foot braces was a process that took time and energy. At night, I had to wear the braces on my feet, but I could only tolerate them until one or two a.m. Then I would have to call my mother and have her take them off—every night, unless we decided to have a night where I wouldn't have them, which didn't happen often. They really followed the protocol that they were told to follow. So there's mom going through all these stresses of having to be there all the time, or make sure she was available when I needed to go to the bathroom. She couldn't go away a lot. Besides that, she had four more kids My siblings were pretty wild kids. In a way, I was easy, in the sense that I was a little goody-two-shoes kid. Mary Sunshine, as one teacher used to call me—I hated that, but it was nevertheless the case that I learned how to conduct myself in a way that would be successful with those around me. Many disabled kids learn that. So I was easier in that sense, even though I was physically more work.

I was one of two wheelchair users in a school of a few hundred. I felt very much the odd one out. It took 'til my third year in middle school to have what I would say was a group of friends, and that was very hard. It got a little better in high school. I tended to hang out with the geek group—the science/math group. Some of us also were able to hang out with the group of people that was engaged in creative writing, [but] I studied too hard to be acceptable to the counterculture group in high school. In college, that changed. You could be a good student and still be accepted in the counterculture in college, so that made it easier.

Barbara Oswald
"I had black and blue marks all the time because [the non-disabled] kids would beat me up."

Barbara Oswald was born in December 1953, in Burbank California. Her father was a sound effects editor at various Hollywood studios, and "a gentleman farmer who had three thousand laying hens when he wasn't busy at the studios." Her mother worked inspecting aircraft parts during World War II, but like many women lost her job when the war ended, returning to the traditional roles of wife and mother. She also did what Oswald today describes as "social justice work" with Mexican immigrants and migrant workers, inspiring Barbara at an early age to develop a "social conscience."

Oswald is currently a program staff member at the Disability Resource Center at Bellevue College in Washington State.

I was born three months premature. I was in an incubator for two months, because I weighed two pounds, and basically they kept you in an incubator until you weighed five. There was too much oxygen in the incubator, and that destroyed my retinas.[12]

I don't think I was aware of my disability until I was taken in for eye surgery when I was five, but I was very aware of my brother's disability. At the time the term was "mentally retarded." Now, one would probably say he was "brain damaged" or "developmentally delayed." And that was because he was also three months premature.

He was seven years older than I was, but I helped him with lots of tasks. It was an interesting situation because, had I been an only child, and with severe vision loss, I think people would have paid more attention, but because I had a brother who was much more severely disabled than I, I was looked at as the one who was going to help. In fact, I remember when my mother was trying to teach my brother to read. He might have been ten and I might have been three, and she would sit there and lose her patience, and I would counsel her that she shouldn't lose her patience with my brother. And I would tell him the words. We had *The Cat in the Hat Comes Back* and I knew it by heart, and so when he wouldn't know the word, I helped.

As for my own disability, my parents ignored it, by and large. I mean, I had glasses when I was very little, but there was not a lot of attention paid to it. And it wasn't really until I got into school that I remember being told, "Well you can't just walk up to things and look at them, you have to go sit down," because when I wanted to see something I just went up and touched it. And they don't like that in the classroom.

I went to public school for kindergarten, first and second grade. And that was just a normal classroom. And I excelled academically. And then

I went to a Catholic school. They were just starting up the school, so it only had two grades, and they'd add a grade, and then the next year they'd add another grade. And there were only eight kids in a class. So, in a way, there was a lot more individual attention, but I would say that the instructors, the teachers, were not as well educated. It was at a time when there weren't enough religious vocations, so you couldn't have a school that was run just by people in the religious orders, you had it augmented by hiring the nice lady who thought she'd like to teach but didn't really have a degree.

In the third grade I had a nun who actually spotted me and said, "This kid is smart, she needs to skip the fourth grade." So I went from the third grade to the fifth grade. And then from the fifth to the eighth grade I had what I knew at the time was a terrible teacher, and it was just survive and get through it. And then I went to Catholic high school. That was a pretty good school, and I did well. My world became much more scholarly.

My brother went to public school, the William S. Hart High School, in Newhall, California. He was in "special ed." At that time "special ed." was gluing peas on cardboard, and cleaning the windows of the high school. There wasn't really much attempt to provide remedial education or alternate teaching methods for reading, writing and arithmetic. It was, "If you can't learn the quote normal unquote way, then we won't even try."

He was terrifically abused because of his disability. He had fourteen broken bones in four years time, by kids beating him up, and taking his arm behind his back and twisting it until it broke. He'd be out of a cast and back to school one day, and the kids would push him down and he'd fall and break something else. That's why I say there was a lot more attention focused on him, because he was abused.

I was getting beat up at school as well, because of my disability. There were two ways I got around that. One was, I'd go to Mass in the morning so the kids couldn't get me before school, and then after school I'd run to the library and stay there until my parents picked me up. And so, prior to the fourth grade I read every book that I could get my hands on, because it was in large print, and then once the print got smaller, I didn't have any accommodations, but I still persisted. I'd just stare real close to the page, hold it up to my face until I could figure it out. Anyway, I think I love libraries to this day because the library was a safe place for me.

And I had an interesting reaction, also because of my disability. I had black and blue marks all the time because kids would beat me up, but I saw that my parents didn't really do anything about what was happening to my brother, so I knew it wouldn't do me any good to say anything. So when they would say to me, "Well, jeez, how come you got that black and blue mark?" I'd say, "Oh, I fell down." And the kids would say things like, "If you tell anybody, we'll beat you up even harder tomorrow."

As for my brother, when he went to the doctor, they'd say, "Oh, he must have brittle bones. Plus, he's not well coordinated." In fact, at one point my mother did go to the principal of the school, and say, "What's going on here?" And the principal defended the students, and said, "Oh they're just saying 'Hi buddy.'" You know, like they were repeatedly breaking his arm because of over-friendliness.

I was about ten by that time. And I remember watching all this very carefully, and thinking to myself, "When I grow up I'm going to be in a profession that never lets this happen to anybody. I may not be able to do anything about it now, but just wait."

2

Institutions, Part 1

THE ACTIVISTS PROFILED IN CHAPTER 1 WERE AMONG THE MORE fortunate of their contemporaries. For although some of them endured extended hospitalizations or stints in rehabilitation institutions and all were affected by disability-based prejudice and stereotypes, all of them spent the greater part of their childhoods at home with their families. From the late 1800s well into the twentieth century, however, this was not the case for millions of people with disabilities. Because the consensus of "expert opinion" during that time was that people with disabilities, particularly those labeled "mentally retarded" or "mentally ill," should be institutionalized, having a disability often meant virtual lifelong imprisonment.

The nation's first residential institutions for people with disabilities were founded in the mid-nineteenth century by reformers such as Samuel Gridley Howe and Dorothea Dix. As Dix demonstrated in her fact-finding tours of Massachusetts in the 1840s, it was not uncommon for people with cognitive disabilities in particular, as well as people with cerebral palsy and epilepsy, to be abandoned by their families and end up as wards of the state, kept in prisons or almshouses or farmed out to those willing to provide for their care at the lowest possible cost to the taxpayer. Dix documented the result: instances of people chained to barn walls, locked into basements or attics, or kept in outdoor holding pens.[1] In contrast, state-run residential schools for the blind and chronic care facilities for people diagnosed as mentally ill or mentally retarded were meant to offer some modicum of physical comfort and safety, perhaps even the possibility of an education or treatment.

The impetus for the massive expansion of these institutions at the turn of the twentieth century, however, came from those who saw people with disabilities as a threat to the social order. For followers of the pseudo science of eugenics, these included those "feeble-minded" "moral imbeciles" who were by their very nature bound to be antisocial, not to mention sexually depraved, and thus likely to propagate more of "their kind." The "threat" posed by these individuals was believed to be exacerbated by the increasing urbanization and diversifying of society. "What is to be done with the feeble-minded progeny of the foreign hordes that have settled and are settling among us?" asked Walter Fernald, a leader of the Association of Medical Officers of American Institutions for Idiotic and Feeble-Minded Persons.[2] For Fernald and others like him the answer was obvious. Children with selected disabilities were to be isolated in institutions where they could be controlled and where they were to remain for the rest of their lives.

By the mid-twentieth century this institutional system had grown into an insular and extensive disability gulag. It was also absorbing a major part of public funds budgeted to provide for people with disabilities, creating both a physical infrastructure and—since it employed tens of thousands of non-disabled staff—a professional lobby that actively impeded the development of community-based services and integrated public school education.[3] Side by side with institutions for people labeled mentally retarded were those for people labeled mentally ill. Although their approach was perhaps more medical (few MR facilities purported to offer "treatment" for mental retardation), the institutions for the mentally ill were often equally brutal and dehumanizing. And for those people with disabilities who were not swept up into the state institutions and private mental hospitals, there were nursing homes and chronic care facilities, all of them isolated from the outside world, most if not all of them daily infringing on the civil and human rights of their residents.

This, then, was the context in which American disability rights activists came of age during the 1940s, '50s, and '60s. It was this reality that shaped the parents' movement of the 1950s and '60s and the independent living and psychiatric survivor movements of the 1970s and beyond.

Gunnar Dybwad
"You have no idea how awful it was."

———

Born in Leipzig in 1909, Gunnar Dybwad was one of the first people in the world to perceive disability as a civil rights issue. Earning his law degree from the University of Halle, Dybwad and his wife, Rosemary Fergusson Dybwad, left Germany after the rise of Hitler, moving first to the United Kingdom and then to the United States, where he studied at the New York School of Social Work. His first career was in penal reform, advocating for the humane treatment of children and juveniles caught up in the criminal justice and child welfare systems. But even as early as the 1930s, Dybwad saw what happened to people with disabilities who were consigned to state institutions. He wrote about one experience, a visit to the Letchworth Village Institution in New York in 1938: "On one adult ward I saw incontinent 'untidy' men lying in boxes of sawdust," while children were confined to "dormitories with 100 beds and 125 children in those beds." He described how the residents of such "state schools" were denied an education but were required to work on the institution's farms or in its workshops. "Here was my first object lesson that persons committed to a mental deficiency institution were denied the protection of the law, a lesson I would have to face time and again."[4]

Dybwad's immersion in disability rights began in 1957, when he was appointed executive director of the National Association for Retarded Children. Over the next five years, together he and Rosemary turned what had been a loose-knit network of parents' organizations into a national player in the disability rights movement.

After his official tenure ended in 1963, Dybwad maintained close contact with the NARC as he went on to a series of government and academic positions. In the late sixties and early seventies he earned an international reputation as one of the principal voices for deinstitutionalization and provided key testimony in a series of crucial disability rights suits filed in the federal courts. In the eighties and nineties, Dybwad became a mentor to the self-advocates movement, seeing it as altogether natural that people formerly labeled "mentally retarded" would want to shape their political as well as their personal lives.

Gunnar Dybwad died on September 13, 2001.

You talk about "mental disabilities," that's too fancy. This was a crude system, a crude system. I was complicit. I participated in some things I would be horror-stricken by today. But those were the early days, and what went on in those institutions is hard to imagine!

The overcrowding, first of all. All of the institutions had a dormitory and doors into the toilet. Then there were doors on the other side, and they opened to the day room. The day room was simply where you were during the day, the dormitory is where you were during the night, and that's the only difference. The day room had benches and heavy tables. There were some people who were naked all the time, although in the earliest days, that was less frequent. The staff in those days [the 1930s and 1940s] felt more responsible, so they kept people dressed. There was more discipline. Later on the staff began to feel less responsibility. "The hell with it!" And so you saw naked people.

I remember one Illinois institution where my colleagues took me on a tour. They had made a bet that I could not stay fifteen minutes. It was that stench. There was feces all over the place. However, I had more experience in these things than they thought. I knew that women's institutions were generally better, so I went to the women's part. It so happened that on that day there was a meeting of the cottage. There was a young, very attractively clothed headmistress, surrounded by forty or fifty naked women. It was an absolutely absurd situation.

Look, you get used to anything. You get used to the fact, for example, that these people have this horrible food to eat. It became an accepted pattern. In all these institutions there were social workers, PhD psychologists, who saw all these things. But they never said a mumbling word. It was just accepted. I have since pointed out that it might be appropriate if [mental retardation professionals] started each annual meeting with a session where they would confess their sins. Because they all knew what was going on, and they never did anything about it.

These mental deficiency institutions were, in most states, completely isolated. You have to understand that you didn't have departments of mental health with institutions carefully separated between juveniles and adults, and between mentally retarded—they would say mental defectives—and people with epilepsy, and those [with other disabilities]. Nobody cared about such differences. They were locked up in these dormitories, and they went down in the mornings—different institutions had different systems— but some people at the end of the day went down into the basement, got undressed, and then they went upstairs naked to the dormitory where they got the nightclothes. That way nobody could smuggle anything in.

Then also the concept was quite different, because in some places they were not only "disabled" people, but they were "wrong," so you treated them in a negative way, as if they had done something wrong.

You must not try to look too much for any, quote, system, unquote. Each state worked out its own system. You have no idea how awful it was in these old-fashioned dining rooms with the food as unappetizing as could be. It was a noise level that was unbelievable! It was tolerated. Nobody thought anything about it. You would search in vain for any kind of standards. You'd say, "What about the state department [of mental retarda-tion]?" Hell! There was no state department. In general, these people got an institution to run, whether through political influence, or not, makes no difference. They were to run these institutions as cheaply as possible, and as long as they didn't cause any trouble, nobody interfered.

Every once in a while there were some decent people, and they were not bothered by anybody, so they could have a very, we would now say, progressive system. There were cottage parents, and these tended to be married people, and they had this house within the larger institution, and if the woman was good, she usually was very, very good. It was an immaculately run place, pretty, with pictures on the wall and so on, and decent meals. In another institution, the famous Fernald School, where the Howe system[5] was still being used, the bell would ring, and the resi-dents came from the day room into the dining room. The bell would ring, and they would sit down. The bell would ring, and they said a prayer. The bell would ring, and the food was served. No word was spoken. Yet that was, in a way, a better system from the completely disorganized scream-ing mob I saw in other institutions.

Remember, parents were not allowed in the institutions. There were leaders in the parents' movement *who had never seen the dormitory where their child slept.* It boggles one's mind.

I know a story about one institution, where a parent took his child back from a home visit, and he delivered him to the door. Driving off, he saw, suddenly, in the rear-view mirror, a little package the mother had given the boy, still on the back seat, so he went back to the institution. Since the people knew him, they allowed him in, which the superinten-dent never would have done. And there was his boy naked, with the oth-ers. This father suddenly was in another world. The one thing you have to understand: the idiocy of it all. They were two different worlds, and there he was, naked without any reason.

The Partlow case[6] is one of those things that is hard to discuss. Com-mon decency kept me from really discussing what was going on. The residents had minimal services. They were let loose in these day rooms, and of course, weaker ones were continually abused—sexually abused, and so on. I was the lead witness in the case. That is where I made the statement that you couldn't possibly speak of "custodial care"—that was a famous statement by me—because "custody," in the minimum, implied a sense of safety and security, and nobody in that institution was safe and secure.

So you have to constantly keep aware that you're dealing with perverted circumstances which are incomprehensible to [ordinary] citizens. They can't understand it. One of my close colleagues had a son who is autistic. This son was beaten *every night* by staff in the institution. Brutally beaten. And you tell this to somebody [who isn't involved in the system], and they just say, "Eh. It's another guy who's spreading propaganda." They won't believe you.

Robert Perske
"We were utterly brilliant about breaking up parents from their kids."

Robert Perske was the chaplain at the Kansas Neurological Institute from 1959 to 1970. The KNI was officially founded in 1960 ostensibly to do research and therapy with people with cognitive disabilities, but Perske saw it develop into yet another residential "custodial care" institution. By the time Perske left, he was a fervid believer in deinstitutionalization and community-based services.

Since then, Perske has written novels, young adult books, and nonfiction, all of which explore some aspect of living with a cognitive disability. His work on behalf of people labeled "mentally retarded" who have been abused by the criminal justice system, chronicled in his book *Unequal Justice* (1991) was featured in a 1995 PBS documentary, *A Passion for Justice*.

Today, Perske continues to work as an advocate and, as he puts it, a "renegade reverend."

In those days doctors advised parents of so-called defective newborns not to take them home but to leave them at the hospital. Social workers would help to get those kids admitted to the institution, but of course promised no support at all to parents who wanted to keep their kids in the community.

Our reception and diagnostic unit would bring the parents of older kids in, and try to talk them into leaving the kids there. In departmental head meetings they'd say, 'This mother and father, how masochistic can they be? They want to keep their kid at home. . . .' I was brought in quite often by the superintendent, because I represented God. And so I'd sit at these meetings where the superintendent is talking to Joe and Mary about leaving their kid, and I had a pat statement that was effective: "Well, Billy is in *our* family now. You go on with your other kids and live a good life. Billy is in *our* family and he's fine."

These kids would pretty much stay there their entire lives, and over the years the institution got larger and larger. We had "A Ramp" for the severely and profoundly handicapped, we had "B Ramp" for the more ambulatory youngsters, we had "C Ramp" for the people who were pur-portedly severely mentally handicapped. One thing that puzzles me when I think back now is the fact that in those days almost every evaluation would say that this person is "mentally retarded, etiology unknown."

In "A Ramp," in the day room, there were large mats, like wrestling mats. People could be lifted out of their beds or cribs and laid out on the mats, so that if you came in there to visit, at eleven o'clock, they were all out there on the mats. And we didn't have air conditioning in those days, we had fans. We had a lot of open windows, and one of the things that I remember about that are the smells, oh God, and the flies.

We had a dining room, noisy as hell. Either people were wheeled in, or else they'd have the food cart brought to them. On "A Ramp," we'd feed everybody from the food cart. Not the kind of warm, enriching meal that you and I might have, and talk, and share. It was just, jam the food in his mouth. They did "bird feeding." I can't explain exactly how it's done, but that's where you hold the guy's chin back, and just pour the gruel down his throat. The only trouble with that is that with some of the kids, it entered the lungs, and a lot of these people died of pneumonia. Life was as close as the suctioning machine in some cases.

In each of these buildings, they had an area for beds. If there were forty people there, forty beds. There would be a kind of a partition be-tween it, and that was the aid station, and then in front was a day room, with benches or chairs or both, so that everybody had a bed, everybody had a seat. But they had no personal things, and the clothes they got were not always their own. I remember one kid who got postcards from his family, and—smart guy—he kept a rubber band around them, and put them in his back pocket, because there was no place for him to have any of his stuff that would be safe. The clothing and the washing, they didn't care too much if it was his or not. So that's all in that mix.

I remember one of the aides taught this one guy, a seventeen-year-old kid, to play chess. And he could beat anybody. He couldn't speak, but he could move his fingers. The aide trained him to do this right under the noses of all the "experts," the psychologists and everyone else. We had another guy there, who's now in a wheelchair, who had muscular dystrophy, and it was pretty obvious to all of us that he was a throwaway kid, and he was sent there to die because his mom and dad couldn't handle it. We had a lot of kids like that.

We didn't understand people with autistic spectrum disorders, but we had them all over the place. We didn't know what autism was. We didn't know what ADHD was. We certainly didn't know what fetal alcohol syndrome was, and Lord knows our institution had a lot of them, all of the behaviors that are symptomatic of people with fetal alcohol syndrome and fetal alcohol affect. We had no idea. We had a lot of people who were brain damaged from accidents, falls—they were jammed in there too. They all pretty much got the label "mental retardation."

I had three different chapels, and I insisted that they would be happy places where the kids could come. We did a lot of singing and a lot of laughing. I should write it up some day, but I can't look back that way. I just can't.

When one of our guys died, all that we'd have would be a graveside service. I would do my damnedest to get some of the caregivers to come out and be at the funeral, but the chief nurse of the place raised hell, and spouted a bunch of stuff about how that wasn't professional, and it never happened. So the way this would be done is that the undertaker, whom I got to know personally, would come up with the body in the limo, and we'd go to the cemetery, and he'd be saying things to me like, "Now Bob, this guy was a nonentity. Let's not take a lot of time." I'd stand at the head, and he'd stand at the foot, and I got a hold of a prayer book that had all kinds of prayers for the dead, and I read him that entire book while he just stood there. But I don't think he was mad about it. He knew I cared, and it was so wrong to not have any sort of service.

There were parents who came on weekends. It got better, because later on we were hoping the parents would keep contact, but in the very beginning we thought if the parents didn't come around, they were happy, and so we didn't have to deal with them. I mean, we were utterly brilliant about breaking up parents from their kids. And I had a hand in all of that.

Early on, about 1960, we had a nativity scene out on the lawn for the front door of the institution, where some of the kids from "B-Ramp," the, quote, "higher functioning kids," would sit out in the cold. One would be Mary holding the baby, and then there would be a Joseph, and some farm people brought in some sheep, and there were some bales of straw and some lights. The idea was that people could drive up this long lane up to the front building—and there were these kids—sometimes in real cold weather. There was a big gift box there, which people could drive by in their car, and drop gifts, of which we seldom saw, mainly because most of the gifts didn't fit our kids, like balsa wood model airplanes. Once in a while some sort of evil person would pack up something that was offensive, like a box of dog shit, and it would show up. I don't know what the goal would be, really, except that we had a lot of lights up there, and people could drive by, and maybe they would say, "Isn't that nice?" and look at those teenagers there, and maybe leave some gifts. It was a kind of a Christmas pilgrimage, and I did with a few expletives tell this particular supervisor what I thought about that nativity, and for a while I thought I was going to get fired.

There was a little kid who died in the dental chair. We had a dentist who came from outside, and this kid wouldn't sit still. He did all of this hyperactive stuff, which none of us really understood, so the dentist over-sedated him and killed him. And I had to go to his funeral, and have the service.

I remember one of our psychiatrists did an examination of some of the older kids transferred from Winfield [State Institution] and was blown away to find out that all of the males had been castrated. It was kind of a secret thing that we heard about. They had a place there where they used to keep the gonads in jars, and in our institution we had an area where we kept the brains of kids who had died in jars along a wall, in an area that was off-limits to inmates. But they knew what was in there. I remember when the kid died in the dental chair, there was a guy we called "Shotgun" because he was a sparky little guy. He kind of nudges me and says, "They got his brain in there yet?" And we did have some qualified researchers come in, and they had a brain-slicing machine, and they were doing some of the earlier work on Down syndrome.

There was a case where there was an abuser who was working sodomy on a kid, and the kid kept saying he was doing it, and nobody would believe it because, after all, he was disabled. And then the guy was caught. I gotta tell you, they didn't call the police. They fired him, quietly, and he turned up in another institution in the system.

In those days you never called the police, you never did anything, you just kind of covered it up. That reminds me of another one. He was on the night shift, and he had a cigarette lighter, one of the old square lighters made of stainless steel. And he used to heat that up, and we were finding a lot of people being branded on their buttocks. It was so incomprehensible. I was the department head, being the chaplain and everything, and I remember that they just knew that they had to get that guy out of there. But they didn't want any press, so they just quietly fired him.

Terry Schwartz
"They controlled everything we did."

Terrell Schwartz spent most of his childhood and young adulthood as a resident of the Fairview Training Center in Salem, Oregon. He left the institution in the mid-1960s to live in the community. His case manager, Dennis Heath, was instrumental in steering Schwartz into what would become People First of Oregon, at the vanguard of the self-advocacy movement. Schwartz became the second elected president of People First and together with Heath would, after the mid-1970s, spread the message of self-advocacy across the United States and later overseas. Schwartz is retired now, and continues to live in his own apartment in Salem.

I was born on March 7, 1947. My parents? Well, there's not too much I can tell you, because I haven't seen them in over twenty-one years. They dropped me off at Fairview when I was a kid, and I grew up out there.

Fairview's an institution, okay? The first place I lived there was like a dormitory. You had bed after bed. You could see it from one end to the other, side to side, on both sides, just a straight dormitory all the way through. That's all we had out there.

We didn't have no freedom, we didn't have no rights at all. They decided when we go to bed. We weren't allowed to take naps. We couldn't go to lie down on your own bed if you wanted to relax or take a little nap or something. They controlled everything we did. We're not allowed to have money. Or we're not allowed to do this, we're not allowed to do that.

I had to sneak off the cottages to do what I wanted. And I didn't care if I got into trouble or not. I mean who cares? They're not going to *kill* us.

They're not going to injure us, they're just going to spank us, that's about all. I mean, I snuck off the cottage so many times. So we're going to do what we want, as long as it's not wrong. Sneaking off the cottages was not wrong. I didn't care what they said.

There was a lot of abuse out there too, that was not supposed to be done. If they wanted to hurt us, they could hurt us. If they wanted to slap us down, spank us, why, it doesn't matter. If they done something real wrong, it's no big deal. They could do what they wanted and abuse people, whatever they wanted to do.

In 1961, they changed the rights of the residents there. We could talk about what we wanted, say what we wanted, or go do what we wanted, as long as it's not wrong. They trained people for different jobs, they drove them to work, out in the community, and then they go get them, and come back to Fairview. You had to work, you had to have a privilege if you want to go downtown. If you want to walk downtown on weekends, you can't. That's what I mean by control.

I didn't get out of there until 1965 or '66. They said back in the fifties, "You're never going to get out of Fairview. You're going to stay here for the rest of your life." And they found out we're smart enough—we took over Fairview. When most staff don't know how to work, a lot of times we do. And so they said, "Hey, these people are smarter than we think they are."

I was in a group home for a while. I was in a foster home for a while, like two years. And then after that I was in another group home. People came along, they wanted me to move into another group home, so I moved in there for a year and a half. And then I finally got out and got myself an apartment. That was in 1974, and I've been in my own apartment ever since.

Ted Chabasinski
"I would roam the hall looking for something . . . anything that would make the time pass."

———

Ted Chabasinski, born in March 1937, is something of a legend in the psychiatric survivor movement. Despite being abandoned as a child, despite the horrific brutalization he experienced during a childhood lived on the back wards of Bellevue and Rockland hospitals (the same Rockland Hospital, and during the same period, that provided the setting for Allen Ginsberg's *Howl*), he has been able not only to rebuild his identity and assume a place in the community but to advocate for others. Since 1971 he has been a nationally prominent activist and organizer, eventually becoming the directing attorney for Mental Health Consumer Concerns (MHCC), a group founded by Jay Mahler in Martinez, California. Along the way he was also the lead organizer of the 1982 campaign to convince voters in Berkeley to ban the use of electroshock "treatment" within the city limits.

Chabasinski is retired from his position at MHCC, but continues to live in California and remains active in the psychiatric survivor movement. What follows is an excerpt from his first-person account of his childhood featured on the MindFreedom website, www.mindfreedom.org. Mind Freedom International, based in Eugene, Oregon, is a coalition of nonprofit and grassroots organizations dedicated to winning "human rights and alternatives for people labeled with psychiatric disabilities."

Psychiatrists and social workers had already decided before I was born that I was going to be a mental patient. My natural mother had been locked up just before she gave birth to me and was locked up again soon after. The social worker from the Foundling Hospital told my foster parents that my mother was "peculiar," and Miss Callaghan soon had them looking for symptoms in me too. Every month Miss Callaghan would come and discuss my "problems" with my foster parents. If I only wanted to stay in the back yard with my sister and make mud pies, this was a sign that I was too passive and withdrawn, and my mommy and daddy were supposed to encourage me to explore the neighborhood more. When I started to wander around the neighborhood, I went to a neighbor's garden and picked some flowers. The neighbor complained, and Miss Callaghan held a long session with my parents about curbing my "hostile" impulses.

When Miss Callaghan had discovered enough "symptoms," I was sent to the Bellevue children's psychiatric ward, to be officially diagnosed and to be made an experimental animal for Doctor Bender. I was one of the first children to be "treated" with electric shock. I was six years old.

It took three attendants to hold me. At first Doctor Bender himself threw the switch, but later when I was no longer an interesting case, my tormenter was different each time.

I wanted to die but I really didn't know what death was. I knew that it was something terrible. Maybe I'll be so tired after the next shock treatment I won't ever get up, and I'll be dead. But I always got up. Something in me beyond my wishes made me put myself together again.

I memorized my name, I taught myself to say my name. "Teddy, Teddy, I'm Teddy . . . I'm here, I'm here in this room, in this hospital. And my mommy's gone." I would cry and realize how dizzy I was.

I spent my seventh birthday this way, and my eighth and ninth birthdays, locked in seclusion at Rockland State Hospital. I had learned the best way to endure this was to sleep as much as possible, and sleeping was all I could do anyway. I was in a constant state of exhaustion, and I began to have colds that lasted all year because the more sadistic attendants would turn off the radiator and open the window, even in December. Doctor Sobel said it was a sign of my sickness that I didn't like fresh air.

Sometimes the attendants would leave the door to my room unlocked while the rest of the kids went to the dining room. I would roam the hall looking for something to read, something to look at, to play with, anything that would make the time pass, anything I could use to keep myself distracted. I would save part of my food and think for hours of when I would eat it. Sometimes mice would run through the room, along the walls, and I would watch them carefully and try not to scare them. I wished that I were small enough to run under the door like they could. Sometimes there was nothing to eat in the room, nothing at all, and I would lie on the mattress and cry. I would try to fall asleep, but I couldn't sleep twenty-four hours a day, and I couldn't stand the dreams.

I would curl into a ball, clutching my knees, and rock back and forth on the mattress, trying to comfort myself. And I cried and cried, hoping someone would come. I'll be good, I said. And the attendant would stare at me unexpectedly through the little window with wires in it so I couldn't break the glass and kill myself. Every few days, Doctor Clardy would come in surrounded by attendants and tell me that I had to learn to "adjust." "Well adjusted" was a phrase that Doctor Clardy used often. By the age of ten, I had adjusted well to being in solitary confinement.

And so I spent my childhood waking from nightmare to nightmare in locked rooms with scraps of torn comic books and crusts of bread and my friends the mice, and no one to tell me who I was. When I was seventeen and the shrinks thought they had destroyed me, they set me free.

I was free.

3
Discrimination, Part 1

BEFORE THE ADVENT OF THE DISABILITY RIGHTS MOVEMENT, DIS-crimination against a person with a disability, regardless of skill or circumstance, simply on the grounds that he or she was "handicapped," was legal in the United States. This meant, for example, that public schools could—and routinely did—refuse to allow a child with a disability to attend classes, even though by definition they had an obligation to educate "every" child in the community and even though the child's parents might still be obligated to pay school taxes. It meant that a landlord could refuse to rent to someone because that person was blind or deaf or because his or her spouse or child had a disability. It meant that employers could, and did, fire people who may have been productive employees, simply because that employee's epilepsy or mental illness had somehow become known.

Beyond this overt bias, people with disabilities faced (and to a large extent still confront) forms of discrimination unique to their situation. It may not be the intent of a business purposely to exclude someone who uses a wheelchair, but the fact that the business is located at the top of a flight of stairs effectively precludes such a person from shopping, visiting, or working there. Similarly, in the years before the movement, municipal mass transit systems believed that they were under no obligation to provide mainline access. In an era before curb cuts, even sidewalks were obstacles to navigating a wheelchair literally from one block to the next.

Finally, people with disabilities were and sometimes still are subjected to another, more subtle type of discrimination in the form of condescension, the patronizing attitude that allowed non-disabled people to pat a disabled adult on the head or otherwise treat people with disabilities like children.

Many of the early leaders of the movement endured years of such treatment before realizing that what they were experiencing was what we now term "ableism"—and that it was the product of societal misconceptions and attitudes rather than any personal shortcoming of their own.

Denise Karuth
"If you're blind, what are you doing in this class?"

Like Barbara Oswald, Denise Karuth was born prematurely and emerged from her months in an incubator with damage to her eyes, rendering her legally blind. Like Johnnie Lacy, whose story is told later in this chapter, she wanted initially to be a teacher of children with disabilities. Thwarted in that goal by discrimination, she thought of seeking employment helping in the rehabilitation of people with visual disabilities. But here, too, she was stymied by the attitude—prevalent at the time—that people with disabilities were the least likely to know what was best for themselves and for those in their peer community.

Karuth was born in 1954, in Buffalo, New York. She moved to Boston in 1976 and began her involvement with the disability rights movement there. She became a wheelchair user in the early 1980s because of multiple sclerosis. A self-taught expert on the issue of accessible mass transit, she was appointed by Governor Michael Dukakis to head his Commission on Accessible Transportation from 1984 to 1988. She was also a founding member and chair of the Massachusetts Coalition of Citizens with Disabilities and a former member and chair of the Massachusetts Statewide Independent Living Council. Karuth now works as a grant writer for the Stavros Center for Independent Living in Amherst, Massachusetts, and is studying to become an ordained minister with the United Church of Christ.

When I was an undergraduate I decided to do a major in what was then called "exceptional education." A lot of this came out of the way I'd been treated as a legally blind kid in the public schools. Basically I wasn't offered any accommodation at all, at least not consistently. I was always a good student, but in math or science, if you can't see the blackboard it's a real problem, and in English or history, if you can't read the books or take the tests in the allotted time, it doesn't matter how hard you try to study. There wasn't even the admission that I was at all disabled until the end of my junior year in high school, when I took the New York State Regents' Exams in large print without time limits. I did really well!

I didn't learn that I was legally blind until I was in college, even though I wore these incredibly thick glasses, even though I was having accidents, like falling down stairs and almost walking into the side of a school bus. When I was little my ophthalmologist told my parents, "She'll never drive a car, but she can see," and that's the last thing anyone said about it. Everyone treated me like a tremendous klutz, like I wasn't paying attention. When I was in fourth grade and took an eye test in school the nurse threatened, "You'd better do better next year or we'll send you away to the school for the blind."

Anyway, when I got to college I started getting services from the state Office of Vocational Rehabilitation. I had some mobility training, learned how to use a guide cane, started learning Braille, started using readers to read my textbooks, and using what was then called Recordings for the Blind, which was this private nonprofit that loaned out tapes of textbooks, and even recorded textbooks for you, providing you sent them two copies, of which they would keep one.

I enrolled in this "introduction to exceptional education" course. I was actually a music major, but I thought maybe I could combine the two. There weren't any public colleges offering degrees in "music therapy" back then, but I had this notion that I'd like to use music as a way to reach out to kids like myself, kids who were "special"—meaning disabled—and as a result were having problems in school, and socially. Because another big part of being blind—and having no one acknowledge it—was that I was a social pariah. The other kids knew I was different. My team almost always lost in gym class until I figured out how to avoid taking my turn at bat. And having thick glasses and asking to sit in the front row in class didn't help—it made the other kids resent me. In junior high, kids learned they could beat me up in the halls providing they didn't make any identifying sounds. People did all kinds of mean things to me. There were times I was humiliated enough to want to kill myself, especially when I was a little kid, except I couldn't figure out a way to do it that was guaranteed to work.

So I enrolled in this college class, and during one of the sessions there was some discussion about kids with visual disabilities, and what to do about a kid who had a progressive eye disease and was gradually losing his sight. The textbook said that the best thing you could do was not to tell the child at all. I wish I could remember the exact words. It was something like, a) it's too horrible to tell a kid that they're going blind, b) modern science is improving all the time, and who knows? they might come up with a cure, and c) besides, the kid probably realizes it anyway.

I thought this was terrible advice, and I said so in class. The instructor and I got into a big argument about it, where I said if no one says anything about it the kid is going to be confused by her experience. They may think they're losing their mind, because the world is disappearing. And that the earlier kids know what is happening, the earlier they can begin acquiring the skills needed to make their way in the world. I said that it's better to use large print books and do well in school than to pretend to be "normal" and flunk out, better to use a guide cane or an assistance dog than to walk off the edge of a subway platform. And the teacher argued vehemently against that. Expert opinion, he said, sided with always keeping this sort of bad news away from a child.

After the class I went up to him and I said, "You know, I'm legally blind. I've been through this. This textbook is really wrong." But it was his response that really shocked me. He said, "If you're blind, what are you doing in this class?" He all but told me I should quit right then and there. That he was skeptical that I could do the work (though I had been all term), and that, even if I could, I'd never be able to get a job in "the real world"—and besides, I was obviously "too emotionally involved" in the subject to be able to be of much help to disabled kids. Except of course nobody talked about "disability" or "children with disabilities" back then. It was "exceptional children."

I stuck it out for that course, but I began to worry about my prospects as a teacher. So I told my counselor at the state voc rehab commission that I wanted to get my Master's degree in rehab counseling. He told me the state wouldn't fund it. They didn't hire blind rehab counselors, he said, because they couldn't drive to visit their clients.

So I ended up getting a BA in music. Then I moved to Boston, partly because I'd learned that the Mass. Commission for the Blind hired blind people. So I got my Masters in rehabilitation counseling in Boston, and ended up running a peer counseling organization for people with disabilities and chronic illness.

What I remember most is that feeling of outrage, that people—future teachers—were being taught essentially to be cruel, to withhold information from kids like me, to keep them in the dark about their own lives and realities, instead of giving them the help they needed. And second, that my input, my experience, could be dismissed like that: "Oh, you're too emotionally involved," or "The state doesn't hire blind rehab counselors."

At the time I didn't see how I had any recourse. And probably back then, I didn't, since [Section] 504 [the anti-discrimination clause in the Rehabilitation Act of 1973] was pretty new, and there wasn't good enforcement. Nowadays, to write and say such things would be, I would hope, completely unacceptable. But back then, lying to disabled kids, and discriminating against disabled adults, was just par for the course.

Mary Lou Breslin
"They're keeping you out because you have a disability."

Mary Lou Breslin is one of the premier disability rights advocates of the 1970s and '80s and a cofounder of the Disability Rights Education and Defense Fund (DREDF) in Berkeley, California. Breslin is not an attorney, yet she likely knows as much about the ins and outs of disability rights law as anyone. She is a senior adviser with DREDF and one of the nation's leading disability policy advocates.

Breslin was born in October 1944; she contracted polio at age eleven. Although her family was affluent, Breslin nevertheless had to confront the usual attitudinal and physical barriers faced by people with obvious physical disabilities. Without the framing narrative of a national disability rights movement, it took her some time to realize that what she was experiencing was, actually, discrimination. Once she had this epiphany, however, Breslin, like others of her generation, moved to absorb the lessons and adapt the strategies of the African American and women's civil rights movements that had come before.

We all have a million stories. Mine were almost always barrier kinds of issues. I applied at one time to be a juvenile probation officer because it was one of those things that I met the qualifications for. I went through the whole application and the initial series of interviews, and I went in for the last interview—the third in a series of interviews—and met with a woman who was going to be making selections for a final, small candidate pool.

I was pretty confident I could handle the tasks of the job, most of which were administrative, and almost all of which had to be done in an office and did not involve a lot of traveling. What I recall of the interview was really the interviewer's belief in her own perception of me. And that perception was that I was too fragile, too vulnerable. How could I cope with a bunch of bad-ass kids, juvenile delinquents?

This was not what was said, but she did say she thought that because of my handicap I would not be able to handle the job. And we discussed some of the details of what the day would look like on the job, and the majority of it, as I say, had to do with working in an office and dealing with phones and having people come in for their appointments. There would be some court appearance requirements, working up investigations into kids' backgrounds, and so on. None of it was the kind of thing that I couldn't absolutely have done, and only a few occasions where I would be required to go someplace. I could certainly have done that as well—I was driving, and I could have gotten there.

I was a client of the Department of Rehab at the time, and there was nothing they could offer me other than job placement services, which were fairly pitiful and ineffective. I remember that my rehab counselor was in the same building as the interviewer for this job, and I went downstairs to my rehab counselor's office and said, "Can you believe this? This thing came up, I was interviewed, and I wasn't hired." He said, "That job probably wouldn't have been appropriate for you anyway, because there might have been some question of your being in danger." Where am I going to be in danger? Some kids are going to come in my office and shoot me? I'm not any more in danger than anybody else.

I guess I make that point because those perceptions were widespread within the rehab profession as well as among employers.

My friends and I used to go to the late movies on the North Side [of Chicago]. A little theater with great first-run art films; you couldn't see them anyplace else. We had such a hard time there. We would steel ourselves, the three or four of us, because every time we would go there would be a fight over, number one, just selling me a ticket, and number two, where I could sit. I was forced to get out of the chair and sit in a seat, and they took the chair away, and if I refused the manager would come and physically haul me out into the street.

I remember standing on the street with my friend one evening, and it was late and raining, and we were probably stoned. We were gnashing our teeth getting ready to go to battle because we really wanted to see whatever it was that was playing. My friend said, "You know, this is discrimination. This is plain old discrimination." I remember saying to him, "What are you talking about? That's stuff that happens to black people. It's not applicable to me." He says, "You're wrong. This is a place that you should be able to go in. They're keeping you out because you have a disability."

It was a very insightful moment that came and went, and twenty years later I figured out that he was right. I didn't get the analogy—I understood discrimination in race, I even understood it pretty much in gender. I didn't get it in disability; I just didn't get that it was the same thing.

Carolyn Thompson
"We can't use somebody like you."

Carolyn Thompson has what she calls "a facial difference." Some people, certainly the medical texts, would call it "disfigurement." In medical terms Thompson was born with "a cavernous hemangioma, a tumor of the blood vessels" on the left side of her face. Because the tumor was pressing against her eye, and made it difficult for her to nurse, the doctors in Corpus Christi, Texas, decided to treat it with radiation.

"In the early 1940s radiation was seen as the new magic cure for many things," she recalls. "The radiation zapped the tumor cells, and the whole thing receded, and I went home after six weeks. But the radiation affected the growth on that whole side of my face, resulting in asymmetry, partial paralysis, and complex dental problems. Otherwise, I developed fine, walking, talking, all those things."

Indeed, aside from a slight speech difference, some difficulty chewing food, and the loss of central vision in her left eye, Thompson might not be considered "disabled" at all, if disability is defined as a physical or mental difference significantly affecting a major life activity. Rather, it has been the response to her difference by others that has proved to be for her the greatest difficulty.

Carolyn Thompson was born in December 1940, in Freer, Texas. She returned to school in her mid-fifties to earn a Master of Divinity degree and works with

churches and ecumenical organizations on disability and access issues. Now retired, she also spent many years as Disability Project Coordinator at the Cambridge Commission for Persons with Disabilities in Cambridge, Massachusetts.

I know my facial difference had an impact on my ability to get jobs. There
were certain jobs I never even considered applying for because I just figured I wouldn't get them. Like a front office receptionist, which at least
in the past was basically, "we need a pretty woman in this position." A
smiling face, you know? I tried a few times to get jobs, like sales clerking
during the holiday season, and never got anything.

After college I taught fifth grade in a rural county school for a year
and took courses for certification in elementary education. I got married
and moved to Austin, Texas. I went to work for the IRS, but I wanted a
job teaching. I applied for a job opening and took time off from work to
go for this interview at an elementary school. I went and I talked to the
principal. I had my resume, and he asked some questions, and somehow
in the conversation it came up that I'd spent time on the Texas coast. After that he went on and on about going there fishing, and stuff like that. I
finally wrapped up the interview myself. It was like he didn't know how
to wrap it up, how to bring it to some closure, and was avoiding talking
about the teaching position.

I had been told by the superintendent that the process was that you
went and interviewed with the principal, and then he got back to the superintendent, and then they would call and let you know. And they were
supposed to call me that afternoon.

I got home from work, and they didn't call, and they didn't call. I tried
to call the office, and first I got no answer. I called back again thirty minutes before they closed. And then I called again. I was told that the people I needed to talk to weren't there. So I said, "Well, I had this interview
today with the principal and I was told that they would be in touch with
me this afternoon." And they said, "Just a minute." And then some man,
I want to say the superintendent but it may have been somebody else, got
on the line, and he said, "Miss Thompson, we can't use somebody like
you." And I think he said something like, "with your appearance." And,
you know, they were trying to avoid getting back in touch with me.

I see that very clearly, the discrimination against me because of how
I look. That was also back when they would fire any woman if she got

pregnant when she was teaching. You could not appear in the classroom pregnant. So there were a lot of ideas about what you had to look like, and how you had to be.

There are different mannerisms, there are different things people sometimes do when talking to me. I remember I was talking with this man who came as a speaker to our church back in Austin, and we were chatting, and the whole time he was talking to me, he had his hand up and was feeling the side of his face. And I've noticed that with some other people. I don't think they realize they're doing it, but I think subconsciously they're looking at somebody, and their face looks differently, and they're feeling their own face because some part of their brain is trying to figure out how their face is different from my face, or mine is different from theirs.

Johnnie Lacy
"The only reason that you are able to take . . . advantage is because I have a disability."

Johnnie Lacy, born in 1937, experienced discrimination several times over: as a girl and a woman, as an African American, and then, after contracting polio in 1956, as a person with a disability. She was in nursing school when she became ill, after attending racially segregated schools in Arkansas, Louisiana, and California. It was these experiences of racial discrimination in particular that motivated her to become a civil rights and anti-poverty activist.

Her disability rights awareness would come later. As for many activists of her generation, for Lacy the idea of disability as a civil rights issue was sparked by the HEW sit-in in San Francisco in 1977. It became clear to her then, but only in retrospect, that she had been discriminated against because of her disability, and continued to be.

Lacy served as the first executive director of Community Resources for Independent Living in Haywood, California, from 1981 until her retirement in 1994. She died on November 15, 2010.

I started at San Francisco State in the spring semester of 1958. None of the buildings were accessible. I was pushed, literally pushed, initially by my cousin and then by people that I hired to push me. They would push me to my class, leave me there, and then they'd come back and push me to my next class.

I learned to drift downhill in my push chair. It was right-arm drive. At that time, right-arm drives had steel bars that ran from one wheel to another, and sometimes this bar would kind of work its way out. Unluckily for me, my bar came loose just as I was going past the administration building, and an administrator must have looked out as I stopped the chair with my one hand and kind of was struggling with it a little bit, but managed.

The following week, in the student newspaper, there was a letter from the chancellor saying that students who used wheelchairs were not any longer allowed to be on the campus by themselves, and since I was only one of two people in wheelchairs on the campus, it had to be me that they were referring to. . . . I ignored it and proceeded to continue, without even a second thought. I got really good at that.

. . . At first [the discrimination] was subtle, I think mostly because I had the attitude that I would give people the benefit of the doubt. I'd prefer to believe that they believed in me as opposed to that they didn't believe in me. It became much clearer as I went through my classes that this was not always true. As part of my preparation for special ed, for example, I had this special ed teacher, and I learned later on that special ed people are probably the most prejudiced in terms of disabilities. She insisted on calling disabled people "cripples" because the Masonic Hospital for Crippled Children used the name and therefore it was a bona fide name. I objected to it, and I did it loudly and in class. When she used the word "crippled," I would raise my hand and I'd say, "I don't want to be identified as crippled. I want to be as identified as handicapped," which was the word of choice at that time.

I did very well in all my special ed classes. I had taken a class from the director of the program, and had done well in that class, and he knew that I wanted to major in speech therapy. He started a campaign to discourage me. He said that the conditions for people in wheelchairs were not good, that a person with my severe disability would not be able to drive. They would be expected to go to the dark corners of schools and buildings that had stairs, there would be no accommodation, and he couldn't see any way in which I would be able to successfully become a speech therapist.

When I insisted, in order to convince me, he called together a panel of experts in the special education field from all over the Bay Area. I can remember people who were heads of special ed departments, professors in special ed, just a myriad of folks. The purpose of this group was supposedly to examine my potential as a possible speech therapist. What it turned out to be was a panel to discourage me from applying to the school. After I met with this panel, they all agreed that I could not do this. And the head of the department by this time said, "If you apply, I will not accept you. And the only other alternative you have is that you can take graduate courses on your own and work on your own, but you will not become a part of the department."

So it made me bitter in terms of the way I was treated, and not given an opportunity to show that I could do it, in spite of the fact that I reminded them that I had spent two and a half years on this campus and that nobody expected me to succeed in that and that I had. I reminded him also that I had done well in all of the special ed classes that I had taken. And so if I could do that, I could certainly do other things. I said I could learn to drive, even. He doubted that very seriously.

My final and departing shot to him was that if I were just a woman, he could not do this to me; if I were only a person of color, he would not be able to do this to me; and my conclusion was that the only reason that you are able to take this unfair advantage is because I have a disability. And he got really upset and walked away. But that was my final shot with him.

Tony Coelho
"No son of ours has epilepsy."

When the National Council on Disability needed a member of Congress to introduce its first version of the Americans with Disabilities Act in 1988, it turned to Rep. Tony Coelho (D-CA). First elected to Congress in 1978, by this time Coelho, as House Democratic whip, had become one of its most influential members, known for his ability to shepherd bills through the intricacies of the legislative process.

Anthony Coelho was born on June 15, 1942, in Los Banos, California, and grew up working on the family's dairy farm.

"We had three hundred dairy cattle, which is a lot of cows, and we had an old fashioned tail-to-tail barn. We'd get up at two-thirty in the morning and milk until eight o'clock, and then have what I used to call 'a Portuguese bath.' You take a wash cloth and wash off real quick and eat real quick and drive into school, which started at nine."

Coelho's Portuguese background would figure prominently in how his family responded to the onset of his epilepsy. His epilepsy again became an issue when, during his first campaign for Congress in 1978, his Republican opponent charged that a Congressman with epilepsy might embarrass his constituents by having a seizure at the White House. Asked by the press for a response, Coelho famously replied, "In the thirteen years I have served in Washington I knew a lot of people who went to the White House and had fits. At least I'd have an excuse."

Coelho left Congress in 1989 but continued to push for the ADA until its passage in 1990. Since then he has continued to be an advocate for disability rights.

What happened is that on the dairy farm one day I was with this hired hand we had. Walt was driving, and we were going down the canal bank, and he was speeding. We were going around a curve and he overreacted, and the pickup flipped and went into the canal. I hit my head on the windshield, and I remember the passenger side window was open and when the pickup went down I floated out that window. But we both were alive. I had this headache, and he didn't get hurt. I always joke about I wasn't worried about that end of my anatomy; it was the other end, because we totaled the pickup and I knew what that meant.

We didn't go to the doctor. You didn't do those things. And the headache went away in a day or so, and then a year later, about my junior year in high school, I was in the barn milking in the afternoon. We didn't have automatic feeders in those days. You had to reach down in a big wastepaper can, and you'd pick up a scoop of grain and put it in the bin for the cow to eat while you're milking her. And I remember going down, and that's all I remember. I just passed out in the grain can. My brother was in the barn milking at the same time, and he noticed me go in, and he started screaming and picked me up and carried me to the house.

My mother called the doctor. I'm waking up and a doctor is sitting on me. I thought that was rather strange. But I was having a seizure—having convulsions—and so the doctor was sitting on me. When I came to, he got up and I felt suffocated and I was exhausted. I asked what had happened, and so they told me I had just passed out. Now what I didn't know is that the doctor had told them that he thought that I had an epileptic seizure.

And so the next day I went in for tests, and the tests supposedly were inconclusive, which they weren't. My parents didn't tell me; and the reason they didn't, I found out later, was that they believed that if you had epilepsy it meant that you were possessed by the devil. It's a cultural thing, and it's something that people in a lot of different cultures still believe.

And so I continued to go to doctors, and they supposedly didn't know. And then all of a sudden I went to witch doctors. The Portuguese believed in witch doctors. The first one I went to was a black woman in Merced, and we go up to this house and go in, and it's a real small, poor little house. I walk in and it's scary to begin with. I had never been in a black person's home. When I got in there my mother and the woman talked. They didn't know each other but she was recommended by a priest. My mother paid her, and so the woman pulls down all the shades and has me lay down, and she has some candles lit, and then she pours hot oil on my forehead and opens my shirt and pours the hot oil on my chest and gets a candle and puts it on my chest to burn and then starts praying in strange tongues. And it was scary as hell. I wasn't frightened of her, but I was just frightened about the unknown—what was this all about?

It was just so contrary to everything I believed in. All of a sudden there was something wrong with me. I mean so I had seizures; I didn't think there was anything wrong with me. I'm seventeen, and I'm a good student, and I'm student body president my senior year. I milked cows and I danced, I partied, I went to school, I got good grades, I was active. I was a *normal* human being and all of a sudden I'm put in this place and told I'm abnormal—something is wrong with me. And it was a very negative experience for me.

Then I was told I had to drink a bunch of teas and junk, and so I did all that. Went back I think twice, but of course the evil spirits were still there. I didn't know they were evil spirits, but I was still having my problem—whatever my problem was. Went to another witch doctor because obviously this one didn't work. Then I went to a third one, and it was a Portuguese guy, who only spoke Portuguese, and basically the same thing, the candles and the room dark. One witch doctor had you take a chicken egg and you had to keep it covered and rub it and put it on your chest. And if it turned rotten, then the evil spirits were still there. If it didn't turn rotten then they had left. Well, you know, give me a break; the egg is going to turn rotten. I mean, there's no way around it, so the evil spirits never went away.

All of a sudden I realized what was going on here, and I thought, "Geez, they're saying in effect that I'm possessed," you know? So at the end of this session he says to my mother in Portuguese, "I can't help him." And in Portuguese, she says, "Why?" "He doesn't believe in my power to heal him. And I can't help somebody who doesn't believe."

So that was it. We walk out and get in the car and my mother says, "What's wrong with you?" And I said, "What do you mean?" "How come you don't believe?" I said, "I just don't, and I don't want to ever go back to another one again." And that was it; I never went back to another one.

During that period I was suddenly excluded from public events. My brothers and I used to show cattle at county fairs. For some reason, my mother never filled out my forms in time. "Oh, I forgot; I didn't know you wanted to go." So all of a sudden, I'm no longer going to public events where I could have a seizure. What was happening, which I didn't know until much later, is that in the Portuguese culture, the reason you're possessed is because somebody in the family has committed some major sin. It's a reflection on the family. God has punished this family through the individual—in this case me—for something they did that upset Him. The suspicion was that somebody in the family had had sex with an animal; and if you think that through—my God—that's a hell of a burden for the family to have. And of course, I knew none of this. I had no idea that all this was transpiring with my family, but I can understand now why they didn't want me to have a seizure in public.

When it comes time to go to college, my family is saying, "You can't go." They can't afford it—blah, blah—but a lot of it was dealing with the epilepsy. They didn't want me to have seizures in public. Little did I know, because I never took my seizures that seriously. I still didn't know it was epilepsy. So I'd pass out and after I'd get up, I'd function. And so I graduated from high school and went onto college.

I continued to have seizures. I'd have them with my roommate or if I was out with people, and I would tell people that I pass out periodically, and I'd laugh—no big deal. It never stopped me from doing anything. I still had great grades. I was active in student government. I ended up being student body president and so forth, and so nothing prevented me from doing what I wanted to do. I dated and all that stuff.

My first traumatic experience was the assassination of John Kennedy, in my junior year. I wasn't political. I just loved John Kennedy—the fact that he was young, that he was Catholic, a Democrat of course. I loved that he was so articulate, and it made me proud. I was social chairman at the school, and I went into the dean's office. We understood that Kennedy was in the hospital, and they were trying to save him. And so the dean and I decided to all go into church, and we had the bells ring. And the chapel was full and out onto the street outside and the gardens below and the lawn—everybody kneeling and praying. And of course we were told he died. I didn't do anything for five days. I just watched TV, as most Americans did. But at the end of it I decided that if he could give up his life for the country, I needed to do something to help people as well. I decided to become a Catholic priest.

I remember a couple weeks after graduating from college going for my physical to go in the seminary. I go into this doctor's office—Dr. John Doyle, Sr., about seventy years old. He's doing all these different tests and so forth. He says at one point, "Tony; have you ever had headaches or passing out spells or anything like that?" I said. "Oh yeah, all the time." "Have you ever been to a doctor for them?" I said, "Oh yeah, I went to a lot of doctors and none of them knew what it was." He said, "Did anybody ever tell you that you have epilepsy?" I had never heard the word. And so he explained to me what it was. "You have epilepsy." He said all the tests showed it.

And he said, "Let me tell you some good news and some bad news. The good news," this is June of '64, "is that you're 4-F, and you can't serve in the military. The bad news is that you have epilepsy and under Canon Law, the Church says you can't be a priest. So you can't go in the seminary." It wasn't like he was giving an opinion; it was a fact.

I remember very vividly walking out of the doctor's office thinking. "Okay, so I just go on with my life." I was disappointed because being a priest is what I really wanted to do—I wanted to help people. But I remember walking out of the doctor's office and going to my car and thinking that nothing had changed, and what I didn't realize is that at that very moment I hadn't changed, but everything around me had.

And then it started coming at me. I called my parents and said, "I know what my problem is. I went to this doctor and I have epilepsy." Well, my mother immediately said—I probably just got the words out of my mouth—she said, "No son of ours has epilepsy." And it was absolutely just not discussable. It was not how are you feeling or—. Just, "No son of ours has epilepsy." And I of course had no idea about the stigma. I had no idea.

So I remember hanging up the phone, devastated and mad, but I already had grown a little bit apart [from my parents]—I did care, but I didn't really care. But then a week later I get a notice in the mail that my driver's license was revoked. I had not been told that that would happen.

I had just turned twenty-two and I was told about my epilepsy on my twenty-second birthday, June 15th, as a matter of fact, and I remember saying the hell with that; I'm going to drive anyway because it's Los Angeles. You can't get around Los Angeles without a car. So I drove without my license. My insurance was taken away, and all of a sudden I realized there was something going on here—that it was serious.

I had been student body president and doing a lot of things. I had people recruit me to go to work after I graduated, until I made a decision to go in the Jesuits. All of a sudden, the word *epilepsy* was on every job application. I had never seen the word before, and all of a sudden it was everywhere. So I checked it, and nobody wanted to talk to me after that. I never got the callback, and I knew that it was because of the epilepsy.

I started drinking at this point, and I would be drunk by 3 o'clock every day. I'd go to Griffith Park in Los Angeles, and I'd be thinking "woe is me," which was so unusual for me because I don't believe in "woe is me." I was feeling sorry for myself. I thought that everything I had ever loved in my life had turned against me. I loved my church, and I loved what it symbolized and everything about it. But I thought God and my church had turned against me, and I couldn't understand that. And there was really nobody to talk to; that's what was shocking.

I internalized it all. It just came on me and really strong.

4
Institutions, Part 2

N OT ALL OF THE PEOPLE WHO WERE INSTITUTIONALIZED ENTERED the institutions as children. Nor were they all institutionalized against their will. And though the worst of the massive state institutions offered only "custodial care," or in the case of the larger mental institutions "milieu therapy" (just being confined in such a place was alleged to be therapeutic), other facilities did indeed offer needed services—rehabilitation from spinal cord injury or polio, education, even peer support.

Nevertheless, the potential for abuse was always there, along with separation from family and segregation from the community. Before the disability rights and independent living movements the approach of even the most enlightened rehab facilities was to treat people with disabilities not as consumers who knew what was best for themselves and could therefore make informed decisions but as essentially flawed people who needed "structure" and "direction" and "therapy"—even if, sometimes especially if, the individual thought differently.

Leonard Roy Frank

"If ever I had the chance to stop the use of shock 'treatment' I would do so—whatever it took."

There are few disability documents as disturbingly comical as "The Frank Papers." These are the collected psychiatric records of Leonard Roy Frank, who, beginning in the fall of 1962, was diagnosed as "paranoid schizophrenic," institutionalized for eight months, and subjected against his will to fifty rounds of "insulin coma therapy," with powerful electric shocks administered to his brain during thirty-five of those sessions. The papers, which Frank obtained twelve years later, were published in 1976 in neurologist John Friedberg's *Shock*

Treatment Is Not Good for Your Brain, by which time Frank had become an outspoken critic of the psychiatric system, most especially of electroshock and forced drugging.

Part of what makes the documents both comical and disturbing is the fact that the "symptoms" on which the diagnosis was based included such "crazy" behaviors as Frank's becoming a vegetarian, growing a beard, and immersing himself in the works of Mohandas Gandhi, Henry David Thoreau, and Arnold Toynbee, not to mention the Hebrew and Christian scriptures. Frank's "experiments in truth"—as Gandhi might have described them—would become familiar to mainstream America as part of the counterculture that emerged during the middle and late 1960s. But in October 1962, while the "sane" world came close to nuclear Armageddon during the Cuban missile crisis, Frank's interests and alternative lifestyle were seen by mental health professionals as symptoms of a psychotic condition. Who else but a lunatic would give up his occupation as a real estate broker and undergo a period of study and reflection with the aim of becoming a better human being? As for his claims that eating meat not only undermined a person's health but also harmed the environment, well, that, the doctors concluded, was just plain nuts.

Leonard Frank was born on July 15, 1932, in Brooklyn. A graduate of the University of Pennsylvania's Wharton School, he has lived since 1959 in San Francisco, where he continues his activism in the psychiatric survivor movement. In recent years he has edited books of quotations, eight of which have been published by Random House, most notably the *Random House Webster's Quotationary* (1998).

———

I lost my job in real estate in 1959, after which I lived off my savings. Eventually, however, I had to sell my car to make ends meet. It was during this time that my parents became concerned about the changes in my lifestyle. Soon they were urging me to see a psychiatrist because they believed there had to be something seriously wrong with me. The psychiatrist they consulted agreed. It was a "personality change." To call it a negative personality change would have been redundant, because to psychiatrists all such changes are negative. The "treatment" goal was to get me back to the person I had been before.

I was not interested in that. I liked the person I was becoming. I had done some reading in psychology—Freud and Jung mostly, and Erich

Fromm as well—and had decided that overall their approach was not for me. I came to believe that psychiatrists, psychotherapists, and psychoanalysts were filling the role of priests in a secular society, and I didn't feel the need for any priests or teachers. What guidance I needed was supplied by the books I was reading and from within myself during my journey of transformation.

Toward the end of this period I ran out of money and was on the verge of becoming homeless. My parents saw the fact that I wasn't working and that I wasn't looking for work as the ultimate sign of my "mental illness." I believed then, and believe now, that we human beings were not put on this planet just to work. It's true, we have our responsibilities. But our first responsibility is to ourselves, to follow our own path, and that's what I was doing.

I don't remember any of this directly; the shock procedure blotted out my memory for this period. Based on a few, vague recollections from the start of this period, and from what others who knew me at the time have told me since, I'm just assuming that was what I was thinking. I chose to go my own way and wasn't at all influenced by what other people thought. If it was necessary for me to be homeless for a while, that was okay too. In retrospect, it couldn't have been worse than being imprisoned in a psychiatric institution and forcibly shocked and drugged. Homelessness was kid stuff compared to that.

Beginning in late October 1962, I was committed to Mount Sinai Hospital in San Francisco, and according to the records I stayed there for two or three days. I was then transferred to Napa State Hospital, which is located about forty miles northeast of San Francisco, for about seven weeks, and was finally sent to Twin Pines Sanitarium in Belmont, about twenty miles south of San Francisco, where I remained for the next six months. The records indicate the "symptoms" observed in me included "bizarre behavior," "impaired judgment," "condescending superior smile," "vegetarian food idiosyncrasies," "negativism," "piercing eyes," "religious preoccupations," "uncooperative" and "passively resistive." The last two items are of particular interest to me because under Gandhi's influence, I had become a believer in "non-cooperation" and "passive resistance," forms of political activism and nonviolence. Once institutionalized, I apparently put these principles into practice.

For about a month following my arrival at Twin Pines, the psychiatrists pressed me to consent to shock "treatment," and when I refused they obtained a court order authorizing them to administer the procedure against my will. The next day, according to the records, the treatments began.

Insulin coma treatment is the technical name. The coma does not come on suddenly. There is a lead-up period lasting about four hours during which the subject experiences increasingly intense hunger as well as heavy perspiration, chills, tremors, headache, sometimes convulsions, and what I would describe as the pangs of dying. All the while, the insulin is absorbing sugar in the subject's body, including the brain. Starved of sugar, the brain goes on strike and begins to feed on itself, eventually causing brain-cell death and coma. The coma lasts about an hour, at which point emergency measures are used to bring the subject out of the coma. And apparently, it was while I was in these induced comas that the psychiatrist would also apply the electroshocks to the frontal lobe area of my brain.

In theory, the way the treatment "works" is through brain damage and disablement: the individual is returned to the person he or she had been before "going crazy." The surest sign of brain damage is memory loss. In my case, the brain damage caused me to forget the three years preceding the last insulin session. I recall nothing about the treatments other than waking up from the last insulin coma.

It was the most horrible and painful experience of my life. Opening my eyes, the first thing I remember was four or five strangers standing around the bed I was strapped onto and holding down my arms and legs. I was fading in and out of consciousness as one of the strangers asked me to count backwards from one hundred. There were some injections. I was ravenously hungry and was fed orange juice loaded with sugar to bring me out of the coma and without which I probably would have died. Breathing was extremely difficult. I felt like I was drowning and feared for my life. Today I think of the detainees in Afghanistan and Iraq and at the CIA black sites who were waterboarded. This method of torture is effective because those who go through something like that are almost always going to do what they're told. I can only imagine what I said and did as I tried to get the psychiatrists to stop the insulin sessions, but I have no memory of any of it.[1]

Much of the immediate post-shock period is hazy as well, but two memories from that time stand out. After re-orienting myself as to time and place, and getting some sense of who I was, I remember thinking that something dreadful had just happened to me. Although I didn't understand the why and wherefore of it all, I was keenly aware that something really important in me had been destroyed. Then and there I made up my mind that if ever I had the chance to stop the use of shock "treatment" I would do so—whatever it took. That I remember as clear as a bell.

The other strong memory that I have is this: The "patients," myself included, would go to occupational therapy in the mornings and then return to the living/sleeping area for lunch. On one occasion we got back a bit early and were waiting around in the day room, which also served as the dining area. This was adjacent to the treatment area (several rooms off a short hallway), separated from it by a thick, heavy metal door. The door had been left ajar for some reason, and suddenly I heard this scream, the likes of which I'd never heard before. It was loud and it was prolonged. It must have came from a very deep place inside the person whose scream it was. One of the nurses saw what was happening and my troubled reaction. She immediately closed the door, but I continued to hear it. The screaming person, an 18-year-old, was someone undergoing the insulin coma treatment. And I imagine that that's what it must have been like for me during the fifty sessions I went through.

My beard was a huge issue with my parents and the psychiatrists. The photograph taken when I was first institutionalized showed me with the beginnings of a beard, which I continued to let grow while locked up. The psychiatrists thought that my shaving would be an important sign of "recovery" and urged me to shave off the beard, which I refused to do. So one day while I was in an insulin-induced coma a member of the staff shaved off my beard. Beard-removal therapy! Soon after that I began shaving myself. The "treating" psychiatrist sent my father a letter noting that I was making progress, because I was now shaving on my own. There were other signs of progress which the psychiatrist noted in his letters to my father. I began to eat some non-vegan foods and had become more sociable.

To the end of their lives, I believe my parents thought they were acting in my best interests. They were angry with me: my conduct was a source of embarrassment to them among family and friends. That I had not turned out to be the kind of person they wanted me to be was a great disappointment to them. It was that fact, more than any other, that had caused the rift between us. Rather than accepting me for the person I had become or choosing not to have anything further to do with me, they brought in the psychiatrists to root out the "disease" they believed had caused the problem.

From their point of view, the treatment worked fairly well. I was probably less objectionable to them after the procedure than I had been before, or at least they felt better about themselves having done what they could to "help" me. In my eyes the treatment was a disaster. It damaged me body, brain, and soul, and left me a shell of what I had been. It is like I've had two lives: one life before the shock and another after.

But the shocks didn't kill me. They injured my spirit, but failed to crush it.

Lucy Gwin
"The world shrinks when you're in a place like that."

"I've had a lot of lives," Lucy Gwin says. "A lot of good lives." Born in 1943, Gwin, at the time of her car accident in 1989, had already been a dairy farmer, an advertising and corporate writer, an antiwar and civil rights activist, a deckhand on ships servicing offshore oil rigs in the Gulf of Mexico, and the single parent of two daughters. Her account of life on the off-shore rigs, *Going Overboard,* was published by Viking Adult in 1982.

Gwin has also played a lot of roles in the disability rights movement: muckraker, advocate, editor, publicist, provocateur, humorist. As the founder, publisher, and editor of *Mouth* magazine, she also provides a forum for up-and-coming writers and investigative journalists and connections for advocates across the United States and Canada.

She currently resides in Washington, Pennsylvania.

It was a head-on collision. The other guy was drunk, and driving a Chrysler or something, and I was in a brand new Toyota. I saw my car many months later. I went to the junk yard and there it was, turned inside out, but the guy who hit me was perfectly all right. It was during rush hour, and no, they didn't charge him with anything. But the police report had it that bystanders were saying—"He got out [of his car] and threatened her." I don't remember a thing about it.

I was knocked unconscious. The next thing I knew, I woke up, and I was in the back of an ambulance. It turned out this was weeks later. I moved my head up and looked out and I could see the headlights shining on a corn field, and the guy who was driving couldn't figure out which way to go. And the woman sitting next to me—I was lying down, and she was sitting up—she couldn't quite come out and say, "You're lost, schmuck"—but I remember ragging on them, because I wanted a cigarette. She gave me one of hers, and then shushed me, because we weren't supposed to be smoking in the back of an ambulance.

We pulled up behind this old Victorian House. It was like a dream. They propelled me to my feet and pulled me out of the ambulance. I had on a hospital gown, they propelled me to the back of this house, up a concrete ramp, and I'm watching all these boys sitting out the back of the house at this picnic table under these really bright mercury lights, smoking cigarettes and laughing, looking at my butt, because it was hanging out of my hospital gown. A woman comes to the back door, and I'd already figured out that this was one of those places they put people, but I'm thinking, "This is all a dream, remember this is still all in a dream," because it can't be anything else.

The first thing I said was, "I want a copy of your patients' rights document." And she said, in this really cheery voice, "Oh, you won't need one of *those*."

They took me up to a bedroom in the dark. I got some clothes from somewhere, a bathrobe or something, and went back down. Sat down with the boys outside in back and smoked cigarettes. I mean, this is typical Lucy, you know? I didn't even know my name then, I didn't have any memory of life whatsoever, it was just a blank. Except I knew things, like "patients' rights document." I didn't know where I knew that from. It's something the brain will do for you. It can't be bothered to remember details like what your name is and stuff, but it'll remember something like "patient's bill of rights." The official name for it is post-traumatic amnesia. I had terrible swelling, my forehead was really huge, but otherwise I had no injuries at all.

New Medico had two facilities there in Cortland, which is a small town about two and a half hours outside of Rochester, New York. They had a giant nursing home, maybe four stories, four hundred beds, and then they had several "community re-entry centers" which were in these old Victorian house group homes, with about ten or eleven people living in each. They also had a day care center, where they'd ship us in buses every weekday. The only other industry they had in that town was the State University. Other than that it was a dead town.

I was there for three weeks. They called it a community re-entry center, but there was nothing there to prepare you to re-enter the community. There was a little bitty gasoline station/mart across the street, and I was allowed to cross the street and buy stuff, a piece of bubble gum, but other than that none of us were allowed to go into the community at all. And some people had been there for so long, that they would never even ask to get out. That was their home. The world shrinks in a place like that, and there's no way out. The world shrinks.

Each of us shared a bedroom with somebody. I shared a bedroom with a woman who'd had a stroke during some minor surgery. A black woman, the wife of the man who wrote [for a famous children's television program]. She obviously had had real class, she had the posture of someone who had lived well. She couldn't speak—she was aphasic.

She was basically the target of the attendants. There was one attendant who, when everybody signed out at night, he'd say, "Oh, I'll watch out and I'll say you were here," and then he'd bring his buddies in and they would rape her. They'd pull her out of bed, take her out to the banister and bend her over and fuck her in the butt. And I definitely saw that, just looking out the door. And I'd say, "Stop that right now!" And they'd say, "Nobody will ever believe you." And they were right, nobody did. I reported it. The first time, I thought they'd do me next. I hid in the bushes all night and came out in the morning and tried to tell the attendant, and tried to tell the guy who ran the day care center, and tried to tell the case manager. "No no no, you're imagining things." I couldn't even call 9-1-1 from the payphone.

And the time-out room ought to be on the record too. I only went there once. I was standing in line for my meds, the chloral hydrate and some other stuff to knock you out, and if you don't take it they put you on the floor, and stuff it down your throat. So, I don't want to take this, I had tears dropping down my cheeks, I thought, nobody knows I'm here, nobody gives a shit. Naturally I was quite upset by all this, and they said [like an alarm announcement] "*She's going labile! She's going labile!*" That's when you have a head injury, and you cry, or you show an emotion, they call it "emotional lability." Anyway, they put me in the time-out room. The inmates called it "the white room," because it had been painted this hideous super-reflective white, and it had florescent lights, a whole bank of them—a closet with these big lights on the ceiling, and no door knob on your side of the door. And deep scratches in that white paint, where people had scratched it with their fingernails. I'm glad I'd had some Zen, because I knew what to do in situations like that. Like when I was in the oil fields, I knew what to do when things were unbearable—you go do your Zen.

Man oh man, there was every opportunity, and I mean *every* opportunity, to go insane. And they watched you all the time. Randy, that's the guy who raped Delores, he was the behavior monitor. Oh great! One afternoon, out at the picnic table, this kid just suddenly jumped up. He never talked much, but all of a sudden he just jumped up and made a break for it, and Randy tackled him, and got him down on the ground, and then stood up and kicked him. This was a kid with a brain injury, and Randy *kicked him in the head.* Admittedly this kid was a big guy, but he wasn't struggling anymore, he was down on the ground.

The whole time I was there, I never saw a doctor. I never saw a nurse. I never had any "therapy." There was nothing to do, so we all sat around the picnic tables talking. The only time I got therapy was when I complained that there wasn't any, and then they made up this silly game that was a rip-off of Trivial Pursuit, where the staff would quiz the inmates on whether or not something was "appropriate behavior." Other than that, nobody got nothing.

It was a total scam, and everybody working there knew it. There was this game going on between New Medico and the insurance companies, and the staff had to be real careful and do their paperwork. All day everybody was nagging everybody else, "*Have you got your paperwork done yet?*" And they'd sit down at the end of the day, the little front-line workers, and say, "Can I say I spent six hours with Juan today, or did you say you spent six hours with him? We can't *both* say it." And they would figure out their lies while they were doing their paperwork, because nobody spent six hours with anybody.

All my people on the outside had been told to stay away. Plus it was two and a half hours away from my house, in this town that nobody had ever been to, or heard of, even. They told all my friends, "The best thing you can do for the first six weeks, just don't come, don't visit, don't call." They were told, "She's going to need lifelong, 24-7 monitoring, because she's dangerous." We were all of us isolated, and removed from our families, and then bad things were said about us to our families, so our families didn't want us back.

Nobody left. They got shifted around to different New Medico centers, but nobody ever left. They had forty-three facilities in nineteen states, all doing the same thing. The woman who founded the National Head Injury Foundation, her daughter, last I heard, was in her twenty-second year of "rehab." It's like bread, when does it come out of the oven? If it's rehab, surely at some point you're rehabilitated! You don't go on rehabbing a house forever. You don't go rehabbing anything else forever, but brain injury rehab? They say, "Oh it's very *complicated,* it's very *difficult.* People have to relearn how to walk, how to talk." Well, I didn't have to relearn to walk or talk.

Maybe the third or fourth morning I was there, I woke up, and all of a sudden *images*—not sounds, not names, none of that came back—it was just images, just beautiful scenes from my life: a piece of barn wood from our farm back in Wisconsin, and that's just a split second, and then the oil fields, a gorgeous piece of orange scaffolding against the purple sky, just amazing images. I went downstairs to the person who was on duty and I said, "I just *remembered my whole life.* I remember my name and my children and my home, I remember *everything.*" And she said, "Oh, that's nice honey, now what do you want on your pancakes?" I went to my case manager and said, "I remembered my life today, it all came back to me," and she said, "Oh, that's nice."

The only person who befriended me there was a person in the town, the wife of one of the attendants. Her name was Midge DeMartino, and she's still a friend. She believed me when I talked about Delores being raped. She was there to pick up her husband, and I just told her everything. She believed me. She knew it must be true.

One night she and her husband invited me to come home with them, got it *approved* for me to come home for dinner with them. I had determined that I was going to leave, and I confided in them. "I am going to get out of here one way or another." And Ed told me, "Well, you'd better honey, because they have you scheduled for surgery next Wednesday!" They had told my family that I had uninterrupted seizures, that I was epileptic, and that I had to have brain surgery. They had me scheduled at Cortland Memorial Hospital for brain surgery. Can you imagine? That's what had been done to Delores, after she'd had her stroke, and that's what had made her aphasic. New Medico had recommended it, and the hospital did it.

So when I got back, I said, "I'm going to get out of here," and they said, "Well, whoever signed you in has to sign you out." And I said, "Well, who signed me in?" and they said, "We don't know that. You have to call the main office, and you don't have a dime to call the main office."

My friend Frank, who at that time drove a Medicab, came to visit me in his Medicab uniform. They had told him not to visit, but he had paid no attention to that. Frank had worked for me when I had the restaurant, so we were good friends and old lovers. I'd been to that dinner [with the DeMartinos] on Friday night, got frantic because the surgery was supposed to be on Wednesday, and here on Sunday comes Frank, visiting me. And he said, "Hey, you look great! When are you getting out of here?" And I said, "Right now, if you'll drive the getaway car." And he said, "Hop in, let's go."

A company man stood in Frank's way, and threatened him. He said the police would find us, and he would go to jail. And so Frank was really afraid all the way back to Rochester. He stopped on the freeway for me to call a lawyer, to assure him that he could not be arrested for taking me out of there. The lawyer really knew nothing about this, but he assured him that it was safe to take me home.

Frank deserved a lot of credit for saying, "Yeah, sure, hop in." Otherwise I'd still be there.

Fred Fay
"This is like the Berlin Wall."

———

Dybwad, Perske, Frank, and Gwin show us the darkest sides of "the total institution"—those places where a resident surrenders day-to-day control of his or her life for as long as "the experts" deem necessary. But there were alternatives, even before the advent of the disability rights movement. Among these was the polio rehabilitation facility at Warm Springs, Georgia, founded by Franklin Delano Roosevelt in the mid-1920s. As a polio survivor, FDR was keenly aware that it was people with disabilities themselves who are the experts on disability and rehabilitation. As a result, unique among such facilities, Warm Springs employed polio survivors as staff, teachers, and mentors. By the time Fred Fay entered Warm Springs in 1962, the facility—though adhering to Jim Crow segregation policies—had begun admitting people with disabilities other than polio.

Born in September 1944, Fay was sixteen years old when he fell from a trapeze while doing gymnastics and broke his neck. After being stabilized in the spinal cord injury unit at the National Institutes of Health in Bethesda, Maryland, he was transferred to Warm Springs in 1962, the same year Leonard Frank was being "treated" at Twin Pines in California. By contrast, Fay's experience at Warm Springs showed him the benefit of peer support for people with disabilities, while making him more keenly aware of the effects of racial segregation and discrimination.

Fay, a founder of the American Coalition of Citizens with Disabilities, the Boston Center for Independent Living, and the Opening Doors counseling center for people with spinal cord injuries in Washington, DC, was a primary advocate for the inclusion of key provisions of the Rehabilitation Act of 1973, including section 504. A prominent voice for disability rights in the Democratic Party, he also played a crucial role in passage of the ADA, and cofounded Justice for All in 1995 to oppose attempts by congressional Republicans to weaken the ADA and other disability rights law.

Fay settled permanently in Massachusetts in 1977, and he was living in Concord with his companion, Trish Irons, until his death on August 20, 2011.[2]

––––––

We pulled in in an ambulance in the middle of the night, and I remember thinking the entrance looked a little like the entrance to the White House, these big white columns you see in front of old mansions. And it was really accessible, but I didn't know a whole lot about accessibility. I knew I didn't have to go up any ramps or bumps in the stretcher to get in. They loaded me into a hospital ward with three other people with major disabilities. The staff seemed very knowledgeable, very friendly. The second day I was there, I realized that some of the teachers were in wheelchairs: my English teacher, my physics teacher, and my German teacher. That had an impact: There was a lot of stuff you could do from a wheelchair.

A week after I got there, a young quadriplegic from Minnesota, a kid named Larry Kegan[3] rolled into the room. He was there to learn to put his socks on. He could do everything else, as a fairly low-level quadriplegic, but the darn socks. He arrived on a weekend. There wasn't a whole lot for him to do. The rehab staff were off. One evening we ended up talking for about three or four hours, and he told me about his life as a student at the University of Minnesota. It just sounded great. He had a hand-controlled car. He could drive to campus. He played the bongos with his thumbs—holding the bongos between his knees. And he was a singer in a local band. Later I learned he had sung with Bob Dylan. He was dating girls and going out and drinking with the guys and living a typical college life. To me, it was just so hopeful and positive.

Later that night, as we talked, he at one point confronted me and said, "You know you'll never walk again." My immediate reaction was to change the subject. I didn't want to deal with it. And three or four times he dragged me back. He said, "Sure, they're doing research, but it's going to be years. You'll probably be in a wheelchair the rest of your life." And I finally said, "Okay, I guess I'll never walk again." And then he let up. But later he left the room, and I was alone at that point, I started letting some of the things he talked about sink in. I just found myself, out of the clear blue, just sobbing hysterically, about the most convulsive crying I had ever felt in my life, crying over the loss of the use of my legs, the same way you cry over the death of a parent or a spouse.

Up until that point, any rehab stuff I'd done was strictly because other people had told me to do it. I wasn't invested really at all in strengthening my arms or learning to do stuff. That next morning, when I went to physical therapy, I had this totally different attitude. I was trying to lift weights, not because I was being told to do it, but because if I lifted weights I'd develop strength in my triceps to be able to slide a sliding board under my butt and park it next to the seat of a car and then transfer over into the car seat and then fold up my wheelchair and pull it in behind the passenger seat, slide over to the driver's seat and work these hand controls, where you pull up for gas and down for brakes, and then be able to drive off to campus and go drinking and dating and enjoy life.

It was my first experience with peer counseling. Larry's role model had a more profound impact on me than I think anything else in the whole course of my rehabilitation. Generally, I've learned more from other people with disabilities than I've learned from all the other doctors and nurses and physical therapists, occupational therapists that I've seen over the years.

[I wasn't able to leave the place] for the first few months I was there, in part because I was in the Stryker frame,[4] but I remember wanting to go on an outing in the autumn, and they said it was too early for me to be doing transfers into a car. Finally my parents came down for a visit, and we went out to a local restaurant. My parents pulled my chair out, and

I was getting out into the wheelchair, I remember looking around and I saw three or four people standing, just staring at me. I remember feeling a little annoyed, "What do they think, I'm a freak or something?" It hit me that I would face a lot of people over the years, and I could react to their reaction and get angry and chase them away, or I could decide it's their problem and view my situation positively, that I'm getting a chance to educate them as to what somebody with a disability can do. I got on with it, and never thought about it hardly at all when people would stare at me, which was frequently the case in the sixties. You didn't see many people in wheelchairs out and around.

The [only time] black people mixed [with white people was when] they served dinner and they emptied urinal jugs and stuff. But there was very little mixing on a social level. I didn't understand why they called the black staff by their first name and the white staff by "Mr." or "Mrs." whatever. But Willy and Cecil and Otis were the black aides. I don't think any of them graduated from elementary school. When I was first there, I thought they were speaking a different language. It took me a while to decipher their version of English. But I also remember thinking how unjust it was. I remember seeing a black paraplegic over in another building and thinking, "Gosh, why don't we see him in therapy or in the dining hall or anything?" There were separate bathrooms, separate dining halls, separate everything. Economically it didn't seem to make much sense to have to duplicate every single facility.

But it was still '61, '62. We were aware of the civil rights movement for blacks, but it wasn't really until I got back to Washington that spring and went downtown with a friend and saw curbs at every corner that I thought, "Jeez, this is like the Berlin Wall." The real world, outside of places like Warm Springs and later the University of Illinois, was just so totally different from these islands or oases of accessibility.

Marilyn Saviola
"I guess that I didn't think I had much of a future."

It is probably safe to say that most people institutionalized in the United States before the 1960s were done so against their will or at least without their consent.

Some people, however, acquiesced to their confinement simply because they felt they had—or indeed did not have—any other option. Marilyn Saviola was one such person. Living in an inaccessible home, surrounded by a society that refused to make accommodations, she entered an institution because it was the only way she could experience any semblance of a community where she could and would be accepted for the person she was.

Marilyn Saviola was born in 1945, contracted polio in August 1955, and became an activist with the direct action group Disabled in Action in the 1970s. She was director of advocacy for Independence Care Systems, Inc., in New York City until 1998 and continues to live in Brooklyn.

———

I woke up one morning when I was ten years old with a horrendous headache and stiff neck. We didn't know what was wrong. That night I had a high fever, and the doctor came to the house and said I had to be admitted to the hospital. At the time, they didn't know if I had polio or meningitis. They took me to this place called Willard Parker Hospital, which had a contagious disease unit on it.

I was in this huge room where I guess there were maybe four or five other people, and they would always die—apparently I was one of the few people who ever survived in that room. And since I was a kid, they wouldn't tell me they died. They told me they went to rehab.

I stayed there until I got over the contagious stage and was weaned from an iron lung and was able to use a chest respirator, and then I went to Goldwater [Memorial Hospital] for rehab. I spent maybe a year and a half or two years there. Then I went home to live with my parents and grandparents in a totally inaccessible environment.

The house that I lived in was what they call a mother-daughter house. The basement was converted into an apartment and my grandparents lived there and we lived on the main floor which was thirteen steps up to get into the house. I used a wheelchair in the house, or I sat on a chair in the living room, like a wing chair.

It wasn't bad when I was young and "carry-able." My parents would carry me up and down stairs like a sack of potatoes, or as I got bigger two people would carry me in my wheelchair, bouncing me on each step. But as I got older, and it was harder to get out, and as I wanted more freedom, it became a real issue. My father would either have to come home from work to carry me downstairs, or the kids in the neighborhood would do it. [But] the kids in the neighborhood weren't always around anymore because they were at an age now where their horizon expanded beyond the block. This meant that I was stuck inside.

I received home instruction, three days a week for an hour and a half a day. I think I had some very psychotic teachers. This one woman would spend her time telling my mother all her troubles. I had a math teacher who was very nice, and an art teacher, but I don't know how I learned anything. All I remember the teachers doing was assigning homework and reviewing it. I have no recall on ever having actual classes, although this was supposed to happen.

I don't think my friends really saw me as an equal. I was someone whose life was a tragedy. I know my family never accepted it. They thought if I prayed enough, and they were good enough, if they said enough novenas or whatever, I would be cured. So this was never seen as a permanent situation. They never accepted it. At that point, I honestly don't think I did, either. Because, I never thought about the future. I guess that I didn't think I had much of a future. I never saw myself beyond today.

Going on sixteen or seventeen, I would go into Goldwater for check-ups. My parents, especially my mother, thought that if I used the respirator less, then I would get stronger and would need it less. So they were constantly weaning me off it. And I began to have problems because of that. I wasn't getting properly ventilated, so what they call your CO_2, your carbon dioxide level, would go up so high that I almost died a couple of times. I almost went into heart failure twice because of this, so that I would wind up in Goldwater, back in an iron lung.

Goldwater was a long term care rehab facility in the middle of an island in the East River, between Queens and Manhattan. The wards at the time were huge—where they would have one, two, three, four patients of different sexes and ages sleeping in, living in the same cubicle. They had three large rooms and four beds or five beds in each area. So you had [your own individual] cubicle, which was your space, [enclosed] with a curtain. A length of a hospital bed plus maybe six, or twelve inches, and maybe an additional foot or two on either side of the bed. They tried to keep the younger people together. This was early on before they had a special unit for us. And sometimes you had someone right next to you.

The staff was either the greatest or the worst. There were very few people who were just regular people. You had some people who were really, really not good people, and a lot of great, great people who took an interest in what you were doing, talked to you, became friends with you. However, there was always this boundary, that you weren't supposed to be friends with the staff. I can tell you how actively this was discouraged and how hurtful this was. And then they would have all these volunteers who were also teenagers—like the candy stripers, Red Cross volunteers—we all became friends with them. So you developed peer groups that way.

On the unit that I was in at the time, most of the people had had polio and had either never left Goldwater or had gone home and had not good experiences and came back in. There was Virginia, Mary, myself, Bibi, and Bruce. I guess we had eight or ten people. We were all in our teens and early twenties.

I was always very envious of the kids in my neighborhood because they would talk about their school activities, their social activities. I felt left out. Not only wasn't I getting the education that the kids were getting, I was not getting a social life. At that point, I began to realize that I was much happier not being home but being in an institution, because there were other activities. I was able to get in and out without being carried, and I saw other people there. I began to think about wanting to do something with my life.

At least in Goldwater I had a peer group, and I got out. So, they became my peer group and my family of choice. There was another friend of mine who was in a similar situation and every summer they would bring us in together for respite. And we kind of stretched that out. If there was something wrong, if I had one of the episodes and I wasn't breathing properly, we'd stretch it out for months sometimes. And Dr. Alba [my doctor at Goldwater] knew it. She knew that I was very unhappy at home, although it was never a stated thing. [So my staying at Goldwater] was kind of worked into, [even if it was] never discussed that I would stay there.

5
The University of Illinois

T HE SERVICEMAN'S READJUSTMENT ACT OF 1944 (COMMONLY CALLED
the GI Bill of Rights), provided every American serviceman or -woman
honorably discharged after World War II with the opportunity to pursue a
college education. Among those eligible were veterans disabled as a result of
their service. However, although they wanted to attend college like their non-
disabled peers, they found that, almost without exception, American schools
were either unwilling or unable to accommodate them.

The principal exception was the program for students with disabilities at
the University of Illinois. Established by Timothy Nugent in 1948, the program was first housed at a makeshift campus at Galesburg, before moving to
its permanent home at Urbana-Champaign, where it would become alma ma-
ter of an entire generation of disability rights leaders, including Fred Fay, Kitty
Cone, Mary Lou Breslin, and others.

Timothy Nugent
"What would they do with a college education anyway?"

Timothy Nugent was born in 1923 in Pittsburgh, Pennsylvania. Disability was
an integral part of his childhood. His younger sister had "severe visual problems," and his father had both hearing and visual disabilities. As a child Nugent
himself was diagnosed with a heart condition, and his parents were advised to
limit his physical activities. Nevertheless, he volunteered for service in the US
Army during World War II.

Virtually everything Nugent did at Urbana-Champaign those first years
was innovative. Faced with his students' need to navigate a large campus, Nugent oversaw the construction of a fleet of lift-equipped buses—the first in the
nation. Curb ramps—virtually unheard of—were built initially on campus and
then in the larger community.

In 1959, Nugent became the first director of research and development at the American National Standards Institute Project A117, with the goal of setting standards for ramps, curb cuts, door widths, and other accommodations. The standards developed by the ANSI project became the basis for subsequent architectural access legislation and regulations.

Nugent was also an early advocate of wheelchair athletics. In 1949, he founded the National Wheelchair Basketball Association, and served as its commissioner for the next quarter century. He personally toured with the teams, going out into communities where people with severe disabilities often had never been seen in public.

In some ways, Nugent appears to have accepted and incorporated into his program the "whole man" rehabilitation philosophy of the time. Fred Fay recounts what he calls "hell week"—an orientation during which students with severe physical disabilities were expected to fend for themselves to the extent possible (and then some), with no expectation that the community had any obligation to provide accommodation or assistance. On the other hand, Nugent's championing of curb ramps, lift-equipped buses, and architectural access went far beyond the approach of most rehabilitation professionals of the era, who often ignored any need for society to make accommodations for people with disabilities.

Nugent, then, might be seen as a bridge between the paternalism of the vocational rehabilitation movement of the 1940s and '50s and the modern era of disability rights. Clearly, without his vision and persistence, an entire generation of advocates might not have received the education that enabled them to be more effective political activists.

———

Galesburg was a brand new hospital that was used briefly but then not needed when the war ended. It was built like most of the army hospitals in those days, a series of one-story buildings connected by corridors. Once you were in, you could go to almost any part of the facility without having to encounter steps or go outdoors. There were, I think, 126 wards, connected by corridors. Some were turned into classrooms, some into labs, some were turned into dormitories. And so the American Legion and others thought, "Hey this would be a good place to try and get some of our disabled veterans in." And so I went down in a quasi-consulting role, and was offered the directorship of the program. I went down there during the '47–'48 school year, but I joined the faculty officially in September of 1948.

I'm going to guess that there were about three thousand students that first semester, with about twenty-three or twenty-seven disabled students. They were housed intermixed with other students. This is also a guess, but I think of that about twenty-five individuals in wheelchairs were veterans and maybe three or four were not.

Very definitely there were people who didn't think we belonged there. One of my own faculty colleagues said, "These people belong in trade schools or nursing homes." I remember one instance that was quite traumatic and stuck with me. We went out to a place in the north end of Galesburg, a famous bar and eating place. I wheeled in with Harold Sharper [one of Nugent's early students] and his wife. His wife was an attractive able-bodied lady, and I remember a couple of couples sitting at the bar, and one of the women turned around and said, "They don't allow those people in here now too, do they?" And she said it loud enough that Harold's wife heard it, and it was one of the worst fights that I ever had to break up.

They threatened to close Galesburg, the whole campus, in an effort to cut the university budget. We immediately tried to get into the University of Illinois in Champaign, and were denied. And then we surveyed universities all over the country and they all denied us the opportunity to bring the program there, to bring our students there. We had the fear that our fledgling program was going to come to an end.

So we marched on the capital in Springfield. When we got there, we were greeted by the Veterans of Foreign Wars, the American Legion, the Disabled American Veterans. All the veterans groups got behind us. We went to the governor's mansion first, and the governor left by the back entrance while we were out in front. It's kind of a humorous thing to discuss now, but it was dead serious at the time. Then we went to the state capitol building, where I met with one of the lieutenant governors and with Senator Thompson, who was from Galesburg and was the ranking senator in the state [legislature] of Illinois. And I met with the director of public welfare. In fact, if you were to go to the *Chicago Tribune* in April of '49, you'd find a picture that was probably twelve inches by twelve inches edged in black and it had the caption "For Whom the Bells Toll." And it was a picture of me and the director of public welfare, Fred Hoehler.

We also took a good number of our students to Champaign for a demonstration. We took planks from a paint scaffolding and we laid them up over some steps to show that these guys in wheelchairs could get into that building. The building was Lincoln Hall, which at the time had about four steps leading into it. We did crazy things like that, and of course as we wheeled around campus, people would see us.

But we still didn't get a positive answer. The positive answer only came when Dr. Hirsch, medical director of the Veterans Administration for this area, got behind us, and the American Legion got in behind us. The DAV [Disabled American Veterans] got in behind us and Dr. Hirsch himself came to campus to argue on our behalf. Eventually we were allowed to come here, but as "an experiment."

I received no appropriation from the state or the university for the program, including my salary, for the first eight or nine years. That was the attitude. A lot of the faculty and administrators at the time were hoping I'd fail. In fact, I published a paper for the American College Health Association back in '52, in which I described the attitudes of most administrators and ranking faculty and that was that these [disabled] people would be an extra cost, a distraction, and what would they do with a college education anyway?

Jack Chase
"I would wheel as fast as I could to come and go. I never went slow anywhere."

"Franklin Delano Roosevelt was our president when I was growing up," Jack Chase remembers. "We never thought of him as being in a wheelchair, because he hid his disability from the media. It was covered up."

Chase was born in early 1927 in Washington state, where his father was a logger. He went into the military in June 1945. "They dropped the bomb on Japan, and the war ended while I was taking basic training, so I did occupation duty in Korea for ten months." He returned home from the service and was trying out for collegiate basketball at Western Washington College of Education when he contracted polio in October 1946. After 122 days at St. Joseph's Hospital in Bellingham, Washington, Chase began exploring his options for continuing his college education.

What he found was Tim Nugent's program at the University of Illinois at Galesburg. It offered him not only a chance to earn a degree but also an opportunity to renew his love of basketball. During his college years, Chase, described as "one of the smoothest and swiftest players of all time,"[1] would go on tour with the U of I wheelchair basketball team. He made the All-American Wheelchair Basketball Team six times, traveling around the world as a spokesman for the game, coaching teams of young wheelchair athletes. "The greatest satisfaction I've had was not from playing," he said, "but watching a team of young kids, seeing that first glint of competitive zeal come into their eye, and then having [their] mom and dad come out and see them play."

Jack Chase is now a retired minister, living with his wife in Corvallis, Oregon.

————

I arrived on campus in the spring of 1949. I was still in a state of shock from my original affliction. I'd had a wheelchair for just a short time, and I hadn't wheeled it around in my little town—there weren't any sidewalks. So I was elated that I had found a place where I could move around, once inside the building. I lived with my wife in an apartment complex right across the street. We had one little daughter at the time. Once I was inside I stayed there all day for all the classes, and did not have to leave. So it was a tremendous facility for wheelchairs.

I would say there were about fifteen of us disabled students, but there were more disabled people that were not necessarily confined to a wheelchair. I would say that we had a dozen people in wheelchairs attending the campus in Galesburg at that time.

I met Professor Nugent in 1949, practically the first day I was there, because he was directly connected with the disabled people. Tim liked to talk to the people, he was a very people-oriented type of man, and you hardly thought of him as a professor, he just was there as one of us. I remember sitting in his office, and he suggested that I play basketball. That's the first time I'd heard about wheelchair basketball. And so I went down to the gym, and to my utter amazement I found myself playing basketball again, and it became a good part of my life.

The first national wheelchair basketball tournament was played during those few months that I was in Galesburg. We invited seven other teams to come, and I think only one of the teams didn't show. And I saw people do things in wheelchairs I didn't think was possible to do. Popping wheelies and whatnot. I got up there to play ball against these fellows, and didn't do that badly. We took third place and I made all-

American the first year. It just came natural to me—the wheelchair—I just seemed to be able to move it very well.

I remember these "cardboard shacks," barracks from World War II, Tim had occupied as his office. He had constructed this adjustable ramp so he could determine how steep the incline should be for this person or that person, or for disabled people in general.

We were at the Galesburg campus just that short time. I come in in January, and they closed it June the 30th of that same year. So I went through this trauma of saying, "Hey, I had a place to go, and now it's gone." And I didn't know what I was going to do.

I don't know if we had a precise gathering of disabled students. We were such a small number, that any time we got together, we were all together. I'm sure it was discussed that the Galesburg campus could not be closed, and we decided to go down to the state capitol by a convoy of cars to see the governor. I remember that the convoy was led by a guy named Wolf, who was disabled, but he got around on crutches. He knew nothing about convoys and he drove rather fast, so we had a wild ride down to Springfield to make our appeal to Governor Stevenson[2] to keep the campus open.

Well, the police were very nice to us there, very accommodating. And they took us by convoy to the capitol and whatnot, to try to get an audience with Governor Stevenson, which we were unsuccessful in attaining. And so they convoyed us through the city with their sirens—it was quite an excitement. I don't know if anyone in the town knew what we were there for. We didn't have flags or banners, we didn't have a lot of publicity to proceed or follow us. Since then we've learned how to protest, we're better now at protesting than we were then. But for our place and time, we thought, "Man, we are really making an impression here."

All I knew from my end was: let's keep this campus open at all costs, because it meant everything to me, as far as my education was concerned. And I think that there probably was quite a bit of pressure on Illinois, and the main campus at Urbana-Champaign, and [University of Illinois] President Stoddard's staff down there, to do something. Tim was so persuasive. He cried for us, in front of people, making our case. I think so highly of him, and what he did for us. So we moved from Galesburg to Urbana-Champaign during the summer.

They gave us housing, and it was already ramped when we got there. The apartments were leftover World War II, almost barracks-like. And it wasn't well constructed, it was just temporary housing from the army's point of view, and they took over those and they converted them into apartments. I did not have a car, and I had to wheel a mile and a half to school.

And so I wheeled to and from class, quite a shock from Galesburg. I would wheel as fast as I could to come and go. I never went slow anywhere in the wheelchair. I was in tremendous shape because of that, for wheelchair basketball. So in a certain sense it was good for me. In another sense it was pretty tough because you used a lot of energy, and you'd get home and you would be pretty tired.

Timothy Nugent (continued)
"I've seen people afraid to shake hands with a person with a disability."

Although Nugent and his students managed to save their experiment from closing, the shift from Galesburg to Urbana-Champaign brought new challenges. Not only were there additional physical barriers, but the prejudices of administrators and faculty had to be confronted if Nugent was to achieve his goal of providing his students a quality education.

The move from Galesburg to Champaign definitely changed the program. Whereas accessibility was relatively easy in Galesburg, it was very difficult here initially. I used to transfer as many as three hundred class sections a semester from one building to another, because we ramped just a few buildings originally. We arranged a system of preregistration for our disabled students, where the sections wouldn't be filled and they could make out a program that was reasonable for them to physically access. Of course we were making things accessible starting from '49 on, that's why I was asked to be the director of research and development and then the secretary and eventually the national chairman of the American Standards Project.

In Champaign, my building was a tarpaper shack, which had been moved onto campus with hundreds of others like it, and they became dormitories for able-bodied students and also for my wheelchair students. We filled four of those tarpaper shacks with wheelchair men and then eventually two of the buildings became our rehab center. And the new Lincoln Avenue Residence Hall was just being completed. It was the first major residence hall built on campus after the war and even there we had a problem.

Shirley Sayers was a wheelchair student at Galesburg, and then came here with us. They didn't want to make Lincoln Hall accessible and they gave me an estimate that it would cost about $10,000 to do it. And so we argued and argued and finally I went to Shirley Sayers's father. "I would like to try a bluff if you'll go along with me. Would you make a check out for $10,000 to the University of Illinois and mark it for the ramp on Lincoln Avenue Residence Hall?" And he did and they were ashamed to accept the check. They put the ramp up and it probably cost about $250.

After we started getting a lot of applications, some cowardly administrators put a limit on the number of students that we could have on campus. At that time the limit was ninety. There was a period of time when for every one I accepted, I had to refuse fifteen. I was getting letters from clergymen, medical doctors, school superintendents, congressmen, and others just raking me over the coals because one of their constituents couldn't get in.

Occasionally I would call one of our medical consultants to inquire about this or that or the other thing. Or I would maybe call the parents and ask them a question or two about the person. It wasn't a simple one-item deal, we looked into everything, and we also required a personal visit because I used to get some letters where the parents depicted this person as being unable to do anything. And when I got them down here they could do just about everything. I had one parent actually bring a student down, the student fought to come, and in my office I heard the mother say to the father, "I don't know why we're wasting this money. He's going to die before he gets through the first year anyway." Now that's an actual quote. I've had other situations equally as bad.

We would put the new students through some functional evaluations and some functional training that started two weeks before the semester started. My whole staff, twenty-four hours a day for a full week, would work with them to become physically independent, to learn how to transfer from a chair to a toilet stool and back again. To learn how to handle bowel management. To learn how to dress and undress and all this kind of stuff. It was called functional training. They called it hell. Then we had a week-long orientation, where we would take them about the campus and show them the entrances and the pathways from this place to that place and the bus stops and things like that, and people with vision would lead the blind around campus to orient them so that they could function independently once school started. This was all done before classes so that it did not interfere with their studies.

But then I realized getting about this big campus was a problem and so we had to work on transportation. The father of one of my students knew the founder and president of Greyhound, Orville Swan Caesar, and he arranged for me to meet with him. I explained to Mr. Caesar what I wanted and why, and he liked the idea. He says, "How many buses do you want?" Well, I was afraid to ask for too much, so I asked for two. If I'd asked for ten I would have gotten them, because at that time he was converting to buses that were [built] higher and had two separate engines in the rear. And so he was selling his old Silversides, which weren't really [that] old, to foreign countries, or would give them to me.

Now what happened then, to show what the attitude was—Don Swift, one of my outstanding wheelchair people, the first wheelchair graduate—he and I visited with the Greyhound people at their various garages, saw the buses that we were supposed to get. So we wrote up our estimates, the cost of operation, and I took it to my dean, and my dean said, "You can't give buses to the university." And I said, "I don't want to give buses to the university. I want the president to know that Greyhound wants to give buses to the university."

But it never got past the dean's desk. And so we sat for hours and said, "What do we do?" Well, what we did was form a parents' organization, and they prepared a letterhead. See, I couldn't bypass the dean, but they could. So they wrote to the president of the university who was Lloyd Morey, and Lloyd Morey sent me a letter of commendation within two days saying, "Tim, it's wonderful that you were able to get these," and he sent a letter of acceptance to Greyhound.

In fact, that dean didn't really want us on campus. This was the dean of health, physical education, recreation, on whose faculty I served. Later on, this same dean became a very dear friend, but he just had a misconception of what things should be, and so did the rest of this campus for the most part.

In 1956, I hired my first full-time staff member. And my budget at that time, I think, was about $11,000 a year for everything. The first two years I slept in my office building.

Some of our students came out of nursing homes. Some came out of just having been in the back room of a home for a long time. Some were more recently disabled and didn't have to go through that unfortunate sequence of events. I admitted freshmen that were the age of forty-nine that had been disabled for years. When our program was sixteen years old, the county health nurse went from building to building—they found people sixteen years old with disabilities that the school district did not even know about, I assume because the parents were ashamed or fearful of letting him or her out of the house.

I admitted one boy who had been in bed in Chicago, one of the largest hospital centers in the world, for twenty-one years! And he came down to campus with an attendant. And the first thing I did was say to the attendant. "You can leave, because he does not need you here." And that just frightened this guy to death. The next thing I did is I called one of my wheelchair boys that had a car. I said, "I want you to pick this guy up and take him to lunch." Well, when lunchtime came we went out of my office, went out to the curb of the street next to the office, and he said, "Well, what do I do now?" I said, "I'll tell you what. The guy that's sitting in that car is going to tell you what to do now and I'm going back to the office."

He spent two weeks. He only came down to get functional training, he wasn't intending to come to college. After he went home, he called me up and said, "If I could learn that in two weeks, what could I learn if I came to college?" I said, "Jack, I can't promise you anything except one thing—you won't be the big bum that you are today." And so he came to college. And he graduated in less than four years and became the vice president of a firm in Chicago.

I pretty much disallowed [power wheelchairs]. Many people came with power wheelchairs that I knew could operate a standard wheelchair properly trained. And we ended up with a morgue of probably twenty-five or thirty power chairs that we couldn't even give away. Many times the easy way for the hospital was to get them a power chair and get them out. I even knew of surgical procedures that were done because it made life easier while they were in the hospital, but was not in the interest of their future living potential.

Professors were part of the problem. In the very first year or two I used to have to relocate classes. One instance I was relocating a class from a third floor of the English building to the first floor, and the professor cussed me up and down and said, "I don't think these people belong here. I've been here seven years now and I finally got all my classes in one room." He had his classes one, two, and three o'clock in that same room on the third floor of the English building. And he was objecting to my moving his classes to the first floor of the same building so students in wheelchairs could attend. Can you believe that?

I got responses like this here in town even after we had maybe a hundred wheelchairs in the program. I'd go to a certain building and a fellow would say, "Well, I've never seen a wheelchair in this store." Or "in this bar," or "in this restaurant." I said, "Of course you haven't. They can't get in!"

We had several accessible toilet stalls in Lincoln Hall, which is one of the largest academic buildings on campus. About ten years later, I went over there and I found that some of them had been removed. The reason the college dean gave me is that able-bodied people on the faculty complained they couldn't use them. They were afraid to use them. There was no sign there that said for a wheelchair person only, nothing like that, it was just their own interpretation or concept.

And I've seen a lot of that. I've seen people afraid to shake hands with a person with a disability. I've seen people who are just shy where somebody is different.

The past president of the Wisconsin State Medical Society and past president of the American Academy of Neurology is one of our wheelchair graduates. We have ten wheelchair people who are medical doctors. We have engineers, architects—we've had state legislators, we've had them in everywhere. And this brings about an understanding and appreciation and a respect for people with disabilities that didn't exist back in the forties.

It doesn't happen overnight. It happens because of the fact that these people went out and did something and did it well.

Fred Fay (continued)
"That was really my first taste of political change."

Although the University of Illinois offered a working model of a campus at least somewhat accessible, well into the 1960s few colleges and universities followed its example. Which is why Fred Fay, after leaving the rehabilitation program at Warm Springs, Georgia, found himself enrolling in Nugent's program at the University of Illinois.

———

The first week there I had what they called a functional training week. Basically the PT [physical therapist] checked all of us out and gave us exercises. We had to push our own wheelchairs around campus, just to make sure that the students would be able to make it on their own. A few were told to go back home and given a long list of exercises and stuff they had to do to get into shape to be able to make it.

The first thing I remember was a classmate who was in bed, a quadriplegic, a little bit higher level than I. He had to get into his wheelchair to go down to eat breakfast, and he didn't make it by breakfast. He just kept trying to get in the chair. Got to be lunch. He missed lunch. Got to be dinner. He missed dinner. Still trying to get in the chair. He finally managed by the end of the day to get in the chair, with a little help from the physical therapist, and ate breakfast and went back to bed. But I remember vividly his swearing an incredible stream of profanity, that he really didn't need to go through all this torture. In fact, the woman he later married had a similar experience. She had written her parents each day, pleading with them to come take her home, and they called Tim Nugent and said, "This is too much for her." He'd say, "Give her a chance." By the end of the semester, they were both quite independent, getting around campus fine and so forth.

It was I think '65 or maybe '67 before the first student came in an electric wheelchair, and she had a helper with her. That was the first time I'd ever seen a student with a helper there, which seemed to strike me as an inadequacy of the program, that they should be more receptive to students who needed attendant care. There wasn't a vehicle other than the person paying for it out of their own pocket.

One of my entering classmates had never been to a public school. He practically lived in a closet all his life. It was a major adjustment for him. It was amazing the number of kids who had a disability and who had been given good grades because of their disability, rather than earning them, and had been valedictorian of their high school class, and then they'd flunk out their first semester in Illinois, just because of the condescension that had taken place.

The civil rights movement was growing in the early sixties, very much so. I remembered later, when I was fighting for the accessibility at the Washington subway, inventing the slogan "No Taxation Without Transportation." The spirit of advocacy from both Illinois and from the folks like Martin Luther King [Jr.] and Eldridge Cleaver and Rap Brown, certainly influenced my thinking a lot. One of my best friends from right across the hall was Bernie, who was active in the Black Panthers and very militant. He didn't want to be seen with me on campus because I was white! We were great friends. I was on the front line of several demonstrations. It was a wonderful sense of camaraderie, a feeling that we were working toward the greater good.

The opposition to the war was fervent. At some of the campuses there were bombs. At Illinois they stoned the armory. One of my fellow students, Kitty Cone, got herself arrested and thrown in jail during some of the protests. There was also some activism as part of the black civil rights movement, and some people with disabilities got involved in that. I remember marching with my son on my lap. He was maybe three years old at the time. He was chanting, "End the war, end the war." It was a great education for him early on.

There was a bookstore I wanted to get into. There was a huge curb between me and it. I talked to Tim Nugent about it, and he said, "Why don't you do a survey of campus town? Get input from fellow students, and we'll get you an appointment with the Campus Businessmen's Association." So I got a map of campus and got about sixty or seventy students in wheelchairs to look over the map and indicate which were their top-priority curbs for getting ramped. We came up with a prioritized list, and then I met with the owners of all the stores in the neighborhood, with the Campus Businessmen's Association, and presented our case. To my wonderful surprise, they agreed that they wanted our business. They wanted to make things more accessible. That was really my first taste of political change on campus.

I got into a controversy with Tim Nugent at one point. In the rehab center there was a canteen downstairs, where the bus drivers and faculty would go to get soft drinks and candy bars and sit around and talk. I was interested in working in a field related to rehab. I'd go down there myself and get a sandwich, and I was told that I wasn't welcome, that it was for faculty only. I didn't like that idea. I didn't talk to Nugent about it. I just put on the front page of our student newspaper, that went to graduates and to funding sources as well, a picture of some officials dressed up as Ku Klux

Klan, saying, "Disabled Keep Out." The staff adviser saw that and said, "I better show this to our boss." Tim looked at it and hauled me into his office and explained that I should exhaust administrative remedies before going to such extremes, that donors in the program wouldn't be real excited to see themselves portrayed as hate mongers segregating people with disabilities. So I somewhat reluctantly agreed to take the picture off the front page of our newsletter. Learned a lesson, though: that you can get a lot done through administrative channels, if you take the right approach.

There were political discussions more about the civil rights movement and about the war, but certainly we talked about how different Illinois was from where we all came from, which was cities and towns all over America, and the contrast and the need ultimately to change the world.

Mary Lou Breslin (continued)
"You got yanked in by the scruff of your neck if the staff . . . saw you doing something they didn't approve of."

―――――

Mary Lou Breslin moved from her home in Louisville, Kentucky, to matriculate at the University of Illinois in 1962, the same year that Fred Fay entered. Her take on Nugent's program is more critical, however, informed by her critique of the "jock culture" on campus. She also—in retrospect—sees how the access and accommodations provided on campus—as advanced as they were for the time—fell far short of what would become the standards under disability rights law, standards and legislation that Breslin had an important role in crafting.

―――――

Illinois wasn't the only game in town, but there sure weren't many choices. I applied to a lot of schools. I got admitted just about everywhere because my grades were pretty good. For some reason I had it in my mind I wanted to go to Miami University in Ohio. I can't remember why now. So I got admitted, and I started correspondence about what the classes would be, and what about dorms.

The access issue arose instantly. I got a letter back from the dean of students saying, "We're really sorry. We'd love to have you, but we can't accommodate you. We have no facilities for people like you." I'm like:

"Wait a minute. I got carried up and down the stairs in high school; I can get carried up and down the stairs in college. What's the difference?"

My family opposed my leaving town to go to college. I'm sure they thought of me as a very physically dependent person. They didn't tell me I couldn't go away to school, but they were urging me to make a local selection. Well, the local choices weren't any better. There were a couple of Catholic colleges, and there was the University of Louisville, none of which had any access. My father's argument was, "Well, yes, but we could pay somebody to carry you up and down the stairs. You can live here, it'll all be safe and contained, and we can manage it." I'm seventeen and I'm like, "I don't think so."

Anyway, I applied to the University of Illinois. My brother and sister-in-law drove me up for the interview. They had these two little tiny temporary buildings with these incredibly steep ramps and a little physical therapy room and a bunch of offices. I had an interview with Nugent which was just horrible. He scared the bejeezus out of me. He said, "I really can't hold out a lot of hope that you're going to be admitted. We have many more candidates than we could admit." I had already been admitted academically, but I had to be admitted through the Rehab Center too. He said, "You have some physical limitations that are problematic. You have to be able to function independently. You have to be able to push your wheelchair long distances and through cold and snow." I said, "I can do all that, I can do it!"

I think that his perception of me was that I didn't have the stuff of which success was made. They screened for ability to succeed, because it made the program look good. If people failed, then he wouldn't be able to continue on. He was fighting an uphill battle there at the time, and nobody thought people with disabilities should be going to school. He was fighting against a difficult tide.

I came out of that interview feeling like I had failed, that I wasn't going to get in. It didn't have anything to do with my academic qualifications. Nothing.

My brother and his wife sat in on part of the interview, and I did part of it alone, and then they were interviewed separate from me. They're not my parents, but they got interviewed. Afterward we get in the car and we drive off—we were going to stay somewhere on the way back. We were all completely silent, because everybody had the same impression, that my attempt to break loose was not going to make it. I remember bursting into tears and being completely undone. My life was ruined. I'm not going to get in. Nothing I want to do is going to be possible.

But I got in—I don't know why, but he took me. And I went that fall. But God, that was a terrible experience. He could make or break you in five minutes; people's fates were in his hands. It was amazing. There was no appeal process.

I enrolled in a couple of courses at U of I with a guy named Mike Lewis, who was a somewhat left-wing intellectual who was interested in political and race issues. I loved his courses and took everything he taught. I got turned on to the idea of social change—a combination of political science and history and sociology—which was really my interest.

This is a great revelation—forever recorded in this oral history—I was a cheerleader for the wheelchair basketball team. [Laughs.] That was a very high-status deal in those days. Being a cheerleader meant that we would, among other things, travel between the fall and spring semesters for about three weeks all around the Midwest—Illinois, Michigan, Iowa, Wisconsin. We put on exhibition basketball games. Part of the halftime entertainment would be to drag out these platforms with ramps and things. A few of the women but mostly the men did wheelchair tricks. They would bounce up and down the stairs in their wheelchairs, and they would do wheelies and spin circles and that kind of stuff.

This whole thing was a public relations strategy by the University of Illinois to promote an image of people with disabilities as people who can fit in, people who can be competitive, people who can be physically independent. That idea of physical independence was extremely important, because that's what they thought was the basis for a lot of the negative ideas about disabilities—that people were dependent.

They never understood the whole concept of the level playing field, of how attendants made people physically independent. Yet attendants were anathema. Only people who were physically able to play basketball, do wheelchair tricks, or be a cheerleader were accepted. I was barely able to do this stuff because I had enough limitations in terms of my disability, but I just muscled through it and passed. So we would go to these little towns and we'd stay in people's homes and sometimes in hotels. It was amazing: no access anywhere. There was no bathroom in the world anybody could use, so we were putting coffee tables and dining room chairs in the bathrooms and transferring to a chair and to another chair and to the toilet.

Kitty Cone and I started college together—literally the same moment. We were four doors down the hall from each other in the dorm. Her influence on me took hold instantly. I was being pulled in two directions: one was toward this jock U of I paraplegic thing, the sort of physicality of what they were trying to portray. On the other hand, I was pulled toward politics and social issues and war issues and the kinds of things that she was interested in.

The dorms were humongous. They were gender segregated, except the graduate dorms. Only the first floor was modified. The bathrooms had accessible stalls. I think they must have had wide doors and low toilets. I don't even know if they had bars. And the showers had fold-down stainless steel seats, with a pad on them. There were elevators to the other floors, but there weren't any accessible bathrooms. So they put everybody in chairs or with mobility disabilities who needed the bathroom access on the first floor. It's integrated, yes, because all the public spaces are integrated and the dining room is integrated. But there were a lot of people in chairs on that floor—not exclusively, but there were still a lot of folks. A lot of people switched dorms after the first year or so because they didn't want to be in the ghetto; they wanted to get into some other dorm situation where there were more non-disabled people.

They had maybe three good-sized school buses equipped with hydraulic lifts. They were really narrow little lifts with no protective flaps or elevated sides to keep you from sliding off. It became a game to see how cool you could be on the lift. There was a bar, which was the passenger bar that you hold on to when you're walking up the stairs. You would get on the lift, you wouldn't put the brakes on, and hold on to the bar and be so cool. The thing was really dangerous, and for the people who didn't have the arm strength to do that the drivers would squat down on their knees and reach out as far as they could and hang on to the chair. Or if it was really an unstable situation, if it was pouring down rain or something, they would have to get out of the bus and operate the switches from the outside and hold the person on the lift. One was not cool if one needed to be held on the lift. So there were these levels of coolness . . .

The buses circulated on a time schedule all around the main buildings on campus. You didn't make arrangements for a ride, you just showed up at the bus stop where the bus came. If you needed to get from one building to another where the buildings were far from one another, you had to schedule classes with an hour in between because you would have to get to the bus stop, get on the bus, ride around on the bus until you get dropped off at the next place. So you couldn't actually take classes back-to-back in buildings that were distant from one another on campus. If people had been allowed to use motorized wheelchairs, of course, you could get there in five minutes, but that wasn't permitted. Riding the buses wasn't all that cool, either.

The ramping situation was kind of interesting in retrospect. I thought the ramps were really, really stupid because I used a pushchair, and I had horrible time getting up most of them and needed help and always had to sit at the bottom and say [in a pathetic voice], "Help me, help me." Sometimes I'd try to muscle up them, and I'd get two-thirds of the way and then I'd be done in; I couldn't go another inch.

There was no such thing as a "primary entrance" theory of life, either.[3] You get in any way you could get in. But compared to being carried up the stairs it was heaven. It was a tremendous improvement. There probably were some buildings you couldn't get into at all, but I honest to God can't remember. There were a few that were just too hard to get in because the ramps were so steep. It was so difficult that you tried to avoid them, to get classes in other places. But basically you could pretty much go anywhere on campus, one way or another. For that day, given the state of technology and the understanding of the issues, it was pretty good. Now we would be appalled, but it was pretty good for what it did.

You got yanked in by the scruff of your neck if the staff at the Rehab Center saw you doing something they didn't approve of. There was a whole range of things, including having somebody push your wheelchair. So if it's four below zero, and the snow's ten feet deep, and you cannot get from A to B, and you're seen being pushed—in some situations they turned their heads [and looked the other way].

I didn't fault them at the time because I didn't know to. Then later, when I began to think about and understand my own experience a bit more, I thought about the U of I, and I thought that they should have done better. They should have been able to figure this stuff out; they should not have permitted this patriarch to determine and direct so many people's lives. Particularly in the sixties, where there was so much foment and upheaval going on.

The race issues, the civil rights issues that were exploding in the South, did not reach that campus except through a few classes like Mike Lewis's. So it's no surprise, really, that nobody could figure the disability issues out. Nobody ever said, "Let's start to think about disability as a political issue. Why is it that the Rehab Center is promoting its philosophy that if you can't get in the building you should crawl up the steps? That unless you're willing to make that commitment, you can't come to school here?"

There was something really radically sick about that picture. And I bought into it, too. I believed it and went along. I certainly was not part of the solution.

6
Discrimination, Part 2, and Early Advocacy

A TTEMPTS HAD BEEN MADE BEFORE THE 1960S TO ADDRESS discrimination against people with disabilities. The League of the Physically Handicapped, the American Federation of the Physically Handicapped, the National Federation of the Blind, and the National Association of the Deaf had all, with some success, pushed for changes in how American society treated citizens with disabilities. But by the early 1960s, both the League and the American Federation were defunct, and neither the NFB nor the NAD considered themselves as part of a broader, cross-disability rights movement. Meanwhile, other disability-specific groups, such as United Cerebral Palsy, Inc., and the Muscular Dystrophy Association, were dedicated to providing services to individuals with particular illnesses or disabilities and support for their families rather than to any broader, rights-based agenda.

As a result, people who wanted to take action against instances of discrimination or prejudice generally had to do so as individuals. In the process, they often met others who had had similar experiences. The coming together of these individuals marked the beginnings of the cross-disability rights movement still active today.

Ed Roberts
"If two or three things had been different, I might have had a whole different kind of life."

Edward V. Roberts is most often identified by his biographers as "the father of the independent living movement," in recognition of his role as a cofounder of the Center for Independent Living in Berkeley in 1972 and the most visible proselytizer of "the independent living philosophy." Roberts was also a cofounder (with Judy Heumann and Joan Leon) of the World Institute on

Disability in 1983, using the money he had received as a MacArthur Fellow to spread the ideas of independent living and disability rights.

Roberts often told the story of how, as he was lying in his iron lung after contracting polio as a teenager, he overheard a doctor tell his mother, Zona, that he would be "better off dead" than to live his life as "a vegetable." The statement, callous as it may have been to say in Roberts's presence, voiced a commonly held opinion among medical professionals of the time. To be, as Roberts would remain his entire life, a functional quadriplegic, growing more dependent on a respirator as he aged, is still regarded by many people as "a fate worse than death." Years later he would joke that if he had to be a "vegetable," he would prefer to be an artichoke: "A little prickly on the outside [but] with a big heart. . . . I'd like to call on all the vegetables of the world to unite."

That early moment wasn't the last time that Ed Roberts would be written off by medical and rehabilitation professionals. One of the more ironic twists in Roberts's story is that California governor Jerry Brown Jr., impressed with Roberts and the independent living movement, in 1975 appointed him director of the state Department of Rehabilitation—the agency that little more than a decade earlier had deemed him ineligible for assistance in getting a college education because he was vocationally "infeasible" and thus unlikely ever to get a job.

Ed Roberts died of a heart attack on March 14, 1995. He was fifty-six years old.

———

At home, I'd been virtually a shut-in for years. I remember when a social worker and my mother came to me and said, "If you don't begin to get out of here, you're going to stay here the rest of your life." So they loaded me up in the station wagon and took me to my school [Burlingame High School in California], and they started to unload me. It was lunchtime; there must have been two hundred students, or it seemed like. They were all eating lunch around this court, and every one of them turned to stare at me. One of the reasons that I had not come out was that I was terrified of being stared at. That just indicated to me how awful it was and how ugly I was.

But I remember that day when they were getting me out of the car, and all of a sudden my worst fear came true: everybody was staring at me. And when I'd look up at them, they'd look away. And something remarkable occurred to me while I was there.

The first thing was that it didn't hurt. For people to stare at me did not hurt me. It had been such a fear that I thought it would.

The second thing that occurred to me was that maybe it wasn't all my problem, because when I looked back, they would look away. As I thought about that, why was I taking all this on as my problem when wasn't the fact they stared also their problem? It was an interesting feeling.

The third thing was, oh, it was like being a star! I think that was one of the more important times in my life, that I realized I could enjoy it. I didn't have to feel guilt or all those things that I was feeling—anger especially. Actually, I could enjoy being stared at, if I thought of myself as a star, not just a helpless cripple.

My whole attitude toward school changed. I went from a bad student in grammar school, really not an F student but basically a C student, to becoming a straight-A student in high school. My mother was pretty smart and helped me do a lot of stuff. Basically, I learned through her tutelage, and other students, how to write papers and how to take tests. I was pretty proud of myself.

I filed for graduation like my brother had, because I'd missed two years of school and so by that time my brother's class was my class. What happened then was the school came back almost immediately and said, "You cannot graduate. You don't have enough required credits." We said, "What? I've fulfilled all my academic [requirements]. I've taken college prep, and done very well." They said, "But you have not had driver training and P.E., and these are state requirements." I said, "I don't think I'm going to need driver training." I remember my mother once, in a state of sarcasm, looking at the principal and saying, "Well, we'll put him in the seat, and I will get behind him, and I will drive him"—very sarcastical. "Well, I've had physical therapy," and they said, "No, no, that's not good enough."

They were still going to enforce it. I remember how I felt, really awful, like I was going to have to stay longer. I was twenty-one or twenty years old already—totally age inappropriate.

There was no question that after that, I fought. And I often did it on my own. Well, my mother did this one. I remember the assistant superintendent of schools, the number two guy in the whole district here, he knocked on the door and he came in, and we were talking. We didn't like him at all. Then he looked at me and he said, "Now, Ed. This won't take you long to do this, and you don't want a cheap diploma." Oh, my mother and I were so livid. He wanted me to continue in school for another year. We told him he could leave the house. My mother escorted him out the door. We were so happy to kick him out of the house. These guys had no concept of what it was all about.

We had a friend of my mother's who was on the school board. We picked up the phone and called Mimi Haas. She was a school psychologist, but she had run for the school board and won. She said, "The school board makes that decision, not the school." My mother was—I didn't go, but she was so afraid—she was just scared to speak. Which is a little bit unusual, because she had been president of PTA and all kinds of things, she was pretty well known at the school. But this was so serious, it was so emotional.

She went to go up to the microphone. They didn't even let her start— they said basically, "We've talked about this. It's totally unreasonable. Ed will graduate." So she started crying. I guess they kind of got the message that she was so relieved.

When I applied to go to [the University of California at] Berkeley, after graduating from the College of San Mateo, I went to see a [vocational rehab] counselor. I went in, and they gave me some tests. And I remember this counselor telling me that I was going to be rejected, and he believed it was important to reject me. Within a couple of weeks, they rejected me for service, saying that I was too disabled to go to work, and I was therefore "infeasible."[1]

We said, "Oh, no you don't." My mother, myself, and Phil Morse from the College of San Mateo, and Jean Wirth, [all of us decided to fight this]. The president of the College of San Mateo also knew me, and so this whole countermovement started. "He's doing well. He can do all kinds of things. He can write. That's crazy."

We got the department to change within a couple of weeks. The director in Sacramento was a real tall good-looking guy. Later, he was a head of INS [Immigration and Naturalization Services] under [President] Ronald Reagan. Anyway, he became a kind of a friend, and he reversed the counselor's decision.

One of the things I learned from that [experience] was in dealing with bureaucracies, it helps to shine the light of publicity on them. Here was this brave quadriplegic hero, whose only real future would have to come because of education, getting an advanced degree to make sure he was qualified to go to work, and they're rejecting him. This horrible department was rejecting him based on some weird standard called "infeasibilty." They got some pretty bad articles written about them. It was total media, and the people at the College of San Mateo calling, that made that happen.

You can imagine, if two or three things had been different, I might have had a whole different kind of life. I tell those stories to people, because I want people to know about how important it is to fight for what you believe in.

Ray Uzeta
"Those of us with physical disabilities were getting kind of resentful."

Ray Uzeta was born in San Francisco in 1941 to Mexican parents who had immigrated to California. As was typical of the era, he had had little exposure to children or adults with disabilities before acquiring a disability himself as a young man.

"In the forties and fifties, if you had a disabled child, you basically put them in a coffin. Not literally, but you kept them home. I used to run into this at the Recreation Center, where we had a lot of people, who were in their forties and fifties, living at home with mommy and daddy. Never went out unless mommy and daddy took them out. I think a lot of parents became very protective: 'We don't want our child to be harmed or stared at or ridiculed out there.' But what the parents forget is what happens when mommy, daddy are no longer here? How is that person going to function in society?"

Uzeta moved to San Diego in 1976, where he established the Community Center for the Disabled (now Access to Independence). In 2010 he retired after serving twenty years as the executive director of the Chicano Federation.

In 1965, I got diagnosed with a very significant and debilitating muscular disease, and by September '65 I was basically on my back, and bedrid-

den. I was functionally a quadriplegic, and I had to use personal attendants, and all the government support programs that existed. And that's
really the thing that changed my life.

It probably wasn't until about '68 when I was able, with some assistance, to get out of the house and a social worker got me in touch with
the Recreation Center for the Handicapped. That program was started, I
guess in the sixties, by a woman named Janet Pomeroy.[2] In essence, she
started offering recreational, social activities for people with severe disabilities. And that was my exposure, for the first time in my life, to other
people with disabilities, from people with cerebral palsy to people with
osteoperosis imperfecta, people with post-polio, a wide gamut. So it was
a real shock to me.

My impression of Pomeroy: she was a socialite do-gooder. Now, that's
not to put her down, but that's my impression. She ran in high circles,
and at that time you needed people with those kinds of connections to
raise money. We'd see her around the program once in a while.

They had different groups that met on different days. They had a large
number of people, what we would now call "the developmentally disabled."
Back then they were called "the educable retarded," "the mildly retarded."
The group I was in was for people with physical disabilities. I would say
there were several hundred people. They had vans that would pick you up
at your house. They had drivers, and tons of volunteers. They prepared
lunch and dinner for you, they took you on outings. So it was nice. It was
kind of a protective, supported environment, but also it was a segregated
environment, because if you didn't know the program you'd drive by that
building and have no idea what was going on inside or who was in there.

And then what started happening is, you started getting this advice.
For example, I said to somebody, "Shit man, I can't button my buttons, I
need someone to help me." He said, "Get a button hook." I said, "What's
a button hook?" He said, "Here, I'll give you a catalogue." Well, those
are the kinds of things where people were doing, what CIL [the Berkeley Center for Independent Living, Inc.] calls, "peer support." But they
were already doing it. They just didn't use that terminology. Your social
worker didn't tell you about button hooks, or anything else. And your
doctors certainly didn't tell you. But it made you more independent, so
you wouldn't have to rely on somebody else.

I remember once they drug us down outside the building and they
lined us up all in wheelchairs, like two lines, and then they gave us a

basketball, and they said, "Okay now pass the basketball back and forth." And twenty socialite women came down. "Oh, isn't this wonderful? They're so brave!" And we were all sitting there, and we felt like puking. "What a bunch of shit this is!" Basically, putting on a show for the wealthy donors. So we were getting resentful. Those of us with physical disabilities were getting kind of resentful, being treated as children, being treated as little crippled people who needed to be taken care of.

After a while we got friendly with some of the staff people, and they would start sharing things about Mrs. Pomeroy, her style of management. Finally some of us, more daring people, decided to take on the system. And so I wrote an article in the in-house newsletter, in which I personally attacked her. To which she retaliated. I was basically asked not to come back, and was bounced out of the program. I wrote letters to their board members, including George Moscone,[3] who later became the mayor of San Francisco. And then I got the ACLU involved. I basically said, "They're infringing on my free speech."

So I became a hell-raiser. I used to have a friend of mine drive me to the center, whenever my group met, and I would sit in the lobby because they would not allow me to enter the building or to interact with anybody. I'd literally sit there for two hours by myself, just to embarrass them, right? Finally I got a call, and they said, "Look, Ray, we'd like to talk with you, but we'd like to talk to you off site." They sent a representative to my house to meet with me. And he said, "We'd like you to go find somewhere else to recreate." That was the way he phrased it.

So those kinds of things were going on, and those of us with physical disabilities were starting to get to the point where we were not really happy there at the Recreation Center. That's when my buddy said, "Ray there's another club, the Indoor Sports Club. Why don't you go over there? We run it ourselves, we don't have these do-gooders telling us what to do. It's all self-determination." That was probably about '69.

The Indoor Sports' Club was a big organization, and they had a lot of chapters all over the country.[4] I remember reading in one of the newsletters the origins of the Indoor Sports' Clubs. It was back in the forties, or something like that. As the program grew, they created an auxiliary of non-disabled people called "The Good Sports," because they wanted to be sure they ran their own thing. A lot of the Good Sports were spouses or relatives of the Indoor Sports' members, but it was definitely a separate, support organization. Maybe they'd do social activities together, or do a picnic together. They had annual conventions at the state level, at the national level, but it wasn't political. I got onto the state governing board, and through them I got exposed to a whole different group of people. So it was another social network. You became very bonded to the group. A lot of personal friendships evolved out of that, people got married out of it. If you didn't go to that once a month meeting, you felt like you were missing something.

Then what happened, in San Francisco, they started building the BART [Bay Area Rapid Transit] system. This was in the seventies. The main thoroughfare in San Francisco is Market Street. And anybody who lived there then remembers that—if you were in a wheelchair—you'd have to be a Kamikaze pilot to go off the curbs at Market and Third because they were at least two feet high. We knew that they were going to tear up Market Street, they were going to repave it. That's when Indoor Sports people led by Irv Meyerson out of the Laguna Hospital chapter contacted the Indoor Sports chapters in the area and said, "Hey, guys, they're going to redo Market Street. Why don't we go down to the city council, the board of supervisors, and ask them to put curb cuts in?" This was pre-architectural legislation. So we said, "Yeah! Crap, we can't get off the curbs anywhere in the city. They're going to tear up the whole street anyway. Put curb cuts in, what's it going to cost them?"

So we went down to city council. This is at City Hall. The main entrances were not accessible, but there was a side street where you went down to the basement level, like the loading dock level, and from there it was a straight shot level entry from which we took the elevators up to the board of supervisors meeting. And we just crammed the place—we must have had fifty people there in wheelchairs. It was probably the first time they'd ever seen so many people in wheelchairs in a committee hearing.

And we got a couple of very receptive councilors; in fact, George Moscone was very supportive, once again, and John Molinari, who was a supervisor. Very supportive people. And I'll always remember the director of public works was totally against this whole idea of curb cuts. Actually came to a committee meeting and said, "I had my staff down at Market and Third for three hours and we didn't see one wheelchair, therefore we don't see no need for this." But we won the day, and the board of supervisors said, "We're going to put curb cuts when we do Market Street."

So we won this first major political victory. We all felt great about it. And what happened then, some other people who happened to hear about this popped up, and I met a guy named John Edmunds. John Edmunds was a post-polio. He was an engineer with Bechtel Corporation, which is a major firm in San Francisco. And he said, "I see what you guys do, I'd like to work with you guys because I think we could do more of these kinds of things."

John was one of these, what I call "lone ranger" disabled people. He didn't want to really associate with Indoor Sports Club or people with disabilities as a group—because he was in the business world, he was working, and he didn't want to be labeled, right? He was a wheelchair user, very independent. You could never help him, boy, he resented that. But a nice guy. Anyway, we started talking, and John said, "Look, you guys won Market Street, why don't you go for further?"

So John, me and a guy called Ken Rheims, who was the president of the Golden Gate chapter of the Indoor Sports Club, we got together, and we said, "Okay, let's figure it out." I was in a one-bedroom apartment in San Francisco. We took out a street map, laid it on my little kitchen table, and we literally penciled in [curb cuts in] every major street in San Francisco, and the side streets on each side.

And we said, "Okay, how are we going to get this through the board of supervisors?" "Well, why don't we pull together all the groups: Indoor Sports, the Easter Seals Society, the Blind Center, blah blah blah?" And John put together this really nice, very fancy report, here's the map, laid it out, very professional. And so we made a list of all the disability-related organizations, we called them and said, "Look, we're going to the board of supervisors to push for a long-range curb cut project, over the next five to eight years. We'd like to send you a document that we prepared, and we're going to ask you if you'd be willing to lend your name to the document, and then to testify at city council when we get a hearing." And they all said, "Absolutely." And John said, "Well, we need a name. What are we going to call ourselves?" And he said, "How about the Coalition for the Removal of Architectural Barriers?" The acronym was CRAB.

So we went down to the city council. We got a hearing. We got all our troops down there, everybody testified, and we beat down the opposition from the public works department, and the board of supervisors approved this long-range curb cut project, and started a five-year master plan of laying out curb cuts. You could just see it year after year, one area at a time, they just jackhammered and laid curb cuts.

So when people go to San Francisco now, through the financial district with all these curb cuts, they don't know this, but they owe it to me, John Edmunds, and Ken Rheims sitting in my kitchen in San Francisco, putting together the master plan.

Deidre Davis
"That was my first self-advocacy."

Like Ed Roberts and Judy Heumann, Deidre Davis's first experience of discrimination came at the hands of a public school system, in her case as an elementary school student in Linden, New Jersey. Unlike Roberts and Heumann, however, Davis's exclusion from a mainstream school had at least as much to do with being African American as it did with having a disability.

Born in 1955, Davis was six years old when she awoke one summer morning to discover that she could not move her legs. After being hospitalized, doctors discovered a tumor pressing on her spinal cord. Although benign, the tumor caused enough damage, even after it was removed, to leave Davis with a significant disability, which has grown more pronounced over time.

Graduating from Brandeis University in 1977 and from Howard University School of Law in 1981, Davis has had a distinguished career as a disability rights activist and attorney, both in private practice and with the government. She has served at the US Department of Education and at the federal Equal Employment Opportunity Commission as the director of the ADA Technical Assistance Division. In 1994, President Clinton appointed her assistant secretary for equal employment opportunity and civil rights at the US State Department, where she was senior policy adviser on international disability rights issues to secretaries of state Warren Christopher and Madeleine Albright. In 2005, Davis became the director of ADA Services for the Walmart Corporation.

Davis's parents were active in the civil rights movement before the onset of Deirdre's disability, working with the New Jersey NAACP and participating in the 1963 March on Washington. Davis herself is a founding board member of the National Minorities with Disabilities Coalition, renamed the National Black Disability Coalition in May 2010.

The neighborhood school I first attended was up the street from where I lived, in a town called Linden, New Jersey, which is just thirty minutes from New York City and next to Elizabeth, New Jersey. Black folks lived on one side of the town, and white folks lived on the other. My school was predominantly black. It was an old school with lots of steps.

I came back home after spending a year in the rehab hospital. My parents insisted that I go back to school and be put in with my non-disabled classmates. This would be second grade now, I was seven or eight years old. They also wanted me to go to a school that was free of a lot of steps. They were scared that I would fall down. These are things that happened long before we had terms like "accessible" or "mainstreaming."

The predominantly white school had only two steps, and a banister. It was brand new, just built. That's where my parents wanted me to go.

However, the white people in my town had another opinion. They had no intention for me, both being colored and being a cripple, to show up at their school and go to school with their children. It became a battle, because when my parents found out that the opposition was so big, it made them all the more tenacious to get me into that school.

What the school district wanted me to do, what they wanted my parents to do, was to put me on a special bus and ship me out to Jersey City. Well, my mother being an educator, and very proactive, she took me to that school. We spent a whole day in that school going from class to class. It was a mixture of kids with severe mental retardation, along with students who had mobility challenges.

When we left, my mother said, "What do you think?" And I said, "Well, they're just babysitting those kids. Nobody's learning anything." "You're absolutely right, and you're not coming to this school."

There was no law protecting us, no 504 or IDEA or anything like that. So my parents worked through the administrative process, not through a judicial process.

After a long administrative process and a battle between black and white, the state secretary of education overruled all the lower administrators' procedures. He said, "Of course this child will go to school where she can function the best." There was nothing wrong with my intellectual development. I was completely fine cognitively. That's why we fought, and that's why he made that decision. "She's going there." So I did.

In my first week, you'd have thought I was the circus, that the circus had come to the school. We'd go out for recess, I wouldn't engage. By this time I had braces, but they were now down to the knee, knee down braces. And I still had my crutches; I still had my funny little atrocious looking helmet that I had to wear, in case I fell. So I kind of hung out at the wall. I didn't venture out. And a couple of guys would throw the ball at the wall, towards me. When they'd run by and get the ball, they would say, "Nigger!" and I would be like, "Whoa!" And that went on for a whole two weeks. And then, later on, they figured out, "She's crippled, too." So then they'd throw the ball at me, and they'd run by and pick it up and say, "Crippled nigger!" And that was even more frightening because I hadn't even heard the word. It wasn't in my vocabulary at all. So that was my other "-ism" exposure.

I think the racism was much more intense than the prejudice against disability. But I was working from a disadvantage. My parents were at the civil rights march of 1963, so they practiced nonviolence. So I knew, one: I couldn't whup those guys with my cane or my crutches, as badly as I wanted to. That wouldn't have been accepted. And secondly: I had to figure out some way to exist here, because I wasn't going to go home and cry to my parents about the names I was being called. They had worked so hard to get me in the school, I really never shared with them the type of abuse I was getting on a daily basis.

I approached my teacher and informed her that this was happening to me. And I said I didn't think my parents would appreciate knowing that this was happening to me, and if she didn't do something they would surely be up here to see the principal. So that was my first self-advocacy. The first time I ever remember consciously having to advocate for myself.

I was processing it as, "How did all these little white kids learn all this hate at such a young age?" That was what was uppermost for me. I didn't understand how these kids could call me these things, how they were taught to hate at such an early age. Did I derive a civil rights posture from it? Sure, I did. Definitely. "This is not right, this is not fair."

Once I went in there and told that teacher, she had a conversation with those kids and their parents. She did the right thing. She never checked in to find out afterwards if anything else was happening to me, but I'm pretty sure that she would have known if those kids had kept up the abuse.

There was another part of all this: When I got into the new school, my parents found that the curriculum that I was exposed to there was totally different, and much more advanced, than the curriculum at the school up the street from my house, the predominantly black school. So basically because of me, the black parents in the community had a lot of meetings, and they demanded that black parents, or any parents, be able to send their children to any school that they chose in Linden, New Jersey. So I was an instrument of racial integration. Unintended, but still an instrument of change.

Up until then, I was the only black kid at that school. This was '68-ish, in the middle of all the regular anti-establishment stuff that was going on. Then, at the beginning of fifth grade, that was when the integration by choice happened. Black parents could put their children at any school in the district that they wanted. That's when more people joined me. And it was wonderful! It was wonderful to have other black kids join me.

Judith Heumann
"Even if I had lost, at least I would have been fighting for what I believed in."

Few disability rights activists have had as significant an impact, and in such a variety of roles, as Judith E. Heumann. She has, at various points in her advocacy career, used litigation, street demonstrations, and legislative lobbying to achieve equal rights for people with disabilities, and her impact can be seen in everything from the drafting of the Education for All Handicapped Children Act of 1975 to the HEW demonstrations of 1977 to the disability rights activism of the 1990s and beyond. As a founder of Disabled in Action and cofounder of the American Coalition of Citizens with Disabilities, and as a recruiter of activists such as Johnnie Lacy, John Lancaster, and Deidre Davis, she has had a profound influence on almost every aspect of disability rights activism from the early 1970s up to the present day.

Born in Philadelphia in 1947, Heumann grew up the child of German-Jewish immigrants in Brooklyn, New York, with the knowledge that all of her grandparents had been killed in the Holocaust. She contracted polio at eighteen months. Her family's first experience of disability-based discrimination came when Judy was forbidden to attend public elementary school in New York City, because the principal was afraid her wheelchair would be "a fire hazard." As with Ed Roberts and others, exclusion from or discrimination by one or another aspect of the public education system was a theme in Heumann's early career as an advocate, and "her vision of equal rights and access for all people with disabilities was shaped in early childhood by [these] experiences of discrimination. . . . Throughout her elementary and high school education, before disability rights even existed as a concept, Ms. Heumann questioned the practice of segregation-based special education."[5]

Entering Long Island University in 1965, Heumann was told by the school administration that she would not be allowed, because of her disability, to live on campus. She appealed the decision all the way to the university's president before she was permitted to move into the dorms, and then she fought for the establishment of a campus disabled students' program. In 1969 she passed her licensure test for a teaching certificate but was denied employment by the New York City public schools. Heumann filed suit, and in 1970 won one of the earliest disability-based employment discrimination lawsuits in the nation.

Heumann founded Disabled in Action out of this experience (recounted in chapter 10). In 1973 she moved to the West Coast, joining Ed Roberts at the Center for Independent Living in Berkeley. By 1974 she was working in Washington as legislative assistant to Senator Harrison Williams (D-NJ) as he drafted the Education for All Handicapped Children Act of 1975. She returned to California in 1975, where she became deputy director of the CIL and a leader in the HEW occupation of 1977 (recounted in chapter 14). Given her experiences with education discrimination, it was an especially sweet victory for Heumann to be appointed assistant secretary of education by President Clinton in 1993, with responsibility over the Office of Special Education and Rehabilitation Services.

Heumann remains one of the most respected voices in the American disability rights movement. In 2010 she was appointed by President Obama as Special Adviser for International Disability Rights at the US State Department.

When I was in high school I thought about teaching, because I like children. I actually was interested in theater, but that seemed pretty unattainable, and my parents were definitely focused on my pursuing a traditional career.

So I took my courses, and when I graduated I applied for a teacher credential at the Board of Education. I had to take a written exam and an oral exam and a medical exam. All three were offered in inaccessible facilities, so I had friends carry me up the stairs. I passed the written and oral exams.

Then I took the medical exam, where I had an old woman as the doctor. It was very strange. I think that she really just could not believe that someone in a wheelchair would apply for this position. I know she didn't follow the usual interview format, because I know she didn't ask everyone she evaluated to show her how they went to the bathroom, which she did for me. First, I remember being completely blown away by the question. Then I remember saying to her that I could assure her that if my job was to teach children how to go to the bathroom, I'd be able to do that.

I think she was something of a voyeur, in that she asked questions that I know lots of people wonder about, but are too embarrassed to ask. Children, for example, will ask, "How do you go to the bathroom?" but adults typically don't get the opportunity to do that. So, being a doctor, she no doubt felt entitled to indulge her curiosity.

Then, in taking my medical history, she found out that I used to use crutches and braces. I told her I didn't use them anymore after my spinal fusion, but she said I had to come back for a second medical exam and I had to bring them in and wear my braces because I had to show her how I walked. I remember explaining to her that I would never be safe in a classroom as an instructor using my crutches and braces because I couldn't stand up by myself, I couldn't sit down by myself, it took me a very long time to walk, and I was completely unstable. But she insisted on it.

So I came back for another medical exam. This time I brought the director of the Disabled Students Program at Long Island University, Theodore Childs. He's an African American man and was very active in the NAACP. I wanted him to come into the interview with me so that I wouldn't feel so vulnerable, like I did the first time. But they wouldn't let him in, they made him wait outside.

This time she had two other doctors with her. I didn't bring in my crutches and my braces, and so they wrote down—I remember reading upside down on the form—that I was "insubordinate." At one point, this doctor—the woman—said to these two men, "She wets her pants sometimes." I remember sitting there, thinking, "This is not really happening." It was like she had this fixation on bathrooms. I said, "What are you talking about?" But the truth is I was ready to cry throughout this whole thing because I was only twenty-one or twenty-two years old. I was trying to get a teaching credential, and I knew there were going to be problems with it, but you can't really prepare. I left that interview very much doubting there was going to be a positive result.

I never expected to get a license, because out of 70,000 teachers in New York City, I didn't know anybody who had been teaching in a wheelchair. It's not that I knew the 70,000 people, but I would talk to people—nobody knew anybody who was teaching in a wheelchair. I did find out later that there were a few people who had gotten their credentials prior to having their disability and had MS [multiple sclerosis] or something like that. But even though I was expecting the rejection, it still hurts you, when it finally happens.

I got my notification of denial in February of 1970. After I got the official letter of rejection, I had to figure out what I was going to do. I talked to my parents, to my friends. Things just fell into place. There was a disabled man who was a journalism major in school, and worked as a stringer for the *New York Times*. He wrote an article on a Wednesday about my being denied the teaching credential. The next day there was an editorial in the *New York Times* supporting my getting a teaching position.

That same Thursday, I got a call from a man named Roy Lucas, who was working with a small organization that was doing constitutional law work. He was writing a book and had read the article in the paper, and so called to talk to me about what was happening. While he was interviewing me for the book, I was interviewing him. One of the obvious barriers in trying to decide whether I was going to sue the Board of Ed was finding a lawyer. It's not like today, where you've got disability rights programs that you can call and say, "I've been discriminated against. Have a lawyer for me." There was no such thing as "have a lawyer." So at the end of our interview, I asked him if he would be willing to represent me, and he said he would. At around the same time, one of my father's customers in his butcher shop, a Mr. Schwartzbart, also agreed to represent me. So they were my co-attorneys, filing the lawsuit.

Then I got a call from NBC, the *Today Show*. They set up a debate between me and a man named Bob Herman, who worked for the Office of Special Ed in DC.

We didn't plan any of it, but between the newspaper and magazine articles, the radio and TV interviews, there was something major happening at least once a month. There were some weeks where there were all types of newspaper articles and TV or radio interviews going on. During that whole year, it was amazing the number of people who stopped me on the street. People would be in their car, honk their horns for me to go over and say hello. People would stop me in stores. Some of them would say, "Congratulations. Keep it up." But there were others who talked about people they knew who had disabilities who were also having problems of discrimination.

And so I and my friends decided, when it was apparent we were getting a lot of publicity out of this, not just to talk about the discrimination against me, but to focus instead on the kinds of discrimination that all disabled people face, which I think also made it a more interesting story. I discussed the experiences other people were facing, people I'd met, people who had told me their stories after finding out about mine. I had a conviction, and it was easy for me to fight for that conviction. And it did feel like I was entering into battle. Was I nervous? Sometimes. But not overwhelmingly so.

I had had no training in public speaking or classes on how to present myself to the media, but I really got into it. My parents had done a good job in teaching me not to be a quiet, unassuming person but, rather, to be a New Yorker, and go for it and do whatever you needed to do to get your point across.

I remember the day in court. The judge was Constance Baker Motley, who was the first African American woman to sit as a federal district judge. It was remarkable, it was awesome. When I saw her, she had such a presence, I felt like it was all going to be fine. Everything felt very serendipitous: the newspaper articles, getting an African American woman as the judge. The symbolisms were very powerful for me.

I guess federal judges change benches, but she told the Board of Ed that she fully intended on keeping this case, and so she encouraged them to revisit it. "I suggest that you do what you need to do to resolve the problem," which was that I had failed the medical exam. So they gave me another medical exam. But it was nothing, it was less than a doctor's visit. A younger woman sat at her desk, had some forms, said, "I'm sorry. This never should have happened."

I got my license, but it didn't stop with that. There had been a law passed in the forties, I think, which had basically said a person couldn't teach if he or she had certain types of disability. And as a direct result of my case, that law was repealed.

Public opinion and the media coverage were very important. Opinion was very strongly in favor of my getting a license and teaching, because of the shortage of teachers, and because people felt that I would be a great role model for kids.

Had I not gone ahead with the lawsuit, it would have been a big problem for me personally, because I would never have known whether I was able to teach. It would have meant that I was accepting what the system was saying to me and to other disabled people, about our worth, about our ability to strive and to achieve. And so, by going forward with this one, even if I had lost, at least I would have been fighting for what I believed in.

Had I not gone to court, I wouldn't have got my teaching license. Bottom line.

I still have the telegram from the Board of Ed, telling me I got the job. My father had it framed.

7
The Parents' Movement

IN THE 1930S, PARENTS OF CHILDREN WITH DISABILITIES, PARTICU-
larly children diagnosed with cerebral palsy and mental retardation, began
organizing into small, local support groups to discuss issues of mutual interest. This process accelerated in the mid- to late 1940s, largely because of the
participation of returning veterans, who believed that their communities owed
their families consideration after their service to the nation. All this activity
led, in 1949, to the founding of the United Cerebral Palsy Associations, Inc.,
and, in 1950, the National Association of Parents and Friends of Mentally Retarded Children, which became the National Association for Retarded Children (NARC).

The parents' movement was instrumental in forcing the creation and expansion of federal, state, and local programs for children with disabilities. Private and public recreational programs and summer camps, the first paratransit
systems in the United States, and the movement for deinstitutionalization of
people labeled mentally retarded all in large part were the result of the advocacy of parents' organizations.

The importance, then, of the parents' movement in the history of disability
rights can hardly be overstated. It was the parents' organizations, most especially
the Association for Retarded Children, that filed some of the first and most far-
reaching disability rights litigation, and here again, Gunnar Dybwad was a major
factor. Inspired by *Brown v. Board of Education,* he had as early as the late 1950s
been contemplating some sort of right-to-education lawsuit on behalf of children
with disabilities, searching for the perfect case and a local ARC to bring it. In
1969, the leadership of the Pennsylvania association (PARC), in particular, James
Wilson and Dennis Haggerty, decided to take up the challenge. After a vote of
approval from PARC, they engaged Thomas K. Gilhool, already known for his
welfare rights litigation, to craft the groundbreaking right to due process and equal
protection arguments that would eventually carry the day.

Dennis Haggerty
"God damn it, there isn't any time. The time should be right now."

As Dennis Haggerty describes himself, he is something of a political incendiary. "I figured our job was to run around the country starting fires, and then sit back to see what happened." It was with this object in mind that Haggerty and fellow attorney Larry Kane solicited the original funds for the National Center for Law and the Handicapped, which began operation at Notre Dame in 1971 and closed shop in 1980. And as a stalwart Republican, Haggerty knew just where to turn for the money.

"Larry had gone to law school at Notre Dame, and we knew the president of Notre Dame, Father Hesburgh,[1] who was a friend of Richard Nixon. So we came up with the idea: why don't we see if we can get Father Hesburgh to let us use the law students at Notre Dame to do research for us, because it would be cheap? And if we can get that done, we might then get some money from the [Nixon] administration. So Hesburgh said, 'Fine. Amen. I'm on board.' We got Nixon to come up with $500,000 to help us." With this seed money, the group of lawyers and students that made up the National Center, including Robert Burgdorf and Frank Laski, filed several of the earliest state right-to-education cases, most notably *In re G. H.* (1974), and pulled together some of the first materials on disability rights law.[2]

Born in November 1927, Dennis Haggerty was institutionalized when he was nine years old, after a bout of pneumonia that turned into bronchitis. "It was called the Atlantic City Seashore House, which was private." Haggerty spent a year there, where he saw not only abuse of patients by staff but also the ways institution administrators were able to cover it up. Returning home to his family and school, he discovered that disability "had a stigma attached to it. During the thirties people were trying to hide the fact that they were involved [with disability] at all." Hazed by his schoolmates, he "just sucked it up."

After high school Haggerty served thirteen years in the navy. He earned a law degree from Temple University in 1955, and set up private practice in Philadelphia. He married in 1951, and he and his wife had a son, Dennis Jr., in 1958. "He was born normal but got pneumonia at three months. It lingered until he was nine months old, when they went in to see what was happening. One of his lungs was dead, so they did a lobectomy. He suffered a cardiac arrest in recovery and lost two or three minutes of oxygen to his brain." Confronted with the absolute lack of services—other than institutionalization—for someone with Dennis Jr.'s disabilities, Haggerty was catapulted into the parents' movement of the early 1960s, where he played a pivotal role in *PARC v. Pennsylvania*.

Haggerty is now retired and lives with his wife of almost fifty years in West Chester, Pennsylvania.

After my son was born, it took two years to get a final diagnosis of his being profoundly retarded, because nobody seemed to want to talk about how limited he would be. I got the final diagnosis in 1960.

We were told by the doctors at that time to put him in an institution. I resisted and said, "I don't think I can do that, because I want to see if we can get some help for him at home and in the area." I joined the local Association for Retarded Children, the Del-ARC, which was the Delaware County ARC, and got very active with them, and got him in the day care program. That's when the frustration started about how little there was to try to educate these children. I told my law partner that I was frustrated, and he said, "Dennis, you're a lawyer. If you can't do anything about it, who can?" And so I became the representative for the Del-ARC down in Harrisburg, and in Harrisburg I quickly got involved with the [PARC] committees.

We did institutionalize Dennis at age eight, because we finally came around to the proposition that maybe he would be better with, quote, his own kind, end of quote. It was a typical institution. I'd visit him every month. I'd fly out to the program in Altoona [Pennsylvania], and spend the weekend, and take him out, and he'd be crying when I had to take him back. And I was so frustrated with it. When I came to pick him up one month, his ear was all bandaged, it had been cut. I asked what happened, and they said, "He fell in the shower."

In the beginning you could go back into the ward, and then they stopped that, and that made me suspicious. I got myself a doctor's kit, and I started going back in the ward as if I were a doctor, and seeing crap I didn't want to see. And one time when I sat there waiting for Boomer to be delivered to me—Boomer was his nickname because he'd bang his head against the wall, twenty out of twenty-four hours—I'm waiting for him to be delivered to me, and I started chatting with this kid that was there. After a few minutes of chatting with him, he said, "I'm sorry Mr. Haggerty what I did to

Boomer." I said, "What happened?" He said, "Well, they were teaching me how to cut hair, and I slipped with the scissors and cut his ear." And my attitude was, why the hell couldn't they tell me the truth? The truth was okay. They're trying to teach people to cut hair.

But it made me so suspicious, and set me up for later on when I investigated Pennhurst. When I found out what really happened to Boomer, I took him on vacation and didn't bring him back. The Catholic archdiocese found me a private home in Middletown, Delaware, where he spent about seven years. I took him out when he was nine, so that would be about 1967. That was the year I was appointed consultant by President Johnson, to the President's Committee on Mental Retardation.

In 1968 I became the chairman of the residential care committee at PARC. You had to be voted in, and I was raising such hell in Harrisburg that I was hard to ignore. One thing I insisted was that they change the name of Pennhurst. I couldn't see why they called it a "state school and hospital," since it didn't qualify as either. So they changed it from Pennhurst State School & Hospital to Pennhurst Center.[3]

The former chairman of the PARC residential committee was really pissed at me because he said I was a rabble rouser, and I said, "I'm raising hell because nothing is being done. Nobody is effecting anything, and why aren't you interested in changing what is happening?" And his answer—he was a minister—his answer was, "It takes time." I said, "God damn it, there isn't any time. The time should be right now." We had absolute fights, absolute fights, and I didn't make many friends in Harrisburg or in PARC, but they did line up behind me after they saw that I was moving in the right direction.

There was a death of a boy in Pennhurst, in 1969. John Stark Williams was his name, and the mother never even found out about it for about a year. She didn't have the money to travel from Philadelphia on her own, and didn't own a car, but we had a bus that took people from the Philadelphia ARC to Pennhurst for free. When she got there, after a wait of three hours, she found out that he was dead. One of the boys ran out and said, "Johnny died in a fire, Johnny died in a fire," and she ran back into the ward, which she was not permitted to do, and she was distraught, because the boy *had* died in a fire. But the official story was that he died after slipping in the shower.

His body had been transferred to a medical institution for research, because nobody claimed him. Of course, nobody claimed the body, because nobody had notified the family that their son had died. It turned out his mother had moved since her last visit, but she'd filled out the paperwork the institution required, she'd done her part. So during my investigation, I asked the administrator, "Why didn't you advise the woman?" "We sent a letter, we sent a telegram." "Where did you send the telegram?" "To 29th Street." And I said, "Well, may I see your phone book?" And there she was, in the book, at 33rd Street. He said, "Well these things happen. We've got twenty-eight hundred people here." I said, "But that was important." And he repeated, "Things happen." I mean, he was just so dismissive.

She called the ARC, and I decided to look into this. I found the boy's body at the Philadelphia Medical Institution. It had been on ice for almost a year. I asked to have an autopsy performed. I talked to the Philadelphia coroner on the phone, and he said "Sure, Dennis." But within one day of that conversation things suddenly changed. "We can't do an autopsy because the death occurred in Chester County, and you're asking Philadelphia County to do it." So obviously somebody had talked to him. So on Thanksgiving Day I visited the chief judge of the Philadelphia court at his home, and I plead my case with him. He ordered the coroner into court the Friday after Thanksgiving Day, and on Friday morning he ordered that the autopsy be done immediately.

The body was brought to the medical examiner's office. The records at the center said that he had died as a result of pneumonia, and that he had fallen in the shower and injured himself. "He fell in the shower." The usual crap that you got. I tried to sneak a camera man into the autopsy, but it wasn't allowed. It didn't matter, I ended up getting photographs from the coroner's office. I then hired our own pathologist, and showed him the photos, and he said, "This is evidence of fire damage to the body, in at least six or eight places."

I used the death of John Stark Williams as my lead case, as I'm preparing for the PARC convention in Pittsburgh to ask them to authorize a lawsuit against the state. I asked Gunnar [Dybwad] would he mind coming to the PARC Pittsburgh convention in '69 to speak for me, because I had been up to Brandeis University quite a few times, as consultant to the President's Committee, and Gunnar and I were good friends. He said he'd be happy to do it.

I arranged for a screen, and for the photos to be shown at the proper time. I showed what we had found, and described the attempt to hide what had occurred, and how and why the institution didn't tell the mother.

The response was overwhelming. "Amen, go ahead. Go sue the state."

That's when I got a hold of Tom Gilhool. He'd already been to the Supreme Court, on the issue of when a person moves from state to state, they had to be a resident for eight to ten months before they could apply for welfare. Tom had been there and knocked that out of the park. So I figured the guy's been the route, he's perfect.

I went to Tom's office, and asked him, would he be interested. He listened quietly, and I went through the whole pitch with him. And when I was finished I said, "Tom, I guess now I'm going to have to teach you about mental retardation." He said, "Dennis, you don't. My brother is retarded." I almost fell off the chair. It was like God was sitting on my shoulder. I said, "Thomas, where is he?" He said, "He's in the state institution up in the mountains. Whitehaven. My mother wants him there. I'd rather he didn't be there, but my mother insists, and it's her boy."

And so Tom and I immediately had a great relationship. I drove him out to Harrisburg to meet the board of directors of PARC, and he was met with open arms, and he came with the message of "I can do," and he did. He was the one who said, "If we're going to sue the state, we should go against the education piece first, because it's easier." So we formed a committee, and we went against the Commonwealth of Pennsylvania, and the education piece was first.

Thomas K. Gilhool
"If we can open the schools, then the demand for institutions will fade away."

Thomas K. Gilhool has devoted his career as an attorney to advocating for people who have traditionally gone without representation. A graduate of Yale Law School, during the mid-1960s he worked with Community Legal Services, Inc., in Philadelphia, on a variety of important poverty law cases.

It was Gilhool's poverty law work that brought PARC representatives Dennis Haggerty and James Wilson to his Philadelphia office in 1969, to discuss PARC's options for filing civil rights litigation. Unbeknown to them, Gilhool himself had had several profound experiences with disability and disability-based discrimination. His younger brother Bob had been born with a cognitive disability and was first institutionalized at the Pennhurst State School & Hospital, Pennsylvania's "flagship institution," when Tom was still a child. Gilhool's father was ostracized by his employer for having a disabled child, which led to "a nervous breakdown" in 1947, the treatment for which included electroshock. "I came to understand" says Gilhool, that Bob's disability was considered "the parents' fault; that these things were [believed to be] genetic . . . and I remember the sense that Darlington [the president of the coal company where Gilhool's father worked] had begun to use Bobby against my father."

PARC v. Pennsylvania was filed in 1969 and settled in 1972. The case was part of a broader strategy, not only to force the public schools to accept children with disabilities but to close down institutions such as Pennhurst. That goal was pursued and achieved in *Halderman v. Pennhurst,* a crucial deinstitutionalization case argued all the way to the US Supreme Court, in which Gilhool was once again the lead attorney for the plaintiffs. The consent decree that came out of *PARC*—a decree largely drafted by Gilhool—provided language that would be used as a model for the Education for All Handicapped Children Act of 1975 (now called the Individuals with Disabilities Education Act, or IDEA).

Thomas K. Gilhool was born in Ardmore, Pennsylvania, in 1938. He retired as director of the Public Interest Law Center of Philadelphia in 2008.

———

Jim Wilson and Dennis Haggerty called one day to say, "We've just done an investigation of Pennhurst and we've got this report. And we have had a vote of the association that we want to go to court. Can we come see you and talk about working on it, and what we might do?"

This was '69. And we talked for a considerable period of time, maybe an hour and a half, two hours. They did not know what kind of a case they wanted to bring, [but] they had already voted that they wanted to litigate. They had some ideas that I don't remember, but I suspect were probably articulated in "right to treatment" terms. "Right to treatment" had been in the air.[4]

They had not known about Bob, and I told them about him, and that was edifying both to them and to me. I am quite sure that it was in the course of that conversation that they told me about Gunnar. And Peter [Dybwad, Gunnar's son] had been one or two years behind Gillian[5] and me at law school. But I had no idea of what an ARC was, or of its context or history or what have you. It was just the world opening up, for all of us. And you know, it was so right that we just enthusiastically committed to each other right there.

Gunnar and I pretty promptly became constant intellectual companions, if not being physically together. And he, shortly after that conversation, gave me a whole lot of stuff to read and understand. He had been counseling with many ARCs across the country, through most of the sixties, and within moments of *Brown v. Board* he had written a piece in the ARC newsletter in which he said, "Look at *Brown*. That applies to us, too." His work with ARCs around the country was much about getting that to be understood. And for reasons that I've never been entirely sure of, he spent an especial lot of time throughout the sixties with the Pennsylvania ARC, certainly in the three or four years leading up to '68 and '69. He was there when they decided they would go look at Pennhurst again, and made it happen. I used to kid Rosemary [Dybwad][6] that the reason why Pennsylvania was so lucky as to have him in this way was that we had the best greasy spoon on the East Coast, on the main street of Harrisburg, and Gunnar was a huge fan of greasy spoons.

I disappeared then for about nine months, because it was that long before I gave them a report with the alternatives for litigation. I can't explain for sure how the hell it came to take me nine months, except that I've always been very slow, particularly at this end of things, trying to formulate things strategically.

The power of education here was, of course, unavoidable, because of *Brown v. Board of Education*. And Gunnar certainly would've called attention to it. I mean, all of us at law school, and then after law school, in anything we were doing, were constantly tuned into the several layers of school desegregation lawsuits that were going on around the country and in the Supreme Court.

People with retardation though were new to the courts, so we had to teach them about people with retardation. Having also to teach them about institutions, and [using] the rather new legal doctrines concerning the right to treatment, would've meant we'd have to teach them two big new things. But because of the courts' knowledge and awareness, all around the country, of the Southern school desegregation stuff, [we] felt that they knew schools, and were comfortable with them, and that was a real gain for starting with this case.

It had become very clear—the ARC people knew it, and Gunnar cer-

tainly knew it—that the very greatest number of people sent to institutions were sent in their early teen years, usually to stay there for life. Why
were they sent then? Because their families were alone. There was nothing else, except an occasional ARC or UCP run program. And so, when
their children started acting like teenagers—namely, getting considerably rambunctious and reaching out to take control of their world—the
families were all alone in dealing with it. They didn't even have the relief
in time, of sending the youngsters off to school. And so their vulner-
ability to sending the youngster off to an institution was at its height. So
the analysis was that if we can open the schools, then the demand for
institutions will fade away.

The foul here, the unlawful violations, were the school exclusionary
laws of Pennsylvania, which it turned out every state had adopted in the
first couple decades of the twentieth century. And there were four or five
particular mechanisms in that law whose function and purpose was to
exclude people with retardation, and cerebral palsy, and epilepsy, and a
couple of other disabilities, from the schools. One of them was: you can't
start school unless you reach a "mental age" of five. Well, as mental ages
were calculated, there would be a whole lot of people who would be five,
six, seven, eight, nine, and ten, and not reach mental ages of five. There
was a second provision, very common among the states, which gave
school boards authority to exclude from their schools children whom
they found to be "uneducable and untrainable."

These statutes were all of a cut. The focal point of the statutes in all of
the states were segregation and sterilization. And then sometimes in the
same statutes, but more often four or five years later, the school codes
were amended—sometimes to charge superintendents with seeking out
these people, and taking them to the institutions, whether or not the
parents objected. That was a kind of enforcer for the segregation and
the sterilization; but it was also the tippy edge of the school exclusion
provisions.

And those were the mechanisms that we alleged were unconstitutional. One, because they denied to children who could profit from an
education the opportunity to be in school; and two, because they did so
in ways which denied due process.

So we sued all of the school districts in Pennsylvania. The lead plaintiff
was the Commonwealth of Pennsylvania. By and large, we always named

the Commonwealth of Pennsylvania as the lead defendant, because it was impersonal. That wasn't the governor, it wasn't the secretary of education. You weren't picking on some*one*. It had been my habit—and I think the habit of very many good social change lawyers—*not* to sue governors, the theory being that we wanted to leave the governor free to come to terms with the case without forcing him to be prematurely defensive.

Gunnar made an amazing contribution to this, struggling around the very writing of the complaint, so that it would be understood by the media, and used by them. And the PARC investigation of Pennhurst had resulted in a ten part series on Channel 10 television here. So the suit, with the resulting publicity, was also designed to influence public understanding, to lessen the stigma, and to increase the appreciation of the fact that people labeled "mentally retarded" could learn. It was designed, in some low key way, to affect school people as well, so that they would begin to know that this would be fun and exciting, or at least hopeful. And it was certainly designed to affect legislative and executive decision makers. Tom Lamb, who was majority leader of the state senate during these times, was quoted as saying, the day the decree was announced, "Damn! I wish we'd done that." And of course, it was also designed for the constituency. That is to say, families of people with retardation, people who are retarded, their relatives, et cetera.

I had prepared four witnesses for the first day of trial. The opening witness was Ignacy Goldberg, who did the brilliant historical stuff, which is reflected in the opinion. And Jim Gallagher and Don Steadman, both of whom were then at the University of North Carolina, one of whom, Steadman, was subsequently a provost at Duke. Jim had been the Assistant or Associate Commissioner of Education for the US in charge of disability education, and had just returned to North Carolina. And they both testified to the underlying educability facts. And the fourth witness was Burton Blatt, from Syracuse, whose dissertation was about the changeability of intelligence.[7] They [all] testified at the close of the day. [Their testimony was so compelling, our case was so strong, that at that point the attorney representing the Commonwealth] stood up and said, "Your honor, we surrender." So we never called our other witnesses.

After the August day of trial and his announcement to the court, [Pennsylvania assistant attorney general] Ed Weintraub and I essentially lived together for the next three months, working on the consent decree.

We did some of it at my office, we did some of it in his backyard in central Pennsylvania. I have a memory that I would have liked [the language of the decree] to have been sharper. "Training appropriate to the child's capacity, within the context of a presumption that . . . placement in a regular public school class is preferable to placement in a special public school class; and placement in a special public school class is preferable to placement in any other type of program of education and training."

Which is pretty good, and has some pretty good bite. But, you know, it could have been sharper.

Paul Marchand
"There was no question that discrimination was going on in every state, to a greater or lesser degree."

While Dennis Haggerty was a parent and advocate, and Thomas K. Gilhool a movement attorney, Paul Marchand was, in the early 1970s, a relatively new phenomenon in disability rights: a professional, Washington-based lobbyist. It was Marchand and others in Washington who built on the legal success of *PARC* and similar right-to-education cases, and the grassroots and local efforts of people like Haggerty to pass the landmark Education for All Handicapped Children Act of 1975. Since then, for more than three decades, Marchand has been at the center of efforts to pass federal legislation to improve the lives of people with disabilities, right up to and beyond the ADA of 1990.

Paul Marchand was born in 1942 in Woonsocket, Rhode Island. After working as a "special ed" teacher in Dartmouth, Massachusetts, he "got into the parents' movement in a big way" in 1967, first as the executive director of the Northern ARC of Rhode Island, then as the first executive director of the state's Developmental Disabilities Council.

Marchand moved to Washington in 1973, where he chaired the Consortium for Citizens with Developmental Disabilities—a coalition of parents' groups and service providers—formed to work for the passage of the Developmentally Disabled Assistance and Bill of Rights Act of 1975. Now called the Consortium for Citizens with Disabilities, or CCD, the group has been a major player in every piece of disability rights legislation passed since 504, and was a clearinghouse for information and advocacy during the campaign to pass the ADA.

Marchand retired as the director of the Disability Policy Collaboration of the Arc and United Cerebral Palsy and the Arc's Governmental Affairs Department in January 2011.

———

The ARC's Washington office opened in 1969. I arrived in January of 1973 as the assistant director. There had been five directors from 1969 to 1973. The person who hired me was a former hill staffer, who knew nothing about disability. She resigned within a year, and I applied for the position and was denied the promotion, so they hired somebody else. And he lasted another year or so, and then in 1975 I became the director.

When I arrived the national staff was the director, the assistant director, somebody who did communications, and a secretary. Then there were two other staffers who were working on a federal grant.

Since 1973 we were always downtown, near the White House. We first were at 1522 K street, and it was an office that very comfortably housed the six of us and a conference room. The conference room was critical because we became the hub for what ultimately become the Consortium for Citizens with Developmental Disabilities.

The Rehabilitation Act of 1973 was my first initiation into the federal lobbying process, my first experience watching senators and congressmen at work, seeing congressional hearings, seeing the process of the bill's language evolve over time, seeing the compromising that had to take place, seeing the various disability groups jockeying for position. It was like being thrown into a cement mixer, going round and round, just absorbing everything that I could. I was primarily concerned, of course, with how the Rehab. Act ultimately would serve people with mental retardation, which was always our priority.

When I first arrived here, there was a loose-knit group primarily around the DD [developmental disabilities] groups. The main players then were the ARC, UCP, the Epilepsy Foundation, the Council for Exceptional Children, the state MR [departments of mental retardation] directors, the state mental health directors, the state vocational rehab directors—they were the core. We officially settled on a name in 1973 or '74. We called it CCDD, the Consortium for Citizens with Developmental Disabilities.

It was not incorporated probably until sometime in the 1980s. It was very informal, no dues. All of it was operated on less than a shoestring by the lobbyists for those particular organizations, and most of us had a staff of one or two people. Sometimes we'd meet weekly, sometimes we'd meet monthly, it all depended on what was going on at the time, and what was necessary to do.

The first thing we did was decide on who was going to do what. We had subcommittees, and anybody could join any subcommittee they were interested in. Remember, none of us were getting paid to do coalition work, we were all getting paid by our individual organizations. So the subcommittees took on a life of their own. We had an education group, we had a group doing rehab, we had a group doing housing, we had a group doing appropriations and Social Security. So whoever joined those groups then would decide the priorities in that particular area. That's how we worked. It's still the model that we use today. The coalition has grown from the eight or nine of us back in the mid-seventies to about 115 national groups today. We went from four or five subcommittees or task forces, to now we have seventeen or eighteen.

As I said, the Rehab Act of '73 was the big item when I first arrived, but I was too new to have much to do with that. My first real work along those lines was on the Education for All Handicapped Children Act of 1975, also called PL [Public Law] 94-142, and now known as the Individuals with Disabilities Education Act, or the IDEA.

In any piece of legislation there's always a substantial amount of negotiation. The House bill was clearly different than the Senate bill. We were, of course, trying to get the best of both worlds. Our biggest problem, besides the people who worry about funding, were the various representatives of the school systems. Their song, as it still is today, was "We'll be glad to do what you tell us to do, so long as you pay for it." And so a lot of the conversation was around the financing.

The business of an IEP [Individualized Education Program][8] was new to the field of education. Nobody else has an individualized program except those kids that are in special ed. The bottom line was the recognition back then, as today, that students with disabilities are not a cadre of similar students. There are thirteen different disability category labels embedded in the law. Each one of those have a certain set of academic and other expectations, that are different from each other, for example, someone with behavior challenges, as opposed to someone who has a cleft palate and has a speech impediment. And also, within each of the categories, there would be substantial differences in academic achievement. Parental involvement in the child's education, which is part of the IEP process, was another huge issue for us. So the individualization—carving out for the individual what is best for them to learn—was the number one factor.

The second factor was more along the lines of a right, as opposed to a service. And that is, since so many students with disabilities had been completely denied their educational rights prior to the passage of that law, we pushed hard that the IEP as developed by the family and the school system would be a contract of sorts, an expectation that what's written in the IEP is in fact delivered.

The "zero reject principle" came from several routes. One was experiences like mine back in Rhode Island, where groups like the ARC were forced to deal with the kids the school system rejected. There was no question that discrimination was going on in every state, to a greater or lesser degree. There were arguments about the educability of some of those kids, but it was hard to argue that the school system should be given a pass for some kids, and not others. That was the basic rights principle of "zero reject," and that word "All" was purposely put into the title of the law so that it was clear that we meant "All."

Besides the IEP, the second driving force in the law is the concept of the "Least Restrictive Environment [LRE]." There were in many of the disability categories various beliefs about how instruction is best delivered. Back then, there were a lot more schools for the Deaf. There were a lot more segregated schools for students with mental retardation. Indeed, a lot of the disabilities were segregated. That has changed some. The inclusive school movement has grown over the last thirty-five years. There are still separate buildings where students with mental retardation get educated today, and there are still schools for the Deaf. On the other hand, there are components of the Deafness community that believe in integration in terms of getting educated with their non-disabled peers.[9] And so the LRE component of the law is subject to interpretation and individualization.

The start date—how much time we would allow to give the school systems to come into implementation—was another issue. The law was passed in '75, but it wasn't implemented until the school year that started in '77. So that was a big debate too, how much time do we give, what was an appropriate time to have this launched in all the school systems.

The key was always bipartisanship. We had to get Democrats and

Republicans working together. I don't want to use too broad a brush, but in general, Republicans have been the more difficult group of politicians to get on our side than the Democrats. So every time we were able to garner support from a key Republican was a major benchmark, a huge step forward for us.

The vote count in the end was pretty strong. Off the top of my head, I'm thinking that there were six or seven, eight negative votes in the Senate, and three or four dozen negative votes in the House. So in the end the final passage was fairly overwhelming.

I was in the spectators' gallery for both the House and the Senate vote. There was unbelievable excitement. When you think about landmark laws—you could say Social Security was one of the landmark laws, you could say that SSI [Supplemental Security Income, for people who acquire a disability before they are old enough to work] was a landmark law—but all of those dealt with cash benefits. Beyond a doubt, 94-142 was the first of the landmark laws that were absolutely, positively, and totally disability and disability rights related.

Diane Lipton
"We realized they didn't know what the hell they were talking about."

Diane Lipton's daughter Chloe, born in 1972, was never institutionalized. Even so, because Chloe was born with cerebral palsy, Lipton and her family had to struggle to get Chloe into the public schools and to obtain access to the services needed to keep her in the community.

Lipton herself, by the time of Chloe's birth, was already familiar with the concepts of discrimination and movement politics. As a teenager she was cognizant of and sympathetic to the civil rights movement of the 1950s and early 1960s. Moving to California in 1963 to attend college at Berkeley, Lipton was soon immersed in that campus's Free Speech Movement. "I was out on Sproul Plaza every day, all day." So when Chloe was born, and her family started experiencing the discrimination to which most every family with a "special" child was subject, Lipton was poised to frame what was happening in terms of civil rights.

Lipton's advocacy brought her into contact with the Center for Independent Living, cofounded by Ed Roberts the same year Chloe was born. It also demonstrated the importance of having one's civil rights protected by law, in this case the Education for All Handicapped Children Act. Understanding this, Lipton earned a law degree and eventually went to work for the Disability Rights Education and Defense Fund (DREDF), becoming one of the nation's foremost litigators and experts on the civil rights of children with disabilities, becoming a bridge between the parents' and independent living movements.

Diane Lipton died in August 2002.

———

By the time Chloe was about ten months old, I started to get suspicious that there was some problem. I had no other children, and I didn't have anything to compare her development to, but I was reading books and knew that at three months, babies do this, at six months [they do] that, and so forth. And she wasn't doing those things. The doctors, when I'd raise this, sort of pooh-pooh'd my concerns. "She's very little and needs time to catch up." I know many other parents have had that same experience, of being pretty certain that something was going on, more than what the doctors were either admitting or sensing.

So when she was a little under a year, we took her to a neurologist, which was a horrible experience. This doctor came in, stood over us. I was holding Chloe. And literally within a second, he said, "She's got cerebral palsy and she may never walk. And it's hard to tell her intelligence at this point. And that's about all I can say right now." And he walked out. That was literally the entire encounter with [this] doctor.

I was just completely blown away. Chloe started crying. I called a friend of mine who lived in San Francisco, because we still lived in El Cerrito. I asked her to come and give me a ride home. I didn't think I could drive, I was so shaken. I went home and gave Lenny the news. It was just totally devastating, because I had no idea. I didn't know what cerebral palsy was. I didn't know what to do with her, or how to help her. I never knew anyone with cerebral palsy. I'd never been exposed much to disability, I just had no idea what this meant in terms of her life, our life, anything.

So what is kind of typical for me is when I feel overwhelmed, and things are out of my control, the way I cope with those kinds of feelings and situations is to get into action, to do what I can. So I made some calls and found out that Easter Seals in Oakland [offered] some physical therapy [for children with CP].

That led me to one or two other resources. Until, when Chloe was about a year and a half, I discovered that about five minutes from my house there was this whole center run by the county mental health, for people with severe disabilities. And there was an intensive nursery school program, like an early intervention. They didn't call it that at the time. They took kids from birth on. So I called them. She started to go there for outpatient physical therapy. Then, within a couple of months, they had room in their baby program. This place was called [the] George Miller West Development Center, because George Miller, Congressman Miller's father, had been instrumental in starting these centers. And for their time, they were very progressive. It was all disabled kids and babies. It went from birth to adult. They had different classrooms for different age groups.

My friends were great. I did not experience what some parents experience, of being isolated from their friends, [of their friends] not knowing how to deal with it, and kind of disappearing. My friends, maybe because I had friends who were hippies and freaky and leftists, they were not turned off by it. They were used to dealing with people who are different. It didn't frighten them. So my friends, our friends, were great, and very, very supportive.

I remember us having to tell my parents about the diagnosis, and dreading telling them. I thought they would be so upset and worried and freaked out, because I grew up in an environment where you didn't discuss illness, certainly not with children. You didn't talk about death. And you didn't really talk about disability. Kids were supposed to be protected from all that. So their squeamishness about all of those things made it very difficult for me to tell them that Chloe had cerebral palsy and that she may never walk, and that we weren't sure about her cognitive development, and so forth. When I finally was able to tell them, and I remember sort of telling it to them in little pieces, they were actually fine in the sense that they loved her very much; they were very supportive. But I know it was painful for them.

So the whole thing had the feeling of being just some terrible tragedy that happened to us. That's how I perceived it. Although, when I was with Chloe, I didn't experience her that way. She was just my kid. I enjoyed her and took care of her and loved her. I didn't look at her and think, "Boy, you're a big tragedy, a mess." But I think it was more the situation that felt like a tragedy to me. It was like being blindfolded in a bad dream or something. Not being able to see a future, because I just couldn't imagine, I didn't know what to imagine was in store for her, for us.

It was difficult even going out. People would always stare, especially as she got a little bit older. Or ask stupid questions. More than that, though, I started to get very aware of what other kids her age were doing and she wasn't doing. If I felt depressed and sad and tragic, it was with respect to that. I found it very hard to be around kids who weren't disabled. Because I could see, then, what she wasn't able to do. But she didn't seem miserable. Her reality was her reality. She would smile and laugh. She's very social, always. She didn't have any perception of herself like that. She didn't seem depressed or withdrawn or in any physical discomfort or anything like that. So there was this kind of contrast between her as a person and the way everyone else perceived the situation. . . .

Some [of the doctors] said she'd walk by the time she was three or by the time she was five. Some said she'd never walk. After a few of these experiences, we realized they didn't know what the hell they were talking about. We started to have a whole different relationship with the medical community. We realized they don't know what to do, and we're really in charge of what should happen, which is kind of scary, because it's nice if you can feel like you can rely on experts. But at sometime pretty early on, you realize that these people are more hung up about disability than you are.

The parents [at the center] had kind of a support group. I met people who were totally different from me. I was making Jell-O molds for the parents' meeting. I'd never made a Jell-O mold before. The parents didn't have the same background or experiences I did. A lot of them just seemed much straighter, more traditional or conventional, but there was this connection about our kids that transcended those differences in a very deep way, which was why people who were very different in terms of economics, race, educational background, really became very close. It's something that has such a big impact on families that to find another family that's dealing with those same issues, everything else sort of fades away, not totally, but largely, in terms of helping each other and understanding each other. A lot of the parents had families who had rejected them. I mean literally, just wouldn't have anything to do with them because they had a child with a disability, or they got very weird and distant. And then there are stresses on marriages when you have a child who requires a lot of intensive attention. So it was a very unifying experience, a very powerful connection that parents had with each other. Even now, I could go to a conference on education and meet another parent with a kid with significant disabilities and there's an immediate connection and understanding. . . .

They would have these meetings with parents and all the experts, once a year or something. Those meetings were torture. Parents would dread those meetings. They would have some psychologist who everybody thought was weird himself, and he would make these pronouncements about how smart the kids were or weren't, in a very cold way. He'd come to these meetings and there would be like fifteen people there and you. They would all go around and give a report. The psychologist would make guesses about IQs. You'd sit there and wonder, "Are they talking about Chloe?" Because it would sound like they were talking about someone you didn't even know. They didn't ask for the parents' input, particularly. You just would sit and hear this. I don't think the teachers liked it very much, either. I always remember them seeming uncomfortable with the whole process.

At age three, that was another big sort of traumatic event, because when the kids turned three, they would make a decision about what was going to happen next. In Richmond at that time, they had a school for what they used to call TMR, trainable mentally retarded, that was run by the county. The school district ran a school for orthopedically handicapped kids. It was called Cameron School. Or you could stay at the development center if they thought you were more severely retarded. So there were these three options. And they just decided. This was before [Public Law] 94-142, IDEA [Individuals with Disabilities Education Act]. Or actually, it was about the same time. Chloe was three the year the law was passed. But we didn't know that for a while. It was a well-kept secret. . . . So I was actually really pleased that she was sent to this orthopedically handicapped school—it's also very close to our house—because I thought she would get the most stimulation there. That turned out to be the beginning of my real advocacy efforts.

The first day at Cameron, I brought her to school because it was a new experience for her. I was carrying her into the building and the principal met us at the door and she said to me, "If your daughter can't cut it here, she's going to have to go back to the development center." And I was like, "Whoa." I didn't know why she said that to me, and it seemed like the most unwelcoming thing to say to a new child and parent. She didn't really know if Chloe could understand what she was saying or not. I said, "What do you mean?" She said, "Well, this may not be the right place for her." It was like she was talking about Harvard or something. "If not, we'll have to look at something else." I was like, "Oh, boy, where do you come from?"

Then Chloe went in; she was in the nursery pre-kindergarten, because she was only three. She had a wonderful teacher there. The program was actually really good for the younger kids, as a segregated program goes. They got a lot of attention, it was stimulating. However, it was on the same block as a regular elementary school, they were run by the same district. The schools were divided by a fence, and there was never any contact between the disabled kids and the non-disabled kids at the regular school. Except at Halloween, when there was a parade around the block of the regular school. They would let handicapped kids in their costumes walk at the end of the parade. I thought maybe, because they're all wearing costumes, everyone looks freaky anyway. Other than that, there was no contact.

This was right when the federal law was passed in '75. There weren't regulations for it until '77. I think the school district, at that time, didn't think there was anything they were supposed to be doing. So their attitude was that we should be grateful for what they are providing, and they're doing the best they can. And myself and a couple of the other parents had some feeling that this was some kind of discrimination, because why should the kids get a different school day as everyone else? But we didn't know about the law.

Somehow Pam [Steneberg][10] and I heard that there was a training. We'd seen a flyer, or something. There was a new law, and there was a training in this law. There probably were about fifteen or twenty parents there. It was an all-day training, and we were just totally blown away. We were just completely amazed by it, that our kids had all these rights.

The biggest message that they gave parents at that training was that there was this law with all these very detailed protections, and that we, as parents, were the experts on our kids. It was very empowering. That was the message. Not to be intimidated by these professionals. Not to think that they know more than us about our children. It was very powerful.

So that changed everything, because we didn't have to be grateful anymore for their little program. Our kids had rights; parents had rights. Parent participation was a very critical part of the law. And for a reason. Because the law respected that parents knew their kids.

8
Activists and Organizers, Part 1

Lee Kitchens (continued)
"It's pretty tough to do it all by yourself."

Little People of America was founded in the mid-twentieth century by activists who were weary of being marginalized by mainstream American society purely on the basis of their physical appearance. LPA, along with the National Association of the Deaf, the Paralyzed Veterans of America, and the National Federation of the Blind, ranks as one of America's oldest disability rights organizations in existence today.

Little People of America started in 1957. Billy Barty [the founder] was the most prominent short-statured actor [in America]; he'd been in show business for years with Spike Jones, and the Harmonicats. His parents were in vaudeville; he grew up in show business. Apparently he had been to a show in Reno, and one night after the show, he and some other performers got together and got to talking, and one of the guys said to Billy that he ought to form a club. Another guy that was there owned a hotel, so he offered Billy free rooms for a get-together. Billy gathered up twenty people that he had met and knew, most in show business, and they had a meeting. They got some media coverage, some signs, "Midgets of America." . . . That was the word they used then. They had a lot of pictures of people standing on chairs and stepladders at the gambling tables. Not the kind of thing we would do today, but those people were used to being exploited.

Those twenty-one people spent the next three years as they traveled getting the names and addresses of every little person they ever heard of or knew of or whatnot. Billy and another lady, who acted as kind of Billy's secretary, put together a mailing list and started contacting all of these people. . . .

A bit of history—there had been two previous attempts to organize a little people's group that had failed. Both of those groups had been organized by average-sized people, show business promoters, not organized for the benefit of little people, but for the benefit of the promoters. [And so] Billy, who had a big hand in writing the first set of bylaws, excluded average-sized people. They couldn't be members. They had no role in the organization.

That did two things: it kept average-sized people from getting involved for whatever reason, either for their own interest or as do-gooders; and it forced little people to stand up for themselves. That attitude prevailed for a number of years until the people in LPA grew up, so to speak, and finally recognized that these average-sized parents that brought in their dwarf kids had something to offer to the organization. We gradually, through bylaw amendments, loosened the barriers to allow other people to be involved. Now we have chapter presidents or district directors that may be parents of dwarf children or spouses or whatever. But it took quite a while to build up this infrastructure of competent little people to run the organization, so that an average-sized person coming in would not be a threat. I think it was the right thing to do at the time, so little people could learn how to operate in that kind of an environment.

Back in the early days, in a lot of cases, little people were socially immature or deprived, because a little person would not likely be invited to become a member of a Lion's Club, or a Kiwanis Club, or whatever. So they were denied the experience of working in a group and learning the leadership skills that you needed to be able to manage a large volunteer group.

About 1959, Billy was featured on the Ralph Edwards TV program *This Is Your Life*. I did not see the program, but one of the guys I went to school with that had also gone to work for Texas Instruments came and told me about it. So I wrote Ralph Edwards a letter asking about Billy and that got forwarded to Billy, but in my letter I did not make it clear that I was short-statured, so I got a very guarded response back. Anyway, we communicated back and forth, and Billy was planning another get-together in 1960 in November in Las Vegas. Because of Billy's contacts and whatnot, he had arranged for the meeting to be at the Hacienda Hotel and the rooms were free, it was during the off-season, and the meals would be half price. Well, that sounded too good to us to be true, and we were expecting a fleabag and a greasy spoon, but [Mary and I] drove out there.

By then we had adopted our son, who was supposed to be little. We had the feeling that we didn't need the organization. We'd gotten educated, gotten employed, gotten married, established the household without LPA. We had surmounted all of the obstacles, so to speak, but [we thought] it would be great for our children to have a support organization. So we drove to Las Vegas, and when we heard the Hacienda was at the end of the strip we thought, "Boy, our worst fears are realized." But the reason that it was at the end of the strip was because it was the newest, and sure enough it was first class.

We had 143 people there, many from show business, but not all. The interesting aspect of that is I was only able to recognize six professional people, by professional I mean teachers or—[there were] no other engineers—[or] accountants, people with university degrees, people holding a position outside of show business. At that conference we essentially wrote the bylaws and the articles of incorporation and proceeded to set up the organization called Little People of America. They divided the country up into twelve districts, appointed a director for each of these areas, and I got appointed by virtue of being the only one from Texas, for the director of this area. The first board of directors were essentially handpicked. Billy was the president.

The next year was spent spreading the word, so to speak. In '61 the meeting again was in Las Vegas. Then in '62 they moved it to Asheville, North Carolina, where one of the vice presidents lived. But again, all this was done in November. Well, attendance dropped way down because it was a long way for the show business group and a lot of them didn't show up, and no children were there. Now we took our son out of school for one week because we thought it was important. But at those discussions in Asheville, we shifted gears to the summertime so it could be a family sort of thing and people that had kids could come, and we've been having summertime meetings ever since. Then attendance picked up and has continued to grow. So that's the genesis of the organization.

The history of the organization itself is long—history of spreading the word, letting the general public know about little people, letting other little people know about the organization, developing programs to help other little people; an adoption committee, a scholarship committee, sharing one-on-one issues about how to drive a car, how to modify a house, and that kind of stuff. It easily became, even though we didn't want to admit it, a dating [service] for [little people]. . . . Mary and I were fortunate in having met each other, but a lot of little people never had that opportunity. So it was a chance for people of short stature to get together and develop a social interaction that they'd never had before. . . .

We didn't know how to deal with the media. That was a thing we had to teach each other, and we did that at the 1960 meeting. The media would come in and want these sensational pictures, want you to stand on a chair in front of a telephone. We had to teach our members, "Don't do anything you wouldn't do in normal life." We started putting our foot down, so to speak. I was kind of a stuffed shirt in those days. One of the few professionals, I always dressed up, I wanted to put the best image forward, overdid it to some extent. I had a better education than most people did, a better vocabulary, had some of the leadership skills based on my experience at TI. I quickly became one of the spokesmen for the group and we tried to explain to our members, "If they want a picture of you using the phone, fine, do it, but show how you would do it in everyday life. You would not drag a chair up and stand on it except in an absolute emergency. Let people see how you drive a car. Answer the questions about clothing and the things you do to accommodate or adapt to the environment."

In those days there was essentially nothing done as far as accommodation. You just tolerated it or put up with it or whatever. Later in the mid-sixties the first architectural barriers act was passed [the federal Architectural Barriers Act of 1968].[1] That was a start. There were a number of things that took place all at once; the civil rights movement in the sixties and the success of people gathering together and speaking as one voice, in this case the African American minority, began to make their presence felt. Then various individual organizations; the hearing impaired, the visually impaired, Paralyzed Veterans of America, all were beginning to band together, as we had done, to bring the public and the government [to understand] that discrimination was rampant, prevalent, and improper, and if the racial minority could have an impact, maybe the disabled group could. But the difference was that the various handicapped groups were each out doing their own thing, each fighting their own fight, and because we are all human, different handicapped groups were prejudiced against other handicapped groups. That didn't get any better until the seventies.

As the organization has gotten large enough to be recognized as a viable group, as we have gotten more and more of our people involved in various movements, as we've become a recognized member on ANSI [American National Standards Institute] committees, as we've gotten involved in some issues and have gotten media attention to some of the stupid things that have gone on, as we've gone to bat for people running into problems in the education field, and as more little people have succeeded in the general public on an equal basis, all of those things have helped other little people to see, "Yes, I can do all of this, too." The organization can help you break down barriers or show you a way around the barriers. It's pretty tough to do it all by yourself, and if you just want to have a little help, I think that's where the organization shines.

We do, now, have members that are in roles that are significant. We have attorneys, doctors, nurses that have some influence based on their position, not on their size. Those people are useful. . . . Actually, short stature can be an asset in public life. When I ran for mayor the first time,[2] everybody knew who I was even though I didn't know all of them. The first time you can run on name identification, it's an easy campaign. Now when you run for reelection you have to run on your record, your size is not an issue any more. But that first time around it's an advantage, even against an incumbent. We've seen that happen a number of times. . . .

The accepted terminology now is little people. When you use the term "midget," it has the same connotation to us as the n-word for African American people. The reason is that "midget" was used by kids or anybody to single you out, and many times in a negative way. I've had people come up to me and say, "What do you want me to call you, 'midget' or 'dwarf?'" The answer is, "Call me 'Lee.' Don't put a label on me."

One day I was going into work and I heard these kids' voices holler, "Hey midget," and I looked and saw two little black kids sitting in a car waiting for their mother. So I went over and talked to them and they were kind of surprised that I went over there. I said, "How would you like me to holler at you when I see you, 'Hey nigger?'" Oh boy, they didn't like that and I said, "Well, I don't like 'Hey midget' any more than you like 'Hey nigger.'" I went on my way. Well, those two black boys now know how I feel and I know how they feel, so they won't do that again, and they may tell somebody else. So it's a gradual education process.

Gary Olsen
"We wanted the students to become well-versed in everything that was going on."

"I've been working since I was thirteen," says Gary Olsen. Over the five-plus decades since he worked after school as a farmhand, Olsen has been a student, an educator, an administrator, an activist, and one of the best known and most effective political organizers in the American Deaf community. Through it all he has seen that community grow in political, economic, and social power.

Olsen was born in Grand Island, Nebraska, in May 1941, and became deaf after a bout with spinal meningitis at age seven. Enrolled in a public school during his early years, he was transferred after his illness to the Nebraska School for the Deaf, a residential school in Omaha. In the classroom, students were encouraged to learn to lip-read and speak, as was usual for "oralist" programs of the time. In the halls and the dorms, however, deaf youngsters used sign to communicate, and it was through the use of American Sign Language (ASL) that Deaf activism and culture began to flourish.

Olsen graduated from the Nebraska School in 1960, traveling to Washington, DC, to enroll at Gallaudet. Like so many young people of his generation, he became caught up in the political and social upheaval of the 1960s, struggling to use the lessons of the civil rights and antiwar movements and apply them to the Deaf community. "I wanted to be an agent of change, and that's what I became."

Since then Olsen has been a major force in everything from the National Association of the Deaf (where he was executive director from 1984 to 1989) to the Deaf President Now campaign to passage of the Americans with Disabilities Act. One example of his far-reaching influence is his work with Frank Turk to found and run the annual Deaf Youth Leadership Development Camp, an annual four-week summer program with the goal of educating future Deaf activists.

Deaf people during the early sixties were concerned about the fact that young Deaf people were not involved in the political process. And there

were a lot of people who were very concerned about the future of the
NAD [National Association of the Deaf]. Many of the older Deaf people
had been there for quite some time, and were keeping things in the status
quo. There was no clear vision. And so we young people began to get
involved to provide a push. Dr. Byron Burnes, who was president of the
NAD for eighteen years and a teacher at the California School for the
Deaf, he and his wife decided to create a youth program. And so, in 1961
they set up the Junior NAD. We set up chapters around the country, in
a limited number of states to start with: Montana, California, West Virginia, I think Michigan, and a few others.

There wasn't a national or regional meetings or anything of that sort,
just chapter by chapter, and through correspondence with each other,
word got around. But there wasn't a whole lot of cohesion among the
groups, until 1964, when Frank Turk was offered the opportunity to become head of the group, and I became the project specialist. And that's
pretty much the beginning of how the youth camps happened.

I had studied Saul Alinsky, and what I took away from that was that
coalition was really the key. We thought about some positive things about
community, and organizing, and also individual self-empowerment, that
we could teach to these young people, these Deaf teenagers, who weren't
getting this sort of training anywhere else. Like how to stand up and speak
for yourself, and how to be involved in the political process, and the importance of becoming involved at the local level in your home state.

Frank and I did a search to find kids we thought had the potential
to become leaders and activists. We went to the individual schools for
the Deaf and asked teachers to look out for students who were potential
leaders, encouraging them to help us develop a good cadre so we would
bring them to the first annual Junior NAD convention, which was held
at Gallaudet in 1968. There were about a hundred and twenty students
at that conference, so we had an opportunity to evaluate those students,
and to recommend which ones would be good for the leadership camps.
Then there were follow-up meetings, for instance at the Indiana School
for the Deaf, in November. And that's when we decided that we needed
a four-week summer camp for the program to include everything we
wanted to include.

And so the annual camps started in the summer of 1969 in the Pocon-
os in, Pennsylvania, where a Deaf owner of the site rented us the space.

The staff volunteered, and the students had to pay three hundred dollars for their room and board. After that we moved to Swan Lake Lodge, in Pengilly, Minnesota.

I developed a lot of that program myself, based on what I saw as the needs for the students at that time, what they needed to learn so that they could go back to their schools and spread the word with the other students. We had presenters from different areas of the country. Most of the presenters were activists, or leaders in their field. And one of the school presidents came to share with the kids the need for them to become better quality students. We had the NAD president come, Dr. Fred Schreiber. So there were many great people who came there. We also did field trips, like to NTID [National Technical Institute for the Deaf, in Rochester, New York], and also Philadelphia. We went to Gallaudet. We went to Atlantic City for a little bit of a break, swimming on the beaches and all of that, and then we went to New York City, and spoke with a Jewish NAD group, asking for their perspectives from the Jewish point of view. And we went to the Helen Keller Foundation, to expose our students to the issues of the Deaf-Blind community.

We did role playing, acting out scenarios. And we explained the reasons for the struggle that we were expecting, and why Deaf people were so far behind historically speaking. Basically, we taught Deaf history, which hadn't been done much before. We shared with them our own experiences, our successes and our failures. We exposed them to as many possibilities and as many new concepts as we could. We wanted the students to become well versed in everything that was going on, and to see how they could become active to protect their rights, and to encourage their future. And we wanted them to pick up some of the skills that they would need to become leaders, future leaders themselves.

The president of the Indiana School for the Deaf decided to add a new system for getting involved with the leadership camp, for kids who were not necessarily college bound. I thought that was a great idea. I felt like the students who were not college bound could be and really should be leaders of a grassroots movement. That's what we wanted—a broad, grassroots movement to include the entire community, and not just the academic "elite."

Over the years I began to notice, when I went to Gallaudet, or to the Junior NAD conferences, or various school functions, and when I went to the eastern or western regional conferences of the NAD, that a lot of the new leaders, the up-and-coming activists, were graduates of our program. I'd go to various places and I would see these people who had been through the camps and they would be working, and using what we had taught at the camps. And some of those students became teachers at schools for the Deaf, and in that work were able to continue to spread our philosophy.

Many of our graduates were involved with the Deaf President Now campaign, and then the push to pass the ADA. And since then they've been involved with the push for implementation of the ADA and its regulations. And if you look at Gallaudet University, at the board of directors, many of those people on the board today went through our camps. If you look at the faculty at Gallaudet University, or the administration, you find the same thing.

Basically, we were a galvanizing force, working to get people at the grassroots level involved, and that's how it happened. That's what created the success.

Ray Uzeta (continued)
"We knew how to work the politics."

Ray Uzeta contracted "a neurological disorder" in 1960, but was still able to continue working. By late 1965, however, he "was basically bedridden . . . functionally a quadriplegic," and it wasn't until 1968 that he was able to start socializing again. It was at this point that a social worker put him in touch with the Recreation Center for the Handicapped.

Uzeta, looking for ways to interact with other people with disabilities, went from the patronizing Recreation Center to the overtly political California Association of the Physically Handicapped, and then on to the "militant" Center for Independent Living in Berkeley.

In this section he traces some of the history of the CAPH, and his own growth as a political activist.

CAPH was the California Association of the Physically Handicapped, which was incorporated I believe in 1970. CAPH was literally founded by four guys sitting in a bar in San Raphael. As a matter of fact some of them were Indoor Sports' people . . . the Indoor Sports' club gave CAPH their initial $25,000 to get off the ground. A big leader in this thing was Dick Wooten, and Dick would share the story. "We were all there sitting at a bar, and we were all complaining about architectural barriers, and I said, 'We ought to form an organization and take it on,' and someone said, 'I bet you can't do it.' And I said, 'I'll take you on.'" And Dick single-handedly started to identify other people with disabilities throughout the state, and went around and said, "You know what? We're going to get rid of these god-damned architectural barriers. Pull together a meeting in your community. We're starting a new state organization." And within five years they went from four guys in a bar to five thousand dues-paying members. The key word is the California Association *of* the Physically Handicapped, not *for* the Physically Handicapped. People with disabilities ran the organization.

This was a different group than the Recreation Center. I remember once when I was working for an organization here in San Diego, and went to a CAPH convention with one of my young ladies I used to supervise. Afterwards I said, "What do you think of the convention?" And this was really telling, she says, "It was the first time in my life I've ever been exposed to middle-class crips." So I think there was definitely a different caliber of people who were involved with CAPH, certainly at the leadership levels. And looking back now, you could see some of the people at the Recreation Center, you could see they were kind of meek and passive. And those of us who just got tired of that environment . . . you could just see the difference in their personality.

CAPH incorporated as a 501(c)(4),[3] specifically so they could push legislation and endorse candidates. And CAPH is the organization that got the first architectural barriers law passed in the state legislature. And Dick's philosophy was, you can't ask for the whole world at one time, you've got to take it on a piece at a time, push the door open a little bit, come back next year and push it open a little more—that was his strategy. Now, the more aggressive people with disabilities didn't like Dick's strategy, but thinking back on it, he was right. You can't take on the whole system, but you can chip away at it. So CAPH is the organization, really, that pushed all the architectural access laws in California. CAPH is the organization that passed the rapid transit accessibility laws here in California. CAPH backed the disabled students when they pushed legislation to fund disabled student centers throughout California.

Probably about '75, '76, we hired a part-time lobbyist, but the policy decisions were still all made by the membership. We used to meet once a quarter throughout the state, we'd go to different places to eat, and we had all these committees on education, health care, IHSS [In-Home Support Services], architectural barriers, you know, really dynamic organization. We all supported the organization by paying dues. We had no foundation supporting us.

CAPH was sophisticated. The legislative committee would say, "Okay, this year we're going to push eight bills, these are the bills, and they come from all the committees." And the board of governors, which was like fifty people, they would vote, and say, "Okay, here's our legislative packet for the next session." We'd then give it to our lobbyist, "Okay, you go and find sponsors for it." And so he would find sponsors, then when they'd come up for a hearing, we had a telephone tree, so the legislative chair would contact all the regional directors, and the regional directors would telephone every chapter president in their region, then the chapter presidents got it out to their members. We cranked out thousands of telegrams and letters within seventy-two hours.

We became so powerful that candidates would come to our state conventions, seeking our endorsements. And that says a lot about an organization's political clout. We were able to kill 90 percent of what we didn't like, and we probably passed 80 percent of our legislation. And whether it was it was a Republican governor or legislature or a Democrat, we were very successful.

CAPH wasn't as aggressive, they weren't really into the heavy-duty rhetoric that came out of CIL. Actually, CAPH was a very conservative organization. The leaders were very conservative, and what started happening, I started coming in with some other people, and we were kind of the Young Turks, you know, we were like the troublemakers. They weren't aggressive enough for us. But we all got along, and were very successful in pushing legislation, and then the chapters would monitor the implementation of state legislation at the local levels, and they worked with the city councils. So it really was pretty sophisticated. We knew how to work the politics.

Okay, so I started with the Recreation Center, then I got with Indoor Sports', then I got involved with CAPH. Well, then what happened, I went to Cal Berkeley. I went to school late in life, so I was probably in my early thirties by the time I got out of Cal. I used to use disabled student services, mostly so I could get priority registration for classes, and I met John Hessler.[4] John Hessler was one of the original founders, along with Ed Roberts and some other people, of CIL. So I used to see John every quarter. I was getting ready to graduate, and John knew I was involved with CAPH in San Francisco, doing a lot of advocacy, and he said, "What are you going to do after you graduate?" And I said, "I'm not sure." He said, "There's an organization down on Telegraph called CIL, and they could use some volunteers. Why don't you go down and talk to them?" So I said, "Sure, what the hell."

So I go down there, and I meet Phil Draper,[5] who was the assistant director. And I met with Ed Roberts too. And Ed said, "We've heard about you in San Francisco. We'd like to start a transportation service for seniors and disabled, would you be willing to do some research for us?" I said "Sure." So I used my library research skills I got at UC, and went to the UC Berkeley library and did all sorts of research on paratransit systems, and came back to Ed and said, "Okay, here's what I found out." And he said, "CalTrans [the California Department of Transportation] has a grant proposal out for vehicles, will you write it for us?" So I said, "Yeah, sure, what the hell?" I'd never written a grant in my life, didn't know what the hell a grant was.

So I write this proposal, and give it to Ed, and a couple of months later Ed came back and said, "Ray, that proposal you wrote got funded." I said. "Great, that's nice. Congratulations." And he said, "Do you want a job?" And I said, "Doing what?" "Running our transportation program." I said, "I don't know anything about transportation." And Ed looks at me and says, "Neither do we. So do you want a job?" Literally, that's how I went from a volunteer to an employee at CIL, and started the transportation program.

So then I got exposed to Ed, John Hessler, Phil Draper, Don Berry, all the original people at CIL, Kitty Cone, Hale Zukas.[6] So now I'm getting exposed to a different disability organization and mentality. Where the focus of CAPH was on legislation and architectural barriers, CIL was very big on In-Home Support Services, because a lot of them had to use these. So when they started CIL, the basic core service was IHSS, and helping people to find attendants and accessible housing. Those were kind of core programs because those were basic needs. Your attendant, getting your IHSS benefits, getting your SSI benefits, getting an accessible house and finding attendants.

Now, the genius of CIL and all those young people who were all college educated, wasn't because they were doing something unique, that wasn't already being done by Indoor Sports club people or CAPH people. I think the genius, and Ed's genius, was they coined the phrase "peer counseling." "We're going to do peer counseling." That's what they sold to funders. But they didn't discover peer counseling, it had already been going on for forty years before CIL ever existed.

And so that was really one of the main differences between CAPH and CIL. CIL was really working with the SSI population, not with people with disabilities who were out there working on their own. IHSS wasn't a priority for the CAPH leadership. Their priority was architectural barriers, and Ed [Roberts] was saying, "No no, we need to help people"—so there was that kind of philosophical priority difference between the two organizations.

Norma Vescovo
"We're out there, most of us in wheelchairs, on the freeway.*"*

Born in 1936 in Denver, Norma Vescovo has been an advocate for disability rights and services since she was a young child. "When I was eight years old, almost everyone I knew was getting polio, so when I became ill, that's what they thought I had. They treated me for polio, and come to find out, it was rheumatic fever. So they mistreated me. As a result, I ended up actually in bed for most of my life until I was fifteen. I had St. Vitus' Dance,[7] and then that became rheumatoid arthritis, and later polymalgia rheumatica."

Vescovo's illness damaged her heart; she had been blind in one eye since birth. "But even though I went through all of that, I was always pushing and pushing my family to try to get services which, of course, during that time didn't exist." Vescovo was finally able to return to school at age fifteen, after missing seven years of education. "They could not believe that I was up to grade level so they put me back a year from what I should normally have been. This placed me in the grade with my younger brother."

Back in school, she faced discrimination of a different sort. Her father's family was Latino, but the Vescovos lived in a predominantly Anglo community. "The very first week I went back to school the teacher said, 'We need to keep track of how many people speak Spanish in the class, so will everybody who speaks Spanish please raise your hand.' I was sitting in front of the room because I don't see well, and I turned around and looked and he said, 'What are you looking for?' And I said, 'I'd like to know if somebody speaks Spanish because I've always wanted to learn.' And he said, 'What are you talking about? You're the only one that speaks Spanish in this room.' And then he said, 'You can call it Martines if you want [Vescovo's maiden name, spelled with an 's' rather than a 'z']. I don't care how you spell it, you're still a Mexican.'"

Vescovo graduated high school, and went to college to learn accounting. Just before learning that she was pregnant with her first child, she was in a car accident in 1957, which injured her legs and thus exacerbated her disabilities. Using a wheelchair during her recovery, Vescovo had to stop her education because of the lack of access on campus. In 1958 she married and became a homemaker. She and her husband moved to Los Angeles, where they had their second child, a son, who was born with cerebral palsy. Seeking to enroll him in public school in 1966, she was told that the schools would not accept a disabled child. School officials suggested that the Vescovos send their son away to an institution. Instead, they found a "special education center," opened by a sympathetic doctor. But even here Vescovo, like Johnnie Lacy, encountered a mindset that saw disability as primarily a medical issue.

"They were going to have the buses pull up and then have the people all in white uniforms get off the buses to meet the kids. And I said, 'You can't do that. My kid's coming to school, he's not going to a hospital.'"

Vescovo was a cofounder and leader of CAPH. In 1975, she became founding executive director of the Western Law Center for Disability Rights. Today she is the executive director of the Independent Living Center of Southern California, Inc., which she helped found in 1976.

We did some big demonstrations on transportation in the early eighties. The transit authorities weren't making their buses accessible. They had some buses with lifts, and they actually put the accessible signs on the front of the buses, but they were deciding not to use the lifts because President Reagan was saying that he was going to redo some of the regulations that the transit people had to comply with. So even though they had lifts on some of the buses, they weren't using them.

We started by meeting with the transit officials, trying to get our point across. Then we picketed in front of the bus company. We got press on it. We started the Office on Disability with the LA City and then tried to use that office to try to force them to provide accessible service. We went every which direction possible. It was almost on a monthly basis. We were either picketing, meeting, doing something with them. We had gone through all those normal routines.

I came up with this idea that the best thing to do would be to get on the freeway with everybody in wheelchairs and go downtown to talk to the mayor, to say, "We can't get on a bus, we don't have any other form of transportation. We're just going to go down on the freeway."

We had about one hundred and fifty, two hundred people show up. I had it planned out. I had a person back in my office who would call the police and say, "There's people in wheelchairs getting on the freeway at this location," and then hope that when we started to get up on the freeway the police would come and stop us, but we'd still get all the news coverage. Because I didn't want anyone to get hurt. I know that when I sent out the notices to all the people, all the members of CAPH and everything, saying what we were going to do, I think half of them showed up only because they didn't believe we were going to do it.

Originally, I was going to have one of our Independent Living Center vans go out in the front and go slow and get the traffic away from them so that the people in wheelchairs could come on behind it and we'd have some kind of stability as far as the traffic. But then I thought "No, that's ridiculous. We're going to have to make sure we don't get on the freeway."

Well, we saw the police pull up at the top of the ramp. So I said, "Okay. Now we're ready." We started up the ramp and I was out in front with Lou Nau and his wife Yvonne, and Gale Williams[8] was there and all of these other people. So we started up the ramp and those policemen pulled off, they were there for something else. They didn't see us. We were going up the ramp and onto the freeway, starting down the side of the freeway in the right lane. And cars were coming by weaving and honking their horns, and we have signs and we're out there, most of us in wheelchairs, *on the freeway.* All of a sudden I could see that a couple of people were scared.

A police motorcycle came up and pulled right over to the front of the line and said, "What are you guys doing out here?" And I said, "We're going downtown to see the mayor, we don't have any transportation. This is the only way we're going to be able to get there." And he said, "Ah well, I would suggest that you not do this." And so one of the women in a chair said, "Are you telling us that we have to get off the freeway?" And he said, "Well, yeah, I guess that's what I'm doing. Get off the freeway." So everybody started to turn back but, in the meanwhile, all the police were there, at the bottom of the ramp. The news media were there, all the newspapers, every station. And what was so great was that when we got back to the top of the ramp, it showed in the picture this whole ramp full of people.

A reporter said, "Well, the buses are accessible, you see the accessible signs." I said, "Yes, but they won't use their lifts, they've been told not to." Just then a bus pulled up with a great big accessible sign on the front.

You never know what people are going to do. We stood in front of the bus and asked them to put the lift down and let somebody get on, and they refused to do it. And so we just stayed in the front of the bus, we held that bus up for that whole time. And the people on the bus were furious because they were late and so on and so forth. We gave them fliers. We talked to them about why we were doing this. They said, "Well, the buses are accessible and you can already use them," and I said, "But you can't use the lift." They said, "But there's an accessibility sign and then inside, where the front seats are, they've set space aside for the disabled." "But you don't see anybody there in those seats that are disabled." "Well, yes, but it's just that disabled people don't like to ride on the bus."

The reporter who I'd been talking to walked over to the driver and said, "Can you show us the lift on your bus?" And he says, "Oh no, we're not provided with a key." And so that hit the news, all over it. The next day they opened up those lifts and started using them.

The press believed us. The next time we sent out press releases they were much more rapid to get there. The same when we rallied in front of the governor's house. We literally picketed in front of his house. Now they've made a new law that you can't picket in front of somebody's private home. But, at that time, we could do it, and we did. And we had press every which way, press coverage. And so it's just a question of coming up with new ideas, something that people haven't thought of yet, to get the point across.

Justin Dart Jr.
"And it suddenly hit me that all these children were going to die."

Justin Dart Jr.'s career as a disability rights activist, first in his adopted home state of Texas, then in Washington, DC, would take him and his wife Yoshiko across the country and around the world, pushing his notion of "a revolution of empowerment." Early on during the Reagan administration he was appointed to the National Council on the Handicapped, and in 1986 he became commissioner of the US Rehabilitation Services Administration (RSA), where he alienated many bureaucrats and rehabilitation professionals with his insistence that people with disabilities themselves must have a say in designing and implementing its programs. This tension culminated in 1987, when Dart testified before Congress to denounce the RSA's "obsolete, paternalistic attitudes about disability."[9] Dart was soon after asked to resign, but his testimony earned him admiration from activists nationwide. It was during this time that Dart began advocating full-time for legislation that would eventually become the Americans with Disabilities Act of 1990. Dart's identification with the legislation and his full-bore commitment to its passage earned him the sobriquet "the father of the ADA."

Justin Dart was born in 1930 into a life of wealth and privilege. His maternal grandfather was the founder of Walgreens, and his father, Justin Sr., was a major Republican fundraiser and confidant of Ronald Reagan. As a child Justin Jr. grew up with maids and chauffeurs and was sent to a series of prestigious prep schools. His independent streak developed early on, and when interviewed years later, he would recount with pride how he beat the all-time record for demerits earned by any student at Deerfield Academy, surpassing fellow alumnus Humphrey Bogart.

Dart contracted polio in 1948, when he was eighteen, and he would use a wheelchair for the rest of his life. It was perhaps another sign of his rebellious nature that even this early on, he chose to identify with fellow polio survivor but liberal Democrat Franklin Roosevelt, bitterly unpopular with Dart's conservative father. Years later Dart was invited by President Bill Clinton to be present when the statue of FDR in his wheelchair was unveiled at the FDR Memorial.

Justin Dart's organizing and managerial skills were evident long before he

took up the cause of disability rights. Whether it was opening the first auto-
mated bowling alley in Mexico City or starting up the Tupperware franchise
in Japan, his methods were effective, if often unorthodox. In Mexico City, for
example, Dart became associated with a group of radical university students,
which eventually brought him to the attention of both Mexican and American
intelligence. "The right-wingers thought I was a radical, the left-wingers figured I was a CIA front."

Dart might have spent his entire life as a driven, overachieving entrepreneur. Instead, during a trip to Vietnam that was part research and charitable
work, part public relations photo op, Dart had an epiphany that would change
the course of his life.

Justin Dart was awarded the Presidential Medal of Freedom by Bill Clinton
in 1998. He died on June 22, 2002.

We did all kinds of things on national television, things that Tupperware
didn't do in America and in these other countries where it operated. So
when the Paralympics came to Japan in 1964, I was a visible person already and obviously a wheelchair user. The delegation[s] from America
and from Japan came to me and said would you donate some wheelchairs and do some little things, you know, to support the Paralympics?
They explained to me how it would be good PR . . . so I said, "Well, okay."
And I got to meet some of those promoters and athletes and coaches
then, and I got some reasonable PR out of it.

Then they [the people with Paralympics] convinced me to start a major program of our own at Japan Tupperware, modeled after the Paralympics, and to take some wheelchair users out of institutions. At that
time, all wheelchair users in Japan were in full-care institutions, where
they stayed literally forever. We took ten wheelchair users out of those
institutions and put them to work in our warehouse. We tried to get
some that could learn how to play basketball, since the promoters of this
idea were sports people, and we started a wheelchair basketball team. We
rented a big house in the suburbs of Tokyo where we built some ramps
and lifts and stuff, and we got them a van that they could ride around in,
a small bus or something with a portable ramp.

So then we hired this coach from America who started to teach them
how to play basketball. We got into these extremely visible basketball

exhibitions all over the country and on national television. The Japanese Olympic Team had practiced in wheelchairs to play against us, playing these hospital teams. They came to us before the game and they said, "Mr. Dart, now we are going to play this game in the Olympic Stadium on national television and for the honor of the Japanese Olympic Team," which was a very good team, able-bodied players, and they had just lost to the Soviet Union by one point. And the coach said, "Now you understand we have to win the game for the honor of the Japanese Olympic Team, but don't worry we are not going to embarrass you. We play these hospital teams. We hold our margin down to one or two points. And the fact that the game is so close will make you look good." And I said, "Well, that is very nice of you and we are going to play as hard as we can, but you know, that is very nice of you."

Remember this is on national television and this is in the Japanese Olympic Basketball Stadium, with a full house—we were leading 40 to 1 or 42 to 1 at the half, and my PR man came over and said, "Mr. Dart, you've got to let these Olympic players make a comeback in the second half because you're losing the sympathy of the audience and becoming the villains." And I told him an unprintable thing, "You tell them to go blank themselves. You tell them that we've been trying for hundreds of years to lose *sympathy* and gain *respect*. And if they want to make a comeback, let them come out and do it, but we are not going to pull any punches."

But I did put in the second string and so they did manage to make one basket. And several of them got injured because we played rough, and they didn't appreciate that. They looked upon us as cripples and as hospital patients. They were shocked when we played the game like it was tank warfare. And some of them went off the court bleeding. These were really superb athletes. They could make baskets from their wheelchairs. They had practiced.

So, in a sense, a disability rights perspective was sneaking up on me, and that statement about losing sympathy and gaining respect kind of popped out as a Freudian slip. And I was becoming increasingly aware of the deep resentment that I was provoking, that I was empowering these people to get out and do things. You see the doctors, when I took them out of the hospital, they had no notion whatever that I was going to do anything like that. And I remember the leading rehabilitation doctor in Japan meeting me and saying, "My colleagues have asked me to meet with you and we want you to know," and he got all red in the face, "what you are doing is *not* rehabilitation! You are *hurting* these people!"

When we toured around the country, these athletes made speeches to our sales ladies. And they went around and they started going to bars and having girlfriends. They started having press interviews. They got more press than the doctors. Well, I can guarantee you this did not sit well with the bureaucrats and the government. Here's the patients taking over the asylum. And these people got very confident. They became empowered people. Then I began to give them other jobs. Ones that obviously had some executive or sales ability, I took them out of the warehouse. They had all started out putting stuff in boxes and doing simple hand work, like Goodwill-type work, putting Tupperware in boxes, filling orders. I took some of them out and put them in the sales department and I made one of them one of my staff assistants.

I became increasingly aware that, by god, there is real prejudice here. And then the social worker wife of my coach got irritated with me and said that I was going way too far, and that these boys weren't ready to do this stuff, and I just said, "Bullshit." This was the way I ran the company anyway. People came in and got results, I'd double their salary after one month. Other people came in, even some big elite university graduate or something, and didn't get results, I'd just fire them. In Japan you don't fire people. You give them a job for life. And I hired prostitutes, and farm ladies with teeth missing. I didn't care. If they got results, they got promoted. I had bar girls who were district managers, ex-bar girls, which irritated the shit out of a lot of people.

Eventually I had to resign from Japan Tupperware, and I started a greeting card company. At that time the greeting card business barely existed in Japan, and I had some vague notion that I was going to use the favorable PR I'd gotten for employing people with disabilities, and I was going to use some handicapped people to help make these greeting cards and then to help sell them.

Of course, the major news in the Japanese newspapers, maybe all newspapers at that time, was the Vietnam War. The Vietnam War was raging in 1966–1967. I was becoming more and more aware of disability rights on the one hand, and I also noted that anything connected with Vietnam got lots of PR. So I gathered a small group to go to Vietnam for a couple of weeks and do a study of the condition of people with disabilities in Vietnam and submit it to the World Congress of Rehabilitation International, which they hold every two years or four years or something. It was going to be in Germany, and I would do this investigation and send the results of it to Germany.

So I got this ace professional photographer that had worked for me in Tupperware and did photography for national magazines. I got one of my wheelchair user assistants who had come out from one of those institutions and who was one of my personal assistants, and my then executive assistant Yoshiko, and I think that's all that went.

We did quite a bit of research before we went. We got the listings of all of the rehabilitation places and different government people that had to do with the disability community. There wasn't any disability rights movement down there. They had rehabilitation people and they might have had some government association of handicapped people or something. So we flew down to Saigon and stayed in a hotel, and then we went out and started visiting all of these places, and also doing photo ops throughout the city and taking notes and doing research.

What we found was that a lot of this so-called rehabilitation was just something that was listed and puffed up in the international directories, but didn't really exist. For example, the main rehabilitation facility in Saigon was entirely empty and they had to come and unlock the door to show me around. I came with some fairly heavy recommendations—I was a supporter of LBJ. And I had a lot of strong relationships with rehabilitation people in Japan, even though we had begun to have considerable friction. And so we visited hospitals and took pictures and went from dawn till dusk every day. And, of course, the war was raging around us on the outskirts of the city. You could actually hear the artillery and the bombs at night.

We encountered some increasingly distressing scenes of just numerous, numerous people that had lost legs and arms by land mines. And people in the Red Cross shelter tent laying on the lawn of the Red Cross Headquarters and just sleeping there, and getting some minimal rations every day. These were civilians. And then we visited soldiers, South Vietnam soldiers, who were amputees, wheelchair users, and institutionalized for that. And we dialogued with them through interpreters down there from some volunteer organization.

Finally, I went to this particular place that was listed as an institution for children with disabilities. It was a large pavilion which consisted of kind of a tin roof and metal posts and concrete floor and sides open to the air. Something like when you go to a tropical market, you know? And on the concrete there were laying a very large number of young children. I don't know how old they were but maybe from three or four years old to ten years old. Most of them I guess had polio. There was no vaccine there. And they were all starving to death. It was like the pictures that you see from Somalia, Ethiopia, from Dachau and the German concentration camps—the bloated bellies, the eyes bugging out, the matchstick arms and legs. And I mean regardless of their paralysis, they were all starving to death and they were laying there on this concrete floor, in these loincloths, in pools of their urine and piles of their feces.

So I rolled into this place with my assistant, and my photographer is clicking pictures. And I rolled up to this child, I think it was a girl, and she reached out her hand to me. So obviously, I grasped her hand and she just stared into my eyes. And it was an indescribable expression but she was in—what I could see into it, what I could read into it, is that she was reaching out to me for some kind of solution to this horrible, ghastly atrocity that she was experiencing. And she must have sensed that she was about to die, and it suddenly hit me like a bomb that here is this little girl who is going to die, and all of these children were going to die, and that was confirmed by some attendant there. They bring them in and they all die and they take them out and dump them some place and bury them. It's a continual process.

And she was reaching out for God, that is the way I felt about it. And she just had the most beautiful, serene look in her eyes as she reached out to me. Apparently, she had reached a kind of situation in her mind that had transcended—she had faced the reality that she was not going to live and had achieved some kind of peace of mind, maybe the euphoria you get when you are absolutely starving to death and you're about to die. And here is this child reaching to me, reaching out to God, and what did she find? She found a counterfeit saint.

Here I am, president of a company, down there with my professional photographer, taking a photo op with this person who was dying. A photo op which is going to perhaps be pictured in a Japanese national magazine and will be used to help me increase the sales of greeting cards, and make me more famous. And in a few minutes I will go back to my air conditioned hotel and eat my unimaginably luxurious food, and I will go back to Tokyo and live in a nice place and have a chauffeur and so forth. *And she will die.*

And I realized: This is evil. I have encountered evil and *I am part of it.* I am killing these kids just about as much as the people who are running this atrocious fraud of an institution, this concentration camp. And remember they are raising money for this place under the guise that it is an institution for children. And I am here using this atrocity as a photo op.

I went back to the hotel, and I got absolutely stoned with whiskey, and I got sick. I went to bed and got sick for several days. And we went back to Tokyo and I went from the airport to my home, went to bed without eating the next day, and was still sick and vomiting. I think probably there were some germs there as well as psychology, but anyway, I went to the Okura Hotel, and met Yoshiko there in the lobby.

I still remember the scene. I remember the chair where we were sitting. I said, "We have the freedom to do whatever it is that we want with the rest of our lives, and we cannot continue what we are doing. We have got to give all of our time, and energy, and passion to destroying this evil—this profound evil," and we liquidated the business and went into the movement.

9
Institutions, Part 3

ROBERT PERSKE AND GUNNAR DYBWAD EXPERIENCED THE REALITY of the "state school and hospital" system in the 1940s, '50s and '60s. Dr. William Bronston carries the story into the 1970s, describing his struggle at the Willowbrook State School and Hospital on Staten Island, New York.

William Bronston, MD
"Wretchedness and suffering and insanity and inhumanity."

Willowbrook holds a special place in the history of disability rights, and Dr. Bronston, more than any other single person, was responsible for bringing the horrific conditions there to the public eye. A grand-nephew of Leon Trotsky, Bronston was a political activist as far back as medical school, when he wrote an open letter to President Kennedy protesting the administration's cold war policies. From medical school he went to the Menninger Institute in Topeka, Kansas (where Rev. Perske had been institution chaplain). While there he tried to help its lowest-paid workers form a union. After being fired from the Menninger and branded a troublemaker, Bronston moved to New York City to volunteer at a poor people's medical center run by the Black Panthers in Harlem. Needing to feed himself and his family, in 1970 Bronston took a paying job at the only medical facility willing to hire him: the Willowbrook State School and Hospital.

Designed to hold 2,950 residents, within four years of its opening in 1951 the facility was "home" to 3,600 children and adults with severe and multiple disabilities. By the early 1960s that number had swelled to more than 6,000. Moreover, by the time Bronston arrived in 1970, a state budget freeze by the Rockefeller administration had cut staff to the bone. (The freeze, as Bronston puts it, was "to reallocate dollars to the construction of the imperial new state capitol complex" in Albany). In addition the institution was virtually cut off from the community around it, and there was little or no accountability by staff or administration. The result was that a resident at Willowbrook was statistically more likely to be assaulted, raped, or murdered than in any other neighborhood in New York City. In 1965, after a tour of the facility, Senator Robert F. Kennedy declared the wards of Willowbrook to be "less comfortable and cheerful than the cages in which we put animals in a zoo."[1]

As Bronston put it, "This was a closed system. This was hell."

Willowbrook was a facility of about sixty buildings scattered over this enormous, pastoral, park-like terrain, similar to Topeka State Hospital. I'd already gotten the picture of what state hospitals were all about. They looked like something straight out of a nineteenth-century pastoral painting, but in fact they were places of towering misery and humiliation and violence.

I was thrown into this building with two hundred of the most broken people I've ever seen. One nurse in the day, one nurse in the afternoon, no nurse at night. Two ward workers on each of four wards of fifty people each. Everybody was in these institutional gowns, because there was not enough support to dress them. The minute clothes would be provided from home, they would disappear.

I had never seen anything like it. I just stood there and tears welled up in me. I'd never seen such squalor. The wards were all concrete, with no furniture, nothing to soften the sound. There was a day room in each ward that was a big terrazzo-floored place with these wooden chairs and benches that were too heavy to lift. There were also some fiberglass chairs but those would constantly fly, people would throw them around. It was absolutely like something out of Dante's *Inferno*. These were wretched "shades" in every form of disrepair, misery, withdrawal.

At first you don't get the full magnitude of it. It takes you day after day to fathom this hell. No programming going on, the most token schooling happening, no support or continuity for the schooling. The minute the kid reaches beyond school age, they go deeper into the institution. No school, no future, no exit. They've got to die to get out.

That first day I said to the staff, "How do I find out who these people are? Where are the off-service notes? Did my predecessor leave exit notes describing who each case was?" "Well, no." I didn't even know who the hell the doctor was that preceded me. So I start trying to figure out who these people are that I'm responsible for, what's wrong with them, and where are they going clinically. The fact of the matter was, it didn't matter. It didn't matter who they were, because they weren't going anywhere.

So I began to look at the charts. The charts were four to six inches deep. People had been there for years. They'd been brought when they were three, four, five, and they were now ten, twelve years old. The charts were filled with incident reports, "pink slips." Week after week they accumulated, a cut here, a bruise there. The place was rampant with tropical diseases, some of which had been instilled purposely for study purposes, like inoculating kids with Hepatitis A in order to study how to develop a hepatitis vaccine. They also had every kind of intestinal parasite that you only see in the center of Africa: Giardia lamblia, amoebiasis, worms. We were constantly sending kids for blood work to make these diagnoses in order to put them on these relentless amounts of rare antibiotics in order to knock out all of these diseases that are strictly diseases of hygiene.

The place smells like excrement all the time. Or this incredible sickening odor of Pine-Sol disinfectant, which comes in industrial cans of twenty, thirty, fifty gallons. It's mopped out on the floor by the inmates because there aren't enough staff to clean the place. So the staff would commandeer the labor of the people that are being incarcerated there, even the young ones.

The place operates just a cellophane's width above absolute chaos. Shrieking, physical outbursts, people struggling against the imposition of the tranquilizing drugs that are car-loaded into them. Any excess movement, any resistance, any human anything is immediately met with a two hundred or three hundred milligram shot of Thorazine to knock them out.

The only heat in the place comes from radiators that are built into the walls with metal sheets in front of them. People get their drugs, which they are forced to take so that two people can handle fifty people doing nothing all day long. Then they would drag themselves over to the radiators, and fall asleep in heaps against and in front of them. So they're laying on the floor, which has this veneer of caustic, chemical disinfectant that's not being cut or diluted, this thick, gummy slimy film, and it eats away at the residents' skin, so that they have these huge swaths of terrible rashes and psoriatic-kinds of crusts on them. They have burns on them because they fall asleep against the radiator, because they are drugged out, for maybe a half an hour, or an hour before the dose gets low enough for them to break through the suppressive impact of the medications.

Initially, I worked with children. And I'm fighting the administration every day because I need more soap, more suture material to sew cuts. I'm on once a week through the night. Like doctors, we'd rotate through. Once a week, or every two weeks, I would have to do a night shift where I would be on call for the entire place. All sixty buildings. Little by little, I begin to see it all.

What happened was that after about four months the doctor who was responsible for the Baby Complex finally got fed up with my continuous demands for hygiene help, and they had me transferred to another building. I think it was Building 76. It was a model "hospital improvement program," a federal grant to fund institutions to set up model programs. The state of New York and Willowbrook had this HIP program that took very young kids and put them into somewhat smaller cohorts, around a hundred children with slightly more staff in temporary buildings that were these star-shaped trailers, mobile homes, where they slept and programmed, with kind of a central playroom and a couple, three classrooms.

They put me in charge of one of those buildings. I had 135–138 kids that I was responsible for, twelve to twenty-one years old. They were all ambulatory, and they were all more capable, more mentally competent.

I began to wage a war against disease in my building. I kept duplicate records. In addition to what I wrote in the chart, I kept a log-book of every single treatment that I did, by ward, by kid, by disease. Because there was no way of tracking or following up. If a kid was presented to me with a raging infection, I'd treat that infection, but then I would lose track of that kid, because they would not keep coming in. There was no way to go back to see what was happening. Or if I sent a kid to a specialist to be looked at—a specialist came from the community to look on a consulting basis, it was just part of the act—then they would order a treatment and there would be no necessary follow-up.

So I needed to keep a book to look at the statistics of what was going on with the effectiveness of what I was doing. I urgently wanted to reduce tranquilizers in these kids. These ward workers were lobbying me, forcing all the doctors to just sign off on these car-loads of tranquilizers so they could play cards and do whatever they needed to do because they—the staff—were out of control, too.

Over a period of about eight months, I cleaned Building 76 up, completely cleaned it up. I reduced the illness and infection rate to almost zero, which was unheard of. I reduced the tranquilizing rate to the point where I could actually look at the kids in my building and think how we could begin humanizing their environment, and begin a real developmental training program and maybe get them out of there. So I regrouped all the kids on paper by putting them in proper developmental groups related to training power needed. And I proposed to change the staff around. In the meantime, I had begun meeting with their parents. They'd never been allowed in before, never been talked to.

I became so intimately involved with every single kid in there, they were like family. I dreaded being off-duty because then the other doctors would cover my kids and put them back on tranquilizers.

Little by little, I began to get it. I began to make breakthroughs in understanding what I was dealing with and that the primary source of illness was the place! The place made illness! It made every kind of illness you can imagine! And nothing was what it looked like.

I had a situation where I had a number of people with extremity amputations in their thirties. These were amputations that were normally a result of circulatory problems and chronic infections that you don't see until people get to be eighty. What was happening, I finally figured out, by just seeing so many people, was that these people were developing these incredible fungal infections from the athlete's foot that was just on the floor everywhere, coupled with the erosion of their skin from the caustic detergents used on the floors, creating fissures. They would develop cellulitis of their feet and legs and then superficial vein thrombosis and then deep vein thrombosis, until finally the leg was destroyed within a decade from being in these buildings.

They had a disease that they called "Mongoloid Dermatitis," which was supposed to be some kind of strange skin disease associated with Down syndrome. This stuff would cause this heaped-up, intertriginous rash, like the spaces in between your fingers and on your chest and legs and shoulders, these scaly, terrible, psoriatic kind of crusts and rashes. The minute I saw this stuff, I couldn't understand what the hell was going on and why doctors were treating it as if it were an inflammatory disease, because the distribution didn't fit. So I brought in a gallon of Kwell, which is what you use to deal with skin mites, and the stuff cleared up overnight. Thousands of people in Willowbrook had been treated improperly for years by professional dermatological specialists who never made the diagnosis that the problem was environmental infestation with skin mites. With the right treatment, the shit cleaned up overnight.

That wasn't what got to me. What got to me was that I was alone amongst all my peers, working with a population that was completely invisible. No doctor that I knew, except Dick Koch[2] and then, of course, Gunnar Dybwad, had anything whatsoever to do with mental retardation in the United States. There was not one radical physician, and I knew them all, that was in the world that I was in, in that institutional pit.

What I did find out, little by little, was that there was a whole economic, big money aspect to what the hell was going on. That the institution at Willowbrook, that institutions in general, were major economic centers that hired thousands of people, purchased millions of dollars' worth of stuff, paid very handsome salaries to the concentration camp managers. That these were all "professionals" who had to be properly ideologized in order to be complicit with this scheme and believe that they were doing "good," to operate in compliance with policies of deprivation and reduction of resources.

We were beginning to get at the graft in the building. By reorganizing the building, all this stuff that was going on at night would be exposed. The robbery, the theft of medication, the corruption, the brutality, the perversion was hidden in the way in which people were organized on the wards, in terms of day, afternoon, night shift. God knows this was multiplied sixtyfold in every building in the institution. It was a closed system and people could not survive just on their salary and in a context that was so dehumanizing, so distorted, so perverse at every level. Sexual perversions. Lots and lots of residents in the institution got pregnant. And beatings were going on constantly.

All hell broke loose. My building nurse and the chief nurse in the institution both went to the director and demanded that I be removed. I had this titanic struggle with the director, who brought charges against me for insubordination.

Overnight, they moved me into taking care of two adult women's buildings, that was four hundred people, and to cover another three buildings. This meant that once every four days, I was responsible for a thousand adult women, with a death rate that was nine times the death rate of the city of New York.

I couldn't believe it. I was so anxious. It was such a traumatic, emotional, move. I was struggling to figure out, "What is going on, what does this mean?" Because I always blew ahead, assuming that I was untouchable. And then something happens, and I suddenly realize that there's been these devastating consequences.

So I wound up filing a grievance against the administration on the advice of a beloved friend of mine, Eugene Eisner, who was the leading progressive labor lawyer, a member of the Lawyers Guild in New York. He was willing to take on my case, pro bono. He never charged me a dime, and we must have spent an hour a day together, every day from then on, for about three or four months. We filed a grievance that my move was punitive. It finally came to the administrative hearing, where he and I sat with the director, Jack Hammond, for about five days, going through the aspects of this administrative hearing, with an administrative court judge. Hammond had his New York State Department of Mental Hygiene lawyer. Him, me, my lawyer, a recorder, and an administrative court judge, sat in the administration building at Willowbrook in order to hear my grievance.

So we went through all the work that I had done. I showed all the records of all the disease control operations, talked in detail about the program that I put in place, talked about the responses of the workers, the responses of the administration, the response of the head nurses. And when the hearing was all over, the administrative hearing record went off to Albany. Came back a letter, a month later, denying my appeal.

In the meantime, I was plunged into the two adult women's buildings and began to establish my grip on what the hell this new job was. They put me into the worst possible environment to get me to quit. Because this was truly the last place that these women were ever going to be. There was no developmental anything going on. There was no school programming going on. There was just wretchedness. Wretchedness and suffering and insanity and inhumanity. Short of Dachau, or a concentration camp in Germany where they were actually burning people every day—they didn't have to burn people here. They needed to keep them alive because they needed to make money off them.

Richard Gould
"Sort of like God's waiting room."

Not all institutions were as massive, or as horrific, as Willowbrook. Even so, life in a nursing home or chronic care hospital in the forties, fifties, and sixties was generally tedious, often stultifying, and sometimes even abusive and violent.

Richard Gould was born to working-class parents in Everett, Massachusetts, in 1935. Injured in a diving accident in 1953, he was first sent to the spinal cord injury rehabilitation center at Boston City Hospital, where he stayed until January 1955. From there he went to the Massachusetts Hospital School, a segregated public school for children and highschoolers with severe physical disabilities, in Canton.

"By this time I had been out of school for two years, so it was kind of an odd place for me to be. But they provided me with training in accounting and taxation. They did a terrific job. They brought in a professor—I guess he was working on a doctoral program in accounting—and basically I was his only student. I did that for something over thirty months. I was there until I was twenty-one and a half, or twenty-two, something like that."

Gould returned to the family farm in West Newberry. He was able to rely on his family for personal assistance, but over time this became less and less practical. Meanwhile, without accessible transportation and community access, he found it impossible to build a practice as an accountant.

As a result Gould, like so many others of his generation, eventually felt he had no choice but to enter an institution, with the prospect of spending the rest of his life in a long-term care hospital or nursing home. Not until the advent of the independent living movement in the mid-1970s was he finally able to find a way not only to live in the community but to pursue the education he wanted, earning his PhD in psychology and establishing a practice as a therapist in the Boston area.

———

I finally left home around 1968. I went to a place called Sea View in Rowley. I only spent about two weeks there. It was a horrible place, really terrible. Nursing homes are not for young people. And they had a lot of burned-out schizophrenics there, which made it kind of challenging. At that point, apparently there was some additional monies going to nursing homes if they brought in some form of rehabilitation. So they wanted me and another fellow, Jim Durant, who was actually one of the kids at the Mass Hospital School, now grown up, to try to set up a program there. But it became very quickly clear to us that, not to put too fine a point on it, it was kind of a scam, and that we were not going to be able to survive there.

I ended up at another nursing home in Haverhill. And I spent several months there. My theory was I'd be able to go to a local community college. But, because MassHealth was paying for this, they would not permit me to go to school. I had to stay within the facility. The logic behind that was that if you're able to go to school, you don't really need this level of care. So I wasn't able to do anything with that.

It was a brand new place, nice and clean. There was some friendly staff there and so forth. But it was really for the elderly and sort of like God's waiting room. There were various stages, generally, of confusion, and I had no interest in being there except that I thought I would be able to go to school. But I was not able to do that and I needed to find something different.

I ended up at Lenox Hill [in Lynn, Massachusetts]. I don't know how I found out about Lenox Hill, but you know, it was, again, a big nursing home owned by a corporation. And they had a scheme to make more money through rehabilitation, bringing in people with spinal cord injuries. I suspect they had no idea what they were getting into.

I think several of the nursing home chains in those days, and even since then, were owned by folks who had some criminal Mafia element. I think that place was what they used to call "the Irish Mafia." One of them was supposed to be toting a gun, you know, a shoulder holster type thing. And it was just kind of a crazy place. It was up on a hill, not a good place for wheelchairs, really steep. You couldn't come and go if you wanted to. Most of us were in manual chairs at the time, anyway, because there were few electric chairs available.

I was horrified by it again—a lot of folks screaming, which happens a lot in nursing homes. . . .

They had some good people working there. They did a lot of therapy, and that got me into some problems. In order to stay there you really had to play the game a little bit. So even though I knew better, I let them try to stretch out some contractions in my knees and it sent me into dysreflexia again.[3] So I ended up at Massachusetts General Hospital, and then because of that [I ended up going into the] Spaulding [Rehabilitation Hospital]. I spent the better part of a year there, same routine, same stuff going on.

I was trying very hard to go to school from there. Trying to get the Mass. Rehab. Commission involved. And I finally got them somewhat interested, though they would ask questions like, "Well, what can you do?"

I didn't have much of an idea of just how to go about it. This was still at a point where just wasn't any transportation.

So I really led a very restricted life.

10
Activists and Organizers, Part 2

———

D ISABLED IN ACTION WAS FOUNDED BY JUDITH HEUMANN IN NEW
York City as a direct action disability rights group. This was, in 1970, a radical idea in and of itself, since almost all organizations having to do with disability were either service organizations, run and staffed by non-disabled, medical or quasi-medical professionals, or single disability constituency groups such as the National Federation of the Blind or the National Association of the Deaf. Even the Berkeley Center for Independent Living and its predecessor, the Physically Disabled Students' Program at UC Berkeley, were first established with the goal of delivering services, such as a wheelchair repair shop and accessible transit. DIA, by contrast, existed solely to put pressure on the local political system. In this regard it was most similar to the California Association of the Physically Handicapped, which by 1970 was already quite active—although the two groups, working on opposite sides of the country, were as yet unaware of each other.

DIA (like CAPH) still exists, and has grown to encompass chapters in New York City, Syracuse, Philadelphia, and Baltimore.

Judith Heumann (continued)
"We kept searching . . . where is the power?
Who are the power brokers?"

———

Disabled in Action played a leading role in the campaigns to override President Nixon's veto of the Rehabilitation Act of 1973, to push for enforcement of the act's groundbreaking Section 504, and in the passage of the Americans with Disabilities Act. Moreover, many of the group's alums went on to prominence in the independent living movement, as staff, directors, and in some cases founders of various independent living centers across the country.

All of this came out of Judy Heumann's lawsuit against the New York City

Board of Education, challenging its right to deny her work simply because she had a disability. In the course of pursuing her lawsuit, Heumann had become the center of a group of like-minded young adults with disabilities, people who were angered at the injustice, galvanized by her victory, and eager to achieve more.

———

A number of my friends and I—for three or four years previous—had been going to different meetings of different organizations, trying to find a place that we felt represented our interests in a disability rights political organization. We had been involved in a couple of different groups, but they weren't organizations that spanned cross-disability and cross-issues. So as we were moving forward with this lawsuit, Denise McQuade[1] and I and a couple of other people decided that what we ought to do was to try to start an organization. We gathered up all the names of the people that had been contacting us about the lawsuit, plus friends and other people that we knew, and invited them to a meeting, which happened at Long Island University. We had about eighty-some people who came to the meeting—quite remarkable.

We formed the organization, which for one week was called Handicapped in Action. I hated the name, so I lobbied everybody to change it. I thought Handicapped in Action was much too retro. At that point, in the seventies, "disabled" was not a word that was being used a lot here in the States, but it was a word that was being used in Scandinavia. They had already done their analysis of what was wrong with "handicapped," so it seemed that if we were supposed to be starting a progressive organization, starting it with the word "handicapped" was not exactly on the right track. So we changed the name.

We were always working. We were doing newsletters, we were doing mailings. We were always answering letters because we were getting lots of letters. "My kid has a disability, and they're not letting him into school" or "I have spinal cord injury and I can't get out of the nursing home" or whatever. What did you do with a letter like that? We just answered them to the best of our ability, referring them to people that we thought maybe could help, or giving them information about what we thought they might want to do. We had no staff. We all were working full-time.

As a rule, we didn't start with demonstrations. We wanted always for people not to be able to say that we were "hot-headed." We wanted to be able to lay out and say, "This is what we saw about the problem; this is what we tried to do to correct the problem; and the reason why we were doing this particular action was because people wouldn't meet with us or make the changes we believed needed to be made."

We had a demonstration outside of [then New York governor Nelson] Rockefeller's office. It had to do with some work that was being done on some architectural barriers law. We wanted to have a meeting with him, and they wouldn't let us in. We had this big demonstration—not big in relationship to any other regular demonstration—but big for us. It was the first time that we ever tried to break our way into a place. I remember somebody pushing our wheelchairs in, trying to push in the door and trying to force our way in because they wouldn't let us in for a meeting.

We got involved with the group from Willowbrook State School for the Mentally Retarded. We knew about it, but we didn't know how to get involved with them. Then one day there was a little article in the *New York Times* about a meeting that was going to be held around the Willowbrook situation,[2] so Bobbi Linn[3] and a few people went to that meeting. That was a whole different group of people. They were politically really on the left, not like us, who were just stumbling through and learning as we were doing. We weren't based in any political organization. We were just setting up DIA, and we had progressive views, but we didn't have a political ideology. We wanted the organization to be truly cross-disability and we opposed institutionalization, so working with this group got us involved with Wolf Wolfensberger's normalization and deinstitutionalization activities.[4] We also began to work with Dr. Bill Bronston, who was one of the doctors at Willowbrook and got Geraldo Rivera to do the exposé.

I visited Willowbrook with a reporter and a nun. They weren't going to let me in because I was in a wheelchair. I could get hurt. Something could happen to me. Me, I was afraid they weren't going to let me *out*. That was my fear once I got there. They wanted me to sign a piece of paper to say that if anything happened to me, they weren't responsible. I refused to sign it. I said to them, "You're not asking these other people to sign a paper like that." So I didn't.

It was a pretty bizarre place. I remember they had big a room for babies, like under three years old, and they had these mats laid out all on the floor. They had these kids laying on the mats, laying off the mats.

They had televisions that were mounted on the wall, and the staff was sitting around, doing nothing with the kids. Then there was a wall. I asked what was behind the wall. So they took us in there, and there were all these babies in these cribs, tied in the cribs. Kids with hydrocephalic conditions and just all kinds of kids either tied in the bed or just in the bed. This visit and the relationships that evolved over the years with Bill Bronston, Diana and Malachy McCourt[5] were very important to me.

Neil Jacobson[6] was on the sheltered workshop committee. We hated sheltered workshops[7] because they had tried to get so many of us into a sheltered workshop. Stevie Hofmann was somebody who was also very actively involved, and Carol Camarata. Carol actually was sent for an evaluation at a sheltered workshop. She was a polio quad. They wanted her to do something like stuff envelopes, and she couldn't use her hands. I mean, you'd hear these bizarre stories. Steve Hofmann had cerebral palsy. He was significantly involved, motorically, with his legs, and speechwise. He also was sent to a sheltered workshop for an assessment. Well, first of all, nobody should have been there, period. But the lunacy of it was that they were asking people to do things that there would be no way they could do, and so then you would be evaluated and paid below minimum wage because you couldn't produce the number of pieces that you needed to produce to be competitive. Well, of course not. If they couldn't use their hands, how could they be stuffing envelopes and doing ridiculous things like that? So that was one of the reasons why we were involved in that issue, because some of the people in the organization felt strongly about it. We were dealing with issues around minimum wage, and getting people regular jobs.

I remember one day we went to visit a sheltered workshop in Manhattan. We had a meeting with one of the executives. I remember this guy telling me that people had a choice. No one forced people to come to a sheltered workshop. If they really didn't like it there, they didn't have to come. I remember saying to him I didn't think people were really being given a choice if their choice was staying at home or coming out, at least being here. It didn't seem to me that was a choice.

We were very active. The board met pretty regularly. We had meetings, I believe, a couple of times a year for the bigger part of the organization, and I think we were reasonably democratic. We tried to move our meetings around to different people's houses, for some of those people, like Roni Stier and myself and Jimmy Lynch, who couldn't drive. Then there were people like Denise McQuade, who could.

Basically, I think our method overall was: we identified an issue that we were concerned about, and we would figure out a plan of what we wanted to do in order to be able to bring attention to the issue. It usually would be anything from letter-writing campaigns to meetings with officials, to testifying at hearings. We had kind of a candy-store approach, driven by the interests of the group. Some people would say, "Focus on two issues," but myself and others were more into "focus on many." I think in part it was because we wanted to get exposure. We kept searching, and it was really searching for, where is the power? Who are the power brokers, and how can we influence them? It was a natural evolution to move out of just dealing with city issues. When you looked at things they were impacted on by the state and the federal level.

We were called, by some, communists, literally, which we used to laugh at. We were definitely considered a militant organization, because we were very strong in our actions, because we disrupted things, because we were not status quo people, and because they didn't know any disabled people like us before—at least in our generation. We didn't just come to meetings. We yelled out at meetings, we challenged people.

We also learned how to use publicity. We weren't experts at it, but we did reasonably well for the time. A lot of the coverage of disability issues in the sixties and seventies was much more on the health page and the socialite page. We actually had a demonstration once outside the *New York Times,* because they weren't giving us appropriate coverage. People told us, "You never demonstrate outside of a newspaper because then they'll never cover you." We said, "Well, it doesn't matter. They weren't covering us anyway." But actually I think we had a meeting with them inside, as a result of the demonstration. It didn't make a dramatic change, but it did allow us to get in there and talk with them and explain what our concern was, that they weren't taking our issues seriously, like a civil rights issue, and that's what this was.

Nixon had vetoed the Rehabilitation Act in 1972.[8] There were many provisions in there that we felt were important. We hadn't been involved in the development of the legislation very much, but we heard about what was going on through contacts that we had in DC and the Mayor's Office on Disability, headed by Eunice Fiorito.[9] We decided that we would have this demonstration outside of the federal building in Manhattan. We decided that we would get a coffin, and we would dress and act as though we were having a funeral. We had fliers, thousands of fliers, that were actually shaped like a tombstone, that talked about Nixon killing the Rehab Act and writing on the tombstone what the specific provisions were that were not going to be enacted.

We never sent anybody up there to actually scout out where the federal building was. So we get up there, and it turns out that the federal building is the only building in all of New York City which is on a little island, where no traffic ever comes. We had this demonstration outside, on the sidewalk. Nobody cared. They sent somebody outside. We talked to the people. We had a little bit of press, but it was a nonevent. I thought we worked so hard on this, we cannot have this be a nonevent.

There we were. We looked great, sounded great, had all the right stuff, and nobody cared that we were there. So then we went into the street. Nobody really cared much more that we were there because I think people could either go to another street or whatever, so it was having zero effect on anything. My God, what are we going to do now? The police were there, and they . . . said, "You should leave." We're, like, "We can't leave." So then we asked one of the cops, "Where is Nixon [campaign] headquarters?" So they called in and asked. I think they were told, "Get 'em out of my precinct!" They came back and told us. So we all got in whatever we had gotten to get there, and we decide we're going to go up to Nixon headquarters. When we arrived we decided to sit down and stop traffic on Madison Avenue. It was totally unorganized, but we still had our fliers.

So we took over Madison Avenue. We actually had shut down three streets, but some of the truckers were not happy having three streets shut down on them, so we decided we'd go back to one street. So we just went across Madison Avenue. We stayed there. It was around 4:45 in the afternoon by the time we got there. No one knew we were coming, so no one knew why we were there. Someone came out from the headquarters and said, "What do you want?" We said, "We want to talk to somebody from Nixon headquarters." So they sent somebody out from Nixon headquarters. "What do you want?" "We want a public debate on MacNeil Lehrer [news program on PBS] with the president on why he vetoed the Rehabilitation Act." They said, "You're crazy." I said, "That's what we want. That's why we're here."

We must have stayed there an hour. We really did shut this area of the city down. But we had hardly any press. If it would have been any other group, a) they wouldn't have let them sit there for an hour in the afternoon, and b) it would have been all over the media. Anyway, after we stayed there for about an hour and had done what we wanted to do, we went into Nixon headquarters. We went in, and we took over the floor.

Cripples threw the Nixon people off guard. They didn't know what to do. We were there, and we were chanting, and it's four days before the election. The police were there, but it turned out we had these really nice cops, who were not into doing anything to us because in this particular precinct, there had been a couple of cops who had been shot in the last year, and so some of the guys that we were dealing with had actually been involved in helping to get their friends to therapy at different places, and they totally understood what we were talking about: lack of transportation, etc. About midnight, we left.

We were upset. We didn't get the coverage that we wanted to get. Some people said we didn't get coverage because we didn't have any Vietnam vets with us. So I called a woman named Nancy Amaday, I called McGovern headquarters and I explained what had happened, and I said, "We want to have another demonstration on Monday. We need some vets." Nancy found two disabled veterans—one was Bobby Muller.[10]

We had decided that this time, we were going to meet on Times Square and we were going to march as a group of disabled people against traffic up Times Square. Bobby, if you talk to him, will talk about how he thought this was the craziest thing he'd ever seen or done in his entire life, and he talked to people about how crazy I was, how I was more out there than he was, and Pat Figueroa and all of us. So then we marched up Times Square, shut down traffic again. It was earlier in the day this time. This time we had a lot of press. There are definitely more articles because we had the vets, and again we went to Nixon headquarters.

We talked about DIA and what was going on as a civil rights movement. We did not use terms like "independent living" because that wasn't known yet, we didn't know about CIL. But we definitely talked about the charitable model versus civil rights. I don't think we used the word "model." It was more like charity versus civil rights, human rights, civil rights.

It felt very much like we were creating something new, which I do believe is true. It was something new. We were a new group of people that were coming together, that didn't have a lot of community-organizing background. We weren't, as I said, a part of other political organizations, where we could have learned things. We worked full-time, dealing with our disabilities, and dealing with this organization. I think, given everything, we did a phenomenal job.

Pat Figueroa
"What kind of monster do you think I am?"

———

Born in 1948 with spina bifida and raised in Puerto Rico until he was ten years old, Pat Figueroa's first experience with mainland America came in the middle of winter "on a cold, snowy day" when his family moved to a converted storefront in New York City.

"We were basically very poor. My father was not able to work and he was miserable. 'Access' was a word that wasn't in the vocabulary. It was a walk-up tenement building. Even the storefront itself was a walk-up." A move to an apartment upstairs in the same building meant Figueroa had to be home schooled, since simply getting out to the street was an ordeal. "It was not a building with an elevator, so I spent most of my time looking out the [fourth floor] window on the fire escape."

In the spring of 1962, Figueroa went into the hospital for "amputations of my lower extremities. I was in the hospital for a better part of a year" and then fitted with prostheses. His family in the meantime had moved into a public housing project with elevators, so when he returned home he was able to attend "health conservation classes" in a public school on the east side of Manhattan. "This school was accessible except the 'normal' kids were upstairs and the 'gimps' were downstairs." Like many of his generation, Pat Figueroa's activism began when he entered college, in his case Brooklyn College in the early 1970s, where he also met his future wife, Denise A. Bader. Both started as student activists, graduating to Disabled in Action and the national disability rights movement.

———

I went back to college, after I had bought a car, a Mustang, and had worked for two and a half years designing labels, logos, and other things for a garment district company, which was a very nice group of people, a family-owned business. It gave me work experience. I went back to the school; I knew that I needed to finish my education. I took my car, the Mustang, and I basically traded it for a Chevy Impala from this guy.

He took over the payments; I took his 1964 Impala. That meant I could afford to go back on benefits and get my education underwritten by the state rehab agency.

I applied to Brooklyn College. They accepted me as an evening open enrollment student. Then I had to take a couple of remedial courses, which I did, and passed them. I get into Brooklyn College—I was there '72 to '74.

There was a group called SOFEDUP [Student Organization For Every Disability United for Progress]. The founder of that organization was a fellow by the name of Fred Francis. I don't think there was a brighter person, a more articulate person, a more gifted leader in the community—not in New York State, but across this country—than this guy, and nobody noticed him. He and Judy [Heumann] were my mentors. I mean intellectually, Fred is up there. He was a double amputee, like I am, and had become disabled as the result of an automobile accident. He was very, very well-spoken. I mean, this guy can talk. He can speak in such a way that was mesmerizing. It reminded me a little bit of the things that John Kennedy used to say.

Anyway, Fred Francis was the founder of this organization. He had just graduated and gone on to NYU [New York University]. I became the leader of SOFEDUP because Arthur [Lefkin], the fellow who was the president after Fred, became ill and had to drop out that year. I met my wife Denise through SOFEDUP. Already I knew what Disabled in Action could do—they had gotten me my apartment. I wanted to encourage all the new people, the young people to continue, to become involved. That was my point, to develop new leadership.

We always tell stories about the experiences we had in this school. I remember sitting with one of the engineering architects [talking] about making a building accessible. We said, "We want a ramp to compensate for those four steps." He wanted to do something around the back of the building, which was totally ridiculous, because you would have had to go all around the building that's almost a block wide. I said, "No, you're going to put up a ramp." I think his most disturbing idea was, "That's going to take away from the beauty of the quad." Brooklyn College is a pretty campus. You had the fountains and you had the green area and all the paths crisscrossing. His position was, "Another wooden ramp that's going to interfere with the aesthetics." So he says, "Look, I have an idea. Why don't we compromise? Instead of making this forty-four-foot-long ramp, we could make a twenty-eight-foot ramp. We will ramp the first two steps." I looked at him and said, "And what the heck am I supposed to do with the next two steps?" He just couldn't understand it. The aesthetics came first. The practicality was something that they couldn't comprehend. So those were the people that we were up against.

People like Fred Francis and Professor Harvey Honig—who taught in City University—these guys were determined to make the City University accessible even before Section 504 became the law, and they did. They had three university administrations saying, "Okay, that's what we need to do." It started at Brooklyn College and it moved to the different campuses: Hunter, Brooklyn Technical, Brooklyn Community College, City College, Queens College, Queens Community College. All the New York City University Colleges, CUNY, eventually had a disabled student coordinator, and we had policies in place. "You know, the lab is in a building that doesn't have an elevator. We need to build another building with another lab, but in the interim, it's got to be moved." And ultimately, if somebody said, "No," it was like, "We'll just demonstrate."

What was also interesting is the reputation you got as a student leader. In Brooklyn College, there were white students and black students and Jewish students, Italian students, and Puerto Rican students, and there were all kinds of conflicts there. It was a time when minority people said, "We want a piece of the action too. We decided we're not going to stay behind." The Latino community in particular was, "We're not slaves; we're American citizens. We have the same rights as everybody else." Whenever there was a problem at Brooklyn College, the administration wanted me to be involved. Everybody said I was "a radical constructionist" because I was a positive force. I didn't just say things were bad. I'd say, "This is the way we have to go and resolve this." Somebody asked me to sit on some of these panels and I thought, "Wouldn't that be interesting?"

This was the beginning of myself getting out of the shell, myself being recognized as a leader. Not necessarily things I wanted to do, because I was very shy. I hated to do public speaking. It was what I admired most about Judy and Fred—people who don't have to script anything. If I'm going to make a five-minute presentation, I have to script it because it's like I can't talk and think at the same time. I've gotten a lot better, but Fred was very gifted in this respect. He also was somebody that, when Judy wanted to have a demonstration or something, she would call on him. We were good strategists. Not to take anything away from Judy and all the women that were in Disabled in Action, but we helped a lot.

We learned guerilla-warfare tactics from the antiwar movement, the black civil rights movement. Women were already throwing away their bras. In New York City, gay people were having riots with the police. We also had great leaders like the late Eunice Fiorito, and others at the colleges. We also had an advantage in that many of the people around us were veterans. These men went out and they gave up their bodies for their country. The country is always told that nobody is held in higher esteem than the veterans. There was a fellow by the name of Bobby Muller—he has a group of veterans in Washington. Back then he could generate some of the young vets, the Vietnam vets, because they felt the same thing, "I want to be able to use the subway; I want to be able to park in downtown Manhattan; I want to be able to have an apartment that's accessible." These guys identified with us, more so than the veterans of the Korea era and the veterans from World War II. "You send me to a war that was for economic reasons only; I came back all messed up and I can't find a job; I can't find a house! You want to give me $1,900 a month and this is not enough!" They just realized that that couldn't be, because what is this country but military might?

I think the success of DIA, this small, but very radical group, was something that some of the other groups had not been able to duplicate. DIA was Judy, all about Judy and what she wanted for people with disabilities. Other groups did not have a young woman that was bright, attractive, and a great spokesperson. She was talented. She knew what she wanted to be, which was a school teacher. Very humble, very all-giving kind of a profession. To be denied that opportunity because of some stupid bureaucratic thing that says that she's got to pass a physical, the public was saying, "Oh God, this is the dumbest idea." We needed teachers, there was already a teacher shortage. So you see the Judy Heumann lawsuit against the Board of Education issue on the front cover of the *New York Times* and the *Daily News* and on television. Everybody knows that anything she says is going to be heard by other people with disabilities, and they're going to say, "Yeah, yeah, let's do it. This is the time to change things." That was part of what she did.

The biggest issue in New York City for everybody, not just for people with disabilities, had been, of course, housing—housing being super expensive. But for people with disabilities, transportation was a close second.

The demonstration I organized and the thing that I take credit for was when we took over the Metropolitan Transit Authority headquarters. The disability community was negotiating with them to make the subway system accessible and getting accessible buses. The chairman of the MTA did not want to do this—not with federal funds, not with state funds, not with anything. So there was an advisory committee that was meeting regularly up at his offices, and that group was reporting to a larger group of activists. I was one of the co-chairs of the larger groups and I said, "I think it's time we take action. We have to tell this guy, the chairman of the MTA, Richard Ravitch, where to get off." I said, "Let's organize a takeover of his office."

I was the one that scripted the whole thing out. "We're going to show up. We're going to go up to his floor. We're going to have x-number of people go up at the same time, et cetera." We planned every detail.

We went up to the floor where the chairman had his office. I told the guy who was the receptionist, "We're here to have a meeting with the chairman." The guy says, "You're from the advisory council?" And I said, "Yes." He said, "I thought there was a meeting with the advisory council yesterday?" There's about two hundred of us that are waiting to meet with the chairman. So this guy was like looking through all the papers. He gets up and he goes into the back and he talks to the chairman. Meanwhile, we're bringing people up on the elevators and just like that—I mean it was a mad rush. We had people downstairs take elevators, and once we had enough people upstairs, we jammed the elevator doors rendering them inoperative. Okay, and then it was like two staircases, we blocked them. Those people in the office staff who wanted to leave were told, "You want to leave? Get out now. But we are not going to let the chairman out." That was the way we did it.

We took over the MTA headquarters. We barricaded the elevators; we barricaded the stairwells. The head of the MTA went into his office with his security people. They had guns too; they thought we were going to kill them. We sat there and we got national/international publicity. We had one reporter running up and down the stairs. He was a double agent. He brought us information on what the police were planning to do, and he would give them information through his reports for the radio station and all the other outlets. In fact, I keep saying to myself, "If it wasn't for that demonstration, John Tesh would still be a little reporter on a local CBS station." He was the only reporter I let come in. He would tell me, during an interview, what was going on with the police tactical squad. "Are you aware that they [have sent for] a tactical police force and they're downstairs trying to figure out how they're going to get you out of the building? Do you know that they were going to make an attempt to come back down the rear staircase but they found that you guys had it blocked? Are you aware that they also called the Rusk Institute because they need technical assistance on how to pick up somebody who's got a disability and what to do with them? Are you aware that they're going to send you guys to Bellevue because the court building is inaccessible?" It was funny. His inquiring interviewing questions to me was giving me information. He would bring in sometimes four or five different radio stations and national feeds, tape recorders and microphones. He wanted to bring a cameraman in and we said, "No," because we couldn't open the door too wide because somebody else could force their way in.

I remember being finally carried out of the building by four policemen, and I was yelling to the television camera crews, "We're going to beat you (the MTA) at the polling place; we'll beat you politically; we're going to beat you in the streets; we're going to beat you in the media; we're going to beat you in the courts. We're going to get accessible mass transit in New York City." This gentleman, Richard Ravitch, who was in charge—the chairman—he had said to me one time at a meeting, that this would not happen in his lifetime, not while he was alive. So I said, "I think you're going to die very soon." And he almost literally jumped over the desk and wanted to strangle me.

Anyway, we won the whole thing—politically. I took a position that we were going to help Mario Cuomo[11] get elected if he promised he would get rid of the chairman of the MTA and appoint somebody who was not going to resist making subways accessible. I said we were going to beat them in the polling places, in the court, in the streets and the media. And we did. After the demonstration all the New York City media stations went sour on the MTA. Every night, every station was doing something. Typically they would start with, "Look at this bus. This bus is filthy. Look at this—the pull cord doesn't work. This bus is half an hour late. This subway train is filthy. This subway train is not safe." The kneeling buses, which were supposed to be in place at that time, didn't kneel. So John Tesh, Arnold Diaz, and even John Stossel, they did a lot of reports on the MTA. The media was bashing the MTA.

What happened—to show you how things kind of snowballed—about a week and a half after our demonstration, there was an attempt on Richard Ravitch's life. What bothered me was I got phone calls from the TV stations, reporters asking, "Was it one of your people who tried to kill him?" You sit back and you say, "Oh, my God! Who do these people think we are?" That started bothering me.

That was the beginning of my self-examination saying, "You know, this has gotten too big." Some mornings I would get out of the van or the car and there's people waiting down the street like high-fiving you and they're saying, "That's the way to go." You say to yourself, "Wait a minute, I'm just a private citizen." It's like you no longer are really a private citizen. I was getting tired because I'm really very private. I enjoy staying in my house because I can listen to music that I love; I can do my art work, and I can watch baseball, listen to the news. Although I'm not agoraphobic. Anyway, I began to realize that this media thing was too much.

This thing brought it all home. I had six or seven reporters call me and ask me, "Was it one of your people who shot him?" And I was like, "No. What kind of monster do you think I am?"

11

Independent Living

IN 1962, ED ROBERTS, FINISHING HIS SECOND YEAR AT THE COLLEGE OF San Mateo, decided to transfer to the University of California at Berkeley. Because none of the dormitories were wheelchair accessible (and none could accommodate the "iron lung" he needed at night), Roberts moved into Cowell Hospital, the campus infirmary. His presence attracted media attention (most notably, an article in the *San Mateo Times* with the headline, "Helpless Cripple Attends U.C. Classes"), which in turn drew other students with disabilities to the campus.

Unlike the program at the University of Illinois at Urbana-Champaign, where students with disabilities were expected to define their disability in terms of the rehabilitation model, the students at Berkeley early on began to develop a political consciousness that redefined their issues as social, not simply individual, problems. San Francisco was, of course, the epicenter of the counterculture of the 1960s, with the civil rights and campus free speech movements feeding directly into the antiwar turmoil of the mid- to late sixties and early seventies. Throughout the last half of the decade Berkeley was the scene of student strikes, demonstrations, and civil unrest. It was not uncommon, as more than one disability activist remembers, to see police and students clashing on campus. In such an environment, it was perhaps inevitable that the students at Cowell would come to see their own issues politically.

One result of this new awareness was the formation of the "Rolling Quads"— an advocacy group pushing for campus and community access—and the opening in 1970 of the Physically Disabled Students' Program (PDSP), a pilot project funded through what was then the federal Department of Health, Education, and Welfare (HEW). As word of the PDSP spread, people with disabilities in the surrounding community who weren't Berkeley students began to avail themselves of its services, which included help finding accessible housing and personal care assistants, wheelchair repair, and rudimentary paratransit where no accessible public transit existed. In addition, students who graduated from Berkeley or otherwise left school continued to need and use the PDSP. And so PDSP students began meeting with these consumers to plan the next phase, and in March 1972 the Center for Independent Living, Inc. (CIL), was established.

The Berkeley CIL was the spark for what grew by the end of the decade into a national movement with its own defined "independent living philosophy." At its core was the then-radical notion that people with disabilities were the experts on their experience and could best decide for themselves what services they needed and how to use them. Many of its early proponents, such as Ed Roberts, Hale Zukas, Donald Galloway, Kitty Cone, Gerard Baptiste, Corbett O'Toole, and Mary Lou Breslin, became national and even international figures. Activists in other parts of the country, including Fred Fay and Elmer Bartels in Boston, Judith Heumann in New York, and Max and Colleen Starkloff in St. Louis, heard about the CIL and used it as a model for their own communities, or—as in Heumann's case—moved to Berkeley to work with the center directly.

In 1977, Berkeley CIL activists carried out the most daring and effective civil disobedience action for disability rights of the decade—indeed, perhaps up to that time—the sit-in at the San Francisco offices of the HEW.

The CIL's Disability Law Resource Center, founded in 1978, split off a year later to become the independent Disability Rights Education and Defense Fund (DREDF), cofounded by Patrisha Wright, Mary Lou Breslin, and attorney Robert Funk, its first director. DREDF in turn played a central role first in opposing the Reagan administration's attempts in the early 1980s to scale back the gains made by the movement in the 1970s, and then in getting federal disability rights legislation passed in the late 1980s, most notably the Americans with Disabilities Act of 1990.

The independent living model fostered by the Berkeley CIL was so successful that by 1995 there were more than four hundred IL centers throughout the United States, as well as in Europe, Australia, Japan, Central and South America, and in several nations of the former Soviet Union.

Ed Roberts (continued)
"Within a day or so I realized, I can do this. I can be free."

———

Ed Roberts, transfering to UC Berkeley, experienced all the trepidation and excitement of a young person leaving home for the first time, along with the additional feelings that went with living those first weeks and months as the only student with severe disabilities on a largely inaccessible campus in a largely inaccessible world.

———

I totally surprised [my mother with the idea of going to the University of California]. Her thought was, "Whoa. Just going through the College of San Mateo was a remarkable feat." And then she started hearing me say, "I don't want to stop here; I have to go on." I think I realized before she did that the path to my future and to my working was going to be education, totally. Because nobody was going to hire me the way I was. There was so much prejudice about disability.

The biggest obstacle became [obvious] real soon: where would I live? I think we almost gave up because of that. . . . [We had] a list of places, like the dorms, like International House, like other places. . . . I went to I-House, which was inaccessible, and Jean Wirth[1] went in. Now, you can imagine, this guy from Pakistan or somewhere just looked at her, this huge tall woman, and just kind of freaked out. "Oh, no, we don't have any students who—Oh, no, we couldn't have him." And then he got the manager to say the same thing. It seemed like wherever we went, there was no opportunity.

I had to go to the [campus] hospital. That didn't sound very good to me. I didn't have high hopes about this. Then I remember meeting [Dr. Henry Bruyn, director of Cowell Hospital], and he was so friendly. He knew a lot about polio, and he looked at me, and he thought to himself, he said out loud—I remember it was one of the first things he said—"There must be a lot of people your age from these old polio epidemics that are ready to go on now to college, and they don't have much help."

He said, "Why don't we open the hospital? You could live here," and I started saying, "But I could live there like a dorm, right? I know about hospitals; I don't want to live in a hospital." He said, "We can work those things out." I said, "I want to have my own attendants when I can. But I can't afford to hire twenty-four-hour attendants." He said, "Well, that shouldn't be a problem. You're just one person. If you need help, you can have a button and get help. We always have attendants there anyway, every shift."

[The day I moved into Cowell, I felt] a combination of excitement and fear. I remember the first room I had was in the older wing. It was kind of dark. Most hospital patients' rooms are dark. It was good-sized. The first few days, my mother stayed there with me, which was real good, because it was scary. And my brother came each day, just to say hi and to help out wherever he could, feed me or whatever.

In the meantime, I was beginning to interview some prospective attendants. Within a couple of days, I found a guy that had been an orderly at Cowell.

[When my mother finally left Cowell to go home], it was scary. I just knew it was a monumental occasion, because we really hadn't been apart except for my being in the hospital. Within a day or so I realized—I could do this, I can be free, even though it was a halfway situation. The big skill I had to learn was how to hire [attendants, and] how to describe what I wanted, but I've always been pretty good at talking.

[My brother] was a very good attendant when he was ready. He'd always drink and come in late, so it would be a rush in the morning to get out. I'd be up and ready in fifteen or twenty minutes—washing and everything; it was amazing. So he was important. I could get him if I needed him. If I needed to go get booze or something, he could go get it, until John [Hessler] later came. We figured out all the stores that would deliver booze. That was pretty weird for them, because the hospital was not supposed to have booze. They brought it all the way up. Once in a while, some of the nurses would help a little bit, but it was a conflict for them.

It's funny, because I started hearing a little bit about John. He was trapped in a county hospital. He was smart, he was going to school and was really ready to come to Cal, and I wasn't sure I wanted to give up my exclusivity. So I met John, and John was an imposing figure, let me tell you. He was six foot eight, and he had a huge wheelchair. He had a very slow power chair, but he had a power chair. It surprised me how large it was. I think we got along pretty much right from the beginning. He moved in right next door to me on the second floor there. . . .

By the second semester I was a veteran. I knew the campus, I knew myself more. I loved it, I loved the campus. I went to the football games. Every week, somebody would come and we'd sit out in the field. I went to Harmon Gym, although it was a bitch to get into. They had to carry me in. See, those were the days, my friend—It wasn't until later, after a couple of years, when I went to a history lecture—I think it was California Hall. I was getting pulled up the stairs, and the top part of my [wheelchair back] rest was removable. They grabbed that, and it yanked right out. I started to flip over, and some guys grabbed me and hauled me up. But I remember how afraid I was. I thought, I guess I'm going to survive, but I remember later taking it a lot more seriously and always having four people lift me, always making sure that if I had to be lifted, it was safe.

I began to choose classes based on access. I remember I went to Dwinelle [Hall] and took classes in Scandinavian literature. . . . I remember learning about how to be a university student. My brother had learned a lot about it, but I remember also wondering how to take notes, and then discovering that if you gave somebody carbon paper, they would take your notes while they're taking theirs. Then I started making an announcement at the beginning of class, [asking for someone to make a copy of her notes] and could usually find a good-looking young woman. I'd get to know somebody that way, and they all loved it. Every day, they'd come by and give me the notes.

I had done most of my reading through high school lying in bed with a reading rack and a mouth-stick turning the pages. When I went to Cal Berkeley, I started using the reading mirror. You see this big mirror above me? If you flip it over, it's a reading rack. So I had a new mouth-stick made that was longer. But I had done some of this anyway, after I had my iron lung. So I got the rack from Fairmont Hospital, and we'd just put it up, we'd turn a mirror over, and it had these rubber bands that you attached the book with. They held the pages up there. Then I'd take out fifty pages at a time, and tuck it in. It took a little more time, but not that bad. I could be really free and independent with that, so I could read for an hour or two before I even got to the point [where I had to ask someone to turn the next batch of pages]. It was really nice.

I went all the through college reading [that way]. If you look at my bottom teeth, see how crooked they are, how they're pushed over? Mouth-stick. The mouth-stick did that, but it was worth it. So I could keep up with the reading, and I could keep up on all kinds of things. . . .

But I loved Berkeley. I really got into it.

Cathrine Caulfield
"Berkeley was the place to be."

Cathrine Louisa Caulfield was born on September 5, 1948, in Frankfurt, Germany. Her father was in the military but came from "dairy farmers and teachers in Minnesota," her mother "from railroad and medical people." The family moved back to the United States in 1952.

"I moved to California in 1964, the same year as my accident. I had been in California two weeks. I was playing in the water near the beach when a large wave hit me, knocked me off my feet, and my head hit the sand. The force of the wave crashed me on the beach. I had an injury to my fifth and sixth cervical vertebrae. This paralyzed me from the chest down."

Caulfield went through rehabilitation at Letterman General Hospital at the Presidio in San Francisco, and then at the rehab center in Vallejo, California. "I did almost two years of rehab, which is unheard of now. But I kept progressing so I was able to stay. But as a teenager in a wheelchair, I kind of liked it there. There were other kids my age who were in the same situation that I was in." Aside from the rehab regimen, which was often grueling, "We had bingo night. Then we changed it to beer and bingo night—much more fun!" How does one get beer to a group of teenagers in a hospital? "It takes one cool urologist, and a rumor that beer is good for kidneys, and voilà—beer and bingo night!"

Cathrine's brother and sister both went to college (her brother became a doctor, her sister a teacher), so it was a given that she would go to school as well. Reading about the Cowell Hospital program in the *San Francisco Chronicle,* she decided in 1968 to go to UC Berkeley.

"I had an interview with Dr. Bruyn. At first he said he didn't think so. There were no females in the program. The Cowell program was on the third floor of the hospital. If anyone needed anything—turning at night, help to the bathroom—the male orderly would come up from the second floor. They couldn't let the nurses off the second floor. I assured him I did not need anything at night and let's give it a try. Dr. Bruyn called in a week and said, 'Yes, we will give it a try.' Of course I was thrilled."

Cathrine Caulfield died on December 12, 2003.

———

I moved into the Cowell program September of 1968. I guess that made it the first coed dorm at UC Berkeley. Just me and seven guys, like the Snow White story all over again. John Hessler, Ed Roberts, Jerome Frazee, Donovan Harby, Bill Glenn, and Scott Sorenson. I think Donald Lorence and I came at the same time. Herb Willsmore arrived a few months later.

I was very nervous. Moving in with a bunch of guys is a little nerve-wracking. Everyone ate dinner in an old nurses' station which happened to be right next to my room. They coaxed me out of my room after a few hours. We all became great friends very quickly. . . .

When I first met John and Ed we were basically roommates. I think they were happy to have a female on board. They were both smart, dynamic people. John was the tough and kind of grumpy one. He had a great sense of humor. Ed was the softer, kinder strategist. John got things done by hollering at you and Ed would charm the chicken off the bone. They were a lot of fun to live with and a major influence in my life for years. John was perfect for the director of Physically Disabled Students' Program, and Ed was incredible as the public personality needed for CIL. . . .

Ed introduced me to a friend of his, Linda Perotti. She was interested in working for me. She started working the next day. Linda's friend Barbara Karten was also interested. This was all new to me. But I quickly picked up on the attendant and disabled person relationship. I learned to hire people who could adapt to my needs. It's important to find people you are comfortable with. I was set up in no time.

Living at Cowell was very exciting and very busy. We were all going to school. In the evenings we would get together and discuss everything! We had to attend to our immediate needs, like privacy, curfews, attendants, and how to deal with the nurses from the second floor. I remember when I first moved there, if you came home after nine o'clock, you would have to climb the hill to the back of the hospital and be scrutinized by the staff (Nurse Benedetti) as to your whereabouts. Well, this didn't wash for long with us radicals from Berkeley.

We started organizing. The Rolling Quads were born. We spent many days and nights in Ed's room brainstorming. I remember a few nights breaking open a bottle of Chivas Royal Salute in Donald Lorence's room for his famous reality therapy sessions. This was a mix of how we could live together in harmony in this small wing of the hospital to who had partied late the night before and left incriminating evidence lying around. . . .

Of course, this was the late sixties, early seventies in Berkeley, and we were right in the thick of it. So sure, we might have indulged in a little bit of sex, drugs, and rock and roll. We partied hard but kept the ball rolling as far as the disabled movement was concerned.

We knew two people who were disabled, Jim Donald and Larry Langdon, who lived outside the dorm in their own apartment. They were both pretty low quadriplegics and were doing great on their own. Neither one of them [had ever] lived at Cowell as far as I know. They went right to an apartment. But anyway, we would go over and visit them, and they were great. Then it started—"Let's start looking around and see about accessibility." Well, accessible housing was the pits. That's how programs like PDSP started. If numbers of disabled people are going to live independently, where are they going to find accessible housing? Attendants to work for them? People to build ramps? All the stuff necessary to live each day. Would the landlord rent to you? Would they let you build a ramp? Could you get into the bathroom?

Linda Perotti and I found a place on Parker Street. Ed's brother was moving out. It was a downstairs flat with only three steps and the bathroom door was wide enough for a wheelchair. Yes! The kitchen was awful but hell, who needs to eat?

We all agreed there were certain basic services that people needed as students and functioning members of the community. We needed a place to live, attendants to hire, a wheelchair that didn't break down all the time, and a place to get it fixed quickly if it did. We needed a central spot people could come to find services, PDSP for the students and CIL for the community. New students would come from all over to check out the Berkeley campus and we would show prospective students around.

John Hessler was the obvious choice as the first director for PDSP as he had worked hard getting it all organized. I was on the board of directors and I believe Dr. Bruyn was as well. There was also someone representing vocational rehab on the board. [And then] the idea grew and led to development of the Center for Independent Living.

There was so much going on at this time. People were working on the housing survey. They would go door to door, to every apartment building, evaluating accessibility. Others were working on funding for attendant care which was in jeopardy for a while. Chuck Grimes and Andy Lennox put together a wheelchair repair shop in PDSP. Zona Roberts, Ed's mom, was keeping the place [PDSP] together; Carol Fewell [Billings], my best buddy, was documenting everything, while trying to keep John calm. We had a lot of fun in that rickety old building, the smell of Top Dog[2] coming through the window, maneuvering the old blue van in and out of the parking lot, and assuring everyone our ramp from hell was quite nice. While all this was going on we had to stop the war in Vietnam and keep People's Park alive.[3]

I remember passing out water to people marching against the war in Vietnam. Soldiers with guns were on one side of the street and we were on the other. One day Ed and I were coming out of our poly sci class (Ed was the T.A.). As we were leaving the building, tear gas was dropped on the campus. Luckily we lived at Cowell then, and we ducked in as fast as our chairs could go. . . .

Berkeley was the place to be then. We were attending one of the greatest universities in the world. My professors were incredible. Sproul Plaza was the [Speakers' Corner] of the West. We spent many afternoons at the outdoor cafe on Sproul Plaza breathing it all in. . . .

It helped me realize a full and active life was possible. It renewed my self-esteem. I was living at home with my parents, attending City College, and that was as far as I could see. Moving to Berkeley gave me all sorts of energy. I no longer thought about "being disabled."

It was a crazy, exciting time and the disabled movement was part of that time.

Michael Fuss
"The disabled were very ripe for becoming a liberation type of movement."

"I have been involved with politics since I was probably twelve or thirteen," says Michael Fuss. "I was concerned about nuclear war, I was concerned about the inequality in the country . . . between blacks and whites." Fuss's concern led him to join the Congress of Racial Equality (CORE), to participate in sit-ins to protest job discrimination, and to organize for CORE in the Watts section of Los Angeles, "prior to the Watts riot."

Born in Brooklyn in 1945, Fuss was fourteen when his family moved to Los Angeles. After graduating high school he took a job at the Southern California Gas Company, where he ran their mail machine. He continued his political work however, recruiting for CORE among blacks at the company "who were basically in janitorial positions only." By 1964 he was also a member of "Friends of SNCC" [Student Nonviolent Coordinating Committee], "involved in trying to generate publicity" about the disappearance of civil rights workers in Mississippi. He also began attending night school, transferring to U C Berkeley in 1966.

Needing money, Fuss took a job as a "personal care attendant"[4] at the Cowell Residence Program, where he met Ed Roberts, John Hessler, Scott Sorenson, and others who would become principal activists in the nascent independent living movement. Fuss himself had a profound impact on the development of the "independent living philosophy," helping to organize the Physically Disabled Students' Program and serving as assistant director from 1966 to 1972. In the meantime, he graduated from Berkeley with a degree in anthropology. He did "a stint in the non-profit world," teaching grant proposal writing, after which he earned an MBA and moved on to a career in small business management, fundraising, and consulting.

———

Over the years we talked more and more about the future, and as the program at Cowell expanded we talked about what should be done. I think that John and Ed and a whole number of other people up there felt grateful for the opportunity, but also very constrained by the limitations of living in the hospital and being under a medical model, and of being actively discouraged from attempting to live on their own. Nurses would come up from the floor below, and it was helpful to have the nurses if somebody was in trouble at night, but also they'd come up and tell people to be quiet or they'd start ordering people around like they were sick.

Well, these guys weren't sick. They had disabilities of one kind or another. Most of them were quads—not all of them. They were healthy, late adolescent to early adult, mostly males—though we had two women eventually—who wanted to be like everybody else and explore their life, explore possibilities. Don't forget the time: this is the middle to late sixties, and everything was exploding, everything seemed possible.

The first idea was more of a group home sort of thing to be run by the disabled themselves—by the quads in this case. Put people in apartments, with a place that they could come for wheelchair repair, and maybe a meal, and advocacy with the Department of Vocational Rehabilitation.

A lot was happening in Washington. There was money coming out, mostly for minority students to develop special services out of the Department of Health, Education, and Welfare. Its mission was to help develop programs across the country to bring people to colleges and universities, and to provide services for people who had not had opportunities in the past. There was a certain amount for Appalachian whites, and there were certain amounts for Puerto Ricans, for Mexican Americans, and for blacks. The original concept did not include disabled. My understanding is that Ed had a lot to do with including the disabled in the program. So we had to figure out what we were going to do.

The first step was to set up independent student courses, one every quarter, so that people living in Cowell could work on this and get credit for it. Sometimes they would be in the sociology department, sometimes in political science. Ed was gone by this time. He and Jean Wirth got involved in setting up Nairobi, which was a two-year community college in the black ghetto in East Palo Alto. Most of his trips to Washington seemed to be around that.

John and I basically taught these classes. In those courses we went into things like self-identity, what does it mean to be stigmatized because you're in a wheelchair? How do people treat you? What do you feel about yourself? How did this come about? What can you do about it? What are the barriers in the way of you becoming more independent?

They were independent study courses, basically. We would approach a professor with a course outline and with books, and then John and I would do the research and tell them what we were doing, and they would say, "Oh sure."

The courses were just open to the disabled students. There were some who took advantage of it and didn't do much of anything, but a lot of people really participated, and I think this raised the awareness of what the problems were and created a lot of ferment in terms of the direction to take.

I think as this happened and people started living more independent lives—and in some ways doing riskier things, like trying drugs and having sexual partners—it started bothering the nurses downstairs at Cowell and, therefore, the hospital administration. They started trying to institute more restrictive curfews, and all sorts of things. There was more pressure from Vocational Rehabilitation on people not spending enough time learning or not taking schoolwork or the appropriate courses. There were basically two people they chose to come down on the hardest: one was John Hessler, and the other was Donald Lorence.

John at that point had two quarters left for his master's degree, and they said that they would support him for only one more quarter, and then he would have to leave. Since he already had a bachelor's degree, there didn't seem to be any sense in them supporting him to a master's.

Their issue with Don was his flamboyant lifestyle. He took on kind of a hippie air: he wore wild clothes and let his hair grow frizzy. I don't think he was doing much of anything that other people weren't, but he didn't hide it. So there was an attempt to remove him from the program.

That created a reaction. The Rolling Quads were formed at that point, basically striking back about this. There were all these threats, for instance, of a medicine cut-off. "We're not taking care of you." The nurses from downstairs were told they had no responsibility up there, so they were not to come up.

I think that was kind of the key in terms of group cohesion. It took a little while, but almost everyone came over to supporting Donald and saying, "We've got to do something, we've got to set something up. This can't work this way." There were a few holdouts. A few people just wanted to be neutral and go to school, which was fine. And there were a few people who were very angry at what was going on. I think that gave it sort of the jumpstart—as a community—out of Cowell Hospital, because people started moving out.

At that point the idea of a group home disappeared, because people started moving out and surviving nicely, and it was great for them. The idea of taking the Cowell project and transplanting it out into the community, that just disappeared, because people took this next step beyond, saying, "I don't want to live that way; I want to live the way *I* want to live."

As things got really close to the point—remember they were going to kick Donald and John out—the Rolling Quads informed the hospital administration that they were going to have a sit-in in their offices. Donald showed them how he was going to do it [laughter]. It was the greatest thing—Donald just sort of collapsed in his chair. It was terrific to watch. We called Ed up, and he said he would be able to get media coverage. I was contacting the various groups on campus I had contacts in. We were going through Arleigh Williams [the dean of students], and Arleigh let the hospital administration and Voc Rehab know that he was not taking anybody out of school for non-academic reasons except for violating University of California regulations, which obviously no one there had done. We were working all the channels, which is a hallmark of how I like to operate, which is applying pressure inside the university, publicity, radical movement, the students themselves. The deadline got closer and closer, and they folded. The understanding that there was that kind of support from the university, from the media, from the student movement, and from themselves, I think just made everyone blossom. The idea that you really could fight city hall and win completely.

What did they win? All the threats were withdrawn. They could live their lives the way they wanted within the university regulations and within reason. The university took a more active role in helping develop the PDSP. There was a new nurse, Edna Breen, who was very sensitive to their needs, understanding that they were college students, they were adults, most of them older than most college students, and they should live their lives appropriately.

At the same time, we started writing a grant for this Physically Disabled Students' Program, or PDSP. Basically the writing turned out to be Larry Langdon, myself, and John, with Donald doing a lot of idea creation and help. It turned out that none of us had ever written anything like this before, and it had to go out in the university's name, and they wouldn't put it out. Arleigh Williams was very impressed with Ed, and John met him through Ed. John went down there and talked to Arleigh, and they went over it. Arleigh came up with this guy who was in public health, who was from New Zealand, and who had written a lot of grant proposals. He took our material, talked to us, and then put it into the right format and showed us how he did it. He was at UCB for only two years; he went back to take over the public health for a number of islands that New Zealand administered under U.N. trusteeship.

It was a good program. It was oriented toward the students, and we really felt like we could help students and bring students in from all over. We had money for recruiting. We also decided to put me in charge of non-university CIL type of activities: setting up advocacy sorts of things, political organizing, doing things in the city, doing things for non-students—all of that sort of thing.

John ended up being the director, I ended up being the assistant director, Larry ended up being the counselor coordinator. And we gave ourselves six months before the university cracked down. We said, "No one's going to notice us or do anything for at least six months." Full bore, out there for six months, then we'll deal with what happens.

Now this gets to the role of John as bureaucrat. John—deep, resonant voice—had a real presence. Very controlled. I don't think anybody in the university ever saw him lose his control. I have. [Laughs.] He's reasonable, forceful, very clear mind. We decided my role with the university was to continue as agitator. When we were having problems, I would go in first and ask for everything and be extravagant and crazy. Then John would come in with what we really wanted, as the peacemaker. It was very effective. Behind me was the threat of students coming in in wheel-chairs and sit-ins and all that sort of thing. Which they definitely did not want. They had enough problems with healthy people, physically whole people having sit-ins and being arrested.

After PDSP came into existence, the university really put its account-ing [department] on us. We started understanding that you couldn't transfer between accounts except for minor amounts. We were all fairly naïve at this point. We were all griping that we didn't have free money—soft money I think it would be called today. I have no idea where the idea came up—but there had been an election—the student government was very big at that time, and the students had voted to tax themselves to support some program for blacks. So we said, "Hey, why don't we get some money that way?" Don Lorence was put in charge of that. So it was a Rolling Quad effort. The first slogan was "Nickels for Cripples," and then "Quarters for Cripples." I have some posters.

It worked. It passed. It was twenty-five cents per student, for close to 30,000 students. In 1970 dollars that's a lot of money. That money was soft money; it had no strings attached. It was basically used for starting the CIL. We made space in our office, bought office equipment, extra telephones.

At this point I'm living in a commune, with a total of seven adults. I'm liv-ing with my wife and a number of other people and two kids. People know my home arrangements and are curious, and I talked about it. There were a bunch of other communes around, and there were ways in which people were trying to say, "I'm supposed to live this way, but maybe I don't want to. Maybe I just don't want to go through the university, live in the dorms, graduate, get married, get a job, move to the suburbs and have kids."

We started talking about how to do that and decided that we had to do it with community-based people. And so I made a bunch of phone calls. We decided to have a meeting—the royal "we"—John, Larry, and me. We each made up lists of people who we wanted for this meeting. Not just anybody, but people who could eventually be on a board or something like that. We didn't want it too large because then it wouldn't function. I remember calling Hale Zukas and a few other people. We gave them some material, and left, saying, "Here you go!" [laughter] John stayed. That essentially became a board meeting. I think it was Phil Draper who became the first chair of that.[5]

I think you can start seeing in the lives of the people on the Cowell floor, people choosing to live different lives. We had our hippies up there who dropped acid and smoked pot. We had our beer drinkers who used to get sloshed and sing songs and chase each other and yell. We had our political activists—not that all these categories are exclusive. We had people who were much more like "let me get through, get a job, get married, and live in the suburbs."

All this contributed mightily to the idea of, "They say I can't do this [because] I'm in a wheelchair. Who says I can't do it? What's in it for them to keep me here? They're getting lots of money at the hospital for keeping us, all this money from Voc Rehab, and they're getting status for having this great program helping cripples. I don't want to be helped; I want to live a life." People started wearing their hair longer, and facial hair, and hippie-style clothes, and going to concerts, and doing all sorts of stuff like the other students and non-students around Berkeley.

This was an era of the liberation movements all over the world. Strong anti-colonial feelings. This was the start of the women's movement, this was the start of the gay movement, a culmination in some ways of the civil rights movement, and the start of the black liberation movement. Attacks against any kind of hierarchy, attacks against patriarchy.

The disabled were ripe for becoming a liberation type of movement, wanting to define themselves and live life as they wanted, being people who were more hemmed in than most because of their physical disabilities, because of the medical model, and because of society's view of them. So the time was very critical in terms of the individuals feeling that and the society around them—Berkeley—being very supportive. The idea of people in wheelchairs having sit-ins or people in wheelchairs dancing and partying was a gas. That was just obvious, wasn't it? How come we never thought of that before?

Kitty Cone
"This is the most wonderful thing."

Kitty (Curtis) Cone first became active in the disability rights movement in 1972, when she moved from Chicago to Berkeley. Only twenty-eight at the time, she was nonetheless by then a seasoned political organizer, active since her college days at the University of Illinois in the civil rights, antiwar, and women's movements. Like Michael Fuss, she was perhaps typical in that she, like many activists of the seventies and early eighties—Mary Jane Owen, Bill Bronston, Wade

Blank, for example—cut her political teeth in movements other than disability rights.

What was perhaps less typical was Cone's evolution across so much of the political spectrum. Coming from an affluent and influential family, as an adolescent Cone was a self-described conservative Republican, entering an American Legion essay contest, writing to the FBI for help with an essay on the dangers of communist infiltration. By the time she arrived at Berkeley, Cone was herself a committed communist with several years' experience in the Socialist Workers Party (SWP), a leader in the Students for a Democratic Society, an editor of Left publications, and among those brutalized and arrested during the "police riot" at the 1968 Democratic National Convention in Chicago, where she lived and worked for several years.

"The undercover cops in Chicago were just notorious. There later was a grand jury investigation into the cops, because they were working hand in glove with the right-wing Legion of Justice that was a very racist, violent group that was attacking the different radical organizations. The SWP was under constant harassment by this right-wing group and by the cops as well."

Cone was born in April 1944, and was diagnosed with muscular dystrophy at age fifteen, though she'd been having symptoms for years. She and others around her considered the diagnosis tantamount to a death sentence, and this added an intense sense of urgency to her quest for social justice. Once in California, Cone offered her commitment and her highly honed organizing skills to the Center for Independent Living.

I moved to Berkeley in the summer of '72. I came out to California because I had friends out here. I said to the guy who was the secretary of the SWP at the time, "I'm miserable in Chicago. I'm having a nervous breakdown." He said, "Where would you like to go?" I said, "What about California?"

I was the assistant organizer of the [SWP] Oakland/Berkeley branch for a number of years. I worked in this office on Telegraph Avenue that had one room downstairs. I got this Advanced wheelchair. It was the best wheelchair they ever made. So I had this super chugger wheelchair that I loved, and I lived about a mile away from the branch, straight down Telegraph Avenue. I would leave my chair at the bottom of the stairs, and the organizer, who was a very strong guy, would transfer me into my pushchair I had there and haul me up this flight of stairs into the regular branch, and that's how I dealt with that. I remember that I was very upset that there were no curb ramps on Telegraph Avenue. So I would drive my chair home in the street, and a comrade would follow me home in the car to make sure I didn't get run over. . . .

My wheelchair kept breaking down. I had bought it through Thrifty Rents, and the guy at Thrifty Rents said, "You shouldn't have to wait while we send this piece back to the factory every time," because then I wouldn't be able to use my wheelchair; I'd have to use the pushchair. He said, "Why don't you call up the Center for Independent Living?"

So I called, and someone came down and jacked my chair up and replaced the part. I thought I had gone to heaven. "This is the most wonderful thing. This is the way it ought to be."

I started doing volunteer work at CIL because I was so appreciative of the wheelchair repair shop. So I decided, number one, that I wanted to be involved with this organization, because I thought they were doing good services. Number two, I wanted to earn money—the SWP was paying me forty-five dollars a week or something, and then I had trust funds from my family, which were not enough to pay for attendant care. I wanted a paying job at CIL. I went to Ed Roberts, who was the executive director at that time, and said, "I really am impressed with your organization, and I would like to work here. Do you think that you have a place for me?" He said, "What do you like to do?" I said, "The only thing I know how to do is political organizing." He said, "Well, then you can be a political organizer. Go work with Hale Zukas."

I reported in for work, and Hale was at that time handling everything for CIL from benefits, SSI, the Homemaker Chore program—which was what attendant care or personal assistance services was called in those days—architectural barriers, mobility barriers, anything like that. Hale dealt with all of it. My job in the beginning was to interpret for Hale. He would take me to meetings with him, and I would translate for him.[6] So I would travel to Sacramento with Hale and whether we were lobbying or just meeting with agency officials or developing testimony or whatever, I learned a great deal. Hale knew more than anybody about all of those issues. As a result of working with him, I learned them as well.

Hale was just a genius on transportation. I remember once going to an APTA [American Public Transit Association] conference with him. I believe it was in 1979. And we were going around to the different open houses that were being hosted by different vendors there. And we went to one that was General Electric, I think. Hale got into this technical discussion with somebody who at first probably wasn't going to pay any attention to him. Then they got totally entranced by him because they got into this discussion about what kind of glass there is in the Amtrak train windows, the history of that type of glass and why they chose to use it. I was trying to translate, and I didn't have a clue what the next word that was coming would be.

A whole variety of issues would emerge, some of which I knew very well because I was working on them regularly, and others which I didn't have any knowledge of. I would be told, "Take this on as a project. Organize around it." This has been a positive thing and a negative thing for me. With the exception of the transportation issue, I didn't have a very consistent job. I'm a fast learner, and I can articulate issues well if they're explained to me. So I would be told, "Okay, this is happening; we need to organize around it, we need to have a demonstration. They're going to cut the county funds, or they're going to take the agents out of the BART stations," or whatever. "Go do something." And I would collaborate with Hale or with Judy Heumann or with Greg [Sanders] or whoever.

I loved the CIL from the minute I got in there. I liked everybody a lot and I felt like they all had a lot to teach me, because they had been living independently, in a way that I hadn't, because I had had this built-in support system through the SWP. I was definitely out there in the world doing my thing and making changes; but I didn't have full control over when I was going to take a bath, when I was going to do whatever. And here were these people choosing and hiring who the people were who were going to be assisting them, and really managing their own lives.

The other thing was that it was a coalition. It was people in wheelchairs, people who walked, who used canes, crutches, and people who were blind or vision impaired—so it was not just all people in wheelchairs. And there were people who were severely disabled like Ed Roberts or Greg Sanders, not just people who could push their own wheelchairs. And there were people who depended on personal assistant services, not people who would spend an hour trying to sit up in bed because they were being watched over by the Rehab Center [at the University of Illinois]. People thought of it as a cause—not just a service, and I think some of the friendships that got forged in those early days, even though people were very, very different, had a great deal of meaning.

The staff was so small that we could all fit into this fairly small conference room. Oh, God, when we had staff meetings! I had come from an organization that had these very structured meetings—which I really prefer. People would give reports on their work, and then you'd discuss it and decide where you were going, and then you'd vote to carry it out or whatever. Ed would call these staff meetings, and would just start talking, and he would just roam all over. I would always come with a report on what we were doing, and half the time I never got to give my reports [laughs]. So I would just butt in and say, "We're having a demonstration. Will people please come? See me later."

So when there was an issue, like when the federal portion of the Homemaker Chore money had run out and the state and counties were not willing to pay the whole amount—CIL always took the leadership because they could say to clients, "Your attendant care money is going to run out. We're going to organize a demonstration. We will provide transportation, we'll help you get to Sacramento." So we would just organize caravans. Nowadays things are very different—nowadays people are working regular jobs. Young people get rehabilitated and go out in the world and take advantage of all the gains that we've made. They're not around and available to take their van off to demonstrate in Sacramento, and the will doesn't seem to be there either.

The early seventies was still a period of radicalism in Berkeley. There was this group of people who were real pioneers and considered ourselves a movement. We hung out and socialized together a lot—we were younger—we were in our twenties. You went into CIL, you got your wheelchair repaired, you talked to people, you found out what was happening in the community—like maybe there was going to be a demonstration around attendant care or so-and-so was having a poker party at their house. . . . It was a happening thing.

Carol Fewell Billings
"Being rebellious in an extremely productive and positive way."

Born in 1949, Carol Fewell Billings was a self-described "walky" during the early days of the independent living movement, arriving in Berkeley in 1969. Soon after arriving she married Larry Langdon—then a student at the university and one of the early Berkeley activists—whom she had known since high school in their home town of McKinleyville, California. Like Michael Fuss, she worked as a personal care "attendant" for residents of the Cowell program, and as staff at the Physically Disabled Students' Program. She was there when the CIL went from being "a closet" at the PDSP to occupying a two-bedroom apartment on Haste Street in Berkeley.

Billings and Langdon eventually divorced, and Billings left Berkeley to return to McKinleyville in 1977, where she became a teacher. Now retired, she has visited Berkeley from time and time, and "there are people in wheelchairs everywhere! And we used to remark on that: 'Look at all the crips! Where'd they come from?' Now there are even more, so I think that shows that if you build it, they will come."

I started working at Cowell as an attendant. I can't remember who I first started working for—probably Cathy Caulfield or Judy Taylor. They were my main people.

It seemed pretty hospital-ish, except there were people buzzing around having a good time or studying. I think the rooms were fairly personalized, but I don't remember to tell you the truth. We'd play music or hang out.

It was a job, and it was people I knew, and it was money, and I had worked in Berkeley as a nurse's aid, at a convalescent hospital. So I knew the attendant kind of stuff, bathing and getting people dressed and how to lift and all that. I'd done it. People in convalescent hospitals are fairly passive and it's basically keeping them clean and maybe moving them some. With active people you've got a lot of stuff that—in terms of catheter care or just in terms of getting them dressed—people want to get dressed a certain way and so there was not the passivity that there was in that other kind of place.

I believe Ed Roberts had gone to Palo Alto by then, or maybe to Washington. I don't remember the first time I met Ed, but he was always a presence even before I met him, because he was the guy who started it.

It was like a subculture of Berkeley. I've thought a lot about how much trouble I could have gotten into at that time in that place. I know a lot of people who went down to the Bay Area and got involved in drugs or crime or different things as a way of working against the system. I feel like I was in the best of all possible worlds because I got to have that experience of being rebellious in an extremely productive and positive way and learned so much about so much.

The students at Cowell eventually got a place, and money from the university to start the disabled students' program—the PDSP. You came up the ramp and went into this little small receiving office and then into a large common area which I think of as the lunch room because that's where we always ate. And then there was a little hallway into the kitchen, I believe, which was a very important room, and then into one of the main offices. If you went through the doorway, to the right, the wall on the right was the walk-in closet where CIL started. . . .

I remember thinking that this is so great to work here, because it was almost like not work. I mean, it *was* work: there were things to be typed, there were phones to answer, and people to call and so forth. And during grant-writing time it was always crazy and long hours and cutting and pasting and typing on my old Selectric. I thought I was in heaven! An electric typewriter!

Lunch was the pivotal point of the day. We all gathered. There was a communal atmosphere, because the walkies would cook and the crips would put in money. We ate together and someone had cooked the food and it really added to the feeling of community that we had. We would take turns cooking—each person had a day. And I really loved that.

We must have advertised for assistants. And Zona Roberts [Ed's mother] was really active in the CO thing—the Conscientious Objectors—so she would get people. In fact, she had people living in her house who were COs and it was like this conduit to the disabled community, because they needed service work and here was the perfect work.[7]

A lot of what we did, or a lot of what I remember doing as I became more competent, was working with students who were coming into the university. You've got people coming into Cowell or into the dorms—that's the first place you would look for housing. And we must have had listings or other ways to find it, too, or just to help them if they were looking for a house—help them to get a ramp put in or to modify the place in some way or other—because there were people out there who were willing to do that kind of thing. Maybe they weren't attendants, or maybe they were attendants, but they also would build a ramp, or come in and fix shelves or whatever it was. There were just so many people who were not into working nine to five but who needed jobs.

I started working at CIL when they had moved from the closet up to Haste and College, their first apartment. There was a living room, and I believe there were two bedrooms. We weren't there very long. . . .

There was definitely a need for the CIL, partly because PDSP was doing such a good job of serving the disabled community. At least that was our feeling—that here was a place where people could come, they could live independently, they could be mobile, there would be people to accept them, they could be visible; and so more people would come in and they weren't students. . . .

When I first got to CIL I was married to a disabled man and there was a lot of discussion within the community about personal relationships and how you deal with the different problems. And one of the problems was the way people would look at you and view you as a couple or as a person. And I think as more people became visible as independent human beings or powerful human beings or human beings with purpose or whatever—things sort of organically started to change. Just by being around it, you can't but see things differently.

And then as PDSP and CIL became more of a force in the community, always with the idea that the leaders were the physically disabled and blind and deaf themselves, that was another way of changing people's views. And the other thing was keeping in mind that there are these people who need certain things so that whenever new streets were built, ramps were put in. It seems like a really small thing, but having that in the consciousness in the community was pretty important. . . .

I remember a party at John's where they played this song called "Don't Stop the Music" over and over and over. It was a country western song. People drank like crazy. There was a lot of marijuana. Ed always had the best dope in the world. People would have parties, they'd go places together, we'd hang out together, you know. . . .

It wasn't [just] another job. It was exciting to be working in something on the cutting edge. That was just part of the whole thing. It was like the social life was integrated, the movement was integrated, everything was integrated as far as I was concerned.

Donald Galloway
"We would draw from the civil rights movement . . . but we were not actively involved in the black movement."

Donald Galloway had a different perspective on the early days of the CIL. An African American, he was among the first to call out the CIL specifically, and the disability rights movement in general, on its lack of racial diversity.

Galloway was born in 1938 in Washington, DC, and disabled at age thirteen after being struck in the eyes by an arrow. Lack of proper medical care led to the wounds becoming infected; he was left totally blind. Galloway subsequently spent three years in a residential, racially segregated school for blind children in Overlea, Maryland.

Galloway's first involvement in politics came after his family moved to California in 1954. In high school he became vice president of the local junior branch of the National Association for the Advancement of Colored People. His first efforts in disability rights activism, understandably, were in the blind community, as a junior member of the National Federation of the Blind (NFB). Galloway graduated from high school in 1958, attended college for a short time, and then left school for a career as a folk singer. He returned to school in Los Angeles and San Diego to earn his BA in science and sociology and his master's in social work. From 1969 to 1971 he traveled throughout Latin America, researching the social, political, and economic status there of people of African descent.

Galloway was introduced to the IL movement in 1974. By then he was living in Berkeley and disillusioned with the factionalism inside the NFB. Ed Roberts invited him to work with the CIL as its director of services for blind people. Galloway left the CIL, and California, in 1977.

Galloway became director of Peace Corps programs in Jamaica in 1978, helping to remove barriers to disabled Americans wishing to volunteer overseas. Returning to the United States in 1980, he coordinated Peace Corps efforts worldwide in connection with the United Nations International Year of Disabled Persons. From 1982 to 1987, Galloway served as director of the District of Columbia Center for Independent Living, and from 1987 was the manager of the Special and Demonstration Programs Division at the District of Columbia Department of Housing and Community Development.

Donald Galloway died in October 2011.

———

When I first got to CIL, I was fascinated by the repair shops that they used to have. They used to have a wheelchair repair unit. I thought that was a great idea, to have a portable unit that would go anywhere in the community and fix people's wheelchairs that would break down.

I had to experience working with people that I couldn't understand initially, like Mr. [Hale] Zukas. I couldn't understand him. Ed Roberts would be talking to him, and I just couldn't understand how could Ed be talking to this man, when all I could hear was "Mmmm, mmmm." Then

I found out that Zukas had a PhD in Russian history or something. My whole attitude about people with cerebral palsy or speech impediments changed drastically. Before, I had the same attitudes that other people had, that if you didn't speak well, you were not educated, you were mentally retarded or whatever.

Then I started running into a blind woman named Janet [McEwan Brown]. She ran the newspaper there; she did all the publications; she was totally blind and did all the editing. I started running into people doing all these wonderful things.

I didn't see very many black people. I was the first black person that I knew of at the center, hired on the staff, full-time. Ed was a very casual guy. He was a strategic planner too; he would put people into positions that normally they wouldn't have thought of. He said, "Now that you've got the blind component started, would you be interested in heading up our research team on independent living standards?" So I became the director of the peer counseling research component of the agency.

That was very interesting. I had PhD's working for me, and people that were very skilled in doing research. [But] that was [also] kind of a bummer period, because I was the only black, and I started bringing black people into the center as drivers and attendants, and bringing in professional types. . . . There was just a handful of us that came in, but we came together and decided that we needed some input into this system. . . .

We were in a predominantly black community. The city council was predominantly black, the whole area was predominantly black. The movement was predominantly white. We needed to reach out to the black community in Oakland, get the Black Panthers involved, and any other group that would like to be involved.

So I went to the board of directors and said, "We're going to start a black caucus to make sure we get our voice heard." That went over like a lead balloon, because the attitude was, "We're all one, and there's no need for it. That would be like a blind group trying to say that we wanted the blind to be paid attention to more." It was part of the whole attitude that no special group should be dominant. Although the people in wheelchairs, the people that were physically disabled, basically ran the joint. I don't think it was consciously said, "We run things, and we're not going to let you disturb that," but I think we knew that the emphasis was with people that were physically disabled.

The process was we would meet as a caucus and then the issues would be brought to the board and then it would be shot down. Like, "We are not racist, [but] we do not think we need to change our system to accommodate any particular group." Basically: "Be quiet."

It was ironic. You had the center identifying with the university more than it did with the community, although it was a community-based organization. Most of the funding for the center was because of the black influence on the city council, on the mayor.

All of Berkeley was very radical at the time. We were involved in a revolution not only with disabilities, but that whole drug culture, that whole hippie thing. If you wanted to start a group in Berkeley, right on. It was a place where new ideas could get a real good start. The city council was controlled by blacks, it was responsive to our needs. For example, there was an effort to restrict people in wheelchairs to [the first] floor of buildings, because of fire dangers. The Center moved from a three- or four-bedroom apartment to a small unit on the second and fifth floor of a building. The fire department wanted to move us all down to the first floor, and the disabled community went and testified before the city council and said, "No, we want to take the same risks as everyone else," and they understood it. They said, "You can't restrict people with disabilities to the first floors of buildings." There was a lot of tolerance of our differences in Berkeley. There was a whole bunch of white people who were disabled coming into the city, and people were like, "That's cool, we'll make space for you." The city opened up.

I didn't see a lot of black people being served. I saw a lot of people coming in from Chicago and New York, and all over the country, coming in to go to school. You could come into the center, and 90 percent of the people being served were white. I don't think that was deliberate; it's just that a lot of the people that came in were college students. They would come into the community, and there would be accessible places for them to live, and there was a center, the streets were becoming accessible. It was kind of a mecca for all of America, for people to come in, and most of those people that came in were white. It wasn't that we would go out to the NAACP and talk to them about disability groups or go to the different black groups, churches, and talk to them. That wasn't the emphasis. The emphasis was with the university, with the rehab centers, with the bureaucrats, and with the consumers that were coming into the city.

There was a severely disabled man in the Black Panther Party named Brad, and Brad was our link to the Black Panthers. We would go and provide him with attendant care and transportation because we had a small transportation system going, a fleet of vans going out to the community. Ed made a decision that he wanted us to get more involved with the Black Panthers and with Oakland. So we would go to some of their meetings and explain our programs. Because Brad, one of their members, had a severe disability, we were quite accepted. This would be in the mid-1970s—1975, 1976, somewhere around there.

I think because of Ed having a political science background, he understood that the black movement was very similar to what we were trying to accomplish in the disability community. But most of the people there didn't have that same level of consciousness. I think the consciousness was that we're starting a disability movement, and our main focus was disability. We would draw from the civil rights movement, some of the principles of nonviolence and advocacy and protest. We would borrow some of that, and we would appeal to the black politicians on those levels. But we were not actively involved in the black movement, in a conscious way, other than to use the similarity to bring about some empathy for our struggle.

To be realistic about it, the organized black community did not really identify with the struggle of people with disabilities in the same way. The black movement, in some instances, did not want to include people with disabilities because they thought it would disperse the power, the emphasis on black history. In fact, Senator [Hubert] Humphrey, even back in 1964, when the Civil Rights Act of 1964 came up to be voted on, wanted to include people with disabilities, and the organized black community said, "No, this is a civil rights bill that is going to have to be limited to the minorities. We don't want to include people with disabilities." So, yes, the emphasis on our side was to try to touch base and identify with the movement. But I don't think the black community at the time, the black movement across the country, identified with the independent living struggle.

Corbett O'Toole (continued)
"We're all branches off of the same tree."

Moving in 1973 from Boston to Berkeley, Corbett O'Toole soon made connections with the disabled women's community, and then the Center for Independent Living. In 1974 she got a job at the CIL, working in "attendant referral," helping to link up people with disabilities who needed help with day-to-day tasks with able-bodied people (like Fuss and Billings) looking for work as personal care assistants.

———

What was CIL like? It was a cross between a party, a job-training program, and an office. It was sort of like all three at once. Everybody was a client of the agency. I mean, we didn't have that concept of clients. Almost everybody that worked there was using the services of the agency in one way or another, and the non-disabled people that worked there were people intimately connected to the community. The same people you worked with or the same people that came in for services were people that you partied with and that you hung out with and that you were friends with.

So it was a very free-flowing environment, which I think allowed a lot of things to happen. First of all, it allowed a lot of disabled people that had never thought that they were ever going to be able to work to come into an agency where other people that looked like them were working. There was like a lot of that kind of social hanging around so that people got to see what it meant to be in a work environment. And it allowed people to help out and try out and learn some basic skills—because for those of us that grew up disabled, there was no McDonald's, there were no entry-level jobs for most of the people—certainly the people in chairs that came up to CIL. This was the first time they ever saw people in wheelchairs working, and so it was a really good experience for people to have.

In those days there was no public transportation. BART was not accessible and the buses were not accessible, so CIL also ran a transportation service. It ran a van repair shop and a wheelchair repair shop, so lots of people in the community got to know each other by using those basic services for people that used chairs. Blind folks came to use blind services. That was the only place in town that had a free braille writer and material in braille and information about how to get books on tape. It was the Information Central for the blind folks in town.

So the combination of the services for people in wheelchairs and the services for the blind meant that it was really like a community center, like the way some senior centers function now—the good ones, where people are really involved. There would be classes on independent living skills, classes on basic sign language, but they were informal classes taught by your friends, more or less.

There were parties—every holiday was a party. We were all young in those days, so nobody thought too hard about dying. Nowadays, I'm going to more funerals than parties some years, but in those days you were just going to parties. People got to be outrageous. I think that's the thing that was wonderful for me about being there. I had always been really closeted about my disability because it was not an okay thing to be disabled, and here I was hanging out with a bunch of people like quads who couldn't hide their disability, couldn't pass, and we were just getting crazy.

What I'm remembering was the Halloween parties, particularly, where the wheelchair repair guys hooked up a power chair to be operated by remote control and they put a stuffed animal in it and it started driving around the party. Or Dale Dahl, who was at that point dating Maureen Fitzgerald. Maureen worked at the Berkeley Women's Health Collective, and Dale showed up with a speculum, a surgical mask, latex gloves, and a surgical gown, and then went around to all the women and said, "Oh, you want a free exam?" It was just outrageous, very funny and very silly and very wonderful—just people with disabilities being really off the wall crazy and changing the world.

In a traditional funding sense, we were not fundable by anybody's stretch of the imagination. Yet, the work that we were doing was really important and making a difference. We helped people make the transition from no access and no independent life—living with their parents, or living in an institution, living in a nursing home—to believing that they could make the transition to having their own life, defining their own destiny and then actually helping them to accomplish that. It was not the agency that did that, but it was the act of having a central place for information and resources and community. People could just essentially show up at our door, which they did rather frequently, and sometimes too frequently, and we would help them. The whole community would pull together to help each other, so there was a sense that we were in it together.

There was a real sense that we were doing something that had never been done before, that there was no other model, that we were in a struggle essentially for our survival. A number of people that had come to CIL, especially spinal cord injury people—quads—had already been in nursing homes. Some of the old polios had also been in nursing homes as kids or spent their whole childhood in hospital-schools. And there was a real feeling that they knew what would happen if we didn't succeed, if we didn't create alternatives—that disabled people were just going to end up in nursing homes, or that the people that could pass and survive, would pass and survive in isolation. They were going to do just what they did before—live in isolation, live in their parents' house, depend on other people to get them in and out of a building, out of a home, and not be able to work or have a sex life—not be able to do anything.

We would literally get calls from the San Francisco airport police saying, "We have this person. They're in a wheelchair. They say they're coming to CIL. Could you please come get them?" This was like Friday afternoon, they'd flown in from New York, and we didn't know who they were! They thought that if they physically just got themselves on the plane, we would figure out how to take care of them. And usually they were right and usually something happened.

I came out as a lesbian in late '74. CIL was a place where there were a lot of lesbians. There weren't very many gay men but there were a lot of lesbians and so it was a place where I felt pretty safe. Even the straight men were not particularly homophobic because, like I said, we were all in it together. Although there were lots of things that could have divided us about age or race or income or whatever, we just chose to be in it together and see each other as mutually helpful. So that was one thing it gave me—it gave me a sense of home.

It also gave me a lot of information, stuff that was not available in books. I didn't know anything about spinal cord injuries before I started working there. I didn't know anything about muscular dystrophy. I didn't know anything about deaf people, about blind people. I had gone to camp with disabled kids, but that's really different than hanging out with people and dealing with leg bags, or Braille, or sign language, or going with them to the grocery store and the coffee shop.

It was hanging out with people where you really got to experience in a much more direct way what their lives were like. How did people who were quads physically manage in the kitchen, how did they manage in the bathroom? How do you manage attendants? What's the role of an attendant, how do you balance that? How do you have a sex life? What kind of sex do you have? How do you find partners, how do you communicate about it? How do you have kids? I mean, all of that stuff— because somebody at CIL was doing all of it. Judi Rogers was having babies, Janice Krones had already had a couple of kids. Certainly closer to the beginning of the eighties there was a whole disabled baby boom, but in the seventies that wasn't as true. Certainly people were having lots of sex—I mean, there was lots and lots of sex going around. Kitty [Cone] was having sex and I'm like, "Well, if she can have sex, I can have sex" [laughs].

So there was a feeling that anything was possible because the jocks were off being jocks, and the eggheads were off being eggheads at school, and the teachers were off teaching, and the parents were off parenting, and everybody was crippled.

So it was very educational. You also got the negative ways that society tried to stop people from making choices—how they tried to not give birth control information to people with certain disabilities or tried to take their kids away. You kind of got the whole spectrum.

By the time I left CIL, I felt like I had value as a person, I felt like I had value as a leader. I had had opportunities to plan events, to figure things out, to write. I had done a lot of training, particularly within the non-disabled women's community around disabled women's issues with other disabled women. I had also kept the Disabled Women's Coalition alive and ran it as an office out of UC Berkeley. I was able to work. I had a career.

The reality of my life, now twenty years later, is that many of the people I was friends with in CIL in the old days are the people I'm still friends with. It became a base that's essentially lifelong, even though a lot of us went off in different directions professionally. Because we came through the same door and because we see all the work as intrinsically tied together, it doesn't matter whether people are doing computers or parenting or school work or whatever, it's all the same root, we're all branches off of the same tree.

12
The Disability Press

―――

THE 1970S AND EARLY 1980S, DURING WHICH SO MUCH DISABILITY RIGHTS activism took place, also saw the emergence of an overtly political cross-disability press. This means of communication was especially vital in the days before the widespread use of fax machines—let alone the advent of the Internet, social networks, and e-mail listservs—and when long distance phone calls were prohibitively expensive for a community in which many members were on low or fixed incomes. Among the most widely read of these new publications were *Mainstream: Magazine of the Able-Disabled* in southern California and *The Disability Rag* in Louisville, Kentucky, while *Madness Network News* out of San Francisco was undoubtedly the most influential publication of its time in the psychiatric survivor movement.

Cyndi Jones
"We never missed a deadline."

―――

Mainstream magazine was intended to provide a voice for people with disabilities, according to its founder, Jim Hammett. Established in 1975, *Mainstream* was also a training center for people with disabilities who aspired to be journalists and editors or to work in the advertising or production side of the publishing industry. After 1984, when Cyndi Jones, a businesswoman, and her journalist husband William Stothers rescued *Mainstream* by assuming its debt, the magazine became a for-profit business, competing in the "real world" for scoops, visibility, and the all-important advertising dollar.

Cyndi Jones was born in 1951 in Terre Haute, Indiana. "After I was born my family moved to Carlsbad, California, and my dad was working on a construction project. His father, who lived in Rolla, Missouri, was dying. So everybody piled in the car and we headed back to Rolla. I got polio, and that was the way that went. . . . I think about the AIDS epidemics now, and I think it's very similar to the polio epidemics in my day in the early fifties, because people didn't want to be around anyone who was associated with polio. There were a lot of similarities in the fear."

Jones's family settled in St. Louis, where she was seen at the local March of Dimes polio clinic. In 1957, she was a March of Dimes "poster child." "That year I was in my class—it was first or second grade—and they passed out this flyer [for the March of Dimes]. I remember my teacher saying, 'Oh, this flyer has one of our classmates on it!' Of course, it was me. It was my picture with the frilly dress and the crutches, and I was in my regular poster-child pose, which is this smiling crippled child. There were two other kids running down a hill, and over the picture of the kids running down the hill it said, 'This,' and over my picture it said, 'Not this.' I wanted to slump under my desk."

Excelling in science in high school, Jones majored in biology at the University of California at San Diego, with a minor in religious studies. In an era before Section 504 or any such thing as "disabled student services," at least in San Diego, she struggled to get to her required courses held at opposite ends of the campus, often arriving late and exhausted. After graduating from college, she applied to the Peace Corps but "was denied on the basis of my disability."

Instead, she became involved in the Episcopal Women's Caucus, becoming its West Coast coordinator in 1974. Along the way she also became involved in disability rights work, first with the California Association for the Physically Handicapped (CAPH), then joining the *Mainstream* staff in 1976.

———

Jim Hammitt conceptualized the program because he thought the disabled community needed a voice. Jim, who I had met at Sunshine School,[1] had since applied to Cal State Northridge. He wound up getting his degree in communications, and he's one of the people at Cal State Northridge who produced campus plays, and he's done really well. You think of someone who came up from Sunshine who, because he had CP and a severe speech impediment, really was not educated. He had to teach himself to read even though he was in school. All of the horror stories we know about special education. Jim Hammitt survived special education.

The first two *Mainstream*s were really four-page newsletters—just two pages folded in half. Then they applied to get RETC funding, which is Regional Employment Training Consortium money. *Mainstream* was funded—I think it was $100,000 a year, which is nothing now. On that money they funded the printing and mailing of the magazine and half-time staff positions for twenty-eight people or whatever it worked out to be. Frank McGovern, who was not disabled but was a journalist, was the full-time paid person. I even think Jim was a part-time paid person; I don't think he was full-time staff. They rented this office space in downtown San Diego because the buses stopped downtown and people could get there. There were no curb cuts, and that was an issue, so one of the first things we did was talk about the lack of curb cuts in San Diego. People couldn't get down the street, get off the block.

It was called "work experience." What that meant was people came in and had a job for nine months. Although it was half-time they still had to be there every day, they had to get up and get there. They got a paycheck. Then at the end of the nine months they started phasing people out and helping them find jobs. So they had three months left to help them find jobs. But the important part of the nine months, really, is that it was a birthing process. Now I know why birth takes nine months. It was a change of attitude. A lot of what happened in the course of people working there was just the camaraderie and talking about issues that people don't have a chance to talk about. So it was a really wonderful kind of experience.

So I went down and interviewed, and got a job as one of the disabled trainees of *Mainstream* magazine the first year. I interviewed in late December '75 and got the job and started in January of '76. It was twenty hours a week at minimum wage.

I started working in the production department, doing page layout and typesetting. I can't type for nothing; it's hard. We didn't have one of these new desktop publishing things; we had what was called a Compugraphic. A line in typeset is only thirty-four characters, plus or minus. So you type this line of thirty-four characters and then you have to set this dial and then type it exactly the same way a second time. That was a very hard process, to get the type set. Then we had to spray fixative on this stuff so it wouldn't smudge, because this was like carbon ribbon on paper, and you had to be very talented at this task, because if you sprayed too much it would run. Heaven forbid if you ruin a column of set type. We didn't have any of the high-tech. stuff. This was really loving hands at home.

So we got the first issue out, and we were there all night. But we never missed a deadline; we were always on time and the printer was always happy that we were there when we said we'd be there.

I think the first press run was five thousand, and then it went to ten thousand. It was going to different organizations in town plus any individuals that had sent in their name. I can't remember what the original price was—three dollars a year or something. It was very marginal.

At the end of the first year they had a job counselor come in—that was part of the grant—and she helped everybody get their résumés together and do job interviews. She did training on how to do an interview. Some of the people she actually went with on the interview. She really worked to find places for them to interview. She did her job well. One of the women had been in our production department and she got a job in San Diego Gas and Electric's graphics department. Another guy wound up being in their accounting department. Another guy, Rich Watkins, wound up getting a job as a teller at San Diego Trust and Savings. He is now a vice president of Union Bank of California in their commercial loan department. Carol Vincelett wound up getting a job in a program called Search and Serve, which was to find disabled students. After that, she wound up in the Lakeside School District as a credentialed teacher in junior high. I think she's been there like twenty-something years. She got that job as a result of being at *Mainstream*. It was a tremendous opportunity.

The first year, I should have gotten a job but they couldn't get rid of me because I wouldn't go. The program needed me. They offered me a job full-time, low pay, for the second year. We were working really hard keeping this thing up. Then it got a little bit easier. It got on a regular cycle. I took a few days off and I couldn't go back. I realized I had been working sixty-hour weeks for like two and a half years. I was exhausted. Until you stop you don't realize you're tired. I came back and I gave notice. I was only twenty-three or twenty-four.

I started selling real estate. I sold—I wouldn't say they were adapted houses—but I would say they were easily adaptable houses. I had a really good sense of what was an easy-to-adapt house. Not like what most real estate agents think, "Oh, you can just tear out the kitchen and redo the bath and add another room on the back." I was able to find some wonderful houses for people where they had to do a minimum of accommodations to get it done. That was really satisfying.

In the meantime, Able-Disabled Advocacy—which was the parent organization of *Mainstream* magazine—had asked me to be on their board of directors. That was like a loose commitment, once a month. It wasn't a big deal.

Then a couple things happened. There was a recession at the beginning of the eighties, and the real estate company I was working for went out of business, so then I went over to another firm. It was in an upscale neighborhood of San Diego, although I was usually selling downscale houses. But I was selling a lot of houses. In fact, the year before this one company went out of business, I was the top sales agent in San Diego county.

At the same time, Reagan became president, and *Mainstream* was a work experience program and all work experience programs went unfunded that year. They started turning people over first in six months, then in five months, then in four months. Pretty soon it's not the same program because you don't have the time to establish the relationships where you really get to the heart of some of the core issues that people have about working. Not just working, but being in society. That piece had gone. When you think about someone being in that program for three months, that wasn't really enough time for any real work experience to take place.

In the summer of '82 they were notified that they were unfunded the next year, because the Reagan administration was only going to fund on-the-job training. Well, on-the-job training, as far as I'm concerned, should have been the one that bit the dust. But see, they have good statistics, high numbers. But what is the turnover rate? It's basically get a job, get fired from the job, go back on the [disability] rolls, get a job, get fired from the job. It's just a revolving door, whereas our placements were solid. It was unfortunate. I felt really bad that that had happened.

So now *Mainstream* is unfunded, and they have to do something with it. We had a board meeting. Andy Ozols (the executive director of the program) offered to buy the magazine. I'm still on the board, and we have this meeting in a restaurant, and I thought, "I put too much energy into this to give it to this non-disabled person. I'm not going to let that happen!" The real estate market was crashing, and I wasn't comfortable with the transactions I was being forced to do. So the timing was right because Bill [Stothers], my husband, was working at the *San Diego Union*. He was making a good salary. He didn't care if I worked at real estate or what.

I basically told the board, "You can't give Andy the magazine because you have a fiduciary responsibility to the people who have donated money." I just flim-flammed this whole thing. I threw up all this stuff and they said, "Well, what are we going to do if we don't give it to Andy?" I said, "I'm willing to come in, and I'll volunteer for two months while you decide what to do with this magazine." That was in June. So it was set that I would start right after Labor Day. Their last funding was through October 1.

We'd never had money at *Mainstream,* and we still didn't up until the end. At the time I took over Andy comes into the office and says, "You might as well take this call." It was the printer saying that they couldn't print the magazine until they got money. Then the landlord called and said, "You're behind on the rent." My response was the same to all these people: "Look, we've had a lot of financial things going on. I've just taken over today," which was the truth, "or this week. I am going through everything and you will be paid." One by one we got people paid, little by little. But the two months I said I would volunteer turned into four months. The four months turned into two years.

Now we are at the summer of '84. We didn't have any trainees anymore because that was gone. During the interim when I wasn't there—between '77 and '82—they had taken it from a San Diego magazine to a California magazine to a national magazine. Now when I took over, even though they were selling it as a national magazine, they were not doing national stories. They were still doing these stupid things like a wine and cheese tasting fundraiser at so-and-so's in San Diego. The first thing I did when I took over, besides telling everybody "I'll eventually pay you," was I quit taking local phone calls. "We don't do that anymore." Over the course of the next six months or so we quit getting those calls, which was good because I didn't have time for them anyway.

So we eliminated all the local stuff and we started pushing on the national stuff. That first year we were the first people—it was in '83—to do a head-to-head comparison of all the wheelchair companies—a double spread on all the wheelchair companies that we knew about or could find. We did a photo of their product and we did all the characteristics that we could think of that anyone would need to know to make a buying decision. You need a wheelchair: what are you going to do? You go into your local dealer, and if you don't have the information they're going to sell you what they have on their floor, whether it fits you or not, whether it's the kind you need or not. Our philosophy was always that the magazine, by giving people information, would give people the power to choose. Part of that was political stuff going on, part of that was sexuality stuff going on. Part of it was housing, part of it was products like wheelchairs, vans, computers. We felt that what was lacking was information, and that we could provide a forum for people to either write in and get answers, or to receive the magazine and get answers to their questions, or even [to think of] being a part of a community.

The disabled community is so spread out, and you didn't have buses in those days with lifts, and you didn't have ways for people to get together. Few people had their own vans. The community couldn't gather in one place at one time, and still can't, really. There are no hotels or convention centers that could hold a real meeting of the disability rights movement. It doesn't work. Our idea was that we could provide the information going into the homes, and that would be like a surrogate meeting place.

The magazine was never crazy, radical out-front leadership, because we knew that we would lose the people behind the movement if we were too far in front of them. So we would always put stuff in the magazine to put them in touch with people—not necessarily names and addresses—but groups that were doing things. We'd give them information that would bring them along. It's like teaching: you have to take people where they are and you try to lead them to the next step, and the next step, and you try to get them involved. So that's who we were writing for.

We got wonderful letters from people. This one said, "You saved my life. I was at the end of my rope. I had been to every meeting for my daughter, and I was stark raving angry." I had written an editorial about how I was angry. She said, "You gave me permission to be angry. The next day I called up the administrator," and basically she got it done.

Originally the magazine was for what we would consider the core disabilities: mobility impairments and CP and polio, muscular dystrophy and those things. Blind and deaf. We also, as time progressed, were doing more in terms of developmental disabilities and psychiatric disabilities. We did a whole issue on psychiatric disabilities. But you have to understand that just like you bring people along who are disabled but are not really in the movement, you sometimes have to bring the movement along too.

There's always been this thing in disability culture that has to do with,

"I'm not mentally disabled. I'm just physically disabled." And where you get that from is when you're a child or a young adult and people treat you like you can't think. So in your mind you get real rigid on this fact that, "I'm not mentally disabled." What we felt was that we needed to work on this a little bit in the movement, but that we couldn't do so much on it that it would alienate our readership—like I said—you have to lead people a little bit by a little bit. You start doing a little bit now and then a little more, and that's how we were moving things forward.

Leonard Roy Frank (continued)
"It was a way for people who were voiceless to have a voice."

———————

Leonard Roy Frank, devastated by his incarceration and "treatment" in the mental health system, spent six years trying to rebuild his life. Not only was the memory of his years in California destroyed by repeated electric and insulin shock "treatments," but he encountered the harsh stigma that attaches to anyone identified as a former "mental patient": "There was a very strange feeling when I came in contact, on several occasions, with people I had known before. They would visit me here in San Francisco, and there was a barrier between us."

One of the reasons Frank's parents had had him hospitalized was his unwillingness to find work or continue his career in real estate. Ironically, his "treatment" while institutionalized left him virtually unable to hold a job. "For six years I didn't do any gainful employment. I studied and worked in my apartment, regaining what I thought I had lost, and then of course I went on from there and learned a lot of things that I hadn't known before."

During this time Frank lived on a stipend provided by his parents, while he slowly made his way back to the life he had known. Along the way, he encountered the local psychiatric survivor movement, which was to provide him with a community and a cause, which have both lasted for more than three decades now. An integral part of both was *Madness Network News,* published by and for people labeled "mentally ill."

———————

At the end of this six-year period or so, I went to work for a new friend of mine who owned and operated an art gallery. And I did that for about a year, and then I opened up my own art gallery in downtown San Francisco. And I did that with money that my mother had given me.

I didn't do well financially, but having an art gallery enabled me to make some connections. It was during that period, between 1970 and 1975, that I started a correspondence with psychiatrist Thomas Szasz,[2] which led to my arranging for him to give a talk at a church in downtown San Francisco in 1971. Several hundred people attended, and so began a long-term friendship.

Having the art gallery opened up other doors for me. I met the people who had started *Madness Network News*, which was a countercultural publication put together by survivors of psychiatry, and by mental health workers, including a psychiatrist. There was just a handful of us, five or six, and although I wasn't in at the ground floor, I joined in soon after, I think the second issue. I stayed with that for about twelve years. In 1974, I cofounded the Network Against Psychiatric Assault (NAPA). For several years both organizations used my art gallery as their headquarters, the base for their operations. It was in downtown San Francisco, and so it was easy for people to get to for our meetings and forums. At around the same time we also began holding annual meetings of psychiatric survivors at various places around the country, and also in Canada. So in that way I got to meet and work with people, with opponents of organized psychiatry, throughout the continent.

We were pretty radical, in terms of what the psychiatric survivor movement is today. We wanted to make fundamental changes in the entire psychiatric system, and were opposed to this whole notion of "mental illness." We didn't believe that there was any such thing, in the medical sense of the term. We thought that it was just a construct that was developed as a rationale for depriving certain troubled or troubling people of their rights. We also opposed all forms of involuntary treatment, and involuntary commitment, where people could be locked up on the basis of what one or maybe two psychiatrists or medical doctors thought was going on in your head. We considered it a form of preventive detention.

Almost all of us were survivors, people who had been institutionalized for short or long periods of time. Most of us had been treated forcibly, in one way or another, usually through drugs. A small minority of us had been treated with electroshock. There were very few people who I met, at that time or since then, who had been administered insulin-coma procedures, because that was already going out of style. I had it in 1963, by 1965 they were no longer doing it at all.

We used a mimeograph machine to put out the first issues of *Madness Network News*. Our paid circulation was in the hundreds, but the readership was much larger. We would publish two or three thousand copies, most of which we'd circulate freely at local hospitals which had psychiatric wards. The hospitals were our major distribution channel at the start, and then we built up a subscriber list of maybe seven or eight hundred. The publication schedule was whenever we could get it together, which usually in the early years amounted to three or four or five times a year.

We did it on the cheap. There was no paid staff, and we covered our printing costs through contributions and subscriptions. Every year or so we would send out a fundraising letter. But we're really talking about small amounts of money going a long way. It might have been fifteen hundred, two thousand dollars per issue, in terms of all of our expenses. Informal is definitely the word to describe our operation. Early on there might be six or seven people, later on we could produce issues with just three or four people. There was no editor. There was no one who took primary responsibility for anything, but somehow the things that needed to get done did get done.

There was a lot of positive feedback. We had a letters-to-the-editors column. Ken Kesey[3] was the most famous person who wrote to us. He wrote a very complimentary letter, which of course we published. Most of the letters were from survivors who welcomed the chance to express their views on the deception and the violence they'd experienced or witnessed in the psychiatric system.

After a while *Madness Network News* became the house organ for the NAPA. We were able to publicize our events, not so much before they happened but after they happened, when we would report on what we were doing. The main activity of the NAPA at that time was lobbying for legislation to regulate and restrict the use of electroshock and lobotomy, and we had some success. Joe Kennedy Adams, a psychologist and NAPA member, was a friend of John Vasconcellos, who was a prominent California assemblyman. He was the one who shepherded this bill, regulating ECT and lobotomy, virtually eliminating the use of lobotomy operations, psychosurgery, in the state of California, and placing restrictions on the use of electroshock. It didn't go as far we would have liked, because there was still a way that psychiatrists could force electroshock on people, and it didn't make it really clear that patients were entitled to genuine informed consent. The entire informed consent process, as far as ETC is concerned, is fraudulent because psychiatrists do not acknowledge the very damaging effects that the procedure has, often including irreversible brain damage and memory loss, so how can it be truthful and informed consent? There were hearings in Sacramento in 1975 that received a good deal of media attention, as did our demonstrations at institutions that were known to deliver electroshock. Actually, the Network Against Psychiatric Assault got a lot more attention than *Madness Network News,* because it was more political. It got the attention of the media.

Madness Network News was a terrific thing. There was a lot of infighting, but also a lot of camaraderie. We did our job, and I think we had a positive impact. It was a way for people who were voiceless to have a voice. It was the first time that had really happened, and we said a lot of very worthwhile things, things that society needed to hear. The *Madness Network Reader* (an anthology of articles from the *News*) probably reached more people than the *News*.

While we were an ongoing operation, we had a subtle kind of impact, particularly with the psychiatrists who used shock treatment, because we had the shock doctor roster. I was the one who came up with that idea: pretty much every issue we would list all the doctors, and their affiliations, who were using electroshock. We got a couple of letters from doctors who objected to being on the list, because they were no longer using shock treatment, or they had never used it. And we would take their names off the list, of course.

The Dr. Caligari column, written by a radical psychiatrist, was also very important. He would treat specific categories of drugs, giving the pseudomedical indications for their use, what their short-term effects were, and what the longer term effects were. Now for the first time psychiatric survivors could read for themselves the truth about informed consent, about polypharmacy (that is, "drug cocktails"), and tardive dyskinesia.[4]

NAPA produced a sixty-five-page booklet based on Dr. Caligari's columns, called *Dr. Caligari's Psychiatric Drugs,* which came out in the late 1970s. There was a second edition, and we sold thousands of copies for just a few dollars each. It really gave the lowdown skinny on psychiatric drugs, and what they do to you. There was also an important section on how to withdraw from these drugs. Most people are not aware that these drugs are addictive, and that when you stop using them you're likely to suffer serious, even life-threatening withdrawal symptoms, which is why discontinuing their use should be done slowly, and if possible under medical supervision.

Madness Network News was the movement's educational arm, our way of informing survivors and the public about the abusive practices of the psychiatric system, about its false ideology. We were the voice of an activist movement, of activist survivors, people who knew what had happened to them and wanted to do something about it, and wanted to prevent other people from having to go through the same kind of difficult, sometimes horrendous situations.

Mary Johnson
"People who had things to say to the movement knew that they could say them in The Rag, *and get a national audience."*

Mary Johnson was born in 1948 in Louisville, Kentucky. She is best known as the founder and editor of *The Disability Rag* and of the Advocado Press. Before blogs, before listservs, before the advent of disability studies programs at colleges and universities, *The Disability Rag* was the movement's preeminent journal of political and social thought. From its beginnings as a four-page newsletter in late 1979 to its demise in 2006, *The Rag* (which through the years was also known as *The Disability Rag & Resource* and then *The Ragged Edge*) provided a forum for some of the most cutting-edge discussion of disability politics, culture, and experience.

Johnson came to disability issues in a roundabout way. She graduated from college in 1970, "at a time when we were moving into a recession in this country, and it was fairly difficult to find work. . . . This was before the women's movement, or right at the beginning of it, and most women who graduated from college were expected to be secretaries. So I did my little stint as a secretary. I was a horrible, horrible secretary, definitely something I was not suited for.

"Eventually I ended up working in public relations. The community mental health movement was just starting in the early seventies, and there was a mental health/mental retardation agency started in the Louisville area, and I was hired to work in their public relations department. And I did that for a number of years. Not because I was interested in mental health but because it was a job, and it was the closest thing you could do with an English major: public relations, communications. Ultimately I got a job with the Girl Scouts state organization in Louisville, and did public relations for them. That was pretty much my career at that time.

"I had a friend from college who had a friend who had cerebral palsy, and the woman who had cerebral palsy was looking to start an organization, and for people to put on a board. My friend suggested me because I had this background in public relations." From this relatively casual beginning, Johnson became an important voice within the movement in the 1980s. Though intended more as a journal than a newspaper, *The Rag* provided some of the best reporting on the hot topics of that era. It was, for instance, one of the few publications to examine in depth the rise of ADAPT and its direct action campaign for accessible public transit.

———

I met this woman whose name was Donna Herp, who has since passed away. She was the one who sat me down and talked with me, this must have been 1976, about the whole issue of disabled people—of course, we called them handicapped people then—having rights, and having rights to transportation. Transportation is always an issue for disabled people, and that was the issue that stirred her to begin an organization in Louisville.

The organization was called the Action League for Physically Handicapped Adults (ALPHA). And there was a man named Jim Cherry who got involved with it. Jim was very instrumental in getting me to understand that there was a national disability rights movement. He filed a lawsuit against [F.] David Mathews, who was the head of the US Department of Health, Education, and Welfare [under President Gerald Ford], because Mathews had not signed the regulations for Section 504 of the Rehab Act, which had passed in 1973. I was the president of the board at that time, and so it's my signature on that lawsuit. A lot of activists around the country were using the protest route to reach this goal, and there is some debate, and I at this point in time am not really sure exactly where the truth lies. Of course, to hear Jim Cherry tell it, it was the lawsuit that forced [Joseph Califano, the newly appointed HEW secretary under Jimmy Carter] to sign the regulations. To hear a lot of other activists tell it, it was the demonstrations. I suspect it was both.[5]

I was involved in several organizations, and towards the end of the seventies I was really pulling away from ALPHA. I heard a term the other day, about someone being a "serial entrepreneur," and I thought that was the funniest term. I suppose I was a serial entrepreneur in the nonprofit field, because I kept starting nonprofits. Myself and a couple of other people who were on ALPHA's board left ALPHA to start another organization that ultimately brought in the funding for the first independent living center in Louisville. That was in 1978. It was called the Center for Accessible Living, and it is still going on. And for a brief period I was the director—very brief, six months, if that. Being the director of an independent living center is definitely not me.

We got some community development block grant money that came to our city, to set up a program that would build ramps for people into their homes. And I was much more interested in doing that, because I actually could see something get done. So I ran that program for a year and a half, maybe two years. But during that time, during my quote unquote spare time, I was starting to do *The Disability Rag*.

We had some VISTA [Volunteers in Service to America] money, and three or four very young idealistic VISTA volunteers, and they were quite into community organizing. And of course they wanted to get disabled people to meetings, and this went back to transportation, people couldn't get to the meetings, right? And everyone was very frustrated. There was a young VISTA volunteer named Tim Powers—he has since died—who was very interested in consciousness-raising among disabled people. Tim was a young gentleman who was just coming out as being gay, and I think he really felt the parallels, and he was very interested in people's self-concept. There was an article written by Leonard Kriegel, years ago, probably in the late sixties, called "Uncle Tom and Tiny Tim: Some Reflections on the Cripple as Negro."[6] His article was way before any of this. It was prescient. All of this was sort of floating around.

I kept thinking, "Well, if we can't get people to meetings, maybe we can send something out to people." So in the last week of December 1979, we put out this little four-page publication. There wasn't even Kinko's back in those days, but whatever the equivalent of Kinko's was, we went there and got it printed up, and sent it out to a lot of addresses that we had gotten hither and yon, different agencies and things. We started this and sent it out monthly for about a year and a half.

Another woman who was very influential in my life and in my understanding of disability, Cass Irvin, was by now on the board of these organizations with me. She wanted *The Disability Rag* to be national. She was an early member of the board of the American Coalition of Citizens with Disabilities, and she kept taking *The Rag* around to these national gatherings. And it started to grow, and people started actually to pay money for it, and subscribe, and in a gradual kind of moving over I did less and less with the Center, and more and more with *The Rag* until, at about 1984, I was doing nothing but *The Disability Rag*. It had actually become a real publication, and was bringing in money. We incorporated an organization called the Advocado Press, just so we could have a 501(c)(3), and could get a mailing permit.

It all happened very quickly, and if anyone had said, "You're creating a national publication," I would have just laughed. I never intended it to be a national publication.

Mainstream media was an early issue for us, from day one. Now remember we're talking four pages, so often all we had in an issue was one article. We had some early articles about the images of disabled people that appeared in the media, and how erroneous they were. Our slogan was, "Start reading *The Rag* and start to think." We very consciously selected what went in there, in the hopes that it would get people to start thinking about the experience of being disabled.

We received a lot of really good responses. We got a letter, probably six issues in, from a woman whom I'd never met, I never have met her. She was just someone that had a disability, and we had evidently put her name on the list because she had joined one of the organizations in Louisville. She wrote this really long letter about how what we printed had awakened her. She'd been thinking these things all her life, but never thought anyone else ever thought them, and she'd felt so alone, and now she was discovering a community. And that was really what *The Rag* was tapping into. We did not realize it, but it really was the beginning of the whole national disability rights movement, and people were feeling that. And I think *The Rag* just happened along at a time when people were ready to hear something like this.

It was based in my home, and then we had a small office in a church basement. It was accessible, though. We did fundraising appeals, two or three times a year, and got some money. Certainly never enough to pay a big salary for me, but I didn't need it, so that was fortunate. But we were able to pay a part-time person who would handle the subscription stuff, and all the bookkeeping, everything that wasn't editorial. There was a period toward the late eighties where *The Rag* actually had two or three staffers. We had a succession of people who handled the news reporting, because we did have a news section, very short little news items, and we needed a reporter to handle that. And after I would say about the fourth year we were starting to do fairly substantive stories that required reporting.

At the beginning of 1984 we devoted an issue to the Baby Doe case.[7] By the end of '83 when we were working on the January '84 issue, we knew enough people in the national movement—Paul Longmore,[8] Mary Jane Owen, a few other people—that we certainly were doing interviews and getting the opinions of people in the national movement around the issue of Baby Doe, and that sort of fed on itself. I'm not sure that any other publication had really touched it, certainly not in the activist way that we were doing it. And so I think because of that, the magazine's notoriety—or whatever you want to call it—spread. And right around the end of '83 and the beginning of '84, we did an issue on Elizabeth Bouvia.[9] And then we did the ADAPT issue—so there were three issues right in a row that were touching on things that disabled people all over the country were interested in hearing about and seeing discussed, and I think that gave the magazine a certain boost and a certain cachet.

The first two years it was given away free. We always had a subscription coupon on the back—but I would say subscriptions were well under a thousand. By early '85, I would say we had probably gone up to twenty-five hundred or three thousand. So it was dramatic for us, but certainly it was a tiny, tiny circulation. I think the highest circulation it ever had was between five and six thousand, which is just minuscule. But the impact was greater than just those numbers. In fact, we did a reader's survey. It was amazing the number of people that said that they passed their magazine on. Or they would copy it and give it to other people. I think at one point we figured that every magazine was actually being read by thirty or forty people. So, if you look at that, the impact was well beyond the four or five, six thousand in circulation.

Until 1986, it was almost always a monthly. For the first two years we were getting it printed off at a place analogous to Kinko's, and it was just an eleven by seventeen sheet of paper folded in half. And then in January '83 we started using a printer that printed little community newspapers, so it was printed on newsprint. It had a staple in it, and that had sixteen pages—we got big! And then we went to thirty-two pages, and it was pretty much that size until the mid-eighties. In the mid-eighties we started being bi-monthly. We had some issues that were sixty-four pages, that was as much as we ever did.

We straddled a very interesting time in the history of publications. When we started in 1980 things were being typed on a typewriter. When we ended in 2006 we were completely online. So that's a big chunk of time.

We got so many submissions, just over the transom. Our problem was how to winnow all the materials, because we only had so much money, and money translates into cost not only in printing, but in mailing and postage. We could have done probably sixty-four pages every two weeks, if we'd had the money. But there were an awful lot of good writers. And I think it was a source of pride to me that people who had things to say to the movement knew they could say them in the pages of *The Rag,* and get a national audience. It went both ways. We got very good stuff from people, and people who wanted to say something got a place to say it.

I did some articles myself. A lot of times there would just be stuff going on that I wanted to report on, that I wanted to investigate. So I certainly could pick up the slack and until we got Laura Younkin, I did all of that.

There was always a tension between people who felt very strongly that *The Rag* had to remain independent, and it couldn't be under the aegis of some national organization, and people who wanted *The Rag* to be more an apologist for the movement. In fact we received a lot of heat, and not all of it apparent in the pages, although quite a lot of it *was* apparent in the pages. A lot of ADAPT people became very irritated whenever we wrote anything that sounded critical of ADAPT. And I think people sincerely could not understand how, if we believed in ADAPT—and I was probably one of ADAPT's strongest champions—we could then publish things that were critical. There was just that tension between doing journalism or being part of a movement.

I would say certainly the activists, probably people who worked in independent living centers, were our core audience, because they were people who were involved with disability on a day to day basis. I would say that we were less popular among the older, established organizations. We were most popular, probably, among people who were actually involved in disability rights. Groups like DREDF, organizations like public interest law centers—groups that were really trying to do the kind of work that we were writing about.

We also had a lot of people who were irritated by it. I think we might have been pretty unusual in that period from, let's say 1980 to 1995, we were probably pretty much alone among the disability publications in regularly printing a whole bunch of letters from people who were routinely horrified at what we were writing about. There was a whole strain of complaint from readers who felt we were always being very negative, that we complained about everything. There was another strain that was similar that felt we were too activist, that we felt everyone should be in the streets and everyone should sue—you know, you can catch more flies with honey than you can with vinegar and we were always going the vinegar route. And, I think, probably both of those strains could be coalesced into that point right there—that people really felt that being antagonistic, being critical, being outspoken about issues, and very critical of the status quo, was just not the way that things should be done.

There were no sacred cows, as far as we were concerned. It was one of the reasons people liked us, because they knew we didn't have any sacred cows. And if there was something that really needed to be criticized, we would do it. On the other hand, I think it made organized disability groups pretty leery of us. I know this was the case with ADAPT. I think, for example, Wade Blank,[10] who was probably our number one source at ADAPT till his death—I always felt Wade understood what we were doing. He didn't take the criticisms that came up as personal. But I know certain people in ADAPT took them very, very personally.

I think those people who were involved in putting the ADA together were probably a little bit leery of us as well. They didn't really want us to know all of the inside thinking, lest we either criticize it or spill the beans in a way. It's really the same way the people behind the ADA felt about the mainstream media. I don't think they felt they could really be sure of what we would publish. And it was true, they *couldn't* be sure of what we would publish, and so it made them very circumspect.

It's interesting because *The Rag* had a brief time, in the history of publications. It was around for twenty-six years, 1980 to 2006. And I think the first years were probably its best in terms of creating community. And partly, I think, that's because there was a need. I think after the ADA, people had established their own communities, the Internet was starting up, people were starting to do e-mail. There were a succession of different editors at the magazine, and while it was still very good, I think it was becoming clear to a number of us who were associated with it that its heyday was passing. And I, frankly, am very happy that the board was willing to end it. There are so many things in life, organizations and everything else, that go on and on and on, and all they do is to institutionalize themselves and they're not as needed as they were at one time. And so I'm perfectly happy to know that *The Rag* existed at a time in history, it did a good job—and it is no more.

13
The American Coalition of Citizens with Disabilities

T HE AMERICAN COALITION OF CITIZENS WITH DISABILITIES (ACCD) was incorporated in 1975 to advocate for the rights of people with disabilities on a national level. During its heyday in the late 1970s and early 1980s, it sponsored the founding of state and local chapters, lobbied for legislation, and coordinated national campaigns on issues ranging from the design of accessible buses to the regulations implementing Section 504 of the Rehabilitation Act of 1973.

The ACCD represented a new direction in disability politics. Traditionally, people with disabilities had been divided into various constituencies, usually based on medical criteria. This categorization applied to consumer-controlled groups (for example, the National Federation of the Blind, the National Association of the Deaf), for service organizations (such as the Multiple Sclerosis Society, the Easter Seal Society), and for parents' groups (such as the Association for Retarded Children, the United Cerebral Palsy Associations, Inc.

With the success of Disabled in Action on the East Coast, and the California Association of the Physically Handicapped on the West, by the late 1960s advocates had begun to think in terms of a national organization that would pull all the various strands together. Chief among them was Fred Fay, who began using his contacts within the National Paraplegia Foundation and then at the annual meetings of the President's Committee on the Employment of the Physically Handicapped to push for the creation of such a group.

There were problems, though. For one, organizers soon discovered that people with disabilities were no more immune than the general public to harboring misconceptions about various disabilities and those who have them. Wheelchair users and people with cerebral palsy, for example, who were used to being mischaracterized as "mentally retarded," were often at pains to distance themselves from people with intellectual disabilities. Many people who were culturally Deaf rejected any attempt to categorize themselves as disabled, as did members of organizations such as the National Federation of the Blind.

Then, too, there were instances when different disability groups had what at first appeared to be mutually exclusive priorities. The organized blindness community, for example, confronted with a history of blind people being segregated into institutions and sheltered workshops, pushed for the mainstreaming of blind children into public schools, while the Deaf community was skeptical of mainstreaming if it would result in the closing of Deaf schools where Deaf teachers taught ASL. Moreover, there were differences, sometimes even bitter controversies, within the same disability community. The American Council of the Blind (ACB), for instance, was founded in 1961, in part to break away from the National Federation of the Blind (NFB). The ACB accepted the notion of cross-disability organizing and community and joined the ACCD. By contrast, the NFB never endorsed cross-disability politics and never joined the ACCD.

Despite all these issues, the ACCD was up and running by 1977, and under the leadership of its executive director, the author and activist Dr. Frank Bowe, it would play a major role in melding what had been regional and single disability groups into a national, cross-disability coalition.

Fred Fay (continued)
"Every single group . . . had members who had been discriminated against."

Fred Fay graduated from the University of Illinois at Urbana-Champaign in 1967 with a bachelor's degree in psychology. Having had his "first taste of political change," he embarked on what was to be a lifetime of disability rights activism. Already the cofounder (with his mother, Janet Carolyn Wright Fay) of the Opening Doors counseling center for people with spinal cord injury, in Washington, DC, he became a leader in the National Spinal Cord Injury Association (then called the National Paraplegia Foundation), establishing and serving as first president of its Washington chapter. In the early 1970s, advocating for access on the Washington Metro then under construction, he coined the slogan "No taxation without transportation."

After receiving his doctorate in educational psychology in 1972 (also from Illinois), he worked as a researcher for the Urban Institute before moving to the Boston area to take a position as a professor and director of research and training at the Rehabilitation Institute at Tufts New England Medical Center. Having met Ed Roberts and visited the CIL in Berkeley, Fred was also an early advocate for independent living, and in 1974 cofounded the Boston CIL.

Along the way Fred had also done his share of "street theater." In 1972, as a protest against Nixon's veto of the Rehabilitation Act, he and other activists staged a demonstration in front of the John F. Kennedy federal office building in downtown Boston. "We had [someone] dressed up as Uncle Sam with a top hat and a red, white, and blue shirt. And then we had an old wheelchair, an old crutch, and an old guide cane piled up in front of the building. And with all of the media, all the newspapers and TV cameras rolling, we sledge-hammered the wheelchair and stuff to bits" as a way of dramatizing the impact of Nixon's veto. "I had just come from the University of Illinois, and the antiwar movement. I thought it was really important for us to be out there out front, raising hell, getting the media's attention, and drawing attention to the problems."

The idea of a cross-disability coalition had been germinating in my head for a while, but I think the first significant efforts were at a national citizens' conference, in June of 1969, with the Paralyzed Veterans of America, the American Council of the Blind, the National Paraplegia Foundation, and so forth all there. We talked about how we could be much more powerful on common issues if we could go before Congress as one voice, rather than let Congress divide and conquer. In the late sixties I would tend to drum it up, promoting the idea in talking with people like Judy Heumann, Lex Frieden, and Eunice Fiorito. Instead of fighting over each group's slice of the pie, it made more sense for us as a group to fight for a larger pie, and that in a nutshell is what ACCD did.

Initially, Harry Schweikert with Paralyzed Veterans of America was reluctant, because he had been so successful with PVA and had been their executive director for years and was very good at what he did. But he agreed after a while. The other big opposition was the National Federation of the Blind. They really did not want anything to do with a coalition, not even with other blind groups. The split between American Council of the Blind and NFB has gone on for years. I met Fred Schreiber, who was executive director of the National Association of the Deaf, out at their offices in Silver Spring in 1970, and then at his home with his family. And he got it.[1]

Eunice Fiorito I met at American Congress of Rehab Medicine. Paul

Corcoran[2] had invited her in as a speaker. And she and I spent a lot of time brainstorming. She was at that time director of the Mayor's Office on Disability in New York City. She was really dynamic, forceful speaker, a really astute politician, knew how to manage people and challenge them and bring out the best in them. . . . I think [the phrase "cross-disability"] was invented in that meeting I had with Jim Garret and Eunice Fiorito, who became our first official president a year later. We needed a term that meant bringing together people with different disabilities.

We were mostly in our twenties. Well, Durwood McDaniel[3] was gray-haired. He must have been forty-five by then, fifty. Eric Gentile,[4] from Michigan, must have been in his twenties. Eunice was maybe thirty. Pretty much a very youthful, full of vigor group.[5]

I had cut my teeth in the early sixties, on being part of a national organization. So I thought a coalition of national organizations made the most sense. However, I was also receptive to the idea of state coalitions being part. I thought it was a huge mistake to be an organization of just individuals, in great part on a fear it would compete with existing organizations and undermine them and/or undermine ACCD.

There was a President's Committee [on Employment of the Handicapped] meeting in Washington [in 1974], and I knew that several people from out of state who I had talked to individually were going to be at this hotel. And that included Sharon Mistler,[6] who was a strong advocate for individual membership, Judy Heumann, who had worked with Disabled in Action, two people from PVA, and a couple of reps from the blind and the deaf. I rented a conference room and invited all these people to get together to talk about whether we needed a coalition. And the room was stacked, because I knew 90 percent of the people there thought we should.

Then, to get a broader mandate, we had a much larger group, maybe two or three hundred people, and we presented our ideas and held elections [for] an interim board whose job it was over the next year to draft bylaws and build a structure, with the idea that we would do elections for the actual organization once all that preliminary stuff was set. We next held a meeting at my parents' house, with Eric Gentile, Judy Heumann, Sharon Mistler, Ralf Hotchkiss,[7] and Roger Petersen[8] from the American Council of the Blind, who was really our early staff. He went in each day on a volunteer basis and answered our mail. We rented an office on Dupont Circle in northwest Washington, DC.

The first year [beginning in April 1975] we were on our own in terms of funding. People made contributions out of their own pocket to get to meetings and stuff, but it became real apparent early on that we needed to have money to hire a staff. At that point the funding source I knew best was [the] HEW Rehab Services Administration because I had worked with them on subway accessibility, and on getting the spinal cord injury centers funded and so forth. So Eunice and I went, tape recorder in hand, and sat down with Jim Garrett, who was the director of research at RSA and a very progressive thinker. He recognized the need for a coalition in terms of supporting his budget and RSA's goals and so forth. He had a slight, I think it was post-polio, disability himself. He was enthusiastic about the idea, so I pinpointed him and said, "This is what we want to do. How can we get it to fall under your guidelines for funding?" And we came up jointly with the title, "A Feasibility Study of a National Model of Cross-Disability Cooperation and Communication." I think it was about $72,000 we got, which gave us enough money to hire an executive director, Frank Bowe.[9]

Frank was a great writer. He was extremely talented, a PhD, just an incredibly charismatic guy. Fortunately he had worked at RSA, I think one summer, so he knew Jim Garrett, which didn't hurt when we later told him that we were going to hire Frank. But I think somewhere I have a report that says we did do the "feasibility study" and that "cross-disability cooperation" was a great idea and quite feasible.

There was one meeting after that at Gallaudet College hosted by Al Pimentel[10] that was really helpful. It was our first meeting after the big meeting at the hotel in Washington, and there we really got into the nitty-gritty. We argued vehemently back and forth as to whether it should be an organization of individuals or coalitions or national organizations. And I, being the eternal compromiser, came up with the idea of including all three: with ten votes for national organizations, three votes for state coalitions, and one vote for the individual organizations of fifty or more members, or something like that.

We had board meetings that whole year. I know we adopted the by-laws at the meeting at my parents' house. And then, once we elected permanent board members, they would have had to have been approved by them. I don't remember specifically the vote, but ACCD as an organization must at that point have adopted them in 1975.

There was a very heated discussion about the name. I wanted "national." Eric Gentile wanted "America." He was very patriotic. He was extremely offended that Roger Petersen was singing labor songs and leftist songs. He thought we were a bunch of communists and threatened to storm out of the meeting. It didn't make that much of a difference, so we went with "American." I argued for "persons" with disabilities or "citizens" with disabilities. I liked "persons." Again Eric was this patriotic guy who liked "citizens" because it had more of a democratic ring. We went back and forth but I really preferred putting the emphasis on people, rather than on disabilities. We went from a Friday to a Sunday hashing that out at my parents' house. It wasn't until Sunday night as I recall that we nailed it all down. And there was some argument over dues structure and stuff like that, but we were pretty much on the same track.

The single biggest focus early on was civil rights, and that was a natural because it was cross-disability. Every single group of people with disabilities had members who had been discriminated against. It was a universal issue, as opposed to wheelchair access, or access to information in alternative formats for the blind, or whatever.

Initially we just argued on behalf of common issues, but what was wonderful was that over time you would find blind people arguing in favor of wheelchair access, or paraplegics arguing for greater American Sign Language interpreter availability, or whatever, and that was a whole unexpected bonus of the good communication that evolved between the different organizations. If you're sitting down once a month for a year with somebody who is working on a different goal, but you see the commonality in terms of supporting, I don't know, somehow just being together with people, talking with them over the course of a year, sharing different issues, seeing the similarities in the issues, and the advantage of having a larger voice, it just seemed natural evolution. It certainly wasn't our original intent. In fact, if you had told me when we were getting ACCD off the ground that we were going to focus on getting the blind to argue on behalf of wheelchair accessibility, I would have discounted it. To me it seemed like our greatest success would lie in finding issues that affected every member ultimately. The single one that stood out more than anything else was civil rights.

Fortunately, there had been the Rehab Act of 1973, which included Section 504, which said that if you receive federal money you could not discriminate on the basis of disability. It was like fifty words long and it was just an amendment tacked on to the Rehab Act, but it became a wonderful organizing focus. Frankly, I don't think the vast majority of Congress had any idea of what they were passing. It wasn't perfect, but if we could make government-funded programs free of discrimination, it seemed to me it would be a relatively small step to making discrimination illegal.

But a law by itself is usually pretty useless. You need to have implementing regulations. Those regulations are usually drafted by one of the federal agencies. John Wodatch[11] took a lead in developing them, but then [HEW secretary Joseph] Califano [Jr.] sat and sat and sat on them. Got us thoroughly pissed off. I made a motion at the board meeting calling for national demonstrations to force Califano to sign the regulations. I think it was Phyllis Rubenfeld, who later became president of ACCD, who seconded the resolution.

There was some debate over whether we ought to do it in every state, or regionally, or just national. We didn't think at that point we were organized enough that we could turn out people in every state. We had board members there from each region, so we went with regional demonstrations. . . . I remember copying the flyer that was going to be sent out. It was vague. We called for national actions, demonstrations. We didn't prescribe to people exactly what to do, but the issue was something that people grabbed onto readily. We had several board members making calls. Frank did a lot of it, but from my calls I had a pretty good idea that people were going to do it.

The people in Massachusetts were quite enthusiastic. I've got a photograph somewhere. I was told by a friend who knew federal funding that it was suicidal where I was working, at a research and training center that was getting federal funding, for me to organize a demonstration in front of HEW's regional office. I think that may have been one of the things that got the federal government RSA [Rehabilitation Services Administration] staff unhappy with my advocacy. . . .

[Califano finally agreed to sign the regs, and] Frank and Eunice primarily worked with his staff [to fine-tune them]. This is getting a little bit head of ourselves, but one of the outcomes of that, after he had signed the regs under duress, Eunice thought it would be a good idea to give Califano an award for his leadership. Kind of smooth the waters, and Judy was adamantly opposed to giving him any kind of recognition, where he had been such a pain for so long. The most heated ACCD board meeting I can remember was Judy and Eunice fighting over whether he should get this award or not. Eunice wanted to speak as president, so she stepped down, and I had to chair the meeting when they went back and forth at each other. By one vote, the group decided that we were in essence going to take the award back, or not present it to him, after he had been notified that he was getting it. Eunice and I had the unpleasant task of going over to Califano's office to tell him that, unfortunately, the board had voted not to give him the award. . . .

[But getting him to sign those regulations was] just a wonderful exhilaration. It gave us a real clear victory, a sign that ACCD was a force to be reckoned with and that we could have an impact at the national level.

Lex Frieden
"This was the genesis of the real disability rights movement in America."

"I wasn't frustrated by the idea of my being quadriplegic," says Lex Frieden, recounting his first months of rehab after the car accident in 1967 that resulted in his spinal cord injury. "I approached this disability thing as a challenge. I looked at it as a puzzle. You have to solve pieces of the puzzle. So from that standpoint I wasn't disconcerted."

Frieden was born in March 1949 in Alva, Oklahoma. After being discharged from rehab he returned to school to earn his BS in psychology from the University of Tulsa in 1971, and his MA in social psychology from the University of Houston in 1979. During this time he also became a major voice in the independent living movement, founding Wheelchair Independence Now in Tulsa in 1971. Frieden was one of the early leaders of the ACCD (he was national secretary from 1975 to 1976) and a cofounder of the Coalition of Texans with Disabilities in 1978. The Texan coalition, like many of the statewide coalitions founded under the umbrella of the ACCD, continued to be active even after the ACCD dissolved in the early 1980s. In 1984, President Reagan appointed Frieden executive director of the National Council on the Handicapped, where he became one of the principal architects of the Americans with Disabilities Act.

I had worked with Judy Heumann and Ed Roberts by phone in 1973, try-ing to get disabled support for passage of the Rehabilitation Act of 1973, which had some radical changes from prior rehabilitation acts, particu-larly Title V, which was our first real civil rights provision in law. I was aware of what the California group was doing in regards to development of independent living centers and organizing to be politically active and so on. I had been involved in the founding and the development of the WIN organization in Tulsa before I moved to Houston. And there were a group of us who discussed having an organization in Houston.

At some point, I think around 1974, I decided it was time to start this organization. So I invited all of the people with disabilities who I could imagine might be interested to my home. This was after I'd left a coopera-tive, communal style living arrangement, and moved into a house that I shared with two attendants, one who was a driver and the other one who would help me get up and go to bed.

About thirty people with different types of disabilities, friends of mine, came to the house, and agreed to start an organization which we named the Coalition for Barrier Free Living. We agreed that it would be a cross-disability organization and we assigned one another roles in the development of the organization, including preparation of the bylaws and incorporations and so on and so forth.

As a matter of fact, that's how I met my wife, Joyce. I needed some-body to type some of the corporate papers that had to be filed and I in-vited this woman who came to my home, and later we married. We had one of those beautiful Houston floods and I convinced her that she had to stay overnight with me in order to avoid risk by the floods. So thank God we have floods in Houston.

Fred Fay, from Massachusetts, had invited me and Ed Roberts and Eunice Fiorito and some other people to a meeting in Boston. That was I think in '74 or '75. That meeting was to talk about forming a national organization. I would say this was the genesis of the real disability rights movement in America. . . .

Some time shortly after the Boston meeting there was a [previously] planned meeting of the President's Committee on Employment of the Handicapped. Many of those at the Boston meeting had been invited to go to this meeting, in 1975, in Washington. One of the women in attendance at the Boston meeting was Dianne Latin, who worked for the President's Committee, an assistant to the chairman or something of that nature. So those of us who had not yet been invited and who were not members of the President's Committee told Diane, [and] she arranged to have us sent an invitation.

Prior to that meeting, I knew that we were going to have votes, and that the votes would be determined according to the organizations represented there. So in Houston not only did we organize the Coalition for a Barrier Free Environment, but we incorporated about five other groups that were not—well, they were organizations on paper. So that when I went to this meeting, I had not one but six organizations that I was voting for. I had more votes than most of the people at the organizing meeting, so we could control politically some of the outcomes. We did, in fact, form the ACCD at that meeting. We elected Eunice Fiorito the president, and John Lancaster[12] the vice-president, and I was elected secretary.

So I participated in those organizing meetings of ACCD, and we met in people's homes. Actually, when the board met in Houston, the board members stayed in my home. Fred Fay slept on the floor in my living room, Judy Heumann slept in the spare bedroom in my house. Gini Laurie slept on a bench outside in the back of my house. It was really a kind of a people's organization. It was wonderful, we learned so much. I had a blind friend who was on the board, Roger Petersen, who I discovered could help lift me despite his disability. I learned sign language from Fred Schreiber, who's the godfather of the Deaf movement. In fact, he gave me my Deaf sign name, which is "Cheap."

This was a kind of a kindling bed for advocates who are now around the country. There was a fellow named Will Clark, who made the first film, that I'm aware of, of [a] disability rights action. Will is now in Missouri. A woman named Marilyn Golden,[13] who was involved in the beginning of some of our organizations, who's now an activist in California. Bob Kafka[14] was one of the cofounders of the Coalition for Barrier Free Living, and he's now an ADAPT leader in Austin. Bob Geyer, who later became the chief of the Coalition of Texans with Disabilities [CTD], was one of the cofounders.

The CBFL quickly decided that in addition to a national coalition, we needed to affiliate with a state coalition. I got a grant from a local research institute to "investigate the possibility that people with disabilities could manage state-run organizations in five states." With that hypothesis, I was able to get the money to bring in people from Texas and the four surrounding states and in one weekend we founded statewide coalitions in Texas, New Mexico, Oklahoma, Arkansas, and Louisiana. The state coalition, the Coalition of Texans with Disabilities which continues to exist, as does CBFL.

I think the second national meeting of ACCD was actually hosted here in Houston by that group. This was the first meeting where Frank Bowe had been hired as the CEO of ACCD, and I invited Justin Dart here from Austin and introduced him to Frank Bowe. So again, it was just a group of visionaries, spirited people here in Houston like those that were working in Massachusetts, California, and Michigan at the time. I think those are really the four centers of activism in the disability movement in the early 1970s.

One of the reasons that we formed ACCD was to get regulations for laws that were written and not yet regulated. One of those laws was the Rehabilitation Act. We observed that the government had passed this law in 1973 and did not have regulations to implement it, and it was already 1975, and so why not? This is one of the issues that we raised at the President's Committee on Employment of the Handicapped. That agency, in turn, went to the Department of Health, Education, and Welfare and asked them where were the regulations. They said they really hadn't gotten around to it. The President's Committee took the initiative to sponsor one meeting in Washington, I think it was held at the Brookings Institution, to provide advice about the development of these regulations. As I recall, a few of us had been identified and were invited to come to this meeting. It might have been most of the people who were at the Boston meeting, because this meeting was held shortly after.

The staff of the President's Committee had done some analysis of the law and had some lawyers from the Department of HEW there to explain how the regulations would be written and sought our input about how to define "reasonable accommodation" and "access" and so on. So we had discussions about that over a two-day period and then we left. Then a couple of years later ACCD was still concerned about the fact that there were no regulations, and we planned a major political action to inform consumers about that.

Simultaneously, there was a group of activist people in the Bay Area in

California who decided that they needed to bring to the attention of the public the fact that this law was essentially toothless because there were no regulations for it five years after its passage. I'm not sure where the inspiration of the California leadership came from at that time, but it was coordinated with ACCD's action in Washington, DC, where Eunice Fiorito confronted the secretary of HEW,, and where a group of us carried candles at night outside the secretary's home. According to informed people, it was the secretary's wife who didn't like those people out there with those candles who encouraged him to go ahead and sign the darn regulations. Others would say it was being backed into a corner by Eunice Fiorito that caused him to sign the regulations. Others would say it was the specter of the capitol police removing people with disabilities from the hallways of a federal building. Who knows?

That all stemmed from the '73 Act, but there were simultaneously other issues. The IDEA [Individuals with Disabilities Education Act] was started in 1975, as I recall. That, again, generated a good bit of support. Although I must say, with respect to IDEA, it was almost like the Rehab Act of '73, it was like somebody gave you something you really weren't asking for, didn't expect. We weren't really lobbying for that. There were a couple of people who may have been involved in it, but the community really was more grateful than supportive of those two laws. After the fact, when they were there, there was clearly a resounding effort by the community to say, "Wait a minute, this is [only] rhetoric unless you're really going to enforce the law." That's where the community became active, it was more of a reactionary thing than a proactive action during the seventies.

ACCD did two important things. Number one is they did a phenomenal amount of leadership training, under Frank Bowe's leadership. The little booklets that Frank wrote and some of us contributed to are still on my bookshelf among the most important references that I have. Booklets about how the political process works, and how to get involved in a precinct meeting, that were circulated all over the country to groups of people with disabilities. They basically took what those of us who were in leadership at the time had to learn through practice and translated them into "how-to" so other people could, in effect, model that behavior. They were handed out at training programs that ACCD did. Frank spoke at many of those. When he wasn't available, I and other colleagues were drawn in from the board of directors to speak at the training meetings. Hundreds of people with disabilities were trained at those meetings to be advocates.

The other primary function of ACCD was to coordinate efforts among people in different communities and states and regions of the country. It was also a wonderful model of cooperation between disability groups, because ACCD brought together what I would say at the time were "the big three." That was the NAD, the National Association of the Deaf, under [Fred] Schreiber's leadership. NAD was a very powerful organization in the early 1970s, it was very well run, and had a lot of money. At that time, NAD had a corner on the market of sales of TTYs and TDDs for deaf people.[15] They were earning a lot of income from that, and selling training programs for interpreters and so on.

And then [there were] the two blind organizations . . . and that was the American Council of the Blind and the National Federation of the Blind. ACB was the one that actually compromised its philosophy to some degree to join ACCD. NFB never really did, but they provided a lot of quiet support. The argument of the blind organizations was you will dilute your own influence if you join a coalition, but ACB finally agreed to join. Schreiber's view, on the other hand, [which he shared with] Al Pimentel, who was a leader in the National Association of the Deaf, was that by joining the coalition they could amplify their influence.

The third leg in that coalition was the Paralyzed Veterans of America. They had a lot of money, a lot of influence, they were very powerful politically. They have a building in Washington, DC, a block away from the White House. They were very skilled at lobbying. I believe that bringing those three organizations together with state coalitions and grassroots activists was the primary contribution of ACCD, in addition to the training that Frank did.

The lure of ACCD was, you can maintain your own identity and do your own thing *and* be part of a national organization. It didn't cost much, and we were subsidizing the work of ACCD through the grants from HEW and later the Department of Education. So it wasn't hard to get local groups to join, and we reached out a lot to try and get them to join because we knew, at least we believed, that the more groups that we had as members, the more recognition we would get from political leadership.

The ACCD conversations, unlike those that we had on independent living about social service agencies, were more like, how many of us would it take at a national convention [of one of the major political parties] to be able to get floor time for a speaker? How many of us do we need to claim we have as members before we can get a candidate for president to mention disability in a speech? How do we get invited to receptions so that we can meet a candidate for president and spend two minutes talking with him about addressing a disability issue in a public way?

And that's another aspect of life in the seventies—we were committed to trying every avenue possible. I would describe it as a layered, multi-impact strategy. One time Judy [Heumann] and I had a discussion about being elected to public office, and we discussed each others' experience going to [Democratic Party] precinct meetings and being elected as delegates, going from the precinct meeting to the district meeting to the state meeting to the national convention. We taught ourselves how to do these things. Part of the energy, part of the stimulus, part of the excitement was learning about these things and then trying them out. That's what was fun. I don't think we'd have done it all if it hadn't been fun.

The first time I went to a [Democratic Party] precinct meeting, I got elected as a delegate to go to a district meeting. I went to the district meeting and wanted to go to a state meeting. At the district meeting, my precinct all voted for me. Then the next meeting, the regional meeting, the section meeting for my candidate, who at the time was [Walter] Mondale, was on the stage at the [local] high school. I couldn't get on the stage. So I went down next to the stage and I said, "Excuse me, you're going to have to move this discussion and this election to someplace else." The chairman of the Mondale caucus looked over, peered over the stage at me and said, "Oh, don't worry, this will just take a minute. We're just electing delegates to the state convention." I said, "I know, I want to be considered as a delegate." "Oh, well," he said, "We already have our slate lined up." I started yelling, "This is ridiculous! This is not democracy! Is this what you people stand for?"

They're all looking at me, peering over the edge of the stage there like I'm some kind of a weirdo. I kept yelling. Well, after a while these lesbian women marched off the stage and came and stood next to me and started yelling. The lesbian women, not only from the Mondale caucus but also from the other caucuses, marched out of their caucuses and started yelling. Then the Free America Independent Voters marched off the stage and started yelling.

Pretty soon this union boss who was running the whole thing came over there to negotiate. "Well, what is it you want?" I said, "I just want to be elected a delegate to go to the state convention." He said, "Fine, you can have my spot. Now we have our slate, everybody in favor say 'Aye.'" They all said "Aye" and the protest ended.

I had learned about making resolutions. I introduced a resolution that basically said that all future meetings of the Democratic Party should be accessible to people with disabilities. Passed the resolution. I mean what did that do? Nonetheless, that's the sort of thing we did.

Then I campaigned to go from the state to the national convention, by calling disabled people in other cities around the state asking them to go and become delegates so they could vote for me. So when we had the state convention there were like seventy-five people with disabilities represented, and we had enough people that we passed resolutions and we got ourselves elected to various positions of leadership in the party.

I was not on the board of ACCD during its demise [in the 1980s]. But I was speaking on a daily basis with Frank Bowe, who was the president and CEO, and with some of the board members. In fact, I was trying to make a truce between two different viewpoints. One of them, led by Frank, was that the organization needed to continue to get grants and do this work that can be sponsored by the government because there's not enough money in the disability community to support a national organization like this. Certainly the big organizations that belonged—PVA, ACB, and NAD—weren't going to spend a lot of money subsidizing yet another organization. Their money was staying with their organization. ACCD survived primarily because Frank Bowe was a skilled grant-writer and very successful at getting federal dollars to do advocacy training, which was amazing. Here the government was training people to complain about the government. That was remarkable and Frank was a genius at that.

On the other hand, there was a group of board members who believed that the organization should be more independent; that it should not be dependent on these federal grants, that the organizations' goals were being compromised by the contractual understandings that it had with the sponsors. Frank Bowe, frankly, didn't want anybody telling him how to do what he thought he needed to do and what he could do best. He didn't want the board to micromanage ACCD.

The conflict led to a split, and they never were able to find anybody who could run the organization with the same kind of vision and purpose and energy that Frank had. So it was a paradigm shift, I'd say, that led to the demise of ACCD.

Peter Breughel the Elder, "The Beggars," 1568. People with disabilities have traditionally been marginalized by society, objects of either scorn or pity. (Public Domain)

Theodore Gericault, "A Paralytic Woman." People with disabilities as spectacle. (© Museum of London)

The Feeble-Minded or the Hub to Our Wheel of Vice, Crime and Pauperism. A typical of example of eugenicist literature, customized for reproduction in almost every state for distribution to educators, legislators, policymakers, and the general public. (Courtesy, Ohio Historical Society)

The Willowbrook State School and Hospital on Staten Island, New York, opened in 1951, became a symbol of the brutalizing effect of "the total institution." (Courtesy, William Bronston, MD, *Public Hostage: Public Ransom—Inside Institutional America,* © 1979)

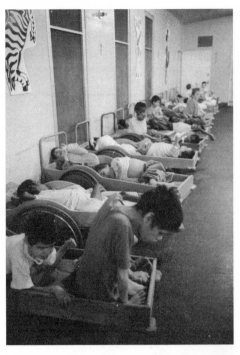

Dr. William Bronston, physician at Willowbrook in the early 1970s, took these photographs to document what he found there. (All images courtesy, William Bronston, MD, *Public Hostage: Public Ransom—Inside Institutional America,* © 1979)

Infants and children crowded two or more in a bed or crib had little or nothing to stimulate their minds and bodies.

An open window was a treasured respite from summer heat and stench. Crowding around radiators for warmth in the winter, medicated into oblivion, residents often suffered serious burns.

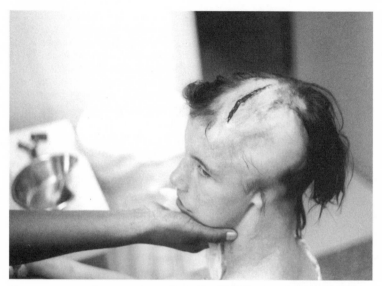

There was no more dangerous place to live in New York City than the back wards of this "state school and hospital."

"Less comfortable and cheerful than the cages in which we put animals in a zoo." —Sen. Robert F. Kennedy, 1965.

A student poses in front of the Rehabilitation Center at the University of Illinois, Urbana-Champaign, the first disabled students program in the country. (Courtesy, University of Illinois Archives)

Among the many innovations at Urbana-Champaign were the nation's first regularly scheduled lift-equipped buses to move wheelchair-using students around campus. (Courtesy, University of Illinois Archives)

Berkeley CIL staff and consumers, c. 1975. *First row, left to right, seated on the ground:* Steven Handler Klein; Linda Perotti; Suzanne Scott; Judith Rogers; Bette McMuldren. *Second row, left to right, seated in wheelchairs:* Joan Johnson; Cathrine Caulfield; William Bash; Nancy DiAngelo; Phil Chavez (immediately behind DiAngelo); Wally Whelan; Mary Ann Hiserman; Frank (Franko) Ramsey; Judith Heumann; Hale Zukas (in helmet); Ron Washington. *Third row, left to right, standing:* Maureen Fitzgerald; Carol Fewell; Deborah Meehan (immediately behind Fewell); unidentified; William McGregor; Vincent Creek; Jim Rowen; Terry Flash; Mary Lester (immediately behind Flash, in shadow); Sondra Thaler (next to and behind Flash); Kari Eis Eeelis; Susan Bateman; Kenneth Stein; Deborah Kaplan; Lynn Kidder; Jerry Wolf; Hal Kirshbaum; Edna Breen; Jan McEwen-Brown; Paul Bendix. *Fourth row, left to right, standing center:* Tom Fussy; Dick Santos; Darcy Coddingham (partially visible, under hat); Jeff Moyer; Eric Dibner (in beard behind Moyer); Eric Morton (next to bus); Gregory Pick (in front of bus). (Courtesy, Kenneth Okuno)

One of the first "Disability Pride" rallies, staged in the late 1970s in San Francisco. (Ken Stein photo)

The parents' movement first used the federal courts and then fought for legislation to win a right to education and community services for their children. (Ken Stein photo)

"The father of independent living" Ed Roberts with California governor Jerry Brown Jr. (Ken Stein photo)

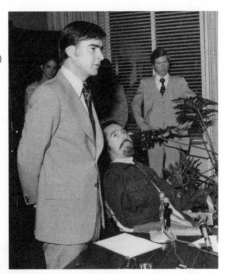

Judith Heumann, deputy director of the Berkeley CIL and a principal organizer of the 1977 federal HEW building occupation in San Francisco. (Ken Stein photo)

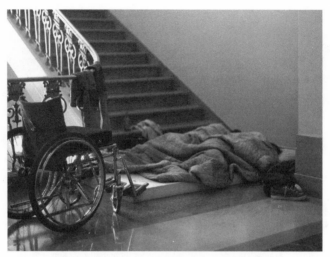

"Sleeping accommodations" for some of those occupying the federal HEW building in San Francisco in 1977. (Courtesy, Hollynn D'Lil)

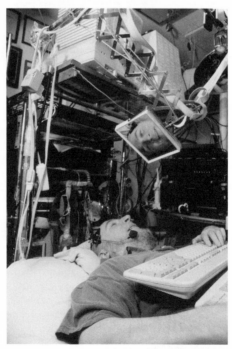

Fred Fay, a pioneer of the IL movement, beneath the array of adaptive equipment he custom designed so he could keep connected to the world, 1995. (Courtesy, Exploding Myths, Inc.)

Cofounder Mary Lou Breslin in front of the newly opened headquarters of DREDF in Berkeley, c. 1979. (Ken Stein photo)

DREDF lobbyist Patrisha Wright with Evan Kemp Jr., commissioner of the Equal Employment Opportunity Commission. (Ken Stein photo)

"Mr. ADA" Justin Dart Jr., speaking to a crowd and leading "a revolution of empowerment." (Courtesy, Tom Olin)

Leonard Roy Frank, survivor of electric and insulin shock "treatment" and a leader of the psychiatric survivor movement. (Courtesy, Gayle Bluebird)

Judi Chamberlin, a leader of the psychiatric survivor movement and author of *On Our Own: Patient-Controlled Alternatives to the Mental Health System.* (Courtesy, Gayle Bluebird)

ADAPT demonstrators barricading a hotel entrance at the American Public Transit Association's 1989 conference in Sparks, Nevada, are confronted by police. (Courtesy, Tom Olin)

ADAPT protesters block a Greyhound bus to protest the
lack of accessible intercity transit. (Courtesy, Tom Olin)

Diane Coleman holds the "Freedom Rider" sign, evoking the civil rights struggles of the
1960s, at another ADAPT direct-action barricade against Greyhound.
(Courtesy, Tom Olin)

Along with civil disobedience, ADAPT used rallies and marches to educate the media and the public and highlight the need for accessible, affordable public transportation. (Courtesy, Tom Olin)

Building momentum for the ADA—an ADAPT march in Atlanta, Georgia. (Courtesy, of Tom Olin)

Students at Gallaudet University gather outside campus as they prepare to march, beginning the Deaf President Now campaign, March 1988. (Courtesy, Gallaudet University)

Gary Olsen, executive director of the National Association of the Deaf, and Bridgetta Bourne-Firl, a student leader of the Deaf President Now protest, address students assembled on campus to learn the response of the Gallaudet board of trustees to the student demands. (Courtesy, Gallaudet University)

The "crawl-up" at the steps of the US Capitol on March 12, 1990, coordinated by ADAPT. (Courtesy, Tom Olin)

Members of ADAPT meet in the Capitol rotunda with Rep. Steny Hoyer, one of the major legislative sponsors of the ADA, March 13, 1990. (Courtesy, Tom Olin)

Victory! President George H. W. Bush signs the Americans with Disabilities Act of 1990. *Seated left to right:* Evan Kemp Jr., President Bush, Justin Dart Jr. *Standing:* Rev. Harold Wilke, Sandra Swift Parrino. (Courtesy, Tom Olin)

"Separate Is Never Equal" (Courtesy, Tom Olin)

14
The HEW Demonstrations

THE ANNIVERSARY OF THE DATE ON WHICH THE AMERICANS WITH Disabilities Act was signed, July 26, 1990, is commemorated in many towns and cities each year as "disability pride" day, but the anniversary of April 5, 1977, usually passes without comment. And yet the signing of the ADA in many ways marked the culmination of the national movement which had begun thirteen years earlier. On that spring day, demonstrators staged the "HEW," or "504," sit-ins, to protest the Carter administration's reluctance to move forward with regulations to enforce what was at that time the most sweeping federal civil rights protection for people with disabilities.

Section 504 of the Rehabilitation Act of 1973, is a single sentence:

> No otherwise qualified handicapped individual in the United States ... shall, solely by reason of his handicap, be excluded from participation in, be denied the benefits of, or be subjected to discrimination under any program or activity receiving federal financial assistance.

But few people fully understood the ramifications of that simple statement. One individual who did, however, was Frank Bowe, executive director of the newly formed American Coalition of Citizens with Disabilities. Bowe described how "the vast reach of United States Government funds, from schools to hospitals to mass transit facilities, meant that almost all of American life would be affected were section 504 to become effective." Bowe also understood how "there was an unwritten rule in Washington: any provision of law that has not been implemented within three years of its enactment is, for all practical purposes, dead."[1] Passed in 1973, section 504 was already beyond that limit and on the verge of irrelevance by the time the newly elected Carter administration took office in January 1977.

Regulations had been written in 1976 by officials in the outgoing Ford administration, staff of the Department of Health, Education, and Welfare, but they had never been implemented. Activists expected more from the newly elected president, but Jimmy Carter deferred to his secretary of HEW, Joseph Califano. Califano, who admitted at a meeting with Bowe that he'd never even heard of 504, refused to issue the regulations. Bowe, after consulting Saul Alinsky's *Rules for Radicals,* decided the only remaining option was civil disobedience. "He's got to feel pressure he doesn't know how to deal with, something coming at him that's outside his experience. There's only one thing I can think of that meets those criteria: thousands of severely disabled people in his own offices." On March 18, 1977, ACCD called for "a massive sit-in demonstration in every HEW regional office coast to coast" to begin April 5 unless the regulations were issued by that date.[2]

Rallies and sit-ins were staged in New York, Boston, Philadelphia, Washington, DC, Chicago, Denver, San Francisco, and other cities around the country. These sit-ins, although they made their point, generally ended after only a single night. In Washington, for instance, the more than three hundred demonstrators sitting in at HEW federal headquarters were forced to leave after the police refused to allow them food, water, and medications.

In San Francisco, however, demonstrators managed to hang on for twenty-five days and nights, a historic record for a sit-in of any federal building. Organizers there, in addition to bringing their own caches of food and medication, were also able to enlist local community groups, labor unions, and even the city government in support. Food was provided by the local chapter of the Black Panther Party, while the International Association of Machinists and Aerospace Workers and Mayor Moscone's office eventually provided logistical and moral support, including mats and portable showers.

The sight of people in wheelchairs, people who were Deaf or blind or who had multiple disabilities, willing to risk their health and even their lives to make a political statement brought national media attention. It also catalyzed disability activists across the country and around the world. The success of the HEW demonstrations, and the San Francisco occupation in particular, evoked feelings of pride and empowerment among people who had for too long been told to be ashamed and silent. As Judy Heumann put it, "There was a real sense of victory and power, which was not an illusion."[3] Mary Jane Owen, a participant in the San Francisco sit-in, explained, "It didn't matter if you were mentally retarded, blind, or deaf. Everybody who came out felt: 'We are beautiful, we are powerful, we are strong, we are important.'"[4]

Judith Heumann (continued)
"We had the civil rights aura.

Judy Heumann, after her successful lawsuit against the New York City school system and her groundbreaking work organizing Disabled in Action, moved to Berkeley at the behest of Ed Roberts, arriving in 1973 to become a member of the Center for Independent Living's board of directors. While in Berkeley she earned her master's degree in public health administration and planning from the University of California, serving her internship during 1974 as a legislative assistant to Senator Harrison Williams (D-NJ), chair of the Senate Labor and Public Welfare Committee. In that position she made important contacts among Washington insiders well-placed to further the independent living and disability rights agendas and became a force within the American Coalition of Citizens with Disabilities while retaining her edge as a grassroots organizer and advocate of nonviolent direct action.

From 1975 to 1982, Heumann was the deputy director of the CIL, and she is largely credited as the catalyst and leader not only of the HEW occupation in San Francisco but of the broader national effort to convince Joseph Califano to issue the regulations enforcing Section 504 of the Rehabilitation Act of 1973.

We had an ACCD board meeting in February '77. People were very frustrated. Carter had been elected, and many of us had worked on his campaign, but still, the regulations hadn't happened.

I believe I was the one that made the recommendation that we set a date specific and have demonstrations. If the regulations weren't promulgated by that day, there would be demonstrations around the country. We planned the date for April. And Frank [Bowe] and Eunice [Fiorito] and the people back East were going to keep doing the work that they were doing, working with members of Congress, and with people in HEW, et cetera.

We recognized from the beginning the importance of 504. We recognized very early that it was a twenty-six-word law that was going to have to get interpreted. We were beginning to work with John Wodatch and others, [knowing] that we had to be able to get in there and make the case for specificity.

But everybody was learning as they were doing. What happened is this law [section 504] came out, and the recipients of federal financial assistance were totally caught off guard. And they started organizing. If they didn't know about it, and they stayed out of this, none of this would have been a problem. But it was their desire to minimize the impact, and to leave the regulations as brief as possible, because that would leave it more up to interpretation in the courts. I'm sure that was their rationale. . . .

I think part of what was going on was a breakdown in communication. Because there were these new people [the Carter administration] who came in who hadn't been involved in the previous process. They didn't know any of us. Califano didn't know any of us. And Califano was, of course, influenced by the lobbyists, and not by the disability advocates.

When we went downtown for the San Francisco demonstration, there were just a few of us who had thought about staying in the building. I think Kitty [Cone] and I had had some discussions the night before about, "Well, should we think about staying? What would we be looking for?" And I remember packing some things in my bag: toothbrush, pair of underpants. I thought, "Well, we'll be there for a night or something." The majority of the planning was for that day. It was to get a lot of people, cross-disability, union, religious community, a lot of press, et cetera. But I would say we absolutely did *not* plan for a long sit-in in the building. Kitty may have thought about it more and not really articulated it. I don't know. But the infrastructure was there to be able to do it.

Berkeley is a small community, period. Ed Roberts lived on the same block as Loni Hancock [a member of Berkeley City Council]. So when I moved into Ed's place for a while, I met her. And that's just the way it is. Brooklyn, New York, you know, there are like four million people in Brooklyn. So in a couple of blocks, you have the whole city of Berkeley. But I think it does go to show that the more intimate relationships you can develop with people, where they can begin to trust you and learn about your issues, then people can use their skills to support what you are trying to do. And we did that over and over and over again.

People had been growing to accept this disability movement that was happening, and this group, the Center for Independent Living. And when [California assemblyman Frank] Lanterman came out [to the sit-in], and when [San Francisco mayor George] Moscone came out, when we were able to get the media, when [journalist] Evan White was doing regular publicity, then it became an international issue. I mean, there was national press coming. And I remember TASS came—the Russian news agency. TASS came into the building to do interviews.

There was the Independent Living Center in San Francisco, Ray Uzeta and that crowd, [the local politicians and media] knew them, because again, San Francisco's bigger, but still not huge. So all of the centers in the beginning had connections to the local politicians. And Ed [Roberts by this time] was the director of the Department of Rehabilitation, a [Governor Jerry] Brown appointee. And Lanterman and Ed obviously knew each other well. I mean, the state was sending down mattresses. Moscone is like trying on the phone to get us showers. I remember when I heard that I'm like, "What?"

The first couple days we were there, there was this same scenario that had happened in New York when we had taken over Nixon headquarters in 1972. There was a bomb threat called in when we were in New York. When there is a bomb threat, your first thought is, "We better get out of this building." But then there was just something about what was going on: if there's a real bomb threat, these police look pretty calm. I know at the end of the day they don't want to get blown up any more than I do, so I'm going to trust the fact that if they really felt there was a bomb, they'd want their butts out of the building. So we just ignored it.

So when there was the bomb threat in the HEW building in San Francisco, we did the same thing. We said, "Well, we could move to another part of the floor," while they did what they had to do. As I recall, I think there actually was something found. But obviously whatever it was, they dealt with it.

We had the civil rights aura, we had the facts. I mean I think the civil rights aura without the facts actually doesn't get you where you need to be. But the facts without the civil rights perspective doesn't necessarily get you there either. So I think there has to be a true resolve that what we are doing is reflective of what a larger group of people agree needs to happen. And then you have to be resolute. It's always been, in my view, for myself, you never walk away from something. I mean "never" is maybe too strong a word, but pretty much never. I will not give up on something that I think is wrong, even if it's something [happening] just to me. Because my thought is, if it's happening to me, it's happening to other people. And somebody's got to take a position at some point in time and deal with it.

I think the 504 regulations and everything surrounding it was a real opportunity for us to think amongst ourselves about what we wanted the regulations to look like. What was too much. What was too little. How to negotiate. We obviously all had good negotiation skills. But it really pushed us. And the demonstrations themselves really pushed us to be able to put forth the strongest argument.

There definitely are provisions in the 504 regs that aren't as strong as we would like. But that was one of the reasons I think why we fought so hard for those regulations. We'd spent years negotiating, and had given up things that we didn't want to give up. So for us that was the bottom line, and we were not going to go below that bottom line. I think we completely believed that we had to go for this, we had to go for broke.

Kitty Cone (continued)
"There was always singing going on in the halls."

Kitty Cone was already a seasoned political organizer when she took a leading role in pulling together the San Francisco sit-in. Her experience as a civil rights, antiwar, and feminist activist would prove invaluable as the Bay Area disability rights community, most especially the Berkeley CIL, crafted its response to the call by the ACCD to make April 5, 1977, a national day of reckoning for HEW.

I thought the idea of a sit-in was a great tactic for a variety of reasons. Organizing people with disabilities to get together to plan an action is sometimes very difficult, and you've got all kinds of issues involved in notifying people through TTYs [teletypewriters for people who are deaf or hard of hearing] and producing materials in braille and getting the word out to all the people. Also, with people with severe disabilities, you've got transportation problems. I mean, can you imagine how difficult it was in New York City—remember, there was no accessible transit; there wasn't paratransit, there was nothing in those days.

A sit-in was much better than a one-day action where you've got people out but there was no response, you lost the momentum, and then you had to try to do it again. Because if you've got people there, with all the support systems necessary—as much as possible—then you had a sustained action, you put the administration into a very difficult position public relations–wise. You had people together and you didn't have to keep bringing them back and forth.

The other thing, which is very obvious, is that a sit-in was a tactic of the civil rights movement, and it was a way of drawing the parallels between this issue and the civil rights movement of the sixties. People all over the country were not thinking of people with disabilities as an op-pressed minority or a group deserving of civil rights; they were thinking of people with disabilities as objects of charity, objects of pity, probably a group of people who were very weak. So a sit-in was a really good tactic to show that we were a civil rights movement and part of the whole his-tory of struggling for progress for our community.

In addition to all these reasons, a sit-in was an excellent strategy because rather than waiting until watered-down regulations were issued publicly and then responding to them issue by issue, this meant the government would have to respond to us.

We held the 504 Emergency Coalition meetings at CIL, and initially we called a meeting of every single organization that we could think of that might be interested: the different independent living centers, dif-ferent organizations serving people with vision impairments, hearing impairments, what was then called Aid Retarded Citizens. We built like a little ACCD in the Bay Area and even reaching beyond the immediate San Francisco area.

At those meetings we never talked publicly about the fact that we were going to have a sit-in. We told people individually to bring their sleeping bags, that there was going to be a sit-in, but [we never mentioned the sit-in] when we were planning outreach, or the rally, or getting medics or getting monitors.

Connie Souci was in charge of getting medics. Judy Heumann always feels we should not emphasize this, because she doesn't want it to have any sort of medical taint to it. But for any big demonstration you always have medics. You don't know what's going to happen—if somebody's going to faint or if the cops are going to hit you on the head. So it's normal operat-ing procedure to have medics for a demonstration. But we also involved people who were rehab docs and who were part of the movement. We knew that if we did stay there any length of time there were going to be issues that we were going to have to deal with—people there were going to be using catheters and needing particular drugs and that sort of thing. But mostly the medics would just deal with regular stuff.

It wasn't a formal coalition. It wasn't something where you pay dues and had official membership; it was something where you came and represented yourself and your constituency. It was like a "one person, one vote" kind of thing. In those meetings we decided who would speak at the rally and who we would try to do outreach to. We knew that we wanted to bring in other civil rights organizations, other constituencies, trade unions, and churches—that we wanted to build the broadest community support that we possibly could. I had a lot of contacts at that time because I was not too many years away from my work that I had done for the SWP [Socialist Workers Party], organizing for CoDEL [Committee for Democratic Election Laws], or the women's movement or whatever.

It was pretty obvious to us who you contacted. The black organizations were the NAACP, the Black Panther Party, different church groups. We contacted the San Francisco Council of Churches and Glide Memorial Church. Of course, [Reverend] Cecil Williams and Glide are an entire force in the city themselves.[5] Also Delancey Street, which is a program for ex-prisoners and a recovery program for people who had been addicted to drugs or alcohol, and which was one of the groups that was affected by the 504 regulations and was the subject of great controversy.

I remember making the leaflet. This was back before the days of computers. I made the leaflet using those little plastic letters that you cut out with an Exacto knife. I remember being at Judy Heumann's house, and we were trying to think of what would be a good slogan. How could you possibly encompass this complex issue in a leaflet to get people to come out? We came up with a slogan: "People with disabilities: The federal government is trying to steal our civil rights." [Laughs.] If you stop and think about it, what the heck does it mean? But then we have a little paragraph explaining that section 504 defends our civil rights, and the federal government is trying to weaken it. Then it said, "Demonstrate April 5," and the time of the rally.

So we had bundles of these leaflets that we were taking around. And Mary Jane Owen was calling groups and saying, "Would you take some leaflets? Would you notify your membership?" I believe Steve McClelland, another deaf guy, was one of the paralegals. They were lining up interpreters, and they were lining up sound equipment. There was a particular group of people who worked on the rally. The speakers, I believe, were decided at the big meetings—who we wanted. Then people would contact them. All the information basically came back through the Center's Paralegal Project telephone number.

I remember being nervous about what was going to happen. How were we going to get in the building? Were they going to close the doors on us as we were going in? I had no idea what it looked like inside the building; I'm sure we had sent people over there to look at it, but I just didn't have any idea what it was like. I remember being up on the stage and looking out and thinking that it was a very good size crowd and that it was very broad in terms of disability and race. And then I remember that we all raced for the door. I think we all went in one door, but that can't be right. All the wheelchairs went up this ramp on the side of the building. Judy Heumann gave the signal, and we all just went in.

A lot of people had come with a sleeping bag. I brought a couple of pillows out of my van. My attendant stayed for a few days and then left. Some attendants stayed for the entire time; they were absolutely incredible—like Avril Harris—she was just fabulous. Avril had a schedule: every morning she came and brought me two cups of coffee, and she would say, "Here, drink your coffee. I'll go get Judy up and then I'll be back for you." Then she'd go get Judy up—didn't take too long because there was nowhere to take a bath or anything. [Laughs.] Then she'd come get me up, and then she'd get up a few more people. Nancy Di Angelo was the person that she had come in with.

In the beginning, we were sure that the police were going to come in. We would discuss how we were going to react if the police came in. Were we going to engage in passive resistance? Were we going to just go out?

One thing that amazes me is the physical stamina—I think we were all operating on adrenalin overload for a month. We would have these mass meetings of everybody in the building, every evening, to discuss how we should respond strategically, and sometimes they didn't end until one or two in the morning, and we'd go to bed and then we'd get up at five-thirty in the morning so we could clean up and be prepared for when the workers came into the office the next day.

I slept the same place every night. I slept in this closet off the main conference room. I had to be turned over at night, so my attendant was turning me the first few nights, and then somebody else was doing it. Debbie Stanley, this blind woman, began to do it at a certain point, and I was sleeping on those cushions that I had brought out of my van. I was actually probably more comfortable than a lot of people. I remember I was wolfing down sleeping pills to get through the pain from sleeping on the floor and from just sitting from five-thirty in the morning until sometimes three o'clock at night and getting like two-and-a-half hours of lie-down sleep time.

Most people were sleeping on the floor in the big conference room, and then some people were sleeping in different offices—somebody would climb up over the transoms and go inside and unlock the door. Judy was sleeping in the elevator. She had her own little private bedroom, and so did I. I remember there was a lot of card playing that went on. During down times, people would play cards. I don't recall ever having one minute of down time myself, personally.

We sang a lot of freedom songs, like "This Little Light of Mine," and "Oh, Freedom," and "We Shall Overcome." A couple of people had brought their guitars: Jeff Moyer[6] and Debbie Stanley. Debbie Stanley had a voice like an angel—a very, very powerful voice. We sang "Amazing Grace." Judy has a nice voice. Debbie had a nice voice. There were a couple of other people who had nice voices, but when we sang "Amazing Grace" we really sounded like a caterwauling batch, I must say. But the singing was something that kept up our morale and reminded us that we were a civil rights movement. There was always singing going on in the halls, and whenever the press came we began to sing too.

We had televisions. We would watch the news and listen to the news on the radio. We would go through the newspapers and we would see what kind of coverage we had gotten. In the beginning, it was "an army of crippled and deaf and dumb people went into the federal building." So we decided that we were going to have to educate the press. On day two we held a news conference and talked about terminology. I remember that we didn't like the term "crippled." We didn't like the term "deaf and dumb." We didn't single out particular reporters, although I can remember which ones used them, to this day. We would say, "Well, we got coverage on this but it's focusing too much on the state of the demonstrators, so we want to make sure that the issues get out," and we would pick a particular issue.

Here's a concrete example. One day we were going to focus on why you need to have interpreters in hospitals. So we organized a news conference, and the press was just hungry for anything that they could use to add information to the story other than just the fact that we were there. So Dale Dahl spoke to the press about his personal experience when he broke his neck, that he was deaf, he broke his neck, he was in the hospital, there were no interpreters, he had no idea what was happening, no one could communicate with him. There he was in the hospital, he didn't know whether he was going to get well, he didn't know why he couldn't feel, he couldn't communicate with his nurses. It was very compelling.

Corbett O'Toole (continued)
"I think the secret history of the 504 sit-in is that we never, ever would have made it without the Black Panthers."

Corbett O'Toole, by now a staff member at the CIL, was one of those who stayed through the entire twenty-five-day occupation.

The bureaucrats at HEW laughed at us. We were nothing to them. I mean, we were like an insignificant nothing: we were not the AMA lobby, we were nobody; we didn't exist. We were gnats on the face of the earth—not even gnats, we weren't even up to the level of gnats.

So ACCD said, "Fine," and issued an ultimatum, which was being ignored. And groups affiliated with ACCD around the country made the decision that they were going to go in to the federal regional offices of HEW, set up a meeting with the federal people in advance on April 5. Because of course the government forgot that we issued this ultimatum, so they allowed us to come into their buildings and have meetings with them. And we weren't going to leave.

So groups of disabled people went into all ten federal regional offices of Health, Education, and Welfare and held sit-ins. In a few cases, some groups decided not to hold sit-ins but just to have meetings with the regional director, but in other cities these people decided to stay—just camp out, sleep over, whatever. Some people lasted a couple of days, some people lasted—I think the longest ahead of us was about four or five days. The people in the Bay Area lasted the whole time.

A whole bunch of things happened very quickly. One is that the [HEW San Francisco] regional director went home for the day and essentially never came back, so we took over his offices. Somebody went out and scrounged an old refrigerator box, and taped it to the director's air conditioning machine to create a refrigerator for people that had medications that needed to be refrigerated. The building went into a shut-down mode—the FBI showed up after a few days and shut the building down. They allowed the employees in, but . . . we couldn't come and go because we wouldn't have been allowed back in.

So there were 150 of us inside the building and we're not able to leave the building, but we could wander within the building. The first week was really when they put the thumbscrews on. They figured, "Oh, this is a group of disabled people, they're going to leave in a couple of days," so they didn't give us any access to the media. They thought they'd get rid of us. The media did a blackout on us for a few days. Everybody was in the blackout mode—you know, ignore them, they'll go away, it's no big deal.

What they didn't realize was because of the diversity of people with disabilities, we had lots of communications channels. We were up on the fourth floor and the phones were cut off, so we couldn't call out, people couldn't call in, and people couldn't get information. We just went to the windows because every day the people in the disabled community—a whole bunch of people that didn't want to live in the building and that wanted to be involved—came every day. It was a beautiful building and there was a giant quarter-acre plaza right in front of the building and every day there was a demonstration outside. There were protesters and there were speeches and there were microphones.

What would happen is we would be on the fourth floor and we would sign the news of what was happening in sign language to the people downstairs. Then an interpreter downstairs would tell the media what was going on up in the building and that's how we avoided the communication blockade of the FBI and the non-disabled people thinking that we couldn't figure out how to survive.

The second big issue that we had was food. We could carry in only so much food and there wasn't a cafeteria in the building, or if there was, we didn't have access to it. They figured they would starve us out, which is actually what they did in a couple of other cities. One of the people with us was a black man who was part of the Black Panthers. He called up the Panthers and said, "I'm here in this demonstration." So the Panthers turned on the news and saw that we were occupying a federal building, which they thought was really nifty. They thought that anybody that challenged the federal government's domain over their lives and were fighting for self-sufficiency and rights were cool people. And they had one guy in there and so they showed up.

They were running a soup kitchen for their black community in East Oakland and they showed up every single night and brought us dinner. The FBI was like, "What the hell are you doing?" They answered, "Listen, we're the Panthers. You want to starve these people out, fine, we'll go tell the media that that's what you're doing, and we'll show up with our guns to match your guns and we'll talk about who's going to talk to who about the food. Otherwise, just let us feed these people and we won't give you any trouble"—and that's basically what they did.

I think the secret history of the 504 sit-in is that we never, ever would have made it without the Black Panthers. The Black Panthers fed us dinner—they fed 150 people of which only one was a Panther—every single night for the whole demonstration. We never would have survived without them.

The first week was the toughest. We're sleeping on the floor, there were no shower facilities whatsoever. I think the feds figured, "Oh, they'll fight [with each other], or people will get cranky and get tired of sleeping on the floor, and get tired of sleeping in their sleeping bags." What they really underestimated was our determination. We were high. We were ecstatic. A lot of us who were disabled as kids had gone to crippled kids camp—we thought it was camp! [Laughs.] We didn't care. You know, we survived surgery! We survived hospitals! This was nothing! We had choices here. We could go to that inaccessible bathroom or *that* inaccessible bathroom. We could go down the halls by ourselves, we were with our friends, I mean, they were never going to get us out of there!

Then they kept thinking, "Okay, we'll just wait for the leaders to screw up." What they didn't realize was we, as a community, didn't function by leaders. . . . The feds were looking for a model, a traditional power structure of one leader, preferably a man. What they found instead was . . . two men and six women who were primarily the leaders of the 504 sit-in—just kind of talking to the community and hanging out and helping us all.

We would have meetings where we would make decisions as groups:

Okay, the feds are saying this to us, do we want to do this? Or the feds are saying things like, "There's a bomb in the building, you have to get out!" We're like, "Yes, right, okay, fine." Or, "It's really dangerous for you to be here." "Yes, okay, fine." But they'd tell Judy or Ed, and Judy or Ed would tell us, and we'd all go, "Okay, fine, we're just going to hang out here."

By about ten days in we were doing things like walking into employees' offices with people when they showed up for work in the morning. We picked up the phone when it rang and would say, "Hello, 504 sit-in," before handing the phone over to the employees. So we were impacting a lot of aspects of the building and the business. So cutting off the phones hadn't worked. Cutting off communication with the outside world hadn't worked. Denying us access to bathing hadn't worked. The disabled people knew they were going to be in for the long haul, and had brought plenty of medications and stuff. We realized about five days in that they couldn't beat us.

About ten days in, the media realized that this was a great story. We were breaking the record for a sit-in. There was no media downside to this drama. In the past—at Pine Ridge[7] or wherever—there were guns or whatever, so that the whole aspect of what the struggle was about was really ousted by the media point of view of guns and stuff. But we didn't have any guns. I mean, we had wheelchairs, you know. . . .

The next thing you know, [George] Moscone, who was the mayor of San Francisco, shows up and says, "Oh, this is an emergency housing situation." So they invoke some emergency housing regulations. And the next thing you know, the guy that's the head of the state health department shows up, because the local and state folks are having a blast making the feds look bad, and say, "Oh, it's an emergency shelter." They treated it like a Red Cross place and the next thing you know we had blankets, pillows, a little kid's bathtub with a hose that you could hook up to the sink so we could take baths.

The health guy said, "These guys have to have access to health care providers." He considered attendants to be health care providers, and suddenly we started getting passes to be able to come and go from the building. People could come and go—say "I'm an attendant"—and suddenly new people could come in, which was the feds' worst fear—to have these people show up: "Oh, I'm blind, and I'm an attendant," and they come in the building with a backpack and food, not to leave. So the tide started to turn in a pretty dramatic way, which was great for us.

CBS started to show up in the hallways. And while our physical survival went up a minuscule—in terms of we had blankets and beds, mattresses instead of nothing—it was more our emotional support that went up really dramatically because people felt like we were winning. And we were. We had outlasted them and nobody was going to shoot us and all these things were happening. . . .

The government realized at this point that we had won the sentiments of the press, and the disabled community was all in agreement that the previous regulations from the previous administration were livable and that Califano had to sign them. So finally, on May 4, Carter just said to Califano, "I don't give a damn. Sign the regs and then get this thing over with. . . ."

Then we had a wonderful, victorious, fabulous exodus—there's actually some [film] footage of us leaving the building. It was wonderful to get out of that building. Nobody was physically injured on either side—not the guards, not the FBI, and not us. No weapons were used. It was all a battle of words and a battle of wills, and it was very successful. Now, I believe—someone had told me this as a historical fact—that we actually hold the record for the longest occupation of federal property, certainly the most nonviolent occupation of federal property, but I believe it's also the longest.

Mary Jane Owen
"She ended up by saying, 'I've always wanted to be beautiful, but now I know I am beautiful.'"

Mary Jane Owen was born Evanston, Illinois, in June 1929, "but I used to lie about my age. There's a tremendous amount of age prejudice, and I figured it was enough to be blind, and to bear that sort of discrimination. To add my age was just too much. But I'm out of the closet now."

Owen, a leader and mentor in the disability rights movement, especially for younger women in the 1970s and '80s, comes from a tradition of political activism. "Both of my parents were ministers, and both were early advocates for civil rights. If I ever saw anyone of dark complexion in the little town where we lived, I knew they were staying at our house." In addition to being a minister, her father was also the publisher of the local newspaper.

Owen herself was involved in the civil rights movement well before she became a disability rights activist. As a young woman in the 1940s (before becoming blind) Owen was a student of Gandhism at the New School for Social Research in New York City. In 1951 she moved to Albuquerque, where she became a founding member of the city's chapter of the Congress of Racial Equality (CORE), going to Los Angeles during the summers to attend CORE's training and action program at Chapman College. She remembers being "slammed by a fire hose through a plate glass window" when she and others tried to integrate a racially segregated swimming pool in Los Angeles. By the mid-1960s she was refusing to pay her federal taxes as a form of protest against the Vietnam War, as well as working toward her master's degree in social work, which she received in 1966 from the University of California at Berkeley.

Owen's work in the cross-disability rights movement began in 1972, as her eyesight deteriorated and she took a position as a paralegal at the CIL's Disability Rights Center, the precursor to the Disability Rights Education and Defense Fund. With her experience as a civil rights and antiwar activist, she was well placed to be a major participant in the occupation of the San Francisco HEW offices in 1977.

Most people bedded down in the big conference room because it had a rug on the floor. I ended up in a little room off the big room, with Kitty Cone and her attendant. My mobility teacher was also there, and so the four of us had this kind of cubby hole where we slept for a couple of nights.

There wasn't a lot on television or in the newspapers about what had happened in DC. But that first full day, when we found out that they were being starved out, I said, "Well, my civil rights are more important to me than food. I'm going on a hunger strike." My mother was a great one for hunger strikes, so that wasn't something original with me, that was just a family tradition. And I invited anybody who wanted to join me to do so. There were probably ten of us that ended up on a hunger strike for the complete time, drinking only fruit juice during the day. I think that, in many ways, that was another inspiring kind of thing to those who didn't go on the hunger strike, that there were some of us who were there for the long haul, no matter what happened.

I can't remember how many days later that Ed Roberts came down with a load of mattresses, but when that happened I switched to sleeping on a mattress behind a couple of piled up desks. A young woman post-polio who had braids, braces, and Canadian crutches was sleeping crossways, along with the young man who had come in to be an attendant, and they fell in love at the foot of my pallet. I became an attendant for one of the guys there, and that was an interesting experience for me because, of course, I was blind, although I didn't have any movement or mobility problems. I had never been an attendant before.

About midway through it all I fell and hurt my foot. There were people who wanted me to leave, but I refused. There was a sort of infirmary set up inside the building, an informal free clinic. I stayed there for a while, but the people there finally prevailed upon me to leave to see a doctor. But I was able to get back in, but in a leg brace. So I started the occupation being blind but able to walk, but ended it using a wheelchair. If you see the film of us marching out of the building in triumph at the end, you'll see me in my wheelchair.

Jeff Moyer was there, playing his guitar, tooting on his harmonica. We had already decided that we were going to sing the workers into the building, which we did, every morning. I had my collapsible white cane and I would beat rhythm. I had to get another cane because I broke the rubber elastic in my old cane from my energetic beating. You know, just singing songs. "We Shall Overcome" is the one that sticks in my memory.

Parading around, singing our defiant songs every morning—no matter how disheartened I might get in the middle of the night—that just empowered me. I remember how, as Easter approached, we got yellow daffodils. I don't know who paid for them, but it was great, especially since I was such a great believer in flower power. We had these yellow daffodils and handed them out to all the staff people when they came in the Friday before Easter. And there were these two priests with us, who were wonderful. I was not Catholic at that point, but I was certainly Christian. And they did a Good Friday service. Judy held some Jewish services, Jewish gatherings, so there was a certain spiritual sense.

I'm also very, very impressed with touch. There was a time when a lot of people were feeling the strain, and so we formed a big, long chain of people on the floor. Everybody got down on the floor, one in back of the other, and we gave each other neck and shoulder massages. And that was great fun. We did different things like that, to help us feel like a community. So we felt like brothers and sisters, all of us struggling together.

As the days went by, and I continued not to eat, I did grow weaker. And I think all of us that ended up maintaining the hunger strike, we did get quite weak toward the end, and were not as a vital as we might have been in the beginning. I can remember one press release that I was working on, I was really, really fatigued, and so I had to redo this press release like six or eight times because my brain just wasn't working that well.

There was an older woman, or at least back then she seemed like an older woman. Maybe she was in her fifties, and she was involved with transportation in San Francisco. I don't remember her name. But one time when we were all sitting around in the circle drinking our juice and talking, strategizing, she said, "I'm your fairy godmother. I can grant you one wish. And what is your wish?" And so, we all went around the circle, saying what we wanted. And there were probably as many people that said they wanted the 504 regs to be signed as there were that said they wanted a hamburger or something like that. It was just each person speaking from their heart and speaking with passion.

But, I'll never forget this young girl that was sleeping on the pad at my feet. She told a story about how she had always hated being on crutches, and she had always wanted to be beautiful. And she talked about what that beauty meant to her: it would mean not having to wear the braces, not having to use the crutches, not being ridiculed by her classmates, and all of that. And then she ended up by saying, "I've always wanted to be beautiful, but now I know I *am* beautiful."

And that was a very, very powerful instance for me, what this wonderful young woman was saying. I know I'm beautiful now in spite of the fact that I'm disabled, in spite of the fact that I'm small or blind or what-have-you. I'm beautiful. But I think that that's something that transpired in some way or another for everybody that was in the building.

Kitty Cone (continued)
"It was the public birth of the disability civil rights movement."

Several weeks into the sit-in, many of the protesters became frustrated that negotiations between the ACCD leadership and the Carter administration had stalled. The group decided to send a delegation into "the belly of the beast"—

flying to Washington to put direct pressure on Califano personally. Judy Heumann, having worked as a congressional aide, still had contacts on Capitol Hill, while members of Kitty Cone's extended family actually lived on the same street as Secretary Califano.

I think our feeling was that things weren't changing in Washington, that we needed to add some West Coast pressure. . . . I think Frank Bowe and Eunice Fiorito—who was another one of the major leaders of ACCD— were doing the best that they could. But they had not been able to break into the *Washington Post,* they weren't getting any coverage, and we felt like if we came in as a contingent that we could bring a fresh force that could demand—with the moral authority of the sit-in behind us—to meet with the president, to meet with Califano, to meet with congressional leaders who had been involved in writing section 504, which is exactly what we did. I would imagine that it was Judy who was the primary person involved in making that decision, but I honestly can't remember.

One of the things that we did that I feel kind of ambivalent about was that when we decided to send a contingent to Washington, we had this election to elect a committee to choose the delegation. We felt like if we voted just on the delegation itself we didn't know what we were going to get. We might not get a racially representative group, not all the different disabilities represented—we wanted a representative group. Of course, Judy was elected to that committee, I was elected to the committee. Different people were elected to this committee, and we met and we chose a delegation which was a very good delegation.

I don't remember who arranged for us to sleep at this church. In any case, they allowed us to stay there. So some of the people slept in the pews, and some of us slept where they have the coffee receptions after church services. We slept in a big room, again on the floor. At this point, Debbie Stanley began to be my attendant. It was kind of neat because I would guide her, and she would take me to the bathroom and help me get dressed and get me up and down off the floor. Actually, I think it took a couple of people to get us up and down off the floor.

We had this meeting, and I always thought this was Frank Bowe's idea until I read an article where he said that he was distressed that we had gone and picketed Califano's house. So I guess it was actually Ralph

Abascal's[8] idea. Ralph says, "Why don't we go picket Califano's house?" And so we say, "Great idea," so they get out the phone book and they look up the address, and it's 25-something-something Springland Lane. And I go, "Oh, my God," because I know that Springland Lane is a street that's one block long—it's a cul-de-sac. My cousin, Jimmy, and his wife and kids lived on that street. Jimmy had just retired from being a general in the army. Then my great-aunt, his mother and father—who was also a general in the army—lived up the street. It turned out that they lived literally directly in front of Califano's house. To get to Califano's house, you had to kind of go around Aunt Mary's house.

We go out, and we sat there with our candles, and we very softly sang hymns and freedom songs or something. Then it was very early in the morning, and what happens but there goes my cousin Jimmy jogging past—the younger one. He sees us there, and he sees me. He comes over and he says, "This is really lovely. You're having a prayer service." [Laughs.] So I just keep my mouth shut and pray for him to go away. . . .

Califano always slipped out the back door. This was a tactic of ours: the Carter administration was calling itself the Open Door Administration. We attempted to utilize tactics that would either force them to come out the front door and meet with us and be confronted by us, or else would force them to go out the back door. Numbers of times when we were talking to the press we would say, "This is not an Open Door Administration; they keep going out the back door."

We had these meetings in the church every evening, and we continued to have our regular mass meetings where we would decide things. We had a number of different tactics that we were utilizing. One was that the contingent—primarily the California contingent but sometimes with the addition of Frank and Eunice and the people from Philadelphia and sometimes pretty much by itself—were just tagging around trying to get press coverage. We were also attempting to set up meetings with people in the Congress who we thought were important to the process, and we were attempting to get a meeting with Carter or somebody high up in the White House.

And another thing that we were doing was organizing larger demonstrations. I can't remember if we had one or two. We organized one at Lafayette Park across from the White House. A stage was built, and I remember that congressmen came and spoke. I remember realizing that it was much harder to organize in that area [Washington] because there wasn't transportation. A lot of people arrived in vans from group homes, I think. There weren't a lot of people in motorized wheelchairs who lived close to a transportation area, who had services, who were living independently in the community—people with physical disabilities—like we had in the Bay Area. When we were calling around to the different organizations, and I was asking somebody, "What's this group? And what's that group?" I realized that there was something akin to an independent living center—but it wasn't anything like the CIL in Berkeley—and that we weren't going to find a whole lot of people like ourselves. I know that a lot of the demonstrators at this demonstration and at the earlier sit-in that had been starved out at the HEW building in Washington were Deaf students from Gallaudet. So I think they must have come out to the demonstration as well.

I remember only two things about the flight back to San Francisco. I remember that the pressure in the cabin was so bad that Bobbi LaNoue started to cry because her ears hurt so badly, and that when we got to the airport I did interviews with the press about what we had accomplished. Then we came back to the building. When we got back to the building, I realized that the people in the building were very glad to have us back because I think that they had been feeling a little bit cut off, although we were calling them from Washington every day and giving them a report. They would report to the larger group what was going on. But some people were getting kind of stir-crazy.

It was very shortly thereafter that the regulations were signed—very shortly after we got back. The regulations contained the concepts of equality and integration, and the affirmative steps that must be taken to achieve those for people with disabilities. In fact, the HEW Section 504 regulations established the basic principles that became the basis for legal compliance with the ADA [thirteen years later]. It established the right of an individual who has experienced discrimination to pursue an administrative remedy . . . as well as go to court.

Everyone was absolutely jubilant. We held a news conference, and we talked about how happy and proud we were that for the first time there was a federal civil rights law that was going to be implemented covering people with disabilities and that we felt that we had been victorious.

We planned this victory rally, and it was something else. All the media

was there, all our supporters came out, and we marched out of the building and down through the UN Plaza and held a rally. You can see tapes
of people coming out of the building, and they are so happy, and everybody's carrying their sleeping bag. It was probably one of the highest
moments in many of our lives.

I would say that there were victories on many levels that came out
of the sit-in. For one thing, it was the public birth of the disability civil
rights movement. People's image of themselves changed, and people felt
so proud of themselves. I'm trying to remember who it was—I think it
was Hollynn Fuller—Hollynn must be slightly younger than I am, and
she still looks like she could be a cheerleader. She's sort of the traditional
beautiful woman who wears high heels and has a lovely face and is so
ladylike. I think Hollynn Fuller said to me, "That was such a pivotal time
in my life. For the first time I felt okay about myself as a disabled person." Many people said exactly the same kind of thing. People who were
involved in the sit-in really were transformed.

15
Psychiatric Survivors

J UDI CHAMBERLIN CITES AS A FUNDAMENTAL PRINCIPLE OF THE
psychiatric survivor movement the belief that "all laws and practices which
induce discrimination toward individuals who have been labeled 'mentally
ill' need to be changed, so that psychiatric diagnosis has no more impact on a
person's citizenship rights and responsibilities than does a diagnosis of diabetes
or heart disease."[1] Indeed, many advocates reject the entire concept of "mental
illness" as socially constructed and having no grounding in any demonstrable
physical illness or pathology. These advocates contend that those individuals living through "altered" or "extreme states" are in fact responding to extreme stress
or trauma or experiencing profound religious or spiritual transformations which
our current era has come to define as symptomatic of a "mental illness."

However one defines the experience, it is an inescapable fact that those labeled "mentally ill" are among the most oppressed people in our society. Popular culture and mass media often portray them as strange, dangerous, and violent. These misconceptions are then used to justify many of the degrading and
harmful "treatments" that have been developed to "cure" people of their mental
illness, treatments which have included insulin-shock and electro-convulsive
therapy, incarceration for extended periods, isolation from family and friends,
and forced drugging. Certainly, before the advent of deinstitutionalization, hundreds of thousands of Americans labeled mentally ill were incarcerated for much
of their lives in massive state hospitals where neglect and abuse were rife.

"For centuries psychiatric inmates wanted to organize," says David Oaks,
a prominent voice in the movement. "In the 1800s there was a group called
'Friends of the Allegedly Insane' in England," and various support groups, such
as WANA (We Are Not Alone) in New York City, formed in the 1940s and
early '50s for current and former patients. But it wasn't until the 1970s that
"the infrastructure," as Oaks calls it, began to develop which enabled people to
think in more political terms.

"We had an analysis, that we took from the left, that had looked at economic oppression, and that was important. There were the examples of the civil rights movement, the women's movement, the prisoners' rights movement for us to draw on. Portland, Oregon, had one of the first survivor groups to form—1970—the Insane Liberation Front. It was gone before I started in the Mental Patients' Liberation Front in Boston, but we were in touch with Project Release, in New York City, and the Network Against Psychiatric Assault in Berkeley, which put out a publication called *Madness Network News*. So there was, as I like to put it, the sunlight, soil, fertilizer, and rain to make our organizing happen."[2]

Among the most influential of the early organizers was Howard Geld (1952–1995). Institutionalized when he was thirteen or fourteen years old (accounts vary), Geld spent more than a year in a facility for "disturbed youth." By age seventeen he was living on the streets of New York City, where he played his harmonica for change, earning his nickname "Howie the Harp" (or "Howie T. Harp"). Geld was a founding member both of Portland's Insane Liberation Front in 1970 and of the Mental Patients' Liberation Project in New York City in 1971, as well as Project Release, the nation's first client-run residence for people labeled mentally ill. The MPLP drafted and distributed a basic mental patient's bill of rights which articulated the core principles of the movement. "You have the right not to be treated like a criminal. . . . You have the right to refuse to be a guinea pig for experimental drugs and treatments," and so on.[3]

Geld, like David Oaks, believed that the struggle of psychiatric survivors was part of a broader movement for civil and human rights, encompassing prisoners and ex-prisoners, women, people of color, poor people, gays and lesbians, migrant workers and immigrants. Like Chamberlin, he was also involved in forging links to advocates in the independent living and disability rights movements. To this end, Geld in 1981 took a staff position with the Berkeley CIL, so that when advocates at DREDF and elsewhere began pushing in 1988 for an Americans with Disabilities Act, people labeled "mentally ill" were among those whose civil rights were to be explicitly protected.

Judi Chamberlin
"It all comes down to these very simple issues of human dignity."

Judi Chamberlin was born in 1944 to parents who were both "leftists." Her father "worked on the factory floor as a union organizer"; her mother was an office worker and, after returning to college, a school teacher. They both lived and worked in New York City. On one occasion, she recalls, "my father was involved in a strike, and I remember walking picket lines with my mom to support my father."

Chamberlin followed the typical path for a young woman in the early 1960s. By 1965, she was married, employed as a secretary, and expecting her first child. Devastated when she miscarried, she saw a psychiatrist who labeled her mourning over her lost child, her unhappiness with the general course of her life, and her inability "to function" as symptoms of schizophrenia. In 1966, Chamberlin was "treated" in a series of mental hospitals, both private and public, including Mount Sinai, Montefiore, Bellevue, and Rockland State, where she was drugged and confined, sometimes as a "voluntary admission" but often against her will. This was, as she wrote in her book, "the worst period of my life. My struggle to overcome the effects of this experience was what led me to become involved in the ex-patients' movement."

On Our Own, published in 1978, was Chamberlin's account of her journey through the mental health system. It cast her experience in a decidedly political light, contrasting the authoritarian way mental health services had traditionally been structured with "patient controlled alternatives" which Chamberlin saw as not only more humane but also as far more effective in addressing people's needs. Together with Frank Bowe's *Handicapping America,* Chamberlin's *On Our Own* stands as one of the most influential documents of the disability rights movement of the late 1970s.

Chamberlin, together with Rae Unzicker,[4] would also be instrumental in building bridges between the psychiatric survivor movement and the general disability rights movement of the 1980s and beyond. Among the organizations she cofounded was the National Empowerment Center in Lawrence, Massachusetts, often described as an independent living center for psychiatric survivors.

Judith Chamberlin died on January 16, 2010.

———

In the summer of 1971 I found out that there was a group in New York City that had just started a few months before, called the Mental Patients' Liberation Project. I found out about it through one of those little announcements in the *Village Voice.* And it was like, "Hey, wow, this is what I've been looking for." That was the first I knew there was any kind of organized opposition. And it just felt so wonderful to find other people.

People introduced themselves, and talked about where they'd been hospitalized and how long they'd been there. Most of the people that I met at that meeting had been through much more horrendous things than I had—people who had been locked up for ten years, for twenty years, been given shock treatments, all sorts of awful things. My experiences were tame compared to what a lot of those people had gone through. I remember one guy said, "I was in such and such a hospital, and I escaped." And everyone went "Yay!" and that felt so good. It was just a sense of, here I'd been thinking these things all by myself, and not even knowing if anybody else in the world thinks these things, and all of a sudden I'm in a room full of people who think these things. It was just so thrilling.

It was also pretty disorganized. Probably more men than women, but there were definitely women. A pretty broad age range: twenties, thirties, forties, maybe some people in their fifties. Most people were pretty poor. But it was just a real mix. We didn't use the term at the time, but it was half political meeting and half support group, meeting in a church basement.

It wasn't one of these organizations where everybody sits very quietly and seriously. A lot of people talking, a lot of general hubbub and trying to get some things done. Like, we wanted to write a flyer, and things like that. And how do we get more members, and collect a little money? Nobody had any money.

We put together this thing over the next few weeks called the Patients' Bill of Rights. We talked about becoming more visible, so one of the things we did was to stand outside Bellevue Hospital, and give this flyer with the Patients' Bill of Rights on it to people going in to visit, and ask them to bring it in to their relatives. Then we got invited to speak on a talk radio show. Nobody was willing to use their real name, everybody had a pseudonym. We went and spoke on one of those call-in shows, and the host really liked us, and invited us to come back for the following week. So I remember sitting outside the steps of the studio, deciding that we were going to use our real names—that this isn't anything to be ashamed of, and why are we hiding behind pseudonyms? I remember being asked to speak to a psychology class at NYU. So it was just different things, trying to make ourselves visible.

We used the term "mental patients." We said that we have to use that term, not in the sense that we acknowledge that there's an illness, but in the sense that that's what the world calls us. And I remember we were doing some stuff cooperatively with a group of gay guys who called themselves "the Flaming Faggots." And they were saying, "We're not going to let other people take these terms and hurt us with them, we're going to throw it all back at them." And that made a lot of sense. So we were saying: "We're mental patients, or we're ex-mental patients." Not embracing the ideology behind it, but embracing the term.

There was a lot of infighting. And a lot of that I think in retrospect had to do with how we were a group of people who had been so mistreated, so abused, and there was so much anger, that a lot of it began to come out against one another. You get caught up in the minutiae. So over the next year or two there were groups that split off from other groups. You know the scene in *Life of Brian*, where they're arguing the difference between the Liberation Front of this, and the Front for the Liberation of that?—that kind of stuff. A lot of badmouthing.

At some point—in 1973 I guess it was—we were contacted by a professor from Michigan. He wanted to put together a conference on the rights of people in the mental health system. I don't know how he even heard about us, or had the awareness that he should do it in conjunction with people like us, but it was certainly the right move. We thought it was a great idea, except he wanted to call it "The Rights of the Mentally Ill." We said, "No no, that's a horrible title. You can't call it that." So he said, "Okay, what should I call it?" We had this meeting where we sat around kicking around different names, and came up with the idea of "The Conference on Human Rights and Psychiatric Oppression." And that was held in Detroit in the summer of '73. I didn't go because I was working and couldn't get away, but a number of people from our group went and people were there from Detroit, from Kansas, from California. It was really exciting to us to know that this was happening in other places.

Then in '74 there was a second conference on Human Rights and Psychiatric Oppression, that was held in Topeka, Kansas, and Howie the Harp, Ted Chabasinski, and I went to Kansas about a month before to help with the organizing.

This was the beginning of networking, and at that time it was really difficult. Not only was there no Internet or e-mail, but even making a long distance phone call was a major undertaking economically. You made a long distance phone call for a couple of minutes, it cost a couple of dollars.

I ended up going to Vancouver in 1974 to see about this place called the Mental Patients' Association, because what we heard was that they were getting government funding, and that seemed so totally impossible. So I went there to see what that was all about, and ended up staying in Vancouver for a year. While I was there I had a very severe depressive quote unquote psychotic episode, and went to stay in a crisis facility that had been set up by a group of, not ex-mental patients, but semiprofessionals, maybe one or two of them had some degree. But it was an alternative crisis center, the Vancouver Emotional Emergency Center, and it was a place of real healing.

From what I learned about it afterwards, this was a group of people who had had very positive experiences themselves with alternative therapy, and wanted to make it available to people whose only other recourse was to end up in the mental health system. People were doing massage and yoga and there were different kinds of what we now call body work and emotional expression. I mean one of the things that happened in the traditional mental health system is that you really can't express strong emotions. If you cry or scream or whatever, you're considered to be out of control, and you're drugged or put in seclusion. And here was a place that said, "If you feel like crying you should cry. If you feel like screaming you should scream, and if you use those painful experiences in a positive way, you'll get through them."

And so I went to stay there, and had a very affirmative, life-changing experience. And it was after that that I decided I wanted to write, because I wanted to contrast what happens to people when they were diagnosed and put into mental hospitals and given drugs and have all their rights taken away with what happened when you treat people with dignity and allow them to determine what they need for themselves, and give them support. So that was really where the idea of writing the book came from.

I came back from Vancouver, and moved to Boston in 1976. I became involved with the Mental Patients' Liberation Front, the MPLF, which was started around the same time as the Mental Patients' Liberation Project in New York—two groups with almost the same name developing totally independently of each other. MPLF was formed in that early seventies period, and the original members came out of the political left, and definitely the name was meant to sound like the National Liberation Front [of Vietnam]. It was meant to shock, it was meant to get people's attention.

The MPLF was held out in the movement as being unique because of the organizing they were doing *inside* the hospitals. Primarily Boston State, where a group of people who were in the hospital and people from MPLF met once a week. And that coincided with a legal rights effort through Greater Boston Legal Services to develop a lawsuit to try to improve conditions in the hospital, mainly around the issues of forced medication, restraint, and seclusion. And the people who became the plaintiffs in that lawsuit were all or almost all people who were active in the patients' rights group, because they were becoming empowered. So we were involved as supporters of those folks, and attended a lot of the court hearings. And some of the people who were plaintiffs in the suit were retaliated against and one guy was kicked out of the hospital. Although it sounds like a good thing, it was really hard for him. He had been there for years and had no place to go, so we got involved in trying to help him, making sure that he wasn't abandoned.

The Rogers lawsuit took years.[5] We had some demonstrations around the case in the early eighties. When the decision came down we considered it a victory, but it has since been perverted so that it's now really another instrument of repression. What the court said was that you couldn't medicate somebody against their will, unless there was a court procedure, what was called a "substituted judgment," which have now become these totally rubber-stamp hearings, in which the hospitals win ninety-five point something percent of the time.

In 1976 the Conference on Human Rights and Psychiatric Oppression was held in Boston, and we did a demonstration in front of the Mass. Mental Health Center, which was an inpatient facility. Boston State Hospital had these big grounds, with a wall around them, but Mass. Mental Health Center was located on a street, so we could gather right in front. One of the traditions of the conference was there was always a march. It was a pretty big demonstration, we had like a hundred people, and we marched and then rallied in front of the center.

I remember a bunch of the Mass. Mental staff were gathered blocking the door, like they were afraid we were going to storm the place. And the patients were able to look out the window and see us. We were having conversations with them, yelling back and forth, and there was this one woman who was in a seclusion room, yelling out the window to us that she had been yelling for the staff to come unlock the door so she could go to the bathroom. And so we began chanting: "Let Selma go to the bathroom! Let Selma go to the bathroom!"

It was really a very exciting moment, because it all comes down to these very simple issues of human dignity. Eventually they started moving people out of the rooms that were facing the streets, taking them out of those rooms and moving them to other rooms. That made us feel very powerful. You could see that they were really scared of us.

A group of disabled people in Boston kind of modeled themselves on us, and called themselves the Disabled People's Liberation Front. We used to meet together, and that was the first real awareness I had of a connection with the physical disability rights movement. That was maybe 1977. And it was really neat that they kind of saw us as role models, and organized themselves along the same lines. These were two separate organizations, but we saw each other as sister organizations, supporting one another's issues. There was some overlap. I remember one of their members, a woman who used a wheelchair, got put in a mental hospital, and one of the ways they controlled her was they took away her wheelchair. So we could see our issues as connected.

Whenever I've been exposed to anything that was cross disability, I've always found it very exciting. But a lot of people in the psychiatric survivor community at that point, and to a lesser extent still to this day, were skeptical of cross-disability stuff. You know, "We're not really disabled." And that's where a lot of the hassle around, "Are we part of the disability movement?" comes in. Because for people who define it as: "I don't have anything wrong with me, I've just come smack-up against this system that is oppressive"—they have problems with being part of the disability community, because they say, "Well, other people really do have disabilities, and we don't." I still have a hard time with it, and I continue to fight those battles within my own community with people who don't get it, although there are fewer and fewer of those, as the years go by. And it cuts both ways. There are people in the physical disability community who will say, "We're not crazy." There's still a lot of misunderstanding. But to me, from the very first time I was ever involved in anything cross disability, it just always seemed so clear.

I think that the difficulty we have as psychiatric survivors in getting our story out is greater than probably any other disability. We're so demonized in the press. There's so much about violence, and "the unmedicated mental patient." It's very rare that you get any kind of sympathetic public portrayal of someone with a mental illness. It's not common, but it's not as rare, to get it for people with other disabilities. I just happened to be channel switching on TV last week in a hotel room and I came upon this little half hour show on HBO which was kids talking about living with Tourette's Syndrome. An absolutely lovely piece of film. And we don't have stuff like that.

And then of course there's this whole question of what's stigmatizing and what's not stigmatizing. A lot of what's called "anti-stigma" work in mental health is controlled by people who are trying to medicalize it, and a lot of the money that's spent on what's called "anti-stigma education" is really about getting people into treatment. "We have to do away with the stigma so people won't be afraid to go for the treatment that they need." So I don't even like the word "stigma," I prefer to talk about discrimination. Stigma says, "There's something wrong with you, but I'll overlook it because I'm such a nice guy." And discrimination says, "The law protects people's rights."

It's like racial integration. You don't have to like me, but I have the right to live next door to you, whether you like me or not. And so the question is, do you change public attitudes first, and the law will follow, or do you change the law first and public attitudes will follow? And my feeling is if you wait for public attitudes to change, you're going to be waiting for a damn long time.

Ted Chabasinski (continued)
"'You can't let these disturbed people have a voice in what happens to them.'"

Ted Chabasinski was released from the Rockland State Hospital in April 1954, after turning seventeen. He had spent most of his childhood in institutions, where he was physically and sexually abused and subjected to repeated electroshock "treatments" as part of an experiment to see what effect they would have on a child. He spent some time as a "board and care" resident, living with a family who were paid by the state to take in people with "mental illness" or disability.

"There I am in Sloatsburg [New York], because I had a job there, packing groceries in an A&P. I remember I was on the bus and there were these two teenage girls behind me. One of them was saying 'Oh, that's that new boy in town.' The other girl was saying 'No, he's not a new boy, he lives with the Davises, he's one of *those* people.' The Davises being the board and care operators. 'He's not a new boy,' in other words, I'm not a human being, so there was no reason for this girl to get excited about me. I'm one of the people that the Davises take in. I remember that really clearly.

"We're talking about the fifties, the age of the zombies. There was no group I could join, so I just had to put up with it. I knew I wasn't crazy. How could I be crazy? I'd seen plenty of crazy people, I knew what being crazy was like. The fucking ironic thing was, after spending eleven years of my childhood in these fucking loony bins, I was just as sane as they were."

Chabasinski then found work at a wholesale fabric company, and with the assistance of the state vocational rehabilitation program was eventually able to enter first New York University and then the City College of New York (CCNY). Once on campus he became politically active, joining a local chapter of the NAACP in 1959.

"A lot of northern liberals and progressives organized to support the black people in the South, who had to sit in segregated lunch counters. We were organizing sympathy picket lines, and I became kind of a leader in that. I did it because I recognized that their oppression was just like mine. Here are these people being pointed to, 'They're not human, they don't deserve any respect, we're going to treat them like dirt.' By this time I was twenty-two, just turning twenty-three in 1960. That was the beginning of my political activity." Chabasinski graduated from CCNY in 1961, after which he worked as a welfare case manager and a probation officer.

"In 1971, I found about this group called the Mental Patients' Liberation Project in New York, founded by this guy, Howie the Harp." By this time Chabasinski had become the New York City organizer for the Young People's Socialist League, but was eventually disillusioned by what he saw as the divisiveness and petty politics, not only in the league but in the mental patients' liberation movement as well. His work life, too, left him less than satisfied. "I wasn't cut out to be a probation officer, because I wasn't authoritarian enough. I felt I was wasting my life, I was not accomplishing what I wanted to accomplish." And so Chabasinski moved west, first to Vancouver, where he worked for a while with the Mental Patients' Association, and then south to California.

In April of '74 I went down to San Francisco, where my friend Jan and her husband Barry had invited me to visit. They were really nice to me and they let me stay there in my own room for two months. They were political people, both socialists. We are all still friends.

I was going to come down to San Francisco with this brilliant idea for the people there which was, "Why don't you form an activist organization?" Well, I arrived in San Francisco and they'd already thought of it. They had started the Network Against Psychiatric Assault (NAPA) just a short time before, maybe even just a month before, and it was thriving. It was like an idea whose time had come.

The first night I arrived, I turn on the radio, and Wade Hudson[6] was talking about the ideas of the movement. It was KPFA, and I thought, "Wow, they've reached the Pacifica station."

I turn on the television, and there's Leonard Roy Frank giving a speech in front of some shock hospital. He's got this long, grey beard and he looks like an Old Testament prophet. I'm thinking, "Oh my God, these people are really getting somewhere."

So I just jumped right into it. I was so excited. And Leonard Frank took me under his wing because we shared this history of shock treatment. This other fellow, Wade Hudson, was very nice to me too.

Leonard and Wade were inspirational people. Everybody respects Leonard, and recognizes him as a man of great integrity. He was focusing on shock treatment, which everybody recognized as a great abuse. *Madness Network News* had created a sort of ideology, which basically disseminated a lot of ideas to a lot of people, so that people were already familiar with these ideas.

Meanwhile, I started working with the local left-wing political party. There was the All Berkeley Coalition who were really like Clinton Democrats, and then the Berkeley Citizens Action who were like the Social Democrats in Europe. So I started working with BCA in their office, and I would raise our issues. They were very receptive—it's Berkeley, after all. And so they invited me to actually write the mental health plank in their platform. So I did, and everybody was impressed by that, and it gave us even more credibility with them.

Then this guy who was famous in Berkeley—Marty Schiffenbauer[7]—

single-handedly put something on the ballot that changed the date of
the city election, so instead of April when there'd be low turnout, it was
switched to November where it would be merged with the general elections where people voted in higher percentages, which of course always
favors progressives.

Meanwhile we had had a demonstration in front of Herrick hospital
about shock treatment. We were always having demonstrations about
shock. That was NAPA's specialty. This local city council member came
who had already heard about these issues from me, and she says, "Has the
city council done anything about this?" We said "No." She said, "I can get
you a hearing with the Human Relations and Welfare Commission." So
we had this hearing, and for some reason, even though it sounds pretty
trivial, the local media took it up. There was this great picture of me and
Leonard on the front page of the *Oakland Tribune*. It got TV coverage
and everything. We had dozens of people testify about shock treatment,
and its harmful effects, and the shock therapists couldn't come up with
one person who would testify *for* it. And it made us look very good and
them look very bad. And the next thing that's happening is Marty has got
this change of the city election going on, and I'd been thinking a lot about
having things on the ballot, and so we said, "Let's put it on the ballot."

We needed 1,400 signatures, and we got 2,600. It was fantastic. One
of the things people would say, which we put into our leaflet, was "Shock
treatment? You mean they're still doing it?" So it was pretty easy to get
people to sign. However, to get 800 signatures you had to talk to about
3,000 people. I got hoarse, talking to so many people. And people got really turned on to the idea that we were actually going to be on the ballot
doing some real political stuff. And so there were probably 50 to 100 of
us who circulated petitions. Some people just got a few signatures, and
we put them in. I got more than anyone. I got 800 and it took two weeks
for my vocal chords to recover.

So there it's on the ballot, and the next thing you know, some local
stringer for the *New York Times* calls up Sean Gordon, who's the aid to
Berkeley mayor Gus Newport. He said, "Is there anything interesting
on the Berkeley ballot this year?" 'Cause you know how it is, Berkeley,
"Berzerkeley." And Sean says, "Well they're putting this thing on the ballot to ban shock treatment here." And the *Times* stringer says, "Is it serious?" And Sean goes ahead and speaks for his boss and says, "Well, I

guess it's serious because my boss, the mayor, has endorsed it." And then the *Times* got real interested. I think they did a front-page story. After that the phone never stopped ringing.

We're now talking about I think April of 1982. The hearing was in January or February. I think Marty must have put the election change on the April ballot but there wasn't a city election, there was just some kind of local election. So it was in April when the city election schedule was changed to November. Anyway, people heard about this, and we'd already started the Coalition to Stop Electroshock.

It started off as a coalition of groups. I just remember the Free Clinic, but I think there were five groups that joined the coalition. But what happened was as we started to have meetings, since we never really had any structure, the coalition really became a bunch of individuals who came to the meetings. The organizations that had signed off on being in the coalition helped us, but it wasn't in practice a coalition of organizations. It was really a bunch of individuals who were interested in this issue. So we would have meetings of twenty to thirty people, maybe more, depending on how exciting things were.

We were in a small but very liberal city, which was important. We probably could have done it in San Francisco, but we weren't in San Francisco. We certainly couldn't do it in New York, because they don't have the initiative and referendum anyway. But even if they did, you'd require tens of thousands of signatures, and that would require hundreds of people being active, and it's hard to pull that together. We probably had about fifteen or twenty people who were really into it.

I'd say maybe a month after the *New York Times* story ran, the doctors realized they'd better take it seriously. Up until then they were just pooh-poohing it. Like this thing that Gandhi is supposed to have said, "First they ignore you, then they laugh at you, then they fight you, and then you win." So we went through the stage of being ignored, and then for a short while they just laughed at us. Then they realized this was something serious, and they started fighting us. They put $15,000 into their campaign, which was a lot of money at the time to spend in a fairly small city. But it was a pretty inept campaign on their part.

For instance, they were using Jessica Mitford[8] as an endorser of their side. The guy I was working with, David Oaks, said, "This doesn't sound right. I kinda know Jessica Mitford. She wouldn't support electroshock."

So he calls her up and says, "Do you really want to do this? I thought you supported us." And she said, "I didn't say my name could be used." So she called them up, and they had to throw away all of their literature that had her name on it. We just chuckled there, it was so funny.

I had a debate in the *Daily Cal,* which is the student newspaper here (at UC Berkeley) which people read for local news. I had a debate with this shock doc at Herrick, who I must say did a pretty good job of defending himself, so it was actually a very interesting debate. And I did a pretty good job, too. But that really got a lot of attention. But basically, they couldn't come up with anybody who *liked* shock treatment, that was their problem. So they would say, "Shock treatment is life-saving" and, "Don't deprive us of this wonderful tool to help people" and blah blah blah. But the average person on the street thought it was barbaric.

So in November we had the election. We couldn't afford to do a real poll, but people are telling us, 'I'm not voting for Gus Newport, but I'm voting for measure T.'" Gus Newport was the black mayor of Berkeley, and this was in the black neighborhood that this guy was telling me this, and I was thinking, "Well, if there's people that aren't going to vote for Gus but they're going to vote for our measure . . ." Everybody picked Gus to win the election—which he did handily—but we ran ahead of him in the black neighborhood. Because just like I identified with black people way back when I was eight years old and in the institution, they identified with us.

It was just fantastic. I was in the mayor's campaign headquarters when the early returns started coming in, and I knew right away that we had won. They counted the absentee ballots first, which at that time were only well-off people, and the absentee ballots showed Gus getting about one-third of the vote and us getting about 40 percent. As soon as I got the first results, I was saying, "We won! We won!" The vote was 62 percent for the ban. We even carried some of the hills precincts, where the more conservative people live. And then later—I'm sorry if this sounds like an ego trip, but it kind of is—the *New York Times* ran this editorial mentioning my name, and Marty said he was jealous! They said they were not sure if Berkeley was a century ahead of the times, or a century behind the times, but they quoted me as saying whatever it was I was saying. It was very exciting.

The next thing that happened was the American Psychiatric Association—maybe it was the California Psychiatric Association—brought it to court on a whole bunch of grounds. The real grounds were, "You judges can't let these nut cases do something like this. We're doctors!" But the grounds on which the court ruled were that our initiative was unconstitutional. There's something in the state constitution that says that "municipalities can't enact ordinances that are contrary to general law." If the state says possession of marijuana is criminal, and a city passes a law to decriminalize it, they can't do that.

If we had been pillars of the community, all wearing suits and ties, the judge wouldn't have ruled against us. But basically the real argument against us was—and in fact it was actually made openly in the press by the lawyer for the CPA—"You can't let these disturbed people have a voice in what happens to them." And the judge basically bought that.

Then, as sort of a side show—before the judge made his final ruling and while the case was proceeding through the courts—we wanted to intervene. "Intervening" in a legal case means if you're not originally a part of a case but you have a vested interest in how the case is decided and you believe that the attorneys in the case are not representing your interests, then you can go to court and say. "We want to be added to the defendants, because we have some arguments that aren't being adequately made by current attorneys." So our thing was that the city wasn't completely representing our interests, and because we were the group that put this thing on the ballot, we should be able to intervene.

But it took a long time to find a lawyer to do it. And by that time, the case had proceeded, so the judge ruled against us on the grounds that the request for intervention wasn't timely. And now that I'm a lawyer, I know that he ruled correctly, because you can't allow the case to continue for a while, and then have other people just jump in at the end, because they'd have to re-do everything.

That was the thing that made me want to be a lawyer. I thought, "If only I was a lawyer, I could have been *our* lawyer and intervened in time." We're already into 1983, and in 1984 I went to law school. So that's how I became a lawyer.

David Oaks
"Forward goes the vanguard of the lunatic fringe."

David Oaks was born in September 1955, and grew up on the South Side of Chicago. "All of my grandparents came from Lithuania, and both of my grandfathers were coal miners in rural Illinois, so I grew up in a working-class family and was very affected by Lithuanian American culture. My parents were clerical workers. My dad worked for the trucking and rail industry as a clerk, and he was in the Teamsters union. They were a very supportive family, very loving."

Oaks graduated from a private Catholic high school, winning scholarships that enabled him to enter Harvard. He did a double major in government and economics, and in an effort to lessen the financial strain on his family, he hoped to complete his undergraduate degree in three years. "Above all, I wanted to make sure that I got into a profession that was economically secure, and that created a lot of stress."

Oaks cites this stress as a major reason he began to experience what he calls "altered" or "extreme" states of mind. "I saw and heard things that other people didn't . . . where I would think a space ship was in front of me, or a neighbor was with the CIA, or that the TV was only talking to me. This would go on for weeks at a time. For instance, I would get into a state of mind—this was very common for me—where I would look at technology as kind of an alien force on the planet: electricity and telephones and computers and radio and machinery. I would be riding in an airplane and become convinced that my mind could somehow affect the bolts in the airplane. That I had these super-powers." The doctors at Harvard had Oaks committed to McLean, a presti-gious private psychiatric hospital in Belmont, Massachusetts. "I was locked up five times, from a few days to five weeks."

In his senior year Oaks discovered a local group—the Mental Patients' Lib-eration Front—that was on the cutting edge of the psychiatric survivor move-ment. Though he would at times become immersed in other political causes—for example anti–nuclear power activism—his involvement with the MPLF proved to be the beginning of a lifelong commitment to campaigning for the rights of psychiatric survivors. At the time of this interview Oaks was the exec-utive director of MindFreedom International, based in Eugene, Oregon.

The MPLF had just had kind of its peak, about a year or two before I joined in the fall of 1976. They sponsored one of the national confer-ences, which were called the International Conference on Human Rights and Against Psychiatric Oppression. They were working with a group of radical leftist mental health workers that put out a magazine called *State and Mind Journal,* originally called *The Radical Therapist,* and then *Rough Times,* and they'd had a number of activists that worked together and put out a publication called *Your Rights as a Mental Patient in Massachusetts.*

This kind of organizing didn't just come out of the sky. It didn't come out of thin air. The way we ran our meetings was informed by leftist organizers, and also by women organizers, who were putting out material about how women should be more respected and given more leadership roles. The Haymarket Fund, in the Boston area, were also radicals, and they helped fund us. When we put out notices it would be the alternative weekly newspapers that covered us. In fact, when I first joined there was an article about how MPLF had helped somebody escape from a psychiatric institution. A group of MPLFers went to a local institution and parked a car nearby, and then visited somebody and then, as they left, a big guy held the door open and the inmate ran up the hill and got in the car and left. And I remember reading this and going, "Wow!"

One more example of the kind of great support we had from other social change groups, is that around '81 or so I took a week-long intensive class on the basics of community organizing, based on Saul Alinsky principles. This was run by ACORN,[9] which is one of the main groups to apply Saul Alinsky principles. They found a scholarship for me. And it was a great workshop.

We applied those lessons, and so we began picking our issues with a strategic purpose in mind, and we began recruitment drives for members. We negotiated with the mental health system as a group, we filled their office with people and negotiated, and said, "You guys should be funding some of these alternatives" and that eventually led to the funding of the Ruby Rogers drop-in center by the Mental Patients' Liberation Front, which is still around in Somerville, Massachusetts.

We were very tolerant. I always remember this one fellow at a meeting, he would just show up and go to the back of the office and play his saxophone. He was very noncommunicative, but I knew from his writing that he was really brilliant and very informed about the issues, and very concerned about the use of psychiatric drugs. He was locked up, and we heard that he died in solitary confinement. And I don't know how true this was or not, but they said that he had fought really hard and that there was blood on the walls, and that he had fought to the death against the forced drugging. And so I heard about those things, and I realized how difficult it would be to organize when someone isn't communicating like other folks are communicating.

Back then we'd do what was called "the rotating chair." What it meant is you went to the workshop, and whoever speaks is the presenter, and they speak until they pick the next person who puts their hand up, and then that's the presenter and chair. And the whole workshop would be done that way, and there's never anybody in charge.

I recognized that this was a reaction to extreme trauma. And that's why I got very interested in the power issues, because I recognized that these were people who had been hurt on such a fundamental level. When the "helping professional" is the one to do the trauma, it's a profoundly intrusive level of violation, similar to going to a priest and experiencing sexual abuse. When some of the most well-off, most powerful people in our society have absolute, unchecked control behind closed doors over one of the most powerless, marginalized, discredited populations, everything we know about humanity will tell you there's got to be some extreme abuse in that context. So at these meetings there would be such sensitivity toward any kind of intrusion about one's power that we would sometimes go overboard.

And then another thing that came from the super-left was self-criticism, and that's when we really were in danger of just falling apart, and becoming like one of these splinter groups, like a Maoist-Trotskyite troupe or something. Ted Chabasinski used to joke about this because he was very familiar with leftist organizing. One of my favorite toasts to this day, if you and I are ever at a party and we toast, I'll say, "Forward goes the vanguard of the lunatic fringe, overthrowing the running dogs of normality."

At the Toronto event in 1982, the annual International Conference for Human Rights and Against Psychiatric Oppression, we marched over to the American Psychiatric Association, and we were accompanied by Royal Canadian Mounted Police walking with us. One of our participants who'd been especially angry during the conference had a whisky bottle with her, and she smashed that on the ground during the march. I was very appreciative of the police officer, he didn't break up the march, he didn't arrest her, he just said, "Okay everybody, let's calm down, let's keep going." And then when we got to the site of the protest, one of our participants did a headstand in front of the entrance to the APA, and then another participant sat down next to him and laid out a Tarot reading, and I watched with fascination as she announced as she laid out the cards that "justice was in the outcome position."[10]

A good number of our folks, I'd say about twenty-five, went to the lobby of the APA conference, and gathered in a circle to do a silent protest. It was very moving. It was in this very fancy hotel, and they sat there surrounded by psychiatrists. And I was trying out journalism at the time, and I covered it for *Phoenix Rising*. I went around and interviewed some of the psychiatrists, and I was really struck by how mocking a number of them were. They would stand there and say, "That one I would put on Haldol, and that one on Thorazine." And they would be laughing and mocking, similar say to whites at an African American protest. And that always struck me, because I was impressed by the bravery of our folks.

Our main connection to other political movements was to the prison justice movement. Our original terminology was that we are inmates, because our liberty is taken away, so that was kind of like our sister movement. But every other movement we could possibly connect with, we did. Women's movement, people of color, third world, you name it, we were connecting. But in terms of disability, that connection wasn't really made until the era of Rae Unzicker and Justin Dart and Judi Chamberlin, who just flung open the doors between those two movements. You have to remember our number one issue was *rejecting* labels. If you had walked into a meeting of *Madness Network News* or the Network Against Psychiatric Assault in the late seventies or early eighties and said you wanted to write an article about how we were "disabled," I'm afraid that article wouldn't have been published. The label itself, the word "disabled"—that alone was a big barrier for people to recognize our common ground. And it still is challenging, and people can get stuck in that.

Mouth magazine was one of the main breakthroughs, because *Mouth* was started by a head injury survivor, Lucy Gwin. Head injury survivors are a bridge for this movement, because a lot of our more radical people will be saying, and I say this too, "What I have is *not* a biologically based condition. Don't tell me it's a chemical imbalance and that it's medicalized and everything." But then we can point out, "Well, head injury survivors say the same thing, and even when you can see a physical difference on an MRI scan, a lot of the issues are the same." So some amount of medicalization is fine. You know, tape up my wound, thank you. But then 95 percent of the recovery is not medical.

I will hear long-term key radical leaders identify as having clinical depression, and wrestle with whether they should be on psych drugs. And then I'll hear others that utterly and totally reject all that. So there's a real diversity in how folks are approaching these issues. And I think that's true in the broader disability movement. You know I love it that some individuals without legs are now being disqualified from running matches because their prostheses help them run faster than the so-called normal person. So there's this fascinating complexity, these real questions about, "What is disability anyway, and what does it mean to be disabled?" The real struggle is uniting the people that reject the mainstream's definitions and the ones that accept it. That's the really tough coalition to build.

My feeling is we're connected to all the movements. We're not a wholly owned subsidiary of the disability rights movement. We're maybe a close cousin of the disability movement, and the disability movement itself has a lot of complexity. So it takes time for people to talk about it, and to find some common ground.

16
Working the System

———

SIT-INS AND DEMONSTRATIONS WERE ONE ASPECT OF THE GROWING movement but were by no means the only tools available to disability rights advocates. Some attained positions of relative power within the social services and rehabilitation systems that had such an enormous impact on the day-to-day lives of people with disabilities and sought to use their growing influence to empower their constituents. Perhaps the most notable example of such an advocate/administrator was Ed Roberts, who in 1962 had been deemed "infeasible" as a client by the California Department of Vocational Rehabilitation and in 1975 was appointed director of that agency by Governor Jerry Brown.

James Donald, also on the West Coast, and Elmer Bartels in the East are two further examples of this "outsider/insider" development. Like Roberts, who found a sympathetic ally in the unorthodox Jerry Brown Jr., Bartels worked for Massachusetts governor Michael Dukakis, who in the early 1970s had cut his political teeth as a "good government" reformer. Dukakis, like Jerry Brown Jr., was willing to take the then-radical step of choosing a person with a disability to head his state's rehabilitation commission.[1]

James Donald
"You can change public morality with the law."

———

As a Cowell Hospital resident at the University of California, Berkeley, in 1967, James Donald witnessed not only the very beginnings of the independent living movement but also the tumult and violence that marked much of campus life during the mid-1960s. "Riots were so frequent there, I used to carry a gas mask on my [wheel]chair just so I could sit and watch them." Neither his stance as a "noncombatant" nor his disability protected him from the violence, however. He remembers one incident: "I was at the steps at the Student Union, watching the riot on a cold day. The students were across the street and the police were sweeping the campus. There's five or six steps there that fade down into Bancroft [Street]. There were about three or four of these blue jumpsuited cops without badges, with gas masks and other masks on, and gloves, and clubs. They came up to me from behind and said, through their gas masks, 'Get off campus.' Basically, they were motioning toward the steps, toward Bancroft, for me to go.

"I had my hands in my pockets, and I started to laugh at them. I said, 'What do you want me to do?' And one of them whacked me on the back of my head, me just sitting in an electric chair. And another one grabbed my chair. I was doubled over by then. I couldn't get up. The other one pushed my chair, and he was just about two feet from the edge of the steps, going full speed, and I looked up and I saw this student storming the cops. The cops let go of my chair, ran, and about five or six students surrounded me and carried me down."

Donald was a Cowell resident for only a brief time before moving off campus, but he kept in touch with Ed Roberts and John Hessler as they organized the Physically Disabled Students' Program, and then the Berkeley CIL. He was also, during his two years at Berkeley, a member of the Rolling Quads. After finishing law school at the University of California at Davis, he served in the California attorney general's office for two and a half years before being appointed deputy director of the state's Department of Rehabilitation under Governor Jerry Brown.

His boss at this new job was an old friend: Ed Roberts. Together, they made fundamental changes in California's rehab programs and drafted major revisions in state law.

James Donald died February 24, 2003.

———

Jerry Brown was the kid governor who had all these new ideas. Disability was becoming a huge issue. And so I applied to the governor to become the director of rehab. And then I called Ed [Roberts] and said, "Ed, I want your support. I want to be the director of rehab." And he goes, "That's funny. I've applied for it, too." And then he says, "Well, if you get it, you appoint me deputy director; and if I get it, I'll appoint you." So that was the deal. Then, of course, Ed got it because he had all the political clout and he was the better person anyway. And so when he got it, he appointed me as the deputy director for legal and legislative matters. So then I was back to being the professional crip. Which was a wonderful opportunity.

It was basically a blank ticket for what we wanted to do. After we started wanting too much, of course, his people started reining us in, and we had fights, not ever with Jerry Brown so much but with his financial people and his legislative people.

Jerry Brown was a governor who allowed a lot of experimentation. That's why he appointed Ed—because Ed was a failure for the Department of Rehab. Brown's philosophy was to put the two extremes together and make them come up with a solution. So they did that with Ed. And then Ed brought in all these quads, myself and John Hessler.

My background with rehab became an issue when I got my appointment. When I [had] applied for law school, my rehab counselor said, "I want to see your grades to see if you're qualified," and I basically said, "I'm not going to [show you my grades]. If I get accepted, you sponsor me because that's your job."[2] I basically rattled him along those lines, made my non-negotiable demands, and I got him to reverse his position. And so when I became the deputy director over all these people, they didn't like it very much. As well as Ed, because he was rejected, too. So they got all these rejects in there that all of a sudden were their bosses.

Ed reversed the history of rehab by focusing on rehabilitation services for the most severely disabled first. I think the Rehabilitation Act already required it, but nobody was paying attention to it because it was easier to get successes with people who had a few fingers missing, or maybe needed new teeth, and get them a job, rather than taking a quad who had a broken neck and very limited function. So that was the battle within Rehab. [The old guard] didn't appreciate it one bit. They saw us as the enemy. And that's not an overstatement. There was tremendous, tremendous resistance. You don't know what institutional resistance is until you get into a situation like that. They just would not listen to Ed.

All of a sudden I embodied the problems that I wanted to solve, and so in that sense it was a wonderful experience. It was a perfect political appointment, because if I had a problem personally, I would try to legislate it and solve the problem for everybody else. For example, I got a van that I could drive from my chair, which was one of the very first, in fact, it was the prototype for driving from a wheelchair. I couldn't get auto insurance because of my disability, so in a fit I went back and wrote a draft law and got one of the legislators whom I was getting to know to sponsor it, and they just jumped on it. And it became law the next year.

If we wanted to get a bill passed, I would write it, or one of my staff would write it, and then we would take it to a community group, like CIL. Depending on what the topic was, we'd take it to a different group that had legislators here [in Sacramento] who had influence in that area. And then they would introduce it, and after it was introduced, we would seek to get administration approval. And that's how we got most of our legislation passed.

After a few of these, the administration said, "Wait a minute. You can't do it that way. You have to get approval from the governor's office *before* you promote any of these." So I tried that two or three times, and the governor had a new legislative coordinator called B. T. Collins. He became a very famous fellow after a while. He was a Vietnam-era veteran who refused to be recognized as a disabled person, even though he had one arm and one leg blown off from a land mine during Vietnam. He was an irascible, foul-mouthed, hard-drinking Irishman. After a while, I found out he wasn't going to let any of my ideas through because they conflicted with other loyalties that Brown had with other legislators who were against what we wanted.

Another obstacle I had in getting legislation approved by the governor's office was finance, because it always cost money, and they always said no. Several times I had to take it up to the governor directly and get his approval. I remember Brown was never on time, and we had to wait and wait, and one time I had to wait about seven hours to get this one bill approved. He never did understand it, but he approved it, in opposition to his finance director and everybody else.

[Then came Proposition 13],[3] where all of the local funding went out the window. Local funding was the source of a lot of the independent living programs and the student programs that we had established or that were being established. At the time, there was a big government surplus, $7 billion, I think. And the question was what was the governor going to do with it? It was called the Bailout Bill. Prop. 13 came through, and the Bailout Bill was a list of items that were guaranteed for funding from the state to the local entities. The one we wanted was that the local entities had to maintain funding at the same historical level for all these programs if they were to accept any of this bailout money.

Couldn't get it through finance. Couldn't get it through. And so the word was passed out to the community groups to do a protest and to picket the governor. I think there were two or three hundred people that showed up to picket the state capitol and the governor directly, and a few legislators were giving speeches on the lawn. It was well-orchestrated through Judy Heumann. The strategy was [to have Ed and I, as state officials] mediate between the disabled and the governor. Ed was sick that day, so I had the privilege of doing that. I went over to the governor's office and met with his chief of staff. "What do they want?" Of course, we had it all orchestrated. "They want this and this and this."

And then the governor comes out. He says, "What do I do?" So I said, "They think you're cold and impersonal, so what you have to do is call in five or six of the leaders, go around and shake their hands, and then listen. That's all." So he did. And it worked like a charm. He went in and shook everybody's hand. Basically, we got 100 percent of what we wanted.

One of the laws that we implemented said that you can't be kicked out of places because you're disabled. I remember once I was not allowed to sit where I wanted to in a San Francisco restaurant, Castanoglas, on Fisherman's Wharf. The waitress made me sit by the coffee maker, and I said, "I'm going to sit where I want to." So my friend and I went over and picked an empty table by the window. The waitress came over, yelling at us, "We told you you couldn't sit here." So we left. And we sued. And the newspaper called it the "Out of Sight Lawsuit" because we couldn't get the table with a view. We settled that one.

The changes [that came] in Washington basically occurred because of what was happening here. California was the one state that started all of these concepts, and everybody said, "Yeah, let's do that." And they were good concepts and they seemed to be working well. A lot of it happened because of Ed's status and his visibility and his personal appeal. People just liked him. And he had the type of personality where he didn't hide anything. He lived in his iron lung, and if you were there long enough and he had to get on the can, he'd do it in front of you. That's just the way he was.

One thing that really was demonstrated by this movement is that you can change public morality with law. If you change the law, society starts changing, and then it becomes the norm. Can you imagine now saying that the disabled aren't allowed into a public accommodation because they're disabled? It's inconceivable. But it changed because of the laws. And maybe the laws were appropriate because of the changing attitudes. There's an interplay there.

When I was first injured, it was still considered to be an unsightly thing, sort of a shame on the family, that old biblical thing that if you're disabled it must have been the sin of your mother type thing. "Shut-in" was a common term. I remember it was not uncommon to be in public and see the little kid, two- or three-year-old, saying, "Hey, Mom, look." And point. And the mother, embarrassed, forcing the kid's face back so they wouldn't stare, or they'd go another way to avoid the wheelchair. I recall being a spectacle. I recall gathering two or three people every time I got into my van because they were so amazed at the technology of a lift going into a van.

So things have changed tremendously. People don't pay attention to me at all, even though I go around in an electric chair, [in a van] with electric doors and electric lift. They don't even look twice. They don't even look. Which is fine.

One time, years later as a lawyer [in private practice], I was helping somebody evict some tenants who wouldn't pay their bill, and it was a rough neighborhood. We were giving the eviction notice, and the guy came to me and said, "I'm going to ignore you." I said, "Ignore me, and I'll own your truck." He grabbed my shirt, and he was about to belt me in the mouth, and my immediate thought was not fear but "I've integrated! He's going to hit me! I'm nothing special!"

And I remember thinking: "I've finally integrated the disabled into society."

Elmer Bartels
"You don't have one of your people appointed commissioner unless you have . . . the ability to make things happen."

While West Coast advocates were working first through the California Association of the Physically Handicapped and then through the Center for Independent Living, in Massachusetts, Fred Fay, Vivienne Thomson, Tim Foley, and others were forming the Massachusetts Council of Organizations of the Handicapped in the early 1960s and the Boston Center for Independent Living and the Massachusetts Coalition of Citizens with Disabilities in the 1970s.

Among these Massachusetts activists was Elmer Bartels. Born in Newton in 1938, Bartels had an early interest in mathematics and science. He studied physics in graduate school at Tufts University and then took a position at the Massachusetts Institute of Technology Laboratory for Nuclear Science in 1964 and at Honeywell Industries in 1968.

Bartels sustained a spinal cord injury in a college hockey game in 1960, and after his initial hospitalization spent time at the Spinal Cord Injury Center of

Boston and then at the Rusk Institute in New York City. While in rehab, he encountered activists from the Paralyzed Veterans of America and the National Paraplegia Foundation, which led him to think about forming a local activist group for civilians with spinal cord injuries. In 1964, Bartels and others founded the Massachusetts Association of Paraplegics (MAP), focused on influencing legislators and policymakers on Beacon Hill—the State House.

By 1977, Bartels was prominent enough to be offered the position of Massachusetts commissioner of rehabilitation, in charge of both the state vocational rehab program and the Social Security Administration's determination service.

***

The summer of 1976 is when the story begins. The commissioner of Rehabilitation, Russ O'Connell, and his boss, the secretary of Human Services, had a bit of a falling out. The secretary, Jerry Stevens, asked Russ to leave. The search committee was made up of none other than Fred Fay and a guy by the name of Webb from the Executive Office of Human Services, and another guy by the name of Duncan Yagee. Jerry thought highly of Fred, and rightfully so. There was an initial look-see as to who would be interested in being commissioner at the Mass Rehab Commission. They looked around, they didn't find anybody they were particularly interested in.

In the summer of '76 Fred called and asked me if I would be interested in being commissioner. I didn't grow up to be commissioner of the Mass Rehab Commission. I was happy at Honeywell. I had been promoted to department head, I was making a little over $30,000 a year at the time, and the job of commissioner paid twenty, so I would have to take a pay cut to do it. I said, "Well, I'd be willing to talk about it."

I came home and talked to [my wife] Mary about it, and wheeled around my backyard, and figured out that here is an opportunity to run a state agency, and to continue to do things that I thought were important for people with disabilities in Massachusetts. I would finally have control over the budget. I decided that I ought to try to do it, if there was any way to do so. So I took a two-year leave of absence from Honeywell and accepted the appointment.

There was Fred Fay in the background, coaching me on how to approach being a viable candidate, and also the stuff we had been doing here. Why does all this stuff work? You don't have one of your people

appointed commissioner, unless you have got some political clout somewhere, and the ability to make things happen. Fred and I would figure
out what I would say at the meetings that I went to with Human Services.
He would give me the lay of the land, and we would scheme on how to be
a good candidate. Lo and behold, I was appointed.

Mike Dukakis was governor at the time. I remember the swearing-in
ceremony. One of the reasons why I was sworn in on January 31 was I was
aware that Jim Jeffers, a spinal-injured para from Illinois, was going to
be appointed on February 1 to be the Illinois state director. If Ed Roberts
was going to be the first, I was going to be the second. So January 31, 1977,
became the date I was sworn in.

At the beginning, there was a shaking out. One of the advantages I
had was that I had been managing a department in the private sector,
at Honeywell, for five years, so I knew a lot about managing people and
getting my point across. Ed had not had such an experience, had not
had that in his background. Ed was more of a visionary, I am more of a
manager. There were three or four people at the top, including the chief
legal counsel, who left the agency upon my appointment. That was just
fine with me. I think they saw it was a new day, and they wanted to do
other things. So it was not a matter of me firing them, it was a matter of
me organizing the agency the way I wanted it, and having them do what
I wanted. I wanted to downsize the organization, to live within available
monies while at the same time serving people with the most significant
disabilities. We had too many managers, too many offices, and too many
regions that we couldn't support with available dollars.

I saw my role was to use the position that I had to help promote the
things that we had been working on as disability rights advocates for the
prior fifteen years. Granted, as a public official, there are certain things
you have to do, that may not directly relate to those priorities. But the
Voc Rehab program has an awful lot of flexibility in it. I saw it as an
opportunity to use the bully pulpit of the commissioner's position to get
new money and new programs. One of my philosophies is, "Get bucks,
serve people." So we got the head injury dollars serving people with traumatic brain injury; we got the home care program serving people with
homemaker services; we got state and federal independent living money,
ultimately amounting to $3.2 million, and then another million from the
feds [on top of that]. How did we do it? We worked on it with the legis-

lature, the disability constituency, and the administration to get the new money.

In the seventies, the expansion was very much physical disability based. It really wasn't until the mid-eighties and beyond that we began to look at other populations that could benefit. For example, the mental health community, people with mental illness, they are where we were in 1960, in terms of getting organized and having an impact on their service delivery system. Part of it has to do, I think, with the stigma of mental illness.

Independent living centers have developed, probably from the mid-eighties on, with the idea that IL centers should be available for *all* people with disabilities who need the services that an IL center offers: peer counseling, housing advocacy, program advocacy, access to the PCA Medicaid program. Also, we began to see that the IL center boards have people with other disabilities on them.

So what started out as a two-year leave of absence from Honeywell has turned into a life's work. My goodness, the time has gone by fast. The opportunity, when you are an agency head, to do that which you want to do, is tremendous. No one really tells me specifically what to do. You have your law, you have your budget, and then you figure out how to get from here to there. But if you are persistent enough, you can get things done. It just takes longer, and persistence is a virtue.

17
Institutions, Part 4

———

W HILE PHYSICALLY DISABLED ACTIVISTS ON THE WEST COAST WERE organizing the first Center for Independent Living and those in the East were working to build Disabled in Action and the ACCD, the struggle to shut down the massive state institutions for those labeled mentally ill and mentally retarded continued all across the country. The "right-to-education" litigation filed by the parents' movement in the early 1970s was followed by lawsuits designed to force states to provide community services to people released from the institutions, who had suffered the most horrific neglect and abuse.

William Bronston, MD (continued)
"There's never been an official apology . . . about these crimes against humanity."

———

Among the most famous of the deinstitutionalization struggles was the one fought at Willowbrook State School on Staten Island in New York City. The key person in that fight was Dr. William Bronston, who had taken a position at Willowbrook because his reputation as "a troublemaker" precluded his being hired anywhere else. Ironically, this put him in precisely the place where his radicalism, energy, and finely honed skills as an "outside agitator" could be used to the most far-reaching effect.

———

> I'd been inside Willowbrook now between a year and a year and a half, clear about the fact that I'm in there to bring the place down. And the way I've been doing that is by developing as much of a relationship as I could with the community-based parent organizations, especially the Down syndrome organization of Staten Island, whose chairman had a

young boy, Bobby, with Down syndrome. He also had Hirschsprung's disease, which is a condition where a baby is born without neurological enervation of the distal end of his colon and rectum, and so he can't poop. What happens is that feces builds up and builds up and Bobby had to be evacuated by hand. The kid's pediatrician just assumed that was part of the picture, didn't know enough to know that Hirschsprung's disease is a very common part of Down syndrome, which I knew instantly. So the kid was four or five years old when I met the family, and the mother had been pulling out this kid's poop by hand once every week or so. The kid was ashen, terribly sickly, thin little spindly arms and legs and this just huge, distended belly and the hair not growing, Kwashiorkor-like.[1] This family was just in hell. The family's name was Marcario, and Mark Marcario was the dad.

Mark became my salvation while I was in Willowbrook. He came to pick me up almost every day. We would have lunch together. Anyhow, what happened was that I urged he take Bobby to Columbia Presbyterian and they'll fix him overnight, which they did. They walked into Columbia Medical School Hospital, and they put him through a real pediatric examination. They made the diagnosis instantly, and they operated instantly, and the kid became normal, overnight. And the parents couldn't believe what had happened.

The point I was making with the family was, once a professional sees your kid as "not human," as not a valued kid, then they're not going to be thinking about service or care the way they would if it was their own kid. This doctor would have known Hirschsprung's in a minute if the kid didn't have Down syndrome. But the fact that the kid had Down syndrome, it was missed by the doc. Then, he blamed the mother for not being a good enough mother, of not being willing to handle this terrible task of regular evacuation, when the mother knows that something is gravely wrong, and has to internalize the sense of sorrow and oppression of having to deal with this terrible problem.

What came out of that was that through Mark, who ran a heating oil business and was a remarkable, civically oriented guy, I got introduced all over Staten Island to the Italian community, and to the parent community. I began connecting with and explaining to the community, through informal gatherings, the terrible toll that the existence of Willowbrook had on the evolution of community-based services, and talking to them like from another planet on what community-based services were like, talking to them about Children's Hospital in Los Angeles, about Child Development Clinic, and the fact that the dominant mode of service in California was community-based services and home-based services with a multidisciplinary team providing the support. But the really important issue here was the politics of disability. Being a part of a devalued minority created a prejudicial and discriminatory relationship that was towering in every aspect, not only of the individual's life, but of their family's. Their families were "retarded" also, by the society and the institutions.

So it became clear that we had to begin reinforcing in the parents the sense that their young person, their son or daughter, their relative that was in the place, was being savagely mutilated in every aspect, by the way the place treated the family by keeping them at arm's distance, keeping the families outside the buildings, keeping them groveling, supplicating for the least aspect of connection to their kid, starting right away when the kid came into the place. The rule was that the family could not see the kid for the first three months as a way of breaking that bond between the family and the kid and imposing a dehumanizing condition on the family. These practices were all part and parcel of trying to get the family to accept the old "professional knows best" paradigm.

Elizabeth Lee was a social worker who was working in Willowbrook, assigned to Mike Wilkins's[2] buildings, the young men's buildings. What happened was that there was a whole series of exposés in the *Staten Island Advance* by this remarkable woman journalist named Jane Kurtin, who had been following the struggle. She should have gotten the Pulitzer Prize, because her stories led to the administration firing Mike and Elizabeth for allegedly leaking information to the press.

Michael [Wilkin] had been working with this lawyer, Jerry Rivers, around the struggle that we were waging at the same time at the US Public Health Hospital, also on Staten Island, to unionize that hospital and defend a group of Native American vocational nurses seeking pay parity. This lawyer had just gotten a new job with ABC Television, and had changed his name to Geraldo Rivera. So Geraldo, Jerry Rivers at the time, was helping us with a lawsuit that Michael had organized on behalf of these Native American licensed vocational nurses who were not being paid the same as Caucasian workers at USPHS. So Mike was very close to Geraldo, who had gotten this job maybe a year or a half a year before, and was struggling as a news reporter.

Mike called him and said, "I've been fired and this place is absolutely abysmal, you've got to come and see it." Geraldo came with a team, a flying camera, lights. Michael had the keys, of course, and walked him through the place in the middle of the night. There was no security, the shit hadn't hit the fan yet. Mike took them to two buildings, number six and number eight. The next day he walked him through more.

The stuff hit the New York and national ABC News audiences like a bomb. It was *the* sensational story in New York, and the country, for about two weeks. Geraldo's ratings went off the chart. It became the great humanitarian story, the great scandal of the day.

What those TV audiences saw was the nakedness, the filth, the inhumanity, the lack of any comfort, the unwillingness of the staff to be seen. Like opening up a dank cellar and finding human beings that had been stored there to live for twenty years with nothing, and have become reduced to absolute wretched souls, out of the worst nightmares that you could possibly imagine in fiction books of drawings of Bedlam.

So here's the governor, here's the commissioner of mental hygiene at the point of the knife. The truth comes out; that hundreds of millions of dollars are being spent, and everybody mindlessly thought everything was okay. And then, you open it up and see this festering, purulent, wretched reality, this miserable, this violent, this savage way in which the State of New York is taking care of its own. The state couldn't allow that kind of truth, that kind of reality, to spill out, because there's no telling where it's going to go when it comes to the ballot box. You just don't want scandal.

We had Senator Jacob Javits on the grounds, we had everybody on the grounds. They came to put the fire out. This was a serious fire in the Republican camp. They were aiming at us every drop of red-baiting they could. The clergy at Willowbrook were given thousands of three-page stapled, unmarked, red-baiting allegations against Mike and I—that we were Maoists, that we were going to poison the water supply of Staten Island! The clergy gave out thousands of these fliers on Sunday morning from all their churches in Staten Island. Staten Island is like the paragon of reactionary politics in the United States. All the largest Mafioso families had homes on Staten Island. Staten Island never was won during the American Revolution and always remained a Tory stronghold. During the Second World War, there were Nazi organizing offices on Staten Island. This was a bad place to be indicted as a leftist in public. And we lived in a big wood frame house, and I expected the house to blow up. We had children there, we had like five families living there. So we had to figure out how to contradict this thing.

Literally overnight, within three days, Malachy McCourt [whose daughter was in Willowbrook] was able to get us on the *Dick Cavett Show.*

Malachy was a television personality. He was a bartender. He was an actor. He's Frank McCourt's younger brother. Frank wrote *Angela's Ashes,* Malachy wrote *Two Monks Swimming.* The two brothers are these incredible Irish ball-busters who are theatrical. They're poets and writers. We got on the *Dick Cavett Show.* Geraldo was sitting there, Diana McCourt, Malachy's wife, Bernard Carabello, who Michael had somehow pulled out from the pits of one of the buildings, who had severe CP but had typical intelligence, myself, and Mike Wilkins. There's five of us. The state sent a bureaucrat by the name of Robert Hayes, who was the new State Commissioner of Mental Retardation, and a guy by the name of Wolf, who was the Public Information Officer for the State Department of Mental Hygiene. These guys came in spats, black suits and vests. They looked like morticians. We were all thirty-somethings, in soft sweaters, hair down to our shoulders, beards. Diana McCourt, this beautiful dark-haired mother, was there, and Bernard was accompanied by his very heavyset Puerto Rican mom. Here we all are, all on this couch, this bunch of gypsies, talking about life, talking about love, talking about decency. And these New York State old boys are talking about their bureaucratic reasons why this place is a tolerable and excusable shit hole.

We read the red-baiting sheet on national television. Cavett said, "Is this true?" I just roared with laughter. I couldn't answer it, really honestly, because it *was* true. I mean, we weren't trying to poison the water supply, but we were communists, we were Marxists, we were self-conscious revolutionary organizers. What that meant was to do the right thing by people, to make sure people don't suffer, and to challenge state power.

Once they couldn't play the communist card against us they had nothing left because the facts were what they were. The place was absolutely inhumane in the extreme. It had been that way for three or four decades. There was a group of people sitting at the top who drove around in chauffeur-driven limousines and black suits, all the way up to the governor, in league with the banks making millions and millions of dollars on the suffering of all these people. And on the other end of the spectrum was the horror that Geraldo was hammering into people day after day on the television.

It was over for them. They had lost the big fight. Now all they had left was to temporize, was to try and stall and to maybe try and put "under new management" banners on the front of this concentration camp. They made a lot of cosmetic changes. They brought in a little more soap—but nothing significant really happened. Whether they fixed something for one kid or three kids, it didn't really matter. The thing that was so desperate to me was that the more we hammered at how bad the place was, the more money would come in to fix it. And we didn't want it fixed. We wanted it closed once and for all.

So there was a whole set of administrators that they'd put in there to try and hold the ground, assuming that people would lose interest, would forget about the situation after a while and that we would ultimately leave. But we locked the federal suit in, and the federal suit became the perpetual ground for revisiting the problem. And a judge forced the whole system under a federal master's hands in order to clean the place up, but it took twenty-five years before the place finally was closed.

The Willowbrook suit was decided on the narrowest constitutional issue, the Eighth Amendment of the Bill of Rights, the right to freedom from cruel and unusual punishment. It was not a sixth amendment or fourth amendment suit. It was a very rigorous, laborious, punishing trial. I testified. I showed the scores of photographs that I had taken of atrocities on the inside, and explained each one of them, and explained the whole strategy of the institution. I knew the institution better than anybody, because I had struggled to change it, so I knew why it did what it did, and how implacable the paradigm was. How unrehabilitatable the workers were, how intransigent the administration was, how locked in the system was.

There's never been an official apology to the families about these crimes against humanity that were waged by the politicians and the bureaucrats and the professionals on behalf of their self-interest. There has never been a tangible memorial set up for the losses that occurred, both real and spiritual, amongst the populations that were involved in that struggle.

Willowbrook has been converted into Staten Island Community College, with every conceivable attempt to eradicate any history of the infamy that existed there. There is not a sign, there is not a memorial. I was there just about a year, a year and a half ago for the twenty-fifth anniversary where the three New York governors that ministered the transformation of the place from a concentration camp to the community college were honored. It was very powerful.

We were so close. So many scores of families were so close when we fought for closure and lived such an incredible struggle with such hopefulness. And here, two-and-a-half decades later, these families are still alive, and they're rusting to death. They're now being confronted with being put into nursing homes themselves. Their children are now themselves in their forties and fifties, potentially confronted with being put back into institutions, back into nursing homes because they're old, and because Title XIX is still in place.[3]

There is still no progressive, radical leadership to articulate what would be the solution. The centerpiece of that struggle has to be universal, comprehensive, single-payer health care in the United States. That is the single most significant social policy breakthrough that could fundamentally change the status of life for all Americans, and especially all Americans with disabilities. No other single policy issue, no other institutional change could have the humanizing consequence that that struggle would deliver, were it waged, as the front end of the disability rights movement. Because it would unite my family community with the rest of the country's struggles for security and decency.

But nothing has changed in national policy except that the whole financing system for medical services has gotten incredibly more greed- and profit-driven. The scandal that exists now is seen in the underlying sadness, the despair, the somberness of the collected families, and how any strong challenge by them to the system has been beaten out of them by all these years of struggling against this implacable bureaucracy that moved as slow as it could in rectifying the situation. It was like wiping your behind with wax paper, spreading the problem from Willowbrook, a single concentrated place, where you could see how bad it was, to five hundred smaller institutional places of ten and fifteen and twenty people.

The problem was our federal suit jurisdiction was only confined to Willowbrook per se, and you had these other fifty-nine New York state institutions that were still cooking along fine. The state was able to temporize indefinitely, in terms of, "give us a year to work on this problem," a year would come around and the problem wouldn't be solved. "Give us another year . . ."

But the important thing here is that, at least at one level, the mortal spear was in the heart of the beast.

Lucy Gwin (continued)
"If you can find forty people . . ."

Lucy Gwin, in the months after her escape from the New Medico Brain Injury Rehabilitation Center in Cortland, New York, began an effort to expose the abuses she'd encountered and to challenge the entire "brain injury rehabilitation" industry.

I had the names and phone numbers of some of my co-inmates, and I'd call their families, and tell them, "Hey look, this is really all a scam." And of course most of them thought I was nuts. I mean, after all, I was a former inmate and had escaped, but a couple of them listened to me, and brought their family members home.

Some of them I kept up with quite a long time. Jim, for instance. He'd lost a quarter of his brain, and had all these surgeries, and so his family dumped him in New Medico because "he wasn't the same." Well, of course not. And they'd call me and say, "We left him alone for five minutes today! We left him alone for an hour today! And it was okay! He went out by himself today! Oh my god, we were so frightened! But he came back with a newspaper!"

He's disabled now, okay? And it takes a while for someone to get used to that, and to figure out how you're going to accommodate yourself to the world, and how the world is going to have to accommodate to you. But these so-called rehabilitation centers would use up everybody's insurance, so if you used a wheelchair now, there was nothing left of your insurance to build a ramp. There was nothing left to do the things that you have to do, once you have a disability.

In September of that year [1989], after I'd just escaped, I found out about this national conference about brain injury. They were inviting people from the disability rights movement for a workshop. And I thought, well, that's interesting. I knew there was a disability rights movement, which nobody else around me seemed to know, and so I flew to Austin, and I went to their workshop. And only eleven people attended, and so we were way outnumbered by the people who were there to lecture to us. And the disability rights advocates were just amazing people, like Alan Bergman, who now runs a brain injury association, but he was working for United Cerebral Palsy, Hank Bersani, Judith Brann from PILCOP [Public Interest Law Center of Philadelphia]. She and Tom Gilhool were the people who did that wonderful Oklahoma suit, another one of those tear down the walls suits.[4] So I made the most useful connections. Lex Frieden was there, and he told me the most helpful thing. He said, "If you can find forty people who believe what you do, who have experienced what you have and want to see the same changes you want to see happen, if you can find forty people like that, you can change the world."

So I set out to find my forty people. I was on the phone long distance all day long—it cost a fortune—to find the other people who had been screwed by New Medico and were willing to say so. People who were former employees, or who knew former employees, parents and other family members, anyone I could find. I made a two-thousand-card rolodex that was nothing but New Medico contacts and the like. And not only New Medico, because there were plenty of other chains like it, like the Greenery.

After that, I started networking with those people. Some of these famous people would call me and say, "My son was in such and such a place." I went to the local meetings of the Head Injury Association—that was such a farce. These people had nothing in common. They had head injuries, but they didn't have the same problems. Anyway, I'd go to these meetings, and then we'd all go out to Howard Johnson's afterwards and talk, and that's when I got connected with people who had been in there, or they knew somebody who had, or someone once came to one of their meetings, or they got this number somewhere, or that kind of thing. And I eventually made a huge network of people who were basically feeding information to me, and I was taking oral histories, transcribing them.

I got invited to speak at a couple of places. I became like, the brain injury survivor of the millennium. Everybody was organizing brain injury conferences and they were embarrassed to note that they hadn't invited anybody who had actually survived a brain injury, so I got invited to a lot of places. And I found out I was being paid fifty dollars, plus expenses, and these "experts" who didn't know anything were getting paid three thousand dollars, and I hollered and howled and made quite a fuss. That was pretty funny. At one of these conferences I made everybody repeat the Pledge of Allegiance until they *got* it, got the part "with liberty and justice for all." Now did we all hear that? "With liberty and justice *for all*." We all grow up thinking this is the way it's supposed to be, right? And then we ignore it when somebody gets hurt? I didn't get invited back to any places, but a lot of places, all kinds of universities and whatnot, had me once. The Head Injury Foundation wrote me off as bitter and seeking revenge. They went on referring people and saying there's nothing wrong with New Medico, and that went on for quite a while.

I did immediately try to report New Medico to the local sheriff, the local police, and to the FBI, anybody, anywhere, as soon as I escaped. Later on I brought people to testify to the Commission on Quality of Care in New York State [in Albany]. People really poured out their stories. I didn't do much talking at all, it was the parents and the former inmates who were weeping and telling terrible, terrible stories that would break your heart. And the commissioners sat there, all listening, and they took notes, and whatnot, but afterwards one of them took me aside and he said, "Now, my daughter works for New Medico, she's in their marketing department, and none of this could be true." So they did nothing.

I was writing on average forty letters a day, to members of Congress, to anybody I could think of, just trying to say, "Here's what the problem is, who do I see about this? Help me find somebody I can turn these guys in to. They're scamming the insurance industry, they're scamming everybody." So people sent me to the Health Insurance Association of America, and Vicki Stephans, and Jim Spall, who is also a brain injury survivor and also a juris doctor, the three of us went to the Health Insurance Association headquarters in DC, and made a presentation about what was going on in the brain injury rehab industry, how it was all a shuck, how it was all screwed up. They all listened very politely, and one of them, this guy from Aetna, took me aside afterwards and said, "You don't really understand our industry, do you? The more we pay out, the more we can charge. So you're not going to find anybody here who's working against fraud." And that was an important thing to know. He was telling me, "You came to the wrong place."

Meanwhile, I was also seeing attorneys constantly, and I got myself an attorney, and then had to get another one, because none of them really believed me. I wanted to sue New Medico. I wanted to bring a class-action suit, I wanted to bring a whistle-blower suit, based on all this fraud, the Medicaid and Medicare fraud that was going on. I wanted to use the Lincoln Law, which says that if you bring to the government's attention some way in which the government is being defrauded, and stop the fraud, then you can get 10 percent of it. I didn't want 10 percent of it for me, but I wanted a tool, a vehicle to undo some of the damage they had done to people. The Lincoln Law is not much used anymore, and all the attorneys said, "No, you have to be an employee." Well, by that time I had more information than any employee had about this company and how it worked.

And I had run into some reporters who were working on the same story. One of them in Boston worked for a weekly paper there, he drove all the way to Rochester, because he was on this story for a long time, but couldn't get anybody to pay attention to it. He'd write things and nothing would happen. And so he brought all of his research to me in the trunk of his car. And he had done some really good research on the money, on where it came from, and where it went, and how it got there. I got another guy interested at *Probe*—a little newsletter for investigative reporters. He did something on it, and because of *Probe*, a producer guy from *NBC News* called me. As it turned out a committee in Texas was investigating a New Medico facility, so I sent everything I had to them. So I was getting these letters out every day.

One day I sent Ted Weiss—he was the congressman from the Upper West Side of Manhattan—I sent him one like I sent everybody else—and his aide called me the day she got the letter, and said, "We've got to talk, this is interesting." And this aide, Ann Marie, she got the FBI interested. In the meantime I was putting out the magazine,[5] and making a lot of contacts through that. That's how I met Sharon Mistler and Phil Calkins, that's how I met Ed Roberts, that's how I met just so many glorious people who helped.

And so, it's like everything converged there in 1992, because I got NBC on the line, they're gonna do the story. They've done all the interviews, and I was interviewed, they're holding it, because they know there's going to be this congressional committee hearing, it was a subcommittee of which Weiss was chairman. They got the FBI involved. I'd say to people,

"Look, I'm going to have the FBI call you," and they'd think I was nuts, and then the FBI would call and say, "This is special agent so and so." So all that converged at once, and we got the front page of the *New York Times,* the day after the hearing started, and that was another reporter who'd been on it a while, apparently, and then *NBC News Presents* had a special one-hour deal on it. It all happened at the same time.

The New Medico in Texas, I helped put that one out of business entirely. They had a guy there, in the Texas New Medico, near Tyler, Texas, as I remember, because Tyler news was covering it, I worked with that producer too. They had a source at the place who called me, so I got his name and number for the FBI. His job was, when somebody ran away, his job was to chase him down in a pickup truck and jump out and tackle him, wrap him up in rope, and throw him in back—just like he was a cowboy. He was a behavior technician cowboy.

It was just unique to see the cockroaches scurry off into the woodwork when we turned on the lights. It was really something. The empire folded, but it took a couple of years for the empire to fold.[6]

18
Self-Advocates

GUNNAR DYBWAD WAS FOND OF TELLING AN ANECDOTE THAT PER-
fectly illustrated the progression from the parents' movement to self-
advocacy. In the 1950s,when he became its executive director, the Association
for Retarded Children published a pamphlet titled *We Speak for Them*—"them"
being people, particularly children, labeled "mentally retarded." Thirty years
later a group of those now-grown children formed an organization called
Speaking for Ourselves—one of the many groups that comprised the burgeon-
ing "self-advocates" movement of the 1970s and 1980s.[1]

"It [was] a most natural thing," Dybwad remarked. "Originally, the persons with mental retardation were not only young, but the older ones were
awkward. They didn't have good schooling." But with deinstitutionalization,
"normalization," and "mainstreaming"—all reforms fostered by the parents'
movement—people now labeled "developmentally disabled" began to speak
out for themselves. By the mid-1970s many thousands of people formerly consigned to institutions began to enter the community, where they confronted
new challenges and new choices. In Salem, Oregon, a loosely organized group
of people who had been recently released from the Fairview Training Center,
with the Reverend Dennis Heath as their mentor, formed the nucleus of what
would become a national and then international movement.

Dennis Heath
*"I didn't realize that was called 'stirring things up,' getting the
people involved . . . and speaking for themselves."*

Born in 1940 and educated as a minister and a social worker, Dennis L. Heath
spent much of his professional life as the "fieldwork manager" and "social

work supervisor" at the Fairview Training Center in Salem, Oregon. Opened in 1908, Fairview was another of the massive state institutions in which people with various disabilities (however loosely defined) and other "undesirables" were incarcerated, many of them for their entire lives. Those committed to Fairview included "orphans, hitchhikers, promiscuous girls and people with mental illness."[2]

By the time Heath arrived in 1972, the institution held several thousand people, ranging in age from infants to the elderly. "There was a guy who was kind of blind in one eye, and he kind of limped. There was no testing, no distinction between 'mild' 'moderate' 'borderline.' It was like, if you were different, you needed to be in Fairview." There were other holdovers from the past besides the vague criteria for admission. As part of his job, Heath sat on a board that made decisions "around the issue of whether women [residents] would be sterilized. It would meet monthly, and review cases of who was to be sterilized, and who wasn't. I think the sterilization board stopped around '74, '75."

People First began as an extension of Heath's work tracking those Fairview residents who were beginning to move out into the community. Founded in 1974, it would become both a catalyst and prototype for self-advocates around the world. "The embryo was people talking, and running the meetings themselves, and sharing about their lives, and listening to each other."

After more than thirty years, Heath is still in contact with many of the movement's first leaders. But although the closing of institutions like Fairview has been a definite leap forward, the benefit has also come at a cost. "In the very beginning it was easy to have these support groups, because there were all these people who were identified as having been in the institution. We've always had a hard time reaching out to younger people, bringing in people that have never been in the institution, that lived at home."

At the time of our conversations Heath was still active as an advocate and counselor in the Salem area.

They called us field-workers. Field-workers provided follow-up to people that had been released from the institution and were living in group homes, or foster homes, around the Salem area. So I had access to people who had once lived in the institution and now were living in the community.

I've seen pictures of the early days. When Fairview started it was crib to crib to crib. There was an inner circle of cottages and then an outer circle, and the cottages were divided by the disability. Profoundly severely retarded, developmentally disabled folks, lived in the intensive care cottages. Originally it was outside of Salem, and they had crops all around, a community in and of itself. Everything they ate, they grew there. They had hogs, they had chickens. But by the time I got there, there were homes all around, it wasn't isolated anymore, but there was still this feeling that the community wouldn't tolerate having people that were different. It was like this group of people are helpless, and can't take care of themselves, and they need to stay at Fairview. Like Terry Schwartz, he said he was brought there when he was two years old. When I came there, he was one of the first people that I followed in the community.

The former residents lived in group homes, or foster homes. None of them could be called just living on their own. So there were lots of group homes and foster homes, and the foster homes had up to five people, they could have up to ten when I first started. There were also what they called board and room facilities, where people were placed from the institution, and board and room providers were given money for their board and room.

One of the things that the people from Fairview taught me was the language of the people, and how those communication styles worked. I recognized the fact that people who had lived in the institutions felt very uncomfortable in making decisions for themselves. They couldn't do anything unless they had a staff member's okay. And they felt very uncomfortable in the sense of who they were as people, and did they have rights? It was like the sense of who they were had been held back.

I saw it at the institution because I would roam around and look at some of the cottages, and I noticed some of the cottages had people that were ready to go into the community, but they were still asking the staff permission to do this, to do that. So when they got into the community, I started asking, "How do you feel about that? Do you ever think about making a decision on your own?" And they talked about how fearful that was, how they just felt uncomfortable doing anything without the okay of the staff person. They were very articulate about that. The early members of People First, the founding People First members were all very verbal. And they had a sense of what was going on.

One of the things that I tried to do was to use the group setting to help them learn how to be more powerful in and of themselves. They could run the group, they could choose what they wanted to talk about, and they could ask each other for opinions. A lot of times, the early times, they would look at me to see what I would say. I'd say, "Why don't you ask the guy sitting next to you? Or the person across the circle?" So in that small setting I was helping them maybe unlearn some of those behaviors that they'd learned for so long at the institution. . . . They found out that they were much better when they were in a group, all dealing with the same issue. That there were many ideas, and suggestions, and they were all coming from non-staff-related people. And that was so important to them. They actually developed that sense of pride.

I always wanted to make sure that everyone in the group had a chance to talk. To start off, we always—introduce yourself, where do you live, what do you do? You see in the early days too nobody had anything to do. There weren't even activity centers or sheltered workshops—only in a few outlying communities were there sheltered workshops. People were placed in board and room facilities, but they had nothing to do. Where at Fairview they had lots of stuff to do. So developing a lifestyle in the community was a big challenge for several years until they really got going with activity centers, workshops, and real work for people, not just fake work.

One day Larry Talkington, the superintendent, called me up to his office. He'd gotten this flyer from Vancouver Island, British Columbia, and they were going to have a convention run by the retarded. He'd made me a fieldwork supervisor, he wanted me to run the community process. And so he brought me up there and said, "Dennis, I want you to go up there with a couple of people from the institution and a couple from the groups in the community, and participate in this." This was in October of '73.

And so I drove up there with three people from Fairview, my wife, and my little son. And the Association for Retarded Citizens was hosting this, on Vancouver Island in British Columbia. It's a resort area, and they had a conference.

My whole thing was to really look at this process, because I had this foundation of groups already, these small groups of former Fairview residents now living in group homes. So I was looking at, how are they going to do this? Well, during the two-day event, not one identified person, not one—as they called them in those days "mentally retarded person"—said anything. The teachers, parents, the ARC members, they did all the talking, and the "mentally retarded" people sat and rocked and looked at each other.

And then we broke off into little clusters, into other little groups that talked. I got in a group, and each of my people got into a group. They introduced me, "This is Dennis Heath from Oregon." "Oooh, that's a long ways away from where we're at!" And I asked, "How come none of you have gotten up and said anything?"

The room was just quiet. There were twenty people in the room. And I said, "I read the brochure and it said people from group homes, and wherever you were from, were going to run this convention." And this one guy laughed and he said, "Well, you can see how much we're running it." And since it was billed as from the Association for Retarded Citizens, I said, "What do you all think of the name 'retarded'?" And there was like a unison of people who said, "We hate that name! We hate that!" And I said, "Have you ever told anybody? Have you ever said anything?" "Well, nobody will listen to us." And then I said, "Well, in Oregon we've started having groups where the people themselves who used to be in the institutions, who now live in the community, they run the groups and they talk and they share, and they've started to feel good about themselves."

So when that session was over the people went out into the general meeting. And a teacher said, "Well, I'll summarize" what happened in our little group, and I said, "Why don't we let this gentleman here, who's got some strong feelings, summarize?" I tried to get one person up there who wasn't a teacher, or a parent, or from the Association for Retarded Citizens. And he said, "You know, we were kind of wondering in our group why none of us have said anything yet." And then he said, "We also said that we don't like the word 'retarded,' and we think the Association for Retarded Citizens should change its name." Oooh, did that ever—they really got pissed at me then. This guy that was the head of Bevin Lodge on Vancouver Island, he said that he didn't appreciate me stirring things up. And I said, "Oh, I didn't realize that that's called 'stirring things up,' getting the people involved in their own lives, and speaking for themselves. I didn't realize that that was such a problem."

Then we got together, the other three people from Fairview, and they said that they were surprised that of all the people in these groups, that it was a teacher or a parent or somebody else that was doing all the talking. And that people just sat and listened. I came back to Oregon, and told Larry that it was a good idea, what they had planned, but it gets an F for how it played out.

That was my first look outside of Salem, looking at what other people did, and I thought, if that's what's being done—so I said, "Larry, we need to get some people together from both the institution and the community, and talk about this. Let's have something here in this state where people that have lived in institutions can get together and have a real convention where *they* are in control, and *they* do the talking, and have the microphone." Having the "mic" was always a big issue with our folks. Who has the microphone? Because who has the microphone has the power.

That's when the core group started meeting. We met at the institution the first couple of times, then we met in the community at group homes, and the groups were getting larger and larger. I remember we had a massive group one night, and everyone voted—and they were running their own meeting by that time—and they said, "We want to have a convention. We want to get everybody together."

Then we had to go through all the steps. Where do you have a convention, and where do people sleep, and what do they eat, and how do we get there? So it took us six or seven months to get those details worked out. We came back from Vancouver in October of '73, and People First had its first conference in November of '74, at Otter Crest off the coast of Oregon.

And during that year the name "People First" was born. "What are we going to call ourselves?" "Happy Guys" or the "Sunshine Group"— they were having fun with these different names. And one guy stood up and said, "You know, Dennis says that we really are people, and that our handicaps come second. I think that we should call ourselves People First, and then our handicaps are secondary." And everybody thought, "God, that was like a thunderbolt."

We had about five different committees. One was to pick a spot and bring back ideas—and people visited all these different places. One wanted to have it on the top of Mount Hood, one wanted to have it at Oregon State, and one at the Willamette football field, and you know we tried to—if you're going to spend the night you can't sleep in a football field. But they had to work through it all—that was like problem solving. . . .

There were about five hundred people at that first People First convention. Most of them were from Oregon, but a few from outside of Oregon, from British Columbia. The *Oregonian* and the *Statesman Journal* ran a couple of great articles about the convention. They had pictures and they described the personalities.

After our first convention the People First box got more mail from all over the country, and then it started to come from all over the world, because it spread like wildfire. Great Britain, New Zealand, Australia,

Germany. I mean we got letters from India, China, Russia: the mail just poured in. The word got out that People First belonged to the people, it was *their* group, it was *their* officers, and they ran the meetings.

We made a decision early on that no helper would ever go to one of these conventions, that it would always be the People First members and officers, so that professionals weren't passing on this word, but it was the people themselves. We thought that was a critical message. I promised myself at the very beginning to be the guy that's behind the curtain, quiet, helping. Suggesting, not telling. Showing options, but not leading. So I always stayed to the back. I was the official driver because I was the only one that had a driver's license.

With a little help from our friends, we started a how-to book at that time, like how do you do it? Everybody wanted a copy of that. Everybody wanted to know, how do you get it started? How do you do this? There were about ten of us, both People First members and a couple of helpers. It was a very basic book.

And I remember that people from California and Washington came to the second annual convention we had at the Inn at the Seventh Mountain, which was another resort. McMillan and Sons had these convention spots, one was at Otter Crest the other one was at the Inn at the Seventh Mountain. And so we had our second one, because they gave us I think it was a thousand dollars to help us. They were saying, "Thank you for having the event at our facility, and we want you to have this money."

When the word started to get out, and the letters started coming in, people wanted to have a convention like Oregon had had. So that was a big issue. In the first five years our folks went to several different states, and brought the message. And they brought the book with them, and we were sending that book out all over the country. It went to activity centers, workshops, ARCs, everybody wanted to know how do you do this? And it would usually be some helper at a workshop level or a group home level. It was very few people higher up in the echelons of different states that really connected with this. It was always somebody who worked directly with the people.

None of the helpers were paid. It was all volunteer case managers in Portland, Eugene, Salem, Eastern Oregon. We were all people who just did this as part of our jobs. And that was very fortunate for the first ten years of People First—there was no outlay. The money always went for stamps, envelopes, information sharing, telephone fees, and that kind of stuff. And every convention we charged a dollar [per person] that came to the organization itself.

The rest of the money went to pay for the convention, because the cost of spending the night and the meals was all—I mean now it looks very reasonable. The cost to have a convention now is almost prohibitive, because the developmentally disabled, number one, are generally poor people, and they don't have that kind of cash to go waltzing off to a high-level hotel and have a big meeting. So that kind of affected the organization after, oh, I would say twenty years.

But we found that some of the states started by getting the mental health division to pay for people to go to the convention, and we kind of were giving this feedback that that's not going to last forever, and the people need to figure out how to get to these conventions on their own finances. And that meant even having day meetings, or not having a full-blown convention, but having a time to get together. You know, Salem, our chapter, was so large that we started having once a year meetings in Salem with all the People First members, and we'd have three, four hundred people in the Salem area meet at a Red Lion motel, and we would start in the morning and we would go through the night, and we would have breakout sessions and dinner and a dance, and that was much more cost-effective.

The breakout sessions would be about issues like transportation in the city, or the right to talk to your guardian, to get rid of your guardian if you needed to. The guardian issue came up a lot, because the guardians could say whether they could get married or not. They could say they could live outside the institution or not. You know in Oregon you're a guardian both of money and body. It's a dual kind of guardianship, a holdover from the past. And parents were always encouraged to become the guardian, that way they would have a greater say in what went on at the institution. I remember at the disposition board, that a lot of time guardians came to the disposition board and said, "I want this for my son or daughter, I don't want this for my son or daughter." They were given a lot of power within the system.

Then there was the issue of marriage. A lot of our folks had boyfriends and girlfriends, and they moved into the community, and they got married.

All this was upsetting to a lot of folks because, number one, the professionals had to face the fact that they had to look at the quote client a little bit differently than just as someone they could control. There was a lot around the issue of control, who was in control of what? I mean if you had a client now starting to speak up and say, "Well, I want my advocates to come and help me deal with this issue"—a lot of times it wasn't the parent that they asked to come with them, it was someone out of People First. So People First was in new territory and had a new political stance with both the parents and also the professional providers. And I sensed a lot of the professional service providers didn't like giving up that little notch of power they had.

Gunnar [Dybwad] came out to an ARC convention in Oregon, and People First gave him a People First T-shirt, and he talked about he and his wife Rosemary and all the work they had done. He said, at last in my lifetime I have seen the people come to the proper stature, and the proper place, in being able to speak for themselves. He said all of his work was not in vain.

When I see People First groups around the world are still meeting, and still dealing with issues, I can kind of say, "The seed of that all began right here in Oregon." So if I have a legacy at all, it'll be just that comfort in knowing that what we started here has reached a lot of folks.

Terry Schwartz (continued)
"We're all people . . . we all have rights."

Although Terry Schwartz had left the institution where he'd spent most of his life, he continued to be in touch with his friends still there and with others who, like he, were now living in group homes or in their own apartments.

Schwartz is retired now, but during the 1970s and '80s he was active as a leader of People First.

People First started way back then. I was there at the beginning, and we just kept going, and we've been going, like, fifteen to twenty-five years—I don't know. Anyway, it was long ago. We had all these conventions and everything going, and this and that, and I got to go on some trips. I got to go to Canada, California, Nebraska, Kansas City. I got to go to Japan! Me and Dennis Heath got to go to Japan for a week. We had people from Japan come here, I was the host to them. And then, it was about a month later, and they wanted us to go down there, and so they paid for our plane trip, meals, motels, food, you name it, they did it all.

We are all human beings, we are all allowed to speak up, and we have a right to do what we want: a right to get married, a right to vote, just like regular people. And you know, because we were at Fairview so long, I mean it was hard for us to get going, to get used to being out. And that's what People First was about, to let us know that we had just as much rights as anybody else. So if we *can* do a job, we have the right to *do* a job. You know, and all these different things . . . we might not get it done as quick as others, but at least we get it done.

It was easy at some points, it was hard at some points. Number one, transportation, it was kind of rough on that one. We didn't have that many buses then and it was hard to get around.

I used to work in a sheltered workshop. Now here's the thing. They have a disabled person work on the job, the problem is they work on what's called piecework. You've probably heard about that. What they do, the faster they work, the more they put out, the more they get paid. See, the less work they do, the less they get. You see what I mean?

To me, it's just not right to do that. I just think they need to get better pay, just as much as other people get paid, and by the hour. And at the workshop they only get a small amount a month. They don't get like four hundred dollars, or six hundred dollars, or something like that. It's something that cannot be helped, because it's just too late, it should have been done long ago when they made up that contract, and that's what they got on the contract. When I used to work in the sheltered workshop, that's how much I'd get. I've been working in a restaurant for twenty-five to thirty years. Right now I'm retired.

The most important thing about People First is it just kind of reminds everyone that we're all people, and they ought to treat us just the same as anybody else. We're all people, we all have rights. We can speak out the way we want, we can do what we want, and live where we want, get married if we want, because back then, we weren't allowed to do all that.

Nancy Ward
"That saying about 'sticks and stones may break your bones but words will never hurt me' is a bunch of crap."

———

Unlike Terry Schwartz, self-advocate Nancy Ward was never institutionalized.

She was, however, segregated into a "special education" program in junior and senior high school. Born in 1950 in Lincoln, Nebraska, she was one of the leaders in organizing the People First chapter in that state.

———

I've never lived in an institution, but I've lived in large group homes, which are basically to me the same thing. It's out in the community but we really didn't get to be a part of the community. There was an apartment complex and there were three bedrooms, six people in each apartment. So you know, I didn't have my own space. I had no place to go just to be, so to speak.

It was independent enough that we could decide when we wanted to come and go for ourselves, and people got to go home. But at that time I didn't know how to do the bus, and so I had to stay there until my parents came and got me.

I worked in a sheltered workshop, and to understand the story you have to understand that the workshop was separate from the main building. My boss became ill, and so when she would go to her doctor appointments I would supervise the contract we were doing. We did all the mailing for Cushman golf carts. Eventually she had to quit work, and people tried to convince me that I should become the supervisor, but no matter how hard people tried to do that, they couldn't convince me, because even though I was doing it, I didn't see that, because of how people in the sheltered workshop are treated.

So, finally people got me convinced that I should at least go down to the main building, which was downtown, and fill out an application. So I did go down there, but they wouldn't even let me fill out an application because I was a sheltered workshop employee. Even though people at the sheltered workshop were telling me that I should do it. But [the administrators in] the main building didn't see people with disabilities, so of course they didn't think that people with disabilities should be able to do that. And so I went back to work, and a couple of weeks later there was somebody new on the staff, and so they introduced me to the new supervisor. And then the new supervisor and I were standing around talking. And as we were all standing around talking one of the other staff told me I was going to have to train the new supervisor. Well, that really pissed me off, so I quit and went and got my own job.

I went and worked for our [social] service system, what we call the

Service Advisory Committee: the SAC. Nebraska is divided into six different regions, and the director at the time for Region Five, she and the assistant director, were teaching the people that they served self-advocacy skills, how to advocate for themselves. Well, it's hard to have the person you see as your boss teaching you how to advocate for yourself, because of course you're not going to talk back. And so that's why they thought that it would be a good idea to hire me. The thing that I liked about it, and what Lynn said she really wanted me to do, though I didn't understand at the time, was to teach people how to close the sheltered workshops down. [Laughs.] I loved having that kind of power.

I became involved in the disability rights movement through Bonnie [Shoultz],[3] in 1980. Bonnie and I are both from Nebraska, and the first time that Bonnie and I worked together she made me mad. So, that's a good way to get to know somebody.

She was the adviser for Project Two, which was the first People First chapter in Nebraska. They called it Project Two because the ARC [the Greater Omaha Association for Retarded Children, and its Eastern Nebraska Community Office of Retardation, or ENCOR] was Project One. So the parents' had had *their* time to say what we were going to do, now it was time for *us* to say what we wanted. So that's why Ray Loomis [founder of People First of Nebraska] called it Project Two.

I think people who have been in an institution have a really hard feeling about the ARC I think that it's really hard for kids—and they're now adults—to see that that was the only option that parents had at the time. And the other part of it is, is that that was what doctors told them was the right thing to do. And surely a professional person knows what they're talking about. So I think there are some that are never going to work it out with their parents. And that's sad because, you know, some people who were in an institution had their family, and some people didn't. And some people found their family afterwards, like one of the People First members, my friend Al, found his family after he had gotten out of the institution, and now he has a relationship with his brother and his sister.

I think it is just as important for somebody to get up in a meeting and say their name as it is for somebody to give some big speech. It takes the same amount of courage. And so when I first started, I didn't speak out for myself.

We talked about Baby Doe, so we did an amicus brief. The Baby Doe case was where people with disabilities weren't seen as people, and they were allowed to starve to death. And of course people had to explain to us what that was, an "amicus brief." People First did it, we did it at a board meeting. We wrote the whole thing.

When we had the first international conference, it was at Puget Sound, and people from all over the world came together, and we had the same issues. And maybe we had problems with President Reagan, and other people had problems with Margaret Thatcher in England, and other people around the world had other problems, but the issues were the same. And that really amazed me, because it was people from all over, and I thought that we would have different issues going on. And one of the things that I really liked about that conference, there was this guy, his name was John O'Brien, and he's a person without a disability, but he facilitated part of the conference. And people got in this big fight. And he just sat there and let us work it out. And because of the conflict, some people left, because some people don't like conflict, but the whole point is that he could have done that for us, but it wouldn't have had the same impact that it did for us doing it ourselves.

Sometimes it was hard for some of our people to live and do things in the community. Right across the street from our [SAC] office was a KFC. We had gone to lunch together, the staff, and the people that they serve. And one guy in our group was standing in the middle of the counter, just staring, looking, because people who had been in the institution weren't allowed to make choices for themselves, and then he's got this whole list of choices that he has to make. And the staff person comes up to him and asks him if he couldn't hurry up. And I go, "You know, people who are in the institutions don't even get to make the choice of whether they want a hot dog or a hamburger, and if they want ketchup or mustard on it, and you're asking him to hurry up when he's seeing all these choices?"

People First in Nebraska at the time was doing this piece of legislation, because they had *moron, idiot,* and *imbecile,* all the kind of words that we really *love,* in our state statutes. And so People First had written legislation to get rid of the offensive terms. We asked the director of the ARC at the time what we needed to do, because we had testified [at the state house] before, but we had never written legislation. And he goes, "You're going to have to ask one of the senators to sponsor the bill for you." And we go, "We're going to have to do *what?*" Because you see senators as somebody way up there. So we were really scared, but we went and asked Senator Seek. He had a child with a disability, and so when it came time to introduce the legislation, Senator Seek let me do the introduction, so that was very cool for me to be able to do that. Everybody was nervous and scared, but he made people feel comfortable, because he knew how we felt, because of having a child with a disability.

We talked to TV and reporters about the legislation. It was the first time people had done that. Now I do it all the time, but when you've never done it before it is really scary. And when People First was started, we didn't have any role models. And it took me five years to learn how to speak out for myself.

We practiced in front of the mirror. We also did mock press conferences, where reporters would ask us questions, while our people would be playing like they were reporters.

There were senators who didn't want the legislation, and eventually we had to end up doing a compromise. So it has, I don't know if it still does, but when we did it, it had "people with mental retardation." So at least we have the person put first, but it still had "with mental retardation" and I don't know if they've changed it, because I haven't gone back there for eleven years.

When we first started self-advocacy, and it's definitely not this way now, so I hate to say it, but there was a pecking order within the disability community, and people with a cognitive disability were on the bottom of that order. And so nobody wanted to associate with us. I think that people finally learned that there's power in numbers, and so if we work together that we're going to accomplish more. Like now ADAPT and SABE [Self-Advocates Becoming Empowered],[4] which is the national self-advocacy organization, do stuff together all the time. But that relationship took time to build.

We had Justin Dart come to one of our national conferences, and he saw what people with a cognitive disability could do. I asked him, "You didn't think that we would be able to put on a big conference like this, did you?" And he said, "No." And so even somebody as high as that, who wants to work with people, still has that preconceived idea. After that we worked with Justin a lot. He helped get people on—then it was called, but it's not called this now—the President's Committee on Mental Retardation.[5] He helped self-advocates to get on that.

We did a lot with ADA. We did rallies, and we got people to understand what the Americans with Disabilities Act is, and we also pressured the senators and representatives. We attended conferences, and the people who worked on ADA nationally taught us different ways to do different things. Like how to lobby, except we call it "educate." And they taught us how to do rallies. They taught us a lot of different things.

When we were in Washington for ADA we did the ADAPT rally. Of course, ADAPT's radical, so there were a lot of things that were radical going on. One of the things that I think was ironic was that when people were hauled off, the jail wasn't accessible. And so they had to put people in a parking garage. And I thought that was pretty ironic. I don't have the courage to get arrested like that, but a lot of my friends do.

I think the biggest issue that we have is how to come together even more. Because I just think that our country is in big trouble. And we need to have the disability voice heard. I think even within the disability community there's issues of us working together, but I don't think it's like a pecking order. I think it's just that people with cognitive disabilities don't understand things sometimes. And society doesn't know how to work with something that they can't see. With people who have a physical disability, you can see it, so you can tell that they need the door opened, for example. I mean, I know it's a lot deeper than that.

I'd like to see the ADA have more teeth, and I'd like to see it define accessibility to help people with cognitive disabilities. Meaning that accessibility doesn't always mean a ramp, it could mean that people need to understand something, because big words are being used. My point being, that you can ask us the same things, but put it in language that we understand. It could be that people need to have signage to find something, because it's hard for them to navigate things. So different things like that. And the accessibility part of ADA doesn't have that. And so I wish we would have spoke out more when it was being passed.

The one thing that I would have for a final thought is that the saying about "sticks and stones may break your bones but words will never hurt me" is a bunch of crap. Because they really do hurt, and I just think that people need to be judged as people, and that you shouldn't judge a book by its cover. And I know those are clichés. But I'm a real sensitive person, and I get hurt real easy. It took me a long time to develop a thick skin, and to learn that you have to educate people about people with disabilities, and to let them know how it makes you feel when they do stuff like that.

And I think that it's real important to listen to people, even if they don't use words to communicate. We have to figure out how people communicate, and then it's up to us to figure out what they're saying.

19
DREDF and the 504 Trainings

B Y THE LATE 1970S WHAT HAD BEEN ALMOST ENTIRELY SEPARATE
streams of disability rights activism had begun to flow together, with a
synergy few could have predicted less than a decade before. Here, again, the
Center for Independent Living in Berkeley was a critical nexus, not only as a
catalyst for other independent living advocates across the country but also in
founding what was to become the nation's preeminent cross-disability legal
practice and public policy think tank.

Activists at Berkeley in the mid-1970s had already started the Disabled
Paralegal Advocacy Program (DPAP)—an office within the CIL staffed almost
entirely by volunteers—to work on behalf of CIL clients. It soon became clear,
however, that what was needed was an organization with a national focus that
was both cross-disability and civil-rights oriented, to litigate or offer assistance
in cases with the potential to impact disability rights case law (reported judicial decisions used as precedent by the courts in interpreting the meaning and
scope of written law) and, ultimately, to help craft and lobby for passage of
additional national legislation.[1]

A major step was taken in 1978, when the CIL received federal funding to
convert the DPAP into the Disability Law Resource Center (DLRC), which
in turn received funds from the Legal Services Corporation. The DLRC grew
rapidly, from a staff of eight volunteers to more than forty-five paid employees, but it continued to be a part of the Center for Independent Living, with
as much a local as a national focus. Finally, in 1979, the attorney Robert Funk
and activists Mary Lou Breslin and Patrisha Wright cofounded the Disability
Rights Education and Defense Fund, or DREDF, as an independent nonprofit
national law and policy center, analogous to the NAACP's Legal Defense Fund.
Bob Funk became its first executive director.

Meanwhile, the Department of Health, Education, and Welfare had invited
proposals for programs to train advocates with disabilities about their rights
under 504. Three different organizations set up what came to be known as "the

504 trainings"—workshops conducted in the late 1970s and early 1980s—designed not only to educate people about this provision of the Rehabilitation Act of 1973 but also to introduce political advocacy to an entire generation of disability rights activists and organizers.

DREDF took the lead in designing these workshops, and together with the Public Interest Law Center of Philadelphia (where Thomas K. Gilhool had already made a reputation as the chief litigator of *PARC v. Pennsylvania*) and Barrier Free Environments (founded by Ron Mace, the architectural access guru, in Raleigh, North Carolina), it created a cadre of thousands of trained activists that was to prove invaluable as the movement fought to keep what it had won and build on its mounting successes.

Mary Lou Breslin (continued)
"That basic shift in how you look at the issue—that's what we did."

———

Having earned a degree in sociology from the University of Illinois in 1966, Mary Lou Breslin pursued graduate studies at Roosevelt College in Chicago and the University of Oklahoma, Norman. She left school in 1971 and worked as a psychiatric social worker, a peer counselor, and a tutor. Breslin moved to Berkeley in 1972, where she became coordinator of the Disabled Students' Placement Program at the University of California and with others at the CIL was an organizer of the 1977 HEW occupation. Breslin, Patrisha Wright, and Robert Funk founded DREDF in 1979. Initially deputy director, Breslin became director in January 1987 and today is a senior adviser with DREDF and one of the nation's leading disability policy advocates. She has taught at UC Berkeley and the University of San Francisco, and has written widely on disability topics, most recently on health care equity for people with disabilities.

———

Bob Funk walked in, historically, when he should have walked in. Bob wanted to do public interest law. He walked into Phil Draper's office at CIL, and Phil had all these federal Requests for Proposals on his desk and didn't know what to do with them. Phil gave them to Bob, and that's it. Bob sat down and in two months wrote about $1 million worth of grants and got them all.

That was a really important moment. The Legal Services Corporation, which funded all the legal aid offices around the country, was not
convinced that disability was a legitimate civil rights issue. Bob, though,
understood that a public interest practice was needed in disability, and
he came up with the idea of DLRC.

I started working for Bob, running this western regional program to
train people with disabilities about 504. There's no staff, there's no office,
and there's no phone, there's no physical place to put anybody. The back
room at CIL was a concrete slab—just a garage. It was November. It was
freezing. It was raining. We dragged in space heaters and put a couple
of doors on two file cabinets and strung in a phone line and the project
was running.

Meanwhile, Bob rented space across the street in an old warehouse.
He was trying to hire people to run these projects, who in fact were also
building office space, because we had no money to pay anybody to do
any of it. So he's got everybody hanging sheet rock and answering the
phone at the same time. It was completely chaotic. You've got forty-five
job descriptions on the street, trying to hire lawyers, trying to hire clerical people, trying to hire program directors—there was nobody to run
any of this stuff. It was insane.

I had the biggest chunk of money to manage, in terms of this federal
contract. It was the biggest and most volatile political issue. These HEW
guys didn't have any confidence that we could do it. They're setting up
site visits and saying, "We're going to be out on such-and-such date, and
we want to meet with your advisory board, we want to see your brochure." I'd never done any of this before. I didn't even know how to generate an invoice, and CIL sure couldn't help me do that.

Bob was absolutely king of the mountain in terms of holding it all
together, telling everybody what to do, putting his soul into the thing. I
was the first disabled person to come on, working for him, but I ended
up much more in a partner relationship with him. Pretty quickly, it was
real clear that he and I were compatible in terms of our ability to work
together.

The idea was that we would send out to various cities a team of
three people with disabilities. They would be the training team that
would work with anywhere from fifty to a hundred people over a four-
day period, to teach the law, to help people develop analytical skills, to
develop communication skills and negotiation skills.

The training curriculum that we worked up had many components in addition to the actual teaching of the law itself. We set out to train trainers, which was never conceived of in the original proposal. But once the contract came in, we realized, "Who's going to do it? Does anybody know anything about training?" Here we are; we're just a bunch of Berkeley hippies, and we don't know anything. So we had to figure out, we had to train ourselves to be trainers.

So we learned the regs, we developed a training team, we learned process and substantive skills, and we went out and traveled for the next year, which was fall of '78 to fall of '79, to twelve or fifteen cities—recruiting people from the disability community to come in and talk about 504. We were pretty raw at the beginning, but we got better and better. By the time we got done with that first year we were pretty good at it.

That contract was renewed in the coming year, and expanded. Later, we ended up also being awarded the training contract for the midwestern region, and we did that for a couple years. We sold all our materials and consulted with groups in the East who used the same model—all the same manuals and curriculum and whatnot.

Every single bit of this was new, conceptually, and the idea that you could take this information and use it as a tool in the community, to make something happen, also required that you develop some other skills to go along with it. How do you talk to the guy who's in charge at the social service office, or whatever it is? If you want something, and they don't want to give it to you, how do you negotiate it, if that's an option? If it's not an option, what do you do next?

The first year we trained grassroots people with disabilities—people who were selected because they had some activist role in their community. The idea was that they would take the information and go do something in the community. The goal would be that they would pick some issue that they could resolve based on 504. It was an implementation strategy, because the regulation had this one sentence in it calling for knowledgeable consumer input into the decision making. That was the hook that all these trainings used. It didn't exist in other civil rights laws; it was a completely new thing. It got stuck in there because a handful of people at HEW realized that 504 ain't going to work if disabled people in the community aren't empowered at least to know about it. So a lot of money flowed, based on that one sentence in the regulation. It's hard to believe some of these things happened the way they happened.

We were really committed to having people with various disabilities: people who were blind, people with hearing disabilities. That entailed, of course, every kind of support you could imagine, none of which was budgeted for initially. We were about four or five weeks into the contract, and we realized there was no way anybody ever thought about what it was really going to take to do this. We realized that we had to travel with attendants, that we had to travel with [American Sign Language] interpreters. We thought about hiring people at the other end, but realistically, there was no good way—particularly with interpreters—to hire local interpreters when we're dealing with such arcane material.

So we traveled with this road show. We made a video because we decided that it was going to be real hard for people who were accustomed to thinking that blind people had different issues than people who used wheelchairs; we needed some way to transcend those perceptions of difference. So we did this video, *As We Are,* which actually still stands up now so many years later, except for the haircuts. It was a little talking-head thing with people with eight or nine different disabilities, including somebody who had a history of substance abuse and somebody with a psychiatric disability. It was making the point that the issue was not their particular disability; the issue was the way they were treated, the discrimination which prevented x or y or z from happening.

So we made the video—it was not originally budgeted. We traveled with interpreters—that was not originally budgeted. We did braille, we did tape, we did attendants—not budgeted. We traveled with wheelchair repair people who ended up doing ten other jobs. We traveled with our own audio equipment. We decided it was cheaper to buy it and take it with us than it was to try to rent it in each city, because we needed so much of it because of all the interpreting and all the stuff that was accommodation-related.

Mostly we would travel together, but sometimes people would come in from different locations depending on where we were. It was a scheduling nightmare. We ended up having to hire a scheduling person who did nothing but pre-preparation. We realized we couldn't verify any hotel access, so we sent people out to visit all the hotels, because there were no accessible rooms anywhere. One or two, maybe, and they'd be questionable, and we had thirty people in wheelchairs or something. We had to negotiate with every hotel to agree to let us pull the doors off in the bathroom and build ramps. It felt like the Pope was coming into town.

I was running this 504 project, so I was always heading up the thing in some way or other in terms of being the lead trainer or the manager or whatever. But mostly we just would divide up tasks by skills and interests, and I usually did technology and wheelchairs, and somebody else did women's stuff, and somebody else did management and whatever.

I was always the lead trainer in the cities that I traveled to. That meant you opened the thing, watched the clock, you do your pieces, you pay attention to everybody else, you make sure everybody's on time. You moderate any disagreements which arise between people who are attending, and deal with any politics or press or whatever.

What I learned from all is that it's the same thing everywhere. The same things that I'd experienced here or anywhere, were going on everyplace. We knew there was discrimination, and we knew people were having all sorts of experiences that were just exactly parallel to what we all personally knew about.

The people who were trained ended up comprising this grassroots national network that DREDF relied on and built and continues to add to even as we speak. This was the basis for our grassroots lobbying efforts when the Reagan administration came into office, intending to gut the 504 regulations. So that was the first example of where it really paid off.

There is a legacy of those trainings, but I didn't think there was for a long time. After I got done with it I was very cynical about it for many years. Now I have changed my tune. I got a call from somebody in the late eighties who portrayed a problem in civil rights terms. I realized in the course of that phone conversation that that person would never have used that civil rights concept in analyzing the situation they were telling me about, if we hadn't been out there spreading this gospel. It was like some kind of messianic thing we did. "The problem is the inaccessible city hall, not that I can't walk up the steps." That basic shift in how you look at the issue—that's what we did. I underestimated its ultimate impact because I was too close to it at the time.

Really, it wasn't about 504. 504 was a tool, a way of embodying that principle and giving it to people in a way that they could make it be personal and could use it. They shifted the game; 504 shifted their own thinking.

The trainings had a real powerful impact over time. It didn't happen instantly. It had kind of a ripple effect: after we trained 5,000 or 6,000 people around the country, it started to resonate. So its legacy is an important one, especially as the idea of the ADA began to evolve.

Arlene Mayerson
"So she can't do it, but it's discrimination?
Why is that discrimination?"

Patrisha Wright—herself a legendary disability rights lobbyist—once called Arlene Mayerson the movement's "secret weapon." By "secret" Wright meant perhaps that Mayerson is less well known than Ed Roberts, Justin Dart, or Judy Heumann. Nonetheless, it's difficult to overstate Mayerson's role in and contribution to the development of disability rights law.

Born in 1949, Mayerson received her BS in political science from Boston University in 1971, her JD from Boalt Hall School of Law at the University of California at Berkeley in 1977, and her LLM from the Georgetown University Law Center in Washington, DC, in 1978. It was during this period that she clerked with W. Arthur Garrity, the federal district judge who ordered the desegregation of Boston public schools by busing, whom she called "a great historical figure." The experience allowed Mayerson to see first hand the impact a civil rights suit could have—in this case, one filed on behalf of Boston families by the NAACP.

Mayerson became a staff attorney in 1979 at the CIL's Disability Law Resource Center, staying with the center as it evolved into DREDF. Mayerson's first significant success came as counsel for people with disabilities and parents who sought the withholding of federal education funding from the state of California in response to its failure to comply with the Education for All Handicapped Children Act, a first-of-its-kind victory in disability rights activism. From there she went on to become a key player in Washington in everything from the fight to keep the Reagan administration from "deregulating" (that is, gutting) Section 504 of the Rehabilitation Act of 1973 to passage of the ADA in 1990 and beyond.

The Disability Law Resource Center [DLRC] was this big building across the street from CIL. It was a big warehouse, and [when I first arrived] people were just laying carpets. Bob [Funk] was the head of the whole place, and Mary Lou Breslin was the head of the 504 training component, and then there's this little legal services office. It looked like a prison [laughter]. It was this enclosed area behind bars, and it was me, Paul Silver, and Shirley Nakao. Paul Silver was a great guy, but he wasn't exactly into being a directing attorney or supervisor, so we were on our own, trying to figure out what to do with this new organization.

Clarence Hart was my first case. He had been turned down as a counselor at Almeda Juvenile Hall because he couldn't drive due to epilepsy. I called Prudence Popink, from the Employment Law Center, whom I didn't know and who was much more senior than I was, and asked her to co-counsel the case. DLRC didn't really have a strong definition of what we were doing, so we would go from doing Clarence Hart 504-type cases, to [dealing with] just anyone who happened to walk in, trying to make phone calls and seeing what we could do to help them out.

I was just finding my own way. I didn't even have a desk at first. I was in the back room, kind of sitting on the floor. I have a very anarchistic feeling of the ambiance of the place. People were working on their own projects, and gradually people got to know each other in various ways, just depending on personality. My general view of the place was that Bob Funk was basically finding talented people that he could then leave alone.

The parent project at DLRC was very dynamic, and was meant to provide something similar to legal services to parents. People called up asking questions about what their legal rights might be. It quickly developed into a place where there could be some accounting of problems that were being heard over and over again, and therefore a source of information for community organizing. Even though it started out as just, "Let's answer the calls," when the three-hundredth call came in about, for example, occupational physical therapy services not being provided, it became clear that this was some place to make a focused effort.

Another thing that happened when I was at DLRC was we had our overnight sit-in, or protest, when the US Department of Transportation regulations came out.[2] Everyone that was at DLRC would be involved in something like that. It wasn't exactly civil disobedience, but demonstrations and protest. Going to the Department of Transportation, we all stayed overnight.

That is when I first met Pat Wright, that night at the Department of Transportation. I don't know if she was there as anyone's particular attendant, but I met her because something happened to somebody; they fell or twisted their leg or something. I went over to the scene, and she said she would take care of it. She acted very authoritative and seemed to know what she was doing.

I think just the idea of being a part of something that was bigger than the law, working with people who weren't lawyers, who were doing all kinds of other things that felt like something that was bigger than just being a lawyer. I was part of a movement. That was pretty unusual in 1980.

[An example of what I mean when I say "bigger than the law" is the DLRC response to the *Davis* case].[3] Basically, that case was the first [Section 504] case heard in the Supreme Court. It involved [Francis B. Davis], a woman who was hard of hearing/deaf, who did have some hearing but relied a lot on lip reading. She wanted to be a nurse, [but] there were parts of the clinical training program that were considered inappropriate for her to do because of her not being able to hear normally. So, the question was whether there was an accommodation that could make it appropriate, or whether it could be waived, or whether she was just not going to be able to be admitted [to the program].

I'm thinking this is a great example of 504 because this woman wants to be a nurse. She's qualified in every way. The idea being that she could still be a nurse, and that there are many things that nurses do that don't require one to hear in the normal range.

Well, I think the Supreme Court thought the whole thing was pretty bizarre, because they were used to a model of discrimination where the plaintiff could do absolutely everything that the other person could do. The black person could do everything the white person could do. The woman could do everything the man could do. It was the mere fact that they had the status of being black or a woman that was being used to prevent them from doing it. To the Court, that is what discrimination was.

So, being given a case where, "Wait a minute, so she can't do it, but it's discrimination? Why is that discrimination?" That was a concept that was too hard for the Supreme Court to get. Consequently, they came out with a very negative decision, which kind of negated the whole premise of disability-based discrimination in the regulations for 504, which was that in order to have equal opportunity, you had to have accommodations, and that sometimes, in order to have an equal opportunity, you have to be treated differently. That was way beyond their grasp, and they didn't like it, and they rejected it. After *Davis,* the whole notion of a meaningful anti-discrimination law was in question.

I'm just starting. I'm a lawyer, and there are all these community activists who formed this movement, made this movement happen. The person I'm thinking of particularly, as I remember that incident, is Kitty [Curtis] Cone.

Everyone was saying they want to do a protest. They want to say it's outrageous. They want to say the Supreme Court doesn't understand 504. From a lawyer's point of view, and me, at the time, being just a young punk, when the Supreme Court speaks, *that's the law*. You don't really want to talk about how it devastated your law because the next case is around the corner. But the community activists were outraged, because it was outrageous.

I remember trying to assert a point of view that maybe it wasn't the best idea to give quotes and to be reacting to the case as though there was nothing left of the law. From a lawyer's point of view, it was like admitting defeat, even in addition to the defeat that actually happened. It sent a message out that the law had no teeth. But from a community organizing point of view, it was just one more institution screwing over people with disabilities, and you want to respond to that.

Thomas K. Gilhool (continued)
"They tended to be gentle and shy. It was their adaptation to powerlessness"

———

Thomas K. Gilhool, fresh from the victory of *PARC v. Pennsylvania* and already involved in the Pennhurst deinstitutionalization lawsuit, also took a role as the director of the 504 trainings undertaken by the Public Interest Law Center of Philadelphia.

———

The logistics were a nightmare. You know, this was before most hotels knew what accessibility was, and it was not easy. There would be fifty, plus or minus, people from the disability world, and there would be the advisory committee of ten, and the six, seven of us, so sixty-seven, seventy people, and partly that was for all the obvious reasons, but also, to make the role-playing exercises real.

The group of fifty was divided into four or five sections and given a scenario. Then they had to plan the negotiation, including their purposes and how they were going to get there, and then, they actually conducted the negotiation, played it out. At various places we rented actors or college students to play officials on the other side. And each role-play was attended by a coach, who observed all the way through and then engaged conversation among all of the players in evaluation of what had happened. We developed six or seven scenarios that we used, and at various times we also role-played meetings with editorial boards of newspapers.

In the role-play negotiations, in the first run, people would not press. Somebody playing a school bureaucrat or a state bureaucrat would offer a dodge, and sometimes people would not take it, but sometimes they would. And when we asked people afterward, "Why?" it became apparent that it had to do with the unpracticed life as a citizen that many people with disability had led to that point. I mean, for many people, the 504 demonstrations were the coming out. And while there were many people who had been at it for a good while, and had significant experience, many people were young, or maybe even middle-aged people with disability who had not had the opportunity to push public officials and the bureaucracy around to achieve their purpose. They tended to be gentle and shy. It was their adaptation to powerlessness.

Well, at some point in the design of the thing, significantly influenced by the conversations with the board of disabled persons who were already veterans, we formulated three teachings that we wanted people to get, not just in the head, but at the tips of their fingers. Number one: Never take no for an answer. Number two: If one way doesn't get what you want, try another way. And number three: Always go to the top.

There was a lineage of the design of this training in legal services, but there's another lineage that is just as important. And that is the welfare rights organizations, whom I represented here in Philadelphia in the late sixties. In Pennsylvania, they negotiated a recognition agreement with the Department of Public Welfare that gave them access to every public assistance office, to assist people in seeking public assistance benefits, and shortly thereafter, they began to say to people, "We will help you if you will agree that you will help others and that you will join us in training"—now I'm sure it wasn't put that way—"to know public assistance law and the regulations and the system and in the ways and means of getting stuff for others." And that happened pretty much all across the country. California, Chicago, all over the country, there were welfare rights organizations in the late sixties, usually functioning in some relationship to legal services programs, and they had an extraordinary effect. And then the Reagan revolution, of course, and the Clintons, crushed all of that.

The trainings were done on a statewide basis. In some states, like Pennsylvania, we did two or three, probably also in New York State. Sometimes, we did a training and then the leadership at that training did trainings elsewhere in the state. [We also did a section on] the political history and the contemporary politics of a state. We pulled this together from a series of books that were available at the time, running down state by state who the major players were, in terms of making things happen. Not just economic, but also bureaucratic. I do not know of a current analogue, by the way, of those books, but they were invaluable. In advance of the training, we'd put the relevant chapter—Massachusetts, New Jersey, etc.—in the hands of all of the people who were coming, and the only other materials we put in their hands, I think, were the 504 materials.

The [next portion] concerned public actions, whether these be demonstrations, or newspaper or media strategies, or what have you, public opinion strategies. And what we played with, in the exercises and in the conversations and so on, was what is now called "framing." Typically, we would start the training session with the history of disability, of the state-imposed segregation and degradation rivaling—even exceeding—that of Jim Crow. And then the other side of it, the triumphs of the movement, in order to get to things like nearly every extended family has the experience of disability, and why you can't count on how any given person from such a family will regard questions of disability, and you're going to need to find that out.

But the primary emphasis of the training was not so much the uses of the law in formal proceedings, courts, or even administrative proceedings, but it was the uses of the law in public action, and in negotiation. César Chávez never went into a negotiation without at least the same number of people at the table for his side as there were people on the other side of the table for the other side. And if possible, one or two more, and that was for several purposes: one, to match the power, in a very important interpersonal sense, and two, they would assign responsibility for watching and gauging the thought, the reaction, where each individual on the other side was coming from. They would assign one of their team to watch one of their team. And in the unpacking after any negotiation, they would report, "What did you see? What did you conclude about whether Agent Y of the growers," in that case, or of a department, or a town council, or what have you, in our case: "Where did Agent Y come from?" And you'd be looking for people who looked like they might come with us, and why. What had moved them to do so? That was all a part of the debriefing, the unpacking of any given negotiation.

And then [after the trainings] we would provide technical assistance [to the local organizations]. All of us participated, and we tracked actions and victories across the states. The effects were pervasive, virtually from the beginning. Remember, going on at the same time, was the Transbus battle,[4] which was both national and local. The other thing that was going on was the Pennhurst trial and the first [Pennhurst court] orders.[5] And 1978 was the effective date of the Education for All Handicapped Children Act, and so you had such very significant activity, state by state and around the country, that arose after the clarion call of the 504 demonstrations on all of those fronts: transportation, community services, education.

All of this was significantly infused and buoyed by the networks that came out of these trainings. I'm sure our reports and DREDF's reports and North Carolina's reports probably recite some of that, which would allow you to track the growth of the movement, from the 504 demonstrations and trainings, to those extraordinary numbers of the state-by-state hearings conducted by Justin Dart [for the Task Force on the Rights and Empowerment of People with Disabilities, leading to the passage of the ADA]. It's much the same people as attended those workshops. The movement continued to grow and grow.

Johnnie Lacy (continued)
"I left with that sense of righteous indignation."

After graduating from San Francisco State University in 1960, Johnnie Lacy, at the suggestion of her state vocational rehabilitation counselor, volunteered at Easter Seals as a way to try to work herself into a job market that offered few opportunities to an African American woman with a disability, even if she did have a college degree.

"I thought I was going there to practice my typing, and I practiced my typing, yes: but it was in a fishbowl, where they set me up right in the middle of the center of the rehab floor. The idea was that I'd be a role model for other disabled people and they could see me practicing this skill and they would be encouraged. And I hated that."

She started her first paying job in 1962, as a secretary and order clerk for a drapery and upholstery manufacturing firm in Los Angeles. She worked there until the firm relocated to San Francisco, at which point she began working as a clerk at the Alameda County Health Department. She was eventually fired from this job after she "cussed out" her supervisor.

"It doesn't matter somehow that you're disabled when it comes to ethnic identity. I discovered that ethnic identity was something peculiar unto itself. I also discovered in later work that many African Americans consider being black as having a disability, and so they didn't really identify with disability as a disability, but just as one other kind of inequity that black people had to deal with."

In 1965, Lacy began working at the Oakland Economic Development Council, a Great Society program aimed at empowering people of color and people in poverty. It was here that she first began consciously integrating all her various identities: as a woman, an African American, and a person with a disability, trying to tease out how best to define herself, and how best to make changes not only in her own circumstances but in the society around her.

This dawning self-awareness, in turn, led her to take her first steps as a disability rights activist, enrolling in one of the first 504 trainings.

———

I believe that African Americans see [people with] disabilities in the same way that everybody else sees us—worthless, mindless—without realizing that this is the same attitude held by others toward African Americans. This belief in effect cancels out the black identity they share with a disabled black person, both socially and culturally, because the disability experience is not viewed in the same context as if one were only black, and not disabled. Because of this myopic view, I as a black disabled person could not share in the intellectual dialogue viewed as exclusive to black folk. In other words, I could be one or the other but not both.

I think [this] left me feeling like I was out there, hanging somewhere, not a part of anything because there was no disability group at that time, and every other disabled person I had ever met was in the same situation— they were trying to identify with something ethnic or some other thing. There wasn't a lot of disabled pride in those days because there weren't a lot of examples of disabled leaders and people who were really out there at the time, in the late fifties, early sixties, from a disability perspective.

One of the things that I've learned is that I cannot allow myself to fall into the trap of being identified by others, that I have to have a sense of my own personal identity. And that sense is very much tied into who I am as a woman of color and as a disabled person, and I try not to distinguish between the three identities anymore. It's almost like what's happening now with multiracial youth who in the sixties were described as having an identity problem when they became frustrated and angry at other people's perception of who they were.

[I found out about the month-long sit-in at the HEW building in San Francisco] mainly by television and the newspapers, and I followed that very closely. I had a really strong sense of pride, like, "Wow, these people really have it together. They're really organized." But at the same time, I think I felt some sense of detachment. It was the first time that I had heard the issue around disability rights articulated in a way that made sense to me, and that was because of Judy Heumann, I think, as the spokesperson.

She just fascinated me. I think more than what she said was, I think, the dignity with which she delivered the message. I felt that here a bunch of disabled people were defying a whole system, and it was fascinating. It was scary in a way because they were putting themselves out on a limb to demand something that they thought was their right. They were confronting people who heretofore were considered powerful people, like when they went to Washington, DC, and surrounded the secretary of HEW's house. I think that was the first time that that had ever been done by anybody, let alone disabled people. I thought this was just really something to see and to experience . . . because at that time I was scared to go to San Francisco by myself. I never rode BART [Bay Area Rapid Transit]. It was just a totally—it was a world far away for me—and it was just amazing that all these folks could get there. I just often wondered where'd they come from? How did they get there?

[I finally met Judy Heumann] at the Hilltop Mall in Richmond [California]. It was just a chance meeting, where I happened to be shopping. It must have been around the holiday time because it seemed like I was shopping for potential Christmas gifts or something. I think I saw Judy Heumann in the hallway at first. And of course I recognized her because I had seen her in the news practically every day for several months. As it turned out, we were both heading into the same shop. I was trying to be cool and pretend, like, she was just another person, browsing around. And then I realized that she was really focusing on me for some reason or another, and I thought, "She doesn't know me, does she?"

She approached me, and she introduced herself and I introduced myself, not ever really saying, "I know you! You're the one that's been on TV all these years." And being the very abrupt and straight-to-the-point kind of person she is, she asked me if I was interested in being in the 504 training. She explained that they were really having a hard time recruiting people of color. And this was always a problem at CIL anyway. And she asked me if I was interested, and I told her, "Well, yeah, I might be." So she asked me for my phone number, and she said, "Well, somebody will get in touch with you and send you an application." I didn't think this was politically incorrect. Obviously, it was not. But it's one of the things that I've often admired about Judy, that she takes risks. . . . She sent an application, and I think I was looking for a job at that time, too. So all of these things came together.

[My first 504 training was at the Claremont Hotel]. I was just overwhelmed by—well, number one, I was overwhelmed that this luxurious kind of place was being occupied by a bunch of disabled people. That was the first thing. And this comment was one that I heard throughout the place—that it was the first time I had seen so many disabled people in one place in my life. I met some people, for the first time, who became lifelong friends with disabilities.

I think [that training] changed my life. It gave me a sense of pride as a disabled person, not as a black person and not as a woman. It brought the three together to me for the first time, and made me feel like a whole person in terms of these issues that I hadn't had the opportunity to deal with. So I think it really shifted my life, and it brought into play something that I had not been able to think about very much.

It was feeling like the first time that a door had opened up to me, that I could identify myself with a whole group of people that I had never identified with and that I didn't really know existed. It was sharing my experiences as a disabled person for the first time, sharing my insights and all of the various humor, senses of humor. It was like being with a group of people who saw themselves as people, not as objects of pity or losers. . . . People, like I say, were being empowered and they were not blaming themselves. They were placing the blame where it correctly belonged, and that was a societal misfortune or attitude toward disabled people. It was just really a very proud moment for me. . . .

I left with that sense of righteous indignation that, "How dare people look at me in a way that made me feel as though I was less than they as a result of my disability?" Because I think I had mastered that righteous indignation of a black person, a poor person, and now I saw that applying again.

20
Activists and Organizers, Part 3

———

T HE 504 WORKSHOPS WEREN'T THE ONLY PLACE WHERE PEOPLE WITH disabilities were educated to be community organizers. Kitty Cone was able to bring to the disability rights movement her experience as an activist with the Socialist Workers Party and other groups on the Left. Other leaders, such as Wade Blank and Michael Auberger, received their political education through religious groups, including the social justice wing of the Catholic church.

And as John Lancaster demonstrates, not all aspiring activists had to be prompted to feel entitled to their civil rights or to show anger at how society had treated them.

John Lancaster
"I was mega-pissed, and it was really easy to express that."

———

John A. Lancaster is a Vietnam-era Marine Corps veteran who has been active in the disability rights movement since the mid-1970s as a lobbyist and an attorney, first with the Paralyzed Veterans of America, then with the American Coalition of Citizens with Disabilities and the President's Committee on Employment of People with Disabilities. Most recently, he has been working on the international scene, returning to Vietnam beginning in the 1990s to work with disabled veterans there.

"I got shot in a firefight on May 5, 1968. I took an AK-47 round through the chest cavity laterally. It punctured two lungs, just missed my heart, and clipped the inside of my spinal column, at thoracic five and six." After surgery at a MASH and transfer to a hospital still in Vietnam, "some navy doctor came up to me and said, 'Lieutenant, we're awful busy here, and I've got a lot of surgeries to do, so I'll make it sweet and quick.'" Lancaster, he said, would most likely be paralyzed for the rest of his life, but he "shouldn't worry because 'they can do

355

wonderful things with rehab these days, and I don't think they institutionalize paraplegics anymore, so you should be able to go back to work doing something. . . . Your family is being informed. Good luck.' And then he moved on.

"My first real interest in civil rights came while I was in Vietnam. We had a very racially mixed platoon, and when Martin Luther King was assassinated a lot of my troops, particularly the black guys, were like, 'What are we doing over here? Why are we here fighting this silly war?' We were having a hard time getting a handle around why these people were a threat to the United States, because all they were doing was fighting to unify their country, and to have a better life for their family and kids. So it started me thinking about a lot of things.

"The day after I arrived at St. Albans Naval Hospital [in Cleveland, his last stop before returning to his parents' home in western New York], Robert Kennedy was assassinated. I remember watching that on a TV they had in the room that I shared with another fellow. That was really something."

————

While I was at the spinal cord injury center a guy came into my room by the name of Peter Lassen. He came in with some other fellow who lived in the Cleveland area. They were both in wheelchairs, and they were going around introducing themselves, talking about PVA and trying to get people to sign up for membership. They talked about their service program to represent veterans with disabilities before the Veterans Administration, to make sure that they're getting everything that they're entitled to, and that they're getting the proper health care, and that they're getting supported in a way that allows them to live productively and successfully in the community. And they also told us about a sports program that they ran, and some other things. And they were interested in spinal cord injury research and research on better treatment methods.

It made a lot of sense to me, so I joined.

I went home and moved back in with my mom and dad, until I could figure out what I was going to do. They had modified our house with a mechanical lift so that I could come in off the driveway and get on the lift and either go up to the first floor of the house, or go down into the basement where my parents had set up a bathroom with a roll-in shower and grab bars and all of that, and a bedroom. Tiled and paneled it, and lights, and made it nice. I was twenty-three years old.

In those days, other than a few of the modern shopping centers, and a few businesses right in the downtown part of the village, I couldn't get into any place without help. There weren't any ramps or lifts on buildings then. They just didn't exist. I purchased my own car, and I bought the hand controls with the help of the VA, and got the car dealership that sold me the car to put them on properly so that they'd be safe. So I got around in my car, and I would just make people pull me up steps, or whatever they had to do to get me in where I needed to go.

I didn't stay home with my parents long. I decided to go to grad school, so I applied using the GI Bill and VA benefits, and started in September of '69 in Notre Dame, working on a PhD in philosophy. I did that for a year-plus. My thesis was going to try to relate Martin Heidegger and phenomenology to classroom pedagogy. After a while I started thinking, "What am I going to do with *that*? How the hell am I going to make a living?" So I decided to jump to the law school, which I did.

In law school I took Marci and Bob Burgdorf's course called "The Law and the Handicapped," and at that time was when they had started the Center on Law and the Handicapped.[1] I got to know them fairly well. They were the first ones in the law school to have any sort of focus on that [aspect of the] law. The Architectural Barriers Act of 1968 had just been passed, and that was about the only thing that even began to resemble a civil rights law for people with disabilities on the federal level at that time.[2] So most of what they were teaching was some developing case law around people with developmental disabilities, and the right to be out of the institutions. There was also starting to be some case law being brought by people with physical disabilities through attorneys—PVA was involved in this too—to start establishing the right to use transportation systems, public transit, Amtrak, the airlines, all of that.

I started to define disability as a civil rights issue when I took that course. Pardon my French, but I was fucking pissed off. I'd gone and done what my country wanted me to do, and fought the supposed bad guys, the commies in the rice paddies and the jungles of Vietnam, and had gotten shot up, and saw friends die, and guys that were serving under me die. To come back here and be told that I can't get on the bus, that I can't go into the court house, that my university, which was getting a ton of taxpayer money, was for the most part inaccessible to me; to put it bluntly, I was fucking pissed. I was coming out of anger.

I remember not being able to take the train, which I'd always done when I was an undergraduate, to and from Buffalo to go home for the holidays. I can remember a number of incidences where I was refused flights, to fly some place, especially on my own.

But I think that the worst things that I can remember were in the employment arena. I graduated from law school in 1974. I had a strong interest in criminal law, and wanted to be a prosecutor at a county or city district attorney's office. I'd gotten married in law school and my wife was also an attorney, so we were looking for areas where we could relocate together, and still both do what we wanted to do. I can't tell you how many county prosecutors' offices I applied to, and district attorneys' offices. I also applied to some law firms that had reputations for doing criminal law.

I got some interviews, mostly because my résumé didn't say anything about a disability. And then when they saw me in the wheelchair, the questions would start. "Well, we don't think you have the endurance to become a lawyer. How are you going to get down through the book stacks of the law library in your wheelchair? How are you going to go to the county courthouse to file papers and argue hearings and cases if you can't get up the steps?" I'd say, "Well, I figured out how to get through law school, I'll figure this out too, if you give me the job." They were looking for excuses, not looking for a way to do it, because they didn't want to hire someone with a disability. And I wouldn't get the job.

All together I applied to more than fifty places, and the only one that was willing to hire me was the Veterans Administration, which was the job I wanted least. My first job was as a staff legal adviser, a law clerk, in essence. I worked for administrative law judges, reviewing claims folders and reviewing files.

I was in my office one day at the Board of Veterans Appeals, a little over a year after I'd started there. This was in 1975 now, and barging into my office late one morning, unannounced, were Judy Heumann and Jim Maye, both in wheelchairs. Jim Maye at the time was the executive director of the Paralyzed Veterans of America, the national organization. And they literally came into my office and Jim Maye blurted out to me, "I hear that you're a Vietnam vet, and obviously you have a disability. Judy and I would like to talk to you." And so they took me out to lunch that day, and two weeks later I was working for Jim Maye.

At first I was just hired to be the assistant service director, but my duties were to do the legislative work on the hill. I worked on a lot of veterans' issues, related to employment and veterans' benefits, veterans' health care. We started getting into the area of various laws for people with disabilities in general. A lot of the things that we did were working on accessibility issues and regulatory issues and transportation issues. We were doing a lot of work to try and influence the administration at the time to write regulations on Sections 504 and 503 and 502 and 501 of the Rehab Act. And we were also working very hard to get regulations written on Section 402 of the Vietnam Era Veterans' Readjustment Act. So we did a lot of things on those laws.[3]

It was a pretty conservative organization. There was a big dichotomy between those who wanted to stick exclusively to veterans' issues and issues pertaining to our members, and those who wanted to pursue a broader agenda focused on people with disabilities in general. One of the reasons I left and that my boss at the time was fired was because more conservative elements wanted to stick to just dealing with veterans' issues and issues pertaining to our members. Fortunately, we had gotten too far down the road in terms of a broader approach, and so it never really went away. PVA just gradually shifted and now they're a really great advocate in Washington, DC, for issues that are well beyond just veterans' issues.

Personally, I thought veterans signed up to serve, and what better way could we serve our country than to improve the lives and the inclusion and the employment and the access and the participation of citizens that were being denied that access, and being severely discriminated against? So it's that simple. I represented PVA on the board of directors of a brand new organization called the American Coalition of Citizens with Disabilities. There was another organization at the time called Disabled in Action, and we worked a little with them, but not a lot. We pretty much did our own thing. We worked heavily with the other veterans' organizations, like DAV in particular, and the American Legion, the VFW, and those organizations.[4]

Access to mass transit was huge. Air line travel was huge. Access to inter-city rail transportation was big too. So we were working on all of it. I remember one of the big issues at the time was we were trying to push the Department of Transportation to issue regulations mandating the bus companies to buy a prototype bus called Transbus, which was the low-floor bus that would have had a ramp. And the manufacturers and the American Public Transit Association ultimately beat us and killed those regulations. The manufacturers kept saying, "Oh, it can't be done, it can't be engineered," and now all the accessible buses that are hitting the streets are low-floored buses with ramps. They didn't want to retool. They would have saved themselves maybe hundreds of millions of dollars if they'd retooled then and gotten with the program, but they resisted.

We weren't into demonstrations and that sort of stuff. It wasn't our style to march around in the streets and chain ourselves to buses. We were more into letter writing campaigns, advocacy, testifying before Congress, that sort of stuff. But we had a pretty compelling argument, and made a lot of progress.

At that time the Capitol wasn't accessible. We got them to build some goofy wooden ramps that people would still have to help you up, but we worked with them to make the Senate and House office buildings accessible. You know, even to this day you rarely go over to the Capitol, you're usually in one of the Senate or House office buildings when you go to the Hill.

I think we got to them out of embarrassment. Here we are, veterans who put our life on the line for the country, and did all this fighting. We come back and through no help from the laws or employers or anything, we have some jobs that we're basically generating through our own organization, and we're paying taxes and contributing to the economy and to the society, and you're trying to tell us we don't have to right to get into buildings, and ride buses and subways that are paid for with tax dollars? If it wasn't for the armed forces that keep the country free, you wouldn't even have those things, so what right do you have to keep us off of them?

When it comes to an issue that veterans care about, they are tough advocates. To start with, they're not impressed by someone because he or she is a senator or a congressperson. They could care less. They're impressed by fellow veterans, and even then, you're just talking to a peer.

I was very angry. Christ, I couldn't even get into polling places and courthouses without people hauling me up steps. I was mega-pissed, and it was really easy to express that. And fortunately we were smart enough so that we did it articulately and had some good legal bases for what we were saying, and made cogent economic arguments about the benefits of opening up society to people with disabilities.

People started to buy it. They were either embarrassed into it, or they saw the logic of it. And we did have some supporters, many of whom, interestingly enough, were veterans themselves. It was then a question of getting them to do the political thing with their colleagues too.

The resistance generally came from the financial argument, and the "It's too hard to do" argument. Particularly when you were talking things like transportation and architectural barriers. The resistance in the employment arena was more a prejudice, a discriminatory sort of thing. "We don't think you can do that," the kind of that old-fashioned thinking about what people can and can't do. "You sit in a wheelchair, you ought to go repair watches, or something like that."

Michael Auberger
"It all started from the want of a Big Mac."

Michael Auberger is best known as a cofounder of ADAPT. He was born in 1955 in Munich, West Germany, where his father was stationed with the US military. He spent much of his childhood in Cincinnati, attending Catholic schools first, and then a public high school.

He became spinal cord–injured in a bobsled accident in 1971. After rehab he went to Xavier University, where he earned a BA in accounting. He spent several years as an accountant with the Internal Revenue Service, where he was named "Employee of the Year." His commute from his home in Cincinnati to his workplace in Kentucky demonstrated the need for accessible mass transit.

"Lots of people commuted from Cincinnati to Kentucky to work, or vice versa. They either drove their own cars, or they took the bus. Well, I couldn't drive, and none of the buses were lift-equipped. There was 'Access-A-Ride'— the paratransit van service—but the Cincinnati vans wouldn't take you across the river into Kentucky, that wasn't part of their service area." And so, every day, Auberger had to take his power wheelchair onto the six lane highway that ran across the Ohio River. "There was no sidewalk, I had to ride in traffic."

Because of health problems related to his spinal cord injury, in 1982, Auberger moved to Denver to be seen at the Craig Hospital. He spent nine months at Craig, where he first heard of the Atlantis Community and Wade Blank. "Staff at the hospital told me to stay away from 'those radicals.' It made me want to meet them all the more."

Auberger was soon hanging out and then working with the Atlantis Community, where he was hired to do community organizing "using the Saul Alinsky model."

I was hired through the Campaign for Human Development, CHD, which was a project of the Catholic church.[5] As part of that grant we said we would bring in people that had disabilities from different parts of the country that were interested in community organizing. The Access Institute is what it was called, and the issue we were going with was public transportation.

We did three workshops in total. The first one was here in Denver, in the spring of '84. We were training at an old synagogue on the east side of Denver, in the basement that was accessible, and several of the people that we brought in were from Syracuse, New York. Part of the workshop involved talking about how to choose, and then how to organize around, a particular issue. One of the gentleman had gone to a McDonald's, and couldn't get in. He wanted to get a hamburger, but he couldn't get in the door, and they wouldn't let him use the drive through because he wasn't in a car.

Somehow that evolved into a demonstration here in Denver at the McDonald's at 15th and Colfax and Pennsylvania. We ended up actually going to the McDonald's—that probably would have been the twelve or so people from out of town plus the local group, which might have been another twelve to fifteen people. We ended up doing it at lunchtime on a Friday, very close to the center of downtown, so it had a lot of both foot and automobile traffic.

The manager came out and said there's no way they're going to make this place accessible, and so we ended up closing the McDonald's down. We had people positioned in the drive-through, we had people positioned so you couldn't drive into the parking lot. We ended up placing people in front of the doors so that people couldn't go in. We had emptied out the MacDonald's so that it wasn't doing any business, and people couldn't go in to get hamburgers, and then the police were brought in. I believe there were six arrests that day.

So that was kind of a first push at training people on community organizing, and how to affect the system. It was real clear that sitting in front of a door saying, "No, I'm not moving," was an interesting dynamic, because all of a sudden you had people with severe disabilities out in public, asserting themselves. That one gentleman from Syracuse would drive his wheelchair with his foot, he had CP that involved his speech as well, so he didn't speak really clearly, and the more they would not listen to him, the more angry he became, and the harder it became to understand him. What's interesting is the dynamics of people with severe disabilities, all of a sudden, saying. "If I can't, you can't," and the public having to deal with that, and not understanding disability at all.

They brought out a regional manager from McDonald's to deal with the media. McDonald's just kept escalating the situation by putting their foot more in their mouth, saying, "We have no control over what our stores do." But we knew that you can't put any other kind of food in there that McDonald's doesn't approve, that no McDonald's restaurant can be built different from whatever the designs are that they had at the time. So it was real clear that everything that he was saying was contrary to the facts.

And so it became an issue. We were still doing the training into the next week, and we went to another McDonald's that was in downtown Denver. It was actually down a flight of stairs. We ended up blocking the stairs and the entrance to the restaurant, and the media just jumped on it right away. And the story got bigger because McDonald's, again, escalated, saying that there's no way that they're going to make their stores accessible.

The irony was that all of a sudden we had an issue that was worth creating a group around. People were fired up, people could understand the issue. So they went home at the end of the training, and we asked, if they could, to work on the issue there. The one gentleman who had the Big Mac attack was from Syracuse, and he worked with a small group of folks there. They did a McDonald's in Syracuse, and that action made the AP wire, and picked up some TV attention as well, and so we could see it was going somewhere. So what we did next was we took three van loads of local people from here in Denver to Colorado Springs, and demonstrated at a restaurant in the Springs, with the same issues, the same demand that they make their restaurants accessible.

All of a sudden it was a national campaign. We'd been to Denver, the Springs, and Syracuse, and so the McDonald's management was sure it was happening all over. Then Wade [Blank] took a van load of folks to Kansas City, and I took a couple of van loads up to Cheyenne, Wyoming, which is a hundred miles north of here. Did the same thing, but the whole reaction in Cheyenne was so much different.

By this point we had graduated from just sitting in front of the doors, because people would push us away, push our wheelchairs out of the way. So I started chaining myself to doors. I bought some chains and padlocks at a hardware store, and wrapped them around my wheelchair and the door handles so they couldn't be opened very easily. We did this on both sides of the doors, and we blocked the parking lot so people couldn't come through, and we blocked the drive-through.

People were driving around the people blocking the street entrance, and people on the highway were running over water puddles—it had rained the evening before—and actually getting the people blocking the street entrances wet from the street. People would crawl over us and fight to get into the doors, three and four people moving people's wheelchairs and then crawling over. And then there was actually a woman that went in and came out with a large soda and poured it on one of the people demonstrating. It escalated from there. We had somebody blocking the drive-through, and a woman in a car actually pushed his wheelchair with her car, and moved the wheelchair probably about two feet. She damaged his motorized wheelchair, flattened all the tires.

And all this time the police of Cheyenne were there, watching all of this happen. A police officer came over to me and said, "We're going to leave here in about an hour, it's going to be getting dark, and we're not going to be able to protect you after that." So, it was an interesting dynamic, and it reminded me of the Old West, "I'm going to do anything for a McDonald's, and you're not going to stop me." That was, as I say, the first time we used chains. It was physical but definitely nonviolent, at least on our part. What's interesting is the lengths people would go to, to get a hamburger. These were people who were *serious* about having lunch, and their right to have it, never mind that someone in a wheelchair couldn't get into the restaurant, or sit at the table, or use the bathrooms. We left at dusk, we didn't wait until sundown.

Next we drove two van loads down to El Paso. We were driving overnight to do these things. We're not staying in hotels. We drove to El Paso because there was somebody there that had been in the training, that had put a small group of local folks together. For whatever reason the restaurant there had an accessible bathroom inside the restaurant, even though someone in a wheelchair couldn't get into the building. There was no rhyme or reason: in some places, you'd find that a McDonald's had an accessible parking place, but didn't have a ramp into the store. So there was this inconsistency around access, plus just the absolute refusal by the corporate headquarters to do anything about it.

It was such a great issue. And one thing we were able to use was the fact that even though McDonald's made a big issue out of all the money they were raising for "Ronald McDonald's kids"—the Ronald McDonald Houses and all that—"Ronald McDonald's kids" couldn't eat at a McDonald's. So here they're raising money from the public "to help" these disabled kids, but they weren't allowing these same kids into their restaurants.

We started to say that every Friday at noon, we'd be at—and we would announce the McDonald's—to demonstrate, so the press would be there. We went back to do one in the Springs, we said we'd be there at noon, and we got lost and were a half hour late. The police were there, the TV was there, the newspaper was there, and we *weren't* there. When we finally arrived we saw that they were waiting for us to show up, and that the police had pretty much closed the McDonald's down, before we had done anything.

All of a sudden we're seeing people with disabilities in a whole different role that you'd never seen before. And that was what you really worked for, when you're community organizing. You go back to the Black Panthers and their leather jackets and berets—they used that blackness as something that white people were uncomfortable with. You didn't have to say anything, you didn't have to do anything. You could just *look* militant. All of a sudden now you have people with severe disabilities who are doing these god-awful things, not letting me go into a McDonald's, blocking my entrance, blocking my car. So we were taking that old disability [prejudice] and using it, if you will, as a weapon, that, god forbid I might catch a disability, god forbid I might know somebody with a disability. You know, all those things would go through people's minds, there was no question about it.

By the time we came back from El Paso we'd had contacts from McDonald's corporate office in Chicago that they wanted to sit down and talk, because the press was just eating them alive. The images were not pretty for them. They said, "Fine, we'll come in and we'll sit down and we'll talk with you." They came in from Chicago with lawyers and some high-ranking people who could make decisions.

It may have been the end of July when this happened, the beginning of August, because before we started negotiating I remember watching the summer Olympics in '84, and constantly being bombarded with Ronald McDonald commercials, and all this fundraising for kids with disabilities, and for Ronald McDonald Houses—just watching this, and becoming more and more irritated about how "good" McDonald's was. And somewhere in that period there was a story that McDonald's was the single largest advertiser in the world, dollar-wise. So they had all this marketing money to sell themselves. So everything fell into place, and you couldn't have planned it if you'd tried.

The negotiation turned out to be little me, and the three of them: two lawyers and an executive vice president. The irony is nobody in our group wanted to stand up to them! "I'm not going to sit down and meet with *lawyers*."

One of the things that we were working on was being able to negotiate. There's always the idea that you've got several key demands that you're not willing to give up, and then you've got what are basically throwaways, things that you could live without. It was real clear that we wanted parking spaces, we wanted to be able to get into the doors and use the rest rooms. Those things were not negotiable. Then, after watching all that TV, I came up with a couple of things that I ran by our folks before the meetings. I said that a throwaway demand was that ten percent of all their advertising include people with disabilities as consumers. And then the other piece was that the "McJobs" program was to hire people with disabilities to work behind the counter. Those were the two issues that we were willing to give up right away to get them to make a commitment that their stores—almost eight or nine thousand stores at the time—as they were remodeled, or as they built new stores, would all be made accessible.

So we sat down for three days of discussions. We probably went a total of five hours a day, morning and afternoon. It was in a hotel downtown, they had a meeting room that they had rented, with all the niceties. And ironically the job piece and the media piece were the easiest pieces. They jumped on those two. I would never have bet in a million years that they would have had anything to do with those, but those were two things they figured would make them look good.

And then we hammered out the other pieces. We agreed that we wouldn't do any more demonstrations, they agreed that wherever they were remodeling, or were going to build new stores owned by McDonald's, they would make them accessible, and that as they redesigned stores for newly purchased franchises, and in any remodeling they did, they would strongly suggest to the franchise that they do the same. So we suspended the campaign, with the understanding that if they reneged, we'd be back out on the streets, doing more civil disobedience.

About a year later, I was watching TV, and I see this commercial about McDonald's, where they included somebody with a disability in the ad. And it was done beautifully. One of the first was a person going into a McDonald's who was using a manual wheelchair. It was a group of people, you don't see the person with the disability again, but you saw him going into the restaurant. And then the next thing you know, there was an AT&T commercial with people with disabilities, and then Levi's started doing one—a macho looking young man wearing Levi's in a wheelchair. It was interesting how it evolved. That McDonald's, with all its money, figured out a way to make people with disabilities ingrained in the commercial, and then within six months or so other businesses were doing the same thing, so that even before the ADA people with disabilities were in all kinds of advertising as consumers.

Think about the far reaching effect that has, and the message it sends. It's much more subliminal than carrying a sign and being chained to a door, but it was a whole image change. And because McDonald's did it, because of its magnitude, and its stature in the community, other businesses said it was okay to do. It was definitely nothing that we planned.

The whole campaign involved probably a total of forty to sixty people. You talk about David and Goliath. They could have ignored us, but they chose instead to escalate it. And the media loved the issue. By taunting McDonald's, by saying, "This Friday we're going to be here," the chains, the signs that said, "I can eat in the bathroom but I can't eat at the table." "Ronald's kids can't even get into the store"—that just created theater around it. You talk about a media-sensitive corporation!

And it all started from the want of a Big Mac, from one guy wanting a Big Mac and not being able to get one. That's why I love the story. It all took less than six months, from beginning to end, but it had such far sweeping effect. There was no way to comprehend that at the time, but it was fun to watch, to see how it just kept evolving, because they never had a clue about us.

Karen Thompson
"Finally . . . Sharon was allowed to move home. It took us eight and a half years and over $300,000 . . . to get that ruling."

Sharon Kowalski became disabled in November, 1983 at age twenty-seven, when her car was struck head-on by a drunk driver near Onamia, Minnesota. She was on her way to her hometown with her niece and nephew, who had spent the weekend with her and Karen Thompson. Kowalski emerged from the accident, and the resulting coma, unable to speak, and with much of her body weakened. Very soon after regaining consciousness she expressed her desire to return to the home she and Karen Thompson had made for themselves in St. Cloud, Minnesota. Kowalski's parents, however, refused to believe that their daughter was a lesbian. Eager to collect in the ensuing lawsuit against the drunk driver, they also refused to acknowledge that their disabled daughter might be able to live outside the confines of a nursing home.

"She's better off dead than living like that," Thompson recalls hearing members of Sharon's family say immediately after the accident. "'This is not the way Sharon would have wanted to live.' And they continued throughout the following years to see only Sharon's limitations, how she wasn't like she was before, instead of getting to know the new person Sharon had become, and moving from there."

Karen was deemed "abusive" and "deviant" by the Minnesota courts for wanting to bring Sharon home with her, while Sharon was sent by her family to a nursing home in Hibbing. This separation, and Sharon's virtual isolation from the community, continued for three and a half years, despite Sharon's clear wishes, typed out during rare interviews with attorneys from the Minnesota Civil Liberties Union and local disability rights activists, that she be allowed to go home with Karen. During this time Sharon was also denied any rehabilitative care that might have helped minimize the impact of her injuries. Karen Thompson, with no other options, filed for guardianship.

The resulting years-long legal battle pitted Sharon, Karen, and the local gay rights, women's rights, and disability rights communities against Sharon's family and the Minnesota courts. It garnered national and even international attention, and also brought together national leaders from the women's, gay rights, and disability rights leaders in ways that would have an impact far beyond Minnesota.

Sharon lost all of her rights when she went into coma, but she came out of the coma, and she wasn't tested for competency. Minnesota law says every six months to a year the person must be retested for competency, and as I was fighting for her right to be tested, Jack Fena, the Kowalski family attorney, was standing there in the courtroom with a Bible in his hand saying that to test her for competency would cost her hundreds of thousands of dollars in the personal injury suit, because it says here in the Bible homosexuality is a sin. I thought he looked like a fool. And yet the judge said it would be in her best interest not to pursue the testing until after the personal injury suit case was settled.

And that case took five years, so Sharon wasn't tested for competency until over five years after the accident. So while Sharon was typing out words, phrases, and sentences, they continued to say that Sharon was incompetent, and didn't understand what she was saying. A judge said in the courtroom that she can't understand nor communicate in any way, and he had in front of him an eight-page typed conversation from a disability rights group, who had asked Sharon, "What did you do before the accident?" She typed, "Teach." "What did you teach?" She typed. "P.E., health." "What did you coach?" "Basketball, track and field." "What kind of a car did you drive?" "Toyota." "What's your favorite flower?" She typed, "Columbine." And a judge ruled that she couldn't understand anything, nor could she communicate in any way.

The Minnesota Civil Liberties Union by that time was involved, and they had had a conversation with Sharon. They asked Sharon, "Were you with Karen?" and she typed, "Yes." They asked, "What are you and Karen?" and she typed, "Gay." And her father said on the stand for her to ever use that word probably means she was having a gay time. She doesn't know what that means now. And yet, when they asked her what it meant, she typed out, "To love someone of the same sex." And they asked her if we had considered ourselves married, and she typed, "Yes." They asked her why. And this woman, who supposedly could not understand or communicate in any way, typed out, "Because we love each other." So in spite of all the well-documented evidence of Sharon's ability to communicate, the judge completely ignored it, and the line that they took was, until she was tested for competency, she was incompetent, and couldn't understand or communicate, and they didn't have to listen to anything Sharon wanted to say.

They wouldn't even let her be in the courtroom. I was fighting for Sharon's right to be there, where her future was being determined, and the judge ruled she couldn't be in the courtroom because of her physical condition. She could be anywhere you could get a wheelchair, and yet she wasn't allowed to be there.

In the meantime, Sharon was not getting the proper care. In the nursing home in Hibbing, the doctor in charge of the case said to give her occupational therapy is a complete waste of time, because there's no way she'll ever hold down an occupation. That's not even the purpose of occupational therapy. So we filed through the Vulnerable Adult Protection Act, and I was sure we'd win. Sharon was not getting proper care. But, of course they found that as long as the nursing home is giving her the care ordered by the doctor in charge of the case, then there's no violation. And of course the doctor in charge of the case is this same doctor who regularly testified for Jack Fena in personal injury suit cases against people like drunk drivers. They worked together. And I kept saying, "There needs to be a doctor appointed for Sharon, a neutral doctor. There needs to be a physiatrist, a rehab specialist, not a general practitioner who doesn't work in this area." And we couldn't get that to happen.

The people at the Independent Living Center here in St. Cloud were the first disability rights activists I contacted. And then I called every disability rights group in the country. I can't remember the name of the group right now, but the people there in Washington, who had some money to work with disability rights, the first thing that was said was, "We can't afford to get involved in a gay rights issue." And I said, "You can't afford *not* to get involved, because what's happening here is going to affect the rights of people with disabilities."

So it took a while for the disability community to come on board. NOW got it pretty quick, that this is a women's rights issue, and so the

National Organization for Women passed a resolution to pursue this case. And then the irony is, that I was so homophobic and had so much internalized homophobia, I didn't want the lesbian/gay rights groups involved, because I thought it would hurt us. We'd never been a part of that community. We weren't like *them*. So I had to work through my own internalized homophobia before I could understand; this community was fundraising for me, and I didn't even want to be one of them. And to come to an understanding of who I am and who Sharon and I are, and to learn to reach out and accept help from a community that, as I said, we didn't want to be part of, was humbling.

We were told, when we finally sat down with national leaders of the disability community, with the women's community, with the lesbian/gay/bisexual/transgender community, that it was the first time that they'd ever all come together and rallied around one case. And that's staggering. I felt like we were such little people, and all of a sudden it just snowballed, it got bigger and bigger. At the beginning, I had no comprehension of the bigger issues, or causes. I was in it for Sharon.

It's just mind-boggling, the connections with so many different groups. I would fly out of here on a Thursday night after teaching, because I had no Friday classes, and I might be in Washington, DC, at George Washington University there, I might do eight programs, some of those in Washington, and some of those in San Francisco, and I'd be back teaching my classes on Monday like I hadn't been gone. I lived in a time warp. Nobody here at St. Cloud State knew or understood. At the same time I was being recognized on the national level, people were going to the other side of the hallway not to speak with me here at St. Cloud State. I was totally isolated. The only time I was spoken to was when it directly pertained to some class, a professional issue that they had to talk to me about.

By the end of the campaign there were twenty-two different Free Sharon Kowalski committees, in twenty-two states. Judy Andrzejewski, the person who coauthored the book with me,[6] was really one of the main people behind this, and Tacie Dejanikus, who did so much, out of Washington, DC, was one. And then there was a woman with a disability in New York City, Harilyn Rousso, and then Connie Panzarino[7] in Boston—I have met so many thousands and thousands of people, I just can't hang on to the names, but I wish I could. Many wonderful people put forth hours of time, and then one of the things that helped break the case was we organized, as a media hook then, a national Free Sharon Kowalski Day. And so we created events the media would cover, to try to break the case a little bit, to try to get it out there.

The main thing that legally helped to set things in motion was finally in 1988, September, Sharon won "the right to be tested for competency." She was moved to Miller-Dwan Polinsky Institute in Duluth, and the team there found that Sharon could understand and communicate many of her basic life choices. And they also said Sharon wasn't getting proper care. So she was moved back after that testing to that nursing home in Hibbing, and finally, in January of 1989 she got moved to Miller-Dwan Polinsky Institute to receive rehabilitation.

Once she got moved there, the rehab psychologist put together the team, the medical team, the OT, the PT, the speech therapist, and she made sure she had people who would advocate for Sharon. And so they documented everything that happened, like when I was there in sessions, they documented how much better Sharon did, and responded.

Of course, some of her responses caused me embarrassment. We were in a speech therapy session, and I came in late. The speech therapist said, "I asked her to work on this or this or this and she doesn't want to work on any of it." Because I had worked very hard with them, I said, "Give Sharon choices. Everything is being done *to* Sharon, she perceives she has no control—give her as many choices as possible." So they were giving her choices. So there I am, and then the speech therapist made the mistake of asking Sharon, "Well, what would you rather be doing?" And Sharon promptly typed out on her speech synthesizer, "Making love to Karen." I turned red, the speech therapist turned red, and then she looked at Sharon and she said, "I guess it does sound more exciting than any of the options I gave you." Immediately Sharon interacted for the rest of the session with her. Which shows you just how important it is to recognize people's families. And of course, with traumatic brain injury, she doesn't have the same inhibitions that we have, and she'll say the first thing that comes to her mind. Which is kind of nice, because then you don't play games.

What I fought for all along was that she needed a less restrictive form of guardianship, conservator-ship, or something else. But the bottom line was that they were going to make her have a guardian, because Sharon's never going to be clear on what day of the week it is, what the date is, who the president is. Anyway, the team at Miller-Dwan Polinsky testified in court that there was no reason why she couldn't live at home and go in for therapy. Then the judge said, "Well, what's home? She's lived the last three and a half years up here, this has become her home." And they went on the record to say, "Well, Sharon's very clear about that, it's St. Cloud with Karen Thompson."

But the judge wouldn't let her move home, because he was afraid that her biological family wouldn't come to visit her, so he ordered her moved to Trevilla of Robbinsdale, which is one of three nursing homes in our state that has a young adult rehab ward. So once she was moved there, in June of 1989, they said, Sharon needs to be able to go out on passes. So then of course the court said, "Yes, but everybody fears sexual abuse." So the judge finally ordered that I could take Sharon out on pass as long as I had a staff escort. But you know it's so upsetting, like people with disabilities, you snap your fingers and all of a sudden they're asexual, for them to have an intimate relationship with anyone must mean it's sexual abuse, right? Or because I'm a lesbian, I'm more likely to sexually abuse? And of course let's not worry about the facts and statistics, that we're one of the least likely groups in our society to do that.

But, actually it helped us, even though I was furious that, we had to find somebody who'd like to go to a basketball game, or a volleyball match over at the University of Minnesota, or who wanted to go to San Francisco with us to get the Women of Courage award from NOW, or who would like to come home and spend the weekend with us here at the house, so Sharon could come home for the weekend. But we had people who did. So we had all these staff escorts who documented how responsive and motivated Sharon was outside the institution, how they saw a different Sharon than they saw in the nursing home.

In the meantime her father withdrew, saying he that he hadn't wanted her moved, hadn't wanted her to see me, hadn't wanted her going out on passes, so he essentially dropped out of her life. So I re-filed for guardianship in that summer of 1989. But I couldn't win guardianship even when I was the only party of record. The judge *still* found that I wasn't qualified to be her guardian, and he appointed a supposedly neutral third party guardian. And he found that my taking Sharon out was putting her on display, was using her for my own political agenda, stating she was better off not going out on passes. Even though all the medical people said she

could live outside of an institution, or at least we should be *allowed to try,*
the judge ruled that she couldn't be cared for outside of an institution.
He said that I didn't understand "the Iron Range Mentality," which, of
course, means I don't understand sexism, ableism, and homophobia.

It was just outrageous, certainly the most homophobic, ableist, het-
erosexist order we'd ever read. This was in April of 1991. We appealed,
and in December of 1991, we received the appellate court decision which
found that the judge had abused his discretion, that he can't make findings of fact that aren't substantiated by the court record. In essence, what
the appellate court of Minnesota found was that Sharon has the right
to be heard, she has the right to see whomever she wants to see, has
the right to go wherever she wants to go. Sharon has the right to live in
the least restrictive environment, and Sharon has the right to the best
possible medical care. And then they went one step further, and used
unheard-of legal language. They found that the judge had made findings
of fact that not only weren't substantiated by the court record but were in
total contradiction of the court record. And they ordered that I was to be
appointed guardian with unlimited powers.

And so I thought it was over. It went back to the district court, and it
took until May of '92 to get them to award me guardianship as ordered
by the appellate court. And then it took until August of '92 for me to get
letters of guardianship, to act as guardian, and then finally I got to turn
my attention from a legal system that doesn't protect a person to a health
care system that would rather keep people in institutions than to enable
them to live in less restrictive environments.

Finally, in April of 1993, Sharon was allowed to move home. It took us
eight and a half years and over three hundred thousand dollars in legal
fees to get that ruling.

I think our case is still being quoted in a lot of other situations. The
appellate court found that Sharon and I were "a family of affinity"—that
we should be accorded respect, that we had the same rights and privi-
leges as other families. That, I know, has been quoted, even though it's
a Minnesota ruling. Judges look to similar cases in other places, to see
how they were handled, and it's been used a lot. I've had lots of e-mails,
phone calls, letters from people, telling me how this case affected their
cases. Just the thousands of people who have taken out durable powers of
attorney, living wills—the National Gay and Lesbian Task Force has doc-

umented it, the National Center for Lesbian Rights out in San Francisco has. They just say literally thousands of people have made inquiries, and stated our case was the reason why.

It's mind-boggling. I thought it would be over when Sharon came home, but it's more pertinent today perhaps than ever before, around the whole gay marriage issue, and we continually get asked for quotes about gay marriage.

And when we're talking about people with disabilities, the traditional one person doing everything for another person doesn't work, and so people need to be open to forming a new type of a family, or different types of living situations that enable everyone's needs to be met, and to live to our highest quality of life.

I've just grown so much, from that conservative, Republican, naive person I was when all this happened. I voted for Ronald Reagan, to help you understand, I voted for him twice, and yet in four years I went from voting for him for president to thinking he should have been impeached. So once I started learning, I learned volumes and I learned it rapidly, and I was forced to question everything I believed to be truth.

We're both very different now. Sharon is very different than she was before the accident, just like I'm very different than I was before the accident. But people shouldn't need to be sacrificed for other people to learn, for other people to grow, the way Sharon was sacrificed.

21
ADAPT

I F THE INDEPENDENT LIVING MOVEMENT, FOUNDED BY UNIVERSITY students and graduates, represented an educated elite among Americans with disabilities, and if groups such as CAPH represented more working-class disabled, then the rank and file of ADAPT brought to the issues of disability oppression the perspective of those at the bottom of the educational, social, and economic ladder. As ADAPT organizer Mark Johnson says, many ADAPT members "can't read or write, many have had little or no education at all." Many—and this was certainly true of the original members of the mid-1980s—are alums of some of the nation's worst institutions and nursing homes and often rely on Supplemental Security Income for their livelihood, meaning that they live at or below the federal poverty line.

On the one hand, this situation could make the task of ADAPT organizers such as Mark Johnson and Stephanie Thomas—themselves college-educated professionals—more difficult. On the other, that ADAPT members often feel they have little or nothing to lose makes them more likely to participate in the confrontational, direct-action methods that have come to be ADAPT's trademark.

ADAPT—which originally stood for American Disabled for Accessible Public Transit—traces its origins to Colorado's first independent living center, the Atlantis Community, Inc., and its founder the Reverend Wade Blank. Although not himself a person with a disability, Blank had had experience in the civil rights movement, marching with Dr. Martin Luther King Jr. in Selma in 1965. Born in Pittsburgh in December 1940, Blank was educated as a Presbyterian minister and was called in 1966 to serve a congregation in Akron, Ohio. His wife, Molly Blank, remembers, "Before then, he was a traveling minister to several small churches in small towns in Ohio. And then he went to Akron and became involved with the Kent State SDS people, and let them use the mimeograph machine in his church. When the shootings happened—he knew some of those kids.[1] He spearheaded a big demonstration after the shootings. And he and two others—an ex-priest and a Congregationalist—founded a radical bookstore in Akron." Blank also helped to smuggle anti–Vietnam War draft resisters into Canada. "Because of his support for the SDS, the FBI went to his church and said, 'You need to find yourself another minister.' He got fired, and that was the last congregation he ever had."[2]

Blank arrived in Denver in December 1971 and found work at the Heritage House nursing home. Conditions at Heritage House were typically awful, with substandard food and few meaningful activities for the residents, many of whom were younger people with disabilities. The "work activities program," for example, involved being bused to a sheltered workshop where participants counted fishhooks. Wade described the atmosphere as "like a morgue," with residents consigned to waiting for death. "I was going to work every day and asking myself, 'If I was disabled, is this the way I'd want to live the rest of my life?'"[3]

Blank began pushing for change, organizing meetings of the younger residents. Over the course of the next four years he managed to negotiate some relatively meaningful reforms—getting the administration to allow residents to have pets, for instance, and to keep TVs and stereos in their rooms. But when Blank suggested that some residents might actually be able to leave the nursing home altogether to live in the community, he was promptly fired. "They came in and they took all the stereos and TVs . . . had the dog pound come by and get all the animals, and in one day it went from everything I'd built for four years—to that."

Within six months of being fired Blank helped eighteen residents to leave Heritage House, moving them into apartments and assuming direct responsibility for their care. These residents in turn formed the nucleus of the Atlantis Community. A number of them and their families sued Heritage House for fraud and abuse (among other issues, it was alleged that the nursing home had for years illegally appropriated residents' Social Security checks). These suits were eventually settled out of court (as described below).

In January 1975, Atlantis began its campaign to force Denver's Regional Transit District (RTD) to make its bus system totally accessible. The choice of accessible mass transit as the issue to organize around was highly astute, as it addressed a need felt by the majority of people with more severe disabilities, not only in Denver but across the country. Many, if not most, are not able to drive (indeed, even if they could get a license, many ADAPTers can't afford the cost of their own vehicle). As transportation advocate Denise Karuth put it, the availability of reliable, affordable, accessible mass transit therefore can mean the difference "between living in a community and being imprisoned there." Making workplaces, schools, grocery stores, houses of worship, government offices, and voting polls accessible serves little purpose for people who can't get to them to begin with.

The issue also had deep historical resonance. Blank was no doubt conscious of the role the Birmingham bus boycott had played in the history of the civil rights movement, and advocates would often point out that while people of color in the Jim Crow South were forced to ride in the back of the bus, people with disabilities couldn't get on the bus at all.

And so, on July 5, 1978, a group of nineteen Atlantis activists surrounded and immobilized two buses at an intersection in downtown Denver, keeping up their protest for two days. The RTD eventually agreed to 100 percent access in all future bus purchases. The demonstration, now immortalized by a city plaque on the site, would become the prototype for future ADAPT actions.

ADAPT was founded in July 1983 at a meeting at the Atlantis Community office. Adopting the slogan "We Will Ride!" the group over the next seven years focused its efforts on the American Public Transit Association (APTA), both because of its belligerent anti-access stance and because its annual national conferences provided a ready-made vulnerable and highly visible target for mass civil disobedience.

The Atlantis Community, Inc., still exists as an independent living center in Denver. ADAPT, after 1990, shifted its focus from accessible mass transit (provided for by Title II of the ADA—in no small measure owing to the ADAPT campaign) to home care assistance, changing its name to American Disabled for Attendant Programs Today. Although the organization files and lobbies for legislation and has gone to federal court to advocate for change, its primary tool remains direct action/civil disobedience, with the American nursing home industry as its new target.

Rev. Wade Blank died on February 15, 1993, at age fifty-two, in Todos Santos, Mexico, while attempting to rescue his eight-year-old son Lincoln, who had been swept from the beach into a rip current. Lincoln was also drowned. Blank's memorial service in Denver was attended by more than a thousand people.

It is a testament to Blank and the other original ADAPT organizers that, two decades after his death, the group is as active, and as relevant, as ever.

Larry Ruiz
"Once the home got wind of our ideas of independence, things began to get ugly."

Larry Ruiz was in the original cohort of people the Reverend Wade Blank helped to leave (Ruiz might say "escape") the Heritage House nursing home. He has been active in disability politics and ADAPT ever since and is something of a legend in Atlantis in Denver and ADAPT nationally.

Ruiz uses a speech synthesizer to communicate, typing out his replies to questions with a mouth-stick. For this reason this interview is somewhat different from most others I conducted; I e-mailed my questions to him, asking Ruiz to call me so I could record his reply.

My name is Larry Ruiz. I am fifty-four years old and I have lived on my own for thirty-four years. I was institutionalized until the age of twenty-one.

My mind is completely intact. I have physical impairments. I lived at Ridge [Home, a state institution] until I was eighteen. In 1972 I was sent to live in a nursing home in Lakewood called Heritage House. I lived there on a huge wing with other children and adults for three years. Most of the people in the youth wing also grew up in institutions, and we did not realize that we were living in substandard conditions. We were treated poorly, and all of our state benefits went straight to the nursing home. We were given an allowance of twenty-five dollars per month.

We had an activities director for youth named Wade Blank. He helped us form a residents' council. Wade discovered that there were a lot of things we could do for entertainment. We saw shows such as Elvis, the Who, and the Grateful Dead. Our eyes were opened to the outside world, and we began to grow restless. Wade had the vision of us being able to live on our own. He helped us realize this possibility.

Once the nursing home got wind of our ideas of independence, things began to get ugly. We were treated worse. We were even threatened by the administrator with a middle-of-the-night eviction. Wade was fired and a restraining order was taken out against him. He used this time to look for an alternative for us. He found a group of apartments. He then came back to Heritage House one last time, to break us out. It was June 1975, and the Atlantis Community was born. Wade named our little community "Atlantis" after the lost city.

We went on to demand accessible public transportation. We did this by going to Colfax and Broadway, one of Denver's busiest intersections, and throwing ourselves into the street to block the buses. We also entered a class action lawsuit against Heritage House. It took ten years, but twenty-two people received $2.2 million in the settlement. With this money, several people were able to build homes. I bought my own home and lived there for ten years.

Atlantis continued to grow, and continued civil disobedience across the country. I myself have been arrested about fifty-seven times.

Mark Johnson
"You pushed. You pushed hard."

Mark Johnson is a veteran of ADAPT actions from its inception in 1983 to the passage of the ADA in 1990 and beyond. He is, in fact, familiar enough with the nuts and bolts of civil disobedience to refer to the chains and padlocks used at ADAPT demonstrations as "jewelry, part of the action kit."

His first action in Denver, however, preceded ADAPT. It was in 1982, not too long after he had arrived in the city from Charlotte, North Carolina., In a public meeting, after months of lobbying by the Denver disability community, the board of directors of the Regional Transit District voted to proceed with the purchase of another fleet of inaccessible buses. The audience of disability activists responded with shock and anger.

"They were hollering and screaming their disapproval. 'It's not over yet! We'll see you again!' and so on. They knew what the next step was. It was going over to Wade's house to plan a protest. . . . Intellectual persuasion didn't work, so we had to create some emotion."

"Some emotion" would lead Johnson, during his next encounter with the RTD, to chain himself and his wheelchair to a railing at the authority's headquarters in downtown Denver. "It was a big open atrium. I remember hollering up into it, when people started coming out of their offices and hanging over the edges to see what was going on, saying, 'Yeah, that's what my tax dollars are paying you to do!' You have to understand how graphic this was. Every piece of garbage I ever had in my system, every paternalistic situation—it all came out that day." Blank and the others at Atlantis stood by "and let me have my catharsis."

Mark Johnson was born in June 1951 and was disabled at the end of his sophomore year in college in a diving accident at age nineteen, becoming "a C5/6 quadriplegic."[4] After two months in an acute care hospital and three months in a rehab hospital, he returned to school to earn a BA in psychology in 1975 and his master's in guidance and counseling in 1977 from the University of North Carolina, Charlotte. After working as a rehabilitation counselor, he married and moved to Denver in 1981, where his wife Susan had already lived. Johnson quickly became active in the local disability community, both as chair of the Colorado Coalition of Citizens with Disabilities and as the Transitional Living Coordinator of HAIL (Holistic Approaches to Independent Living). In 1986, Susan got a job in Atlanta, and so she, Mark, and their two-year-old daughter Lindsey moved back to the Southeast. In 1988, Johnson was the accessibility coordinator for the Democratic National Convention in Atlanta, where he now works as the director of advocacy at the Shepherd Spinal Center.

Your best bet is getting right in their face. In other words, create your own playing field, with its own rules. The way Wade talked about this, it's basically creating a situation that you control, versus them controlling it. People don't like having to deal with something they're not used to—"All of a sudden these people are all in my face, and they're *angry*." That's what ADAPT did for the seven years leading up to the passage of the ADA. What did we do? We blocked buses that didn't have lifts. If you think about it, that was the most visual way to dramatize the issue—to say, "If I can't get on, then *you* can't get on either."

I tend to refer to ADAPT more as a network than a national organization, because it's not like we have a national office. We don't have a building, we don't have staff, we don't have a board. What we have is just a group of people who are committed to doing whatever it takes. And so, yes, as a network, we would always encourage people to push wherever they needed to push, on whatever they needed to push on.

We eventually won the battle there in Denver. We got lifts on all the buses, being used on all kinds of services. And people began to call us from around the country, asking, "How did you get that done?" So Wade and I, and some other folks, began to think, with all these independent living people coming to town—they were just starting NCIL [National Council on Independent Living][4]—why don't we go present to them this idea of using transportation, in particular getting lifts on buses, as an organizing tool to really develop the skill to organize? So we went over to NCIL's meeting in Denver to make this presentation to the NCIL board, and they basically said, "We have a position on transportation, thank you very much." And we left that meeting a little bit disillusioned, and frustrated, but then we sat in the back room, and had our own meeting, and that's when ADAPT was born.

We talked about the different wrinkles to nonviolence and people with disabilities. For instance, if you have CP and you get excited, and you begin to spasm a lot, how that could be misinterpreted as resistance. Or whatever. You've got to understand Wade. Wade always pushed the envelope. So it was the probably the most aggressive nonviolence that you'll ever see. You pushed. You pushed hard. You didn't just go up to the front door and go limp and say, "Take me off to jail." You didn't do that. You went up to the door, you blocked it for a while, and then you handcuffed yourself to it.

Some of it was to dramatize it, some of it was to push the envelope, and some of it was, knowing the authorities will be asking themselves, "What do you do with all these people in wheelchairs?" It's kind of like getting in the front of the line at Disney World. If a group of non-disabled people had done what we did, they might have been wiped out in ten minutes, hauled off, whereas we'd be there for hours. "What are we going to do with them? These folks don't want to leave, in fact, they're pushing on the door, and they're chained to this, and chained to that."

People in ADAPT didn't read Gandhi or Martin Luther King. You're talking about folks here who didn't get any formal education, or even if they had—these were *really* disabled folks. If you went up to somebody and said, "Why are you doing this?" "I want to be able to get on the bus." That's it. And to be honest, that's what it's really all about. So, I don't need to know Section 504, I don't need to be able to describe the law. "George. Why are you involved in this?" "I want to be able to get on the bus." That pretty much captures it, doesn't it?

At any of our actions, if somebody wanted to stay back, they could. Back then you had to understand too, that if you appeared non-disabled, you usually stayed back, because you could get knocked off, arrested, just grabbed in a hurry. Or, you would get approached about, "Would you please go talk to that man, and convince him to move?" Very paternalistic. You know, I'd come in, and they'd be talking to the non-disabled person beside me, and going, "Yeah, you need to move." And if we didn't, they usually grabbed *him*. With me alone, they'd tell me I need to move, but then I'd stay, and I could buy a lot more time.

We'd meet at Wade's house, and play it out, well this is what *usually* happens, and this is what *did* happen last year, and this is what *could* happen, but you never could totally predict it. So a general rule of thumb was, if you're not disabled, you probably need to step back. If you've got to be somewhere tomorrow, you need to step back. If you can't spend the night in jail, you need to step back. If you only want to hold a sign, that's fine. If you only come in the building, that's fine. Whatever role you want to play, we need it played. At the same time, we usually had a head count, who was going to be a hard head, and who was not. So you tended to know ahead of time, who was going to do civil disobedience.

This was all Saul Alinsky stuff. You had this core of experienced people. And then you either trusted them and followed them, or you didn't. It didn't mean you had to. I never saw any pressure. I mean it's interesting, when people say, "All you do is ask to get arrested." Well, first of all, that's not what the majority do, and the second thing I can tell you is any pressure you feel is self-imposed, because of your own discomfort with, being in the Boston Tea Party or something.

You always knew certain people who reacted to stress differently than others. I can remember a guy named Clarence who would get real emotional about stuff, and if you got near him he'd take a swing at you. Clarence got involved in some of the group stuff, and some of the emotions, the stress related to the group stuff, he just didn't respond well. And so you always knew you had to have someone with Clarence, to keep Clarence away from some of that stuff, or else. In Phoenix, he cold-clocked a cop. We were just so lucky to talk our way out of that one.

Sometimes Wade used to talk to the police ahead of time, but not often. There's something about the game in this, just doing it as a surprise, kaboom! It's much more fun. So it wasn't like, "Would you please close off this intersection so we can be there?" No no no. There was always that little element of the unpredictable, that you wanted to create. Right or wrong, ADAPT has always had that. We'd hide out in an alley, sometimes, and pop out—but how do you hide a hundred people in wheelchairs? It's pretty hard. And now there is a little more of—"No, we don't have a parade permit, but don't you think five hundred of us marching down the street here in the far right-hand lane is a lot better than us going up and down sidewalks, some that don't have curb cuts?" I mean, there is a lot more negotiation, now, with security, than there was in the early days, because it's pure size.

For the first ten years it was small, but dramatic, and as a result people tended to think it was bigger than it was. But it really wasn't that big, as far as the hard-core people. When the Million Man March happened, people said, "Oh, let's get a million people with disabilities in DC," right? But let's look at it: what are some of the barriers to making that happen? One is the diversity of the disability community, the isolation, the pure amount of resources people have, or don't have. So you have people out there who are doing everything from praying for us to sending us a dollar. But they couldn't themselves participate, for a lot of good reasons.

When I moved from Denver to Atlanta in '87, Wade paid me a couple of hundred bucks a month to organize, and he gave me some time, so I could make phone calls, right? And the first thing I did was I asked Mary Johnson to give me the list of people who subscribed to *The Disability Rag*. Because the whole idea was, *The Rag* had been one of the few publications in general, mainstream or disability, that covered ADAPT. It wasn't always as good as we'd have liked, but it was coverage. And so my guess was, if I sent out a solicitation to the people who subscribed in Georgia, and it was a very small number of people, at least, when I mentioned ADAPT, it wouldn't be something foreign to them. And that's how loose and community-based it was. You only had several hundred people, in the first ten years, that could really go out and do this stuff. There weren't the resources to bring as many people as wanted to come.

At each action, you never knew for sure how the police would react. Ninety percent are fine, 5 percent are macho, 5 percent get frustrated. Macho—you run into those every once in a while. "You're breaking the rules, all of you." "Okay, then, arrest me." Whereas most of them will tell you, "I have a mother," or "I have a dad, I have a brother or a sister or a friend of mine, you know . . ." After the initial tension dies down, they ask, "Why are you all here, what's exactly going on?" So we make personal connections. And in their minds they're thinking, "These people aren't bad. They're passionate. They care about what they're doing, and we're going to give them a little bit of leeway."

In the early years APTA tried to portray us as crazy, as violent, and using our wheelchairs as weapons or what have you, using the chair as a battering ram. If you look at some of the old APTA footage, it's taking the worst of twenty years and trying to frighten the police into a frenzy. That went on for years, maybe it's still going on with the nursing homes now that the nursing home industry is our number one target. They had their own film, of maybe someone who would run around the corner and empty their leg bag into the gutter, that became, "They throw urine on you."

So when you go to a newer city, sometimes they freak. St. Louis freaked. And then in 1989 we thought we were in Reno—unfortunately, we were in Sparks, Nevada. They didn't freak, they kicked our ass! They just took us all in, and put us in jail. It was a one-judge town, under one casino, a very *big* casino, and they didn't appreciate anything that interfered with business.

So you see all kinds of stuff like that. But then you go to DC, where they're so used to demonstrations, it becomes almost hard at some point to keep coming up with something that will be a little different, to grab the public's attention. And so we have to constantly improvise, constantly come up with new tactics and techniques.

Barbara Toomer
"We were pretty edgy, for Salt Lake City."

Barbara Toomer was born in California in 1929, to a working-class family that did not approve of President Roosevelt's "politics or his disability." Toomer's own political views were developed before her disability, during the anti-communist hysteria of the McCarthy era. She was attending school at Santa Monica Community College, hoping to become a nurse, when one of her college professors refused to sign a loyalty oath as required by the state. "He gave us reasons why he didn't want to sign, and they seemed reasonable to me. My father and I had a huge argument about that, about how he was a communist and teaching me wrong. Basically, at that point, I decided there's something wrong somewhere, that there was discrimination going on."

The onset of polio in 1956, after which she became a wheelchair user, furthered this family rift. Toomer was by then married and living in Tennessee, and although her father by that time had business in Nashville, only fifty miles from where Barbara was receiving rehab, he refused to visit her because "he couldn't stand to see me that way." It wasn't only her family, however, who had problems accepting who she was after polio.

"My very dear next-door neighbor, who I thought was a really good friend made arrangements to meet me when I was in the hospital, and I waited and waited and she didn't show up. Later I got a note saying that she also just couldn't stand to see me that way. So I had some inkling that I was not welcome everywhere, or that people didn't want to see me. But my husband never ever did that. He visited me every single day.

"That feeling still exists, that disability is the most awful thing that could possibly happen to a person. And it's really difficult to overcome that pity emotion."

Toomer's introduction to the disability rights movement came two decades after she became disabled, by which time she and her family had moved to Utah. "That was when Justin Dart went around to all the states trying to get a feel of what was going on in the community. At that point we organized what was called Advocates for Utah Handicapped, as a result of that meeting with Justin."

Toomer cofounded the Utah Independent Living Center in 1981, and was deeply immersed in its operation two years later when Wade Blank called for a meeting in Denver of disability advocates interested in organizing around the issue of accessible mass transit. "We'd been working on transportation here [in Utah] for quite a while. We were met at the Denver airport by some of the Atlantis people, and while we were waiting for other folks to arrive they gave us signs saying, 'We want a ride just like you.' I'd come with my friend Deb, who was an extremely conservative woman, but the two of us were sitting outside the airport with our signs. We were in our suits, and looking pretty elegant, now that I stop and think about it."

Since then Toomer has been to dozens of ADAPT actions and continues to be active in the movement.

———

Always, the purpose of the actions are to change the mindset of the individuals we're after. So we were trying to change the mindset of APTA, because after President Carter had issued an executive order that said that all buses should have lifts on them, APTA went to court and got a suspension of that executive order. And so APTA was the target, because you can't ride a bus if you can't get on the bus. And it was really essential that we get to ride the buses, especially those of us who didn't have the ability to drive or the ability to afford a vehicle.

Our demonstrations could take many forms. The one I really remember was a regional APTA meeting here. It was virtually inaccessible, so what we did was to take a really teeny tiny elevator through the kitchen up to probably the second floor of this hotel and gathered in a little anteroom and then just stormed into the meeting room and handed out flyers basically saying, "We want you to think about putting lifts on the buses because you're discriminating against us." And I particularly remember because one of the young women who was handing out flyers was pushed by one of the members—whether it was a guard or, I don't know who it was—but it was somebody who was in the room, and she fell down. And the press here made a big to-do about it, which was only right. But what it did was gain us more publicity to alert the public that there really were not lifts on the buses and there was no way that we could ride.

We were pretty edgy, for Salt Lake City anyway. They were completely out of the black civil rights movement because—I mean—what have we got, 2 percent black or something? As a whole, the population of Utah is extremely conservative. And so any disturbance at all was a big shock to them.

The biggest problem we had was when we stopped the buses. This would've been probably '88, '89. We had been working with UTA [the Utah Transit Authority] for several years to release those twenty-three lifts for public use, and to order more. And they just were adamant that they weren't gonna to do it. We had been on advisory committees and task forces and you name it. We'd tried hard for years to work within the system, so what we finally decided to do was to stop, or at least slow their buses down.

Now, Salt Lake City revolves around South Temple Street and Main Street. It makes a "T." That's where the big department stores are, it's where everything is. And the buses all go down there. And so what we did, for two weeks, we did a "crawl on," where you kind of guppy up the stairs and someone throws a wheelchair on, and then you get down to the next stop and you crawl off. And it slows the system down. And we kept talking to the head of UTA and he was not going listen to us, and he wouldn't have anything to do with us.

And so we sent out a call to Colorado and Idaho for help, and I guess we had maybe fifteen people who were ADAPT members, and they came down. So now there were about thirty-five or forty of us, and we went out on Main Street at five o'clock and stopped every bus in the system. We had alerted the mayor and the mayor said, "It's okay, I'm going to protect you." And we know that he had detectives going up and down Main Street when we had the buses stopped. We had flyers, "This is why we're here" type things. "Sorry for the inconvenience, but we've been waiting for a long long time."

We stood on First South, which is the street below South Temple. We stopped the buses at First South, and halfway between First and Second South. So every bus in this city was stopped. And I remember some young man who went out into the street before me, who used a board to communicate. We had to go off the curb because we didn't have curb cuts, so I remember going out and being next to him in traffic to try and protect him. And he said, "What are you doing here?" And I said, "Stopping a bus and helping you." And he said, on his board, "I don't need your help, but thank you for coming." So, you know, at that point I got a better respect for people who could not communicate easily. I mean, this kid was wonderful.

As a result of that, the next time the UTA put in an order for new buses it ordered that 50 percent be lift-equipped, and then they also worked with us to release the lifts they had already ordered. When the Americans with Disabilities Act was passed, the order [directly] before had been 100 percent lifts. And so they really didn't even have to worry about complying with the ADA in their August [1990] purchase of buses, because they had already done it.

Babs Johnson
"They deliberately broke this one woman's leg."

Babs Johnson was born in Cheyenne, Wyoming, in 1952. She met Wade Blank in the 1970s, when he visited a mutual friend who was a United Church of Christ minister in Rock Springs. In 1980, Johnson, now a single mother looking for work, moved to Denver, where Blank offered her a job as a personal care assistant for some of the more severely disabled clients at Atlantis. Johnson quickly found herself immersed in disability politics, and was there when ADAPT was founded in 1983. In all, Babs Johnson has helped to organize more than fifty national ADAPT actions, and in 1999 she became the lead organizer for the group's Colorado chapter. In the meantime she continued to work at Atlantis Community, Inc., where she is now assistant director.

She begins her account here with the action in Montreal, where APTA held its annual conference in October 1988. One could speculate that APTA, having already experienced ADAPT's in-your-face style of civil disobedience, chose Canada and leaving the country entirely as a way of avoiding another confrontation. If so, it was to no avail: with this action ADAPT proved it could organize effective civil disobedience in the face of the additional barriers implicit in being in another country.

———

Montreal was one that we went out ahead of time just to scope things out, because it was so different and we didn't have a [local] group there. One of our members was a travel agent, and had booked a hotel there. They evidently figured out who we were and they backed out on us. So we were scrambling to get a hotel, and then we met with a lot of local people with disabilities. So, it was a lot of preparation setting it up.

To me, it was a whole new world. I'd never been to Canada. People primarily spoke French. They didn't like to speak English, and so that was a challenge for us. I was very concerned about getting across the border. We lined up this really great lawyer who agreed to go down to the border when the group got there and make sure that they all came across safely. Everyone made it without a problem.

We ended up staying at a really old hotel. One night the electricity went out and Wade and I were so concerned that this would be a way to really mess with us, because if the electric goes out, the power chairs don't work because we can't recharge the batteries. And also, how would we get the power chairs down the stairs if the elevators aren't working? That was a worry, but then the lights went back on.

We had a great action. We had a lot of local support, a lot of local people showed up.

The APTA conference was at two hotels, the primary conference center and then a backup one. We went to the backup hotel after dark one evening. It was raining. They blocked the front doors with luggage racks so we couldn't get in. We just pushed our way through the luggage racks.

But the other part of us that weren't in power chairs, people in manual wheelchairs able to push themselves, went through a back door that Wade had put a matchbook in to leave open. It was a fire door. Those of us who were ambulatory carried people down the stairs in their manual wheelchairs, and then came up the main elevator at the same time that our other people broke through the front doors. So we're coming in from two different directions at once into the lobby of this hotel, and that took them really by surprise.

They ended up arresting quite a few people and sent them to this old, old jail that was a little bit outside of town. They separated the men from the women. They had court in the middle of the night and kept these folks. But we continued having protests through the rest of the week. We did one in a park where APTA went for some kind of a social event and then we ended up in the Montreal subway system, which was not accessible, climbing down the steps. This was a little outside of town so that we weren't in the same district or area of where we had been arrested before, so they couldn't count it as two arrests.

That was one where I and my husband were arrested, so while we were in jail my daughter, she was about fifteen at the time, stayed with Wade and some other people at the hotel. Someone from Montreal called her up in the middle of the night and said, "Social services will be after you because your parents are both in jail." That scared her to death.

[Sparks, Nevada, 1989]

Sparks is just outside of Reno, and it was very scary. They played real hardball. First of all, that particular year [1989] the APTA conference was at a hotel/casino. A lot of the really violent stuff that happened was from the security in the casino. Everything's a casino there, and so the hotel where APTA was also a casino. We went to the doors and they wouldn't let us in, so we blocked the doors and they got real angry.

We had maybe seventy-five people. They had tried to actually block us with a barrier on the sidewalk as we left our hotel at the end of the street, not thinking that we would jump the curb and go right around it. We got to the casino and blocked the doors and that's where they went after Wade. He was carrying his son, who was just a baby at the time, in a backpack on his back. Wade is on the sidewalk and they said, "You'd better get rid of that baby because we're going to arrest you." He said, "But I'm just standing on the sidewalk." And they said, "You didn't hear us. We are *going to arrest you,* and you'd better get rid of the baby, or we'll take him to social services."

You know, those security guards don't mess around and they're really big, macho men. They deliberately broke this one woman's leg. It was real obvious that her legs did not bend, and they just bent it and broke it. When they arrested people—after they had arrested them—they sent one man out a door—it was dark and there were steps there. He was in a wheelchair and he couldn't see the steps, so he fell off the steps in his wheelchair and broke his leg.

After we were arrested the regular police put people in different jail cells and separated everybody—separated people with really severe disabilities from their PCAs—so one woman had seizures over, over, and over again. They put another person with a spinal cord injury in a cell all by himself, and he couldn't go to the bathroom, and so he started going into hyperflexia [autonomic dysreflexia] which a person can die from, stroke out, because you're not able to go to the bathroom.

They were rough with anybody that would not exactly do what they wanted. There was people that they drug on the ground, a blind man, another man in a wheelchair that was out of his chair and they dragged him. They were very violent.

We changed what we were doing then for the next day, doing some more theater rather than the direct-action in-your-face sort of stuff. And the next day people in jail went on a hunger strike and a lot of them ended up in the hospital over that, or in the jail infirmary. I can't remember if it was the infirmary or the hospital, but I do remember they got sick.

We couldn't even get a lawyer there. We were trying to get a lawyer, as I remember, and some guy walked out of a bar, after our protest, and said, "Do you all need a lawyer?" and he offered to help us out. He was the only lawyer we could get there.

Michael Auberger (continued)
"They put us in segregated housing, with the Hillside Strangler on one side and a child molester on the other."

After prevailing over McDonald's Corporation, Michael Auberger went on to cofound ADAPT with Rev. Blank and the other activists who had gathered in

Denver. As an ADAPT organizer, he was at the center of the group's campaign for accessible mass transit.

———

The first day of the APTA national meeting, in October 1984, they had barricades around the convention center. There were forty-two of us at the time, that were part of that first group in DC. They had the barricades up, and so we marched around the whole perimeter of the convention center and held up traffic. The police didn't do anything. We pushed and we pushed, the DC police weren't real interested in having to deal with us. And so I ended up taking my wheelchair and literally pushing the barricades away from the front entrance so that everybody could get through. There are some funny pictures of me hitting the barricades to move them with my motorized wheelchair. That was the last straw, that we'd gotten through and closed the main entrances by putting wheelchairs in front of the doors of the convention center. The transit association had had enough and told the police to arrest.

The police weren't ready for that. They had to find a vehicle that they could put people in. So they ended up finding, an hour or two later, an accessible school bus that was used for the special kids going to school. There were thirteen of us under arrest, and it took them three hours to get us to court [to be arraigned]. They had to take us out of the bus one at a time. Then we had to go down through the basement parking lot, because they didn't have an accessible entrance, take the elevator up to the jail, over on Indiana Street in DC.

They got all of us out of the elevator, they had this wall of bars with a door in front of the entrance to the jail. And so they tried the first person; they couldn't get him through the jail door, because the wheelchair was wider than the door. So they hadn't a clue what to do. One of the police officers had the bright idea to take us out of our wheelchairs. They took the person out of the wheelchair, put him in a desk chair, wheeled him through, and tried to wheel the wheelchair through. Well, the wheelchair still didn't go through. We tried to tell them the first time it's not going to work, and tried to tell them the second time it's not going to work. They actually tried it three different times, and they just couldn't figure out that the wheelchair was wider than the door. This is something the police had never done, so moving even a group of thirteen or so was not anything that anybody had ever thought about how to do. And so what they did was they took the three people that they'd gotten out of their wheelchairs, took them back out the other side of the jail, put them back in their wheelchairs, went back down the elevator, had to go around through the back of the building, single file with an officer accompanying each person in a wheelchair, out to the front of the building, then into the court to be arraigned.

Everybody pleaded guilty. Everybody had agreed ahead of time that that's what would happen, and everybody would be very clear about why they were breaking the law. There's all kinds of irony, and serendipity, throughout everything we did. The judge happened to have a brother who used a wheelchair, and he was no longer alive, and the judge told us the story of all the complications his brother had had with public transportation. Then he finds everybody guilty, and he fines everybody court costs, and he suspends everybody's sentence. And then he says, at the end of it, that he'll pay the court costs out of his own pocket.

It was just amazing, the places you went. There was the LA County Jail, where three of us were arrested. That was probably the most horrendous experience. We were put into the general population. It was surreal. I'm a C4/5 quad, there was Bob Kafka, who is a complete quadriplegic, and then there was Ken Heard from Syracuse, who had cerebral palsy, spastic, his speech was involved. So we were stripped by trustees and put into jumpsuits.

We were taken to the infirmary to see the doctor. We sat there probably for a good six hours, waiting like everybody else. They were making the point that jail wasn't a fun place. That was the whole idea: to treat you like everybody else.

So we waited there. You get all kinds of characters in jail, for sure, and while we were in the infirmary they bring in this one guy in a wheelchair. He obviously had a physical disability, but he didn't have his own chair. They brought him from his cell in a wheelchair, and made him transfer onto a bench and sit and wait for the doctor, and then took away the wheelchair. It was obvious he had pneumonia, and was just profusely sweating from the high fever, and coughing so much he falls off the bench. The officer tells him to get up, and he says, "I can't get up." And the officer kicks him a couple of times. The guy tries to tell him again that he can't get up. We're telling the sheriff that he physically can't get up, he needs help. "If I want any shit from you, I'll ask for it." It was just that clear. "So shut the fuck up, stay over on that side of the orange line, and don't say anything until you're talked to." He finally figured it out, and he got a couple of people to put the guy back on the bench. But you got the exact treatment that everybody else gets in jail. It wasn't like a lot of the other jails, where you were segregated, and so the stories are a lot different.

We got through to the doctor, and so the doctor made sure that you had whatever urinary equipment, catheter stuff you might need, and minimal medication that they had—it wasn't what you needed, it was whatever they had that was *close* to what you needed. Again, you were reminded that this was a jail, it wasn't a hospital. And when they kept us overnight they put us in segregated housing, with the Hillside Strangler on one side and a child molester on the other.

It was real in the LA jail, but all these experiences about the jails are interesting stories. We've also been in what I would call some "five-star jails" across the country. One time we were in Phoenix, and the Phoenix jail has its own bakery. And so we're sitting in jail, and every evening the trustees would bring over fresh cookies and bread and cake to us for snacks. The trustees would do the attendant services, but it was an interesting kind of thing. In the Long Beach jail they ordered in pizza.

The people who they perceived as leadership at the time they would keep longer, and they would dump everybody else out. But we worked out strategy, and made sure that we always had people out every day. As the numbers got larger, it got more difficult for the system to deal with us, no matter where we were. What do you do in a jail with sixty people who have physical disabilities? The system wasn't meant for any kind of number of people with physical disabilities at the time, and probably still isn't.

One of the realities that was explained to new ADAPT people was that we can't guarantee what's going to happen in jail. We'd tell them, here's what happened in these places, but you need to understand that you're breaking the law, and you're going to jail—that you may get this, or you may get nothing, and if you get nothing, you get nothing. Like in the LA jail, one of the things that ended up happening, with them taking my shoe strings from my shoes, and me not getting my medication for the spasticity of my legs, was that the spasms were bad enough at times that my feet were banging on the pedals of my wheelchair, and created some open wounds that I still have. I've been healing my feet off and on for twenty-five, twenty-six years now, an old problem that keeps coming back from the LA jail.

Again it goes back to how the system wasn't used to dealing with us, and that could be good and it could be bad. Clearly, civil disobedience was not something that people with disabilities usually did on any kind of regular basis. Being arrested, sitting in front of buses.

One of the most empowering things that happened was to convince somebody that they could stop a bus. Here's a sixty-ton bus that all of a sudden doesn't move because somebody's sitting in front of it, somebody's sitting behind it so it couldn't back up. (That was another of the things we learned early on, that you can't just block the front of the bus, because they will back up). You can talk about putting lifts on buses, and all the other things that came out of what we did, but I think the most amazing thing was the empowerment and the self-esteem that people ended up taking home with them. To watch someone who had been institutionalized, is now out in the community but still struggling to survive, and accepting the handouts, to see somebody in that situation sitting in front of a bus and telling a police officer "No, I'm *not* moving." You had to tell people, "Don't smile when you're saying these things, this is a serious issue," but all of a sudden you've got somebody who's feeling their oats, who's feeling like, "Wow, I just told a cop 'no, I'm not going to,' and the bus is not moving, and it's not going anywhere because *I* can't ride it." As far as I'm concerned that had more value than all of the other things that we did and accomplished. People went from feeling powerless to being truly empowered. And those were the people that went back home, talked about what they did, and organized around the issue, that felt like now they were somebody. You know, Jessie Jackson is always repeating the "I am somebody" chant. Well, it's one thing to *say* it, but it's a whole 'nother thing to *feel* it, and to actually *do* it.

It was part of that whole organizing problem: having somebody who's oppressed recognize that they're oppressed. And I think even more so for people with disabilities. You were supposed to say "please" and "thank you," you were supposed to smile. It was the Jerry's Kids mentality, that's how you'd get things. And so in community organizing one of the things you want to do is to get people who are oppressed to recognize their oppression, number one, and number two to take that oppression, and to take that anger, and to focus it, in a demonstration, in sitting in front of a bus and saying, "Hell no, I'm not moving . . ." To get people to the point where they say, "I've got a *right,* I've got a *right* to be angry, I've got a *right* to be like everybody else. And I don't have to look like them to have that same right. I don't have to have the same *things* they do, but I have the same *rights.*"

What makes you so different? Because you have cerebral palsy? Because you've had a stroke? Because you've acquired a disability for whatever reason? There's nothing that says you don't have that right to ride a public bus, to be in the community just like anybody else. You have that basic right as a person. That's what you're selling, and it was a tough job. "What happens when I go back to my community and try to do this?" "Well, it won't be as easy. That's why you want to get other people. We'll help, we'll come to your local community, and we'll help you organize," and that was part of what we did as ADAPT.

That's what civil rights are all about. That's what Martin Luther King talked about with African Americans. You have that basic right as a person, to be equal. And equality for us meant riding the bus.

22

Deaf President Now!

I T WOULD BE DIFFICULT TO OVERSTATE THE IMPORTANCE OF
Gallaudet University to the American Deaf community. Established in
Washington, DC, in 1864 (with a charter signed by Abraham Lincoln) it was
and remains as of this writing the world's only liberal arts college for people
who are Deaf. Since its inception, virtually every Deaf political leader of note
has received his or her college education at Gallaudet, and virtually every Deaf
scholar has at one time or another studied or taught there. After the advent
of oralism[1] in the 1880s, Gallaudet remained the most visible and prestigious
stronghold of Deaf culture, where Deaf people, using American Sign Language
(ASL), could live and study in an environment with complete communications
access. Its library contains the archives of American Deaf history, and it was
at Gallaudet, in the early 1960s, that scholars such as Dr. William C. Stokoe
conducted their groundbreaking studies of ASL, contributing to what would
be by the latter part of that decade a renaissance in Deaf culture.

And yet, for the first 124 years of its history, not one of Gallaudet's presidents had ever been Deaf. So when, in September 1987, Dr. Jerry C. Lee, the
sitting president of Gallaudet, announced that he would retire the following
spring, Deaf community activists across the country began a campaign for a
Deaf President Now (or DPN). Articles appeared in the Deaf press arguing
that, with so many eminent Deaf educators to choose from, the appointment
of a hearing president would be a setback to Deaf people everywhere, while the
choice of a Deaf president would be both an affirmation of Deaf people and a
rejection of the stereotypes that continued to plague them. Jack Levesque in
California and Barbara Jean Wood in Massachusetts[2] were among those making this case, while in the Washington area a loosely organized group of Deaf
professionals and recent Gallaudet alums, who styled themselves "the Ducks,"
began agitating on and off campus. Gary Olsen, president of the National
Association of the Deaf, and his assistant Fred Weiner (who had just left a
position with the Gallaudet Alumni Association), both played pivotal roles in

the campaign, appearing on campus numerous times to enlist students in the fight they saw coming.

On March 1, 1988, all of these people came together for an on-campus rally that featured many of nation's most prominent Deaf leaders. The estimated fifteen hundred people who attended—students, alums, activists, even some Gallaudet faculty and staff (who faced the possibility of retaliation from the administration)—looked around and saw a community united as never before.

Then the announcement came that Dr. Elisabeth Ann Zinser, the only hearing finalist interviewed by the search committee and someone with no prior experience with the Deaf community, had been chosen to replace Dr. Lee. Adding insult to injury was the way the announcement was made: late on a Sunday night, communicated via a mimeographed press release distributed on campus.

The student strike that resulted—lasting from that Sunday night, March 6, to Sunday, March 13—has been called "The Week the World Heard Gallaudet."[3] The board of trustees was presented with four non-negotiable demands: (1) Dr. Zinser's resignation and the appointment of a Deaf president; (2) the resignation of the board's (hearing) chairperson, Jane Bassett Spilman; (3) an increase in Deaf representation on the board to at least 51 percent and (4) no reprisals against anyone taking part in the protests.

Dr. Zinser resigned on March 10. On March 13, the board of trustees placed a TTY call to the student leaders at their headquarters on campus, announcing that they had agreed to the other three demands. On that day, Dr. Irving King Jordan, dean of Gallaudet's College of Arts and Sciences, became Gallaudet University's first Deaf president.

The repercussions of DPN were felt by Deaf people around the world, while in the United States the campaign and its attendant publicity brought disability discrimination and disability rights to the public's attention at the time that Congress had begun to consider the first version of what would be the Americans with Disabilities Act of 1990. Coming when and as it did, the victory at Gallaudet generated both a buzz and a momentum that would be enormous assets to the nascent ADA coalition.

Jeff Rosen
"We'd been conditioned to live in a mental ghetto."

On March 1, 1988, Jeff Rosen spoke before the crowd gathered on the campus of Gallaudet University to demand the appointment of a Deaf President Now.

"People have died in the civil rights movement. People were jailed in protesting the Vietnam War. I stand here in 1988 asking: What do you believe in? What is your cause?"[4] It's no accident that Rosen would cite the civil rights and antiwar movements in his speech. Born in 1962 and coming of age after their high tide in the mid- and late sixties, he nonetheless had an abiding interest in both, not to mention personal experiences with the discrimination, disempowerment, and violence often visited on deaf people in twentieth-century America.

"Often I was teased and hurt because of being deaf at a mainstream middle school. That put a stigma on me and I became a target to some kids. And so I tried to respond the best way I could. I was a fighter, but not much of a fighter, not a good fighter, anyway. So that was difficult to deal with and it became a problem for me. You know, kids are very straightforward with how they feel about those sorts of things. One time this one kid confronted me, said, 'I'm going to fight you.' And that kid was ten times bigger than me. He really beat me up bad. I got punched in the face, got a broken nose. . . .

"I'm a very avid reader, and as a teenager I read Zora Neale Hurston, Eldridge Cleaver, Malcolm X, and other people who opened up my mind about what it meant to be oppressed in America. And, you know, some of the issues that we faced in the Deaf community, they dealt with also."

Rosen himself had spent a year at Gallaudet before matriculating at the University of Washington in Seattle. After passing the bar in 1985, he returned to Washington, DC, where he took a position with the federal Equal Employment Opportunity Commission, first under Clarence Thomas, then under Evan Kemp.

Rosen today is general counsel at The Z, the nation's first video relay service provider.

———

Both of my parents worked at Gallaudet, and my mother at that time was dean of continuing education. Their community, the folks that they would socialize with, were Gallaudet people: professors, administrators, staff, faculty. At the time that Dr. Lee's resignation was announced, I heard all about it because my parents were just so involved with that group of people. So I overheard conversations, that people knew that the next president would be a hearing woman, named Elisabeth Zinser. The

chair of Gallaudet's board of trustees, Jane Basset Spilman, had already
gone to North Carolina to meet with her before the process even began,
and then came back with a report about her wonderful impressions of
her. So this Deaf group that my parents socialized with all had the feeling
that she would be chosen as the new president.

But then one morning I was on the Metro on my way to work and I
was thinking: "Nothing is ever final." And so I thought it was just awful that people were already resigned to this fact. So I got to work and
I called on my TTY to a friend of mine, whose name is Paul Singleton,
and I said, "You know what? This is really bullshit, what's happening at
Gallaudet." And Paul was working at Gallaudet at the time, doing some
work in the financial office.

The two of us then were part of a small group of friends who happened
to call ourselves, for some reason, "the Ducks." James Tucker was in that
group. James is now the president or the superintendent of the Maryland
School for the Deaf. Stephen Hlibok was a member, he's now a vice
president for Merrill Lynch, and his brother Greg was one of the four
student leaders of what would become Deaf President Now. Another
member was Mike O'Donnell, who was a former teacher at Gallaudet
and was working with the Congressional Special Services Office, and
moved around Congress. Each one of us were in different areas. I was in
advocacy. Paul was with his office in Gallaudet. Fred Weiner was involved
with the NAD [National Association of the Deaf]. Mike O'Donnell had
good PR skills. Stephen was very important with his connections among
the student leaders. So this group got together and we discussed the idea
of a rally to let students, let faculty know that it was not inevitable for us
to have a hearing president.

There were many students at the time, and a lot of people at Gallaudet, who did not believe that a Deaf person *should* be president, that it
would be impossible for Deaf people to lead. And a lot of people asked
questions like, "How can a Deaf president communicate with Congress
or with politicians or people to do fundraising?" But there were also a
lot of people who started to feel very angry, to realize that they'd experienced this kind of oppression year after year after year, that we'd been
conditioned to live in a mental ghetto, and that our expectations had
been lowered. And for myself, I felt a very strong determination. It was a
very tough, emotional time, changing a whole mindset.

It was a problem to arrange anything on campus. They would not allow us to use any of the campus organizations because the Gallaudet administration was very strictly controlling of all that. In fact, they fired Paul because he was helping with the arrangements, to make the reservations for the field that we used to hold the first stage of the rally. What we were going to do was have a march around campus, with seven hundred, eight hundred people involved, but they fired him. So there were no campus organizations involved, it was really all outside of Gallaudet. We would get together in somebody's kitchen, sit around at the table and draw up our plans.

There was no Deaf press back then and there's very little even now, but the NAD did publish a wonderful *Broadcaster,* their newsletter, and there were articles about the Deaf President protest. In California there was an advocacy organization called DCARA [Deaf Counseling, Advocacy, and Referral Agency], headed by Jack Levesque, and he wrote articles about what was going on at Gallaudet: "Why not a Deaf president?" But that's just a very limited sample of media. It's not like today with the Internet and video and stuff like that. It was all word of mouth, all across the US and really across the world because people across the world did know about it. But it was all community networking.

What it boiled down to was educating the students. We told the students over and over again: no students, no university. We told them that they *do* have the power, that *they* were going to decide the future of the university, not the administration, not the faculty, not the staff. That was our strategic approach. The faculty, the staff were all afraid to get involved because if they got involved they would be terminated and they didn't want to risk that. And the administration, of course, was following the board's directive.

The first rally started at the football field and then there was a march around the campus. There were several points where it stopped and there were speakers. And it ended at the Gallaudet president's home, where I spoke. And I explained the fact that this was analogous to the civil rights movement and that I myself was determined to go to the president's house to prove that there was no accessibility for a Deaf person to go into that house, that, in fact, even the door bell didn't have a strobe light. There was nothing in the house that would make it a comfortable place for a Deaf person to live. The students were all jumping up and down, it was very emotional. They were very angry, they were ready to go.

I think that during the next week a lot of people hoped, even I had some hope, that this profound expression of the community's will would influence the board, that people's minds would open, that people might understand how important this was to all of us. We had daily meetings. We had candlelight vigils. We had daily events, and letter-writing campaigns to the board. So there were all kinds of things going on. But it was all very much in real time, in the flow of the moment. There was no sitting down and developing thoughts or strategy about what to do, because it was all so new. We'd never experienced this before. Everything that happened, happened in a very spontaneous way.

I was at the Gallaudet press office when the announcement was made that Zinser had been chosen. And there were three stacks of press releases for each of the three final candidates. So I was with Jeff Bravin, whose father was on the board at the time, and we went in and the press person there was on the phone. He looked at me and gave me this big stack that had the name "Zinser" on it, and he said, "I'm sorry Jeff."

I just felt like smashing my hand on the ground and having it bleed. But I sat down and thought, "Okay, I have to go talk with the group," which was now assembled in front of the Gallaudet Gate. There was quite an uproar going on, quite a turmoil. People weren't sure what to do and somebody said, "Let's go directly to the Gallaudet board and demand an explanation." We knew the board was meeting that night at the Mayflower Hotel [in downtown Washington, DC]. I would say there were a hundred and fifty, maybe two hundred people on the march that Sunday night.

The police came, saying, "You can't march, you don't have a permit." But the police weren't able to communicate with anyone because they didn't have an interpreter. They kept trying to interrupt us, but we ignored them and we kept marching. They decided to close all the streets so that no cars could come in and hit Deaf people. At the very, very back of the crowd there were some people with multiple disabilities, people with mobility issues. And so I went back to be with that group because they were slower.

It was interesting, marching through those streets, past all these apartment buildings. People were looking out the windows and everybody was interested to see what the march was all about, even though it was dark at the time. And there were black people who were cheering from their windows, even though they didn't know exactly what was going on. They were cheering for us anyways.

We arrived at the Mayflower Hotel, and people were looking for me, wondering, you know, "Where is Jeff?" The reason why they asked for me was they felt that with my legal background I'd be a good representative. There were two others, besides me, who were picked to meet with the board. So it was Greg Hlibok, Tim Rarus, and myself.

Greg was the Student Government leader and he explained to the board why it was so important that a Deaf president be selected and what it meant to the student body. And that was what the first few minutes were about. It was very calm, very straightforward. This was the first time that the board had had the opportunity to see us face to face, the first time we really looked each other in the eye and gave our views and our reasons why. Spilman's response was that she was aware of all of our reasons, and she felt they were very compelling, but she thought that Zinser was truly the better choice.

Then the next part of the meeting Spilman started to talk about her conversations with the executives of Merrill Lynch and about the challenges that the Deaf community faces in the hearing world. So she talked about that experience and made some comment, that Deaf people, in her opinion, were not ready to function equally in the hearing world. And at that point I got up and said, "I am finished with this meeting," and that I wasn't going to continue any conversations if that was going to be the tone. "How can we work with this? Her decision's already made." And Tim said, "Maybe it was an interpreter error, maybe we need to sit down and make sure we're clear." And I was like, "No. She made it very clear. There's no point in talking any more." And Tim really had to sit with me and calm me down, to get me to return to the meeting. I got back in my seat and we continued.

This went on for about forty-five minutes, and at that point we went back to the lobby. About 80 percent of the group had already left. They were not feeling that they'd gotten what they wanted, so they were heading to Congress, to the Capitol. Again, this is in the middle of the night, but they went anyway. Everybody kept saying, "We cannot miss this opportunity. We need to go to the Capitol, we need to explain our situation, we need to explain what happened and we need to know why Zinser was picked and we need to make it known why we were looking for a new candidate."

I didn't go to the Capitol. I went back to campus. So now it's maybe three, four o'clock Monday morning, and there was a crowd on campus, students who'd come back from the Capitol, and others. There was a lot of anger. The students were young kids. Some wanted to be violent, they wanted to destroy things. They were upset, they had been oppressed. So there was a lot of discussion about nonviolence. We talked about Gandhi, we talked about Martin Luther King and their approaches to nonviolent movements, instructing them as a group. "Come on, don't do any damage, don't do anything that's going to discredit our cause." And people respected that.

About four or five in the morning a group of students went to the front gate, and that's when they proceeded to block all the gates. People were pulling fire alarms so all the students had to evacuate the dorms, and we saw that the whole school had been barricaded. And to barricade the front gate, a group of students had hot-wired a school bus, parked it in the gate, and then let all the air out of the tires.

Now, there was this stereotype that Deaf people weren't supposed to be mechanically inclined. And so when I saw how these college students had hot-wired the bus, I remember thinking, "Wow! I never knew Deaf kids could be mechanically inclined like that." [Laughs.] Really, that just surprised the hell out of me.

Greg Hlibok
"We had each other's backs."

———

The face and voice of the Deaf community to the hearing world during the Deaf President Now student strike was twenty-one-year-old Greg Hlibok. His appearance on *Nightline* was for millions of Americans their introduction not only to Gallaudet and Deaf President Now but to the idea that Deaf people could be discriminated against and that they felt the same way about such discrimination as members of other oppressed minorities.

Like Jeff Rosen, Greg Hlibok was born into a Deaf family, and ASL was his first language. And like Rosen, Hlibok takes issue with the idea that deafness is in and of itself a disability.

"I didn't consider myself disabled as a kid, and I still don't. Not even for a moment, ever. Not even when I was confronted with my hearing friends, neighbors, and such. I knew that I was Deaf, and I would try to communicate. Every once in a while, of course, I would be frustrated, but I didn't blame myself for the situation, or feel, 'Oh, I'm disabled.' I was born with this, and it was a part of me, and so I didn't give it any thought."

Born in 1967 in Flushing, New York, Hlibok attended the Lexington School for the Deaf in New York City, which at the time was an "oral" school committed to teaching students to speak and read lips. "That was the mentality in the 1970s." He also attended a mainstream public school for a short time, receiving nothing in the way of services or reasonable accommodation. Through it all he knew he would eventually attend Gallaudet. "My two [older] brothers had gone, my mom was an alum. By the time I was in elementary school I had already decided that that was where I would go."

Hlibok, like many other Deaf people of his generation, attended one of the Deaf Youth Leadership Camps, in his case in 1982. He was also active with the Junior NAD, and as a youth met both Gary Olsen and Frank Turk, cofounders of the Leadership Camps.

He entered Gallaudet in 1985, majoring first in engineering, then in government. By spring 1988 he was the elected president of the Gallaudet Student Body Government (or SBG), and thus was a natural choice for a leadership role as the strike unfolded.

Hlibok is now the chief of the Disability Rights Office at the Consumer and Governmental Affairs Division of the Federal Communications Commission.

Ducks was a group that formed before the protest, and they believed that we were ready for a Deaf president, and they decided to get more people involved for the cause. I was just elected president of the SBG, so we'd meet and discuss the possibility of having a Deaf president. But it was beyond our imagination that it could happen, and that we could do something about it. We didn't think that we had the power. We were just students at that time, we thought, but the Ducks, they said, "You *can* do something about it, you can take action."

So me being SBG president at that time, I decided, "Okay, let's take action." But we needed full support from the student body, and so I went and took over the bull sessions in the cafeteria during that time. Some of the students came from a "mainstream" background, they weren't really fully understanding the meaning of having a Deaf president. Unfortunately, lots of Deaf students don't have a lot of confidence in themselves, and because of that, Deaf people always feel that they're not ready. So we really had to empower them, and to explain, and say, "Yes we can, we need it."

Everything was based on a short-term plan, and the process was really quick. We didn't really start planning until the middle of February, when we started planning for the rally on March 1st. Our goal was to get as many students as possible to go. I had a bull session in the cafeteria, and that's where we discussed everything. It was four straight nights of discussion, trying to convince students to come on and join us, come to the rally and support the cause.

And then we had the rally, and oh wow! It was really a surprise. We had a great turn-out, there were so many students there, there was around three thousand students during the middle of the day at our school, it was amazing. At that point I knew that we had enough support.

Our goal, of course, was to convince the board, to send a message that they should pick a Deaf president. And so we started sending letters. I sent letters to the board, on behalf of the students, and I sent a letter to Zinser who had applied, and I suggested that she resign. We had a suspicion that the board was kind of fixed, so to speak, to have her as president.

That next Sunday night we were expecting someone from the administration, or some of the board members to come to the Field House, I think it was about seven at night. But my friend was hungry so we decided to drive and order food, and by the time we got back, the announcement had already been made: they made it earlier than scheduled. They had printed up flyers, and there was a stack of flyers there, and the papers announced that they had picked Zinser as the first woman president.

So we were really confused. It was all turmoil, and everybody was so upset, and they had gathered outside of the Florida Avenue entrance in front of Gallaudet, and we had maybe an hour discussion about what to do. And some suggested that we just trash the campus, and other folks said, "No, we don't agree with that. We need to see the board members, and we need to ask them, Why?" We needed an answer.

And so we decided we would go to the hotel, and meet the chairperson of the board, Jane Spilman. And when she announced that Deaf people were not ready to function in the hearing world—that was the quote—we just—we decided to protest. We decided to march back to Gallaudet campus. We arrived there, and we had a meeting at the gym. We set up a strike committee, and we agreed to boycott classes, and that none of the staff or the administration would be able to get on campus. One guy flipped his hat over, took donations, gathered the money. We bought locks and chains from the hardware store, and we were able to chain and lock up the seven gates that led onto the campus. It was very spontaneous. We didn't have a formal plan.

The whole time, during that week, we were emphasizing that there was to be no violent actions, to keep things under control. Some suggested that we throw rocks at the windows of the admin. building, or break in, but we were against that.

We were really learning to take advantage of the media. The interviews just kept going during that whole week: the *Washington Post,* the *Times,* ABC, NBC, CBS, all those were there. We had so much exposure, we were welcoming as much support as we could, and the last few days we had a lot of support.

I was chosen to be the spokesperson because I'd been in the meetings all that week, I'd already been doing the interviews. I guess it just kind of came naturally, a part of who I am. I was so fully involved, the answers just flew, they just came right from my heart. And that's one of the reasons why the protest was so successful, because our message was able to go through so smoothly. We didn't go off the point, we didn't have any confusion.

This was a one-time chance, to make it or miss. But we had each other's backs. We were strong, and a very close group of people. But I wasn't sure of success until Wednesday, when things started to change. Before that we were a little concerned, and also overwhelmed with so much of the media exposure. We weren't expecting that. Monday morning, we didn't see any reporters standing anywhere on the campus, so we didn't expect that at all.

Going on *Nightline* on Wednesday was a turning point, because it had millions of viewers all over the world. And in the interview it was obvious that Zinser had shot herself in the foot. When Ted Koppel asked her, "Are you a puppet of the board?" she just froze. And after that interview she was gone. That following morning she decided to resign. That was the turning point.

Zinser resigned on Thursday, but now we were concerned that the board would announce that they would do another search, and start the process all over again, instead of picking one of the other candidates. We were in strong support of either of the other finalists, because they were both Deaf.

The board was pretty much trapped. On Sunday we heard that the board had flown in again, Sunday, March 13th, and all day there were meetings. I was at the gym waiting for the announcement, but a few people came to the gym asking for me to go to the "Ole Jim"[5] alumni room, that's where the alumni offices are. So I went there, and we got a phone call, at that time a TTY, from Phil Bravin, one of our supporters on the board. He was typing us the message to let us know that all four demands had been met, and to let us know that he was the new chair of the board.

Phil and I. King Jordan[6] and I met at the president's office in the morning to discuss a few issues, and the three of us were there without an interpreter. It was the first time that the board chair, the president of Gallaudet, and the student body president were able to meet without an interpreter. It was pretty cool. There was the final press conference right after the meeting, we walked directly to the RV—we had liberated an RV—we all got in the RV. There was a sign [we'd had made] that said, "Pah!"—that's a Deaf term meaning "Victory!" or "Finally!" It said, "Deaf President Now Victory!" on one side and on the other side it said "Pah! Deaf President Now."

So we were all very excited, everyone was cheering the RV as we passed. That was a great day. That's history. And after that, the celebrations began.

Bridgetta Bourne-Firl
"We knew we were going to be in the spotlight."

Bridgetta Bourne-Firl was born on the last day of 1967 into a family that understood firsthand how important it is for Deaf children to be rooted in a Deaf culture. "My mom grew up in an all-hearing family. She didn't have any communication at all until she was six, when she went into the Washington State School for the Deaf. She finally started her language there. She didn't even know she had a name until she was six years old." Bridgetta's father, by contrast, was born into a Deaf family, "and so had his language from the beginning."

"My dad went to the Iowa School for the Deaf, and mom to Washington State. They were really nice schools, for back then, but they were oral schools. In the classrooms you had to speak, but when they got back to the dorms you could use sign language. Growing up, ASL wasn't considered a formal language. It was just everyday talk, is what they called it. They both went to Gallaudet University in Washington, DC, and met and married. And then they had me."

Bourne-Firl entered Gallaudet herself in 1985. A serious student, at first she didn't think much about Deaf politics or the Deaf President Now campaign.

Once the student strike began, however, she found herself at the center of the action, and became one of DPN's student leaders.

Bridgetta Bourne-Firl is now director of Outreach Programs at the Outreach Division at the California School for the Deaf.

It started with community leaders who went into fraternity meetings on campus. The most energetic group was a group of young men around thirty years old, that really pushed it, and encouraged the Gallaudet students to do *something*. At that time my future husband was president of the fraternity, and one of those men's wife was a member of my sorority. So they came into our meeting and tried to do the same thing. But this woman was not really convincing, I thought. I didn't know who this woman was, I didn't know who they were. But then, at the same time, we students all talked in the dining room. There was no e-mail or anything like that, so we depended on visual communication, on face-to-face meetings.

Jeff Rosen was the most radical person in this group of thirty-something men, who called themselves "Ducks." One of the Ducks was John Yeh, a successful Deaf businessman who funded the first rally. And NAD, in the *NAD Broadcaster*, carried many articles on the need for a Deaf president. So people were talking about it everywhere.

I really didn't pay attention at that time. I would see things going on, but I was focusing on my studies. At that time I also had a job—I had to work my way through college. I was working at the National Academy [Center] for Continuing Education, which was a part of the college. My boss there was Dr. [Roslyn] Rosen.[7] And I really looked up to her. She was like my mentor, one of these strong Deaf women that I used back then as role models.

The rally on March first was when I changed my position, my thinking. Dr. Rosen was one of the speakers that day, and Jack Levesque, he flew in from California. And I thought, "Wow, this really is bigger than just Gallaudet students, you know."

Well, we were close to midterms at the time, and like I said, I was a good student. If I could chose between studying or partying, then I chose to study first. So when the choice of Dr. Zinser was announced on Sunday, I was studying in my room. And I was trying to think of what to do, should I go or should I stay? And I felt like God kept telling me, "You go." So I decided just to run out of the building, and just take a break, and run on over there, and into the gym. There was no one in the gym. I saw the papers all over the ground, and I couldn't figure out what was up. One of the students told me, "Go to the street, go to the street, it's all over the university." So I picked up a paper and went running out into the street, and saw Gary Olsen. At that time he was the executive director of the NAD. And he was standing up, and saying, "We'll march to the Mayflower Hotel."

I went to the street, and marched down to the Mayflower. When we got there, we waited and waited for the board upstairs to come down. Greg Hlibok, who was the student body government president at that time, and Jeff Rosen, those two, and Tim Rarus, as former SGB president, the three of them went upstairs to meet with the board. And the hotel security came out and pushed us all away, they didn't want all of us going into the building, they made us stay outside. People began talking, and then other people wanted to talk, and I saw—it's not really in control, everything was going crazy. So I decided to stand up and take over. I was a cheerleader at that time, so we did some chants. I was like a crowd control person.

We marched to the Capitol, and gathered there, and talked a little bit until it got dark, and we couldn't see in the dark to talk any more. So we decided to go back to the old gym—it was always open for students to play basketball or whatever—and a group of us met to plan for tomorrow. It became the core group, and then we went back out, and I was still the crowd control leader. That became my role, and I had that role all the way through the strike.

It was a day-by-day thing, really. Every night, we planned what to do, and then the next day we would do it. And we repeated over and over that this *had* to be nonviolent. We knew we were going to be in the spotlight. We didn't want to show the public anything that was violent or destructive. A few things did happen, for example, that first night people had set the trash cans on fire. But right away people went over and put them out and said, "We can't do this, we can't do this." We didn't want to destroy anything on campus, any buildings or any property or anything like that.

There were students who felt like this was something they shouldn't be involved in. We tried to convince them, to explain to them that they needed to support the protest. Most of the students gathered with us and supported us, but not all of the student body was involved. Most of the graduate students were not Deaf, and they didn't show any support for us.[8] We had some graduate students that we did convince, that had good friends who were Deaf, who did participate and support us. But as for the faculty and staff who arrived Monday morning, and Tuesday—all week long when they arrived at the gates—the students would ask them, "Do you want to support what's going on?" And if they said "No," then we wouldn't let them in. If they said they were in support, then we would let them onto campus.

People had agreed to lay down in the streets if the police tried to force their way in. For necessities like food, any kind of medication or medical needs and things like that, we would let people come in and bring that in. If there was an emergency, if an ambulance needed to come in, of course we would let those people come on campus. We'd stand at the gate when the police would come. They would say, "Now you make sure if there's a fire or something, make sure that the trucks can get through," and we agreed.

In the beginning there was a lot of confusion, because we didn't have any interpreters. Then some of the grad students who weren't Deaf came to interpret for us. As the week wore on, we became more organized. The faculty and staff got on board and became involved and were able to find interpreters to come help. Some of the agencies around the country volunteered to send interpreters.

The DPN council came to meet with the student leaders two times a day, in the morning and in the afternoon. But other times we were at the gate with everyone else, and then other times we were doing interviews with media. Mostly Greg did that, because he was the student body president at that time, so he was our spokesperson and he did a great job in that role.

I can't remember which day it was, Wednesday or Thursday, one of the faculty came up to talk with me and Tim Rarus. And he said, "Now, don't say anything about this to the others, but Zinser wants to meet you in North Carolina tomorrow morning. A car will come to pick you up to take you to the airport." Now me and Tim, we were naive. We were young, and we didn't [tell others what had happened], because we were just busy with other things that had been happening through the day. And it seemed that people found out about this. The faculty [those who were supporting the strike] of course were older. They called me and Tim into one of the teacher's offices. Dr. Allen Sussman, and Dr. Rosen was there, and Nancy Bloch.[9] And they asked us, "Did someone tell you to leave campus tomorrow?" And we said "Yeah." And they said, "Well, don't do that—this is divide and conquer." And we were kind of naive about it, we didn't realize what the administration was trying to do: it was trying to split up the four leaders. And so the older people warned us: "You have to talk with the DPN council, and tell everyone what's going on." We were really kind of shocked. And I'm wondering why they picked me and Tim. Maybe they thought that we were the most naive—I don't know.

There were meetings with groups of people—senators, representatives, politicians. At the same time the media attention was starting to really grow, and those at the state level that were interested, state commissioners [for the Deaf] were all becoming involved. So there was just a lot of focus on the campus, and that started having an impact. And Jessie Jackson lent his support to the protest, and there were many important well-known political figures that started lending their support. And so that really was a turning point, I think. As the support grew bigger and bigger, the university was no longer just an isolated school for the Deaf.

The following week was spring break, so we were concerned that everybody was going to go home and on vacation, and we wouldn't be able to continue the protest. But thank God the protest did end, just before spring break.

I remember Greg went to the SBG office to get the call, and then people were signing to everyone and explaining what had happened, and telling the whole crowd that the four demands had been met. But then we got the news that Phil Bravin had become chair of the board of trustees, and that wasn't even a part of our original four demands. So that was like a gift, like the icing on the cake. And everyone was jumping up and down. There was so much excitement.

After that I just felt such exhaustion. Later I asked Greg and Tim if they had felt that—you know, the thrill of the moment was over, and they said they felt similarly. There was just such high emotions, first that anger, and then once the anger was gone the excitement was still there, and it lasted that whole week. But afterwards, it felt like there was a void. I don't want to call it depression, I guess it's just human emotions. I think it was just such emotional relief that it was over, that we'd won, that it was almost a letdown afterward.

DPN impacted the world. Newspapers published information about sign language, about Deafness, all over the world. Deaf people became inspired, they became more confident. It was realized that Deaf people could have jobs and lives and work in the community just like everybody else.

23
The Americans with Disabilities Act—
"The Machinery of Change"

THE PASSAGE OF THE AMERICANS WITH DISABILITIES ACT OF 1990 remains, as of this writing, the high-water mark of the American disability rights movement.[1] Never before, and not since, has such a broad coalition of disability groups and activists united around a single issue. The goal was to pass a federal civil rights act to extend basic protections against discrimination, and thus ensure equality of access to employment and the public arena, to all Americans with disabilities. It might have sounded a simple-enough goal, but writing a bill that would do all this while garnering the support necessary to pass both houses of Congress, with their Democratic majorities, and the signature of a Republican president was a test of both the movement's savvy and its political clout.

At first glance, the 1980s would not appear to have been a hospitable moment for such an effort. If the Carter administration had to be pressured into signing the 504 regulations, the election of Ronald Reagan in 1980 promised, and soon delivered, even worse times for proponents of expanding the federal role in protecting civil rights. Indeed, one of the new administration's first moves was an attempt (under the direction of Vice President George H. W. Bush) to gut the very same enforcing regulations of Section 504 that the movement had fought so hard to enact in 1977.

There was, however, a silver lining to what seemed to be a very dark political cloud. This attempt to revisit 504 galvanized the activist network so recently organized across the country by the 504 trainings and the ACCD, demonstrating to the Reagan administration, especially to the vice president and his staff, that there was, in fact, a constituency that could be readily mobilized by disability rights leaders. Faced with a deluge of letters, phone calls, and demonstrations, the vice president relented, and Section 504 was declared off-limits as the administration "de-regulated" other aspects of the federal government's presence in American life.

During this same period, a ruling by the Supreme Court, which impacted not only disability rights but also limited the scope of the Civil Rights Act of 1964, Title IX of the Education Amendments of 1972 (protecting women's rights), and the Age Discrimination Act of 1975, brought together for the first time representatives of all these constituencies, resulting in passage, over the president's veto, of the Civil Rights Restoration Act of 1987. The ad hoc coalition formed to pass the CRRA introduced African American and women's rights leaders to the idea that disability was a civil rights issue, and fostered relationships between these leaders and the principal activists in the still fledging, but now growing, national disability rights movement. All this would be crucial to the passage of the ADA three years later.

Thrown into this mix was a new federal agency, the National Council on the Handicapped (eventually renamed the National Council on Disability). Created by Congress in 1978, the NCH was made an independent federal agency in 1984, and its fifteen-member panel, appointed by the president, was charged with reviewing and evaluating federal policies related to disability. The NCH, chaired by parent activist Sandra Swift Parrino and vice-chaired by Justin Dart, would produce two documents: *Toward Independence* (1986), which explicitly laid out the need for federal civil rights protection for people with disabilities, and *On the Threshold of Independence* (January 1988), which offered a detailed section-by-section summary of exactly what such an act should contain. A complete draft of the bill, titled the Americans with Disabilities Act of 1988, was introduced into Congress by Senator Lowell Weicker (R-CT) and Congressman Tony Coelho (D-CA) in April that year.

Patrisha Wright
"The golden age of disability legislation."

Patrisha A. Wright is often referred to as "the general" who led the campaign to pass the ADA. Wright herself eschews such labels: "I'm not into top-down hierarchies," she says. She traces her roots as a disability rights activist to the 1977 HEW occupation in San Francisco, where she acted as a personal care assistant to Judy Heumann, then traveled with Heumann to Washington to participate in the demonstrations there. "It's funny how DREDF is seen sometimes as this 'insider' lobbyist organization, when really we were a bunch of Berkeley hippies coming to Washington to shake things up."

Born in 1949 in Bridgeport, Connecticut, Wright earned her master's degree in health services administration from Antioch University in 1976. Having by that time moved to the Berkeley–San Francisco area, she set up community programs for people with developmental disabilities, and then directed the graduate Psychology of Physical Disability and Health Services Administration program at Antioch's San Francisco campus (which has since closed), running it both on campus and from an office at the Center for Independent Living.

In 1979, Wright, along with Bob Funk and Mary Lou Breslin, founded the Disability Rights Education and Defense Fund. Together with Breslin and attorney Arlene Mayerson, Wright became the point person for DREDF's lobbying efforts in Washington.

If Wright isn't comfortable with her rank as "general," it is nonetheless true that she served as the overall coordinator of the broad effort that culminated in the passage of the ADA. As DREDF's lobbyist-in-chief, she had previously spearheaded the campaign to include people with disabilities under the Fair Housing Amendments Act of 1988, and represented the disability community in the coalition that pushed for the passage, over President Reagan's veto, of the Civil Rights Restoration Act of 1987. Also active in HIV/AIDS advocacy and a board member of the Leadership Conference on Civil Rights, Wright was well placed to tap into not only the existing national and (through Breslin) the grassroots disability rights organizations but also the more established (and far more experienced) African American civil rights groups belonging to the LCCR.

Wright was disabled "when I was fifteen or so by a head injury which caused me to be unconscious for close to six weeks. When I woke up I had amnesia, and later it became obvious that I had a neurological issue with my eyes. I have double vision all the time." Wright had wanted, since early childhood, to be a surgeon. Instead, "it was suggested to me by rehab that, as a legally blind person, I could make screen doors for a living. That was not something that I had ever thought of as a profession. Not that I have anything against people who make screen doors . . ."

Wright's experience as a person with a disability, like that of many others, overlapped her exposure to other forms of discrimination. "I was discriminated against on the basis of being a woman, and on the basis of being gay." Famously reticent about granting interviews, Wright now lives in rural Mexico, "twelve miles off the grid." Needless to say, her home is completely accessible.

———

The opening of the DREDF office [in Washington] was a result of a civil rights meeting that DREDF had in 1980. Bob Funk, Mary Lou Breslin, and I had spent a couple weeks in Washington, DC, asking all the traditional civil rights leadership about who they thought was critical for the civil rights movement. We invited the people whose names came up the most often to a meeting out in Berkeley, offering them a free trip to San Francisco. Most people can't turn that down, no matter what they're doing.

We told them, "We're starting a legal defense fund for people with disabilities. We're coming to you to say, essentially, 'Please be our guide, and give us a primer on what we should do, and what you would and would not do if you were starting it all again.'" And one of the suggestions that came out of that meeting was to open an office in Washington, DC, because they felt that nobody could do public policy from afar. So we looked around the group, and I joke and say that I had the blonde hair, and Arlene Mayerson had the clothes, so together we made a team able to become Berkeley-hippie-Washington-lobbyists.

So Arlene and I went and opened the Washington office and started meeting with the traditional disability groups, as well as the civil rights groups, to say that what we were going to do was disability civil rights, which was, historically, not what the lobby for disability had done. They did what I would refer to as "benefit boosting." They were interested in getting more money into programs, and we weren't into that at all. We were into civil rights.

We all came to Washington right with Reagan. One of the things that was great about the Reagan years, and I always used to kid Boyden Gray[2] about it, was that they did more to help organize the disability community than any other program ever. Because the Reagan administration targeted all the disability laws for review and to deregulate. The Education for All Handicapped Children Act was targeted, Section 504 was targeted, so it became a great organizing tool. There wasn't a day when there wasn't something new that came out from the administration that you could send out an announcement saying, "Look what they're doing to us."

DREDF was originally part of the Disability Law Resource Center, the DLRC, coming from the Center for Independent Living, which after the 504 demonstrations held the federal training contracts to do training on Section 504 and civil rights for people with disabilities. Mary Lou Breslin had spent five years or so of her life traveling around the country teaching civil rights theory to people with disabilities and to the parents of disabled children. So we had contacts in every single state who had gone to those trainings.

We also had relationships that had developed as a result of those contracts with a number of federal employees, who were willing to "accidentally" slip us some information as to what was going on, because they were appalled. We were able to provide cover for their identity, so we were able to develop a set of excellent sources in all the federal agencies. Anything that was happening around disability, people would call us or leak information to us.

When we would get a piece of leaked information, I would send it back to Mary Lou and Bob at the Berkeley office, and then Mary Lou would get it out on fax machines all across the country. It was essentially a war room, responding as soon as we heard anything was coming down. So that was basically how it worked.

Evan Kemp[3] was an invaluable resource for us to be able to get to people in the White House, to talk to them and to line up meetings. Here Evan would come in his three-piece suit, and the Berkeley hippies would trot not far behind. It was interesting because Evan knew all the Bushies on a personal level. There was a level of trust as a result of that. If Evan was saying these guys were okay, then they would trust us. But there was little or no contact with the Reagan side of that White House. Basically, the Bush side of that White House couldn't stand the Reagan side of that White House, and so even some of the lower-level people in the vice president's office were willing to leak us information about what they were doing.

I remember at one time they [the Reagan White House] came out with this understanding of what the new 504 regulations should be, which would be a cost-benefit analysis of people with disabilities. It was basically determining what your value to society was based upon their assumptions and stereotypes of what people could do, and the more disabled you were, the less civil rights you got. I remember being so appalled by that. I think that was really the critical turning-point in the deregulation.

The second part was that every time we ran into a member of Congress who was giving us problems, we were able to use the network Mary Lou had put together, to pull somebody in from the community who was able to organize cards and letters. And so this rapid response network made people think that the movement was humungous, when it was probably initially forty or fifty people. The numbers grew as the issues became more popular, but initially it was really smoke and mirrors to make them think how powerful we were.

As a result of the deregulation effort, I took a seat on the board of the Leadership Conference on Civil Rights, and developed a very close relationship with LCCR executive director Ralph Neas.[4] Ralph had had Guillain-Barré,[5] and so he had somewhat of an understanding of what we were talking about. It wasn't as big of a leap for him as it was for most people. He and I formed quite a lobbying duo, and he was our personal tutor on how to lobby, and had contacts into the traditional civil rights community, and to the members of Congress who traditionally voted in support of civil rights.

In terms of people's attitudes in the administration, we were starting from ground zero. The only person at the White House who uniformly hung in there was Boyden Gray, who talked about how he "got" disability by being a Southern boy having to go to a Northern prep school, and how he was tall and skinny and awkward and had a Southern accent and was shunned. I used to tell him he was probably shunned for his politics, not for his height, but, you know, Boyden and I had that type of relationship.

The third piece was that the *Grove City* decision[6] came down from the Supreme Court. Brad Reynolds's[7] actions were the key to organizing the disability community. *Grove City* was a decision on federal financial assistance affecting women in colleges and universities. Reynolds said that, because all the laws are written similarly, "as assistant attorney general, I'm going to apply it to *all* the civil rights laws across the board." So he lumped us in with race and gender and age, and so we became, by fiat, a part of this broad civil rights group. And so, as we were starting this other fight on deregulation, the other front was doing the Civil Rights Restoration Act,[8] and that was the precursor to doing the ADA. A lot of decisions were made around the ADA based upon the years that were spent trying to overturn the *Grove City* decision.

My goal and my task in doing the Washington office was to develop those relationships, and for the first few years, before we even got to the ADA, I pounded the halls for every single race and gender legislation and amendment that was up there. I was part of the lobbying team for the traditional civil rights community, and you know, you pay your dues.

And that's how we were able to put that large coalition of race and gender and religion together.

The LCCR, historically, had never worked with the disability community. Disability, up until the Civil Rights Restoration Act, was never viewed as a civil rights issue. It was always viewed as a welfare issue or a benefits issue. So for the first time you had the race groups and the women's groups and the church groups and the unions all supporting a civil rights bill, and all interacting with the disability community. And the disability community is not a rich community. We didn't have the five hundred dollars to go pay for the grip and grins for the various members [of Congress], like a lot of the unions and the other lobbying organizations do. And where we as the disability community could not get in, by having Ralph Neas or a member of the unions call to ask for a meeting with a member, we were able to bypass the staffers and get in to meet directly with the member. And that was a change for the disability community. It's not to say that there had not been members of Congress, historically, who had supported disability programs. But again, they were benefit boosting programs, they weren't civil rights issues. So this was a big, big change in the whole concept of how disability was viewed legislatively. And the ADA could not have passed without that whole relationship between the disability lobby, and DREDF and LCCR and Ralph Neas in particular.

For us—"us" meaning the disability movement—that ushered in what I refer to as the golden age of disability legislation. Because we were then hooked in with traditional civil rights. It gave me room then to argue in the LCCR meetings, when the Fair Housing Amendments[9] came up, that disability should be included, when it historically never was there.

That's why I'm saying that Brad Reynolds, whether he wants to be known for this or not, turned the key to open the door to civil rights for people with disabilities.

Arlene Mayerson (continued)
"In Washington, you're in as long as you're winning."

When the leaders at DREDF decided the organization needed a Washington office and a national voice, they chose Patrisha Wright as their lead lobbyist and Arlene Mayerson as their legal expert to make it happen. Mayerson had lived in the city before—during her time at the Georgetown University Law Center when she was a supervisor in a clinical law program. She was now returning to the nation's capital determined to change national law and policy.

———

We went to Washington pretty green. Pat [Wright] had had some prior experience and she knew some people from a completely different context. For me it was just civics 101, learning as I went along. When I think about it now, it's the courage of youth or something, because I was just gung-ho, ready to do anything. And so when the deregulation effort took place, I would go to these meetings. I would be the lead lawyer [for DREDF] and I would be sitting at this meeting with Brad Reynolds, and the head of OMB (the Office of Management and Budget at the White House), and all these various people, and I would be the lead lawyer. When I think back on it now, I think it's amazing.

When Pat and I first came to Washington to establish the Washington DREDF office, we got space from Evan Kemp. At the time he was running the Disability Rights Center.[10] He had two rooms, basically, and one big room with a double desk. And Pat and I sat on either side of the double desk and he sat in the other room. We came there specifically to fight the deregulation. Well, it turns out that Evan's bridge partner was C. Boyden Gray, who was the counsel to the Vice President, and it was the Vice President's Task Force that was doing the deregulating. So, we were able to get access at a very high level, to talk to administration officials to say why this was a very poor idea.

It was a fantastic entree to have Evan and his relationship with Boyden. What it meant was, when we met other people from the White House— from the Department of Justice or from OMB—they had to bring people of comparable status. So, normally, we would have been dealing with just the lowest possible staff person. But instead, we were dealing with the highest people in the administration in these various agencies because, as a matter of protocol, you don't have Boyden Gray come to a meeting and then send your little lackey. So, we were meeting with Brad Reynolds, and very high up people at OMB as well.

Those meetings were, I think, very successful from a legal argument and negotiation point of view, but I don't think we would have ended up where we did unless we were also able to show that we had a very big political and community-based network. The other thing about those meetings and about what was happening was that nothing had ever been announced. There was never any public announcement that there was going to be deregulation. There was certainly never any public draft. . . . But we would always know what was going on inside the government because a lot of people had worked for ten years getting the regulations to begin with.

We would get the information from inside the government. We would then send it out to our network in these action alerts. The network would respond tremendously, because it had just been trained that they had a new right and it was being taken away. . . . So, when we went to the meetings, it was always after this community-organizing effort had taken place. I remember one meeting we went to where they had literally just received 40,000 letters at the White House about a deregulation that had never even been announced. It was a very impressive thing.

It was also impressive to the civil rights community, because this was a time when the civil rights community was being completely closed out [of the White House]. Access was nil. And the disability community was having a lot of access to the administration. So we let it be known that disability wasn't going to be a side issue or go on everyone's coattails.

I think the biggest change happened with the advent of the Civil Rights Restoration Act, which was a response to a very negative Supreme Court ruling, which affected minorities, women, and people with disabilities equally. Normally, what would have happened was representatives on race and gender, who were very established and esteemed lawyers, certainly people I liked and looked up to, would have gone to the meetings by themselves. And when we came into town and started working on that bill, we wanted to do our fair share of the work. And so, because of that, we started meeting the people on the Hill that were also the allies of the civil rights community and establishing those relationships and, at the same time, being able to open certain doors that weren't open to the civil rights community. And that was a very long fight. To get that Civil Rights Restoration Act took several years.

Shortly after that, there was a very big negative decision involving the rights of kids with disabilities in special education. *Smith v. Robinson*[11] took away the right of parents to recover attorney's fees in those cases.

And that was another whole interesting phenomenon, because in DC, there was an organization called the CCDD, the Consortium for Citizens with Developmental Disabilities.[11]

That coalition had been working on a response to *Smith v. Robinson*. And we came in and wanted to expand what was happening because we wanted to take a very strict civil rights perspective. The traditional way of working on the Hill was more of—there was always something special about disability. There was always a benefit overlay. And we came in and said, "We want at least as much as any other civil rights group. And, no, it's not any different to deny a disabled kid educational rights than it is to deny someone any other kind of civil right." And this is the whole general history of the eighties, which is DREDF's view that we should go on the civil rights track.

And in that struggle, we formed a very close relationship with Bobby Silverstein,[12] who at the time was over on the House, working for [Congressman] Pat Williams (D-MT), the head of the Education Committee. And we worked very closely with him to develop the Handicapped Children's Protection Act.[13] He later moved over to the Senate. So, he was positioned at the time of the ADA to be the key staff person, and we knew him very well, and we had already established a lot of trust. . . .

So by the time anything was happening with the ADA, there had already been a lot of credibility-building on the Hill. Not only that, there had also been a lot of wins, because the Bush Task Force on Regulatory Relief had now said it was going to drop its deregulation attempt for 504.

I remember one late-night, three-o'-clock-in-the-morning conversation with Evan Kemp, where he told me that "in Washington, you're in as long as you're winning." And so, by the time we got to the ADA, we were in, we were winning.

Lex Frieden (continued)
"All the stars were aligned."

———

The demise of the American Coalition of Citizens with Disabilities in the early 1980s didn't end Lex Frieden's advocacy for disability rights. To the contrary, he moved to Washington to become the director of the newly created National

Council on the Handicapped, as it was then called. In this section, Frieden describes how that council came to be, and how it came to champion the idea of a national civil rights act for Americans with disabilities.

———

In 1983 there were hearings on amendments to the Rehabilitation Act right before the passage of the bill,[14] and I was invited to testify on behalf of independent living centers. Jim DeJong[15] was the other person invited to talk about independent living centers. Jim, as I recall, made a very nice presentation about the development of the independent living centers and how the Congress needed to continue supporting them. At the time we were defending the fact that they were a demonstration program, and Jim made a very nice defense that the demonstration needed to continue.

Then it was my turn. I got the impression that Jim had sold the deal. I didn't need to push the issue any more. Besides that, the House members who were there were sort of losing interest and beginning to make notes in their books and so on, so I thought, "Let me just throw something else in here while I'm at it." I said, "It seems to me that now is the time to create a blue-ribbon committee of leaders with disabilities to define for the Congress what the primary needs in policy pertaining to people with disabilities are. So that when you have your next hearing and your next bill, you'll know what the issues are that people with real needs have."

Many of these guys kind of perked up. "There's a clever idea." The congressman from California looked up and the congressman from Dallas, Texas, Steve Bartlett, he looked up, and the congressman from Illinois, he looked up. And, one of them asked, "Do you mean to suggest that we should appoint people with disabilities to advise us on what the issues are?" I said, "Who could better do it?" He said, "My constituents will surely support that."

The chairman of the committee said, "Well, we've heard enough great ideas today, we've got our work ahead of us," so all the committee voted in favor of passage of the rehabilitation act reauthorization bill. Well, the guy from Texas, Bartlett, said, "I want to add [to the bill] this concept of this blue-ribbon committee." The chairman said, "Okay, we'll include that in it. Mr. Bartlett, you work out the language and the details of it, thank you very much, the meeting's adjourned."

So Bartlett came over to me and he said, "Well, we've got a little job to do here." I said, "What do you mean?" He said, "The chairman just told us we could write words in the law to include your ideas about this blue-ribbon committee." I mean, I'd been around a while, but I hadn't seen things move that quick before. So we went off to his office and he got an apple out of his refrigerator and he called his staff in and we started talking about how we could do this. We wrote a beautiful paragraph on this blue-ribbon committee that was going to advise the Congress on what the primary disability policy issues were. And I was so pleased.

Then the Senate passed their version of the bill, which did not have this provision in it, because nobody suggested it. The bills went to the joint committee between the Senate and the House, where they worked out the final bill. When they got down to do side-by-side comparison, Senator [Lowell] Weicker's staff said, "Wait a minute now, the Senate is not going to have the House throwing in some blue-ribbon committee here. There's not a need for another advisory group." Bartlett stepped out and phoned me, and he said, "Things don't look good, this is what the Senate's doing." I said, "Try and challenge them and see if they're willing to say that people with disabilities shouldn't have a voice about the policies they enact." Bartlett went back, and then Weicker's staff said, "No, we're not going to do it."

This was a thing between the House and Senate more than anything else. Weicker's staff said, "No, we're not going to have this, we don't care what kind of gracious arguments you make. There is already this advisory committee in the Department of Education for the rehabilitation programs. Consumers can be on that advisory committee."

Then Weicker's staff guy whispered to Weicker—I heard this from John Doyle who was a staff person at the time—"Why don't we make this committee a presidentially appointed independent federal agency?" Weicker gave this speech about how the House didn't need to invent something new, because all we need to do is take this committee that already exists in the law and promote it. It's not effective now anyway because all the stuff it produces is made in the basement of the Switzer Office building and nobody listens to the [members of the committee anyway]. He said, "I was going to sunset them anyway because they're not doing a darn thing. Let's give them one more chance," he said. "Let's promote them, make them presidential appointees. We'll tell them they have to report to us, just like the House wants. They have to make a report in two years about the status of policies affecting people with disabilities in the United States, what the priorities are, and if they come back in two years to get reauthorized and they haven't done a damn thing and I don't expect they will, then we're going to sunset them." So in the 1984 amendments to the Rehabilitation Act, the National Council on the Handicapped was established as an independent federal agency. Nobody knew what that meant at the time, but that was how the two bills came together.

Shortly afterwards, the council set up its offices. The first acting executive director of the council was Weicker's staff person, Doyle, who suggested the compromise, which was a good thing because Doyle knew how to work within the rules. So he effectively wrote the regulations to strengthen the role of the council, to make it, indeed, independent. He's the one who knew how to use the senators' influence to get space on Independence Avenue. He's the one who understood that in Washington perception is reality. He was brilliant, and he single-handedly set the council up in 1984.

When it was established as a federal agency it was called the National Council on the Handicapped. In 1988, to conform to a more current semantics, it was renamed the National Council on Disability. But it was essentially the same agency.

When Doyle was ready to go back up on the Hill, the council hired me as its first full-time executive director. I took a two-year leave of absence when I left the university where I work because I knew we had two years to write the report, that was going to be my deal. The chairman [of the council][16] told me not to tell a soul that I was on a two-year leave, because she believed that if people knew that I was a short-timer they wouldn't pay attention to me. It was very good political advice.

I did a lot of traveling in those [first] twelve months. We had public hearings and invited people to talk. In addition, we commissioned one of our members, Justin Dart, to go state by state and do little mini-hearings. We paid his expenses, but not a salary. We used his data as part of our data set. We hired consultants to analyze the data and summarize it. We put all that into a report. The fat report, the one I'm describing now, is really the appendix to *Toward Independence*.[17] By the time we had the report written, it was two hundred and some-odd pages.

At a meeting of the council I said, "We've done a great report here, but there's not a member on the Hill who's going to read a two-hundred-page report. So what we need to do is make our report thirty pages, and everything else is going to be the appendix." Even today, I believe the appendix to *Toward Independence* is far more important than the report itself. The report itself is simply a summary that Bob Burgdorf and I did on a weekend in the latter stages of the process. The real data are included in the appendix, which were written by the consultants.

We invested a lot of effort in details. We got advice on the report from members of Congress. We expected them to say, "Include provisions for the rights of people with disabilities." No, no. One of them told us to make the cover a pleasant color. Another one told us to use graphics. "Make it a book that will sit on my coffee table." "Put it in language that I can read without having to use a dictionary." "Make the print big enough for me to see without my glasses."

We followed that advice. We contracted with a graphics design artist to help us with the color. Federal agencies often just put the seal of the agency on the front. We hired an artist to find and draw an eagle representing independence to go on a blue cover. We invested a lot in making sure that that report was significant, and we printed, ultimately, maybe fifty thousand copies. It was delivered in ceremonies to people all over the country. The report was distributed in its entirety to the members of the South Carolina legislature in a ceremony in the state house. The governor had people with disabilities take to each one of [the legislators] a copy of the report. The governor of Texas received it on the steps of the state capitol in Austin with hundreds of people with disabilities in the audience.

In Washington, we hired the same public relations firm that had advised President Reagan during his election campaigns. They coached the members of the council on how to speak to the press, what to say, what not to say. They arranged a private meeting with the president to be covered by the world press for the presentation of the report. The meeting was scheduled to occur on January 28; the spaceship Challenger blew up two days before that. The president canceled all his meetings. We had to meet with the vice president, George Bush, a few days later. As we left the meeting with Bush, he said, "You know, I'm just the vice president, but if I ever have a chance to support you on this, I'm going to do it." Four years later, in his inaugural remarks, he said there ought to be a law protecting people with disabilities from discrimination. That goes into your "Don't burn your bridges" category, I guess. Or, "Don't underestimate whom you're talking to." Or, "Not every politician forgets a promise."

We presented *Toward Independence* at a reception on Capitol Hill. A number of senators and members of the House of Representatives came to the reception and we had a little stage. We introduced them, and they would come up on the stage and Senator Weicker took the report and waved it in the air and said, "This is the Emancipation Act for people with disabilities." One, the senator from Illinois, Paul Simon, said, "We are going to hold ourselves accountable for taking responsibility for each one of the recommendations made in this report." That was an example of the kinds of things that members of Congress said.

After the report was presented, we watched what was happening on the Hill. Nothing was happening, just a lot of platitudes. So we decided that our next report would be on how the Congress acted in response to our first report. We did an inventory of the recommendations, and in a couple of cases there had been—in fact, we had planned it this way— there was some legislation already in the works that quite naturally met the requirements of our recommendations. So we said, "Here, they've achieved this and this. These [actions] were recommended, they were done. But the main recommendation in our report has yet to be acted on." So that second report, *On the Threshold of Independence*,[18] provided further justification for an equal rights bill for people with disabilities. Not only that, it gave an example of what we thought an equal rights bill ought to look like. That was pretty gutsy, in a way, because a federal advisory agency doesn't write legislation. Congress writes legislation.

Well, that achieved the desired effect. Shortly after that report was issued, three senators met and four representatives met and decided that there ought to be an introduction of the legislation. So the thirteen-page bill that the council drafted was introduced by Senator Weicker before the end of Congress in 1987. It was introduced, purposefully with the knowledge that it would never be passed, just to make a statement.

Congress reconvened. Senator Weicker had lost his seat and [Senator Tom] Harkin (D-IA) had agreed to become the champion of the disability community and the chairman of the Senate Committee on Disability. Harkin had his staff work purposefully on a version of the ADA patterned after the proposed one. He introduced it early in the congressional session, with time to have hearings on it and time to have action and, indeed, that's most of what we did in late 1987 and 1988. The council prepared testimony and appeared at all the hearings. We assisted members of Congress to provide information for their constituencies about the impact of the ADA. So that process was begun and continued until final passage, basically, eighteen months later.

That's the way things are supposed to happen. You have a problem, have a solution, have the legislature act on it, and have a resolution. Now, it often doesn't happen that way. But in this case, ADA followed a fairly straight-line course. All the stars were aligned in the right direction. Here you had a presidential election where the president in his final campaign speech talked about disability and disability rights, and where in his first inaugural address talked about disability and disability rights. In his first statement before Congress, said he wanted within a hundred and eighty days to sign a civil rights bill for people with disabilities. I mean, the timing, and the personalities, everything just more or less just fell into place.

24
Drafting the Bill, Part 1

Justin Dart Jr. (continued)
*"Not only is the President not going to oppose this,
he is going to support your proposal."*

F OLLOWING JUSTIN DART'S 1966 EPIPHANY AT THE CHILDREN'S "REHABIL-
itation" center in Vietnam and several years of self-examination and medi-
tation, he and his wife Yoshiko left Japan, and their business interests, moving to
Texas to become a part of the disability rights movement there. The Darts, however, did not leave behind their background, most especially the Dart family's
Republican connections. With the election of Ronald Reagan in 1980, the Darts
were poised to become leaders in the national disability rights movement.

We did a long-range policy for Texas which was very radical, in that we
did not confine ourselves to policy that we thought we could get implemented in the political reality. What we thought the governor wanted
was a real radical proposal to do the best possible thing, and then let
the governor and others decide which part of it they thought they could
actually get implemented.

One of the things that we proposed was that the civil rights of people
with disabilities should be mandated by law. And that was the first proposal of such nature or formal proposal at that period that I know about.[1]
Then we spent three years writing this thing and several of the things
that we proposed did get implemented into law in Texas.

I first attended meetings of the National Council wherever they were
held and a lot of them were held in Washington. I moved to Washington
about twelve or thirteen years ago [in 1985]. That was when Lex Frieden

came up here and when we were writing ADA. We put a bunch of our computers and files and a few pots and pans in the back of our pickup truck and came up here supposedly for two months, and we never went back. I mean we had a home in Texas, but we never moved back, and eventually we sold our home there. And [seventeen years later] we are still in the same apartment that we rented to stay a very short time.

When the Reagan administration came in I was appointed vice chair of the National Council on Disability, probably because my father was a major player [in the Republican Party]. We eventually managed to get Lex Frieden put in as the director of that National Council, and then I asked Joe Dusenbury, who was the chair, to let me go out and start working on a national policy for people with disabilities. He said yes, and that was our first trip to every state, holding forums.

By the time I came to Washington any thought of passing any more national disability rights legislation was pretty well dead. When I went around and visited the fifty states as a preliminary to writing this national policy, people would tell me, "Justin, how could we possibly have full civil rights when we can't even implement 504?"

This national policy was written by, it was edited by advocates in almost every state. We started out with a draft which was a nationalized draft of the Texas policy. I thought it was pretty perfect the way it was, because we had been working on it for years. I thought I was going to take it around to every state more or less to discuss it and have them approve it. But we did say, "If you have some suggestions, then we would be glad to consider them." And in forty-eight out of fifty states, they made specific suggestions, which I could immediately see would improve the document. I learned plenty about the wisdom of the disability rights advocates in the United States.

Then when Lex Frieden came up to Washington we decided to write *Toward Independence*. And this was in answer to a federal mandate that we do a special report on the state of federal disability legislation and policy, and we report to Congress and the president. We didn't have a lot of hearings but had a lot of consultations with service providers and with disability rights people, and did a lot of research and so forth. And I think that is when we did the first Harris Poll on people with disabilities, a rather vast undertaking, under the directorship of Lex Frieden, who did an absolutely magnificent job of steering this agenda through the baroque maze of the federal bureaucracy and of Washington politics, because it could have been shot down at any point.

There were numerous suggestions in the council to send our drafts over to the White House, to have meetings with the staff and to get some approval of what we were doing. I opposed that. Lex and I opposed that on every occasion, because I knew that they would tell us not to do it. Now the way I looked at it, they had delegated to us the responsibility and the authority to do this [report]. And that the biggest favor that we could do them, was to report to them not what they already knew, not to replicate the stereotypes that were in their own minds, but to give them a real progressive and productive disability policy. And if we went up there and asked them, "Is this your idea of a disability policy?" they probably would have said "no" to about half of it.

At some point in writing this thing we asked the question, "Are we going to recommend civil rights coverage?" And, of course, we had Bob Burgdorf working for us—a law academic and a lawyer—and he had studied the civil rights situation for thirteen years at that time. And I was the civil rights fan and so we had a meeting in the conference room of the National Council there on Independence Avenue, and I recall it vividly. And he and I were sitting alone there (with Yoshiko listening to the conversation). Lex Frieden for some reason couldn't come. And the subject of the meeting was what we do about civil rights in this historic report. And so I said, "Well, I think we ought to include it." And he said, "Well, Justin, obviously I am a passionate advocate for civil rights. I have been doing this for thirteen years and I haven't been getting much of anywhere. I think it might turn people off about the rest of the report. So maybe we ought to pass on this." And I said, "Bob, we have a mandate from Congress to recommend what needs to be done to the president and to the Congress, and you and I are going to sign our names to this thing, and Bob, will we be able to sleep nights if we don't do it? I think we ought to do it no matter what the consequences are." And he said, "Well, you know, Justin, you're right."

And so we did it and we went forward. And with his guidance, Lex Frieden and others decided that the notion of including people with disabilities in the Civil Rights Act of 1964 was not terribly practical. It was not practical in the context of the reality of disability rights discrimination. The discrimination takes far different forms and the Act of 1964, by just including us without any further measures, would leave a lot of the solutions to the imagination. You don't just have to open the door; you have to rebuild the door. I had not thought about that. So they wrote the proposal for the Americans with Disabilities Act.

We sent it over to the White House and very shortly we got a call from somebody over there to Lex Frieden. And he said, "Lex, we have your draft of your policy *Toward Independence* and I have got halfway through the first chapter," which is ADA, after the introduction. And he said, "What in the world are you people thinking about up there? The President is not going to touch this with a ten-foot pole. This goes even farther than Kennedy." [Senator] Ted Kennedy at that time was sponsoring the Civil Rights Restoration Act [of 1987], which Reagan was in opposition to. Reagan finally vetoed it, but they overrode the veto. Remember now, that we were all fifteen Reagan appointees. And he said, "You've got to fix this." And he hadn't even bothered to read the rest of it.

So, here is Bob Burgdorf's prediction coming true. So Lex was really upset and he called me and told me about this. So I said, "Well, what can we do?" He said, "Well, maybe we can talk to Bradford Reynolds." Reynolds was the assistant attorney general for civil rights, and he had expressed himself informally as supporting some kind of rights for people with disabilities. He was also an adviser to Reagan, closer to Reagan than his title might suggest.

So we set up this meeting with Bradford Reynolds, and Lex said, "Justin I want you to go and talk to him." Madeleine Will[2] came to the meeting, and Bradford Reynolds and Gordon Mansfield [a mutual friend of Dart and Reynolds, who helped set up the meeting]. We were in Reynolds's office. And I said to Bradford, "Have you read it?" And he said "Yes." And I told him the story about the call from the White House and I quoted this White House aide exactly. I didn't try and cover it up or put any kind of spin on it. And I said, "Here they have told us that the President is not going to touch it with a ten-foot pole. They have told us that this goes even farther than Ted Kennedy and that we ought to change it." And I said, "Bradford, all we are asking for is that the promises of the Declaration of Independence, the Constitution, and the Bill of Rights be kept for people with disabilities. And I don't think that President Reagan wants to go down in history as being the president that opposed keeping the promises of the Declaration of Independence to 35 million people with disabilities. And Bradford, they say we go farther than Ted Kennedy. Wouldn't we be embarrassed if we didn't? Because he has not proposed full civil rights for people with disabilities." And that was my entire speech. It was about three minutes.

And he thought about five seconds or ten seconds and he looked back at me. And he said, "Justin, I agree with you." He said, "Not only is the President *not* going to oppose this, he is going to support your proposal, and you are going to get it in writing. And I am going to call the White House when you leave here." Now he did, and we *did* get it in writing. Reagan supported the concept of the entire report including the ADA. So when the report was published there was a very strong statement in it by Ronald Reagan, where he says, "I agree with you that this nation is founded on the principal that each human life sacred and inviolable. People with disabilities have an absolute right and responsibility to participate fully and equally in society and to maximizing their quality of life potential in manners of their own choosing." And I was, by the way, the author of those lines, but he chose that in all of those documents that we sent him to quote back to us.

Now, I think that one of the key things that I said, besides referring to the Declaration of Independence and the Constitution and Bill of Rights, was that I did not offer to take the ADA out of the recommendation. I simply said that I don't think the president is going to want to go on record as opposing it. In other words, we were going to make an issue out of it, and he was not faced with the choice of having us take it out or leave it in. He was faced with the choice of approving it or opposing it in public, and going down in the history books as having opposed it. So that is a key conversation that I have never seen in any history of ADA.

And you see if it had been shot down in that point, it would not have been in *Toward Independence*. It would not have been introduced in the Congress of 1988. It might have been written by somebody else or separately introduced, but it might not have happened when it happened. And had we come into the "Contract with America"[3] period without having passed the ADA, it is my impression that it would not have passed. We would not have an ADA.

Lex Frieden (continued)
"It was like we'd gone from the pony league baseball players to the pros."

"Everything" about the ADA, as Frieden put it, may have "more or less just [fallen] into place," but, of course, that doesn't mean there wasn't a lot of hard work that needed to be done. Frieden started the ball rolling in Washington, in his role as executive director of the National Council on the Handicapped, and then left that position to return to Texas, where he resumed his advocacy in retail politics.

———

When we first [made] our ADA proposal, the real advantage of doing this with a group of conservative Republican presidential appointees was that if we could convince them this was a good thing to do, we could convince anybody. One of those conservative presidential appointees happened to be Jeremiah Milbank. Mr. Milbank is a very well-endowed individual from a monetary standpoint, from a very wealthy New York family. He's got not one, but two foundations named after him. He was the treasurer for the Republican Party when President Nixon was elected. He's also the principal patron of Boys Clubs of America. He just comes from a wonderful family, and he's a wonderful man. He's very conservative from a fiscal standpoint.

Milbank said, "You know, doing all this work is fine . . . but if you're going to do more than just come up with a proposal, you're going to have to sell the public on it. You're going to have to do the same thing that other businesses do when they're trying to get laws passed. You're going to have to have data.

"What data do you have that you can show me that people [with disabilities] aren't getting jobs? I haven't seen that data, you're just saying that."

"Well, Mr. Milbank, what would we have to show you to convince you?"

He said, "If my buddy Lou Harris does a poll of people with disabilities, and he tells me that most of them aren't working, I'd believe it. You could publish that in the *New York Times* or the *Wall Street Journal* and everybody else would believe it."

"Okay, can you arrange us a meeting with Lou Harris?"

"Sure, next week."

So we went to New York and we met Humphrey Taylor, who was president of the Lou Harris company, and we asked Mr. Taylor if he could do this. He was personally interested in it. There were about six of us who worked as technical advisers to the Lou Harris Poll and came up with the questions that were asked. . . . Predictably, he came up with answers that we expected him to come up with. I say "predictably," because we knew which questions to ask to get the right answers.

And then Milbank said, "You know, somebody's going to ask how much all this is going to cost."

"Well, what are we supposed to do about that, Mr. Milbank? What could we do that would make you feel comfortable?"

He said, "Why don't we do an economic analysis of this legislation?"

"How do we do that?"

"I'll call you next week."

Next week he called me, wanted me to come to New York that night. I took the train to New York. Eight o'clock that night in Milbank's office in New York City, I was introduced to one John Raisian, an economist from the Hoover Institution. I was in shock. I was frightened to death, because I knew the Hoover Institution was the most conservative public policy think-tank in America. I felt like I'd been set up, in a way. Here, Milbank has us, has me paying the bill for an economist who's going to tell us that this cannot be afforded, and this is going to be the end of the ADA. At the same time, I knew we needed Milbank's support. . . .

So Mr. Milbank left the room and left me and Raisian together. Raisian is kind of an imposing figure. He said, "What am I supposed to be doing here anyway?"

I said, "I think Mr. Milbank wants you to do an economic impact study of this bill that we've drafted."

"Well," he said, "Whatever Mr. Milbank wants."

So Raisian worked for several weeks, he came down to the [National] Council once or twice a week, and Bob Burgdorf and I would sit with him and we went piece by piece through this thing. He'd go away to California for a while and work on it and then come back and bring these results of his research, and he was always puzzled. He would say, "How can we tell how many people with disabilities in this country need public transportation? I need data like that before I can do my work." Burgdorf and I looked at each other and winked and said, "Don't think you can. So we might as well assume that every person with a disability in this country needs public transportation and that would be, at this point, about thirty-six million." He put his pencil down, and he said, "Well, that won't cost too much per person."

So we produced a study that said the ADA was feasible from an economic standpoint. I may have a copy of that report somewhere. We didn't publicize it very much, because I didn't think it was very good research.

It's kind of funny because Raisian is a renowned economist and it was very helpful for us to be able to say, when the Congressional Budget Office wanted to know how much this bill was going to cost, that Dr. John Raisian had done this economic profile.

There was a reception on the evening of the day when we introduced *Toward Independence*. They had people with radios in their ears who were standing outside the reception room who would tell Ms. Parrino and I in a hidden earphone in our ears the name of the senators and the House members who were coming in, their wife's name, their children's names, and something pertinent to each one of them. So when a senator that I'd never met came up, "Hello, Senator, we're so happy to have you here. How is Mrs. Dadada? I heard your son was in an automobile accident last week, is he okay?"

To me, now, it's kind of amusing. That's the way things are done. When the disability movement started in 1972 we were like kids playing around at a little game. Now, in 1989, 1990—it was like we'd gone from the pony league baseball players to the pros.

I left the [National] Council [on Disability] because, as a federal employee, I could not lobby for the ADA. I did a good job, I think, writing testimony, presenting it as a government agency on behalf of ADA, but I was frustrated because I couldn't organize and lobby. So I left in 1988 and came back to Texas.

The first thing I did when I got back to Texas was ask Congressman Major Owens, who was responsible for the committee in the House that had principal jurisdiction over ADA, if we could have a field hearing on the ADA in Houston. He agreed, and thus we organized the first hearing on the ADA outside of Washington. I thought that was very important because one of the criticisms of the ADA to that point was that this was a bunch of Washington lawyers and lobbyists who've worked on this. It was generally accepted that the Washington-based national advocacy groups would support the bill, but what about ordinary people?

Well, there's no place with ordinary people like Texas. I think it was a defining moment in the history of the ADA, that hearing. Because Owens came. He brought Don Paine, a member of Congress from New Jersey who was African American and part of the Black Caucus and supported the ADA for philosophical reasons. The ranking member on that committee was Steve Bartlett from Dallas, who was a very conservative

Republican. He did not like the ADA bill that was presented, the Harkin bill. He thought it was too liberal and too aggressive, and he felt there would be backlash against people with disabilities if the bill were enacted. In fact, Bartlett at first said he wouldn't even come to the hearing. I called him and I said, "Mr. Bartlett, this is *your* state. You're going to have your constituents here. I'm not asking you to support the Harkin bill, but I *am* asking you to take part in this hearing." So he agreed to come.

That hearing was very well organized. I have to recognize Congressman Owens and his staff. Not often does a member of Congress give an individual or a group of individuals the authority to organize a public hearing on behalf of a bill as their proxy, but he did that. We lined up the transit administrator; the superintendent of schools (who was an African American woman); the mayor of Houston, who was a woman who had established the first women's rights office in the mayor's office; the county judge, who had a disabled guy working in his front office as an attorney; the vice president of Southwestern Bell telephone company, who happened to be on the board of the independent living center. We didn't advertise that these people were well-informed. The congressmen came down, and they saw the vice president of the largest telephone company in the country at that time, the mayor of one of the four largest cities, the largest transit system administrator, the largest school district chairman in the country, and the county judge of the largest county in the country. That's what they saw. One by one these people offered testimony.

We invited people from all over the state of Texas to come, and we said that after the official hearing, nine in the morning to eleven, there would be a people's hearing. Our plan was to have a group of ordinary people with disabilities from outside Washington talking on the record so we could forward their testimony to the Congress later on. We got 550 disabled people into this big auditorium. It filled up.

In his opening remarks, Bartlett was amazed, overwhelmed, to see that many people with disabilities. He said, "I understand you're going to have a people's hearing after we finish our formal hearing here. You all are my constituents. I'll stay here as long as it takes to hear each one of you. I don't want you to feel like I come here just to hear these high-ranking officials."

So the mayor, the county judge, the telephone company lady, they all spoke and said they supported the ADA. Bartlett just sat there and acted like this was a rigged up deal. The Democrats came down and got their people to come and testify. Then the chairman of the school board, nice young attractive African American woman, stood up and said, "I realize this bill will not have a particular impact on our schools because we already provide assistance to people with disabilities under what is now the IDEA. However, many of our disabled children find it difficult to get jobs once we spend all the time and money and love preparing them for work when they leave. I feel like this law is important from that standpoint."

Bartlett had some notes that his staff has prepared for him. He said, "You may say this doesn't have any impact on you, ma'am. You may not be aware of it, but this bill will require your schools to spend 'x' amount of money"—and he had it figured out—"to provide new accommodations to meet the requirements of this law, in addition to that which you mentioned. Do you believe that your board and members of the school district are willing to bite the kind of bullet that will have with this bill? Do you understand the budget impact this bill will have on your program?" She said, "As clearly as I'm standing here before you, sir, that's exactly what I'm saying." Bartlett's response to that was, "Well, us old Baptists up in Dallas have a phrase that says, "Be careful what you pray for, because you just might get it."

Then it came time for the transit administrator. Bob Lanier talked about his original view that there were better ways to do this transit thing than to make the buses accessible. He said, "I still believe that door-to-door service for many people with disabilities is better than buses running on Main Street, and we're going to provide that door-to-door service. We've got a paratransit system and we're going to make it better. But I also believe that we need to make our buses—and everybody in the United States needs to follow suit on this—accessible to people with disabilities, because it should be their civil right. And therefore, I support this legislation."

Bartlett stood up and said, "I think I've heard it all now. The tough old bird that was the head of the Texas transit agency and the State Highway Commission is standing up here telling me that he's in support of this legislation! Have you lost your mind, Mr. Lanier?" Lanier said, "In response to your question, Mr. Congressman, let me quote poetry." He recited a poem. It was a moving poem about waking up in a morning and not knowing who you are and finding—'In a Graveyard' or something, I can't remember. Bartlett said, "In my wildest dreams, I never expected to hear, you, Mr. Lanier quoting poetry." Lanier said, "That's how I feel." Thunderous applause, it was incredible.

Bartlett later said that poem is what changed his mind about the ADA. That was very important because Bartlett was [in] the conservative leadership, he was the ranking Republican, the one that all the small business groups were depending on to block the ADA. He turned around and became a proponent, and worked as hard as any of the other members, the Democrats, who were more logically in support of it after their leadership came to it.

In my opinion that was one of the turning points in the passage of the ADA, that hearing in Houston. But it was a well-staged activity. I mean, we had disabled boy and girl scouts bring the flag in. We had a trumpeter who was disabled, from San Antonio, who composed an original fanfare that was played. The entire hearing, all eleven hours of it, was broadcast live on public television, and it was taped and played over and over again for the next six months.

Everything that I had observed and learned in Washington, I applied to organizing here [in Houston]. Members of Congress had hosts and hostesses, people with disabilities who met them at the airport and escorted them to their hotel, escorted them to the hearing, escorted them back to the airport. Owens and his staff came over to my house for dinner. In fact, two of his staff members stayed in our home. It was a charming event that was a lot of fun.

ADA was enacted because of a whole series of activities like this.

Patrisha Wright (continued)
"Our biggest fear was somebody was going to realize what an impact this piece of legislation was going to have."

Patrisha Wright may describe herself as a "Berkeley hippie" but as a lobbyist she was a savvy pragmatist of the highest degree.

It was a great thing, strategically, to have the first version of the ADA done by a Republican administration, a Republican appointed National

Council. It was the best thing that could possibly happen. Because once the Republicans arrived, it'd be easier to get the Democrats on. So that's always a good sign.

When actually seeing the legislation, and being someone who had spent years doing traditional civil rights stuff on the Hill, I knew the problems we were going to bump into. And that's not to say that it wasn't a wonderful piece of legislation. It's just coming after the throes of four years of trying to do the Civil Rights Restoration Act, it would be next to impossible to sell it as it was. And it really is a case of selling. Lobbying is marketing, nothing more than that. Buy my toothpaste.

When DREDF first raised questions about the bill as it was drafted by the National Council, that was a pretty difficult time for me. There were a lot of accusations made back and forth, that, from my perspective, were not valid, nor true. And part of the discussion I had with Justin Dart at that time was trying to decide whether or not I was actually willing to take it on, because you have to be willing to be the person that everybody hates. If it passes and they like it, then you're "the mother of the ADA," but if it passes and they don't like it, you're the person who killed the world's best bill. So it was a difficult issue because of the struggles that were going on.

DREDF was viewed as belonging to nobody—we weren't in the consortium's camp, we weren't in NCIL's camp, we weren't in that National Council's camp. We were an independent, lone ranger group. But what we were committed to doing was civil rights. I can remember sitting on the couch at Mary Lou's house basically saying, "I don't know what we're going to do, I don't know if I have the intestinal fortitude to put up with it again." But as long as I had Arlene Mayerson and Mary Lou Breslin at my side, I felt like we could do anything. You know, I get a lot more credit for the ADA than I deserve, and most of it should go to Arlene and to Mary Lou. I might have figured out a strategy or two, but they were great wingmen, is all I can say.

Evan Kemp pulled off a coup. Bush One [President George H. W. Bush] was trying to find an example of what "kinder, gentler" meant.[4] Evan rolled forth with the ADA and said, "This is 'kinder, gentler.'" We happened to be at the right place at the right time with the right person, Evan, to go in there and peddle it. That [presidential] campaign [of 1988] was desperate to find something that was kinder and gentler. And ADA became the vehicle for him to explain what kinder, gentler meant. So from then on throughout his term we had that card to play. On the other side, the Democratic folks with Phil Calkins[5]—who was working for the Dukakis campaign—everyone was recommending that the Democrats *not* go on board, which further forced the Republicans out to talk on the issue. Which was a great strategy.

This second part of the marketing strategy was decided shortly after we started. It turned out that every time somebody was getting interviewed by the press, it caused us to fall three or four steps backwards, because people would use an analogy like, blind people will now be jurors, and so the four members who were scared that a blind person would be a juror would then ask, when we were at lobby day, "Was that really true, would this force juries to be wheelchair accessible and to have blind people?" So we said that no one should talk to the press at all about the ADA. Now that is, from a marketing perspective, a plus and a minus. It enabled us to pass the bill, because we then weren't fighting a large number of counter-amendments. But the minus side of it is, once it gets passed, nobody really knows what's in it. I remember at the signing ceremony, I sat with Senator Kennedy, and Teddy Jr., and the senator leaned over to me and said, "I had the worst nightmare last night." I said, "What is that, Senator?" And he said, "I dreamt that George Bush read the bill." We all laughed, but it was true: our biggest fear was somebody was going to realize what an impact this piece of legislation was going to have on the United States. I don't think we all got the impact it was going to have on the world, but we did understand that the line was drawn in the sand and the United States would be different from that time on.

I had worked with Congressman Tony Coelho originally. Way back when, Bob Funk and I and Mary Lou put on a benefit at the Kennedy Center with Itzhak Perlman, for civil rights, and we got Tony involved. We had done work with Senator Lowell Weicker throughout the years, on 504 stuff, up to the Civil Rights Restoration Act. His committee had the jurisdiction for 504. And his staffers, like Jane West, were all people who understood disability. Lowell was instrumental in deinstitutionalization, Willowbrook, that whole genre of legislation. So he had the first step of understanding, that people were falsely imprisoned and held against their will, basically in the spirit of taking care of them, quote-unquote. And again, I had met all these people through my work with the Leadership Conference, so that was my entree to these folks.

In the initial draft that the National Council put forward, health insurance was covered. You know, insurance never made it into the ADA, to the extent the community, including myself, would want insurance covered. It would never have passed had it remained in the bill, because, as you can see with [President Obama's] health care [reform legislation], there seems to be a problem with the insurance companies insuring people who quote, unquote aren't of perfect bodies and minds. So that was one of the tensions: the community really felt that insurance was one of the major issues that prevented people from getting jobs and being able to live in the community. But the trade-off is, do you pass the rest of the protections and drop the insurance protection? Part of it was, when the original sponsor was Lowell Weicker, who came from Connecticut, which was the insurance capital of the country, asking him to do that would be asking him to totally take on the health insurance industry himself. And he couldn't do it. As radical as Lowell was, and I love him dearly.

We set up weekly meetings. Liz Savage did a weekly lobbying meeting, and then I and/or the lawyer that was working on a particular section or language would appear every Monday morning and brief everybody about what the agenda was for the week. The infamous agreement between Justin and I came out at that time, which is here are the principles that we'll abide by in any discussion about legislation, and we'll never sell out a principle.

Basically we said that we would not separate anyone from coverage under the act. Meaning, they couldn't decide that this week the disease of the month was AIDS or mental illness or lupus or whatever. It was going to be one for all and all for one. And that, unless you agreed to one for all and all for one, you shouldn't be a part of this coalition, because today you may be the favored disability, but, with Congress, tomorrow you may not be. So that was the first principle. And the second principle was about basically not selling out people's civil rights. That we would, instead of dropping transportation or dropping employment, we would extend the period that it would take to implement it.

And our mantra became that we wanted equal protection under the law, the same protections that race had. We had all these catchphrases that we would use that were used historically in the civil rights movement, such as "a right without a remedy is no right at all." From a strategy point of view, Ralph Neas was my mentor and guide through this process. So he came with a lot of the past history and knowledge of the civil rights community. It was a major focus and it was the primary focus, again, to right the wrongs.

The joint congressional hearing on the bill came when we knew we couldn't go any farther that first session. It was the end of the session type of thing, but [it was still important] to have a real, pardon me the expression, opening show of cross-disability issues, [to demonstrate] that the bill wasn't just limited to the phys dis biz. We were able to give that broad spectrum, that panoply view of where we were going with it.

I organized that hearing. I had never seen a bicameral hearing. So that was the first impression, seeing both House and Senate members sitting there was really a wonderful experience for me. The second experience was having that room filled with people with disabilities. I'd never seen that many people with disabilities in Congress at one time, advocating for their rights. So just from a typical, across-the-board view, it was really kind of awe inspiring to me. Plus, we had a range of witnesses at that hearing from people from within the community, leadership like Judy Heumann, and people who weren't. And it really—it makes a difference. It kind of set the scope and stage, so to speak.

I remember that that was the first time Tony Coelho publicly told his story. Tony had privately told his story to various groups that he had met with, but that was the first time he told it so publicly. It's always a very moving story. But everybody's disability story, for the most part, is a moving story. To actually have a member of Congress say, "This is what it is for me," and then Kennedy's story, too.

I remember Kennedy saying to me and Harkin after that hearing that he thought it was going to be an incredibly moving couple of years.

25
Insiders, Part 1

P EOPLE WITH DISABILITIES, AS HAS BEEN NOTED BEFORE, BELONG TO
an "open minority," that is, anyone can acquire a disability at any point in
his or her life, no matter what that person's social or economic status. This flu-
idity can work against the efforts of disability rights activists to organize their
constituency, since it means there is generally no shared culture or consciousness implicit in the simple fact of having a disability. It can also, however, be
an advantage, as certain individuals with disabilities have access to centers of
political influence that are usually unavailable to people in other oppressed
minority groups. These individuals, then, connected by family or friendship
to large fortunes or impressive political connections, can mobilize these resources for the community.

Evan Kemp Jr. was one such individual, born in New York City to "old
money." Diagnosed at age twelve with Wohlfart-Kugelberg-Welander syndrome, or Kugelberg Welander spinal muscular atrophy, a disease related to
polio, Kemp began using a wheelchair after an accident as an adult—the
direct result of being refused reasonable accommodations—while working
for the Securities and Exchange Commission. He was close friends with
C. Boyden Gray, conservative attorney, member of the Federalist Society,[1] and
a confidant of then Vice President George H. W. Bush. In 1987, President
Ronald Reagan appointed Kemp a commissioner at the Equal Employment Opportunity Commission (EEOC). When President George W. Bush
appointed EEOC chairman Clarence Thomas to the federal bench, Kemp
took Thomas's place.

Kemp's position inside the political establishment enabled him to play a
crucial role as a bridge between the ADA coalition, C. Boyden Gray (who by
that time was White House Counsel), and President G. H. W. Bush.

Janine Bertram Kemp
"In Washington, nothing happens by accident."

———

Janine Bertram Kemp, Evan's wife during the campaign to pass the ADA, came from a background far removed from old money and political insider status. She made her first effort as a disability rights advocate a little more than a decade before she became involved with the movement.

"There was a woman named Janet Fox with CP who was my brother's age, graduated at his high school the same year he did. I ended up getting to know her, and then ran into her years later in Seattle, where I lived. This was probably 1974 or '75. We went out to eat, and they threw us out of the restaurant because of her cerebral palsy. They said their customers didn't like drooling.

"I was appalled at that level of discrimination. And so I called the media contacts I had, we went home and made a few signs and held an impromptu picket in front of the restaurant."

Disability as an issue of civil rights may have been new to her, but this was hardly Janine's first experience as a political activist. Born in November 1950 in Tacoma, Washington, she came of age during the political and social tumult of the sixties, and participated in the radical politics of the time. Starting as an activist "with a progressive peer-to-peer counseling service called the Tacoma Rap Center, I moved to Seattle and organized Coyote, which was organizing hookers and trying to decriminalize prostitution."

Bertram's politics led her to "go underground, join the George Jackson Brigade,[2] and become a revolutionary. This was the era of Patty Hearst and 'Give Them Shelter' and the Weather Underground and all of that.[3] I ended up with a group that did bombings. I drove the getaway car in four bank robberies. We called them 'expropriations.' I set a pipe bomb in a safe deposit box at Rainier Bank."

Bertram's life underground lasted a year and a half. She was arrested in 1978, and served fifty-two months of a ten-year federal prison sentence. On her release in 1982, she went to college in Arizona to study American Indian law and policy, then moved to the San Francisco Bay area to work with Prison MATCH (Prison Mothers And Their Children), an organization she'd helped to start while in prison. In 1984, she went to Washington, DC, to raise money for the program, where she met her future husband, disability rights leader Evan Kemp.

"Evan was running the Disability Rights Center, which had been started by Debbie Kaplan and Ralph Hotchkiss. When Debbie and Ralph moved to the Bay area, Evan took it over." The two fell in love, married, and became compatriots in the movement.

Evan Kemp passed away in 1997. Janine Bertram Kemp has since returned to her native Pacific Northwest.

———

Evan graduated at the top of his class from the University of Virginia Law School. After graduating he applied at thirty-seven different law firms, and they all turned him down, and said overtly why: "We're not hiring you because your disability will mean you can't travel easily," or "This job needs such and such and it would be too hard for you to do."

And he was shocked. He just never anticipated that. It was really a horribly depressing time for him. He was engaged to be married. He broke the engagement. His cousin, Tyler Abel, was postmaster general under President Johnson and got Evan a job working for the IRS in Washington.

Those thirty-seven rejections were the seminal experience that made Evan a disability rights activist. It was never far below the surface. You could talk to him almost up until he died, and if you would get him to tell that story you would always hear him say, "And I wanted to make sure no young person with a disability would ever have to go through that agony of discrimination again."

Many people think ADA dropped from the sky but there was a ton of sophisticated planning to set up the conditions that would allow us to "play with the big boys"—and at that time it really was close to having exclusively only males in power. For instance, Evan was a Democrat who came from generations of Democrats. In the early 1980s, the national disability movement began anticipating ADA legislation, and Phil Calkins, Pat Wright, and others began an informal campaign to talk Evan into changing parties and bringing key Republicans on board for disability rights. He became a Republican, and Pat Wright agreed to get civil rights groups behind our cause. Evan said the first time he cast a vote after changing parties, it took him four hours to wheel over to the polling place, which was about four blocks from our house.

Evan had been told he'd be dead by age eighteen, and then in his thirties, and that made him fearless. It was key during his fight with Jerry Lewis when Evan was at EEOC. He came out with the statement that no self-respecting person with a disability would look for a job the week after the Jerry Lewis telethon, and then did a whole interview about Jerry Lewis and the pity approach. Lewis and the MDA bigwigs went after him with a vengeance. They tried to get him fired. Sam Skinner was the White House chief of staff. He called Evan up to order him to apologize. Evan said, "You'll have to have the president fire me before I do that." Justin Dart called Evan several times and tried to talk him into apologizing, because Justin thought that it was key to have Evan in that job at EEOC. Remember in the late 1980s and early 1990s there were not a huge number of presidential appointees with disabilities. Evan just absolutely would not budge. It was because he was fearless. He had faced death, and he was un-fazed. That was when Wade [Blank] of ADAPT called him, and said, "If you get fired because of this, I will walk from Denver to Las Vegas before the telethon." So that deepened the link between Evan and Wade, beyond the initial bond of an irrational love of the Cleveland Browns.

After *Toward Independence* was announced, a first draft of the ADA was written and circulated among the disability community. The President's Committee on the Employment of the Handicapped was having their national meeting at the Washington Hilton, and Evan was address-ing the full meeting. I think Justin Dart addressed that meeting, too.

The bill had initially been written with what the Republicans saw as a bankruptcy standard. Basically it was requiring all businesses to make accommodation and remove architectural barriers, no matter what. In his speech, Evan came out against that standard and all hell broke loose.

I had been sitting with Evan, I think at a head table. I was working at the Endependence Center of Northern Virginia (ECNV) at the time, and I walked down to where several of the people from the center were seated. As I walked by, Marsha Mazz[4] said, "Well, Evan Kemp just gutted the ADA!" So there was just huge anger building about Evan taking that position.

I saw what happened and thought, "He needs to talk to people in the disability community more about why he's making a public statement saying that." So I went around and grabbed people and said, "Let's get together and meet." And we went I think to Sharon Mistler and Phil Calkin's room in the hotel. And we were up until one or two interacting.

Evan talked about that afterwards and said, "You know, I've never thought to do that." And for me, I come from a more consensus, leftist background, so I think I brought that to him. I think it was an ongoing process. Far more understanding was built, instead of having this whole group of people going out saying things sort of behind people's backs. There was probably still some of that, but at least there was open communication. So I thought Marsha Mazz did a big service when she said that, and always respected Marsha's willingness to blurt out a perception. That wasn't too common in Washington.

Evan was also worried about the definition of disability being too broad. He felt that in any instance when an employer could hire someone with a hangnail as opposed to someone with a spinal cord injury, that they would choose someone with a hangnail. I'm exaggerating a little bit, but he kept saying, "I don't want this bill to apply to people with hangnails and hernias." And that was quite a major discussion in the community, the narrowing of the definition of disability.

Evan was a very important link between the phys-dis community and the Deaf community, because Evan got Vice President Bush to write a letter in support of I. King Jordan's getting the presidency of Gallaudet. I was at ECNV and saw something about the Gallaudet student strike on the news and ran into Sharon's office and said, "We've got to get out there." And she said, "Go." And I called up Evan and Lisa Gorove.[5] Or Lisa may have already known about it. We brought Evan out to join the week of demonstrations.

There was a huge amount of networking. And I would think that this support of the Deaf President Now movement by leaders of the phys dis community might have been important to [Senator] Tom Harkin, whose brother was deaf. So that might have been a key boost for the ADA. We also developed a very wonderful relationship with Jeff Rosen, one of the DPN leaders. When there were major high-level meetings, at the White House or on the insider level, or when there were high-level meetings with government officials, I know Evan always made sure that a leader from the Deaf community participated.

There were other things that Evan did to make alliances. We began going to Federalist Society meetings, which is a very conservative group in Washington. It actually is for conservative lawyers and law students to make connections, and debate policy informally. That was when

William Bradford Reynolds was nominated for assistant attorney general for civil rights. That required Senate confirmation. Brad was a Dupont family heir. He was a controversial candidate, known for being anti–affirmative action.

Boyden came over for a bridge game one night and said, "Evan, I think you should come out in support of Brad Reynolds for this position." And so Evan did, and we ended up meeting Brad Reynolds and having lunches and dinners with him. We learned that a few years before he had done one of those sensitivity exercises where he spent a day using a wheelchair. It totally shifted his view about the inclusion of people with disabilities. It made him support disability rights, despite his opposition to quotas. He held many of the conventional Republican civil rights positions. But Brad supported disability rights, so Evan came out in support of his confirmation as assistant attorney general.

In Washington, nothing happens by accident. Everything is planned out, at the presidential level, to achieve a goal or send some message. It was very important for ADA that Evan was invited to this first small dinner at the White House after George Bush took office [as president], with I think either twenty-four or twenty-eight people. Evan and I attended, on March 17th, 1989, and it was key because what the president was saying to all of his staff was, "I want the ADA passed." That was the whole point of inviting us.

And there was sort of an interesting aside, because Evan was a commissioner at the Equal Employment Opportunity Commission at the time, and he knew that I had done four years in prison for bombing and bank robbery. And so when he received the invitation he called up the director of the Secret Service. He wasn't available and Evan left a message. So the guy called back and Evan says, "Well, I have this issue that I need to discuss with you . . ." This is on March 15th. "We're supposed to go to the White House, and my partner, Janine Bertram, has a felony in her past and so I wanted to discuss it." And the guy said, "Oh, thank God, I thought somebody was filing a claim against me!"—an employment claim.

So Evan begins telling him the particulars of my charges, and the Secret Service guy keeps getting quieter and quieter. And finally he says, "Well, let me look into it. Patty Hearst was here at the White House just two weeks ago." And so the head of the Secret Service called back and arranged to get me in and said, "This conversation never happened." Of course, Evan proceeded to tell it all over town. So I had that sense that at the highest level, the Secret Service was not freaked out. But the president himself had to approve me every time I came to the White House.

I can't remember the specific problems we were having, but later on I think there was some problem with getting the ADA out of committee. And the White House staff was not working it very hard at all. And that was when the president invited Evan to have lunch with him in the White House mess. There was this whole press bruhaha at that time about the president not liking broccoli. And so they were looking at the menu and Evan said, "I think I'll have the broccoli." And the president laughed and said, "Oh, is that on there?" And, of course, there was no broccoli on the menu.

Evan said it was really interesting because when you were sitting there with the president, all of these people, the upper echelons, White House senior staff, started coming up and treating Evan like he was their best friend. And these, of course, were people who would never take his calls, never speak with him, until he was having lunch with the president.

These events may not seem real significant, but they are absolutely huge in a president's day, in signaling what a president wants. He signaled that he was pro-ADA to all his staff, and things opened up. I think it was after that White House lunch that Steve Bartlett on the House side, who was probably one of the most right-wing conservatives, started pushing for the Americans with Disabilities Act, too.

There were certainly some senior staffers that didn't want to see a major civil rights bill passed. I mean, if you look at the ADA, it's more broad-based and covers more people than any other civil rights act had. In the White House it was the president and Boyden Gray that made it happen. It helped that NCIL[6] was in town [for its annual conference] at the time and we had a huge march in the pouring rain to the White House. Boyden and Lee Lieberman, his assistant, and Ken Duberstein, a top domestic policy adviser, all came out to join the marchers. Boyden commandeered a DC police car and addressed the marchers saying President Bush supported ADA and they were working for the bill.

I think the attitude at that time was to get a bill that made sure that the community's bottom lines were met. I remember there was a fight over HIV, and whether it would be covered. And I remember it as not a fight really, but certainly a strong discussion between Pat Wright and Evan. Because the civil rights groups were adamant that HIV be covered.

And Evan called several disability groups all over the country, leaders of independent living centers, and nobody at that time, I mean this is certainly early on in the AIDS awareness campaign, too, but really, nobody cared. It was not a bottom line issue for the disability community. But it was for the civil rights community. So there was certainly some discussion that the right wing, I mean, the people really to the right of Newt Gingrich, people like [William L.] Armstrong from Colorado, would try and exclude HIV.

And it almost happened that people with psychiatric disabilities were excluded too. That was, again, led by Senator Armstrong. We were all in a room off the Senate side of the Capitol and it was very late night and the Senate was debating it and Bill Roeper, who was the White House staffer detailed to shepherd the ADA, was there too. There was a compromise reached, I know, that excluded people who set fires and I think it excluded transvestites, too.[7] But it was just this knock-down, drag-out, with Senator Kennedy running out and saying, "Will this language work?" At one point the White House was just about to go with excluding people with psychiatric disabilities, and Evan grabbed Bill Roeper's attention and just shook his head, absolutely not. And Bill Roeper got it and got on board.

The day the ADA was signed I actually ended up sitting with Bob Cooper of Rhode Island and Jim Dickson.[8] And that was when the Secret Service said, "We're not letting her in unless she has an escort with her all the time." And so they had to get someone to shadow me. But it really made no sense because there were over three thousand people there at the signing. I was nowhere near the president, while I was right next to him, frequently, at the smaller events. My "guard" was just somebody from the White House Office of Protocol who was a volunteer, some wealthy Republican woman who was told to not let me out of her sight. I told Jim and Bob what was happening and, of course, they kept trying to run interference and keep her busy, just to play with her head. So I think, I either ended up shaking the president's hand as he walked down, or maybe Mrs. Bush, I can't remember which of them stopped. It was just funny to experience—just a fun game.

I think Evan felt that he had achieved his goal, that no other person with a disability would have to go to thirty-seven job interviews and have thirty-seven rejections based on their disability. That was truly his driving force.

Tony Coelho (continued)
"It was an interesting piece of legislation, and I was at the peak of my power."

———

Denied the chance to enter the priesthood because of his epilepsy, Coelho cast about for another calling, struggling both with his damaged self-image and with his use of alcohol to ease the pain of his rejection by the church. His mentor with the Jesuits was able to get Coelho a job as a personal assistant for Bob Hope, and in 1964 Coelho went to live at the Hope family home in Palm Springs, California.

"Bob Hope was a wonderful human being, and he would help a lot of people, and the stipulation was that nobody could talk about it. . . . So one day we're talking, and he knows about my problem. And he said, 'You know, Tony, you really know ministry, but you don't understand what a ministry is. You think that a ministry can only be practiced in a church. And a true ministry is practiced every day. There's a ministry in the entertainment business. There is a ministry in sports. There is a ministry in government . . . One of the really truly good ones is a ministry in politics. You're helping people, you're solving people's problems, you can really be committed to it' and so forth. And he said, 'You ought to go work for a member of Congress.'"

Coelho took this advice to heart, writing to his congressman, Democrat Bernie Sisk, in early 1965, very shortly thereafter becoming the congressman's administrative assistant. Congressman Sisk took the young Coelho under his wing, introducing him to his constituents and, in effect, grooming Coelho to be his replacement. As Coelho puts it, "I found my next mentor." In 1978, Coelho ran for Sisk's seat and won.

Through it all Coelho remembered his experience of being discriminated against because of his epilepsy. As he grew in experience and stature as a member of the House Democratic leadership, Congressman Coelho found himself uniquely situated to make ending disability-based discrimination a primary part of his political ministry.

———

I had been very successful in [the congressional campaign in] '82, and so all of a sudden I become the fifth-ranking Democrat in the House, and it was obvious I was going to move into leadership. . . . I'm raising the funds and targeting [members'] races, as to whether or not unions and political action committees contribute to their races and so forth. And I also then identified candidates for open seats or candidates to run against Republicans. So I could be very helpful to incumbents or people running for Congress. So if I wanted something on disabilities, that's not a big issue . . . that's a small price to pay for what I was doing for them. And I used it all the time; I have no reservations in saying it, because it's what's important to me.

I became whip in '87.[9] At that time I'm counting the votes for every amendment, every bill that goes through the House, and so every committee chair, every subcommittee chair has to deal with me because they have to come to me to get the votes. The majority leader would schedule the bill, but if I said we didn't have the votes it would come off the schedule. So I played a big role in whatever they were personally engaged in. I knew how everything worked, so people had to deal with me just in a legislative way, and as long as I was liked—and I was fairly well liked—whatever was important to me became an easy thing for them to help me with.

I was aware that the National Council on Disability was doing something, but they're Reagan appointees, so that doesn't have much credibility, right? They aren't the type that I'm into—you know, raving idiots: "We want everything *now*." And so I knew what they were doing, but I wasn't interested because I didn't think I'd be interested.

And then one day Roxanne Vierra brings Sandy Parrino by to meet me, and Roxanne's husband and I are very close friends. He's Portuguese, Fred Vierra, and he's in the cable business, and I was close to the people in the cable business. And Fred had done some things politically with me, and he was a right-wing Republican. And Roxanne is more conservative than he is, by the way. And so she walks in and brings Sandy with her and says to me, "Look, we're putting together this bill. Lowell Weicker has agreed to sponsor it, and we would like you to consider being the House sponsor."

And so I listened, and I knew it wasn't what the disability community wanted. A lot of people in the disability community wanted quotas and so forth, to correct the problems. And so I said to them, "I know it's going to be controversial within the community, but if you're really committed to it, let me look at it because maybe this is a beginning, and having Lowell as the Republican sponsor on the Senate side makes sense with me. If you really think you can bring some Republican support, I'm interested. I'm just interested in the concept, but I want to make sure I read the bill and so forth."

My staff assistant, Heidi Hicks, said to me, "Tony, you know the community is going to go bananas. They're going to think you're crazy to be part of this." I said, "Well, they may be wrong. You're never going to get through what they want, so maybe I start somewhere in the middle." So I went through it and talked to some people in the community. They didn't want me to do it, but I talked to Lowell, and he was totally committed to it.

I decided to go ahead and put it in, and I did it primarily because I loved the idea that it was a Reagan group advocating, that the commitment was there from Sandy, and I love Roxanne. I said, "Look, if we move this, I want testimony, I want involvement; I don't think we can move something that's partisan, so I really want engagement," and they both assured me they would. And Lowell was totally committed, and he said he would get cosponsors on the Republican side. And so I put it in and the community was unhappy. . . .

When I put out the "Dear Colleague" letter asking for cosponsors for the ADA, I had people who came to me, not knowing what was in the bill at all, saying, "Look, on your disability bill, put me down as a cosponsor." Some of them had mothers, fathers, wives, husbands, sons, daughters, aunts, uncles, best friends with a disability, and that's why they went on. Others did it just because they knew this would be something that I would like, and I got a lot of Republicans on as well. It was an interesting piece of legislation, and I was at the peak of my power at that point. And we got a lot of people engaged. I left the Congress in June of '89, and I asked Steny Hoyer[10] to lead the effort for me. . . .

I parted with a lot of good friendships and a lot of great relationships. So people still wanted to help, but it was a battle to get it through the House. Getting it through the Senate was not as tough, but getting it through the House we had to go through five committees. The Speaker at the time was Tom Foley, and he decided that it wouldn't go through one committee; it would go through five separate committees, which meant it could easily be killed along the way.

Foley told me that he thought this was like the bill dealing with seniors that the public got so upset at—they were demonstrating and throwing things at Rostenkowski's car—it was some type of reform dealing with Medicare, and they had to repeal it because it was so unpopular. So Foley said this is going to be like this bill—and we're going to end up having to repeal it because it's going to be so unpopular with business. And I told him I didn't care. And he said, well, we had to do the five committees.

I finally said, "Okay, but I want to designate the committees and the order." And he said, "That's fine." That was a mistake on his part, because if he wanted to kill it, which I suspect that he did, he did the wrong thing. So we started off with Education and Labor, which we knew we could win big. The second committee was Judiciary, and Jack Brooks from Texas was opposed. Now I was very close to Jack, and I periodically had to call him and cash in every chit I had. I [had] helped him out a lot when I was campaign chair and when I was whip, and so forth. And I was just very aggressive with him, and Steny ended up becoming an enemy of his as part of this. It was not the most pleasant thing, but he voted for us, and we got it out of there with a decent vote. I knew if we could bring it to a vote we'd be fine. The issue was bringing it to a vote, and I pressed and pressed and finally got him to agree to give us a vote.

Then the third committee was Commerce and that was telecommunications and that was health, and so forth and so on, and that was [John] Dingell. And Dingell and I had an interesting mixed relationship, but I could press Dingell, and I did. And Henry Waxman was one of the subcommittee chairs, and he was a big advocate. Dingell ultimately, his first wife had depression and so forth, and so I was able to aggressively work that and get that done.

Public Works was the hardest; that was the last—well, Rules Committee was the last one, but that one was rather easy to get done. But we went before Public Works and the chairman was a congressman from Long Beach, Glenn Anderson, who used to be lieutenant governor of California at one point, and he was a great friend, and the bus industry was very close to him. And Glenn said to me one day, "Tony, they're really putting a lot of pressure on me." And I said, "Glenn, there's nothing more important to me—nothing." And when Glenn's son wanted to run for mayor in Long Beach, I had raised money for him and helped him. And I said, "Look, I was there when you needed me. I want you here now," and he said, "Fine."

And then we still had Norm Mineta to go to, and Norm Mineta was the congressman from San Jose. He was chairman of the Transportation Subcommittee. Glenn was chairman of the full committee, and Norm was chairman of the subcommittee, and Norm was close to the bus industry, and Norm was basically opposed. And what I did with Norm was, you know, my aggressive, tough way. When the Japanese Reparations Act was before the Congress on the House floor, the majority leader, Jim Wright had it scheduled. There was opposition from, I would say, some racists, and they convinced Jim that it would boomerang on us if we put through this "Jap" bill. Norm was a deputy whip, and he had supported Jim Wright for leader and so forth and his was a critical vote; Jim Wright had won by one vote. So Jim calls up Norm and says, "You know, I don't think we should schedule that bill; I don't think we have the votes for it, and you don't want to lose it. So let's schedule it for next week or the week after." So Norm said, "Let me think about it."

So Norm came and saw me on the House floor and said, "Jim tells me that we don't have the votes." Now I'm the vote counter as the whip. . . . I said, "Norm, it's your decision. Obviously, it's your bill and if you want to pull it you can pull it. But I guarantee you I have the votes. And I guarantee you if you pull it, it won't get rescheduled. So you're going to have to trust me. I can get it through today. If you reschedule it for next week or the week after, I don't know what will happen then. The fact that [Wright] wants to withdraw it means we *have* the votes. So let's do it." So he did. He went along, and we scheduled it, and we won. So Norm is always grateful to me.

So now I'm out of the Congress, okay? Now I'm told Norm's against me on ADA and that we may lose it by one vote. If he voted against me we would lose it for sure, and if he voted for it we'd probably win by one vote, and the Greyhound people were the ones that were working it the hardest. So I go to Norm, and I said, "Norm, I'm going to do something you may not like. But I remember when something was really important to you, and you told me it was, and I gave you advice, and you followed my advice. And you've always been thankful that I told you to go ahead. I'm now cashing in that chit. I want your vote. It's the right thing; you know it's the right thing. As much as you felt that reparations were right for Japanese Americans who were interned during World War II, I think the same in regards to us—those of us who have disabilities needing our civil rights. It's the same issue and you shouldn't deny us that." He said, "Okay, okay, okay."

The Black Caucus was wonderful. They were supportive from day one. Major Owens was the chairman of the Labor Subcommittee and he was a huge advocate. John Conyers was on the Judiciary Committee, number two on the Judiciary Committee. He was a huge advocate for me. And I just had tremendous support from the black community.

It was in the Senate chambers; it was in the Judiciary Committee and I was the lead-off [person to testify]. It was televised, and I was the first member of Congress to publicly talk about my disability in the way I talked about it. And I was very passionate, very emotional about what I went through. I talked about suicide, I talked about what my parents put me through, talked about the Church, and what it did to me as a person and the scar tissue that developed. But I was not deterred; I was determined not to let this scar tissue stop me. And that I was determined to let the scar tissue drive me to try to make changes. And in my testimony I shared all that.

Ted Kennedy was crying, and Orrin Hatch was crying, and Bob Dole; it had a very emotional impact. It also reinforced what I believed in, that if you're willing to be honest, if you're willing to share the hurt, that you can really have an impact. You have to be willing to share the hurt, though; it has to show and it has to come out. And I did that day, and people give that a lot of credit for creating the momentum to get going. And I think it did, but I think that to a great extent I was the culmination of a lot of grassroots. The people here in California, to my view, started it, their willingness to demonstrate, their willingness to put their chairs in the way of commerce and do things, set a tone for those of us with disabilities to have pride in ourselves, to speak out.

Justin Dart Jr. (continued)
"I saw your hat and I thought about ADA."

In addition to traveling across country pushing for the ADA, Justin and Yoshiko Dart also helped to subsidize numerous individuals, organizations, and publications working within the movement. They also made strategic contributions to senators, congresspeople, and presidential candidates, earning "a seat at the table" for people with disabilities to represent the disability community.

Justin Dart was also a savvy PR man, applying to disability rights some of the same techniques he'd used in business. For instance, Dart would never appear at a public function without his Texas hat and cowboy boots—they became his trademark. Before his death Justin donated them, as well as the first pen used by President Bush to sign the ADA and the Presidential Medal of Freedom bestowed by President Clinton, to the Smithsonian, where they remain as part of the exhibit on the ADA.

———

My father was a kind of one-man PAC [political action committee]. One of the roles he played was as a great fundraiser for the Republican Party. And that was one thing that gave him his influence. He would go out and get groups that supported him and get them to contribute to selected campaigns, not only of Republican presidential campaigns, but of senatorial candidates all over the United States, year after year. And so he ended up being one of the leaders of the so-called Reagan kitchen cabinet. But he also advised President Eisenhower, Thomas Dewey who lost, and everybody on down the line. So I grew up with that background, and then I also grew up with LBJ down in Texas, who was a very earthy politician. And he was in a way one of my mentors, not that I knew him personally. I met him a couple of times at some barbecues.

Yoshiko and I noted early on that our movement had no PAC. And so we tried to be a tiny PAC for the disability rights movement. And we noticed that we, the movement, had just about no presence at all in the Republican Party. I had this kind of entree with my father, getting these Republican appointments down in Texas. So, we contributed regularly to the Republican Party, and we headed up these political campaigns. And remember, it has not been terribly fashionable to be politically involved, and go out and actually campaign for people, although there were people in our movement who did campaign, mostly for Democrats. Nobody ever campaigned for the Republicans. So, I headed up People with Disabilities for Reagan-Bush in 1984. And then I was one of the leaders of the Bush-Quayle campaigns in 1988 and in 1992. I forget if I had always had the title of chair, but I did an awful lot of stuff.

And then, at the same time, I was a very substantial contributor to the Republican Party. And I am talking about major money here. I was at the Reagan White House many times, and met President Reagan, because I was a contributor. Not that we can afford that, we are not multimillionaires, but we devote a lot of our money to it because we think it is important. There is a role that contributions play, exerting an influence that cannot be exerted any other way. There just isn't any free lunch. And it's not the best way to run a democracy, but it is the way *this* democracy is run. Until we get a better way, I am not embarrassed to make large contributions that will enable me to spend one minute or thirty seconds shaking the hand of the President of the United States in a photo op, and getting to say those few words to him about ADA.

I knew I was getting successful when I met President Bush in the receiving line [at the White House] for about the twentieth time and he introduced me to the person next to him. I forgot what the person's name was, he was a professor or something. And the president said, "Professor, this is Justin Dart, he is the ADA man." And another time he said, "Justin, I saw you yesterday across the park at the dedication of the Korean War Memorial." He had seen me in the distance. "I saw your hat and I thought about ADA."

26
Drafting the Bill, Part 2

T HE FIRST DRAFT OF THE ADA, INTRODUCED INTO CONGRESS BY Senator Weicker and Congressman Coelho, lapsed into legislative oblivion with the end of the 1988 congressional session. It was obvious to most advocates, especially those with legislative experience, that a new version needed to be written. And so, in early 1989, there began a series of meetings between advocates such as Patrisha Wright, Arlene Mayerson, and Bob Funk (who had left DREDF to take a position in the White House), John Wodatch, a policy expert at the US Department of Justice, and legislative aides Robert Silverstein (staff director and chief counsel for the Subcommittee on the Handicapped) and Carolyn P. Osolinik (chief counsel for Senator Kennedy), working to produce a bill that both met the needs of the community and stood some chance of being both passed by Congress and signed by the president. Others involved in this effort, what one historian called "a line by line" review of the bill, included Paul Marchand, Liz Savage, Ralph Neas from the Leadership Conference on Civil Rights, Robert Burgdorf from the National Council on Disability, Jim Weisman from Eastern Paralyzed Veterans of America, Chai Feldblum, counsel for the American Civil Liberties Union in Washington, and others.

Among the many changes made in the draft, two of the most significant—and controversial—were the exclusion of health insurers from the covered entities and the adoption of a more stringent definition of "disability." Those crafting the legislation decided early on that the health insurance lobby—which was unalterably opposed to being included in the ADA—was too powerful to oppose. And while the previous NCD draft defined a "disability" as "a physical or mental impairment, perceived impairment, or a record of impairments," Wright and others felt that the new version should echo the definition already included in Section 504 of the Rehabilitation Act of 1973 and subsequent disability legislation and litigation: "a physical or mental impairment that substantially limits one or more of the major life activities"—such as seeing, walking, self-care, and learning. The idea, as Evan Kemp often put it, was to ensure that "people with hangnails and hernias" wouldn't suddenly expect somehow to be covered by the new law.

This process of drafting and redrafting would continue even after the bill was submitted, indeed, virtually up until the final vote in July 1990.

Patrisha Wright (continued)
"We had a twenty-four-hour DREDF operation."

In order for the ADA to pass, it was necessary that the law being drafted not only satisfy the needs of the community, but that it also win the support of a majority of the members of Congress. Patrisha Wright, as DREDF's point-person on Capitol Hill, had to ensure that the two needs were balanced in such a way that neither side felt unable to endorse the bill as it made its way through the legislative process.

We probably saw Senator Harkin every single day. During that time Arlene [Mayerson] and I basically lived out of the conference room in his office. He would come in at least once a day and offer us pizza or whatever, because the whole group of us was there for many, many long hours. You know, I can't say enough about the disability legal community. We were really able to garner the best and the brightest, all the people who had previously done litigation related to these various sections of the new bill, to come in and act as the expert whenever the issues were out there. I've felt it was an incredible gift to work with all these lawyers. They were just brilliant, is all I can say. They did the real heavy lifting of getting the language together.

And I have to tell you, we had fun. You talk about being together, that close and for that long. We had a great time. And exciting, intellectually stimulating, trying to solve some of these issues. And Bobby Silverstein, with his ninety-two books filled with everything anybody has ever said in their life, so he could turn to tab number 32 and pull it out. He would come in with his big wheelbarrow full of books. . . .

When [Congressman] Steny [Hoyer] took over for Coelho, he held the negotiations [over the details of the new draft]. Chai Feldblum[1] and myself sat on either side of the table with him and we had negotiations two or three times a week with every single committee that the bill had to go through on the House side. Four to five hours a day, he spent working that bill. These were guys who really understood the content of what was in there, and that made a difference.

It came out in negotiations with Steny that [Congressman John] Dingell's staff had made these sweeping statements that basically said mentally ill people should not be allowed on the trains because they're too disruptive. Which would have opened the door totally. I mean, do you have to have a card to say you're not mentally ill? And does anybody who is in therapy, does that spell mental illness, because insurance is treating it as a mental health condition? Does that mean anyone who has gone to marriage counseling shouldn't be allowed on a train? And how does the conductor determine that? Oh, by looking at you. I see. So by looking at you, I can tell that you're mentally ill, and you're going to disrupt the train. So, I mean, it was that type of discussion. I walked out of the room when this debate was going on and called over to Senator Kennedy's office and he sent Caroline Osolinik over to the House and she walked into the office and sat down and basically said, "Forget it. You don't get to do that." And that was it.

Again, there's the advantage of having DREDF in the coalition. I truly believed I represented every type of disability there could possibly be. There was not another group who would say that. Most of the Washington organizations were disability-specific. So with mental illness, when an active lobbyist was not sitting at the table, those issues were never raised. So I believed it was my job as DREDF to raise those issues across the board, no matter where we were. And when it came to creating a group of people, lawyers that we could turn to for reliable information and past legislative history and case law, the Bazelon Center [formerly the Mental Health Law Project] filled that role, and that was Bonnie Milstein.

In the middle of the campaign Arlene had a baby, Emma, and she wasn't traveling with Emma. She stayed at the DREDF office in Berkeley, and so we had a twenty-four-hour DREDF operation. Liz Savage would have the lobby team out and find out what's the newest problem. We would talk the information over with Arlene. Because of the three-hour time zone change, we'd go to bed, get some sleep, and by morning Arlene would have the new talking points written up for Liz to hand out to the lobby team for the morning. . . .

Liz Savage ran the lobby operation in DC proper. She would pick up information from a staffer that X member was having problems with this or that, and then the legal team would draft the responses that the lobbyists would go in with the next day to combat whatever we were hearing, and also talk to anyone who was on our list the next day to ensure that in case the rumors started going, we would have the talking points to address them. And if there was still a problem, then the call would go back to Mary Lou at DREDF in California, who would then call the appropriate state and get those people on it in that state. So it was a continuous loop of the lawyers writing the points, the lobbyists delivering the points, the grassroots going to various districts to get the local view in there.

This went on, day after day, for two years.

I think the toughest part of the bill to explain to members was the interrelationship of the individual pieces, and then, too, the scope of the bill. This bill was as far reaching, if not farther reaching, as the Civil Rights Act [of 1964]. It would have a profound impact on the shape of society. I think people were overwhelmed by it. But the pieces were so interrelated that you couldn't carve off a part and say, "Okay, this year we'll just do employment," because physical access is there in employment, and communication access, and so you have to do those pieces as well. And if you're doing that piece then you also have to do transportation, because how can somebody get to a job without accessible transit?

But again, that was the brilliance of posing it as kind of an employment issue, because when it gets sold as an employment issue, and you're talking about people wanting to get off benefits and wanting to be tax generating, versus tax consuming, people don't want to then say, "Oh, well no, I think that we should just pay disabled people to stay at home." So they get in a catch-22, trying to back out of certain parts of it.

Part of the problem we had in discussion with the traditional civil rights community was on how best to do this. For example, the disability community for years had talked about an employment nondiscrimination act. The easiest way to accomplish that would have been to amend Title VII [of the Civil Rights Act of 1964]. But, you know, once you have a civil rights piece of legislation you create basically a middle class. And you know, when you got nothing, you got nothing to lose, basically. But when you have *some* civil rights, it becomes very difficult to organize because you're afraid to lose the progress you've already made. So the traditional civil rights groups didn't want the disability community to open up Title VII to include disability.

The other issue was that there's a legal premise in race discrimination, the idea that but for the fact I'm a woman, but for the fact I'm a racial minority, I would be able to do the job. I am being discriminated against, but for my race, but for my gender. In disability civil rights, the traditional civil rights groups argued that it was "equal plus." It was not just but for my disability, because people with disabilities may also need an accommodation. So they referred to our civil rights as being different from their civil rights, because nothing had to change in theirs to get equality, but we might need an accommodation in order to make our opportunity equal. Our basic argument was it wasn't *us* that was unequal, it was trying to live and adapt in an inaccessible society that made it "equal plus." And that once you altered society and you built a society that *everybody* could use, then that equal-plus argument, for the most part, fell out, whether it was having communication barriers removed or physical access barriers removed or denying people health care based on disability removed. If you removed all that, then we'd all be equal. So that was our counter to it.

The toughest part of the bill to explain to the community, to advocates, was the need to compromise. You know, it always is. I mean, look at health care reform right now.[2] Because a lot of the issues couldn't happen that quickly. . . . There was the wish that everybody had, which is you'd snap your fingers and in thirty days the entire world would be accessible. The reality is, that's not practical.

Most of the time, when you pass a piece of legislation, it has a date by which it is to go into effect. "And as of this date, this is what happens." If you look at the ADA, all the different sections had different effective dates. So you could tell how difficult the negotiation was to get that piece, depending on how far out the date was for it to be effective. The sections where it was a horrific negotiation, we agreed not to change our principle on what we wanted for equality, but to move the date out to give people more time to get there.

And that's why the agreement of the principles before we started was so important—to say, "I will never, ever, in any meeting, go back on the basic rights of people with disabilities." That, and the all for one, one for all principle, was the underlying pin to it all.

Robert Silverstein
"It's not just politics. It really is people."

As the staff director and chief counsel for the Senate Subcommittee on Disability Policy, and as Senator Tom Harkin's principal adviser, Robert Silverstein was at the very heart of the effort to pass the ADA. His work on disability rights and civil rights in general goes back to the 1970s, when he was director of the Legal Standards Project for the National Lawyers Committee for Civil Rights Under Law. In the mid-1980s he became counsel to the House Subcommittee on Select Education, where he wrote legislation establishing early intervention programs for infants and toddlers with disabilities.

Silverstein arrived at the Senate in 1987, and apart from the ADA he was also instrumental in drafting and enacting the Developmental Disabilities Assistance and Bill of Rights Act Amendments of 1987, the Technology-Related Assistance for Individuals with Disabilities Act of 1988 ("Tech Act"), as well as expansions of the Rehabilitation Act and the Individuals with Disabilities Education Act (IDEA).

I was on the House side when the Senate was in the control of the Republicans, and then Senator Harkin hired me when he became chair [after the Democrats took control of the Senate in 1989]. So Harkin was chair, Weicker was ranking. But because the National Council and Sandy Parrino were Republican, she went to Senator Weicker and said, "We want to do this civil rights statute." And Weicker said, "Absolutely," and Harkin agreed to be the cosponsor.

So my original involvement was the original ADA that was introduced, that was verbatim from the National Council on Disability. And we had hour after hour of discussion with the council—Pat [Wright] was involved in that, and others—to try to get them to do a bill that was very strong but still reflected some sense of what's possible. And we weren't that successful in terms of our discussions with them because the National Council was in fact going around the country talking to advocates and saying, "We're going to include what we think is right, and the hell with politics." And so the actual bill that was drafted had some rather—I'll call them extreme—provisions. For example, there was a provision that said that businesses must make accommodations unless it would threaten the existence of the business. And there were requirements to retrofit the whole country within two to three or five years unless it would threaten the existence of the business.

We didn't win in some of those discussions, but Senator Harkin was a cosponsor notwithstanding, and the original ADA that was introduced was done for one purpose only: to get it on the presidential radar screen so that we could get both candidates talking about the need for an omnibus civil rights statute. And it worked, because you got a number of statements by candidate [George H. W.] Bush—and then President Bush—which were used extensively in the negotiations when we would say to their staff, "Who are you working for? This is what President Bush says. I thought you were working for President Bush, and your statement seems to be contrary to what the president is saying." So the strategy was to get on the record as many positive statements as possible for use in 1989, when the real effort was going to occur.

One of the things that we did was first of all recognize that this was not the members' bill. This was the disability community's bill. Our principle was to have the strongest possible defensible bill. But there was a notion that we had a window. We had to set up a set of guiding principles that we would not breach no matter what happened, but we recognized that, if you're dealing with bipartisanship—which is the only way to get the civil rights statute passed—we had to recognize the various legitimate points of view of the various stakeholders. But there was a notion that we had a very short time. Because when you pass major legislation, if you don't get it through quickly, it dies because the opponents organize. They're more powerful than we are, and the longer it's sitting out there, the greater the chance is it's not going to pass.

We had to make some judgments—we being the Hill staff, Senator's Kennedy's staff, Caroline Osolinik, Michael Iskowitz, myself—we had to figure out who in the disability community we could talk to off the record. It became critical to figure out who those folks were. Pat Wright was the key person in terms of trying to figure out who to work with. I need to have one person who's a contact, and in the disability community the primary contact was Pat. And she then had to figure out the hard stuff of who to talk to in the community, what to say, when to say it, how much to say. And you don't make a lot of friends when you have to do that, because there were some folks, to be quite frank, who we did not want in these negotiations, because they might have a different notion of how to pass legislation.

We knew we were going to have hearings. We knew we had to be able to answer questions. So what Caroline and I did, before we drafted the ADA of '89, we developed a hundred questions. I said, "We're not writing another bill until we get answers to these hundred questions." And there's a big black binder that still exists somewhere that has the answers to those questions. So that helped us frame what it was we were going to say, how we were going to structure the bill, what was going to be included, what wasn't going to be included, what were the guiding themes.

We had constant contact with Senator Hatch's staff. Senator Harkin and I met with Senator Hatch and his staff before we had anything in writing, because we knew ultimately that Senator Hatch, who was the ranking member of the full committee, was an essential person, and he had traditionally been very positive in terms of disability policy. He has his own [disability] advisory committee back in Utah. So before we were even talking to the disability community Senator Harkin and Senator Hatch had an off-the-record meeting that was shortly after the [1988] election when Senator Weicker was not reelected and Senator Harkin had taken over the helm and responsibility for the legislation.

And then I'll never forget the day that Caroline and I had to defend the draft in front of NCIL. They beat the shit out of us. "Why are you compromising before you even introduce?" And I hope and I believe by the end of the two- or three-hour grilling they understood what was included and why and what was not included from the previous draft and why.

If you're trying to move legislation, you look at the stakeholders. You look at the people that you're trying to affect. You don't use words that you use with your peers. If you're in the independent living centers, you don't want to be talking incrementalism with your peers. But if you're trying to say the words that will work to get something passed, you have to look at the needs of the policymakers, of the politicians. And they may like to talk out in the hinterlands about radical change, but the truth is that's not what they do here. And so you use terminology, you use approaches that are reflective of the audience, the folks that you're trying to affect. And then after it's done you don't worry so much about what you're saying, then you can call it what it really is.

The first obstacle was probably making sure that the disability community functioned as a coalition. In other words, the obstacle was a history of self-destruction. "We have found the enemy and they is us." Too often the factions of the communities—providers versus people with disabilities, people with vision impairments versus hearing impairments, those with developmental disabilities versus physical disabilities—the major obstacle was the lack of unity. And we weren't going to win this major effort unless we stayed together.

The other was to keep the Bush administration on track, because there were the forces of good and the forces of evil—and that's the way we referred to it—within the Bush administration: those who wanted this legislation desperately, the Boyden Grays and Richard Thornburghs of the world, and others within the administration who really didn't, and they were fighting every inch of the way. So even when Attorney General Thornburgh testified in June of '89, nobody knew what he was going to say, because there were two drafts [of his statement], from what we understood, the good draft and the not-so-good draft. And at every turn, the forces of good ultimately prevailed, with the behind-the-scenes work of the Evan Kemps of the world—the Evan Kemps, the Boyden Grays— to keep people on track to deal with the Sununus and some of the other folks who really didn't want to do it at all. But again, the key was that Bush was on the record ten times saying certain things.

It's not just politics. It really is people. It is gaining trust and respect. It is person-to-person dialog and negotiation. We would be giving them information that made sense to them. And so part of it was figuring out these personalities. And they would then figure out the politics with their secretaries and stuff like that. But if we could work with Boyden behind the scenes, get him information, understand what his concerns were and respond to them, we were okay.

Once it passed the Senate I was convinced that it was going to become law. It was just a question of sticking to the strategy, staying together as a coalition, being patient, being persistent, not compromising principle. And then all of a sudden a number of senators who were probably watching it on TV came to the floor. Senator Kennedy had given a passionate speech, giving his family experiences, his son with cancer, other relatives in terms of mental retardation. And then Senator Hatch gave a speech. And remember, we're talking about Senator Hatch. His hair is always cut the same length, every hair is always in the right position. He is as straight as can be. Always under control. He was crying on the Senate floor as he was talking about a relative with disabilities.

It was clearly a very emotional point for a lot of members who understood disability firsthand. And the fact that I could play a role in helping move this was something that I will never forget as long as I live.

27
Lobbying and Gathering Support

———

THE NEW DRAFT OF THE ADA WAS SUBMITTED TO BOTH HOUSES OF Congress on May 9, 1989, and the lobbying effort on the part of the broad disability rights movement began in earnest. The first hurdle was getting it through the Senate—this happened on the night of September 7–8, 1989, with a vote of 76 to 8.[1]

Steering the bill through the House was more difficult. A bill as complex and touching on so many facets of American life had to be sorted through by no less than four separate House committees and six subcommittees, with the potential to derail the entire process in each one.

Here, again, Tony Coelho exerted his considerable influence, not only on a one-to-one basis with various members of Congress but also by recruiting Liz Savage (and, by extension, the Epilepsy Foundation of America) as a central part of the campaign. Savage, in turn, proved to be a remarkable and sophisticated advocate, yet another instance of the community somehow finding the right person to fill the right place at the right time.[2]

Liz Savage
"There was something in it for everyone, and no one group had the power to pull it off on their own."

———

Liz Savage was born in 1955 in Norwich, Connecticut. "When I was about two years old my parents realized that I had poor vision. My vision deteriorated as I grew up, but growing up in the late fifties and the sixties, I was taught to ignore my disability, and the same expectations were made of me as were of other, non-disabled children. . . . The positive part of that is that I was encouraged to be incredibly independent, for which I'm very grateful. I was not patronized or coddled, and I was fortunate in that my parents had the moxie and the wherewithal to ensure that I had the best treatment that modern medicine had to offer, so a lot of my vision was saved. If I hadn't had the access to the specialists I did, I probably would have been blind at age fifteen.

"But there was no assistive technology, there were no support groups for parents, there were no laws that provided accommodations. It was a time when parents didn't really question doctors in a holistic way, so I did a lot of things that in retrospect I shouldn't have done, like contact sports, which for people with low vision have the potential to destabilize your vision by causing a detached retina. So I grew up in a time that was radically different than the life that kids with low vision or other disabilities experience today."

Savage is perhaps best known for her work as chief lobbyist for the Epilepsy Foundation during the time the ADA was working its way through Congress. Currently she is the director of health and housing policy for the Disability Policy Consortium of the Arc of the United States and United Cerebral Palsy, and housing co-anchor of the Consortium for Citizens with Disabilities.

I never went to law school to be a litigator, and that wasn't really my forte. I decided that I wanted to come back to Washington and do policy work. It seemed to me that because I had this personal interest in disability that that would be the most fruitful avenue to pursue. And through people in the [Geraldine] Ferraro [vice-presidential] campaign [of 1984] I met Anne Rosewater, who worked for Congressman George Miller [D-CA] on the Select Committee on Children, who had worked very closely with DREDF, with Pat Wright and Arlene Mayerson and Mary Lou Breslin. I hung out with Pat and learned a lot from her, and did some project for DREDF, the specifics of which I can't remember.

The one thing that distinguishes me from a lot of people in the disability movement is I had a lot of campaign experience before I came to the disability community, and most of my friends were political. I view the world in political ways, which is different from a lot of other people in the community. I was a lawyer and I was interested in civil rights, but I also had a political background, so lobbying seemed like it would be an appropriate avenue to pursue. I had friends in the Ferraro campaign who were hooked up with Pat [Wright] and with DREDF, but there were no openings with DREDF. But then in the summer of '85 there was an opening at the Epilepsy Foundation for an assistant director of government affairs to do lobbying on education and civil rights issues.

Tony Coelho was on their board, and I had met him in July of 1980, during my first summer off, between the first and second year of law school. President Carter was going to [Coelho's] congressional district in Merced to do a town meeting for the Fourth of July, and my former colleagues from the White House asked me to come help organize that. And it was a big coup for Tony, because he was a first-term congressman, to get the President of the United States in his district, and I met him in the context of doing that trip. So he knew me, and we had a lot of mutual colleagues and friends. So when that opening came up I went to talk to his staff, and he wrote a letter of recommendation for me and made it clear that he would like to have me hired, so I was hired.

Tony represented an agricultural district so he was on the Ag. Committee and was very involved in the Democratic Congressional Campaign Committee. He wasn't on any of the committees that considered the Civil Rights Restoration Act or the Fair Housing [Amendments Act], but he would do floor statements. The beauty of Tony Coelho that a lot of people don't see is that he did a lot of his work behind the scenes. The ADA in a lot of respects is due to his savvy and expertise and calling in a lot of chits. . . .

I remember when I first got hired [at the Epilepsy Foundation], I went to thank him and he said, "Well, I want you to raise hell because they're much too conservative and we really need to change that." And I said, "Thanks a lot." They didn't really want to hire me, I don't think, and he really shoved me down their throats. And so I really had to prove myself, in a way. . . .

The Epilepsy Foundation did much of the structural work for the whole [ADA] coalition that wasn't really related to people with epilepsy. I had an assistant, Donna Meltzer, who did a lot of interaction with the grassroots. We sent out many mailings, and not necessarily just to our affiliates but to the whole coalition. The Epilepsy Foundation committed a lot of resources, for which they should be commended. It was thousands of dollars in long distance charges and mailings. There were often times where I was questioned, "Why is this important for people with epilepsy?" and the concern that we were spending much too much time on coalition work and not enough time on work that would benefit the foundation or people with epilepsy. [But] you know, I worked for Tony Coelho. [Laughs.]

Tony was very well liked and so people wanted to be on his bill. The goal then was to show support, and [since] it was a presidential [election] year, to have it on the radar screen for the presidential candidates. And then President Bush in his acceptance speech at the Republican convention talked about the importance of integrating people [with disabilities] into the mainstream, and that was the first time that a presidential candidate had talked about disability issues.

Following that, in September of '88, there was a joint hearing between the House and Senate committees that had jurisdiction, the Senate Labor and Human Resources Committee and the House Subcommittee on Special Education. It was held in this huge room in the Hart Building, and it was the first time that all of the witnesses, with the exception of the chair of the President's Commission on AIDS, either had disabilities or were parents of kids with disabilities. The whole point of the hearing was to educate members of Congress and the public about the extent of disability discrimination. Tony actually testified as the lead sponsor of the bill and told his story.

The gestalt of that hearing was very different. I mean the way he conveyed his story there was different—you know, you get vibes from the audience that are different from the vibes he probably got when he talked to an audience of non-disabled people. I mean historically you'd have organizations who'd had either their executive directors or their non-disabled board members talking about what people with disabilities needed. So this was a dramatic shift, people speaking for themselves, which for them was very empowering. It's the first time that members of Congress heard directly from people with disabilities.

C-SPAN covered it and we took the C-SPAN tape and with Tony's help, I believe it was the film studio of the Democratic National Committee, we got the tape edited down from four hours to a half an hour, and we used it. We had hundreds reproduced and Justin Dart was very involved in this, in funding it, and it was used to educate people with disabilities about discrimination, because they themselves—you know, when you take it for granted you don't see barriers; it becomes part of your life; you don't see it as discrimination.

In 1989 the bill was rewritten to be much more reasonable and was reintroduced in the spring. We went around and got cosponsors, and our basic message was if you were on this bill before, this new version is far more reasonable so there's no reason for you not to be on it again. I think it was early spring and then Tony resigned from Congress in June.

One of the most brilliant things Tony did that nobody knows about is the day he left Congress, he did interviews with the press, and he had talked to President Bush, and he told the *Washington Post* that he had thanked the president for continuing to support the ADA. And at that point there had been no official articulation of the president supporting the ADA. It was a brilliant move that definitely boxed them in.

The ADA was based on two fundamental principles—one, that people with disabilities should have the same civil rights protection, no more and no less, that other minorities enjoy. And then the parallel message was that all of society benefits when people are independent and have the ability to join the social and economic mainstream, and can live, work, and play side by side with their non-disabled peers, and be tax-paying citizens rather than dependent on federal or state or local benefit programs. So that was the essential message, and that's a very difficult message to oppose.

The beauty of the ADA was that there was something in it for everyone and no one group had the power to pull it off on their own. It was not people fighting over their own piece of the pie, to get federal money. We made a concerted effort to make people feel like they were involved and had a role to play. . . . [A]nd I think the one thing about the ADA that was most impressive is that people stood up for each other based on their shared experience of discrimination. Way before the Chapman amendment[3] there were efforts to exclude people with HIV or mental illness, and the folks who beat back those amendments were not the HIV community or mental health community. I did a lot of lobbying visits with people from Paralyzed Veterans of America—quadriplegics—who talked about the kind of discrimination that veterans faced when they came back from World War I or World War II, whether it was attitudinal or in architecture, and they were incredibly eloquent about how discrimination is discrimination and it's just wrong. And members of Congress responded to that, and that was what saved protections for people with HIV and other less fashionable or popular disabilities. And the same thing happened with the Chapman amendment. It was just an issue of conscience, and it wasn't the AIDS groups; it was people like Bob Williams,[4] who had cerebral palsy, who was incredibly eloquent talking about the experiences he had, in a meeting with Boyden Gray at the White House. And you know, there is no comeback to that. . . .

A lot of people did a lot of gutsy things, which if their boards knew about it they probably would have been fired. You come up with a problem like an amendment that excludes people with HIV, and you get a letter that groups can sign onto, and the way you get a coalition letter is you get a couple of mainstream groups who have conservative boards, and if they agree to it then it's easier to get other groups to sign on; it gives you cover, and that's how you form a cohesive message from a cross section of the disability community. Paul Marchand of the ARC was like the dean of the disability community, and he was enormously well respected, and you know if you got the ARC and United Cerebral Palsy and Epilepsy and PVA or Easter Seals on a letter then others would [come along]. . . .

One of the reasons the ADA passed the way it did was because most interest groups just did not pay attention to it. We didn't seek out press attention. In retrospect it was the right decision; the law never would have been enacted [if there had been a great deal of publicity]. I mean there's a divergence of opinion on this; some people think there would have been less backlash if the public was educated on it and if there was more press before it was enacted, but it would have been a totally different bill.

Justin Dart Jr. (continued)
"What you are really talking about is empowerment."

Justin Dart Jr. played many roles in the movement, some public, some behind the scenes. As the co-chair, with Elizabeth M. Boggs, of the Congressional Task Force on the Rights and Empowerment of People with Disabilities from 1988 to 1990, he was an educator, a collector of testimony about the condition of Americans with disabilities, and a catalyst for local activists in all fifty states, providing them with a forum in which to describe their experiences of discrimination and explain their needs and expectations for the new legislation.

Major Owens was chairman of the committee in the House that governed disability policy, and he was very impressed by the statement I made as head of RSA.[5] It was Congressman Owens's idea to form the task force and, by the way, I think that he is one of the most underrated congressmen in the Congress. He is considered to be a far left Democrat. As a matter of fact, the American Conservative Union rated him as zero. I didn't know they rated people zero. They rated Kennedy as 20 percent or something like that, and Major Owens rated *zero*. But he happened to chair the oversight hearing where I made my statement of conscience, and he was impressed with that, so he asked me when I got fired to head up this task force.

I did it full time for several years. Boy, we had magnificent people on that. And I think that was, in terms of federal appointments, by far the most productive contribution that I made. We had people like Pat Wright and a real hall of fame group on there. Elizabeth Boggs was the co-chair. I think she walked on the water, you know. We had people from ADAPT on it, Wade Blank or somebody.

I think for that point in time we had a fairly significant cross-disability group and a fairly radical departure, that had people with psychiatric disabilities, people with AIDS. It took me six months to get the group to agree to have a person with AIDS on it as opposed to an advocate *for* persons with AIDS. They said, "Well, [he or she] will die." And I said, "Of course, they will die, but meanwhile we will have someone from that community on our task force. We are not into empowering paternalists."

Major Owens taught me a lot of things. He is a brilliant person. When I was testifying before him, he and I saw these issues as rights issues. He told me in a public hearing, and then he told me in private, "Mr. Dart, what you are really talking about is not simply civil rights and not simply independence, what you are really talking about is empowerment." So he is the one that said, "Now this is going to be the task force not only on the rights, but on the rights and the *empowerment* of people with disabilities." And he led me into this concept of empowerment.

He was a tough man to work for. Not that he nitpicked, he didn't, but he insisted that I live up to my philosophy. And he would come down and say, "Well, is this constituency represented? How well is it represented?"

And he never tried to use me. Remember, I was a Reagan appointee a lot of this time. Well, not right in the beginning, because I had just been fired. Then I was reappointed to the National Council and so once again I was a Reagan appointee. And I was campaigning for Republicans, and Owens is as devout a Democrat as you can possibly get. And I never felt that he tried to manipulate me. I don't remember a single word he ever said which made me think that he was arguing about politics or trying to tell me to be a Democrat, or trying to tell me to say things which would tend to support Democrats as just opposed to disability and human rights. He is a totally remarkable person.

Theoretically it was an objective task force that went around gathering information. You have public hearings, public forums. Some of them were official congressional hearings in the sense that Congressman Owens would come and hold it. And sometimes he held it with other congressmen. We had one like that in Boston, and we had one in Houston, and we had one in Washington. We did at least one in every state. The public was invited to come in, and not just consumers, but parents and service providers, and even opponents of ADA. Everyone would have five minutes to speak, first come first serve, with some exceptions. Very busy people we put first, outstanding advocates. And we would tape record all of these things. And then they would bring in written documents. They could bring in anything they wanted. Some brought big, thick things. People with all kinds of disabilities, all kinds of levels of expertise, and service providers, doctors, you know just about anybody you could think of.

I remember one place where a couple of people testified who had been incarcerated in nursing homes for years about how their basic human dignity and civil rights were abused every day. And that was impressive. And then some of the testimony about psychiatric disability and the extreme oppression that those people face, and some also having to do with the ghastly institutions that they are sometimes forced to be in and those kinds of things.

I would give introductory remarks and they were hardly objective remarks. I mean I was a 150 percent advocate and so this task force was not nonpartisan. It was bipartisan in that it had Republicans and Democrats on it. But if you had been an opponent of the law sitting there you would not have been confused that we were even partly on your side.

And we have a big pile of cartons, boxes of documents; I think they are still over at the President's Committee on the Employment of People with Disabilities. Now, I don't think that we got as many discrimination diaries[6] as we would have liked to have gotten, but we did get a lot of letters and a lot of stories. Some people did keep some diaries that were very moving and persuasive, and we collected all of these boxes of several thousand documents and we took them [into the Capitol] and symbolically gave them to the Congress. I think there was a photograph from the press of me sitting there with all of these boxes.

The local advocates in these hearings were magnificent. You talk about being empowered—I didn't have advance people to set up these meetings. The local people, the real grassroots patriots, set up these meetings. And many times they paid for the rooms. And they would arrange all kinds of things, depending on the state. A lot of times I just went out there alone and they had set up the entire meeting, all of the microphones, the room, everything. For example, in Chicago, they hired a huge room in some hotel and they had about three hundred and fifty people, people standing up around the walls in there. And the advocates in Chicago paid for that. So I was not the only godfather of this venture. That was a role played by advocates in every community.

Lex Frieden (continued)
"This gentleman here is going to get me a disabled baby to hold and we're going to vote for the ADA."

Lex Frieden recounts two examples of disability rights lobbying. Although he had moved back to Texas after leaving the NCD, Frieden still visited Washington to lobby on behalf of the ADA

On the Senate side Senator Hatch was a leader of the Republicans. Hatch had indicated that he believed it was a Democratic bill and he wasn't going to support it. We were running around all over the Hill trying to meet with senators and representatives to get them to support this bill. Hatch's appointment secretary had said he was too busy even to a meet advocates from Utah whom we had asked to go up there to talk to him.

So I was up there one afternoon, the day before the vote. Hatch was still against it. Justin Dart, who came by, said, "What can I do? I've talked to as many people as I can." I said, "Look, come with me. We're going to go and see Senator Hatch." So Justin said, "Okay, whatever I can do."

We went to Hatch's office.

"Can we see Senator Hatch?"

"Who's calling?" the appointment secretary said.

I said, "Well, it's Lex Frieden."

She said, "Oh, I'm sorry, Mr. Frieden, his schedule is busy."

"Okay, would you please tell the senator that Mr. Justin Dart is here with me and wishes to have a moment."

"Mr. Dart?"

"Yes, Mr. Dart."

Two minutes later she came back and said, "Mr. Dart, if you'll come with me through this door, please."

He went alone. About two minutes later, I mean a short period of time, Hatch came out, shook hands with me. I'm wondering—what's happened here?

He said, "Good to see you all, look forward to seeing you all tomorrow."

I said to Justin, "What happened?"

Justin said, "He agreed with us."

I don't know what transpired, I have no idea. But nobody else could have gotten in to see him. Nobody. So that was just one of those things.

. . .

I went to see a Texas congressman who was the head of the committee where all the civil rights bills go through in the House of Representatives. Congressman [Jack] Brooks from East Texas. Congressman Brooks, while he was a Democrat, was regarded as a conservative Texas Democrat. Many people would say he was more like a Republican than a Democrat. He didn't like this ADA bill. He didn't think that there should be rights for people with disabilities like there should be—and he thought there should be—rights for black people and women and other minorities.

He said, "If you want me to vote to put more money into education for disabled people, I'm more than happy to do that. But, the people are not going to support this. They had a hard time supporting [President] Johnson on the business with the civil rights, and now you want me to support the same for people with disabilities."

I said, "Well, sir, you'd get a lot of votes out of it. Yes sir, I'm a psychologist and I've studied this. There are studies that indicate that companies, for example, that reach out to provide opportunities for people with disabilities have a better reputation than those companies that don't. I can give you an example."

I told him about an oil company in Sweden that had gas pumps that were accessible and another one that didn't. They did a survey and found out the reason people felt like the first company was a better one to trade at was because they had services for people with disabilities.

"Do you think I could get votes by holding a disabled baby?"

I said, "Well, sir, if you get votes by holding a baby, I guess one with a disability would be just as good."

"Yes," he said, "I like the sound of that. I'm in a close race this time, can you get people with disabilities to come down and help me?"

I said, "Yes, what do you want them to do? Do you want them to line up on the street and cheer for you? You want us to give you an award? I mean, what can we do to help you?"

He said, "All those things, but if you give me a disabled baby to hold, that'd be real good."

I said, "Whatever you want, I'll do."

"All right, we have a deal then. I'm going to support your act, you're going to get me re-elected."

We walked out of there and he said to his staff, "This gentleman here is going to get me a disabled baby to hold and we're going to vote for the ADA."

So that was Congressman Brooks, and his committee had to approve it before it could go to the floor of the House of Representatives. In the hearing, Steny Hoyer, who was the principal House proponent, was climbing around on his hands and knees behind these members of Congress, talking to them, trying to answer questions that they had, resolve fears that they had about this law.

At a critical point in the hearing, a bell sounded, calling for a vote on the House floor. Brooks said, "We've been discussing this far too long, it's time to take a vote here and now, before we go to the House floor." The members were saying, "We're sorry, we just had a call, we'll come back and have more debate later." He said, "No, we're taking a vote now. Sergeant-at-arms, lock the doors. Nobody's leaving here until a vote is taken, and it will be taken now. You know my position on it."

The sergeant-at-arms locked the door, the vote was taken, and it passed, probably by a majority of one or two. At that time there wasn't the kind of consensus that the public saw on final passage. On final passage, why would you vote against it if you knew it was going to pass anyway? So we had a great majority by then.

But the key was in these committees, whether we could get it through each one of the committees, one by one.

28
Mobilizing the Community

C IVIL RIGHTS LEGISLATION, WHEN PASSED, IS ALMOST ALWAYS A response to pressure from the public, exerted in a variety of ways. The ADA was no exception. At first, this effort, as some of the ADA point people have been candid enough to admit, was somewhat sketchy, more "smoke and mirrors" than an actual, engaged constituency. But as time went on, and the message spread either through personal meetings such as those organized by Justin Dart and the Owen task force, through the disability press, or by simple word of mouth, more and more people became engaged and then committed to seeing the ADA through to final passage.

Marilyn Golden
"People rallied in a huge way."

One of those most involved in making this happen was Marilyn Golden. She was already an experienced activist, although she considered herself "quite 'green' in terms of national advocacy" when her work on ADA began.

Golden was born in 1954 in San Antonio. After graduating from Brandeis with a degree in sociology, she returned to Texas and became the volunteer social action codirector of the Coalition for Barrier Free Living in Houston in 1977 and, in 1978, a founder of the Coalition of Texans with Disabilities. That same year she moved again, this time to California, where she became director of Access California, an information center "on architectural accessibility run by the City of Oakland. I got to know other leaders and advocates in the San Francisco Bay area." In 1987, she coordinated the involvement of local advocates with ADAPT's protests against the American Public Transit Association, in the course of which she became acquainted with people at DREDF, especially Mary Lou Breslin. "I chose working at DREDF because I would get a chance to work with Mary Lou, and it was the best choice I ever made."

Golden thus wore several hats during the campaign to pass the ADA. As an expert on architectural and transportation access, she was involved with developing the parts of the bill related to these topics, immersing herself in the arcana of over the-road-bus modifications and access requirements for passenger and commuter trains. Golden was also, together with Liz Savage and Breslin, instrumental in identifying and rallying grassroots groups around the country. And so, when a particular senator or congressperson needed to be "pressed," it was often Marilyn Golden who got the ball rolling.

During the Senate portion of the ADA of 1989, which was before the House, we needed grassroots pressure for key senators, and since there aren't that many senators, relatively speaking, I was able to do the calls. Liz Savage, who I was working with very, very closely, had assigned me a lot of the grassroots organizing. And so I would call into a state any leadership that we knew, or call nearby states, if we didn't know anyone in that state. I looked at who I knew and I looked at who my colleagues knew, and we would talk to those leaders, "We need letters going to Senator Dah-dah-dah, letters and calls." And then I would try to assess as best I could, by talking to them on the phone, whether there would be follow-through, and get from them other names, and then call the other people they mentioned. And we would hear sometimes that a certain member, all of a sudden, was getting better. We would hear, anecdotally. So we knew a little bit from that whether it was working. But a lot of it was a guess. But we did get letters coming in and we did have some sense that it worked.

When the bill went to the House, it was far too big for one person to make all those calls, for so many members of Congress. So the idea evolved to develop a system—we called it ADA Regional Contact Persons—that divided the country up into twenty-five groups. It really varied. For example, Texas was one region, but New York was two. There's New York City and there's the rest of the state. And the same with Illinois. There's Chicago and there's the rest of the state, and if you don't know that about that state, you don't know that state in terms of grassroots organizing.

And so in each of these regions of the country, which could be part of a state, one state, or several states, I would find one, or possibly two, but usually one person that would serve as ADA regional contact person. Usually I asked people I knew from working grassroots on the Senate side, or others I knew from the disability community. I tried to find people that were responsible and really together.

Their primary job was to get others writing letters, making calls to particular members of Congress when that was needed, mostly because they were on one of the many committees that considered the ADA— four formal committees considered it, and the fifth, the Small Business Committee, had a role, and then the conference committee.

And it worked, not perfectly, but, largely, and sometimes it worked very well. Sometimes something interesting would happen locally that they fed back to us. Whether it was a wonderful rally that they held, or they made buttons that no one had ever seen before in the ADA, that were passed around DC, or whether some local article came out that had to be countered, or some presentation by a member of Congress saying something negative about the ADA, that needed to be countered. We would hear about it. Certainly, information went out; but it also came in. I would send them periodic updates every few weeks: what's happening with the bill, this committee, that committee, what was needed.

At one point, I think it was with Bob Michel, the Republican House leader, on his position on a particular committee, we needed a lot of pressure, and so we ended up asking the ADA regional contact people in the non-Chicago part of Illinois, to hold peaceful, very polite picketing, continuous, as much as possible, at his offices. And it was really interesting because it worked, and his position softened up fairly quickly. We heard stories about how their staff was bringing coffee in the morning 'cause it was very cold outside. This was not a part of the country that was ready to thumb its nose at protests, and so it didn't take much. I remember getting the assignment and calling the people, and it happened fairly quickly.

The best people in the state would make time in their busy lives to do this. Or at least we hoped so. Largely, I think, they did. Why? Because people wanted their civil rights. It was clear that the community was ready but not organized yet. They needed to be organized. But it was ready, and people rallied in a huge way. We've said during the battle, and since, that the easiest issue to get complete union on in the disability community, nationwide, is civil rights. It's harder on other issues, because this organization will have a stake in one agency or another. We get "turf battles," and there's a variety of conflicts that come up. But the seeds of unity were there, the support was there, not only because every organization agreed, philosophically, that people with disabilities needed civil rights, but because there was this community awareness of what was going on across the country. And so it set the community up, subsequently, to be ardently, vigorously protective of the ADA.

It was incredibly interesting to be in touch with people with disabilities all over the country. I was very fortunate to be the person in that position.

Cyndi Jones (continued)
"People sacrificed a lot to do this."

In the era before the Internet, the one sure way to reach the disability community was through the disability press. Cyndi Jones and Bill Stothers at *Mainstream* in San Diego were an obvious choice, then, to play a role informing and then mobilizing advocates for passage of the ADA.

Justin Dart came to San Diego for a meeting one day, and he invited Bill and I over to have lunch. It might have been '87, '88. He had this idea about the civil rights bill. He wanted to know our opinion. Did we think it could get done? I said, "Well, it's a Republican presidency. I don't know, Justin."

You have to understand people were very frustrated because public transportation still was not accessible under 504. A lot of cities didn't have lifts on buses. A lot of stuff under 504 was not being enforced. Some stuff was being litigated, but basically there was a huge frustration in the community that here we had gone through all of this effort to pass 504, and nothing was happening.

He asked if we would support it and we said, "Yes, if you think you can get it passed, we'll help you. The only concern we have is that we don't want to screw up what little rights we have under 504. We don't want to kill it, even though it's not where it needs to be."

Now they're submitting the ADA to Congress, and the magazine is pushing hard. Almost every issue we have something in there about writing your congressman.

This was between the first round—from '86 to '88. Dukakis and Bush were running in '88, and we ran a photo on the cover of the magazine of the candidates, and we do this debate between the two. In that same issue, September of '88, we ran a listing of everybody in Congress who had signed on to the ADA. We wanted people to know who their congressmen were, if they were supporting it or not. We told people, if their congressman had signed on to the ADA, we wanted them to call and thank them. If someone was running for office, they needed to talk about the ADA. We tried to raise the consciousness of not only our readers but the people in Congress. If they hadn't signed on, they should know it was going to cost them. Every issue for two years or longer we ran something about ADA. It almost got to the point where we were embarrassed. It's like, "Don't you have any other stories?"

In the debates between Bush and Dukakis, Bush said he would sign the ADA. He would bring disabled Americans into the mainstream. We couldn't get Dukakis to make that statement to save his life.

In 1990 we're coming up on the ADA. I went to the meeting that they had. The meeting was with the core group—Paul Marchand and CCD [Consortium for Citizens with Disabilities]. I remember one of the woman staffers at the judiciary committee, who came out and was talking to us. She said, "If we're in a small town and they have two stores, and one of them goes bankrupt because they have to make it accessible, then the town will only have one store. It will basically be a monopoly." I looked at the woman and I said, "If you have two stores in that small town and both of them are inaccessible, then I can't shop in either one." She hadn't thought about it. I feel like she got it. One by one you get it. I just had the right thing to say, and you oftentimes don't have the exact right thing, but that was the right thing. All of a sudden it was like an "Aha!" experience for that lady. I felt pretty good about that one.

During this time period we're working, trying to keep people calling and sending letters. E-mail wasn't so much a big deal yet. People were writing letters. Any time they wound up in Washington they were doing lobbying. This was a real nickel-and-dime thing. You think of the poorest population trying to do this work. The poorest of the poor weren't the ones doing the work. It was the people who really weren't the poorest of the poor in terms of the disability movement; it was the people who had jobs.

There was a lot of sacrifice. Diane Coleman sold her house in Los Angeles, which was a high-priced market, and she went to somewhere in Nowheresville, Tennessee, and spent the money she made from her house doing advocacy work. Same thing with Mark Johnson. Mark Johnson sold his house in Denver, Colorado, and went to Alpharetta, Georgia, and was able to do advocacy for two years on the differential

in the housing market. I say those things because people need to understand that people sacrificed a lot to do this. You probably have tons of
other stories of what people gave up and sold and did.

Diane Coleman and Mark Johnson, they were among the few who
owned a house. Most people didn't own a house. You don't have a job
because you don't have accessible transportation, and you can't get a job
anyway because you're not educated because you had this stupid special
education that didn't teach you anything. You couldn't get a group of people to demonstrate because you could only get two people in your van if
you're lucky. How do you get a hundred people to a demonstration site?
You can, but it's really complicated. So I think that the organizing was really
grassroots, and that's also the reason why a lot of times the media didn't see
the movement. You couldn't see it. You couldn't get people in one location
to be the movement, so people were primarily calling and writing.

Justin went around to all the states and was accumulating stories of
discrimination. One of the things we had to do was educate people that
they were discriminated against. It's like, "You've been down so long it
looks like up to me." You forget that you should expect to go in the front
door of a business. You forget that you should be able to go to the bathroom in a restaurant. You've been using alternative means of getting the
job done for so long that you forget that you should be treated like everybody else. So a lot of that education was not just accumulating stories,
but educating people about what constituted discrimination. That was
all going on during that whole time.

Denise Figueroa
"I was starting to feel like . . . Wow! This could really happen."

———

Denise Figueroa was an early activist in New York City, first as a member of
SOFEDUP, a disabled students' group in the early seventies, then with Disabled in Action, one of the first direct action groups, organized in large part
by Judith Heumann.

Born in 1954, Figueroa contracted polio when she was nine months old, "so
I grew up as a person with a disability. . . . I don't recall not being disabled."
Her family moved from Brooklyn to Connecticut when she started school. "I
was the only kid with a disability in town. They didn't have special education,

and, of course, that was prior to IDEA [Individuals with Disabilities Education Act] anyway, so they really didn't have many accommodations for kids with disabilities. In my case, it actually was a positive, because what they did was instead of me climbing the steps for the school bus—because I used braces and crutches—they just sent a cab for me. They sent me to school every day by cab, and I went to school with all the rest of the kids." When her family moved back to New York, however, Figueroa was put into what were then called "health preservation classes." "That was my first experience with being segregated as a result of having a disability. I was very unhappy, very uncomfortable with it. . . . It was four grades in one classroom, a very poor education."

By the time of the ADA campaign, Figueroa was a seasoned activist, the founder and director of the Troy [NY] Center for Independent Living, and beginning to make her mark on the national scene as a board member (and eventually president) of the National Council on Independent Living. NCIL, founded in 1982 as an all-volunteer, nonprofit organization, had already played an important role in advocating for the passage of the Civil Rights Restoration Act of 1987 and the Fair Housing Amendments Act of 1988. Under the leadership (from 1986 to 1989) of independent living activist Marca Bristo,[1] NCIL then became an important part of the ADA coalition.

———

[The campaign for Section] 504 [in the 1970s] had been so exciting. I was so young, and it was all so new. [But] a lot of years had gone by, by the time the ADA came around. I guess I was jaded by all of the previous experiences, and wasn't so sure that we were ever really going to accomplish this. I wanted it to happen, but at the same time we had been through so much in terms of the Reagan years. . . .

I was up here [in Albany, NY] and Justin came [to hold a hearing for the task force]. We had a meeting at the Marriott Hotel. We brought consumers. It was energizing, and reaffirmed my feelings to hear other people talk about their experiences, the discrimination that they had faced. It reinforced why we had to be doing this. One of our consumers who was there, Roberta Duke, a woman labeled as mentally retarded, grew up in institutions and talked about her experience. She came to do her testimony, and I cried. It wasn't that I cried feeling sorry for her. I was just connecting so much. She was very aware of how much she had been discriminated against, and how poorly she had been treated, and it was the first time she was getting to put into words, I think, that this wasn't fair, and that this wasn't the right way to be treated. It was a tremendously moving experience. Even to think about it now, it's moving.

I think that whole process re-energized me. I had just started the center only in the last three years, and you get bogged down in all the administrative mumbo-jumbo stuff. Even being on the NCIL board was more stuff to bog you down, dealing with their bylaws and anything else that you had to deal with. But this was the stuff you were in it for, and that just gives you energy. . . .

The first march that I remember doing for the ADA was when my daughter was only four months old. I was carrying her in the rain, in the march to the White House with Justin Dart and Marca Bristo, leading the pack to advocate for the ADA. That was in '89. I was on the NCIL board at the time, and I was the executive director of the independent living center, so I was advocating as an independent living center director, as a NCIL board member, and as an individual.

We wrote letters and met with our congressman. We had some pretty positive congresspeople who were supportive of the ADA. New York was an important state, I think, in having so many representatives in Washington. It was important to get the New York state delegation on board with it. At the time we had Senator [Patrick] Moynihan [D] and Senator [Al] D'Amato [R]. D'Amato was a character, and not somebody who was on board so easily. That was a fight. He was from Long Island, and I know the folks from Long Island really had to go after him to get him to sign on. I think he voted for the ADA. I'm fairly certain he did, but he was kicking and screaming all along the way. . . .

I have to say that I was pleasantly surprised—I was amazed at how we had grown as a community, to be able to organize the marches in Washington, and the recognition that we had gotten by that point was impressive to me. We actually were being listened to. When we fought for the Rehab Act [in 1972–73], we were such a small community, we were so splintered. I think the really neat thing was just to see how many people we got out for that march in the rain, and the impression that we made in the White House.

I was re-energized by it because up until that point I was starting to feel like, "Aw man, things are getting really bad here." It was very exciting. So it was easy to write the letters, and it was easy to make the phone calls at that point because it was just, you know, "Wow! This could really happen."

29
Experts

———

THE GERMAN STATESMAN OTTO VON BISMARK ONCE FAMOUSLY declared that "laws are like sausages; it is better not to see them made." Certainly, lawmaking can be complicated, arcane, even sordid. Deals are cut, agreements reached, favors traded, and often no one knows for certain what the final product will be until the law is passed and enacted. The ADA was no exception. Indeed, large parts of it were ground out, sentence by sentence, in negotiations the details of which are for the most part recorded only in the memories of those who were present.

Arlene Mayerson (continued)
"There was never a time when there wasn't a lot of work to do."

———

One of the experts the community turned to during this process was attorney Arlene Mayerson. Mayerson would get "down in the weeds" with senators, members of Congress, and congressional and White House staff to make sure that the actual words of the law did what the disability community wanted them to do and try to steer clear of amendments or other changes designed to limit or even kill the bill.

———

The critical stuff in the Senate happened in a condensed-enough period that I could be there, not through everything, but for those few months when a lot of things happened.

In the House, I was there sometimes, but I was also here [in California] sometimes. The fax, its use as a tool of communication, was somewhat new during that period. Not only did it allow me to be very involved without being physically present, it also allowed us—those on the East and West coasts—to work around the clock, which we did, often times.

I was most involved in the [House] Judiciary Committee. Small business had a hearing that I actually testified at, with a disabled person from the National Federation of Independent Businesses who said that people shouldn't have to have disabled people around them if it made them uncomfortable. That was one of those amazing things where you have someone who is a beneficiary of the bill speaking out against it. [It was amazing to me] that the NFIB would make the decision to use someone who had that much internalized prejudice. It was one of those situations where if you change it from disability to any other group, if you had a Jewish person testifying that he thought people shouldn't be subjected to Jews if they didn't want to be—there's no way anyone would even think that would be something that you would want to promote in a congressional hearing. So I was in the position there of speaking out against his position, with him sitting there, using a wheelchair.

On the House side there were a lot more questions that came up about the actual implications of the bill. That had been done to a certain extent on the Senate side, but on the House side it was really hopping.

Steny Hoyer, majority whip, was in charge of coordinating what was happening in all the various committees, and it was a very unique role, since he wasn't on any of them. So we were working very closely with his office with amendments that were constantly coming up by members [in response to] particular things that were being raised by their constituents. For instance, the police didn't want to have to wait until post-offer [of employment] to do a psychological exam.[1] They thought that they should be able to do that pre-offer. That was a perfect example where he would say, "We need to know by tomorrow how many police departments are in fact doing post-offer psychological exams, because if there are, then obviously it's not so much of a hardship." Every time there was a potential amendment, it would be our job to do [something like] that.

What I would do in response to that kind of amendment was to network really quickly, and call someone who would have contact with people who knew police work. And that is just one example. Sometimes it would be a legal issue, and then it would be more turning to the books. Sometimes it would just be a hypothetical that had really no answer other than what we made up. For instance, "Do you have to get rid of stools at bars?" At the time no one had really thought about stools at bars, so we would get together and think, "Well, let's see, no, as long as there is equivalent accessible seating." Because you wanted to come out with the answer "no," because people wanted to continue to have their bar stools. But you had to have a reason for it. . . .

I went to a lot of meetings, and I did a lot of talking, but there was also a lot of written work that needed to be produced, binders and binders of questions about the ADA and its implications. I'd sit there at a desk with fifty questions and write short, concise, readable answers. And then write a letter to someone who had made an inquiry, and then do a legal analysis, and then get fifty more questions. There was never a time when there wasn't a lot of work to do, when I would ever feel like there wasn't something that needed to be done.

And at the same time, the last-minute negotiations were going on in the White House, and I was very involved in those. A lot of it was so behind the scenes, and is so forgotten, even by people that were close to me. But there were critical things that happened in the ADA then. Just the other day, I had a meeting with someone who explained to me how the ADA covers the lessor and the lessee, and the definition of who was covered by public accommodations. That was one of the things that happened in this last-minute White House negotiation and which I was instrumental in drafting.

What happened was, there were members of the Judiciary Committee, very right wing conservative members, who wanted amendments, and they were really pushing the White House. They thought the White House hadn't carried any water for them as Republicans, and so they opened the door to wanting a few things. They wanted there to be a definition of "direct threat,"[2] because they were trying to appease their own constituencies about that. And they wanted a definition of "undue hardship."[3] The way the 504 regs had been written, it looked like you had to look at the entire entity to determine undue hardship. So they were concerned about multi-facility corporations that had a budget that was unbelievably large nationally, but their local store in some rural town was really operating at a deficit. How much renovation would they have to do? Would you compare their undue hardship to the revenues of that store, or to the entire company?

We, at that point, had discovered that there were actually some things *we* wanted too, and we had already gone to Congressman Hoyer to try to figure out if we could get them. But the rules of the game at that point were that everything was closed. So actually *them* wanting some things was a good opportunity for *us*.

What we had realized was that in the Senate [version] the definition of "public accommodation" had been done very quickly, and it seemed like it covered everyone. Then this incident had come up. Evan Kemp had been asked to speak at an American Bar Association convention. He got to the place and there were steps, and he couldn't get in. It was an outrage, and he was in the cold, etc. etc. We looked at our ADA and realized, because the way the law was written at the time, the ABA wouldn't have been on the list we had made of "public accommodations." So we were like, "Whoa." This was a big omission.

So our goal was to get a different definition of public accommodations. Steny was saying, "We can't just go in there with a whole new thing." At the time the bill said, "A public accommodation cannot discriminate." We thought if we could change it to "Anyone who owns, operates, leases, or leases to a public accommodation" [that that would fix the problem]. We went in saying it was a technical amendment, a clarifying amendment, it wasn't a substantive amendment. And for some reason they bought that, but when you think about it—that's huge.

So we were called to the White House, me and Pat Wright and Chai Feldblum, for this meeting with Boyden Gray and his chief lawyer working on this at the time. We negotiated a deal, one of those things where we walked out, and it was like, "Yes!" because we got things that were so critical to us, and we had given up basically nothing.

Karen Peltz Strauss
"This is incredible, this is exactly the vehicle that we had wanted."

Born in September 1956, in Brooklyn, Karen Peltz Strauss grew up in a family where politics was always in the air. "My parents were socially conscious, very liberal Democrats, probably to the left of most people, and I grew up with a strong social conscience because of them." Although she would eventually become an attorney at Gallaudet University, Peltz Strauss never met a deaf person before becoming an adult. "The only contact that I had with anybody that was deaf was that there were two little girls living in the apartment building across the street from us, and they had deaf parents. And I recall other children being very nasty to them, and making fun of them, because their parents were deaf."

When Peltz Strauss started college at Boston University in 1974, she first majored in special education and then in psychology. She went to law school at the University of Pennsylvania, where she worked for the Penn Legal Assistance Office operated by the university. After graduating, she went to the Institute of Public Representation, a law clinic at the Georgetown University Law Center. "And that's where I really got involved in disability work. They had a thriving disability law practice."

In the early 1980s Peltz Strauss was pivotal in pulling together a coalition to lobby for passage of the Voting Accessibility for the Elderly and Handicapped Act of 1984. This work brought her in contact with the American Coalition of Citizens with Disabilities, the National Association of the Deaf, and the National Center for Law and the Deaf at Gallaudet, where she eventually took a position as attorney and lobbyist. It was in this capacity that Karen Peltz Strauss became point person for drafting Title IV of the ADA, the section dealing with telecommunications for people who are deaf, hard of hearing, or speech impaired. Since then she has literally written the book on communications access: *A New Civil Right: Telecommunications Equality for Deaf and Hard of Hearing Americans* (2006).

I look at the twenty-five years in which I've been involved in these issues and it's like leap years. The gains have been just astronomical. Back then there were no [telephone] relay services, there were hardly any TTYs,[4] even. Some police stations had them, most didn't. Most governmental entities didn't have them, and even if they did, they were the old-fashioned TTYs, one of those six-hundred-pound teletypewriters; mammoth machines that were incredibly slow, incredibly ineffective. And if the place you wanted to call didn't have a TTY, you were out of luck. The only way that you could get to that individual was to literally get in your car and go.

I was constantly going up to the Hill when the Deaf President Now campaign began in March of '88. I had been doing some work on the Hill on hearing aid compatibility—to make telephones accessible to people who use hearing aids. And the difference that DPN made was extraordinary. Before DPN, if I entered a congressional office and said, "I'm from the National Law Center at Gallaudet University," they'd say, "What's that?" even though it was just down the block. After DPN, overnight it became, "Oh, welcome. Come in and let me talk to you."

It was not only a wonderful example of self-empowerment; it also brought the issues of America's Deaf population to the rest of the country and to the attention of Congress. As a result, within weeks, we started seeing pending legislation that affected this community getting enacted. Two examples were the Assistive Technologies Act, and the National Institute on Deafness and Other Communication Disorders Act. Both bills got passed, and then the Hearing Aid Compatibility bill[5] also passed right after DPN.

And our work on relay services mushroomed. We had been pushing Congress to write a bill or do something about the FCC to get them to move on relay services. They weren't moving it. Al Gore actually sent a letter to the FCC urging consideration of a petition for interstate relay services that had been pending. But right after DPN the FCC started responding and within two weeks, by the end of March—this is how fast everything was going—they released a new notice asking for proposals to implement the petition. It was literally overnight.

Then things slowed up a bit, but not all that much, because if you look at when the ADA was introduced and when it was passed, I can't imagine a law like that getting passed so fast now. And I firmly believe that it had to do with DPN.

There was a new respect for the Deaf community, even by other disability groups that had never previously worked with the Deaf community. Up until that point the Deaf community had always been segregated in its efforts on the Hill. I don't think the physical disability community ever made much of an effort to reach out to the Deaf community before the ADA. I think this was because of the huge language barrier. For example, there was never any funding for interpreters at disability meetings. And whether it was the ADA or, in part, the Deaf President Now movement, there's no question that after that the efforts became much more coordinated.

I remember the exact moment I first heard of the ADA. We were working on our relay legislation. We started around 1987 or '88, drafting something that we were going to bring to Congress as a stand-alone bill. And I remember one day being in the office (at the National Center for Law and the Deaf) and Sy DuBow, who was the executive director of the Center, coming in, standing there holding this document in his hand saying, "Look what they're trying to do." And it was from National Council on Disability, basically the ADA blueprint, *Toward Independence*.

The problem was that they were talking initially about revamping all of the Section 504 regs. I mean, they were going to redo *everything*. And given our background with the Reagan administration, we were convinced that this was a ploy. Everybody had worked so hard on getting what we had in terms of those regulations, and we thought, "This is a disaster, they're going to start all over, this can't be." That was my first thought. I remember Justin Dart also had gotten a little bit involved in the voting access issue as well. I really knew nothing about him. I learned about him from afar. "Who *is* this man?" I was concerned about the involvement of some rich Republican who might be working with the Reagan administration to hurt our efforts. Who knew?

The other thought that we had was: "This is preposterous, how could they possibly expect to cover all of these private entities? There's no way this will ever go through." So, while we thought it was a weird concept, we also weren't very worried about it because it was *so* outlandish. I remember walking back into my office and saying, "Eh, I'm not going to worry about it."

Then, in January of 1989, the National Council on Disability came to us and said, "We're going through with this and we need to know from the different disability constituencies what they want." And so we, the Law Center, contacted all of the Deaf and hard of hearing leaders around the country. We had a meeting, March 8th, 1989, at Gallaudet. We worked with various Deaf leaders to put it together, a face-to-face gathering and literally sat around the table to try to prioritize what we wanted.

The list was very, very long. Everyone agreed that relay services was at the top of the list, but the second thing on the list, which was just as important, was closed captioning on TV programming. We actually wanted to go forward with captioning in the ADA, but we were told in no uncertain terms by staffers on the Hill, "Over our dead bodies are we putting this in the bill." The problem was that the Motion Picture Association of

America was very strong, and it had promised to kill the whole ADA if we went forward with a captioning mandate. So instead, we went forward with the Decoder Circuitry Act of 1990, which said all TVs with screens larger than 13 inches had to have decoder circuitry built in to show captions. That was designed to widen the audience of people able to receive captions, and provide more of a business impetus to the television programmers and stations to provide captions on their programming. But we also agreed at this March meeting to include things like sign language interpreters and assistive listening devices and other accommodations.

Of course, we talked about what were the merits of attaching our relay service proposal to this bill and whether doing so would be beneficial or not. But I remember that discussion being fairly short. I remember saying, "This is incredible, this is exactly the vehicle that we had wanted." There was really very little thought given to not joining this bandwagon.

We were a bit concerned about whether our relay demands would fit into a nondiscrimination bill like this. Title IV of the ADA required the establishment of a nationwide relay service system, and we weren't real hopeful that Congress would accept that as a civil right—that you couldn't just prohibit discrimination, you actually had to *do* something to remedy that discrimination. And then we looked around and saw how other segments of the disability community were doing this with transportation, actually requiring something to be done, putting in requirements for buses and trains to be accessible. So we realized our telephone section could fit right in. That was what was so great. We literally took the stand-alone relay bill we'd written and put it into the ADA as Title IV. We had been working on the bill for at least a year or a year and a half, so we had a complete draft.

I was the point person and lawyer in terms of the drafting. I didn't make the decisions on the bill's content by myself, rather I got feedback from a task force that we had created at Gallaudet, consisting of Deaf and hard of hearing people. So I would be the one corresponding with the Hill, but I would communicate on a regular basis with Al Sonnenstrahl who was the head of TDI [Telecommunications for the Deaf][6] and others in the Deaf community.

Mostly we went through Senator McCain's office. McCain had a Deaf person on his staff and was very sympathetic to our issues. Basically, anything we asked for, his office put into the bill.

It was our goal to make clear that relay services were not a social service but a civil right. The best analogy is with people in rural communities who live further away from the telephone public switching stations, the central offices. It costs more to provide telephone service to those rural communities, but no one would expect people in those communities to pay more. Instead, when a public utility commission sets the rates, they gather up all of these costs together so that everybody pays equally. It's all for one and one for all, basically. And so our argument was: do the same thing for people with disabilities. Consider this just another utility service. Just the way people who live in rural and urban communities have an equal right to affordable telephone service, so the same thing should be true for people with disabilities. And if you look at relay services as part of a telephone utility service, then it should not be funded by a tax or government appropriations.

What we absolutely didn't want was for there to be a line item on people's phone bill that said, "Services for the deaf" or whatever. We fought vigorously against this, it became one of the biggest debates: whether surcharges could be allowed for the interstate part of relay services. On the Senate side we won, and got surcharges prohibited; on the House side we lost, and they took out the prohibition. So when it went to the FCC, surcharges were permitted to pay for interstate relay service, but the FCC on its own said, "No, you can't have surcharges." Basically what that means is long distance companies have to incorporate the costs of providing relay services into whatever they charge the general public as just another cost of doing business.

The states, however, by and large, have used surcharges, and there was nothing we could do to stop them. For example, one of the ways that California used to characterize these services on their bill was something like "telephone for the deaf" or "telecommunications for the deaf." Well, what happens when you are hearing, and you get a bill that says this, and you've never talked to a deaf person? You call up your telephone company and you say, "Take this off. I don't have any deaf friends." And that's exactly what was happening. So, anticipating this, we successfully put some language into the ADA's legislative history telling states not to use offensive language to identify relay services on customer phone bills. One of the most important points that we always made, and continue to make, was that every relay call is not only for the Deaf person. It's between two people, one of whom is hearing. So again, looking at it like a tax is like looking at it as a charity only for Deaf people, when in fact it's a utility service that connects Deaf people with hearing people, or speech-disabled people with hearing people, and vice versa.

We had to make some compromises, but what we lost in the House we got back in the Senate. For example, initially Title IV was supposed to be implemented in two years, but it went to three, plus an undue burden exemption, and we all said, "That's ridiculous, there's no way providing relay services could be an undue burden," so we got rid of that in the Senate. The House also snuck in a provision that said that telephone companies didn't have to handle relay calls made to audio-text services, which are pretty much like interactive voice menus, you know: "press 1 for hours of operation, press 2 for location," etc., because they were afraid it wasn't technologically possible. But when we caught this change, I wrote a colloquy that ended up on the House floor, making clear that if technology was developed in the future to handle these calls, they had to be provided. Many years later, the FCC used that colloquy between two congressmen to cover these services. So in the end, we really lost nothing.

It was a different time in Congress. I remember being upset at how long it was taking! This was probably incredibly naive, now that I look back at it, but I remember thinking, "I wish this would just go forward already." I was young, and I didn't realize how hard it was to get legislation passed. Only now do I realize how easily this part of the ADA glided through, and how much it has changed the lives of people who are Deaf, hard of hearing, and speech disabled.

Jim Weisman
"The transportation dude."

"I got involved in disability in the strangest way," says Jim Weisman, often called "the transportation dude" for his part in drafting those provisions in the ADA relating to public mass transit. "I had no disabled relatives or anything. I was a teenager and I was interested in a girl in high school who was working at a camp for disabled kids. I wanted to be near the girl but they wouldn't give me a job so I said, 'I'll volunteer.'

"I don't know where she is now, but I got involved right away and I met people who were my age who were disabled, and it was the first disabled people I'd ever had any contact with. I became friendly with them and stayed friendly with them from my teenage years on up. . . . One of my closest friends [back then] was a guy named Paul Hearn, who passed away a few years ago. Paul was about three feet tall. He was in a wheelchair. He went everywhere. He did everything. He was the president of his high school class. He was the president of the student body in college. He went to law school. He hitchhiked around Europe by himself. And I just thought that he was a typical disabled guy. I didn't realize that he was unusual. Then, of course, I did."

James J. Weisman was born in April 1951 and earned his law degree from the Seton Hall School of Law in Newark, New Jersey, in 1977. By 1979 he was working as a legal advocate with the Eastern Paralyzed Veterans Association (EPVA). EPVA is now the United Spinal Association, and currently Weisman is its senior vice president and general counsel.

———

I got involved with the ADA because I had sued New York City and Philadelphia to make their transit systems accessible. New York City took from 1979 to '84 and I learned a lot about transit. Then I sued Philadelphia, [which took] two years. The settlement agreements for the two cities made all rail systems accessible—at least on paper—so we knew we could get transit systems to agree to do it. And we didn't have a lot of transportation experts on the disability side. Most of the [experts] were aligned against us. It seems silly now but only ten years ago [in 1990] people were adamantly opposed to making even just buses accessible. So [when the ADA came up, the sponsors] called me to come to Washington and argue the case for people with disabilities.

I was the transportation dude but the thing that happens is that every congressional committee can deal with every subject in an omnibus bill like the ADA. So the transportation committee can talk about labor, and the labor committee can talk about transportation. So you had to become an expert in every area of the bill because you'd be talking to the transportation committee and they'd ask you a labor question. And every one of these committees would think they had a great amendment to improve the bill or to weaken it and you had to put out a million fires.

Transportation was a sticky issue and it's silly that it was, because it's the simplest part of the ADA. Everybody knows that disabled people want to go where everybody else wants to go and do what everybody else wants to do, so their transportation needs are identical to the transportation needs of able-bodied people. There's not a lot of special stuff. But for so many years, so many generations, people defined people with disabilities as having "special" transportation needs that had to be met in a "special"—i.e., a different—way. It looked more complicated than it was.

Also, in the late seventies, early eighties, there was a Congressional Budget Office report that "proved" that making mass transit accessible was more expensive than providing paratransit, which was silly, of course, but people bought it and the transit industry ran with it. In fact, it cost them dearly to do that. If you think about it, the bus runs [on a regular route]. It's driven. It's fueled. If it's accessible you can take advantage of it. The van doesn't run [except as a "special service"]. You have to buy it. You have to drive it. You have to pay the driver. You have to fuel it. You have to insure it. You have to replace it much quicker than you replace a mass transit bus. Mass transit buses last twelve years; vans three to five years, probably two years in New York City, with all the potholes. So it made no sense, this Congressional Budget Office report, but the transit industry liked what it said and so they publicized it. They created a consciousness in Congress that paratransit was inexpensive, which was completely false.

I think [a lot of the opposition came out of] arrogance. They'd never had to provide transportation to people with disabilities. History was on their side. The newspapers, the editorial boards, all bought the transit argument and transit probably figured that charities would do this. I don't think people really thought that disabled people would work. Last month in New York City, sixty thousand people took the bus with wheelchairs. That's just one month, and most of those people were peak-hour riders. They're going to work. I don't think people envisioned that. They thought this would be charities, church groups. Maybe state and city departments of social service would provide the rides. "Just keep them off the bus and we won't have to worry about it," was their philosophy, but it backfired because they created a mind set that paratransit was necessary for some people.

The most specific parts of the ADA are the transportation sections. There are no broad mandates in general language that need to be interpreted, or regulations that needed to be written by the Department of Transportation to tell people what to do, and that is because we had history with them. We didn't want to leave it to the Department of Transportation to implement because we'd been abused, so we put it right in the statute, so there wasn't a lot of wiggle room for transit to get out from under.

Probably the most significant opposition to the transportation provisions of the ADA came from a guy who actually voted no in the final vote. There weren't very many of them. It was Congressman [Bud] Schuster from Pennsylvania. He used to tell us that his mother was in a wheelchair, that he knew all there was to know about this. He would always show me his knuckles were scraped from pushing his mother through narrow doorways. And we went to see him over and over again, and he would not change his mind on this. "Lifts don't belong on buses." And he would say that President Bush—his own president, he's a Republican—"doesn't know what he's doing." He'd say that right at hearings. And, of course, I'm not a constituent of Congressman Schuster. He's from Pennsylvania. I'm from New York. And he would say, "You're not even a constituent. Get out of my office." So we brought him a constituent, a warm, live, disabled constituent, who completely agreed with everything we were saying, and he threw us out again with his constituent.

And then people demonstrated outside his office. His office was right next to Hamilton Fish's office, who was a Republican supporter of ours, and we were going to see Congressman Fish, and Congressman Schuster saw people in wheelchairs coming down the hall and immediately called security, who tried to block us because they thought we were going to demonstrate at his office.

There's a few things wrong with the transportation section. The most glaring one is what they call over-the-road buses. Over-the-road buses are the kind with the forward-facing coach-style seat with the baggage compartment underneath, and they usually go intercity like Greyhound. And, of course, Greyhound was the biggest operator at the time the ADA passed.

Greyhound lied. Greyhound testified on a panel in the Congress with the Denver Transportation System sitting at the same table. Greyhound said it would cost $35- to $50,000 per bus to make a Greyhound accessible, and they would lose half their baggage space and eight seats. Greyhound hadn't done it, but Denver had. Denver said, "Greyhound visited us. They've seen our buses." That's the first thing they said. Then they said, "It cost $8,500 per bus, and that includes our research and development money. We did not lose half our baggage space and we lost one or two seats," for the lift equipment and things.

Congress heard it but Greyhound lobbied hard. Greyhound said behind closed doors—Congressman Boehlert [R] from Utica, New York, is the one who told me this—that they were threatening Congresspeople with denying service to their community, that they'll have to cut their service in half and lay off half their staff if they're included within the scope of the coverage. "And if it's you who votes for it, Congressman, it will be you that loses the service. Explain *that* to your constituents. There's one person or none in a wheelchair who live in your community, explain that to them, why they lost Greyhound," which is hard ball, and they got away with it. So they got a six-year exemption, which was extended.

Attitudes about transportation have changed dramatically. In transportation schools where people go to plan mass transit, to be transit operators, they learn how to provide services to elderly and disabled people. Transit is becoming relevant again. If you have no ridership, what's the point of running the bus? The people who need it are the people you should serve. People who use mass transit, by and large, are lower-income people, and that's who transit has to direct itself at.

They got the message. I think the ADA was the catalyst in that regard. There's a new generation of transit management. They have no politics about this. They just want to do a good job.

30
Insiders, Part 2

I T IS A TRUISM OF THE MOVEMENT THAT EVERYONE IS JUST ONE ACCI-
dent or illness away from being a person with a disability. People without
disabilities therefore are often called "TABs," meaning "temporarily able-bodied," and the disability community itself is sometimes called "an open minority"—meaning that anyone, no matter what their race, gender, class, ethnicity,
or politics—can become a member. While in some respects this might be a
political weakness, in that it makes it that much more difficult for organizers to
bring this disparate constituency together, it also means that the movement has
been able to find some seemingly unlikely allies in high places, President George
H. W. Bush being a prime example. Another such ally was C. Boyden Gray.

C. Boyden Gray
"It was an attitudinal thing. That was why we needed the act."

Born in February 1943, Gray is a politically conservative attorney and a member of the Federalist Society, which is generally skeptical of any federal mandate, regulation, or civil rights law. And yet, because of his close relationship
with Evan Kemp, Gray became one of the staunchest supporters of the ADA
within the Bush administration.

Gray graduated from Harvard University in 1964. After serving in the US
Marine Corps Reserve, he attended law school at the University of North Carolina, graduating in 1968. He clerked for Chief Justice Earl Warren and then went
into private practice until 1981, when he became legal counsel to Vice President
Bush and then Counsel to the President from 1989 to 1993. That same year President Bill Clinton presented Gray with a Presidential Citizens Medal.

In 2006, Gray was appointed US ambassador to the European Union, and
in 2008 as special envoy for European affairs and special envoy for Eurasian
energy at the US Mission to the European Union. He has also continued to be

active politically, serving, for example, as co-chair, with former US congress-man Dick Armey, of FreedomWorks, a conservative nonprofit foundation based in Washington.

———

We were embroiled early on in the Reagan administration, right off the bat, with the program for deregulation. I was assigned one particularly thorny issue involving the Architectural and Transportation Barriers Compliance Board,[1] otherwise known as the ATBCB. They had coughed up a rather complex set of regulations on the eve of the inauguration—one of the so-called midnight regulations—and it was my task to unwind all of that. Also on the radar screen were the regulations implementing 94-142—the Education for All Handicapped Children statute. And so I was very early immersed deep into disability issues.

As I got more and more immersed I became more and more intrigued with the issues, and I was given enormous help from an old friend of mine—with whom I had played bridge over the years—named Evan Kemp, who really is, in many ways, the grandfather of the disability movement. I learned that the ATBCB regs could easily be withdrawn and redone. I also learned that 94-142 was not so simple, and was a different issue. And in the process of all this I learned about the power of the move-ment, how big it was—what an ignored civil rights issue this had been, and I ended up spending a great deal of time in the eighties and into the nineties on the issue. But it was that deregulation phase in the early Rea-gan years that got me involved. And my great friend Evan Kemp became my teacher. Everything that I've been able to do I really owe to him.

President Bush had such insights into this—I think in part because his son Neil was dyslexic. His parents were told he could never finish college, and they managed to get around that and he actually ended up with an advanced degree in five years. Or maybe it was because of his daughter, the one he lost to leukemia. His favorite uncle was a leading surgeon in New York—a Walker cousin or a Walker uncle, I guess a brother of his mother's. I knew him too; I played a lot of bridge with him. Wonderful, wonderful man. And he came down with polio or something, and he spent the rest of his life in a wheelchair and could no longer practice his specialty. I think those things worked in the president's mind to teach him about these issues. But he was completely understanding of what was going on and never hes-itated a moment, and took great interest in what was happening.

President Bush liked Evan, and he was involved with his appointments to the EEOC, and I think had him to dinner two or three times in the residence. He was accompanied by Janine Bertram [Evan Kemp's wife], who was a former Weatherman, Weatherperson, Weatherlady—whatever you want to call her—and had served jail time. And this, of course, set off alarm bells at the Secret Service. They just were terrified that "he was going to have a Weatherman in the residence?" But President Bush used to laugh and laugh about that. Nothing could have bothered him less or deterred him from having Evan come to the residence and talk about what they were doing.

It was among the staff where you would have a lot of the [resistance]. It was an attitudinal thing. That was why we needed the act, to change the attitudes foremost. One had to stare down the people who would make fun of the effort. And then later to stare down the conservatives who had criticized it from a programmatic point of view—not an attitudinal thing, but programmatically. And I would always have to say, "Look, if you could understand this as an empowerment, as a welfare reform initiative, I think you'll look at it differently." And eventually I was able to persuade people. . . .

[So] there was a receptivity, clearly, in the Reagan and Bush administrations from the very top, from President Reagan, then Vice President—and later President—Bush. What was needed was someone to connect, if you will, the Pat Wrights of the world with the policymakers. Don't forget, don't underestimate the serendipity, if you will, of having Dick Thornburgh and Ginny involved too. She was one of the great advocates of the disabled, again because of the tragedy Dick Thornburg had suffered.[2] But all these things conspired, if you will, to produce a result which was magnificent.

I suppose my role was simply to alert people to it and force people to pay attention, because once you got their attention, it wasn't all that difficult. This disability movement is all about empowerment, and that is not something that Republicans were going to oppose. As far as the Democrats were concerned, you say "civil rights" and you have an adherent to begin with.

So the convergence of those two in this legislation, and in this movement, was something which, looking back on it, seems easy. At the time it was quite difficult. We were up against lots of obstacles. The attitude about the disabled was really almost ugly—the way people viewed the disabled, not wanting to have anything to do with them. There were occasional jokes in the White House when we first got started on this— quite ugly, quite ugly. So I suppose if I had any personal role to play, it was staring down the people who wanted to make fun of this as they were learning about how important it was.

I don't know that Lee Atwater, who was the political guru of the Reagan-Bush years until he became himself disabled,[3] I don't know whether he ever laughed at me, in front of me, but he certainly was a true believer in the importance of all this by the time the '88 election was over. And it was persuading people like Atwater, the politicians who controlled the way elections are debated, that was really the ultimate triumph here—getting the politicians and political consultants to understand why this was important. Lee completely accepted it, and maybe I had something to do with that. . . .

One of the things which we were never able to persuade the media about is that the ADA in a sense was the first shot at welfare reform, in that you were going to empower individuals to make their own living. And this is what the disability community devoutly wanted, and so it was something that's part of an overall movement to free people up and empower them. That was something that was happening independently, I think, of this political movement. But the politics of the disability movement were made to dovetail very nicely into what was happening at large.

There were two issues that I remember vividly. I want to say here that my capacity to work on the details was curtailed dramatically once [Bush] got elected [president] because I was in charge of White House clearance and ethics and financial disclosure forms and FBI reports [on prospective appointees], and I just couldn't devote much time to the actual drafting of the legislation. But there were two or three big issues in the beginning which I did get involved with. One was whether the legislation would be retroactive. If it were to be prospective only it would be a lot less expensive, a lot more politically palatable, but it would take a lot more time to implement its provisions. But, all things being said, we made the decision that we couldn't justify the expense and couldn't risk the political downside of making it retroactive from day one. And so that was a key decision very early on. . . . [And then] there were some very tricky issues involving gay rights. . . . Would it apply to someone with AIDS? They were quite tense and emotional [issues], and it became political and ideological.

I know a young woman from the South, whose family gave what was originally a plantation to the South Carolina School for the Blind. And she has been a critic generally of my role with the ADA. But then she went back to South Carolina and visited this school at which she had never spent any time. And there was a huge reception there honoring her grandfather and her great-grandfather. And all of a sudden she was in a room full of deaf and blind people, who could communicate with each other but with whom she couldn't communicate. And all of a sudden she was the minority, and the scales fell from her eyes and she understood what this was all about. Of course they were saying that the ADA was the most important modern milestone in helping people who were blind and deaf. And for the first time she understood the power of all of this and why it's important.

And that's one of the reasons why the ADA has been so important. It has forced people who are otherwise not exposed to the problems of the disabled, it's forced people to understand. Evan Kemp used to say that in many ways what we wanted with the ADA was to have it work well enough so that by the time the baby boom generation became aged and disabled the country would be ready. And I think we're going to meet that target even though Evan didn't survive to see it himself. . . .

I don't have any regrets. I just wish that some of our most bitter critics on the right could have been a little more understanding about what we were trying to do.

Richard Thornburgh
"One of the great things about the ADA is that it has a mood-altering phenomenon to it."

Richard Thornburgh played multiple roles in the development of disability rights law in America. As the father of a child with a disability, and the husband of parent activist Ginny Thornburgh, he was a natural ally of the disability rights movement of the 1970s and beyond. As the governor of the Commonwealth of Pennsylvania, however, his administration was the de facto defendant in the deinstitutionalization lawsuit pursued by Thomas K. Gilhool, on behalf of the Pennsylvania ARC, in *Halderman v. Pennhurst State School & Hospital*. And as attorney general under President George H. W. Bush, he was in a key position to help—or hinder—the passage of the ADA.

Thornburgh was born in July 1932, in Pittsburgh. His first wife, Ginny Hooten Thornburgh, was killed in an automobile accident in 1960. This same accident left their three-month-old son Peter severely brain injured. Thornburgh's second wife, Ginny Judson Thornburgh, subsequently became a nationally known advocate in the parents' movement, most especially for her work with the National Organization on Disability, where she became the director of NOD's Religion and Disability Program, working to make religious communities accessible to and inclusive of people with all kinds of disabilities.

Richard Thornburgh was elected governor of Pennsylvania in 1978, and re-elected in 1982. He was appointed attorney general by President Reagan in 1988 and retained in that post when George H. W. Bush was sworn in as president in 1989.

With any movement, any kind of initiative, there's always a magic moment, and I think the advocacy within the disability community during the 1980s was stepped up considerably in tempo. There were more and more people wanting to build upon the Rehabilitation Act of 1973, the education initiatives that were undertaken, and when President Bush came into office in 1989, he very quickly acceded to the suggestions made that he be a leader in seeking to move the ADA out of the Congress and, in a stroke of good fortune for me, asked that I be the point person in that effort.

And so you had two people—the president and the attorney general—who were very much committed to the passage of this legislation and willing to work with leaders in the Congress to get an acceptable piece of legislation forthcoming. I credit a great deal to President Bush's leadership. Very often, major policy initiatives derive from the quality of leadership that is exerted on their behalf. And clearly, if he had not been committed and had not exerted his leadership, we never would have had an ADA, or we would have had quite a different ADA than ultimately was achieved through his signature on July 26, 1990.

The philosophy of the Americans with Disabilities Act says to us as a society: you must make reasonable accommodations in order to empower these people to permit them to make a contribution and to enjoy those aspects of life which they are now denied by reason of discrimination or artificial barriers. And in the employment area, the notion of reasonable accommodation is an evolving process. There have been studies done that indicate that the average cost of reasonable accommodations is quite low.

I remember in the Department of Justice we had an outstanding lawyer, part of the White House fellows program, named Drew Batavia, who was a quadriplegic, and the reasonable accommodation for him—an excellent mind, good lawyer, trained in health care law—was as simple as [installing a] touch pad [for his] computer keyboard [and telephone] and putting them on the wall so that he could punch into those with a stick that he used in his mouth. That to me has always been the quintessential reasonable accommodation, because if that weren't done he could not operate a telephone or a computer. At a cost of $78.75 or whatever it was to have a carpenter come in and do it, he is empowered to participate in his chosen profession. That's not always that easy nor that stark, but introducing that notion of an affirmative obligation on the part of all of us as a society to exert our ingenuity and some minimal expense in order to make a life that is noncontributing into a life that is contributing is very exciting, and represents the signal advance in thinking about rights law in general that the ADA offers.

One of the great things about the ADA is that it has a mood-altering phenomenon to it. . . . When you look around at all the indexia of the disability rights movement—curb cuts, brailled elevators and ATM machines, all of the accommodations that have been made with regard to those with poor hearing or eyesight, things in churches and other types of community, you get an unmistakable signal of concern that simply wasn't there twenty or thirty years ago. And, in fact, some would argue wasn't there ten years ago prior to the passage. I think what ADA has done is accelerate that markedly.

I testified in both the House and the Senate on behalf of the ADA. And there were three things that were in my mind. One was, I suppose you might say, [to] establish a mood, that is to say, to get people's attention, to let people know what we're talking about. We're talking about a lot of people with all kinds of different disabilities, each one of whom is an individual and shouldn't be stereotyped as being hearing impaired or using a wheelchair or whatever. Secondly, as I indicated, [was] overcoming a kind of what I call knee-jerk skepticism about further civil rights legislation. "Don't we have enough civil rights? Haven't we addressed these issues sufficiently?" And clearly that wasn't the case, and clearly, that was a difficult undertaking, but eventually I think people came around.

And the third was to address the concerns specifically of the business community, especially small businesses who really were haunted by the notion that they would be obliged to make enormous outlays of resources to make their facilities accessible. And that is a legitimate concern and one recognized by the concept of reasonableness that pervades the act in almost every respect. If there's undue difficulty or expense required in order to make a facility or service accessible, you're not required to do it. But, for the first time you *are* required to consider it and to make reasonable accommodations in order to permit people with disabilities the same access to a facility or to a service or a program that people without disabilities have. . . .

The role that I played in consideration of the ADA was to draw down on whatever capital I had as a parent, as a longtime advocate, as one who had been committed to disability rights and yet was a Republican and a loyal member of the Bush administration, to try to get people to sit down and discuss their differences and come up with reasonable solutions. Sometimes it was hard. [At] some of these meetings . . . I felt more like a referee than a participant in a negotiating process. But, I was by no means the only one who had those sentiments or those kinds of experiences to share. As I said, there are many, many heroes in this effort and I was very proud to be a part of it, but I don't want to exaggerate my own role.

Most of the discussions that related to the ADA really became kind of set pieces. People with particular points to make would make them, and make them again, and make them a third time, and then we would hear from other persons. And I really was more of a kibitzer. I would occasionally offer something that I thought might help to bring issues of contention to resolution. You very seldom went to a negotiating session that ended in resolution on the spot. What it did was to raise a lot of different considerations that were then mulled over by the parties, who would then come back and say, "What about this or what about that?" This is typical of the process of resolving issues. And it's fun. It's an exercise that is not only worthwhile in terms of the result that's achieved but it's fulfilling in terms of the experience. . . .

We had a couple of sessions up on the Hill that got very heated and personal, and that's a rarity in dealing with these kinds of things. But it got ugly a couple of times and fortunately cooler heads prevailed and we went back to the drawing board and accomplished the goal.

But all things considered, the period of time and the amount of commotion attached to the passage of the ADA through the Congress was unusual. The die was pretty well cast when the president put his support behind the bill, when there was a Democratic Congress that was naturally inclined toward it, and leaders on the Republican side were who very forthright in their support of the ADA. Which is not to say it was a piece of cake, because there is always something that can go wrong. But, in the grand scheme of things, its passage was remarkably smooth.

[After passage of the ADA] I applied a vigorous whip to John Wodatch and his colleagues in the civil rights division to get these regulations [on enforcement of the law] done by the first anniversary of the act. I made clear that I would not tolerate our not having those regulations in place one year after passage of the act, which by the way is some kind of new NCAA record for the issuance of regulations in a complicated area like this. Well, they got the job done and we arranged a ceremony for the Great Hall of the Department of Justice, where I would sign the regulations and they would come into effect. And we obviously wanted to have a replication of the signing ceremony at the White House lawn, and we wanted to invite all the leaders of the advocacy community and the disability community and people who had put their life's work into this.

As we were preparing for this, we realized that the beautiful Great Hall of the Department of Justice, and that magnificent art deco building down there, was inaccessible to persons with wheelchairs. So we embarked on another crash program, to ensure that accessibility was at least enhanced if not totally provided, and at the same time [we] had an obligation to preserve the historic character of the building. We fortunately had the services of a woman named Jane Barton, who had worked at the Department of Treasury on historic preservation, and our own internal staff who worked together to accomplish both goals so that by July 26, 1991—a year after passage of the act—the hall was accessible and yet it still retained its historic significance.

That was a kind of a minor accomplishment, but it was terribly significant. Imagine what it would have been like to sign these very important regulations in a place where people with disabilities couldn't enter.

<h2 style="text-align:center">Justin Dart Jr. (continued)</h2>

"They wouldn't give me the time of day until that demonstration occurred."

To sophisticated advocates, the debate over whether it is best to work inside or outside the political system is moot. They would say, as Justin Dart does here, that both approaches are necessary, that, indeed, the one type of advocate can get no traction without the other and that there are times when even an "in-sider" like Justin Dart needs a little help from his outsider friends.

In chapter 28, Marilyn Golden described how, together with others on the team, she asked for a demonstration to put pressure on a House member who was perceived to be blocking action on the bill. Here Justin Dart describes the impact of such an effort.

———

We were having trouble at one point with Bob Michel, the Republican leader in the House. The advocates in the House were having trouble, especially with his chief of staff, who was opposed to the ADA. They needed his support to get it through and not to have a gutting amend-ment, a Jim Crow amendment. So the Washington team told me to go see Bob Michel. Well, I didn't know Bob Michel. They said, "But you are a Republican and see if you can see him."

So I called a staff member and said, "I would like to see the Con-gressman," and she said, "Well, he is very busy. We just don't think that is going to be possible." "Well, can I see you?" "Well, it's not possible." Anyway I bugged the devil out of her and she finally agreed to see me. And she said, "Well, I'll see you for a few minutes. But the Congressman really can't see you."

He was the minority leader and he comes from Peoria, Illinois. So I called, I think it was Jim DeJong, who at that time was out with the Illinois Coalition of People with Disabilities. And I said, "Jim, we have got a big problem here. We are trying to get through to Bob Michel. Can you all exert any influence there, so that maybe at least this guy's staff would listen to me?" And so they got about thirty people and did a demonstration in front of his Peoria office. And I think it got on the local television.

I went to the meeting the next day and this lady was there. And she was a whole lot more polite than she had been on the telephone. And she said, "You know, Mr. Dart, the Congressman just happens to be here and if he has a minute, he might be able to drop in and just shake hands with you." And I said, "Well, great!" This meeting had been going about thirty seconds and then the congressman walked in the door and he said, "Hi, Justin." "Hi *Justin*," you see. I had never met the man before, and now I am *Justin*. And he said, "I am delighted that you were able to come to see me." And then before he said anything else, he said, "Justin, whatever gave your friends in Peoria the idea that I don't support the ADA?" And he met me for about forty-five minutes. And he listened to the whole thing. And he said, "Justin, I am going to support the ADA, don't worry about it." And I said, "Well, Congressman, the only thing is, we have faith that it is going to pass in some form, but we have got all of these amendments that will gut the intent of the bill. We have got to have a real equality law." And he said, "Justin, listen to me carefully. I cannot bypass the system that we have in this Congress. We hold hearings. Everybody gets their say. It takes a long time. Everybody offers their amendments. There are opponents to this law. You have got to have patience until that process occurs, but if you do, let me promise you this: You are going to get your equality law. You are going to get your full equality." And he said, "I want you to go out of this room and call your friends in Peoria and tell them that. And tell them that I am going to meet with them as soon as I get back there, and tell them what I told you."

And I think that is a great story about empowerment. You know, you hear these introductions of Justin Dart that he—or Pat Wright—that we practically single-handedly passed the ADA. Bullshit. They wouldn't give me the time of day until that demonstration occurred. And suddenly he is all for the law. You know what I mean?

31
Wheels of Justice and the Chapman Amendment

B Y SPRING 1990 DISABILITY RIGHTS ADVOCATES AND THEIR ALLIES HAD shepherded the ADA past its first hurdles in the Senate. After hearings in the Senate Committee on Labor and Human Resources and negotiations between the Senate, the White House, and disability advocates, the full Senate passed its own version of the ADA—S. 933—by a vote of 76–8 on September 7, 1989.

Passage in the House would prove more difficult. As has been mentioned, the bill had to be heard—and approved—by a variety of separate committees and subcommittees, including subcommittees on Select Education and Employment Opportunities, on Surface Transportation, on Telecommunications and Finance, and so on. Even the House Subcommittee on Transportation and Hazardous Materials felt it necessary to conduct a hearing (on September 28, 1989) on the ADA.

The pace therefore was necessarily slower. Although the House Committee on Education and Labor reported out its version of the bill, as amended, on November 14, 1989, the Committee on Small Business was still hearing testimony at the end of February 1990. It wasn't until March 1 that the House Subcommittee on Surface Transportation reported to the full Committee on Public Works and Transportation, which in turn still needed to consider and approve the bill, while such critical committees as Energy and Commerce, Rules, and Judiciary still needed to debate, vote, and report out their versions of the bill.

Indeed, it wouldn't be until May 17 that the full House would begin debate leading to a vote on a House ADA, after which a Senate/House conference committee would need to hammer out differences between the two versions of the bill. Only then could each chamber take a final vote, after which, of course, would come the final hurdle: winning White House approval and President Bush's signature to turn the ADA from a bill into the law of the land.

At each step of the way there was a possibility of delay, not to mention passage of some "poison pill" amendment that might make the entire bill unpalatable to other House committees, the full House, the Senate, the president, or—most important of all—the disability community itself.[1]

Michael Auberger (continued)
"Everybody in Washington . . . was scared to death that we were going to blow it."

Impatient with the process and the pace, ADAPT—by this time well versed in the strategy and tactics of direct action civil disobedience—staged its "Wheels of Justice" campaign. Central to the effort was Michael Auberger, veteran now of dozens of actions and of multiple arrests.

The three days of demonstrations—March 12–14, 1990—particularly the "crawl-up" at the Capitol steps on March 12—provided some of the most powerful images in the history of the movement. For many of those participating, it was, as Auberger himself describes it, nothing less than a "cathartic" experience.

The next day's sit-in in the Capitol rotunda was itself hardly an anticlimax. And it revealed some interesting splits inside a movement on the verge of its greatest legislative triumph, when, according to Auberger, those working more or less inside the halls of power were concerned that those on the outside might do more harm than good.

In the late eighties it started to become chic for independent living centers to participate in ADAPT actions. Wherever we went, from early on, if there was a local ILC, we tried to get local folks there to participate, and typically they weren't going to be part of anything we did. But in the late eighties all of a sudden ADAPT was chic, because obviously we were making progress, and the independent living system had not had much luck in public transportation at all, whereas by 1990 we had an agreement with UMTA [Urban Mass Transportation Administration], . . . to mandate 100 percent lift-equipped buses in all future purchases.

So we felt comfortable enough that it was going the right way, and then the ADA shows up. We agreed to participate in the ADA stuff, because of the public transportation piece. It was clear that policy is one thing, but putting it into law was something that we always wanted, and the ADA was a vehicle for us to do that.

Until we went to DC and did the march on the Capitol and the sit-in at the rotunda, we actually purposely had not dealt with the Washington folks. Pat Wright, and the local disability community, and the leaders of the ADA stuff had all approached us about addressing it prior to us getting there, but when we got to DC it was Pat Wright who took the lead. We had agreed before we went in that we would do the march, and everybody could participate in that if they chose to, and that everybody else in the disability community could also participate in the other demonstrations that we were going to do, but they were going to be around transportation and the ADA.

Before we'd get into a city, a small group, Bob Kafka, myself, and maybe Stephanie Thomas, would go in a week or so early, actually scope out the place, and look at what we were going to do, and come up with a strategy for the time that we were going to be there. It was at that point that we had met Pat Wright, and like I said we agreed to do the march, and that they could have some say over that, but not a whole lot, because it was still our show.

But when we started talking about doing a demonstration at the Capitol, everybody was saying "No no no, you don't want to piss them off." Well, they're not doing anything anyway, so how can we piss off people that aren't doing anything? It was stalled at the time, and there was no getting around that. And so we ended up disagreeing on that.

One of the things we said that we wanted to do, because the ADA was stuck in the House, we wanted to meet with the minority and majority leaders in the Capitol, and that was a no-no, apparently. See, they never met in the Capitol unless it was a state function, a funeral or some such thing, otherwise you'd never see the two of them together at the same time. And so they were all sure it was going to backfire.

We did the march on Sunday. About five thousand people came out for that day. We started at the White House. We met with C. Boyden Gray, and he was kind of spearheading the ADA for the White House. One of the people who had approached us earlier was Evan Kemp. Evan at the time was EEOC chairman, and he was from Ohio, from Cleveland, and Wade [Blank] was from Akron, and so they had that common ground, besides disability issues. And then I was a Bengals fan, which made us even more in synch. And so Evan and Pat had set up the meeting with the White House, and we had agreed that there would be no demonstrations in front of the White House, that there would be no demonstrations at all on Sunday, so that all those people could participate in the march who didn't necessarily want to be part of a demonstration, but wanted to be part of something that felt good. And that was hard to swallow. It was real hard to swallow, to have that number of people, and to have the media that were following it, and not *do* something.

And so we marched, from the White House down Pennsylvania Avenue to the Capitol. It was definitely a pretty day, a very feel-good event, and for all the ADAPT folks it was a picnic in the park, just marching up the streets, keeping people together. And it just kept getting bigger and bigger. As you get up to First Street, you're starting up the hill towards the Capitol, and you end up where you can look back down the avenue. And it was amazing to see the four lanes of traffic going towards the Capitol with nothing but people with disabilities. It looked like a good mile. That felt good to see, and to do. We went to the Capitol, in front on the south side, the direction that faces the Washington Monument, which is where we'd set up for speakers. They had all the regular ADA people speaking, and people from around the country, and myself, and so it just ended up being a feel-good event in which everybody could participate.

But we felt we had to have something for the ADAPT folks that had some kind of significance, other than a march, because otherwise we would have had a riot on our hands. It wasn't ADAPT, it didn't feel like ADAPT, to just march and not do any sort of direct action. So the crawl-up was something that we'd set up to meet that need. Everybody was invited to participate if they chose to, but they didn't have to.

That was a piece that actually played out much better than I could have ever predicted. Part of that speech that I had at the time was about having been in Washington, and been in the Capitol as a kid, walking on my hind legs into the building. It was just this whole sense of irony, that after all these years you still couldn't get into the Capitol using a wheelchair. They always had to install temporary ramps.

So after the speeches, those who wanted to participated in the crawl-up, which was people getting out of their wheelchairs and crawling up the steps of the Capitol. It was definitely theater, but it was also a statement: "As far as you've gone, you're not there yet." Probably about a hundred people did the actual crawl-up. Everybody who started made it up—we made sure of that. And then when people got to the top, their chairs were there, waiting. Of course, it was all prearranged.

I was surprised at all the emotion that came out of it, and everybody at the bottom who watched, they couldn't believe what they saw. I guess it was a catharsis, is the best way to describe it. And I don't think any of the people that actually crawled up thought that it would be that way. Somewhere in there, with all the energy that was expended, it just put everybody right there on the edge of, in touch with, their anger, in touch with a lot of history about access. All the years of oppression seemed to come out right then and there. Tears. People were crying. I was completely surprised by that, that people would feel it in such a powerful way.

Then the next day we did the demonstration in the Rotunda, and at that point the local folks were nowhere to be found. Some of the independent living people that we had been working with for the last couple of years were part of that, but it wasn't the same kind of event. Among the folks in ADAPT the next day, it was an inside joke for sure, that yesterday we went up to five thousand, and now we're back down to five hundred. It's an amazing difference.

One of the things that we did the week earlier, when we were scoping things out, was to actually set up a tour of the Capitol. There's a special office in the Capitol, and I explained to the woman there, we'd probably have eighty people or so that wanted to tour the Capitol. It would be kind of the highlight for people who don't ever leave their city, the first time coming to Washington, DC. So we sold it as a group, and we made up some silly name for it.

And so, we met with the woman, and I said it would make a lot more sense, if we were going to do the tour, why don't we start in the Rotunda, and work our way down, because that way we're only using the elevators twice, instead of up, down and around, their normal tour? Because with all those wheelchairs and just these small elevators, it would take too much time.

Neither the House nor the Senate had ever seen this many people with disabilities. We used every elevator. We used the Senate elevators, we used the House elevators. The Capitol police did everything they could to expedite us, so that "the tour" could happen. They didn't know what was happening either. There were no signs, everybody was very respectful, talking among themselves, and so it wasn't like you knew something was going to happen if you weren't expecting it.

Once we had everybody together in the Rotunda, that's when the signs came out and the chanting started. We had all these people in the rotunda chanting "ADA Now!" We said that we wanted to meet with [Bob] Michel from Illinois, the minority leader at the time, he was a Republican, and Tom Foley, the Democrat who was the Speaker. And initially they were adamant that they weren't going to do it. "We don't ever come to the Rotunda, unless it's some big event. We'd be glad to meet with all of you outside," blah blah blah, you know, the normal rap that happens. And we said that we're not leaving because we have all these people here from around the country, they're all going to see their representatives, and they want to know where the ADA is in the process, so that when they go see their representatives, they want to make sure that they can tell them what they expect to be done.

And as we're waiting for Michel and Foley, the lady came over, the one we'd set up the tour with. You have to understand, everybody's chanting, and there's close to five hundred people in the Rotunda. It's packed, and going out in both directions, to the House and the Senate sides. And so after about forty-five minutes of chanting, she comes over to me—she had to dig through the crowd because I was buried in the middle some-where—she comes over and asks me, "Do you want to start the tour now?" She was having to yell to talk to me. And I said, "I don't think it's going to happen right now, but I'll let you know later."

It was so loud, chanting in the Rotunda. It was the most amazing thing, to be in there and be able to do that. And the way that it's designed, you can say something in one spot and someone on the opposite side of the Rotunda will actually hear it, just speaking in a soft voice. So the sound was bouncing around up there, and it just threw the whole place, that this was going on. We had started right around noon, we timed it for the lunchtime media to show up. We had all kinds of television, from earlier speeches, who followed us the next day, all of the local TV stations from around the country still had somebody following us. They would follow their local people, and they would send the feed back home of their local people at the Capitol.

They [the Congressional leaders] ended up showing up, and every-body quieted down. I'm almost positive it had to be Michel that was the one at the time speaking, laying out where it was. They were getting ready for the [Memorial Day] recess, and they'd come back in June. What we had asked them to do was to vote right after they came back, because Pat Wright, Liz Savage, and whoever else was in the know in DC that was working on the ADA at the time had said there's no way they could get the votes before the break, so in June they could do the vote and actually have it pass. So we said fine, we'll tell them that we want them to vote the first week in June that they're back, no ifs, ands or buts about it.

It was beautiful. Foley and Michel come up, we met with them, and they said, "No, we're not going to guarantee a vote." And then they left, and we started chanting "Vote now! Vote now!"

A hundred and six people were arrested. As soon as the arrests started, several things happened. One is that we brought out the kryptonite locks and chained all the wheelchairs together with kryptonite chains, and put them through everybody that we could put them through, so that they couldn't just cut one link and it would all go away. So they came up with these big four-foot-long cutters, trying to cut the chains, and it doesn't work. They had to go ask, I think it's called the Capitol architect, to go out and find a hydraulic bolt cutter. They didn't have one, and the Capitol police didn't have one. They never had experienced that.

There was one elevator being used for everybody that was being arrested, and two elevators, one on the House side and one on the Senate side, for everybody that was going down that wasn't going to be arrested. So this was a major manpower effort because they had officers at the elevator, running the elevator, and then also at either end, and whoever they took into the elevator had to have an officer with them, and if you've ever been in those Capitol elevators, you know you can barely get two regular manual wheelchairs in there at the same time. And so it took *six hours* to get everybody down.

Everybody that was arrested was brought to the back of the Capitol, and put in a kind of holding area, in the circle between the steps on the Senate and the House side, where maintenance is. They didn't have any lift-equipped vehicles, because we had already told the DC Metro, "If you bring buses to take our people to jail, your bus system will be stopped on Constitution and on Independence. We're not going to be sent to jail with the lifts that we had you put on your buses." So the Metro refused to send their buses, and so the Capitol police had to start lifting people into these vans that the Capitol architect had. They would get two or three people in a van, and would take them over to the Capitol police station—one at a time, two at a time—with four and five guys actually lifting people who were in wheelchairs into the van, and into the back of pickups. Then they had to have a policeman, a Capitol cop, for each person to go with them, in case they escaped. These were regular street vehicles that they had to clean the trash out of, or get their tools out of, or whatever it was, and they didn't hold but one or two wheelchairs at best.

So at some point they made an executive decision to keep sixty people there, and when they got the last sixty people down, they got sixty Capitol Police, and they stopped the traffic, and marched us in single file with officers and sirens and red lights at the front and at the back of this group of people. This is probably at about five o'clock in the afternoon, on Constitution, so there's sixty police officers plus whatever were on the front end and back end, one with each person, single file, marching everybody over to the Capitol Police station.

They took us down there to the station, and then decided there was too many people on the main floor, they couldn't get everybody in on the main floor and still do their regular business. So we had to come back to the first parking garage on the Senate side. So they again marched a hundred and six people, and took everybody over to the garage on the Senate side, in single file all the way back to the entrance to the parking lot. They put everybody in the garage, set up a booking process, held everybody until everybody had been booked, and then at that point released everybody on their own recognizance.

By this time it was eleven o'clock at night. They held the group until eleven o'clock, so that there wouldn't be any more demonstrations that day. And we agreed, that was always something that we agreed with the DC police, if we had done something during the day, we weren't going to do a second one unless they were keeping people, one or two people, that kind of thing. So that ended up being the outcome. Everybody was cited, and booked in that garage.

We went back to the hotel. It was midnight, and everybody had a big party in our meeting room at the Holiday Inn.

Patrisha Wright (continued)
"It ain't civil, and it ain't right."

———

The Wheels of Justice campaign was acted out in public and intended to demonstrate, quite literally with the bodies of people with disabilities, how the Capitol itself, and the Congress it housed, were inaccessible, most especially to those who used wheelchairs. Anyone watching or listening to the event would know exactly why an ADA was needed and would witness the visceral anger of those so long shut out of society.

The struggle around the Chapman amendment, by contrast, took place mostly in meeting rooms on Capitol Hill and in the White House and on the floor of the House and Senate, with the community by and large unaware what was happening until it was over. And yet, it might well be said that from 1988 to 1990 advocates in Washington and around the country never came so close to losing it all, and this only weeks before the bill was finally passed.

The Chapman amendment, introduced into the House version of the ADA by Representative Jim Chapman (D-TX), would have enabled employers to remove people with contagious diseases from positions where they handled food. It is important to note that the amendment did not distinguish between people who actually might put the public at risk and people merely *perceived* or *believed* to be a threat to the public. The clear intent was to enable restaurant owners, among others, to deny people with HIV/AIDS coverage under the bill. As Jonathan Young notes, "By this time, in May 1990, it appeared the ADA would pass; few wanted to stand in its way. But members also feared that being forced to vote on an 'AIDS' amendment during an election year could be damaging: a perfect ten-second sound bite. Moreover, the Chapman amendment was precisely the kind of issue that could kill the ADA. It seemed to represent more than just concerns about contagious diseases: it looked like a way to stop the ADA in its tracks."[2]

After a vigorous and even rancorous debate on the House floor, the amendment passed in a vote of 199 to 187, with 46 abstentions, on May 22, 1990. Despite the amendment's being put forward by a Democrat, most Democrats voted against it, while most Republicans supported it.

The debate then moved to the Senate, which had already passed its own version of the ADA—without language discriminating against people with HIV/AIDS. A conference committee composed of members of both houses met to attempt to reconcile the two bills for a final vote in each chamber, and advocates hoped the committee would reject the new language. However, Jessie Helms (R-NC) went to the Senate floor on June 5 to introduce a motion to instruct the Senate conferees to defer to the House version and endorse the amendment. Helms announced that the amendment had the support of the National Restaurant Association, the National Federation of Independent Business (NFIB), and other important business groups. On June 6, the Helms motion passed.

Here, then, was the gravest challenge yet faced by the ADA coalition, and the acid test for Patrisha Wright's principle of "one for all and all for one."

Would disability rights activists who had worked so hard and fought so long to see their civil rights enshrined in federal law risk it all because one group of people with disabilities had been singled out? Or would they flinch, believing, as most did, that the window for passing an ADA, if closed at the very end of that session of Congress, would likely never again be open in their lifetimes?

DREDF saw AIDS as a disability issue, and so DREDF was involved every time an AIDS amendment came up in Congress, and for all the initial AIDS legislation. So we had developed a pretty strong relationship with the AIDS community as a result of all that work that we'd been doing. Because, again, if we single out any disability today, tomorrow it may be your disability that society decides to hate. AIDS met the disability definition under 504, and right before the ADA passed they tried to pass an amendment on the House floor saying AIDS didn't meet that definition. We were able to beat that amendment.

So we were working very closely with the AIDS commission at that time, and with HRC [Human Rights Campaign].[3] Dr. Jane West worked for the AIDS commission, and she contacted DREDF and asked us to help her draft and review her draft of the civil rights provision in the AIDS commission report to the president. This was about a year before the introduction of the ADA. We had ensured that the AIDS commission talked about civil rights and made the link to disability rights, so that we had the president on record and the AIDS commission on record as saying that HIV/AIDS was covered under 504.

So that report came out and then we were very careful when we had hearings to make sure that there was somebody from the HIV community. In one hearing we used parents who had a foster child who had HIV and had died, and none of the funeral parlors would bury their kid. Liz Savage was a key person in identifying witnesses for us. We would say, "This is the type of witness we want, now go find that person." And I would say to her, "Go watch the soap operas because we want that kind of emotional pull." All along, we knew that HIV was not a comfortable issue for the members of Congress. We were very careful in the type of people we picked, sometimes to the chagrin of the HIV men's community who wanted to be righteous and out there. So we picked a straight woman with HIV from Tennessee to testify about the issue, so as to put up a face that was not a gay man. But that's the difference between being a lobbyist and understanding how far you can push and how far you can't.

The whole saga of the Chapman amendment is an example of giving people in Congress something comfortable that they could vote on. Because doing an up-and-down vote never worked on the House or the Senate side. We had to give people an alternative to vote for in order to make it okay because, again, the myths and stereotypes and fear around HIV were so rampant at that time that you just couldn't get a straight vote.

I remember the first time the vote came down on the House side. There was this little phone booth outside the House chamber where a lot of the lobbyists just stood in the hallway by the elevators and grabbed the members as they came in. I remember being on the phone and calling Boyden Gray at the White House saying, "You've got to call your dogs off, you've got to get me some Republicans to vote with the Dems on this." And he said he couldn't, that the Chapman amendment was more than just contagion under HIV/AIDS and food handling. It was really the last hurrah of the business community to try and put a stop to this bill. And they hunkered down and it was the last great fight: can the business community derail the ADA by using the Chapman amendment? The red herring was HIV, but it was really a business vote.

I called a meeting at the White House. This is when we were going back and forth with votes and to be honest with you, I didn't think we had the votes at that time. But I knew we had to do something, and that something was calling up the White House, saying, "Are you going to be with us, or are you not going to be with us?" And repeating, again and again, that the Chapman amendment was based on myths, on stereotypes and fear.

As I said, President Bush and his team said the ADA was an example of what "kinder, gentler" was. And so we went in to say that the White House had to step up and intervene on behalf of the ADA. So I asked Evan [Kemp] to help us get a meeting with Boyden Gray. Actually I wanted to meet with the president, but we got Boyden.

We were in the Roosevelt Room, and there were probably twenty-some-odd of us in the room. I remember Tim McFeeley, who was then the executive director of the Human Rights Campaign Fund, sat in the meeting because I wanted to make sure that the AIDS community was a part of it. Historically the AIDS community had never attended disability coalition meetings. They were part of the ADA coalition but not at the disability meetings.

At any of these meetings I always sat at the opposite end of whomever I wanted to confront at the meeting. And so I sat at the opposite end of the Roosevelt table from Boyden, because it meant he had to find me in the audience to look at me to talk to me about these things. Bob Williams sat next to Boyden. Bob used a spell board and his lapboard to communicate. Everyone went around the room and talked about why this was a bad thing to do. Bob told this story about how when he was a young kid, his parents used to take him to restaurants. And they were turned away from restaurants because of his cerebral palsy. And the restaurateurs were always very cheerful and nice, saying "Well, we'll serve *you*, but leave the little crippled kid at home. He makes noise and he's not good to look at." And that he could be contagious for all they knew. And Bob is very particular around talking and being verbal. He doesn't shortcut any conversation that he's having. And so he spelled out every single word of this long story about going into restaurants in this incredibly eloquent and powerful statement, and then the last thing he spelled out to Boyden—and Boyden was sitting next to him so he was saying each letter as Bob pointed to the letter—he, Bob Williams, spelled out, "It ain't civil and it ain't right."

At that point Tim McFeeley just started crying, and he later said that it made such an impression on him. He was so used to the gay movement, and people with HIV being isolated, and having to go it alone. And to have this motley group of folks basically standing up like this just moved him tremendously. And today it is still moving. I think it was moving to anybody who was in that room.

We then had a press conference in which we announced that we would take down the entire bill if the Chapman amendment remained. That was a public statement. At that press conference we also had the Flight Attendants Union—the unions became involved, everybody became involved. And so it really was drawing the line in the sand.

The key person on our side around the Chapman amendment was Michael Iskowitz from Senator Kennedy's staff, who was a gay man who had gone up against [Senator Jessie] Helms five thousand times, had done numerous bills with [Senator Orrin] Hatch on AIDS. So he had a lot of experience with both the House and the Senate, trying to find compromises, to be clear about what compromise would work on the Senate side to be able to get enough votes. The other key staffers were Bobby Silverstein and Nancy Taylor. Bobby went to Hatch, and basically said, "We've done eight million disability amendments with you, Senator Hatch. I've worked with you for years. You've got to help us out here. You've got to do something because the rights and lives of people with disabilities are going to fall to the side, if this isn't taken down." It really was unclear as to whether we would actually have a bill.

Nancy Taylor, on Hatch's staff, was on her way to take a leave because she was pregnant. Historically, through the past months, we'd always been able to defeat amendments around AIDS using science as a linchpin. And so Nancy Taylor came up with what was the breakthrough amendment, to be able to (a), give both the Democrats and the Republicans something to vote *for*, as opposed to something to vote *against*, which is the secret to lobbying in Washington. It's almost always easier to get votes for something, as opposed to against something else. The amendment basically said that the Secretary of Health and Human Services should, on an annual basis, prepare a list of communicable, contagious diseases that can be transmitted through food handling.[4]

There was then a lot of jockeying with Senator Kennedy's staff around parliamentary procedure, and where that new amendment should go, and it went back and forth as to what amendment would pass. They rejected Helms, I think it was a 61 to 39 vote. Once they rejected Helms, then our Hatch Amendment came and it was, I believe, almost 99 to 1, with Helms being the only one voting against it.

32
Lobbyists, a Conversation

T HE DISABILITY RIGHTS EDUCATION AND DEFENSE FUND, IN 1999–
2000, sponsored a series interviews, videotaped by Ward and Associates,
to commemorate the tenth anniversary of the passage of the ADA. The series
reunited some of the major players in the campaign to reminisce on what they
had accomplished.

"That was an amazing piece of solidarity. When I think
about it now, it really does almost make me cry."

Paul Marchand, whose account as an activist in the parents' movement is
featured in chapter 7, was the chairman of the Consortium for Citizens with
Disabilities (CCD), which he described as "the Washington-based coalition
of national disability groups working together" to improve the lives "of our
constituency." Karen Peltz Strauss, featured in chapter 29, was the supervising
attorney at the National Center for Law and the Deaf, which has since changed
its name to the National Center for Law and Deafness at Gallaudet University.
David Capozzi was the national advocacy director for the Paralyzed Veterans
of America, and Karen Friedman was the deputy legislative director for the
Human Rights Campaign Fund (now the Human Rights Campaign).

They begin their conversation with a discussion of the relationship between
Section 504 of the Rehabilitation Act, up to that point the nation's most potent
federal cvil rights law for people with disabilities, and the ADA.

MR. CAPOZZI: There was a meeting held by the National Council on
Disability and I think it was Sandy Parrino or Pat [Wright] who talked
about "the donut and the hole." The question was: should we go for a

broad, all-encompassing law, or start with Section 504 and amend that and make that better? I don't know if 504 was the donut or the hole.'

MR. MARCHAND: [It was] the hole.

MR. CAPOZZI: That was the hole, and we went for the donut. . . . That was an important point. . . . I think the National Council was waffling as to which way to go. But I think that [this agreement] solidified everybody's position, and we then all went forward in one unified way, all finally agreeing that this was the approach we wanted to take.

MS. PELTZ STRAUSS: For me, I think the turning point was a meeting with Senator Harkin's staff, [with] Bobby Silverstein. We had been meeting for several years before the ADA to talk about how to get access to telecommunications for people who are deaf and hard of hearing, and had been drafting our own proposals for this really revolutionary concept that telephone companies would start providing relay services on a nationwide basis. We were never quite sure whether or not we had any chance of having [the] telephone companies or Congress go along with this. I remember a meeting that we had with Bobby and I think Senator Harkin, and they said they were going to put it into the ADA. We knew at that point that we had our vehicle, because we knew that a stand-alone law would have much less chance of passage.

MS. FRIEDMAN: From our perspective the fact that we were fighting to get people with HIV infection in the Americans with Disabilities Act during a Republican administration was an amazing thing in and of itself. The fact that the gay rights organizations were able to work in concert with the disability community was a turning point. For me it was a combination of doing grassroots actions and watching how many members of Congress were beginning to support our efforts. . . .

Our opposition, besides some conservative Republicans, were the National Restaurant Association, who had done this campaign saying that it wasn't so much people with AIDS or HIV infection—they knew that you couldn't transmit AIDS or HIV infection through food—but it was *the perception*. It was that argument that rallied so many organizations with us because what we are talking about here was not the reality, but the perception. So for me it was just a wonderful, historic moment in my life, organizing with the disability community this big campaign where we stuffed lunch bags with information, and we said the National Restaurant Association is "out to lunch." There were people with disabilities lining themselves up and down the Capitol steps, and we gave out these lunch bags. I can't say that that was what ensured that we defeated what was then the Chapman amendment that the National Restaurant Association had put forth, but it was definitely something that coalesced all of our organizations and gave it a new energy. When we won, it was just spectacular.

MR. CAPOZZI: It might be a good idea to talk about, besides the highlights, some of the lowlights, some of the real bummers. . . . It is very hard to find a true champion for any legislation. We found two terrific champions [for the ADA], one in the House and one in the Senate, one a Republican and one a Democrat, and they both went down, one through election and one through resignation, very shortly after we launched the ADA. Multiple times more amazing is that somehow those champions were replaced by others equally committed. To think that Tony Coelho in the House would step down and then literally hand us Steny Hoyer, and say, this is the guy who is going to do it for me and for us in the House. Then to lose somebody like Lowell Weicker in the Senate, who was himself a parent of a child with disability, and to be able to carry on from there, was stunning. That was huge.

The other [turning point] that I remember was again very early on, when we were essentially told by our congressional leaders that we had to drop the whole issue of insurance coverage. Discrimination in insurance is very big in the disability community. That could have stopped ADA in its tracks before we even got started. Some very gut-wrenching conversations took place among our community about whether we wanted to proceed without the potential for a good anti-discrimination provision in the insurance industry, and we swallowed hard and said, "Yeah, we think they are right, we can't take on the insurance industry."

MS. PELTZ STRAUSS: The telecommunications section was always seen as separate and apart, and it was also separate and apart in the senators and congressmen that supported us. Actually, we worked very little with either Hoyer or Harkin. We did work with some of Harkin's staff, but primarily we worked with Senator McCain. It was Senator McCain's staff that sat with us and painstakingly wrote this incredible section to require the relay services. The same thing on the House side. It was Congressman Markey (D-MA). We had to swallow hard, too, on not covering broadcasters—at that time cable wasn't as big as it is now, but we wanted captioning and we were told forget it. We wanted, also, movie access and we were told forget it. We remedied some of that. We went back to Congress and got the captioning coverage in 1996, but we still don't have movie access, not the way we want to. But we felt that we were getting so much elsewhere in the act, not only in the relay section but also in terms of auxiliary aids, that we just swallowed hard and said, "Okay, we'll pass up captioning for now."

MR. CAPOZZI:There was another example of significant compromise, and that was the whole discussion about access to over-the-road buses [such as those used by Greyhound or Trailways]. It was very controversial. In the Senate, we did fine. In fact, I can remember during one of the hearings, Charles Webb, who is the counsel for the American Bus Association, got up and testified how expensive it is to put lifts on buses. "It costs $35,000 to $50,000 to put a lift on an over-the-road bus." Senator Harkin asked, "Well, if it costs let's say $8,000, would that be reasonable?" And Webb said, "Well, yeah, that probably would be." Harkin said, "Well, good. I have got a letter here from a manufacturer who manufacturers lifts for $8,000." But then, when it got to the House, we had a much more difficult time, and we had to compromise and wind up with a study that said, "Study access to over-the-road buses. And then, based on that study, the Department of Transportation will issue some regulations and then maybe later you will get access to Greyhound-type buses." It wasn't until late 1998 that DOT finally came out with regulations that we are just now seeing, ten years later, over-the-road buses being accessible.

I think, generally, it was our experience that we had a lot more significant input in the Senate than we did in the House side. I think a lot of us felt like we worked [with] Bobby Silverstein and Senator Harkin on the Senate side, and felt less like that on the House side. The Senate bill was largely crafted by the disability community from the statutory language to the report language to the floor statements to witnesses. We lined up witnesses. We prepped them. On the House side, it was more reactionary than being proactive.

MR. MARCHAND: Part of the reason is the dynamic in the Senate compared to the House. But also remember that, in the Senate, we had one committee to go through. In the House, we had four chairmen attempting to stitch together a bill that came out of four different committees—go to the floor, a fairly unruly place, and get it passed. Again, we were extremely fortunate to have Steny Hoyer there because he essentially shepherded every piece that came through in every subcommittee, in every committee; despite the fact that he had no jurisdiction, no seat assignment in any one of those four committees. His role was amazingly critical because it could have fallen down. Those were other times that it got pretty depressing, when we had two of those committees simultaneously doing some bad stuff, and trying to orchestrate who goes where to do what when. I can't remember how many pizzas we ate in that conference room that Steny purloined in the Longworth Building where we spent many, many moons figuring this out. And he was there with us all the time—just an amazing role.

MS. FRIEDMAN: I remember camping out both in Steny's office and in Harkin's office. I feel like I spent the entire time running down for emergencies, for votes and stuff like that. I am trying to remember by how many votes we even beat the [Chapman Amendment]. I can't even remember at this point, but I remember it was very close. And that would have had just a terrible impact on public policy. Remember, this was ten years ago. Now members of Congress talk about gay rights issues on the floor and they talk about AIDS issues. At that time, AIDS was still extremely controversial, and it would have set such a terrible precedent. It was just frightening.

I even remember a press conference that we held—actually, it was on the Senate side, I believe. It was so interesting because so many people were so nervous about having a gay rights group up front that we didn't even—we put the press conference together, then we didn't even speak at it because people were so nervous about perception. It was a really intense time.

MR. MARCHAND: I am not sure if I ever articulated this with anybody, but certainly in the back of my mind constantly was: If we can protect [people with] HIV and AIDS, we got it made with everybody else. If we can hang in and have nobody walk away for all the reasons that Karen just said, we would be fine. [And] right behind you was the mental health crowd. They took some pretty strong hits during some of the debates, in terms of "dangerous people" working in the community, having their rights protected under ADA.

MS. FRIEDMAN: The disability community had to make a decision: Are we going to fight for people with AIDS, or are we going to have this bill? It was really an astounding thing that the whole disability community came and worked with the AIDS community and the gay rights community and said, "No. If this amendment stays on, the bill goes down." That was an amazing piece of solidarity. When I think about it now, it really does almost make me cry. Because, at that time—we are talking '89–'90—the gay rights movement was in a very different place than it is today, and the AIDS movement was in a different place.

MR. MARCHAND: AIDS was new to all of us from a political policy perspective. It was uncharted territory, and there always has been sort of a pecking order of "cool disabilities" and "not cool disabilities," with mental impairments and mental illness being at the bottom end of the "uncool disabilities" in terms of the public's general perception. AIDS ended up probably below that, when you look at it in that era. As I said, if we could win on AIDS, we could win on almost everything if it was solid policy; and we did—which brings me to mention one member of Congress, now deceased, who I hope we never forget. That is Hamilton Fish, the Republican from New York state who was a conferee and cast what I believe to be the deciding vote in conference, away from his Republican colleagues and with the majority on that issue or one equally sticky. When Ham Fish did what he did in conference, I, for the first time, said, "I think we are really going to get this done."

MS. PELTZ STRAUSS: I remember, during the time that the bill was being contemplated, I gave a workshop in Williamsburg to court stenographers on providing interpreters in court, an issue that cannot be further removed from the AIDS issue. While I was talking about providing auxiliary aids in courts for deaf people, one by one the hands shot up in the audience attacking me for supporting an act that would protect people with AIDS. I never forgot that. They engendered this hysteria around the issue.

MS. FRIEDMAN: President Bush, the Bush administration, completely abandoned us on this [see Patrisha Wright's account in chapter 31]. And

Bush had just made a speech basically saying that unfair discrimination against people with AIDS is wrong, and he even said something publicly about how the idea of discriminating against people with AIDS, even in the food industry, is wrong. So he had said this and he had made it public. Members of the disability community and representatives of the Human Rights Campaign and other AIDS organizations went to this meeting, and Pat was reminding me that it was the disability community, not the representatives of the AIDS groups or the gay rights groups, that argued this to a representative of President Bush. It really was a very emotional, a very exciting time.

MR. MARCHAND: I was certainly most proud of our consortium members. We had organized this consortium in a fairly serious way in the mid-seventies. We had CCD in place and effective and trusting each other—and I am talking then about eighty-five national groups representing providers of services, advocacy groups, parents, distinct disability groups all over the map—absolutely willing and able to work together and knowing how to do it. We met weekly at the Methodist building. We got our shit together. We made sure everybody who wanted to know would know what we had just accomplished that past week and what was coming in the week ahead and what their jobs were going to be. There is, for me, a thrill, an absolute thrill to see the group as a whole working in harmony so efficiently, so effectively. Without it, absolutely, ADA had not a prayer.

MR. CAPOZZI: I still think about that when I go past that Methodist building.

MS. FRIEDMAN: Yeah, I do too.

MS. PELTZ STRAUSS: Yeah, that was great.

MR. MARCHAND: The Methodist building, for those who don't know its physical location, is directly across the street from the United States Capitol, right adjacent to the Supreme Court Building.

MS. FRIEDMAN: A really special moment for me, apart from the politics, apart from passing the bill which, of course, were wonderful moments for me, but a really special moment for me was realizing that I had never worked with or met people with disabilities before, lots of them. I think one of the most amazing moments for me was Bob.

MR. MARCHAND: Bob Williams.

MS. FRIEDMAN: For me, he was one of my special moments in that process—meeting and becoming friends with him because I had just come in. I came in on the AIDS issue, and I remember that I was with Liz Savage, Bob, somebody else. Liz had been doing the spelling for Bob, when he was speaking, and then everybody left. They said, "Karen, do you mind, we have to leave, will you do this?" And suddenly I panicked. I thought, "Oh my God, I am not going to remember how to spell anymore." And I didn't know what to do. So I looked at Bob, and said, "I just have to tell you this Bob. I have never met anybody with cerebral palsy, and I am suddenly becoming completely panic-stricken that when you are speaking I am not going to be able to spell." He was just so delightful and adorable about this. We just hit it off—I can't explain it to you but it was just a moment when I realized, "Wow, this is really cool." It was a really important moment for me, personally.

MR. CAPOZZI: Do you realize that was a tactic on our part? That we used Bob in this way with all the doubters and all the rookies who just needed to get into it?

MR. MARCHAND: I can't tell you how many House and Senate staffers who were very uneasy with us, generally, and we would put Bob absolutely right in the front of them and hand that poor staffer Bob's talking board. And Bob would begin pointing at his board and that staffer, totally ambushed, would have no choice but to work out every letter in every word. But it created an environment where some of them really began to get it instantly, as you did. But that was a tactic—just kidding, was not a tactic for you, but we did it a lot.

MS. FRIEDMAN: Oh, I can see that.

MR. MARCHAND: And Bob willingly lent himself as essentially a tool for us to get some great points across.

Another part, for me—being one of the older dogs in this neighborhood doing his business—was to see some of our rookies in the disability lobby world and even some of the folks who had been there five, six, seven, eight years but who were still fairly young, blossom, take on roles and responsibilities that they probably hadn't thought about doing before. Others who we were hoping would do so, not only did it, but even surpassed what those of us who were in "leadership" thought. That was great to see that. And we continue to reap the benefits of that.

33
Senators

T HE TWO US SENATORS WHO STAYED WITH THE ADA FROM BEGINNING
to end, and who have been identified more than any others with its passage and its influence in American life, are Thomas Harkin of Iowa and the
late Edward M. Kennedy of Massachusetts. Like the original sponsors, Lowell
Weicker in the Senate and Tony Coelho in the House, both had direct and
intimate involvement with disability.

Senator Thomas Harkin
*"There were times when I had my own doubts that
this could ever, ever get through."*

Thomas Richard Harkin was born in November 1939, in Cummings, Iowa. His
father was a coal miner; his mother died when he was ten years old. Harkin
graduated from Iowa State University in 1962 and enlisted in the navy, serving
until 1967. He was elected to the US House of Representatives in 1974, reelected
four times, and then elected to the Senate in 1984, where he continues, as of this
writing, to be a leading figure in the Democratic Party.

I first recognized the need to make changes in law to address aspects
of disability when I was in the House of Representatives. See, I grew up
with my brother, who is deaf, and when I got into the House, I formed
a working relationship with then Senator Jennings Randolph from West
Virginia. . . . Just about the time I got here, I found out that they were
working on providing that line at the bottom of the television screens
[closed captioning for people who are deaf and hard of hearing], and

535

that they were making a decoding implement to go on a television set. So I worked with Jennings Randolph to get Sears Roebuck to make this decoding device, a great big box, and to sell it for cost. If I remember right, it was $179. We delivered the first one to then President Jimmy Carter in the White House, if I am not mistaken, in the year 1978. I think my brother got the fifth one ever made. I began to see just what laws could do to impact people with disabilities and how they live.

Of course, during my time in the House, I was also involved in debates on Public Law 94-142, [the] Education for all Handicapped Children Act, [and] also what would later become called the Rehab Act. Even though I wasn't on the Education Committee, I was greatly concerned about those. Then there was a couple of years there where I didn't do anything [related to disability, until] I got to the Senate and discovered, after I had been here about a year, that there was a move afoot to enact the sweeping comprehensive disability law.

At about that time, in January of 1987, the Democrats had taken the Senate back [and] I was asked by Senator Kennedy to go on his committee [on Labor and Human Resources]. I told him that I would if I could get the chairmanship of the Disability Policy Subcommittee. He said, "Sure."

That is when I first really began to see that disability rights legislation ought to be more than piecemeal. I had always thought of it before as, you do this for the deaf; you do this for the blind; you do this for people with other physical disabilities; you do this for people with mental disabilities. I had not thought of an overarching comprehensive civil rights bill until that time. . . .

Probably one of the biggest stumbling blocks to our getting ADA through was a guy by the name of John Sununu. I remember one time I was down in the White House on a social occasion, visiting with President Bush. I just happened to get on the elevator with [the president] and I said, "You are backing the Americans with Disabilities Act, the bill that we have in the Senate. We are having some real problems and, quite frankly, your chief of staff, Mr. Sununu, is not being very helpful on this and we need some help on it." He immediately got Boyden Gray, and Boyden Gray . . . came in and weighed in very heavily on it, and was sort of [the president's] representative on it from then on. That was a turning point, because we [then] had someone to deal with other than Mr. Sununu. . . .

I think another big turning point was when Bob Dole called all of us

together in a classic historical meeting in a room upstairs in the Capitol.
. . . All the players were there; Mr. Skinner, who was secretary of trans-
portation; Attorney General Dick Thornburgh—who was also very help-
ful in this, by the way—Boyden Gray; Mr. Sununu; Senator Dole, Senator
Kennedy. I was there; Bobby Silverstein, my staff person; and a couple of
House members were also there: Steny Hoyer; Major Owens.

We were sitting at this table, and Sununu was on one side and I am sitting on the other side, just about across from Sununu. Bobby Silverstein
is sitting next to me, and Kennedy is sitting next to Bobby Silverstein.
We are going through the bill. Now mind you, this is at the point where
the House has passed it and the Senate has passed it, but we have got two
different versions. We are trying to work out the differences.

Sununu is there raising all of these points about the bill, and why it
can't work in the fashion that we had it in the Senate. I remember there
was something about a barber shop in New Hampshire, some barber on
the second floor. Every time he would raise a point, Bobby Silverstein
would say, "Mr. Sununu, no, that is not right. Section 'so and so' of the
bill says this," and he would recite it to him and read him the exact language. Well, this happened maybe three times . . . and every time Bobby
Silverstein would correct him and say, "Well, here is what the bill says."
Finally, after about the third time, Sununu blew his stack. He looked at
Bobby Silverstein and he just started yelling at him. He said, "I don't need
any more of this from you. Every time I say something, you always bring
something up. I don't want to hear any more from you."

I am thinking, "Uh-oh, he can't get by with that." I am trying to think
what my response is going to be to this unseemly outbreak by Sununu.
Just about the time I was thinking about it, and Sununu was about halfway through his tirade, I looked over at Kennedy.

Senator Kennedy jumped up and he leaned across the table. I thought he
was going to grab Sununu by the collar. He took his hand and he hit it on
the table, boom, right in front of Sununu's face, and he pointed his finger at
him and says, "If you want to yell at anybody, you yell at me or you yell at
Senator Harkin. You don't yell at our staff. You got something to say, you say
it to me. You want to yell at me? You go right ahead and yell at me."

Sununu just got lower and lower in his chair. I think that was a great
turning point, because the other Bush administration people were there,
who were not in line with Sununu. But no one was willing to dress Sununu
down, and Senator Kennedy dressed him down and that was the end of

it. Sununu never raised any more points after that. That was the end of Sununu's objections.

It was a long, long process. It was emotionally draining. You think it is going to get through, you think it is going to happen, then it drags on and on and on. I know there were times when I had my own doubts that this could ever, ever get through, or if it got through it would be so weak and so watered down it would be meaningless and the disability community would have [had] a cruel joke played on them. That was my biggest fear—that we would pass something that wouldn't do anything. Then people would say, "Oh, isn't this wonderful, isn't this great?" and it wouldn't get anything done. . . .

[But] I was proud when it was signed into law, on July 26th. There is another little story about that. It has been standard practice, before and since, that the president always has the major sponsors of the bill with him when he signs a bill into law. Well, obviously, I was the major sponsor on the Senate side. I was up for reelection in 1990, and I had been hit pretty hard by a lot of the chamber of commerce and the business people, and my [Republican] opponent was making an issue of this ADA thing. So, when Bush signed it into law, he fixed it so that no one in the legislative branch would be on the stage because, if they had to have one, they had to have me up there. So none of the sponsors of the bills were on the platform with him when he signed the bill. It was kind of petty.

But, you know, what made it all right for me was the fact that Justin Dart was there. As long as Justin Dart was there, I could forgive anything because he really was the father of this whole thing. He was always out there. I might have objected to somebody else on the platform but as long as Justin was there, it made it all right as far as I was concerned.

Senator Edward M. Kennedy
"It was a proud moment for the country."

Senator Edward "Ted" Kennedy for more than four decades was such a fixture of American political life that he hardly needs an introduction. Born in February 1932, he was the younger brother of President John F. Kennedy and Senator Robert F. Kennedy. He was first elected to the Senate in 1962. From then, until his death on August 25, 2009, he was involved—and, particularly in the 1980s and '90s, played a leading role—in virtually every significant piece of civil rights legislation passed by Congress, including the Civil Rights Restoration Act of 1987, the Fair Housing Amendments Act of 1988, and the Americans with Disabilities Act of 1990.

Obviously disability was something relatively easy for me to identify with because of my own son, Teddy's, experience. He had lost a leg to cancer. I was able to understand how he viewed it, being very close to him. And I've had scores of small instances as well as larger instances where he'd travel with me, and Sunday morning we'd go to church. And if the church wasn't accessible, he'd say, "Excuse me, Dad," and he'd sit outside and read his prayer book and say his prayers outside till the Mass was over.

It was a constant reminder about the importance of accessibility. He then ran a foundation, that I was very familiar with during the eighties, to try and open up employment possibilities for people with disabilities in Massachusetts. And so I had the benefit of having some important insights and then [also] having the benefit of a wonderful sister, who's mentally retarded.[1] So I think being able to become even more emotionally involved in it was perhaps of some value.

If you look at this sort of globally, if you look in the 1980s, we were making some progress in the area of civil rights. You take 1988, we passed the Fair Housing Act, to stop discrimination on the basis of race. But in that '88 Act, we included discrimination against those who had a disability. They were tied together. This was two years, two-and-half years, prior to the ADA. And so once we were able to get thinking that this was civil rights rather than just special legislation, I think we created a climate and an atmosphere of understanding with our colleagues, that was really the basis of the progress we were able to make on that legislation.

There were several very important and significant moments along the pathway [to passage of the act]. I think one was the time of the actual markup and the reporting out of the legislation. I've been in the Senate for a long time, and generally speaking, if you call a meeting of a committee after the Senate is out, it's rare that you even get two or three members to come, let alone enough to really markup a bill. And as we were going through the evening and marking up a bill, more often than not the members leave because they have engagements in the evening, or they want to go home. And what happened [with the ADA was] at about eleven or eleven thirty at night, there were members of the committee that were opposed to the legislation and taking out books and started reading; I mean a real old-time filibuster. And that is usually a time when people say, "Well, okay, we'll try and bring this out the next day." But, no, people stayed. And so as the night went on, after midnight, almost *all* the members of the committee came. And the press took an interest in it, and so they began to show up, to pay attention.

But what was absolutely extraordinary to me, and what made an indelible impression upon all the members, [was that] the disability community came to that hearing, in wheelchairs, and packed that room, at one thirty or two in the morning. And what it said to every member of that committee, Republicans and Democrats alike was, "We're serious about this, and we're not going to take no for an answer. And it isn't *if* we're going to pass it, but *when* we're going to pass it." And that created an atmosphere and a climate in terms of not only the committee, but I think in the Senate, that said, "This is serious business; we're going to address it later on in the session." And we got the legislation out.

Secondly, there was a very important change in terms of the scope of the legislation. We were really at odds with the administration, and with important groups in the House and the Senate, special interests. But when we were to bring greater focus in the areas of transportation, in the areas of public accommodations, in terms of employment, and in the areas of communication, to bring a tighter scope to this, then suddenly I saw sort of a change in terms of the willingness to engage and talk about these issues. And that was something that took place in the late spring [of 1990].

We were running up against the arguments, you know, "What are you going to do on a ski lift? Are we going to require every chair in the chairlift to be accessible to someone in a wheelchair?" And I can remember others that said, "What are we going to do in a small bookstore, in Keene, New Hampshire, if we have one person in there and a blind person comes in? Will that person have to leave the counter and go back and help the blind person, or will they be able to stay there?"

There was an awful lot of fly-specking from those that were opposed to the legislation, but we were able to overcome that at a very important [conference committee] meeting that we had in the Capitol later on. I think, quite frankly, the momentum [by] then had become so powerful that by that time there was an inevitability about the legislation. There were still important issues to be resolved, but they were resolvable. And the emotions were very hot and heavy. Tempers were frayed and people were tired. And so there was some pretty strong exchanges during the course of the meeting. I'd rather leave that description up to others.

And then we had the other negotiations with the House, the whole debate on the Chapman amendment. If we had yielded on this to ideology rather than science, in terms of what were going to be the conditions of employment, then we would have enshrined in the legislation an ideology. And this legislation was important for the message that it sent, that we were going to free ourselves from ideology on this issue, which was the AIDS issue, and look at sound science, instead of it being wrapped up into a partisan political issue. You could say, "Well, this is just one section, and it only applied to a certain kind of workers"—still, it undermined, in a very important and significant way the basic freedom that this legislation, this declaration of independence [promised] for those with disability. And Pat Wright and the [various disability rights] organizations would not compromise on that principle, and I think it was a wise judgment, although there were people that were attempting to second-guess it at the time. But it was the right decision, and fortunately we prevailed.

This legislation was obviously a benchmark achievement for those with disabilities. If you look at what the conditions were a generation before and compare it to now, it's monumental. And the progress that was made in the eighties and then, I think, achieved with that legislation was [also] monumental. But we still have important ways to go, and particularly in the areas of health care. We still have to try to recognize the special health care circumstances that many of those with a disability are facing. And we still have to make progress in terms of employment. . . .

Certainly the highlight of this whole experience was sitting with my son Teddy and Pat Wright on the White House [lawn] at the time of the signing [by President Bush]. We were, I think, about 55 or 65 rows back. But we were back there with a lot of the people that had made the difference, and that was the place to be.

It was a proud moment for the country. And I think the disability community made this nation a more fair and a better country because of it, and they ought to get the sense of satisfaction from making this country the America that all of us want it to be.

34
Victory

———

WITH THE CHAPMAN AMENDMENT DEFEATED, THE ADA NOW ROLLED toward passage. There was, however, one last problem that had to be resolved before both houses could vote on the final bill.

Patrisha Wright (continued)
"It was an incredible sight to see that many disabled people . . . sitting on the lawn of the White House."

———

In addition to powerful rhetoric and dramatic street theater, the campaign to pass the ADA also saw moments bordering on the absurd. Here Patrisha Wright recounts one of these, coming just before the final vote and the signing ceremony on the White House lawn.

———

There was another amendment put on the floor by our friend Senator Hatch, which led to the most Fellini-esque scene I have ever had in my disability lobbying career. We were in the Senate anteroom, which is this really historic, ornate room with pictures of great orators painted on the wall. In the low periods of lobbying—of which there are a lot—you sit there and wait. You look around that room, and understand that Martin Luther King sat here. It's that type of emotion-filled room. And off to one side is the vice president's chamber, where you could go in and, depending on what your relationship is, watch the debate, because there's no television in that room. You're just outside the Senate Chamber, and so there is a gaggle of lobbyists there, of all shapes and sizes and types, anybody who has a bill pending. And you wait there and you offer technical assistance to the members, if they have a problem on the floor.

We're in this debate on the ADA, and it seems like everything's going along fine and then Kennedy comes out and says he's got a problem with Hatch. And the problem with Hatch is this list of kleptomaniacs and compulsive gamblers, and are we offering them protection? Hatch gave us a list of things that he wanted to exempt, and there were lots of mental illness–type disabilities in the *DSM-III*.[1] So we were going back and forth and back and forth, him saying this person can't stay in, this person can stay in, this person can't. "Are we going to give pyromaniacs, they burn down the building but we give them civil rights?"

So as he's trying to exclude people from protection, in walks the Easter Seals handicapped kid, the "very special" kid of the year. And he props this kid up on the table that's in the room, and does this photo op about being a friend of the disability community and helping disabled children. We're in the vice president's room, debating all these people he wants to take off the list.

And there was always the debate about transvestites. Congress had real problems with trannys at that time. It was difficult because you don't want to be arguing that a person who is transgender is mentally ill, and so therefore should be covered under the mental illness provision. People who were transgender would tell you that they're not mentally ill, they're transgender, they were just born the wrong gender.

The transgender lobby was mixed because they wanted civil rights. We all debated and came to the conclusion that having them be declared a disability would not be the best way to ensure their civil rights. But yes, there were lots of members who were very emphatic about excluding transvestites. And Senator Hatch really didn't like them.[2]

A final version of the ADA was approved by the House of Representatives on July 12, 1990, by a vote of 377 to 28. The next day it passed the Senate by a vote of 91 to 6. Despite these margins, Patrisha Wright and the team around her took nothing for granted until the final vote was cast.

Anybody who does bills does their own whip count. The House and Senate both do whip counts, and you do your own whip count and my count was just about on. I think I missed it by one or two votes. But you're never sure until it's over. Somebody from Sheboygan could call in, and their member says, "I'm voting with you," and then somewhere during the walk from that telephone to voting on the floor, they've been grabbed by two or three other lobbyists, and they vote the other way.

The sad part about it is that historians will look at those vote margins and say, "Oh, it was so easy. They had overwhelming support." That wasn't true. It took a lot of hard work by people in the states, various disability groups, people in the government, everybody working. Each one of those provisions were worked for, they were not an easy vote at all. Although the final outcome looks like it was just a sail through, like it was a sail through in all the House committees. But that wasn't easy either. But then I'll take that final vote. I wouldn't want it to be any closer.

The ceremony on the White House lawn was hysterical. Here we were talking about a civil rights bill being signed for the first time, and if you look at the language that they had drafted for Bush about "the walls of oppression coming down," and then you look at the fight that went on about that ceremony—they were trying to figure out how to get ambulances all around the audience, because there was going to be a bunch of disabled people there and it was going to be hot. So the stereotypes and fears about disabled people were rampant during that whole discussion about, "Can it be outside?" We all wanted it outside because we felt like the more people could come, the bigger the audience we could have, the better.

Sharon Mistler was part of putting it together, and Evan and Janine Kemp, putting together lists of names of people to be let through the door. And it was an incredible sight to see that many disabled people, as somebody said, dressed up and ready to go, sitting on the lawn of the White House. It's a visual that I will never forget.

And it was a wonderful sense, to know that a lot of those people who attended were people who worked incredibly hard in their community to make this all happen. And for them to be able to come to the table and come to the party was just an incredible gift. And I thank Evan for really hanging in there and pulling it off.

The staging was a little different than I would have imagined. It wasn't quite the people I would put on the podium, but there was lots of animosity going on between the Republicans and the Democrats at that time, and to not have any Democrat anywhere near the podium was kind of an insult. But you know, it was okay, because the bottom line was Bush signed it. And the bottom line was that a lot of people from all around the country got to come and share in that event, and that was pretty special.

I think the empowerment of people with disabilities is the biggest effect of the ADA. If I look at the impact the ADA has had globally—and I've spent a lot of time post-ADA traveling to various countries, and talking to people, and working with governments around their disability laws—it was a breakthrough for a lot of people in this country and around the world. I think the ADA really said it in the United States, and then again to the world, that we're a part of society. And that was a real change. I mean, the joy of my life is, every year when Mary Lou Breslin and I go on a trip somewhere, and it used to be a real fight to find an accessible bathroom. And she talks about now being able to go anywhere and pee, and as simple as that is, to be able to travel freely in this country—that's a big change for a lot of people who never had that before.

For a lot of people, internationally, it was the spark and a goal to work toward, knowing that this could happen in their country too. And we've seen people duplicating the ADA, we've seen people going off and doing it in a different way, but still using that jumping off point to say: "They did it there, we can do it here."

Even where I live now, in my remote area of Mexico, I see people understanding that they have to make things accessible. Although Mexican law doesn't require all the things they're doing, when expats come from the United States and open a business here, access has become an integrated part of life. And that's a big change: to know we're going to build a society that is not going to exclude you because of your inability to deal with that society's [in]accessibility.

To have been a part of making that change is just really incredible.

Justin Dart Jr. (continued)
"I went to the celebrations, but I did not feel euphoric."

———

On July 26, 1990, more than three thousand people convened on the White House lawn to witness President George H. W. Bush put his signature to the ADA. On the podium with him were Reverend Harold H. Wilke, a long-time civil rights activist and one of the first people with a severe disability to serve as a parish minister; Sandra Swift Parrino, chairperson of the National Council on Disability during the time the ADA was being debated first at the council, then in Congress; Evan Kemp Jr., chair of the Equal Employment Opportunity Commission during the same period; and Justin Dart Jr., who held many titles but is most widely remembered as "the father of the ADA."

———

At the signing ceremony I sat on the podium with Evan Kemp. And I was upset about that because I was totally embarrassed that Pat Wright and Judy Heumann and all of these other people weren't up there. I would have had thirty, forty, fifty people up on a really big stage, but they didn't listen to me. They did listen to me about the other arrangements, and got three thousand people onto the south lawn. They listened to me and Pat Wright and a whole bunch of other people about that. But anyway, I got there and I didn't even know I was going to be on stage.[3] And then, the president signed the law and gave me the first pen.

Remember that I have been a passionate civil rights advocate since I first read Gandhi when I was nineteen or twenty years old. I was in the movement in the 1950s trying to desegregate a segregated southern university. So civil rights is my dream. And here I am sitting next to the President of the United States as he is going to sign the first civil rights law in the history of the world for people with disabilities. So this is a monumental, historic occasion.

And as I was sitting up there waiting for the signing, there is the United States Army Band playing the "Battle Hymn of the Republic." And I am a red, white, and blue patriot. I remember World War II, when patriotism was in fashion. That's how I grew up. And here's the United States Army Band playing the "Battle Hymn of the Republic," about which I am very romantic. And here I am up there as the great hero at the great event.

I was going to take a vacation the next day. We had been working for ten years on this without stopping. We had worked Christmas and New Year's. We hadn't had a day off. So we were finally going to take a week off.

I thought I was going to feel euphoric, but instead of feeling euphoric I felt oppressed and depressed. And I said, "Justin, what the hell is the matter with you? When you were young you never dreamed anything like this would ever happen to you. And even if you died this afternoon, you have got it made."

But it suddenly occurred to me, and this had never occurred to me before and it really came down on me like a ton of bricks—I looked at these three thousand people, then I thought of the forty-three million people in America with disabilities, and I thought of all of the people in the future with disabilities. And I thought of three-quarters of a billion people with disabilities around the world, many of whom were being murdered, or were beggars on the street. And none of these people ever asked me to bet their life on this notion that this was a good time to have the first civil rights law.

What if we did it too soon? What if we can't carry it off, and it is perceived to fail, and they will not pass another law like this for one hundred or two hundred years? Look at how prohibition failed. Now if you want to get laughed out of Washington, just propose a law that prohibits alcohol. Look at the backlash against emancipation—Jim Crow for decades. And I thought, what if *this* is perceived to fail?

It just hit me like a ton of bricks, and I knew at that point that I would never rest easy. I would be oppressed by this responsibility for the rest of my life, and there would be no vacation.

I went to the celebrations, but I did not feel euphoric. And that has been true ever since. I have just felt the heavy weight of responsibility to make this thing work. Because it occurs to me that if it doesn't work, people will be condemned perhaps to an extra century or two centuries of a very serious oppression which is often the difference between life and death.

And I still feel that way.

35
Aftermath

THE TWENTY YEARS AFTER THE PASSAGE OF THE ADA SAW CONTINUED successes—as well as some significant setbacks—for the American disability rights movement. Yet nothing during those years so galvanized the community as did the struggle to pass the ADA. Nor did any coalition in those following decades approach the broad, bipartisan, cross-disability alliance that had shepherded the act through Congress to its final signature on the White House lawn.

In fact, Justin Dart's fears were to some degree realized. An intense backlash did occur. Critics of the act fulminated in the media, and adverse federal and Supreme Court rulings were handed down—often catching the community by surprise. A virtual industry of conservative and libertarian think tanks, lawyers, journalists, and publications seemingly intent on ridiculing the very notion of disability rights was spawned. Most notable in these efforts was the proliferation of ADA "horror stories," many of which were exaggerated or entirely fictitious, and attempts by, among others, Clint Eastwood to amend the act so as to limit its impact.[1]

Moreover, although many of the groups participating in the push for the ADA continued on the scene, they moved on to work separately on their particular issues. ADAPT, for example, switched its focus from accessible mass transit (which was now mandated in Title II of the act) to the provision of personal care services outside of nursing homes and other institutional settings—a shift reflected in the organization's name change, from American Disabled for Accessible Public Transit to American Disabled for Attendant Programs Today. Other groups, such as those comprising the Consortium for Citizens with Disabilities, largely reverted to their advocacy for increased budgets or various programmatic changes as opposed to straightforward civil rights work.

The midterm elections of 1994, which shifted control of both the House and Senate from center and liberal Democrats to conservative Republicans, seemed then to spell an end to Patrisha Wright's "golden age of disability rights legislation." Once again, as in the early 1980s, the emphasis was on defending rights already won. Justin Dart put it another way, comparing the situation of the disability rights movement to an army "that has seized control of the battlefield, but doesn't have the troops to hold it."[2]

In response to these developments, Dart, Fred Fay, and Becky Ogle in 1995 founded Justice for All, taking advantage of the emerging Internet and allies closely connected to Congress to pull together a rapid response network to foil attempts to roll back the gains made up to 1990. DREDF, recovering from a period of turmoil in the early nineties, returned to the field to litigate important cases and push for further legislation to solidify and extend those gains.

ADAPT and its legal allies, meantime, won what was perhaps the most significant ADA-related lawsuit of the 1990s. *Olmstead v. L.C and E.W.* was brought by two Georgia women with disabilities who had asked that the state provide them the community-based services they needed to live outside the nursing homes where they were being kept at state expense. They filed suit when the state refused. The Supreme Court ruled in July 1999 that the ADA required states to provide, wherever possible, community-based services rather than institutionalization. ADAPT also began lobbying for MiCASA [the Medicaid Community Attendant Services Act] and then for the Community Choice Act, efforts through legislation to force federal and state governments to direct significant public funding away from nursing homes and into independent living services.[3]

There were new groups arriving on the scene as well, though these tended to focus on specific issues not directly addressed by the ADA. Not Dead Yet, put together in large part by Diane Coleman, Carol Gill, and Steven Drake, tackled the issue of physician-assisted suicide. To them, the notoriety, even acclaim, which former doctor Jack Kevorkian received for what advocates perceived as the murder of people with disabilities, the majority of whom were not terminally ill, was an indication that the passage of the ADA had done little to change public perception of disability as "a fate worse than death." Jerry's Orphans, founded by Mike Irvin and his sister, Cris Matthews, confronted what they (and others, including Evan Kemp Jr.), saw as the paternalistic and demeaning stereotypes fostered by Jerry Lewis and his annual Labor Day Telethon to raise money for the Muscular Dystrophy Association.[4] The National Council on Independent Living and the National Council on Disability meanwhile devoted significant energy to spreading the message of independent living around the world and ensuring that new technologies, most especially the fast-expanding World Wide Web, would be accessible to all people, including those with visual and other disabilities. Finally, people with autism, Asperger's Syndrome, and learning dis-abilities emerged as a newly empowered constituency, building on the successes of the "phys-dis," self-advocates, and psychiatric survivor movements to assert their own place in the loose-knit disability rights coalition.

But where some groups saw progress, others felt they were losing ground. Title IV of the ADA may have provided hitherto unprecedented communica-tions access for people who are deaf, hard of hearing, or speech disabled, but many Deaf activists regarded the impetus to integration and mainstreaming under the Individuals with Disabilities Education Act as compromising the integration of deaf children into the Deaf community, tossing them instead into an all-hearing environment where they were less likely to succeed aca-demically. The economic and fiscal crises of the twenty-first century only exac-erbated this problem, with residential schools for Deaf children facing drastic budget cuts, to the point where some faced closing entirely.[5]

Then, too, many of the individuals highlighted in this account have died—Justin Dart Jr., Rev. Wade Blank, Evan Kemp Jr., Ed Roberts, Judi Chamberlin, and Fred Fay, to name only some—and many others have retired from the scene for health or other reasons. Disability rights activists are no less prone to "burn out" than those in any other social justice movement, while younger people with disabilities who might in earlier years have become politically active have instead availed themselves of the progress made and have gone to school or into the workforce relatively unaffected by the barriers and attitudes their forebears fought to overcome.

But the struggle for the civil and human rights of Americans with disabili-ties continues—in the courts, in the halls of Congress and the corridors of state houses, in the streets, and in the court of public opinion. New cohorts of activists now use tools and technologies inconceivable in the sixties, seventies, and eighties—the Internet, Listservs, YouTube—to apply the legal, political, and social leverage made possible through *PARC v. Pennsylvania,* Section 504, the Individuals with Disabilities Education Act, and the ADA.

It is indisputable, then, that despite whatever setbacks, the gains made by the movement in the second half of the twentieth century have been profound and enduring. They have, indeed, physically altered the American landscape. Every ramp into a school or shopping mall, every sidewalk curb cut or acces-sible voting booth, every ATM or elevator marked with braille signage, every lift on a public bus or elevator in a subway station, every television program with captioning, every ASL interpreter available in a courtroom or hospital emergency room, is testimony to this fundamental change. Perhaps even more profound has been the change in attitude, more difficult to measure, impossible to touch, but crucial nonetheless. The very idea, for example, of locking hundreds of thousands of children into massive state-run warehouses because they walk, talk, see, communicate, or think in ways different from some more or less arbitrary standard of "normal" is today virtually unthinkable.

Which is not to say that there are not still occurrences—sometimes widespread—of disability-based oppression or discrimination. Nor does it mean that people with disabilities don't continue to face many deep-rooted problems, including staggering rates of unemployment and poverty. But individuals facing these problems today are not alone—at least not legally or conceptually. They have a legal standing and political and social analysis unavailable, if not unimaginable, to those in similar situations in the 1940s and 1950s, at the far edge of the movement's living memory.

Denise Karuth (continued)
"I've waited twenty-two years to take this train."

Denise Karuth, who in the early 1970s faced discrimination in an undergraduate program in special education because of her disabilities, went on to become an advocate for "safe, reliable, affordable, accessible transportation in all its forms." Karuth knows firsthand how important an issue this is. She and scores of people she knew were, in the era before the ADA, unable to work, worship, or receive needed medical care because they couldn't drive, or afford their own vehicles or drivers, and because the Massachusetts Bay Transit Authority, like most others, did not consider access for people with disabilities a priority. Karuth herself, among other privations, missed an opportunity for a last meeting with a dying friend, *and* his funeral, because the Boston-area paratransit system, known as The Ride, insisted on three business days' notice for trips. "A subcontractor for The Ride refused to take my friend Rosemarie Ouellette to a funeral home on the day after her mother's death to make arrangements because Rose only gave twenty-four hours' notice." Karuth also worked with the Massachusetts Commission for the Blind in the early 1990s to document more than forty instances of blind individuals' falling from MBTA subway platforms into station pits with unshielded high voltage third rails. Shortly after this survey was submitted, Peggy McCarthy, a blind advocate with multiple disabilities, died after falling from an unmarked platform. "Now," Karuth says, "because of the ADA, people can schedule trips the day before they need them, the buses and trolleys are required to be accessible, and all platforms have tactile stripping to warn people that they are near the platform edge."

Karuth returned to Boston in 2003 from her new home in western Massachusetts and took the Green Line above-ground trolley on Beacon Street in Brookline. She and others had spent decades trying to persuade the MBTA to make the Green Line accessible. Now, at last, she had a chance to use the service for which she and others had fought so long.

It was a beautiful summer day. I was so thrilled to finally be able to do this. But of course, there was a glitch. To save money, the MBTA had opted to provide access to the trolleys using these rolling, hand-cranked lifts, stored at each accessible stop, which were designed for intercity trains that linger at platforms rather than trolleys which make many brief stops. The operator [of the trolley] had to jump off the train and run to get the ramp, which he had difficulty moving, deploying, and stowing.

I could tell there were people who were getting impatient, people who obviously needed to get somewhere, and were upset that we were taking so much time to get one person—me—onto the train. Some were beginning to step off the train, deciding to walk the rest of the way. When I finally got on, and saw that people were checking their watches and grumbling, I called out, "I'm sorry for the delay, but I've waited twenty-two years to take this train."

Some people probably had no idea what I was talking about, but there were others who did. Maybe they'd heard about the movement, or maybe they put it together for themselves. A couple of people said they were happy for me, and for what we have done. Several were surprised that people who used wheelchairs hadn't been able to ride the trains all along. I had to wonder about that. Didn't they ever notice that we were never around, that we never used the trains or the buses? What did they think, that we just didn't want to?

Despite the hassle, it was one of the best days of my life. After all that work, all that disappointment, all that struggle, I was finally *on* a trolley, looking out instead of always looking in. I was getting directly to where

I needed to go instead of driving my power wheelchair miles out of my way to catch buses with limited service, each and every day. I was Sisyphus, and I'd finally pushed the rock to the top of the hill.

I can't begin to tell you how good that felt.

Mary Lou Breslin (continued)
"I don't think people with disabilities, particularly people with visible disabilities, will ever have to live in the shadows again."

Finally, there is the experience of Mary Lou Breslin. As much as anyone in this volume, Breslin, as a founder of DREDF and the principal designer in the late seventies and early eighties of the "504 workshops," was one of the most prominent catalysts for the conceptual change that has taken Americans with disabilities "from caste to class."

Like Karuth, Breslin remembers the days when disability-based discrimination was quite literally written in stone—in the bricks and sidewalks, the buses and bathrooms of the entire nation, and she has a hundred stories about having to spend each day trying to work around these obstacles. There was, for example, "the time a friend of mine was arrested and asked me to bail him out of jail. So I go down there and of course there are a hundred steps up to the county facility. And I just had to sit at the bottom of the stairs and wait until somebody walked by who looked like they were hefty enough to drag me up. And that was very common—where you just waited until somebody came by who looked like they might be willing to do whatever needed to be done. Every single attempt to go out some place was affected by the presence of architectural barriers."

Even worse, perhaps, was how all this was accepted, not as discrimination, but simply as they were things were, the way they were meant to be. "I interpreted the problem as residing within myself. I had to figure out a way to overcome these barriers, rather than find a way to remove them."

Breslin is now the senior policy analyst at DREDF and lectures widely on disability rights issues and history. Every year she and Patrisha Wright take a "road trip" to celebrate their friendship and the progress the two of them have seen—progress they helped bring about.

If you work in the movement day to day, you tend to focus on what the present needs are, and not necessarily on what's working. But I think that there has been a shift in the way society perceives people with disabilities. There is less distance between them and us, and that's just a function of participating, of us actually being out in the community. I don't think people with disabilities, particularly people with visible disabilities, will ever have to live in the shadows again. I think that that is owed to the disability movement, to the legislation the movement has been able to engineer.

That doesn't mean there aren't huge challenges ahead, and much yet to be done. It's not even for a minute to suggest that we've gone where we need to go on all these issues, but I don't think, ever again, that somebody with a visible disability won't be able to go out on the street. Someone may glance at them, but they are much more a part of the diversity of communities and the nation, and perceived that way, than ever before. Now whether or not they can get around, or get in and out of places, or get jobs, or not still be experiencing a certain amount of stigma, continues to be a question. But I think the idea that people with disabilities have the right to live in, to work, and to participate in the community is really permanently embedded in the national psyche. And that, to my mind, is an extraordinary accomplishment, and one that is worth marking and noting.

This accomplishment is embodied in the built environment which people see and use every day. No one will ever again think there shouldn't be a ramp to a building now, or that there shouldn't be an accessible bathroom. Not to harp only on the physical access issues, but the built environment educates, it instructs, it stands for something. It's there, and you see it every single day. And, so, you'll never think again that you shouldn't be able to get into a place you want to go as a patron or as a participant. The world expects it now, it expects for access to be there.

For example, on Friday I spoke at an employment lawyer's conference. And it was just so interesting because they have a 700- or 800-person membership in California. About 30 percent of them do disability employment discrimination law, and they're doing all kinds of fascinating cases that have to do with accommodating people with multiple medical problems and all kinds of things that are covered as disabilities under the state law. As the ADA sets the pace nationally, some of the states are going further, and California is one of them. So we're seeing progress beyond the

ADA in California. The definition of disability in California since the early 2000s has been "a person with a limitation," not a "substantial limitation" as we have under the ADA. And that covers a lot of people. Of course, you still have to prove that you've been discriminated against, but you can try to use the law for your benefit. So the whole idea of taking the focus off of the person and putting the focus onto the adverse action, either by the built environment, or through employment policies, or through educational issues, that, to me, is the real shift. It's not perfect, and it's not working everywhere, but that is the shift that is happening.

And that's the civil rights paradigm. And these employment lawyers are doing this every day. They don't know anything about our history as a movement. Some of them do, but most of them don't. They're younger, they're practicing an area of law they've learned through their interest and through law school, and they're using it: this living, organic belief system that's resonating everywhere. And it was exciting to observe what they're doing and how successful they are at it, and how important it is that the law keep pace with what we're experiencing, and how we're defining and redefining the issues.

We can't go back. It's like driving over the little prongs in the parking lot, and you better not back up or you're going to get your tires blown, you know? It's like the arrow of time: it's going forward, it's not going to go backward. And the ADA specifically has been the impetus for that. I suppose it could be undone through some cataclysmic social or environmental event that we can't anticipate, where everything gets suspended. But short of that, we may lose ground on some court cases, or there may be some backsliding, but there isn't going to be a return to the ways of forty or fifty years ago.

This last fifty years have seen an extraordinary change. And one would hope that it can only get better.

Notes

Preface

1. The phrase also forms the title of a history of the disability rights movement by James I. Charlton, *Nothing About Us Without Us: Disability Oppression and Empowerment* (Berkeley: University of California Press, 1998).

2. There have, of course, been first-person accounts by people with disabilities, Helen Keller's *The Story of My Life* (Garden City, NY: Doubleday, 1903) being perhaps the most famous. These have generally been personal stories written to explain how, through individual exertion or perhaps with the support of family, friends, therapists, and/or physicians, the author has been able to "triumph" or "overcome" or otherwise accommodate to their disability. In contrast are autobiographies told from a disability rights or movement perspective, for example, Frank Bowe's *Changing the Rules* (Silver Spring, MD: T. J. Publishers, 1986) and Connie Panzarino's *The Me in the Mirror* (Seattle: Seal Press, 1994).

3. Paul Longmore, "Disability Scholar and Activist, Historian of Early America," interview conducted by Ann Lage, 2006, DRILM Oral History Project, Regional Oral History Office, The Bancroft Library, University of California, Berkeley; © 2008 by The Regents of the University of California, 161–62.

4. For the history of this convention, see Carol Padden and Tom Humphries, *Deaf in America: Voices from a Culture* (Cambridge: Harvard University Press, 1988), 2.

Introduction

1. Leon Friedman, ed., *Argument: The Oral Argument before the Supreme Court in Brown v. Board of Education of Topeka, 1952–55* (New York: Chelsea House, 1969), 51.

2. Thomas K. Gilhool interview, 53.

3. For a discussion of how these terms were used, see James W. Trent Jr., *Inventing the Feeble Mind: A History of Mental Retardation in the United States* (Berkeley: University of California Press, 1994): "At the [American Association for the Study of the Feeble-Minded] meeting in 1910 . . . Goddard presented the committee's new scheme. . . . In it . . . *[i]diots* referred to individuals with a mental age of two years and less; *imbeciles,* three to seven years; and *morons,* eight to twelve years" (161–62).

4. Buck v. Bell, 274 U.S. 200 (1927).

5. Mark A. Largent, *Breeding Contempt: The History of Coerced Sterilization in the United States* (New Brunswick, NJ: Rutgers University Press, 2008), 102.

6. Harry L. Laughlin, "The Legal Status of Eugenical Sterilization," a supplement to *The Annual Report of the Municipal Court of Chicago,* 1929, 17.

7. For a more detailed history of the case and discussion of its impact, see Stephen Trombley, *The Right to Reproduce: A History of Coercive Sterilization* (London: Weidenfeld and Nicolsen, 1988). The rate of coerced sterilizations after *Buck v. Bell* "skyrocketed. In 1925, just under 6,000 compulsory sterilization[s] had been recorded, but within ten years that number would top 20,000." Largent, *Breeding Contempt,* 102.

8. Floyd Matson, *Blind Justice: Jacobus tenBroek and the Vision of Equality* (Washington, DC: Library of Congress, 2005), 117–18.

9. For a discussion of tenBroek's personal experience with employment discrimination, see Matson, *Blind Justice*, 86–99.

10. Friedman, *Argument*, 62–63.

11. Robert Funk, "Disability Rights: From Caste to Class in the Context of Civil Rights," in *Images of the Disabled, Disabling Images*, ed. Alan Gartner and Tom Joe (New York: Praeger, 1987), 9, 24.

12. Sharon Barnartt and Richard Scotch, *Disability Protests: Contentious Politics, 1970–1999* (Washington, DC: Gallaudet University Press, 2001), 3.

13. John Vickrey Van Cleve and Barry A. Crouch, *A Place of Their Own: Creating the Deaf Community in America* (Washington, DC: Gallaudet University Press, 1989), 1.

14. Nora Ellen Groce, *Everyone Here Spoke Sign Language: Hereditary Deafness on Martha's Vineyard* (Cambridge: Harvard University Press, 1985).

15. Justin Dart Jr., "An Open Letter from Justin Dart to the Disability Community," *Mainstream: Magazine of the Able-Disabled* 22, no. 6 (March 1998): 27.

16. Aliki Coudroglou and Dennis L. Poole, *Disability, Work, and Social Policy: Models for Social Welfare* (New York: Springer Publishing, 1984), 13.

17. Nancy L. Eiesland, *The Disabled God: Toward a Liberatory Theology of Disability* (Nashville: Abingdon Press, 1994), 70.

18. James I. Charleton, "Religion and Disability: A World View," *Disability Rag & Resource*, September/October 1993, 14–16.

19. William Blair and Dana Davidson, "Religion," in *Encyclopedia of Disability and Rehabilitation*, ed. Arthur E. Dell Orto and Robert P. Marinelli (New York: Macmillan Library Reference, 1995), 628.

20. Nancy J. Lane, "Healing of Bodies and Victimization of Persons: Issues of Faith Healing for Persons with Disabilities," *Disability Rag & Resource*, September/October 1993, 11.

21. Melvin Lerner, *The Belief in the Just World: A Fundamental Delusion* (New York: Plenum, 1980); Rosemarie Garland-Thomson, *Extraordinary Bodies: Figuring Physical Disability in American Culture and Literature* (New York: Columbia University Press, 1997), 36–37.

22. Henri-Jacques Stiker, *A History of Disability*, trans. William Sayers (Ann Arbor: University of Michigan Press, 1999), 24.

23. Joseph P. Shapiro, *No Pity: People with Disabilities Forging a New Civil Rights Movement* (New York: Random House, 1993, 1994), 117.

24. Stiker, *History of Disability*, 39.

25. Ibid., 40.

26. Robert Garland, *The Eye of the Beholder: Deformity and Disability in the Graeco-Roman World* (Ithaca, NY: Cornell University Press, 1995), 28–29.

27. Carol F. Karlsen, *The Devil in the Shape of a Woman: Witchcraft in Colonial New England* (New York: Vintage Books/Random House, 1987), 16.

28. Leonard Kriegel, "The Cripple in Literature," in Gartner and Joe, *Images of the Disabled*, 33.

29. Martin F. Norden, *The Cinema of Isolation: A History of Physical Disability in the Movies* (New Brunswick, NJ: Rutgers University Press, 1994), 220.

30. George Henderson and Willie V. Bryan, *Psychosocial Aspects of Disability* (Springfield, IL: Charles C. Thomas, 1984), 8.

31. Deborah Kaplan, "The Definition of Disability." The Center for an Accessible Society: Disability Issues Information for Journalists, www.accessiblesociety.org/topics/demographics-identity/dkaplanpaper.htm, 2.

32. Richard K. Scotch, "Medical Model," in *Encyclopedia of American Disability History*, ed. Susan Burch, 3 vols. (New York: Facts On File, 2009), 3:602–3.

33. Kaplan, "Definition of Disability," 2.

34. Funk, "Disability Rights," 9.

35. For a detailed recounting of this transition, see, for example, the chapter "Idiots in America" in Trent, *Inventing the Feeble Mind*, 7–39, and Philip M. Ferguson, *Abandoned to*

Their Fate: Social Policy and Practice toward Severely Retarded People in America, 1820–1920 (Philadelphia: Temple University Press, 1994).

36. Floyd Matson, *Walking Alone and Marching Together: A History of the Organized Blind Movement in the United States, 1940–1990* (Baltimore: National Federation of the Blind, 1990), 5.

37. Timothy M. Cook, "The Americans with Disabilities Act: The Move to Integration," *Temple Law Review* 64, no. 2 (1991): 400. Cook in this instance is quoting Henry H. Goddard, *The Possibilities of Research as Applied to the Prevention of Feeblemindedness, Proceedings of the National Conference of Charities and Correction* (1915), 307.

38. Douglas C. Baynton, "Disability and the Justification of Inequality in American History," in *The New Disability History: American Perspectives,* ed. Paul K. Longmore and Lauri Umansky (New York: New York University Press, 2001), 33.

39. Cook, "Americans with Disabilities Act," 404.

40. Baynton, "Disability and the Justification of Inequality," 34.

41. Cook, "Americans with Disabilities Act," 400–401.

42. Largent, *Breeding Contempt,* 78.

43. Ibid., 8.

44. T-4 refers to Tiergarten 4, the address of the German government office supervising the extermination of people with certain disabilities. Estimates of the number of people murdered by the program—most often by poison gas or lethal injection administered by physicians at designated killing centers—vary from a low of 90,000 to a high of 275,000 for Germany and Austria alone. For detailed accounts of T-4 and other Nazi atrocities against people with disabilities, see Hugh Gregory Gallagher, *By Trust Betrayed: Patients, Physicians, and the License to Kill in the Third Reich* (New York: Henry Holt, 1990), and Robert Jay Lifton, *The Nazi Doctors: Medical Killing and the Psychology of Genocide* (New York: Basic Books, 1986).

45. Largent contends that "contrary to conventional wisdom, the American eugenics movement did not end with the discovery of the Nazi's atrocities during World War II, nor did the practice of coerced sterilization. From the late 1940s through the 1950s, eugenically justified legislation to limit immigration persisted, hospitals and prisons coercively sterilized record numbers of Americans, and educators in high school and college biology courses continued to teach students how 'a great reduction in human suffering could be achieved' if it were possible to 'decrease the number of afflicted individuals born in each generation.'" *Breeding Contempt,* 8.

For examples of the impact of the eugenics movement on particular individuals in just one American community, see Mary Bishop, "An Elite Said Their Kind Wasn't Wanted," *Roanoke Times & World-News,* June 26, 1994.

46. Edward D. Berkowitz, *Disabled Policy: America's Programs for the Handicapped* (Cambridge: Cambridge University Press, 1987), 15.

47. Berkowitz, "The Origins of Social Security Disability Insurance," in ibid., 41–78.

48. Paul K. Longmore, *Why I Burned My Book and Other Essays on Disability* (Philadelphia: Temple University Press, 2003), 238.

49. Ibid., 239.

50. Scotch and Barnartt, *Disability Protests,* 5.

51. For a history of these developments, see Paul Starr, *The Social Transformation of American Medicine: The Rise of a Sovereign Profession and the Making of a Vast Industry* (New York: Basic Books, 1982), especially the chapter "The Mirage of Reform," 235–89.

52. On the history of income maintenance programs for people with disabilities, see Coudroglou and Poole, *Disability, Work, and Social Policy,* 15–24.

53. Longmore, *Why I Burned My Book,* 236.

54. Paul K. Longmore, *The Invention of George Washington* (Charlottesville: University Press of Virginia, 1999).

55. Longmore, *Why I Burned My Book,* 236.

56. In 1986, Congress "overrode SSA[Social Security Administration]'s resistance" to eliminating work disincentives. "With the arrival of Section 1619, the work penalties that had blocked

me were at long last gone. Or so I thought." Ibid., 249. Longmore was eventually able, after years of struggle, to achieve his dream of teaching history, eventually earning tenure as an associate professor of history at San Francisco State University in 1995. He died in 2010.

57. Ibid., 253. See also Cheryl Rogers, "The Employment Dilemma for Disabled Persons," in Gartner and Joe, *Images of the Disabled*, 117–27.

58. Wilma Donahue quoted in Ruth O'Brien, *Crippled Justice: The Theory of Modern Disability Policy in the Workplace* (Chicago: University of Chicago Press, 2001), 68.

59. O'Brien, *Crippled Justice*, 7.

60. "Counselor knows best" is taken from Kelly Buckland, Ann McDaniel, and Jeff Hughes, "The Struggle for Independent Living," *American Rehabilitation*, Special Edition, Summer 2010, 32. The article cites a continuing tension between the "medical and rehabilitation models" and the "independent living paradigm" coming out of the disability rights movement of the 1970s, "an ongoing struggle over the balance of power and authority between VR [vocational rehabilitation] and IL [independent living]."

61. O'Brien, *Crippled Justice*, 5.

62. Jack R. Gannon, David Myers, Charlotte A. Coffield, Richard Johnson, and Ernest Hairston, "The Neverending Legacy of Mary E. Switzer and Boyce R. Williams," *American Rehabilitation*, Special Edition, Summer 2010, 5.

63. Nora Groce, *The U.S. Role in International Disability Activities: A History and a Look Towards the Future*, a study commissioned by World Institute on Disability, World Rehabilitation Fund, and Rehabilitation International, 1992, 54.

64. O'Brien, *Crippled Justice*, 75–78.

65. See Frank Bowe, *Handicapping America: Barriers to Disabled People* (New York: Harper and Row, 1978), 18–22. "When the Senate Special Committee on Aging held hearings on architectural design in October of 1971, testimony revealed that only one community, Owen Brown Village of Columbia, Maryland, then under construction, was designed to be totally barrier free. When Timothy Nugent of the University of Illinois, one of the nation's premier experts on barrier-free design, confronted thirty-five architectural groups with figures showing that doorways to bathrooms and other parts of residential buildings typically were inaccessible to many non-ambulatory disabled people, none of the architects could explain why the buildings had been designed that way, except to say that this was how it had always been done" (19).

66. See Karen Peltz Strauss, *A New Civil Right: Telecommunications Equality for Deaf and Hard of Hearing Americans* (Washington, DC: Gallaudet University Press, 2006). Strauss, in her introduction, gives a vivid description of the difference that telecommunications access in general, and Title IV of the Americans with Disabilities Act of 1990 in particular, has made in the lives of Americans who are deaf and hard of hearing.

67. Jacqueline Vaughn Switzer, *Disabled Rights: American Disability Policy and the Fight for Equality* (Washington, DC: Georgetown University Press, 2003), 31–32.

68. Hugh Gregory Gallagher, *FDR's Splendid Deception* (New York: Dodd, Mead, 1985). *Disability Rag* editor Mary Johnson notes: "Like many successful 'overcomers,' people who 'just happen to have a disability' but who are not seen as 'handicapped,' Roosevelt had managed to cross the line separating 'normal people' from those society considered deviant and had labeled 'the handicapped.' Roosevelt had struck The Bargain society needed, so he was considered OK by society. He was, after all, trying to be 'normal.'" She quotes Paul Longmore's definition of "The Bargain": "The non-handicapped majority says . . . 'we will extend to you provisional and partial toleration of your public presence—as long as you display a continuous cheerful striving toward 'normalization.'" Mary Johnson, "The Bargain," *Disability Rag*, September/October 1989, 7, 6.

69. A vivid example of this can be seen in the phenomenon of "public stripping." Many disabled people recount how, often as children, they were stripped and displayed in hospital and rehabilitation settings to groups of medical students, interns, and others. Lisa Blumberg, "Public Stripping," in *The Ragged Edge: The Disability Experience from the Pages of the First Fifteen Years of the Disability Rag*, ed. Barrett Shaw (Louisville, KY: Advocado Press, 1994), 73–77.

70. Bowe, *Handicapping America,* ix. Bowe can hardly be accused of hyperbole in his statement that people with disabilities have been raped and killed. One study found that 83% of women with developmental disabilities surveyed had been sexually assaulted; another study found that half of those who had been assaulted had been assaulted ten or more times. Switzer, *Disabled Rights,* 167–68. For a discussion of the issue of physical and sexual violence against people with disabilities, see Richard Sobsey, *Violence and Abuse in the Lives of People with Disabilities: The End of Silent Acceptance?* (Baltimore: Paul H. Brookes Publishing, 1994). Sobsey cites numerous examples of people with disabilities being targeted for assault and homicide, including "mercy killings" by caregivers: 1–2, 210–11, 274–76.

Barbara Faye Waxman defined some assaults against people with disabilities as "hate crimes," citing as examples the firebombing of group homes for people with developmental disabilities and the vandalizing of wheelchair ramps. Waxman, "Hate," *Disability Rag,* May/June 1992, 5.

H. Ted Rubin notes that "There are reports that adults with disabilities are more likely to be victims of crimes than adults without disabilities and that the rate of victimization may be shocking while going largely unnoticed." Furthermore, "Law enforcement officers, particularly those who lack specialized training, may choose to terminate an ostensibly valid injury complaint [by a person with a disability] without forwarding this on to a prosecution official." Rubin, "Crime and Delinquency," in *Encyclopedia of Disability,* Gary L. Albrecht, gen. ed., 5 vols. (Thousand Oaks, CA: Sage Publications, 2006), 1:324.

71. Jerry Lewis, "If I Had Muscular Dystrophy," *Parade,* September 2, 1990. For an account of the disability rights response to Lewis, see Mary Johnson, "A Test of Wills: Jerry Lewis, Jerry's Orphans, and the Telethon," in Shaw, *Ragged Edge,* 120–30. For an exploration of the "complete stranger" phenomenon, see, Corbett O'Toole's narrative in chapter 1 of this volume, and Denise Karuth, "If I Were a Car, I'd Be a Lemon," in *Ordinary Moments: The Disabled Experience,* ed. Alan J. Brightman (Syracuse, NY: Human Policy Press, 1985), 11.

72. Katherine Simpson, "Traveling," in Shaw, *Ragged Edge,* 104.

73. Gannon, *Deaf Heritage,* 59–74; Susan Burch, *Signs of Resistance: American Deaf Cultural History, 1900 to World War II* (New York: New York University Press, 2002), 88–89.

74. Paul K. Longmore and David Goldberger, "Political Movements of People with Disabilities: The League of the Physically Handicapped," *Disability Studies Quarterly* 17, no. 2 (Spring 1997): 94–98.

75. Matson, *Walking Alone and Marching Together,* 13–57; Groce, *U.S. Role in International Disability Activities,* 32; Audra Jennings, "American Federation of the Physically Handicapped," in Burch, *Encyclopedia of American Disability History,* 1:37–38.

76. Matson, *Blind Justice,* 116.

77. Ibid., 154–60.

78. Audra Jennings, "Strachan, Paul A.," in Burch, *Encyclopedia of American Disability History,* 3:869.

79. Groce, *U.S. Role in International Disability Activities,* 32.

80. Audra Jennings, "President's Committee on Employment of People with Disabilities," in Burch, *Encyclopedia of American Disability History,* 2:738.

81. Ibid., 2:739.

82. The Library of Congress website states that the committee officially became the President's Committee on Employment of the Physically Handicapped only in 1955, under the same executive order signed by President Eisenhower that established it as a permanent government entity. "President Kennedy issued Executive Order 10994 in 1962 . . . renaming the Committee as the President's Committee on Employment of the Handicapped. . . . In 1988 President Reagan issued Executive Order 12640 which again renamed and reorganized the committee as the 'President's Committee on Employment of People with Disabilities.'" "National Disability Employment Awareness Month," www.loc.gov/law/help/commemorative-observations /disability-awareness.php.

83. See, for example, Fred Fay's description of using committee meetings to help organize the American Coalition of Citizens with Disabilities in the mid-1970s. Frederick A. Fay interview, 105.

84. Kathi Wolfe, "War Work," *Mainstream,* August 1995, 17–23.

85. Richard Bryant Treanor, *We Overcame: The Story of Civil Rights for Disabled People* (Falls Church, VA: Regal Direct Publishing, 1993), 19–20.

86. Groce, *U.S. Role in International Disability Activities,* 38.

87. Fred Pelka, *The ABC-CLIO Companion to the Disability Rights Movement* (Santa Barbara, CA: ABC-CLIO, 1997), 225–26; Polly Welch, ed., *Strategies for Teaching Universal Design* (Boston: Adaptive Environments, 1995), 6–8.

88. United Cerebral Palsy was chartered in August 1949 as the National Foundation for Cerebral Palsy; the name was changed to United Cerebral Palsy in 1950. For a history of the founding of UCP, see Maria Killilea, *Karen* (New York: Dell, 1952). For the founding of the NARC, see Mildred Thomson, *Prologue: A Minnesota Story of Mental Retardation Showing Changing Attitudes and Philosophies Prior to September 1, 1959* (Minneapolis: Gilbert Publishing, 1963). For a history of the later NARC, see Rosemary Dybwad, *Perspectives on a Parent Movement: The Revolt of Parents of Children with Intellectual Limitations* (Brookline, MA: Brookline Books, 1990). For a biography of Elizabeth Boggs, see Groce, *U.S. Role in International Disability Activities,* 135–36.

The evolution of the NARC's name is itself an instance of the evolution and impact of the disability rights perspective. The parents of children labeled mentally retarded who founded the organization in 1950 called themselves the National Association of Parents and Friends of Mentally Retarded Children; in 1953 the name was changed to the National Association for Retarded Children (NARC). By the 1970s many of the children of the founders were grown, and so in 1973 the name was changed to the National Association for Retarded Citizens—thus retaining the acronym. In 1981 the name was once again changed, to the Association for Retarded Citizens of the United States, or ARC. However, the use of "retarded" to describe people with disabilities, whether children or adults, was keenly resented by people with developmental and cognitive disabilities themselves, and with the rise of the self-advocates movement (see chapter 18), the use of the acronym was abandoned entirely in 1991. Today the organization is known simply as "the Arc." See the History section of the Arc's website, www.thearc.org.

89. Groce, *U.S. Role in International Disability Activities,* 150–52; Pelka, *ABC-CLIO Companion,* 189–90

90. Jennings, "American Federation of the Physically Handicapped" in Burch, *Encyclopedia of American Disability History,* 1:37–38; Clarence Averill, interview by Fred Pelka, September 19, 1996, in the possession of the author.

91. Matson, "Civil War: Disunity and the Road to Recovery," in *Walking Alone and Marching Together,* 117–66. For the ACB perspective on this issue, see James J. Megivern and Marjorie L. Megivern, *People of Vision: A History of the American Council of the Blind* (Washington, DC: American Council of the Blind, 2003). For a nonpartisan description, see Brian R. Miller, "American Council of the Blind," in Burch, *Encyclopedia of American Disability History,* 1:35–36.

92. "It should be noted that minority populations with disabilities have been ignored from at least two fronts. First, minority communities have been generally preoccupied with their own particular needs related to survival and agendas such as the elimination of discrimination and racism. Their members with disabilities have not been a priority. Second, within the 'disability community', minorities have not been an emphasis and service delivery to Americans with disabilities has been essentially a movement of the White majority. It may be safe to say that even the passage of the Americans with Disabilities Act (ADA) may not by itself have much impact upon minorities unless both the minority and majority communities become much more aware and sensitive to the minorities with disabilities within them." Tennyson J. Wright and Paul Leung, "Minorities with Disabilities: An Introduction," in *The Unique Needs of Minorities with Disabilities: Setting an Agenda for the Future, Conference Proceedings,* ed. Wright and Leung, The National Council on Disability and Jackson State University, cosponsors, May 6–7, 1992, 2.

The education of children with disabilities, prior to *Brown v. Board,* was as racially segregated as that of non-disabled children. Indeed, the segregation was in some ways worse, since such major institutions of national importance as the Warm Springs polio rehabilitation center (in Georgia) and Gallaudet College for the Deaf (in the District of Columbia) were located in areas where racial segregation was particularly rigid. Within the Deaf community the separation between black and white seems to have had a particularly adverse impact: "The ramifications of deafness, the lack of sufficient Black role models, and the overall racial situation in the schools deprive many Black deaf youth of the strong sense of racial pride many normally hearing Black young people have." Ernest Hairston and Linwood Smith, *Black and Deaf in America: Are We That Different?* (Silver Spring, MD: T. J. Publishers, 1983), ix. Segregation was prevalent in social settings as well. In Washington, DC, the Washington Silent Society was established as an all-black Deaf social club, in part as a response to blacks' not being permitted to join the District of Columbia Association of the Deaf. Ibid., 37.

For a discussion on the confluence of sexism and ableism, see Michelle Fine and Adrienne Asch, eds., *Women with Disabilities: Essays in Psychology, Culture, and Politics* (Philadelphia: Temple University Press, 1988); Esther Boylan, ed., *Women and Disability* (London: Zed Books, 1991); and Marsha Saxton and Florence Howe, eds., *With Wings: An Anthology of Literature By and About Women with Disabilities* (New York: Feminist Press at the City University of New York, 1987).

For a discussion of gay/lesbian/bisexual/transgender issues and disability, see Connie Panzarino, *The Me in the Mirror* (Seattle: Seal Press, 1994), and Raymond Luczak, *Eyes of Desire: A Deaf Gay and Lesbian Reader* (Los Angeles: Alyson Publications, 1993). For a discussion of cross-cultural issues, disability, and rehabilitation, see John H. Stone, ed., *Culture and Disability: Providing Culturally Competent Services* (Thousand Oaks, CA: Sage Publications, 2005).

93. In her review of the film *Malcolm X,* Marta Russell observes: "Malcolm's most important message was to love blackness, to love black culture. Malcolm insisted that loving blackness was itself an act of resistance in a white-dominated society. . . . It is equally important for disabled persons to recognize what it means to live as a disabled person in a physicalist society—that is, one which places its value on physical agility. . . . Our oppression by able-bodied persons is rife with the message: there is something wrong, something 'defective,' with us—because we have a disability." Russell, "Malcolm Teaches Us Too," in Shaw, *Ragged Edge,* 11–12. See also Cris Matthews, "Giving It Back," in ibid., 34–41.

94. Rita A. Varela, "Changing Social Attitudes and Legislation Regarding Disability," in *Independent Living for Physically Disabled People: Developing, Implementing and Evaluating Self-Help Rehabilitation Programs,* ed. Nancy M. Crew and Irving Kenneth Zola (San Francisco: Jossey-Bass, 1987), 42–43; Shapiro, *No Pity,* 41–58; "History of Cal's Disabled Students' Program and Residence Program," http://dsp.berkeley.edu/history.html (Berkeley: UC Regents, 2009).

95. For an in-depth look at the *PARC* case written in its immediate aftermath, see Leopold D. Lippman and Ignacy Goldberg, *Right to Education: Anatomy of the Pennsylvania Case and Its Implications for Exceptional Children* (New York: Teacher's College Press, 1973).

96. Kelly Buckland, Ann McDaniel, and Jeff Hughes, "The Struggle for Independent Living Rights," *American Rehabilitation,* Summer 2010, 32; Doris Zames Fleischer and Frieda Zames, *The Disability Rights Movement: From Charity to Confrontation,* updated ed. (Philadelphia: Temple University Press, 2011), 43–45; Rita A. Varela, "Organizing Disabled People for Political Action," in Crew and Zola, *Independent Living for Physically Disabled People,* 311–26.

97. Judi Chamberlin, *On Our Own: Patient Controlled Alternatives to the Mental Health System* (New York: Hawthorn Books, 1978), 77–85; and Renee R. Anspach, "From Stigma to Identity Politics: Political Activism among the Physically Disabled and Former Mental Patients," *Social Science and Medicine. Medical Psychology and Medical Sociology* 13 (November 1979): 765–73. For an excellent introduction into the politics of the early psychiatric survivor movement, see Sherry Hirsch, Joe Kennedy Adams, Leonard Roy Frank, Wade Hudson, Richard Keene, Gail Krawitz-Keene, David Richman, and Robert Roth, eds., *Madness Network News Reader* (San Francisco: Glide Publications, 1974).

98. Leonard Kriegel, "Uncle Tom and Tiny Tim: Some Reflections on the Cripple as Negro," *American Scholar* 38 (Summer 1969): 412–30, available online at www.disabilitymuseum.org/lib/docs/678.htm. Although Kriegel's essay is generally considered to be among the earliest

articulations of the analogy between people with disabilities and people of color, there are earlier instances. See Roger Barker, "The Social Psychology of Physical Disability," *Journal of Social Issues* 4, no. 4 (Fall 1948): "The minority status of the physically disabled which is due to the negative attitudes of the physically normal majority . . . would seem to be in almost all respects similar to the problem of racial and religious underprivileged minorities" (28–38).

For discussion on the various models or definitions of disability, see also Harlan Hahn, "Civil Rights for Disabled Americans: The Foundation of a Political Agenda," in Gartner and Joe, *Images of the Disabled,* 176–203.

99. Carol Gill lists four distinct differences between people with disabilities and other minority groups: "public misperceptions of people with disabilities are imbedded in a confusing mix of positive and negative emotions"; "in contrast to race and gender, negative ascriptions based on disability can be superficially linked to 'real' human differences . . . such as pain and troubling limitation"; disabled people are often isolated in their experience even from their own families and friends; most disabled people don't see themselves as members of a minority group. Gill, "The Social Experience of Disability," in *Handbook of Disability Studies,* ed. Gary L. Albrecht, Katherine D. Seelman, and Michael Bury (Thousand Oaks, CA: Sage Publications, 2001), 365–66.

Lennard J. Davis also sees a major difference in how "disability confounds the neat borders of identity in that it is not a discrete but rather a porous category. Anyone can become disabled, and it is also possible for a person with disabilities to be 'cured' and become 'normal'. . . . Because the category of disability is a shifting one, its contingent nature is all the more challenging to other identities that seem fixed." Further, "disability is an identity that, while it may intersect with other identity categories, is still mainly divorced from rubrics such as family, nation, ethnicity, or gender. I do not mean that disability has nothing to do with these other identities, but rather that it is generally perceived as being independent of one's identity as a citizen, a woman, or a parent, for example. In other words, disability is perceived by the majority as a nonpolitical identity. Disability activists and theorists have worked hard to make people understand that there is a political history to the body and to the formation of concepts of normalcy." Davis, "Identity Politics, Disability, and Culture," in Albrecht et al., *Handbook of Disability Studies,* 536.

100. As Kriegel writes, "there is no sense of shared relationships or pride. Cripples do not refer to each other as 'soul brothers.'" Kriegel, "Uncle Tom and Tiny Tim," 421.

101. Without exception, every Deaf activist I interviewed at some point (generally at the beginning of the interview) said, "I don't consider myself disabled" or words to that effect. It is in fact possible to see the Deaf rights movement as quite distinct from the American disability rights movement, certainly up until the 1980s and even during the campaign for passage of the ADA. I decided, however, to include Deaf advocates in this book because Deaf advocacy has been so important to the success of the disability rights movement in general and passage of the ADA in particular, and also because one entire section of the ADA, Title IV, was crafted almost entirely by advocates within the Deaf community and their allies. See Strauss, *New Civil Right.* It is also notable that the foreword to one of the first explications of the ADA after its passage was written by I. King Jordan, who became president of Gallaudet University as a result of the Deaf President Now campaign. Jordan, "Foreword: Reflections on a New Era," in *Implementing the Americans with Disabilities Act: Rights and Responsibilities of All Americans,* ed. Lawrence O. Gostin and Henry A. Beyer (Baltimore: Paul H. Brookes Publishing, 1993), xiii–xv.

102. Precisely how many American families have members with disabilities, or had members with disabilities at the time of the passage of the Americans with Disabilities Act, is difficult to know. Among the statistics commonly cited at the time were those compiled by the National Center for Health Statistics, together with its ad hoc cosponsors from other federal agencies, which in 1993 estimated that "4.5 percent of the U.S. population [were] unable to perform the major activity of persons of their age group [thus meeting the NCHS definition of having a serious disability], another 6.1 percent were limited in performance of the major activity, and another 4.9 percent were limited in other activities, for a total of 15.5 percent who had a disability." Since people with disabilities, unlike members of most other minority groups, are to be found

scattered throughout the population, it is safe to assume that most American families have thus had some experience with disability, either congenital or acquired. Gerry Hendershot, "Statistics," *Encyclopedia of Disability and Rehabilitation*, 701.

103. Among the people with disabilities close to Senator Edward Kennedy were his older sister Rosemary, who was labeled mentally retarded and institutionalized, and his son [Edward Jr.] who lost a leg to cancer. President George H. W. Bush was similarly familiar with disability: his daughter Robin died of epilepsy in 1953; his son Neil is learning disabled; another son, Marvin, has an ostomy as a result of colon surgery; and his uncle John Walker was a polio survivor. Switzer, *Disabled Rights*, 103–4.

104. The Education for All Handicapped Children Act of 1975, since amended and renamed the Individuals with Disabilities Education Act (IDEA), mandates that children with disabilities are entitled to a "free, appropriate public education." The law established the "zero-reject" principle, meaning no child could be excluded from a public school education merely because of his or her disability. Pelka, *ABC-CLIO Companion*, 111–12. Section 504 of the Rehabilitation Act of 1973 prohibited discrimination against "otherwise qualified handicapped" individuals by any entity receiving federal funds. Before passage if the ADA in 1990, it provided the most far-reaching federal civil rights protection for people with disabilities. Pelka, *ABC-CLIO Companion*, 278.

105. Longmore, *Why I Burned My Book*, 103–5.

106. There are numerous accounts of the HEW sit-in and its context, including Frank Bowe, *Changing the Rules* (Silver Spring, MD: T. J. Publishers, 1986), 183–96; Longmore, *Why I Burned My Book*, 105–11; Shapiro, *No Pity*, 64–70; and Treanor, *We Overcame*, 61–83.

107. Longmore, *Why I Burned My Book*, 109.

108. Many activists who attended the conference remember simply the fact that they had never before seen so many obviously disabled people in one place at one time. Perhaps typical is the reaction of Meg Kocher-Magnan: "I often dream of a country in which everyone is disabled. I got a glimpse of this in 1977, at the White House Conference on Handicapped Individuals. There were four thousand people there, three thousand of them disabled. I saw every kind of disability imaginable, including combinations of disabilities: people in wheelchairs using respirators and portable iron lungs; short deaf people; and blind wheelchair users. The experience was incredibly rich. . . .

"When the conference was over, I went to a restaurant with a friend. I couldn't believe how *boring* it was to be in a place with people who all walked the same, sat the same, talked the same. None of them used their hands to talk, none had canes or dogs or wheelchairs or respirators. . . . There was no wealth, no richness." Meg Kocher, "I Would Be This Way Forever," in *Ordinary Moments: The Disabled Experience*, ed. Alan J. Brightman (Baltimore: University Park Press, 1984), 109–10.

109. Pelka, *ABC-CLIO Companion*, 322–23.

110. For discussion of Section 504 and its relationship to the ADA, see Jane West, "The Evolution of Disability Rights," and Arlene Mayerson, "The History of the ADA: A Movement Perspective," in Gostin and Beyer, *Implementing the Americans with Disabilities Act*, 11–12, 18–21.

111. Among other initiatives, the incoming Reagan administration began a purge of the Social Security Disability Insurance (SSDI) and Supplemental Security Income (SSI) programs, both of which were intended to provide income maintenance—and perhaps more importantly, health insurance coverage—to people who had been evaluated as too disabled to hold gainful employment. Although this review had begun under the Carter administration, pursuant to passage of the Social Security Disability Amendments of 1980, the process under the Reagan administration was often arbitrary, with individuals receiving news that their disability had been "cured," and they had been terminated from the program, often without having been seen by a physician or caseworker. Some 500,000 cases were "reviewed" in fiscal year 1982 alone, with almost half of all reviewed cases terminated: more than 470,000 people dropped from the rolls in three years. By the end of 1983, more than 90% of those terminated had filed appeals, two-thirds of which were ultimately successful. However, since those appealing were left without income or health insurance during the appeal process, which often took a year or more,

termination still often brought great hardship, with the media carrying stories of people with severe disabilities unjustly terminated, some of whom, in desperation, committed suicide.

In response, Congress overwhelmingly passed the Social Security Disability Reform Act of 1984, mandating that terminated beneficiaries of SSDI and SSI would continue to receive benefits until their appeals were heard (in cases where the appellate was unsuccessful, he or she would be required to reimburse the government for benefits received after termination). Furthermore, the act required that termination of disability benefits must be made on the "basis of the weight of the evidence," and not on the basis of any quota system, as had evidently been the case under the Reagan administration review. Susan Gluck Mezey, *No Longer Disabled: The Federal Courts and the Politics of Social Security Disability* (New York: Greenwood Press, 1988).

112. See chapter 23.

113. West, "Evolution of Disability Rights," 11–13.

114. See Erving Goffman, *Stigma: Notes on the Management of Spoiled Identity* (Englewood Cliffs, NJ: Prentice-Hall, 1963). For a disability rights critique of Goffman's analysis of "stigma," see Gill, "Social Experience of Disability," 355–57.

Chapter 1. Childhood

1. The Industrial School for Crippled and Deformed Children opened in Boston in 1893, as the nation's first day-school for children with physical disabilities. The name was changed in 1974 to the Cotting School for Handicapped Children. Phyllis Coons, "Cotting School's Commencement Is Its Last to Be Held in Boston," *Boston Globe,* June 19, 1988.

2. See Martin F. Norden, *The Cinema of Isolation: A History of Physical Disability in the Movies* (New Brunswick, NJ: Rutgers University Press, 1994). A more recent example of the use of disability to connote evil can be seen in Dan Brown's best-selling novel *The Da Vinci Code,* in which one villain is an albino monk, the other a historian identified as a polio survivor. The notion that albinos in particular either are evil or possess magical power persists. For example, "A court in north-western Tanzania has sentenced three men to death by hanging for killing a 14-year-old albino boy. They were found guilty of attacking Matatizo Dunia and severing his legs. . . . In the past two years there has been a huge rise in murders of albino people. Witchdoctors use their body parts in potions they claim bring prosperity." BBC News, "Death for Tanzania Albino Killers," September 23, 2009. http://news.bbc.co.uk/2/hi/8270446.stm.

3. Neil Jacobson, "Cofounder of the Computer Training Project; Cochair of the President's Committee on Employment of People with Disabilities, interview conducted by Sharon Bonney, 1997, in *The Computer Training Project in Berkeley, Accessible Technology, and Employment for People with Disabilities,* DRILM Oral History Project, Regional Oral History Office, The Bancroft Library, University of California, Berkeley; © 2004 by The Regents of the University of California, 10.

4. Ed Roberts, quoted in *When Billy Broke His Head . . . And Other Tales of Wonder,* film produced and directed by Billy Golfus and David E. Simpson, National Disability Awareness Project, 1995.

5. Telephone relay services provide deaf people and people with speech disabilities access to phone service. Initially, relay service was provided mostly by volunteers or family members and friends of the deaf or disabled person and worked via the use of TTYs (or TTDs), that is, telephone-teletype machines. A deaf person, using the keyboard of a TTY, calls a hearing relay operator who also has a TTY. The hearing relay operator then dials the intended hearing recipient and relays the message, and relays any response back to the deaf caller.

Title IV of the ADA mandates that telephone companies make relay services available to all their customers, with funding to come from the provider's general revenue. (Karen Peltz Strauss, "Title IV—Telecommunications," in Gostin and Beyer, *Implementing the Americans with Disabilities Act,* 155–72). The advent of home computers and the Internet has given rise to video relay services, or VRS. For example, to conduct my interviews with Deaf activists, I dialed the VRS number of the interviewee. My call was routed to a relay service office—one of several providers competing for customers—where an American Sign Language (ASL) interpreter, sitting in front of a computer screen and Web camera, dialed the interviewee and used ASL to communicate my remarks. The interviewee, also using a webcam, was able to sign his or her responses to my interpreted questions.

For a history of telecommunications access, see Karen Peltz Strauss, *A New Civil Right: Telecommunications Equality for Deaf and Hard of Hearing Americans* (Washington, DC: Gallaudet University Press, 2002).

6. Deaf clubs were perhaps the first organizations in America to be established and run by people with disabilities themselves, going back at least as far as the 1854 founding of the New England Gallaudet Association of Deaf-Mutes. In the following decades Deaf people founded a variety of professional, religious, and political organizations. John Vickrey Van Cleve and Barry A. Crouch, *A Place of Their Own: Creating the Deaf Community in America* (Washington, DC: Gallaudet University Press, 1989), 87–93.

7. Established in 1969 by the National Association of the Deaf under the leadership of Frank Turk and Gary Olsen, and held annually since 1970, the four-week Youth Leadership camps have introduced several generations of Deaf youth to political advocacy. Jack R. Gannon, *Deaf Heritage: A Narrative History of Deaf America* (Silver Spring, MD: National Association of the Deaf, 1981), 319–20.

8. Frank R. Turk, born in 1929, was dean of men in the Gallaudet Preparation Department and assistant professor of physical education at Gallaudet from 1965 to 1971, when he became director of Youth Relations at Gallaudet's Office of Alumni/Public Relations. In 1985, he became dean of Pre-College Student Life at the Model Secondary School for the Deaf at Gallaudet. He was a member of the Deaf President Now (DPN) Council in 1988, and in 1991 became director of North Carolina's Division of Services for the Deaf and Hard of Hearing. Matthew S. Moore and Robert F. Panara, *Great Deaf Americans: The Second Edition* (Rochester, NY: MSM Productions, 1996), 239–43. Frank B. Sullivan became Grand President of the National Fraternal Society of the Deaf in 1967. He was a leader in the development of television closed-captioning. Peltz, *New Civil Right*, 218. Malcolm "Mac" J. Norwood (1927–1989) was chief of Media Services and Captioned Films at the US Department of Education and is widely known as "the father of closed-captioning." Moore and Panara, *Great Deaf Americans*, 221–25.

9. *Dorland's* online medical dictionary defines spinal muscular atrophy as a "progressive degeneration of the motor cells of the spinal cord, beginning usually in the small muscles of the hands, but in some cases (scapulohumeral type) in the upper arm and shoulder muscles, and progressing slowly to the leg muscles. Called also Aran-Duchenne disease, Cruveilhier disease, and Duchenne disease."

10. The use of telethons to raise money for disability-related causes has long been controversial within the disability community, with the Jerry Lewis annual Labor Day telethons for the Muscular Dystrophy Association a particular target of criticism. As far back as the 1970s activists in the New York City chapter of Disabled in Action picketed the event. Evan Kemp, director of the Disability Rights Center in Washington, DC, wrote an editorial in the *New York Times* attacking Lewis for playing on public fears of disability and for portraying people with disabilities as pitiable objects of charity. Evan Kemp Jr., "Aiding the Disabled: No Pity Please," *New York Times*, September 3, 1981. In the 1990s the group "Jerry's Orphans" was organized specifically to confront Jerry Lewis and the MDA. Fred Pelka, *The ABC-CLIO Companion to the Disability Rights Movement* (Santa Barbara, CA: ABC-CLIO, 1997), 301–2.

11. "Pre-education law requirements," that is, the situation before passage of the Education for All Handicapped Children Act of 1975.

12. "Retrolental fibroplasia"—also "retinopathy of prematurity" (ROP)—is "a bilateral disease of the retinal vessels present in premature infants some of whom were exposed to high postnatal oxygen concentrations" in incubators. Clayton L. Thomas, ed., *Tabor's Cyclopedic Medical Dictionary*, 15th ed. (Philadelphia: F. A. Davis, 1985), 1486. Oswald was part of a worldwide epidemic of ROP, during which more than twelve thousand babies were blinded from 1941 to 1953, mostly in

the developed world, until the link between ROP and oxygen toxicity was recognized. See William Silverman, *Retrolental Fibroplasia: A Modern Parable* (New York: Grune & Stratton, 1980).

Chapter 2. Institutions, Part 1

1. Typical of the conditions Dix found during her tour of Massachusetts: "Newton alms-house, a cold morning in October . . . the furniture was a wooden box or bunk containing straw . . . protruding from the box was—it could not be feet! Yet from those stumps were swinging chains, fastened to the side of the building. . . . A few winters since, being kept in an out-house, the people 'did not reckon how cold it was,' and so his feet froze. 'Are chains neces-sary now?' I asked. 'He cannot run.' 'No, but he might crawl forth, and in his frenzy do some damage'"; "Barnstable. Four females in pens and stalls"; "Westford. Young woman fastened to the wall with a chain." Dorothy Clarke Wilson, *Stranger and Traveler: The Story of Dorothea Dix, American Reformer* (Boston: Little, Brown, 1975), 119–20.

2. From the *55th Annual Report of the Trustees of the Massachusetts School for the Feeble-minded at Waltham, for the Year Ending September 30, 1902* (Boston: Wright and Potter, State Printers, 1903), 14.

3. "One important inhibiting factor is the tremendous monetary investment your state has in the physical plant of its institutional system and the economic utility this has for certain communities and other interest groups. They attempt to block and effectively delay action for change." Gunnar Dybwad, "Lest We Forget," in *Ahead of His Time: Selected Speeches of Gunnar Dybwad,* ed. Mary Ann Allard, Anne Howard, Lee Vorderer, and Alice Wells (Washington, DC: American Association on Mental Retardation, 1999), 141.

4. Gunnar Dybwad, "From Feeblemindedness to Self-Advocacy: A Half Century of Growth and Self-Fulfillment," paper presented at the 118th Annual Meeting of the American Associa-tion on Mental Retardation, Heller School, Brandeis University, June 2, 1994, 2.

5. "The Howe system" refers to Samuel Gridley Howe, a social reformer who is best known for his work with blind students, but who was also the founder of the Massachusetts School for Idiotic and Feeble Minded Children. He believed that children with disabilities learned best in a highly structured environment, hence Dybwad's recollection of institutions where children responded to signals to sit, eat, rise from the table, and so on. James W. Trent Jr., *Inventing the Feeble Mind: A History of Mental Retardation in the United States* (Berkeley: University of California Press, 1994), 24–25.

6. "The Partlow case" refers to a lawsuit brought in 1971 by the employees of the Partlow State School in Alabama to redress staff layoffs as well as the abysmal conditions at the school. The case was combined with that of Ricky Wyatt, a cognitively disabled man living at the Bryce Hospital in Tuscaloosa. The resulting class action suit, *Wyatt v. Stickney* (503 F.2d 1305 [1974]), concluded with a federal court ruling that people confined in state institutions had "a right to treatment" beyond simply being housed in "custodial care." The decision was an important precedent for other deinstitutionalization cases. Fred Pelka, *The ABC-CLIO Companion to the Disability Rights Movement* (Santa Barbara, CA: ABC-CLIO, 1997), 335; Trent, *Inventing the Feeble Mind,* 257.

Chapter 4. Institutions, Part 2

1. Frank is also the editor and publisher of *The History of Shock Treatment* (1978), a com-pendium of articles dating from the beginning of the use of shock "therapy" by mainstream psychiatry in the 1930s to the time of its publication, by both medical authorities and politi-cal/social commentators. Some of these articles can be, for contemporary readers, quite unset-tling, including those praising the use of shock treatment to "cure" homosexuality and lesbian-ism, and noting its use in patients as young as three and as old as ninety-four years old. Other articles include "Brain Damaging Therapeutics," "Death and Other ECT Complications," "Military Uses of Electroshock," "Four Fatalities," "Shock Treatment and Lobotomy Com-pared," "1000 Convulsions," "Death Due to Treatment," "Survey of Deaths Following ECT," "ECT during the Algerian War," "Entire Wards Were Shocked," and so on. Perhaps among the

most disturbing are "To Inform or Not to Inform," written by a psychiatrist who believes that patients should not be informed that they are about to be shocked), and "Anti-Psychiatrist Groups . . . the Menace to Society," in which the author decries psychiatric survivors' organizing politically and labels those opposing ECT "delusionary, frustrated, maladjusted people." A. E. Bennett, MD, "Anti-Psychiatrists Threat to Society," *San Diego Union*, July 11, 1975, reprinted in Frank, *History of Shock Treatment*, 112.

2. Matt Schudel, "Frederick A. Fay, Forceful Activist for Rights of the Disabled, Dies at 66," *Washington Post*, September 1, 2011.

3. Larry Kegan was a singer, songwriter, and musician from Minnesota who became a spinal cord–injured quadriplegic after a diving accident when he was seventeen. He performed with Bob Dylan (a high school friend) on several occasions, as part of the "Rolling Thunder Review" in 1975 and at the Orpheum Theater in Boston in 1981, among others. He also was featured in the 1995 Billy Golfus film *When Billy Broke His Head . . . And Other Tales of Wonder*. Kegan died at age fifty-nine of a heart attack on September 11, 2001. Billy Golfus, "Life and Death of a Mere Mortal," *Mouth*, no. 69 (January/February 2002): 28–30.

4. A "Stryker frame" is a device that sandwiches a person's body between two slotted metal planes attached to an axis, allowing him or her to be turned or moved by others while keeping the patient's neck and spine immobilized. Stryker is a brand name, but the term has become generic.

Chapter 5. The University of Illinois

1. Horst Strohkendl, Armand "Tip" Thiboutot, and Philip Craven, *The 50th Anniversary of Wheelchair Basketball: A History* (New York: Waxman Publishing, 1996), 59.

2. Adlai E. Stevenson II was governor of Illinois from January 10, 1949, to January 12, 1953. He was the Democratic candidate for president, running against Dwight D. Eisenhower, in 1952 and 1956.

3. Before the passage of architectural access laws and standards, access for people with disabilities, if provided at all, was often improvised and second rate. For example, a wheelchair user wanting to enter a hotel might be required to use a freight elevator at the back of the building; someone wanting to enter a restaurant might have to roll past the dumpsters in a back alley. "Primary entrance philosophy," by contrast, holds that people with disabilities should be able to enter a building or access a service through the same main entrance as everyone else.

Chapter 6. Discrimination, Part 2, and Early Advocacy

1. The denial of services to Roberts by his state Office of Vocational Rehabilitation can be seen as an example of the practice of "cherry picking" people with less severe disabilities, who were perceived as easier to serve and more likely to ensure a positive outcome, which would reflect more favorably on both the individual counselor and the program. It also illustrates the baleful impact of the "whole man" theory of rehabilitation on people with disabilities, since one reason that Roberts was initially denied services—aside from his vocational "infeasibility"—was that he scored high in "aggression" on the psychological tests he was required to take as part of the application process. Edward V. Roberts interview, 28.

2. The Recreation Center for the Handicapped, founded in 1952 in San Francisco by Janet Pomeroy, was born of Pomeroy's own experience with disability. Contracting polio when she was ten years old, Pomeroy was seriously ill for a year but eventually recovered the full use of her body, except for one stiffened arm. In 1951, she volunteered with the Red Cross and worked at a private school for children with cerebral palsy. The experience stayed with her, and while starting her own program at the Fleishhacker Pool in San Francisco, she also worked toward a master's degree in therapeutic recreation, which she received from San Francisco State University in 1962. Her book, *Recreation for the Physically Handicapped* (New York: Macmillan), was published in 1964. In the meantime, her recreation center grew from serving just six teenagers in 1952 to a program with more than two hundred employees, serving some two thousand

people a week, in its own building with extensive facilities on a five-and-a-half-acre site. The facility was renamed the Janet Pomeroy Center in 2003. Janet Pomeroy died on November 26, 2005, at age ninety-three. Heather Knight, "Janet Pomeroy—Helped Disabled," *San Francisco Chronicle,* November 30, 2005.

3. George Richard Moscone (1929–1978) was elected mayor of San Francisco in November 1975 and served from January 1976 until November 27, 1978, when he and city board member Harvey Milk were assassinated.

4. In 1930, Los Angeles radio personality C. Allison Phelps broke his leg and was housebound. The station installed a remote control setup, and he did his daily program of inspirational poetry and stories from bed. Impressed by how isolated he felt, he suggested to his listeners that those who were likewise "shut-ins" write in and he would forward their letters to other "bedfast" listeners. Phelps was deluged with letters, and one correspondent, Edna Enoch, suggested that all the correspondents form a club. Those members of the "Indoor Sports" who could met in one another's homes and eventually began organizing events—boat rides, beach parties, picnics, and trips to the World's Fair. From Los Angeles the concept spread up and down the West Coast, with a San Diego chapter forming in 1931, a Seattle chapter by the early 1940s, and chapters established in other parts of the country thereafter. In time some chapters became large enough to purchase or rent their own clubhouses and publish their own newsletters, and by the 1950s membership in the various clubs was estimated in the thousands. "Origin of the San Diego Indoor Sports' Club" compiled by Mrs. Yancy "Sunshine" Adams, early 1950s, recompiled by Maude Whiting and Marjorie Dillon, September 1982, and recompiled by Lee Wolf, posted online at www.sdisc.org/index.htm.

5. Denise Sherer Jacobson, "Interview History," Judith Heumann interview, vii.

Chapter 7. The Parents' Movement

1. The Reverend Theodore Martin Hesburgh was the fifteenth president of Notre Dame, serving from 1952 to 1987. During this time he was a champion of academic freedom and autonomy from outside authority, as well as active in civil rights, serving as a member of the US Civil Rights Commission beginning in 1957 and as chair from 1969 until 1972, when he was dismissed by President Nixon. Don Wycliff, "Father Hesburgh Honored; He Brought 'Reason to the Fore,'" *University of Notre Dame News and Information,* October 14, 2007.

2. *In re G. H.* (218 N.W.2d 441 [N.D. 1974]), was a "right to education" case argued before the Supreme Court of North Dakota. Like *PARC v. Pennsylvania,* it affirmed the right of children with disabilities to a public school education. Frank Laski was a staff attorney at the National Center for Law and the Handicapped from 1973 to 1974 and continues to be among the most prominent disability rights litigators in cases involving education, institutionalization, and public transportation. Robert Burgdorf was a staff attorney at the center from 1973 to 1976. As attorney/research specialist in the mid-1980s for the National Council on the Handicapped (now the National Council on Disability), he drafted the first version of the Americans with Disabilities Act. Fred Pelka, *The ABC-CLIO Companion to the Disability Rights Movement* (Santa Barbara, CA: ABC-CLIO, 1997), 54, 188–89, 214.

3. The Pennhurst State School & Hospital, often described as Pennsylvania's "flagship institution," was opened in 1908 as part of the national movement to identify and segregate people with intellectual and developmental disabilities. A special commission appointed by the Pennsylvania General Assembly in 1911 reported two years later that "where the mental disability [of a possible resident] is of a degree which renders the afflicted individuals *unfit for citizenship,* or a menace to the peace, they are regarded and treated as *anti-social beings, and may be permanently segregated* in institutions especially constructed for their reception and care." Thomas K. Gilhool, Frank J. Laski, Michael Churchill, Judith A. Gran, and Timothy M. Cook, *Motion and Brief Amici Curiae before the Supreme Court of the United States, City of Cleburne, Texas, et al. v. Cleburne Living Center et al.,* October term, 1984, app. A, 18–19. As with other institutions established during the heyday of the eugenics movement, Pennhurst became more prison than either school or hospital. In December

1977 the federal court ruled that conditions there violated residents' rights under Section 504 of the Rehabilitation Act of 1973 and other federal and state law, and under the Equal Protection Clause of the Fourteenth Amendment. In its factual findings, the court described conditions including "urine and excrement on the ward floors. Infectious diseases are common. . . . Serious injuries inflicted by staff members, including sexual assaults, have occurred. . . . Physical restraints . . . have caused injuries and at least one death." Testimony revealed that one female resident, during the month of August 1976, had been in physical restraints for some 720 hours. After lengthy federal litigation, including arguments before the US Supreme Court, the Commonwealth of Pennsylvania agreed to a settlement in July 1984 to close the institution and provide community-based programs for all its residents by July 1, 1986. Pelka, *ABC-CLIO Companion,* 145–46.

Pennhurst was again a subject of controversy when the abandoned facility was opened in the fall of 2010 as the privately operated "Pennhurst Asylum," "a fright-filled Halloween" theme park, charging $25 to $95 per "patient" to tour the facility and its supposedly haunted wards and tunnels. Among entertainments offered were "an electro-shock therapy scene with a Frankenstein-like monster" and "an autopsy room" with artifacts supposedly found on the property, all presented as "traditional Halloween fun." Disability rights advocates condemned such use of the former institution as exploiting "the suffering that took place there" and as reinforcing "stereotypes and negative perceptions that persist in society against people with disabilities." Peter V. Berns, CEO of the Arc of Pennsylvania, quoted in Arc of Pennsylvania press release by Laura Hart, "The Arc Calls for Boycott of 'Horror' Attraction 'Pennhurst Asylum,'" September 23, 2010.

4. The legal "right to treatment" came out of a series of deinstitutionalization cases argued by advocates for people labeled mentally ill and confined to institutions, notably *O'Connor v. Donaldson* and *Wyatt v. Stickney.* In those two cases, judges ruled that the government could not keep persons in an institution indefinitely unless they were a danger to themselves or others and without offering some form of treatment, thus striking a blow at "custodial care." See Morton Birnbaum, "The Right to Treatment: Some Comments on Its Development," in *Medical, Moral, and Legal Issues in Mental Health Care,* ed. F. J. Ayd (Baltimore: Williams & Wilkins, 1974).

5. Gillian Gilhool is an attorney, human rights activist, and program coordinator for the Women's International League for Peace and Freedom.

6. Rosemary F. Dybwad (1910–1992) was an advocate on the international stage for the rights of people with cognitive and developmental disabilities. She was the author of many articles and pamphlets and of the book *Perspectives on a Parent Movement: The Revolt of Parents of Children with Intellectual Disabilities* (Brookline, MA: Brookline Books, 1990). She and Gunnar Dybwad were married in 1934. Pelka, *ABC-CLIO Companion,* 110.

7. Burton Blatt (1927–1985) was a teacher, professor, and writer who is perhaps best known as the coauthor, with Fred Kaplan, of *Christmas in Purgatory: A Photographic Essay on Mental Retardation* (Boston: Allyn and Bacon, 1966). Blatt and Kaplan secretly photographed the back wards of several major state institutions, providing commentary for the photos. He was a pioneer in arguing for community services for people with cognitive disabilities. From 1969 he was Centennial Professor and Director of the Division of Special Education and Rehabilitation at Syracuse University. In 1971 he, Douglas Biklen, and Robert Bogdan founded the Center on Human Policy, a policy, research, and advocacy center focusing on disability issues. Blatt and Kaplan, *Christmas in Purgatory,* i; Pelka, *ABC-CLIO Companion,* 65–66.

8. The Individualized Education Program, or IEP, is a procedural requirement imbedded within the IDEA, wherein parents, teachers, and others concerned with a child's education come together to formulate and agree upon a specific plan for that child's education. Teresa Garate and Jose Mendez, "Individualized Education Program," in *Encyclopedia of Disability,* ed. by Gary L. Albrecht (Thousand Oaks, CA: Sage Publications 2006), 2, 943–45.

9. The idea of mainstreaming continues to be controversial among some advocates in the Deaf community, who see deaf children better served by being in an environment where

American Sign Language is used for all instruction and interaction—generally best accomplished in residential schools for the Deaf. See Ben Bahan, "Who's Itching to Get into Mainstreaming?" in *American Deaf Culture: An Anthology,* ed. Sherman Wilcox (Burtonsville, MD: Linstok Press, 1989), 173–77, and John Vickrey Van Cleve, "The Academic Integration of Deaf Children: A Historical Perspective," in *The Deaf History Reader,* ed. John Vickrey Van Cleve (Washington, DC: Gallaudet University Press), 2007, 116–35.

10. Doreen "Pam" Steneberg was a parent advocate, the mother of a child with cerebral palsy, and herself a person with a disability. After the passage of the Education for All Handicapped Children Act in 1975, she worked at DREDF to train other parents in how to use the law. She retired in 1997 and died in March 2006. "Children with Disabilities Lose Dedicated Advocate, Doreen 'Pam' Steneberg," DREDF press release, March 28, 2006.

Chapter 8. Activists and Organizers, Part 1

1. The Architectural Barriers Act (ABA) of 1968 required that all buildings constructed, altered, or financed by the federal government after 1969 be accessible to people with disabilities. The law made buildings leased or purchased by the federal government subject to the same requirement, with the exception of buildings intended for non-disabled military personnel. Although this act marked the first time that the federal government required architectural access, it contained no provision for enforcement and thus was minimally effective. In 1973, Congress acted to address this problem by creating the Architectural and Transportation Compliance Board as one of the provisions of the Rehabilitation Act of 1973. The ATCB, however, was seen by most activists as little more than a rubber stamp, granting numerous waivers to entities seeking exemptions from the ABA's requirements. Caryn E. Neumann, "Architectural Barriers Act," in *Encyclopedia of American Disability History,* ed. Susan Burch, 3 vols. (New York: Facts On File, 2009), 1:63–64; Fred Pelka, *The ABC-CLIO Companion to the Disability Rights Movement* (Santa Barbara, CA: ABC-CLIO, 1997), 27.

2. Lee Kitchens was elected mayor of Ransom Canyon, Texas, for a single two-year term in 1987. He was elected again in 1991, serving until 1999. The Ransom Canyon city hall is located at 24 Lee Kitchens Drive. Murvat Musa, City Manager, e-mail correspondence with the author, January 25, 2011.

3. A 501(c)(4) is an organization founded explicitly for social activism; 501(c)(3) is a not-for-profit entity founded primarily for public education, charity, research, or some other form of social service. Contributions to a 501(c)(3) are tax deductible, contributions to a 501(c)(4) are not.

4. John Hessler (1940–1993) was a cofounder of the Physically Disabled Students Program at UC Berkeley, a member of Rolling Quads, and a cofounder of the Berkeley Center for Independent Living. Pelka, *ABC-CLIO Companion,* 151–52; Joseph P. Shapiro, *No Pity: People with Disabilities Forging a New Civil Rights Movement* (New York: Random House, 1993, 1994), 47–48.

5. Phil Draper (1940?–1992) was an activist in the San Francisco area disability community and the second director of the Center for Independent Living, taking the position in 1975 after Ed Roberts left to become director of the California Department of Vocational Rehabilitation. Draper was director of the CIL during the HEW occupation in 1977. Pelka, *ABC-CLIO Companion,* 61.

6. Hale Zukas (1943–) is another of the original founders of the Berkeley CIL. He enrolled at UC Berkeley in the mid-1960s, became a member of Rolling Quads, and was also one of the founders of the Physically Disabled Students' Program. In 1983, Zukas became a public policy analyst at the World Institute on Disability in Oakland, California. See Hale Zukas, "National Disability Activist: Architectural and Transit Accessibility, Personal Assistance Services," interview conducted by Sharon Bonney, 1997 and 1998, in *Builders and Sustainers in the Independent Living Movement in Berkeley,* vol. 3, DRILM Oral History Project, Regional Oral History Office, The Bancroft Library, University of California, Berkeley; © 2000 by The Regents of the University of California.

7. St. Vitus' Dance is the common or folk name for Sydenham's chorea, or Chorea minor,

"a disease of childhood commonly occurring between 5 and 15 years of age; more females than males are affected. Usually associated with rheumatic fever. Characterized by involuntary purposeless contractions of the muscles of the trunk and extremities; anxiety, impairment of memory and sometimes of speech." *Taber's Cyclopedic Medical Dictionary,* ed. Clayton L. Thomas (Philadelphia: F. A. Davis, 1985), 1668.

8. Gale Williams (1938–) joined CAPH in 1973, and was elected its president for two terms in 1979 and 1980. He led in organizing a number of important CAPH campaigns, including a successful effort to force California supermarkets to remove barriers to shoppers who use wheelchairs. He was president of the LA chapter of CAPH for three terms, from 1976 through 1978. Gale Williams, interview conducted by Fred Pelka, May 3, 2007, audio recording in possession of the author, to be deposited at The Bancroft Library as part of its Regional Oral History Office Project on the Disability Rights and Independent Living Movement.

9. Dart testified before Congress as director of the RSA on November 18, 1987. He was asked for his resignation within days. Fred Fay, "Empowerment: The Testament of Justin Dart, Jr.," *Mainstream: Magazine of the Able-Disabled,* March 1998, 23.

Chapter 9. Institutions, Part 3

1. David and Sheila Rothman, *The Willowbrook Wars: A Decade of Struggle for Social Change* (New York: Harper and Row, 1984), 23.

2. Dr. Richard Koch is best known as for his work in researching and treating phenylketonuria (or PKU), a metabolic disease that causes brain damage in newborns and young children if undetected. He was also an early advocate of deinstitutionalization. Professor emeritus of clinical pediatrics at the Keck School of Medicine and Children's Hospital in Los Angeles, he is coauthor with Kathryn Jean Koch of *Understanding the Mentally Retarded Child: A New Approach* (New York: Random House, 1975) and coeditor with James C. Dobson of *The Mentally Retarded Child and His Family: A Multidisciplinary Handbook* (New York: Brunner/Mazel, 1971).

3. Autonomic dysreflexia, also known as autonomic hyperreflexia, is "a condition commonly seen in patients with injury to the upper spinal cord . . . caused by massive sympathetic discharge of stimuli from the autonomic nervous system" often triggered by some form of over-stimulation. Potentially fatal, the symptoms are sudden hypertension, bradycardia, sweating, severe headache, and gooseflesh. *Taber's Cyclopedic Medical Dictionary,* ed. Clayton L. Thomas (Philadelphia: F. A. Davis, 1985), 159.

Chapter 10. Activists and Organizers, Part 2

1. Denise McQuade (1948–), born in Brooklyn, and a cofounder of DIA. An advocate of accessible mass transit, she eventually became the Public Information Coordinator at the Paratransit Division, Department of Buses, at the New York Mass Transit Authority (MTA). Denise McQuade, "Early Activist in Disabled in Action, Advocate for Independent Living and Transit Issues," interview conducted by Denise Sherer Jacobson, 2001, in *New York Activists and Leaders in the Disability Rights and Independent Living Movement,* vol. 1, DRILM Oral History Project, Regional Oral History Office, The Bancroft Library, University of California, Berkeley; © 2004 by The Regents of the University of California.

2. See excerpts of the oral histories of Dr. William Bronston in this volume. See also David Rothman and Sheila Rothman, *The Willowbrook Wars: A Decade of Struggle for Social Change* (New York: Harper and Row, 1984).

3. Bobbi (Barbara) Linn (1950–). See Bobbi Linn, "Activist with Disabled in Action, Counselor at Center for Independence of the Disabled in New York, and Director of Bronx Independent Living Services," interview conducted by Denise Sherer Jacobson, 2001, in *New York Activists and Leaders in the Disability Rights and Independent Living Movement,* vol. 3, DRILM Oral History Project, Regional Oral History Office, The Bancroft Library, University of California, Berkeley; © 2004 by The Regents of the University of California.

4. Wolf Wolfensberger (1934–), a psychologist and researcher at the Nebraska Psychiatric

Institute in Omaha from 1964 to 1971, was the leading American proponent of "normalization." Originally articulated in Denmark by Bengt Nirje, the advocates of normalization believed that children with disabilities should be treated as much like "normal" children as possible. This meant, for example, that parents should be expected to raise their disabled children at home, and that children with disabilities should be educated in as mainstream an environment as possible. When Wolfensberger and others first brought the concept to the United States in the late 1960s, it was met with great skepticism, most especially by the directors of the nation's major disability institutions. Robert B. Kugel and Wolf Wolfensberger, eds., *Changing Patterns in Residential Services for the Mentally Retarded* (Washington, DC: President's Committee on Mental Retardation, 1969); and Wolf Wolfensberger, *The Principle of Normalization in Human Services* (Toronto: National Institute on Mental Retardation, 1972).

5. Malachy McCourt (1931–) is an actor, writer, and political activist. He and his wife Diana were parent activists during the struggle to close Willowbrook, where their daughter Nina was institutionalized. Their role is discussed in Dr. Bronston's oral history in chapter 17 and in McCourt's memoir, *Singing My Him Song*, published by HarperCollins in 2000.

6. Neil Jacobson, born in 1952 in Brooklyn, was an early participant in Disabled in Action and with Judy Heumann in other disability rights endeavors. See his interview cited in chapter 1, note 2.

7. The idea of "sheltered workshops"—that is, workplaces established for people with disabilities and segregated from the mainstream workforce—has been around at least since the 1830s, when Samuel Gridley Howe established a vocational training program at the Perkins School for the Blind. But the system as known in twentieth-century America began with the passage of the Labor Standards Act of 1938. Originally established for blind workers, the act gave exclusive bidding rights to certain federal contracts to companies where 75 percent or more of the workforce was blind or (after 1971) otherwise disabled. The act also waived minimum wage and other federal labor regulations. By the early 1970s there were some 1,500 such workshops, employing an estimated 160,000 workers. With deinstitutionalization, this figure by the mid-1980s had grown to more than 650,000, with many of the workers classified as "mentally retarded" or as having other disabilities.

The modern sheltered workshop system had critics almost from its inception. Among the first was Jacobus tenBroek, and protests against the substandard wages and often demeaning and even dangerous working conditions were major events during the first decades of the National Federation of the Blind. For an early disability rights critique of the system, see TenBroek and Floyd W. Matson, *Hope Deferred: Public Welfare and the Blind* (Berkeley: University of California Press), 1959. For a look at sheltered workshops post-ADA, see Stephen T. Murphy and Patricia M. Rogan, *Closing the Shop: Conversion from Sheltered to Integrated Work* (Baltimore: Paul H. Brookes, 1995).

8. President Richard M. Nixon vetoed two versions of what would become the Rehabilitation Act of 1973, citing the additional costs of the programs included in the legislation. Paul K. Longmore, *Why I Burned My Book and Other Essays on Disability* (Philadelphia: Temple University Press, 2003), 103–5.

9. Eunice K. Fiorito (1930–1999) was one of the founders of the American Coalition of Citizens with Disabilities. Blinded at age sixteen, she graduated cum laude with a BS in education from Loyola University in Chicago in 1954, taking only three years to finish the four-year program. She earned her master's in psychiatric social work from Columbia University in 1960. Like TenBroek, despite her excellent academic record (she graduated from Columbia fourth in her class) she was turned down by more than sixty prospective employers before being offered a job at the Jewish Guild for the Blind in New York City. In 1970, she was named coordinator of the Mayor's Advisory Committee on the Handicapped, persuading Mayor John V. Lindsey to expand the committee into the nation's first Mayor's Office for the Handicapped in 1971, where she served as director until 1978. During that time she used her position to foster disability activism and awareness, not only in New York City but nationwide, particularly in the

struggle for enforcement of Section 504. Fred Pelka, *ABC-CLIO Companion to the Disability Rights Movement* (Santa Barbara, CA: ABC-CLIO), 1997, 123–25.

Fiorito was also an important activist with the American Council of the Blind (ACB) and spent the last decades of her career working in Washington in the Department of Education. "At the time of her retirement, she was vice chair of the Department's Task Force on Section 504—the focus of the sit-in she had organized 20 years earlier." Billie Jean Keith, "Eunice Fiorito: A Voice That Should Never Die," *Braille Forum,* January 2000, 4–6.

10. I contacted Bobby Muller to ask about being interviewed for this book, but he said that his actions with DIA and Judy Heumann were pretty much all he'd done by way of disability rights activism. He has, however, been a dedicated and effective antiwar organizer and speaker. Disabled in Vietnam at age 23, the self-described former "bad-ass Marine" lieutenant founded the Vietnam Veterans of America Foundation, and was a cofounder of the International Campaign to Ban Land Mines, which won the 1997 Nobel Peace Prize. Cecilia Capuzzi Simon, "VFA's Bobby Muller: Transformed by a Bullet from Marine to Peace Activist," *Psychology Today,* March 1, 2006, 72.

11. Mario Cuomo was elected lieutenant governor of New York in 1978 and then governor in 1982, winning reelection in 1986 and 1990.

Chapter 11. Independent Living

1. Jean Wirth was Ed Roberts's vocational rehabilitation counselor during the time he went to San Mateo College, before his admission to Berkeley. She later accompanied Roberts to Washington, DC, as a consultant on independent living. See Jean Wirth, "Counselor at the College of San Mateo and Early Mentor to Ed Roberts," interview conducted by Susan O'Hara, 2000, in *Zona Roberts: Counselor for UC Berkeley's Physically Disabled Students' Program and the Center for Independent Living, Mother of Ed Roberts, An Interview Conducted by Susan O'Hara in 1994–1995, Includes an Interview with Jean Wirth,* DRILM Oral History Project, Regional Oral History Office, The Bancroft Library, University of California, Berkeley.

2. A restaurant on Durant Avenue in Berkeley that figures prominently in the memories of many of the early activists at the CIL.

3. People's Park is a three-acre plot of land, owned by the University of California, which in the 1960s became the scene of a confrontation between those who wanted to develop the land as a park; the university, which had plans to turn it into a parking lot and build student housing and offices; and California governor Ronald Reagan, who saw efforts to build a "people's park" as a leftist challenge to property rights and public order. The university ran out of funds to go forward with its plans for development, and so in April 1969, roughly a thousand people from the campus and community planted trees, flowers, and shrubs, volunteering their time and money.

In the early morning hours of May 15, 1969, three hundred California Highway Patrol and Berkeley police officers were ordered to destroy the garden and erect an eight-foot-high chain-link fence around the site. In the unrest that followed, roughly six thousand protesters confronted the police, some of whom responded by using buckshot when demonstrators refused to disperse and began tearing down the fence. A university student, James Rector, was killed, and more than one hundred others were wounded when police fired on or otherwise assaulted protesters, spectators, and people fleeing the scene.

Governor Reagan declared a state of emergency and sent 2,700 National Guard troops into Berkeley. On May 21, 1969, National Guard troops surrounded and tear-gassed a memorial service for Rector attended by several thousand people. The gas was carried into Cowell Hospital as well as nearby public elementary schools. The situation continued for weeks, with Berkeley occupied by police and National Guard, despite a vote of protest by the city council and a referendum of students and residents that showed overwhelming local support for the park and disapproval of the harsh tactics used by police and guardsmen. Richard Brenneman, "The Bloody Beginnings of People's Park," *Berkeley Daily Planet,* April 20, 2004, available online at www.berkeleydailyplanet.com. Today "People's Park is still a park, but UC did put in a basketball court on part of the land and there are periodic rumors of development schemes." Marty Schiffenbauer, e-mail correspondence with the author, July 25, 2011.

4. Many of the interviewees use the word "attendant" or the term "personal care attendant" when describing those who provided personal assistance to students at Cowell, at the PDSP, and consumers at the CIL. Use of "attendant," with its connotations of a medical model of disability is less favored today; the terms "assistant" and "personal assistance services" (or PAS) are used instead.

5. "A number of years ago I donated some papers to the Bancroft Library. As I went through the material I found a study . . . that I did . . . and a draft John and I wrote for the creation of an organization to be called CENTER FOR INDEPENDENT LIVING. It was created at least six months before the meeting called to create the CIL." Michael Fuss, e-mail correspondence with the author, August 15, 2010.

6. Like many people born with cerebral palsy, Hale Zukas has a speech disability, making him difficult to understand for those not used to interacting with him. People such as Cone would therefore be assigned to help "interpret" his speech for those outside the CIL.

7. This was not the first interaction between conscientious objectors and people with disabilities. During World War II, conscientious objectors were required to perform community service, often by working in the various state mental institutions. Some of these individuals then went to the media in an attempt to bring public attention to the abuses they witnessed. Steven J. Taylor, *Acts of Conscience: World War II, Mental Institutions, and Religious Objectors* (Syracuse: Syracuse University Press, 2009). The conscientious objectors working with residents at Cowell and at the PDSP were presumably doing so as an alternative to serving in Vietnam.

Chapter 12. The Disability Press

1. "San Diego had a policy that if you had a disability you would go to the special school which was Sunshine School. Actually, it wasn't just elementary, it went from preschool through [grade] 12. I don't want to say that all the classes were combined, but they had like first/second as a class, and third/fourth, and fifth/sixth . . . I hated it there." Cynthia [Cyndi] Jones interview, 8.

2. Thomas Stephen Szasz is a psychiatrist and professor emeritus of psychiatry at the State University of New York Health Science Center in Syracuse. An outspoken critic of mainstream psychiatry, he is best known for his book *The Myth of Mental Illness* (New York: Hoeber-Harper, 1961).

3. Ken Kesey (1935–2001) was the author of numerous books and essays including *One Flew Over the Cuckoo's Nest* (1962) and *Sometimes a Great Notion* (1964) and a central figure in the 1960s psychedelic counterculture.

4. Tardive dyskinesia is a side effect of the neuroleptic drugs often prescribed to people diagnosed with schizophrenia or other "mental illnesses." People with "TD" "suffered from jerky, spasmodic motions of all types. Arms, ankles, fingers, toes, torso, neck, and larynx could all be affected. Some patients had difficulty walking, sitting, or standing. At times their speech became incomprehensible." The condition is most often prevalent in patients who have been prescribed neuroleptics over the course of several years. Robert Whitaker, *Mad in America: Bad Science, Bad Medicine, and the Enduring Mistreatment of the Mentally Ill* (Cambridge, MA: Perseus Books, 2002), 190–92.

5. *Cherry v. Mathews:* James L. Cherry, frustrated at how long officials at HEW under Secretary David Mathews were taking to issue regulations for 504, filed suit in federal court on February 13, 1976. On July 19, 1976, Judge John L. Smith found in the plaintiff's favor (Cherry was joined in the suit by the Georgetown Law Center Public Interest Law Institute and the Action League for Physically Handicapped Adults). Judge Smith ruled that the regulations were to be promulgated "with no further unreasonable delays." Richard Bryant Treanor, *We Overcame: The Story of Civil Rights for Disabled People* (Falls Church, VA: Regal Direct Publishing, 1993), 65–66. The regulations, however, were not promulgated until after the 1977 HEW demonstrations described in chapter 14.

6. Leonard Kriegel, "Uncle Tom and Tiny Tim: Some Reflections on the Cripple as Negro," *American Scholar* 38 (Summer 1969): 412–30, available online at www.disabilitymuseum.org/lib/docs/678.htm.

7. "Baby Doe" was born in Bloomington, Indiana, in April 1982, with Down syndrome and a blocked esophagus. Her parents, acting on their physician's advice, decided to withhold the medical procedure needed to remove the esophageal blockage, thus making the infant's death by starvation inevitable. Disability rights groups, most especially People First, believed that the decision to withhold treatment was made because the parents and doctors involved held stereotypical and demeaning views of people with Down syndrome. Advocates urged the courts to intervene, while others offered to adopt the infant and be responsible for his care themselves. The baby died, however, before any such intervention could take place. This case, and similar cases that followed, prompted the passage of the Child Abuse Prevention and Treatment Act Amendments of 1984. Fred Pelka, *The ABC-CLIO Companion to the Disability Rights Movement* (Santa Barbara, CA: ABC-CLIO, 1997), 37.

8. Paul K. Longmore (1946–2010) was a professor of history at San Francisco State University and the author or editor of several books and many articles on disability history and disability rights. Among these are *The New Disability History*, coedited with Lauri Umansky (New York: New York University Press, 2001), and *Why I Burned My Book and Other Essays* (Philadelphia: Temple University Press, 2003). His research on the League of the Physically Handicapped—a disability rights group active in New York City in the 1930s—and his discussion of the Elizabeth Bouvia case were among his many contributions to disability rights advocacy and scholarship.

9. In 1983, Elizabeth Bouvia checked into a California hospital, asking that physicians there give her pain medication while she starved herself to death. Because she had cerebral palsy, the media, the American Civil Liberties Union, and the "right to die" movement all saw her request as entirely reasonable, and the ACLU and right to die advocates entered the case on her behalf, their argument being that it was her disability that was prompting her to reach this decision. In fact, Bouvia had suffered a series of traumatic losses, including the death of her brother by drowning, financial problems, a miscarriage, the breakup of her marriage, and disability-based discrimination at her college, all in the two years immediately prior to her request. Eventually she decided to withdraw her request. Disability rights advocates noted that someone without a disability in the same circumstances would never have received this level of support for wanting to commit suicide. They also noted that, had the law allowed for physician-assisted suicide, Bouvia would never have had the opportunity to change her mind. See Paul K. Longmore, "Elizabeth Bouvia, Assisted Suicide, and Social Prejudice," in *Why I Burned My Book*, 149–74.

10. Wade Blank (1940–1993) was a principal founder and the guiding spirit behind ADAPT, and the group's direct-action, nonviolent, but sometimes highly confrontational style of political activism owes much to Blank's involvement with the civil rights and antiwar movements of the 1960s. It was for these tactics that ADAPT has often been seen as the more militant, even radical, wing of the disability rights movement.

"The independent living movement is into meetings and lobbying and socials. My members are into confrontation. We'll tell somebody what we want, and we'll talk about it once or twice, but that's it. Then we deal with you." Laura Hershey, "Wade Blank's Liberated Community," in *The Ragged Edge*, ed. Barrett Shaw (Louisville, KY: Advocado Press), 149–55.

For more on Rev. Blank and ADAPT, see chapter 21.

Chapter 13. The American Coalition of Citizens with Disabilities

1. Frederick C. Schreiber (1922–1979) was a prominent Deaf activist and a proponent of cross-disability organizing. He took the position of executive director of NAD in 1966, at a time when the organization was floundering and near bankruptcy. By 1979, Schreiber had turned NAD into a financially solvent, dynamic organization with a $2 million annual budget, its own national office building, and a staff of some forty people. He was a leading participant in the ACCD, and a participant in the 1977 sit-in of the HEW offices in Washington. Jack R.

Gannon, *Deaf Heritage: A Narrative History of Deaf America* (Silver Spring, MD: National Association of the Deaf, 1981), 421. For a more complete account of Schreiber's life and contributions to the Deaf community, see Jerome D. Schein, *A Rose for Tomorrow: Biography of Frederick C. Schreiber* (Silver Spring, MD: National Association of the Deaf, 1981).

2. Paul Corcoran, MD (1934–) is a retired Boston-area physician who for most of his career specialized in rehabilitation. His work brought him in contact with disability rights activists such as Fred Fay, Elmer Bartels, and Tim Foley, and with them he was a cofounder, in 1973–74, of the Boston CIL. Paul J. Corcoran, "Physician and Cofounder of the Boston Center for Independent Living," interview conducted by Fred Pelka, 2001, in *Massachusetts Activists and Leaders in the Disability Rights and Independent Living Movement*, vol. 1, DRILM Oral History Project, Regional Oral History Office, The Bancroft Library, University of California, Berkeley; © 2004 by The Regents of the University of California.

3. Durwood K. McDaniel (1915–1994) was one of the principal founders and leaders of the ACB through its first two decades, beginning in 1961. Before that he had been active in the NFB. Bradley Burson, "Dear General—Wherever You Are," *Braille Forum* 33, no. 7 (January 1995): 35–36.

4. Eric Gentile (1943–) was a disability rights student activist at Michigan State University and a leader in the effort to pass Michigan's "Handicapper Civil Rights Act" in 1976.

5. Another activist playing a major role in the early days of ACCD was Max J. Starkloff (1937–2010), founder of Paraquad, Inc., in St. Louis, Missouri, the first independent living center to be established in the midwest. Starkloff and his wife, Colleen Kelly Starkloff, were crucial in rallying support for the ADA, enlisting Senator Thomas Eagleton (D-MO), among others, into the effort. Fred Pelka, *The ABC-CLIO Companion to the Disability Rights Movement* (Santa Barbara, CA: ABC-CLIO, 1997), 290–91.

6. Sharon Mistler was director of the ENDependence Center of Northern Virginia. After helping to shape and pass the ADA, she worked in the Disability Rights Section of the US Justice Department, where she was a frequent critic of (and whistleblower on) the department's lack of zeal in enforcing the ADA and other disability rights laws. Mistler died in 2004. Alcestis Oberg, "Thanks to Her, the World Changed," *USA Today*, November 23, 2004.

7. Ralf David Hotchkiss (1947–) is an inventor whose innovations have revolutionized wheelchair design and construction, especially in developing nations. Disabled in a motorcycle accident in 1966, Hotchkiss has been called the disability movement's "technical genius," advising attorneys and advocates, for example, on the ins and outs of transit bus design. He has traveled throughout the world founding and cofounding bicycle/wheelchair factories and workshops which employ workers with disabilities at a decent wage and provide a product for the local market (bicycle manufacturing and repair), while producing wheelchairs specifically designed to fit the needs of the local disability community. Like Ed Roberts (in 1984), he was awarded a MacArthur Foundation Fellowship, in 1989. Pelka, *ABC-CLIO Companion*, 160.

8. Roger D. Petersen (1942–) attended the Idaho School for the Deaf and the Blind in Gooding from 1947 to 1954. His family then moved to Oregon, where he attended public school. He graduated from the University of Oregon, Eugene, in 1963, receiving a Woodrow Wilson Fellowship to study experimental psychology at Cornell University. While in graduate school he joined the National Federation of the Blind. Moving to Washington, DC, he became active with the President's Committee on Employment of the Handicapped in the early 1970s and was a founding member of the ACCD, serving as the group's staff "until we got the money together to hire Frank Bowe." Because of this cross-disability work, Petersen was expelled from the NFB and became a member of the American Council of the Blind. Roger Petersen, e-mail correspondence with the author, June 15, 2011.

9. Frank Bowe (1947–2007) was one of the foremost strategists of the American disability rights movement, especially during the 1970s and first half of the 1980s. As executive director of the ACCD he was a tireless advocate for cross-disability rights organizing. Bowe held a doctorate in educational psychology from New York University, and initiated and supervised

some of the first and most influential studies of the status of Americans with disabilities and the conditions under which they lived. He was also a central figure in the HEW demonstrations of spring 1977. Bowe published numerous books and articles. His *Handicapping America,* often cited in this volume (see introduction, note 65), is perhaps the single best overview of disability in America in the mid-1970s. Among his other works are *Disabled Women in America: A Statistical Report Drawn from Census Data* (Washington, DC: President's Committee on Employment of the Handicapped, 1984); *Rehabilitating America: Toward Independence for Disabled and Elderly People* (New York: Harper and Row, 1980); and *Approaching Equality: Education of the Deaf* (Silver Spring, MD: T. J. Publishers, 1981). His autobiography, *Changing the Rules* (Silver Spring, MD: T. J. Publishers, 1986), chronicled his experience growing up as a deaf child in an oralist environment, forbidden to use and largely unfamiliar with ASL until he began his graduate studies in 1969 at Gallaudet University. At the time of his death Bowe was a professor in the Counseling, Special Education, and Rehabilitation Department at Hofstra University. Pelka, *ABC-CLIO Companion,* 47–48.

10. Al Pimentel (1933–), like Frank Bowe, was an early activist in ACCD and cross-disability organizing. He was executive director of the NAD from 1979 to 1985, assuming the position after the death of Fred Schreiber. He is also a longtime educator, mentor, and advocate for Deaf youth, initially as a counselor at Northwest Connecticut Community College and then as director of the college's Career Education for the Deaf program. Al Pimentel, e-mail correspondence with the author, July 31, 2009.

11. John Wodatch was the chief author of the federal regulations implementing Section 504 of the Rehabilitation Act of 1973, and of the US Justice Department regulations on enforcement of Titles I, II, and III of the ADA. With more than thirty years' experience as a civil rights attorney with the federal government, as of this writing he is chief of the Disability Rights Section of the Civil Rights Division of the Justice Department.

12. John Lancaster has been the advocacy director of the PVA, project director for the ACCD, director of the Maryland Governor's Office for Individuals with Disabilities, executive director of the President's Committee on Employment of People with Disabilities, and the executive director of the National Council on Independent Living. A disabled veteran of the Vietnam War, Lancaster has also been the director of the Office of Disability Technical Assistance for Viet Nam Assistance for the Handicapped. His own account begins in chapter 20.

13. Marilyn Golden (1954–) is a senior policy analyst at the DREDF. She was the social action director of the Coalition for Barrier Free Living in Houston in 1977, and a cofounder of the Coalition of Texans with Disabilities in 1978. In 1987, she coordinated the local activists involved in the ADAPT demonstrations in San Francisco. Golden wrote the chapter "Title II—Public Services, Subtitle B: Public Transportation," in *Implementing the Americans with Disabilities Act,* ed. Lawrence O. Gostin and Henry A. Beyer (Baltimore: Paul H. Brookes Publishing, 1993), 109–21. Her own account is included in chapter 28.

14. Robert Kafka (1946–) is a longtime national organizer for ADAPT. Based in Texas, he was a board member and president of the Coalition for Barrier Free Living in Houston, an organizer and president of the Coalition of Texans with Disabilities, and president of Texas PVA. He has been involved in every major ADAPT action since founding the Texas ADAPT chapter in 1984. Pelka, *ABC-CLIO Companion,* 177.

15. TTYs—or Teletypers for the Deaf, were the precursors of TTDs, Telecommunications Devices for the Deaf and Hard of Hearing. TTYs were large, cumbersome, and expensive machines, essentially the same sort of teletypewriters used by news organizations such as the Associated Press. "By 1966, only eighteen TTY's were in operation in the entire United States. Karen Peltz Strauss, *A New Civil Right: Telecommunications Equality for Deaf and Hard of Hearing Americans* (Washington, DC: Gallaudet University Press), 8.

Chapter 14. The HEW Demonstrations

1. Frank Bowe, *Changing the Rules* (Silver Spring, MD: T. J. Publishers, 1986), 183.

2. Ibid., 185.

3. Richard Bryant Treanor, *We Overcame: The Story of Civil Rights for Disabled People* (Falls Church, VA: Regal Direct Publishing, 1993), 83.

4. Joseph P. Shapiro, *No Pity: People with Disabilities Forging a New Civil Rights Movement* (New York: Random House, 1993, 1994), 69.

5. The Reverend Cecil Williams (1929–), became minister at the Glide Memorial United Methodist Church in San Francisco in 1963, where he quickly became known as a "controversial and radical" preacher who transformed the formerly conservative congregation. He was "one of the first clergymen to take a revolutionary stand for same sex couples by presiding over their weddings four decades before today's struggle to legalize gay marriage." Glide has "a membership of over 11,000 . . . in the heart of the city's toughest neighborhoods" and is known for its diverse and growing congregation and its eclectic style of Christian worship. "Executive Leadership: Reverend Cecil Williams," Glide United Methodist Church website, http://66.211.107.100/page.aspx?pid=414.

6. Jeff Moyer (1949–) is a singer and activist whose original songs are a chronicle of the disability rights movement. Among them are "For the Crime of Being Different," "You Can't Deny Me Now," and "Just a Home of My Own." In the years since the HEW protests he has been a commentator on National Public Radio's *Morning Edition* and has given performances in forty-seven states and internationally, including several appearances at the White House. "Jeff Moyer Profile," at www.jeffmoyer.com/profile.htm.

7. This is a reference to the Pine Ridge Indian Reservation, home to the Oglala Lakota Nation, located in South Dakota. The reservation was the site of the massacre at Wounded Knee, during which more than three hundred men, women and children were killed by the US Cavalry on December 29, 1890. In the early 1970s the area was the scene of several violent confrontations—including a seventy-one-day stand-off between Lakota and other supporters of the American Indian Movement (AIM) on one side, and the FBI, federal marshals, the Bureau of Indian Affairs (BIA) and local authorities on the other. The stand-off ended with a negotiated settlement, but during the confrontation two AIM activists were killed, and an FBI agent was paralyzed. Peter Matthiessen, *In the Spirit of Crazy Horse* (New York: Viking-Penguin, 1991); John William Sayer, *Ghost Dancing the Law: The Wounded Knee Trials* (Cambridge: Harvard University Press, 1997).

8. Ralph Santiago Abascal (1934–1997) was the founding director of the Center on Race, Poverty, and the Environment, for more than twenty years the general counsel to California Rural Legal Assistance, and a prominent litigator for the rights of people living in poverty, especially poor farmers. Among his legal victories was a lawsuit which forced a legal ban on the use of the short-handled hoe, "a symbol of harshness in the lettuce fields that allowed foremen to assume their laborers were slacking off if they were not hunched over." Other cases led to the end of the agricultural use of DDT, which had been poisoning farm workers. He is credited by many with founding the environmental justice movement. Tim Golden, "Ralph S. Abascal, 62, Dies; Leading Lawyer for the Poor," *New York Times,* March 19, 1997.

Chapter 15. Psychiatric Survivors

1. Judi Chamberlin, "The Ex-Patients' Movement: Where We've Been and Where We're Going," *Journal of Mind and Behavior* 11, no. 3 (Summer 1990): 323–36.

2. David Oaks, interview conducted by Fred Pelka, May 19, 2008, audio recording in possession of the author, to be deposited at The Bancroft Library as part of its Regional Oral History Office Project on the Disability Rights and Independent Living Movement.

3. "Another Loss: Howie the Harp, 42," *Disability Rag & Resource* 16, no. 3 (May/June 1995): 26; Fred Pelka, *The ABC-CLIO Companion to the Disability Rights Movement* (Santa Barbara, CA: ABC-CLIO, 1997), 137; Lawrence Van Geller, "Howard Geld, 42, Advocate for the Mentally Ill, Dies," *New York Times,* February 14, 1995; Sally Zinman, "The Legacy of Howie the Harp Lives On," *National Empowerment Center Newsletter,* Spring/Summer 1995, 1, 9.

4. Rae E. Unzicker (1948–2001) was an activist in the psychiatric survivor movement and a

proponent of cross-disability cooperation and organizing. Her first experience with the mental health system came at age fourteen, when she was diagnosed as schizophrenic and catatonic. Her doctor recommended that she be hospitalized, and Unzicker spent the next twelve years in the mental health system.

Her political education began in 1978, when she read Chamberlin's *On Our Own*. Unzicker began attending conferences on alternatives to the mental health system. An appearance on the *Phil Donahue Show* prompted hundreds of people to write and phone her, and together with Chamberlin and others in 1985 she organized the National Association of Psychiatric Survivors. In 1995, she was appointed by President Clinton to the National Council on Disability. Her appointment was complicated by her status as an ex-mental patient, which required her extensive vetting by the FBI. Rae Unzicker, interview by the author, October 4, 1995, audio recording in possession of the author.

5. In *Rogers v. Commissioner of Mental Health* (1983) the US Court of Appeals for the First Circuit concluded that "a mental patient has the right to make treatment decisions and does not lose that right until the patient is adjudicated incompetent by a judge through incompetence hearings." Although considered a victory at the time, the ruling also contained significant loopholes, for instance, allowing a patient to be medicated against his or her will "to prevent the immediate, substantial, and irreversible deterioration of a serious mental illness." David Oaks, interview conducted by Fred Pelka, May 28, 2008, audio recording in possession of the author, to be deposited at The Bancroft Library as part of its Regional Oral History Office Project on the Disability Rights and Independent Living Movement; Pelka, *ABC-CLIO Companion*, 202–3.

6. Wade Hudson (1944–) moved to Berkeley in 1962 to attend classes at the University of California. Graduating in 1967 with a BS in social sciences, he enrolled at the Pacific School of Religion in Berkeley, where he helped found the New Seminary movement. Hudson moved to San Francisco in 1969 and worked as an intern minister at Glide Church, which in 1977 supported the occupation of the local offices of HEW by disability rights activists based at the Berkeley CIL. During this period and in the years after. he became involved in a wide range of social justice issues, working as staff or as a volunteer with various organizations including the Network Against Psychiatric Assault, the Bay Area Transit Coalition, the Bay Area Committee for Alternatives to Psychiatry, and the Tenderloin Jobs Coalition. He also volunteered with and wrote for *Madness Network News*. See "Wade Hudson's Bio," *Progressive Resource Catalog*, www.progressiveresourcecatalog.org/index.php/About/WadeHudson.

7. Martin Schiffenbauer (1938–) is known in the Berkeley area for his work on various political initiatives, most especially enacting local rent control. In 1982, he "personally drafted and collected nearly all the signatures for an initiative charter amendment to move Berkeley's general municipal election from April to November of even-numbered years. . . . This change would increase turnout of students, tenants, Democrats, and low-income voters." David Mundstock, "Berkeley in the 70s: A History of Progressive Electoral Politics," http://berkeleyinthe70s.homestead.com/.

8. Jessica Mitford (1917–1996), English-born author and journalist, is best known for *The American Way of Death* (1963), what one critic called "a scathing indictment of the American funeral industry." She also chronicled abuses in the American penal system, was an opponent of the Vietnam War, and a supporter of civil rights. She moved to the United States in 1939 with her first husband and eventually became a US citizen. Richard Severo, "Jessica Mitford, Incisive Critic of American Ways and a British Upbringing, Dies at 78," *New York Times*, July 24, 1996.

9. The Association of Community Organizations for Reform Now (ACORN) was founded in 1970. The coalition campaigned for better housing, schools, neighborhood safety, health care, and job conditions for working families. It also encouraged voter registration and the participation of poor and minority people in the electoral process. "Mission Statement," www.acorn.org/about/mission.

10. The 1982 meeting adopted a list of thirty principles, among them: "1. We oppose involuntary psychiatric intervention including civil commitment and the administration of psychiatric

procedures ('treatments') by force or coercion without informed consent; . . . 4. We oppose forced psychiatric procedures such as drugging[,] electroshock, psychosurgery, restraints, solitary confinement, and 'aversive behavior modification; . . . 8. We oppose the psychiatric system because it is an extra legal parallel police force which suppresses cultural and political dissent; . . . 16. We oppose the medical model of 'mental illness' because it dupes the public into seeking or accepting 'voluntary' treatment by fostering the notion that fundamental human problems, whether personal or social, can be solved by psychiatric/medical means." "Statement of Principles from the 10th Annual International Conference on Human Rights and Psychiatric Oppression."

Chapter 16. Working the System

1. Some disability rights activists were critical of Governor Dukakis for being less forthright during his 1988 presidential campaign in his support for the Americans with Disabilities Act. According to Jonathan Young, although Dukakis did give "a mild endorsement of the principles of the ADA, he did not court the disability community as vigorously as [then] Vice President [and Republican presidential candidate George H. W.] Bush." Young further explains how "Bush's leadership [while vice president] of the Task Force on Regulatory Relief and the disability community's defensive effort helped convinced [sic] Bush of the power of the community as a voting block: it commanded respect and could pay high dividends. Bush did not let the opportunity escape him. . . .

"Dukakis, on the other hand, was facing criticism that he and the Democratic Party were too beholden to interest groups, which led him to downplay rather than accentuate direct appeals to specific constituencies such as persons with disabilities. He thereby alienated much of the disability community." Jonathan M. Young. *Equality of Opportunity: The Making of the Americans with Disabilities Act* (Washington, DC: National Council on Disability, 1997), 85.

Ironically, disability lobbyists themselves may have been at least partly responsible for the candidate's unwillingness to take a firm stand in support of the ADA. Marilyn Golden, policy analyst for DREDF, states that advocates "told George Bush's campaign that Michael Dukakis's campaign was about to endorse the ADA any day. However, that was not true. Actually, we were telling the Michael Dukakis campaign not to endorse it," the fear being that any endorsement of the act from a liberal Democrat would alienate potential support from moderate Republicans. Marilyn Golden, "The Americans with Disabilities Act: An Activist's Perspective," in Report of the CIB Expert Seminar on Building Non-Handicapping Environments, Budapest, 1991, posted at www.independentliving.org/cib/cibbudapest11.html.

Cyndi Jones, editor at *Mainstream,* recalls a conversation she had with Tim Cook, a prominent disability rights attorney and the Dukakis campaign's senior adviser on disability issues. "After receiving Tim's article" about the candidate's stand on disability issues, "I spoke with him and he clearly said, 'I can't get him to sign on to save his life.' He was (VERY) frustrated." Cyndi Jones, e-mail correspondence with the author, January 8, 2011.

2. The vocational rehabilitation system, as I discuss in the Introduction, was inaugurated on the federal level following World War I and was vastly expanded under the leadership of Mary Switzer after World War II, especially after passage of the Vocational Rehabilitation Amendments of 1954. As a part of this expanded program, students with disabilities (such as James Donald) who qualified would be "sponsored" by OVR and given assistance in paying the costs related to their education, including, for example, college tuition and the purchase of textbooks. For a detailed history of the program, see Ruth O'Brien, "From Warehouses to Rehabilitation Centers: Restoring the Whole Man," in her *Crippled Justice: The Theory of Modern Disability Policy in the Workplace* (Chicago: University of Chicago Press, 2001), 63–87. For a description of the scope, function, and eligibility requirements of the program as they existed at the time of Donald's account, see Frank Bowe, *Handicapping America: Barriers to Disabled People* (New York: Harper and Row, 1978), 166–72.

3. Proposition 13 was a state ballot initiative, passed in 1978, which capped property taxes and required a two-thirds majority vote in local elections for local governments to raise special taxes. In coming years the initiative became a model for similar measures voted on in other

states, including Proposition 2 1/2 in Massachusetts, which required that municipal property tax increases not exceed 2.5 percent of the assessed value of all the property contained in a municipality, unless an override is approved by a majority of voters.

Chapter 17. Institutions, Part 4

1. Kwashiorkor is "a severe protein-deficiency type of malnutrition in children. It occurs after the child is weaned. The clinical signs are, at first, a vague type of lethargy, apathy, or irritability. Later there are failure to grow, mental deficiency, inanition, increased susceptibility to infections, edema, dermatitis, and liver enlargement." Clayton L. Thomas, ed., *Tabor's Cyclopedic Medical Dictionary*, 15th ed. (Philadelphia: F. A. Davis, 1985), 912.

2. "Mike [Wilkin] was the worker's physician at the US Public Health Hospital [in Staten Island]. . . . Michael stayed at the USPHS, which we began organizing, which was another story. Later I recruited him to come and support me at Willowbrook State School, once I began to realize what I'd gotten into. It was so massive and so impenetrable that I needed another organizer to help me on the inside that knew the score." William Bronston interview, 66.

3. Title XIX of the Social Security Act as amended in 1965 created Medicaid, one aspect of which provides federal aid to states in the form of matching funds for the placement of people with disabilities into residential institutions or nursing homes or chronic care facilities. Diane Rowland, Rachel Garfield, "Medicaid," *Encyclopedia of Public Health,* ed. Lester Breslow, 4 vols. (New York: Macmillan Reference USA/Gale Group Thomson Learning, 2002), 3:740–44. "Disability activists charge that Medicaid is biased toward institutions, reflecting the political power of the nursing home industry, and have proposed radically shifting funds away from nursing homes and toward home- and community-based services." Richard K. Scotch, "Medicaid," in *Encyclopedia of American Disability History,* ed. Susan Burch, 3 vols. (New York: Facts On File, 2009), 3:602. Ending this bias is now the main focus of ADAPT, which seeks to divert at least a portion of Title XIX funds into community-based services.

Bronston, feeling "depressed" and "terrifically exhausted," left Willowbrook in 1973, accepting an offer from Burton Blatt, chairman of the Education Department at Syracuse University to take a post as "visiting lecturer." While there Bronston was able to work with an intellectual mentor, Wolf Wolfensberger, who had coined the term "normalization" and popularized the concept in the United States. From there he moved, in 1975, to become a senior consultant and medical director for the Developmental Disabilities and Mental Health branches of the California Department of Health, where he fought to close down the state's institutions and replace them with community-based services.

The notoriety of the Willowbrook case caught the attention of disability rights attorney Bruce Ennis, who had been co-counsel for the plaintiffs in another landmark deinstitutionalization case, *Donaldson v. O'Connor.* In 1973, Ennis became counsel for the New York chapter of the Association for Retarded Children, which filed *New York ARC v. Rockefeller,* asking the federal courts to close Willowbrook and replace it with community-based services. In 1975 the court ordered the state to reduce Willowbrook's population, at that time some 5,400 people, to no more than 250 by 1981. Although the state took considerably longer to comply with this order, Willowbrook, as Dr. Bronston said, no longer exists as "a concentration camp" for people with developmental disabilities. David Rothman and Sheila Rothman, *The Willowbrook Wars: A Decade of Struggle for Social Change* (New York: Harper and Row, 1984); William Bronston interview, 114–17.

4. "Tear down the wall suits," meaning deinstitutionalization class-action lawsuits such as *Halderman v. Pennhurst State School & Hospital.*

5. *Mouth* magazine was founded by Gwin in 1989, roughly six months after she had been injured and placed in a New Medico facility. Over the years *Mouth* grew from a forum for brain injury survivors (it was first called *This Brain Has a Mouth*) to a publication covering all aspects of the disability rights movement. Fred Pelka, *The ABC-CLIO Companion to the Disability Rights Movement* (Santa Barbara, CA: ABC-CLIO, 1997), 207.

6. New Medico, founded and owned by Charles Brennick, went out of business in 1992 as a

result of what one reporter described as "a flurry of malpractice suits and several federal investigations into allegations of fraud and neglect." Less than ten years later, a central Florida "neurologic treatment center"—the Florida Institute for Neurologic Rehabilitation (FINR)—became the target of hundreds of complaints by patients and patient-advocates, with accusations including everything from lack of treatment to beatings, torture, and rapes. The owner and president of FINR, Joseph Brennick, had nine years earlier been a top administrator at New Medico, the company founded and owned by his father. Bob Norman, "Beaten, Burned, and Raped: Hundreds of Complaints Allege That a Central Florida Neurologic Treatment Center Is a House of Horrors," *New Times Broward/Palm Beach,* August 9, 2001.

Chapter 18. Self-Advocates

1. There is also a book titled *We Can Speak for Ourselves,* a comprehensive history of self-advocacy organizations up to the time of publication. Paul Williams and Bonnie Shoultz, *We Can Speak for Ourselves: Self-Advocacy by Mentally Handicapped People* (Cambridge, MA: Brookline Books, 1983).

2. Sarah Hunsberger. "Fairview: The Closing Chapter," *Salem Statesman Journal,* March 12, 2000.

3. Bonnie Hazel Shoultz (1941–) was an early adviser to People First, beginning in 1974, when she was first the intake adviser and then (after 1976) administrative assistant to the executive director at the Structured Correctional Project at ENCOR in Omaha. From 1981 to 1983 she was a senior research assistant at the Boys Town Center for the Study of Youth Development in Omaha, and then worked as a Community Program Specialist at the Community Support Program at the Department of Public Institutions in Lincoln, Nebraska. In 1985, she moved to Syracuse, New York, to become associate director (and, later, director) of training and information at the Research and Training Center on Community Integration at Syracuse University. In 1995, she became associate director at the Center on Human Policy, also at Syracuse University. Although retired from her position at the Center on Human Policy, she continues both as a mentor and adviser to People First and as the Buddhist chaplain at the Onondaga County Custody Division and also at Syracuse University. Bonnie Shoultz, e-mail correspondence with the author, June 27, 2008, and July 28, 2011.

4. Self-Advocates Becoming Empowered (SABE) was founded during the North American People First Conference in Nashville, Tennessee, on August 2, 1991. Among its goals are to promote legislation at state and national levels to protect the rights of people with disabilities, to support local self-advocacy groups, to close institutions, to ensure opportunities for people with disabilities to work fair wages, and to work with the criminal justice system and people with disabilities regarding their rights. The group also publishes material on self-advocacy and the rights of people with disabilities. Fred Pelka, *The ABC-CLIO Companion to the Disability Rights Movement* (Santa Barbara, CA: ABC-CLIO, 1997), 280.

5. The President's Committee on Mental Retardation had its origin in the President's Panel on Mental Retardation, first established by John F. Kennedy in October 1961. President Kennedy and other members of the Kennedy family, especially his sister Eunice Kennedy Shriver, had a personal connection with the issues of disability through their sister Rosemary Kennedy, who had a cognitive disability and who had been institutionalized when a young adult. The original panel was composed primarily of recognized "mental retardation professionals"—physicians, educators, and psychologists—but it also included parent advocates, notably Elizabeth M. Boggs, one of the founders of the National Association for Retarded Children (now known as the Arc). The panel was empowered to conduct a survey of the conditions and needs of children labeled mentally retarded and to issue a report with recommendations on how their situation could be improved. The panel released its report in early 1966 and was disbanded, but President Lyndon Johnson, on May 11 of that year, established a permanent President's Committee on Mental Retardation to continue and expand the work of the original panel. In 1969 the committee released its groundbreaking publication, *Changing Patterns in Residential Services for the Mentally Retarded,* the printed proceedings of the conference that introduced "normalization" to the United

States. In 1976 it published *The Mentally Retarded Citizen and the Law*, laying out the legal and social changes necessary to ensure full citizenship to people with cognitive disabilities. Nora Groce, *The U.S. Role in International Disability Activities: A History and a Look Towards the Future*, a study commissioned by World Institute on Disability, World Rehabilitation Fund, and Rehabilitation International, 1992, 69–73; Pelka, *ABC-CLIO Companion*, 249–50.

Chapter 19. DREDF and the 504 Trainings

1. The Disability Rights Center in Washington, founded in 1976 by Deborah Kaplan under the auspices of Ralph Nader's Center for the Study of Responsive Law, was primarily concerned with the problems of wheelchair users; the National Center on Law and the Handicapped, in South Bend, Indiana, dealt with the rights of individuals with developmental or cognitive disabilities and had pretty much closed down by the latter part of the decade.

2. Prior to passage of the ADA, the principal legal tool used by advocates to force transit authorities to provide access was Section 504 of the Rehabilitation Act of 1973. At first they were supported in these efforts by the federal Department of Transportation, which during the Carter administration issued regulations mandating that transit systems, in order to comply with 504, retrofit their stations and vehicles to become accessible. In 1979, however, the US Supreme Court, in *Southeastern Community College v. Davis* (see note 3 below), restricted the scope of 504, and in response the American Public Transit Association filed suit to force the DOT to rescind its regulations. In 1981 the US Circuit Court of Appeals, in *APTA v. Lewis*, invalidated the Carter DOT regulations. New regulations, giving transit systems "the local option" to neglect mainline access in favor of "special efforts" to provide mostly segregated accessible service, were subsequently issued by the Reagan administration. Doris Zames Fleischer and Frieda Zames, *The Disability Rights Movement: From Charity to Confrontation* (Philadelphia: Temple University Press, 2001), 65–66.

3. *Southeastern Community College v. Davis*, 99 S. Ct. 2361 (1979). As Meyerson explains, the Court in this decision ruled that Southeastern Community College in Whiteville, North Carolina, did not violate Section 504 of the Rehabilitation Act of 1973 by refusing to admit Francis B. Davis into its nursing program because of her hearing disability. It did, however, acknowledge that "situations may arise where a refusal to modify an existing program might become unreasonable and discriminatory."

4. In 1973 the Urban Mass Transportation Administration (now the Federal Transit Administration), an agency of the federal Department of Transportation (DOT), began to review prototypes of Transbus, a low-floor, wide-aisle mass transit bus with a retractable ramp designed to be accessible to all transit users. Three manufacturers—General Motors, AM General (a division of American Motors) and the Flxible Company—had each been awarded $9 million in federal funding, and had each developed its own working prototype. In 1976 a coalition of disability rights groups, led by Disabled in Action of Pennsylvania and represented by the Public Interest Law Center of Philadelphia, filed suit asking the federal court to order the secretary of transportation to require transit authorities to purchase only buses built to Transbus specifications as they retired their older, inaccessible models. The suit was dismissed when Secretary of Transportation Brock Adams, newly appointed by the Carter administration, issued such a mandate in 1977. By this time, however, AM General and Flxible had both dropped out of the Transbus program, and General Motors announced it would not manufacture Transbus—despite having accepted federal money to develop its working prototype—citing the expense of retooling its factories. In 1981 the DOT, responding to a federal ruling in a lawsuit filed by the American Public Transit Association, reversed the Adams mandate, making the purchase of accessible buses optional rather than mandatory. It would not be until passage of the Americans with Disabilities Act in 1990 that transit authorities would again be required to purchase only accessible buses. Frank Bowe, *Handicapping America: Barriers to Disabled People* (New York: Harper and Row, 1978), 81–83, 198; Fred Pelka, *The ABC-CLIO Companion to the Disability Rights Movement* (Santa Barbara, CA: ABC-CLIO, 1997), 306–7.

5. Federal District Judge Raymond Broderick ruled on March 17, 1978, that Pennhurst "be

closed and suitable community living arrangements and necessary support services provided for all Pennhurst residents . . . that individualized program plans be developed for each resident . . . and that plans for the removal of Pennhurst residents to appropriate community based mental retardation programs, meeting individual needs and structured in the least restrictive, most integrated setting, be developed and submitted to the court." *Halderman v. Pennhurst State School & Hospital,* as quoted in the subsequent ruling of the US Court of Appeals, 612 F.2d (3rd Cir. 1979), 90.

Chapter 20. Activists and Organizers, Part 3

1. Robert Burgdorf (1948–), author of *The Legal Rights of Handicapped Persons: Cases, Materials, and Text* (Baltimore: Paul H. Brookes Publishing, 1980), along with many other books and articles. As the attorney/research specialist for the National Council on Disability in 1988, he wrote the first draft of the Americans with Disabilities Act of 1990.

2. The Architectural Barriers Act of 1968 required that all buildings constructed, altered, or financed by the federal government after 1969 be accessible to people with disabilities. The act, however, contained no provision for enforcement. The Architectural and Transportation Barriers Compliance Board (ATBCB), created by the Rehabilitation Act of 1973, was meant to address this problem, but the board itself was criticized by disability rights advocates as being underfunded and having little actual power. Frank Bowe, *Handicapping America: Barriers to Disabled People* (New York: Harper and Row, 1978), 32–33, 198–99; Caryn E. Neumann, "Architectural Barriers Act," *Encyclopedia of American Disability History,* ed. Susan Burch, 3 vols. (New York: Facts On File, 2009), 1:63–64.

3. Sections 501 of the Rehabilitation Act of 1973 required that the federal government open its agencies and departments to qualified employees with disabilities; section 502 established the Architectural and Transportation Barriers Compliance Board (see note 2 above); and section 503 required federal contractors with contracts more than $2,500 to establish affirmative action programs for qualified employees with disabilities. Section 402 of the Vietnam Era Veterans' Readjustment Assistance Act of 1974 required employers receiving more than $10,000 in federal funds to take affirmative action to hire qualified veterans with disabilities. Fred Pelka, *The ABC-CLIO Companion to the Disability Rights Movement* (Santa Barbara, CA: ABC-CLIO, 1997), 263–64, Jonathan M. Young, *Equality of Opportunity: The Making of the Americans with Disabilities Act* (Washington, DC: National Council on Disability, 1997), 13.

4. Disabled American Veterans (DAV) was established following World War I to advocate on behalf of veterans with disabilities. It was pivotal in the establishment of the first federal Veterans Bureau, the forerunner of today's Department of Veterans Affairs. Pelka, *ABC-CLIO Companion,* 101.

5. The Catholic Campaign for Human Development was founded in 1969. Its "pastoral strategy is empowerment of the poor through a methodology of participation and education for justice, leading toward solidarity between poor and non-poor as impelled by the Church's biblical tradition, modern Catholic social teaching, and the pervasive presence of poverty in the United States." United States Conference of Catholic Bishops, Catholic Campaign for Human Development, www.usccb.org/cchd/mission.shtmi.

6. Karen Thompson and Julie Andrzejewski, *Why Can't Sharon Kowalski Come Home?* (San Francisco: Spinsters/Aunt Lute, 1988). See also Charles Casey, *The Sharon Kowalski Case: Lesbian and Gay Rights on Trial* (Lawrence: University of Kansas Press, 2003).

7. Harilyn Rousso (1946–) is an educator, social worker, psychotherapist, and disability rights advocate who has done landmark work advocating for girls and women with disabilities. She founded the Networking Project for Disabled Women and Girls of the Young Women's Christian Association in New York City in 1984 and has been part of numerous organizations and campaigns, including serving a term as commissioner with the New York Commission on Human Rights (1988–1993), and as executive director of Disabilities Unlimited Consulting Services, which offers counseling and advocacy to people with disabilities and their family. Harilyn Rousso, "Advocate for Disabled Girls and Young Women, Researcher on Gender Issues and Disability," interview conducted by Denise Sherer Jacobson, 2003, in *New York Activ-*

ists and Leaders in the Disability Rights and Independent Living Movement, vol. 3, DRILM Oral History Project, Regional Oral History Office, The Bancroft Library, University of California, Berkeley; © 2004 by The Regents of the University of California.

Connie Panzarino (1947–2001) was an advocate for disability, women's, and lesbian rights. She worked extensively with women and men survivors of physical and sexual abuse, and lectured and wrote on the subjects of disability, homophobia, sexism, and the ethics of genetic engineering. She was the director of the Beechtree, an independent living program for disabled women in Forestberg, New York, from 1980 to 1985, and the executive director of the Boston Self-Help Center from 1986 to 1989. As an antiwar activist, she features prominently in Ron Kovic's *Born on the Fourth of July* (New York: Pocket Books, 1976). Her autobiography, *The Me in the Mirror*, was published by Seal Press in Seattle in 1994.

Chapter 21. ADAPT

1. "On May 4, 1970, at Kent State University, [Ohio National] Guardsmen fired on [anti–Vietnam War] demonstrators, killing four and wounding nine." The students had been protesting the announcement by President Nixon that US forces would invade Cambodia, thus marking a widening of the war. The shootings at Kent State "spurred still further protests. Eventually, students at more than seven hundred colleges and universities declared strikes and many campuses were effectively shut down for the remainder of the semester." Christian G. Appy, *Patriots: The Vietnam War Remembered from All Sides* (New York: Penguin, 2003), 380.

2. Molly Blank, interview by Fred Pelka, December 2, 2006, audiotape in possession of the author, to be deposited at The Bancroft Library as part of its Regional Oral History Office Project on the Disability Rights and Independent Living Movement.

3. "ADAPT: The Movement Takes to the Streets, and Takes to the Media," in *Spinal Network: The Total Resource for the Wheelchair Community*, ed. Sam Maddox (Boulder, CO: Spinal Network, 1987), 295.

4. The spinal cord is divided, in order descending from the brain, into the cervical, thoracic, and lumbar sections. These sections are in turn divided into numbered vertebrae which surround the spinal cord, with the lower numbers designating higher sections of the spinal column. And so, for example, the seven cervical vertebrae descending from the brain stem are C_1, C_2, C_3, up to C_7, at which point the thoracic portion of the spine begins, in twelve vertebrae designated T_1 through T_{12}. Generally speaking, the higher up the injury to the spinal cord, the greater degree of overall paralysis and disability, depending also on the severity of damage to the cord. To say, as Mark Johnson does, that he is a "$C_{5/6}$ quadriplegic" means that his spinal cord was injured between the 5th and 6th vertebrae of his cervical spine, resulting in at least some paralysis of all four limbs. *Taber's Cyclopedic Medical Dictionary*, ed. Clayton L. Thomas (Philadelphia: F. A. Davis, 1985), 1599–1600.

5. The National Council on Independent Living was founded in 1982 as an association of independent living centers. Based in Washington, DC, it advocates on behalf of the centers and the independent living movement and provides technical assistance to centers and other groups in the disability community. Fred Pelka, *The ABC-CLIO Companion to the Disability Rights Movement* (Santa Barbara, CA: ABC-CLIO, 1997), 215.

Chapter 22. Deaf President Now!

1. Oralism is a theory of deaf education adopted by hearing educators of the deaf in the years after an international conference of educators in Milan, Italy, in 1880. It maintains that deaf children should be taught language exclusively through lip-reading and spoken speech and discouraged from using signs or American Sign Language. Its embrace in the United States in the late nineteenth and first half of the twentieth centuries led to the firing of Deaf educators, the de-funding of Deaf schools, and even the removal of deaf children from their Deaf parents. For discussion of the history of oralism and its impact on the American Deaf community, see Jack R. Gannon, *Deaf Heritage: A Narrative History of Deaf America* (Silver Spring, MD: National Association of the Deaf, 1981), 359–67; Richard Winefield, *Never the Twain Shall Meet: Bell,*

Gallaudet, and the Communications Debate (Washington, DC: Gallaudet University Press, 1987); and Susan Burch, "Reading between the Signs: Defending Deaf Culture in Early Twentieth-Century America," in *The New Disability History: American Perspectives,* ed. Paul K. Longmore and Lauri Umansky (New York: New York University Press, 2001), 214–35.

2. John F. "Jack" Levesque (1945–) was educated in the oral method at the Clarke School for the Deaf in Northampton, Massachusetts. He was nineteen years old before he first discovered American Sign Language and Deaf culture. He went to Gallaudet in 1965 and experienced what he called "culture shock." Receiving his BA in sociology in 1972, he went to work for the NAD as assistant to executive director Fred Schreiber. He was then a cofounder and president of the Massachusetts State Association for the Deaf and instrumental in founding Developmental Evaluation and Adjustment Facilities (DEAF), Inc., also in Massachusetts. In the 1980s Levesque became executive director at the Deaf Counseling, Advocacy, and Referral Agency, now in San Leandro, California. By 1988, DCARA, with a staff of forty providing services to "members of the Deaf and hard-of-hearing community—Deaf/Blind, Latinos, the Gay/Lesbian population, Deaf senior citizens, the foreign-born group—you name it," was one of the largest and most influential Deaf advocacy agencies in the nation. "Jack Levesque: Leader and Advocate," in Matthew S. Moore and Robert F. Panara, *Great Deaf Americans: The Second Edition* (Rochester, NY: Deaf Life Press/MSM Productions, 1996), 347–51.

Barbara Jean (or "BJ") Wood (1950–), from Scotch Plains, New Jersey, graduated from the National Technical Institute for the Deaf in 1975 with a degree in social work. She helped establish the Massachusetts Commission for Deaf and Hard of Hearing, and was appointed that agency's first commissioner by Governor Michael Dukakis in 1986. She left the MCD-HH in 2001 to serve five years at the Colorado Commission for the Deaf and Hard of Hearing. She retired as the executive director of the New Mexico Commission for Deaf and Hard of Hearing in 2011. Mabs Holcomb and Sharon Wood, *Deaf Women: A Parade through the Ages* (Berkeley: DawnSignPress, 1989), 61; Barbara Jean Wood, e-mail correspondence with the author, July 27, 28, 2011.

3. Jack R. Gannon, *The Week the World Heard Gallaudet* (Washington, DC: Gallaudet University Press, 1989).

4. Ibid., 25.

5. "The Old Jim" or "Ole Jim" is the Peikoff Alumni House on the Gallaudet University campus. It currently houses the Gallaudet University Alumni Association Headquarters. It is known as "Ole Jim" because it originally housed Gallaudet College's first gymnasium, built in 1881. "'Ole Jim'—the Peikoff Alumni House," www.gallaudet.edu /development_and_alumni _relations/alumni_relations/ole_jim_.html.

6. In addition to being on Gallaudet's board of trustees (and the first Deaf chair of that board), Philip W. Bravin has been a pioneer in and long-time champion of captioning of films and television programs. In the early 1980s, he was the chair of the NAD's TV Access Committee and president of the National Captioning Institute, headquartered in Vienna, Virginia. During this time, Bravin spearheaded street protests involving hundreds of deaf captioning activists at more than one hundred CBS TV affiliates across the country, in reaction to CBS's resistance to offering closed captioning with its programs. The protests were ultimately successful, and in 1984 CBS agreed to follow the other networks in making their programming more accessible to deaf and hard-of-hearing viewers. Karen Peltz Strauss, *A New Civil Right: Telecommunications Equality for Deaf and Hard of Hearing Americans* (Washington, DC: Gallaudet University Press), 218.

At the time of the DPN campaign, Dr. Irving King Jordan (1943–) was Gallaudet University's dean of the College of Arts and Sciences, a position he took in 1986, after becoming an assistant professor at Gallaudet in 1973 and a full professor in 1983. Deafened at age twenty-one in a motorcycle accident, he eventually enrolled at Gallaudet, learning sign and graduating with a BA in psychology in 1970. After graduate and postgraduate studies at the University of Tennessee, he returned to teach at Gallaudet, where he remained as president until his retirement in the 2006–2007 academic year. "I. King Jordan: First Deaf President of Gallaudet University," in Moore and Panara, *Great Deaf Americans,* 335–39.

7. Dr. Roslyn "Roz" Goodstein Rosen was the director of Gallaudet's Kellogg Special Schools of the Future Program, the university's first woman dean, and the director of its College of Continuing Education. She has also been active with the NAD and in a variety of other Deaf organizations. Mabs Holcomb and Sharon Wood, *Deaf Women: A Parade through the Decades* (Berkeley: DawnSignPress, 1989), 86.

8. Gallaudet, as well as being a center of Deaf education and culture, is also a place where hearing people can enroll to study ASL, education for Deaf students, and other fields relating to deafness and Deaf people.

9. Allen Sussman earned his doctorate at New York University in 1973. At the time of the DPN campaign he was director of the University Counseling Center. He has been a longtime advocate of the need for counselors, psychologists, and psychiatrists to become educated in Deaf issues and culture if they expect to meet the needs of Deaf and hard-of-hearing patients. Katherine Delorenzo, "Groundbreaking Conference on Mental Health and Deaf People," *On the Green: A Publication for Gallaudet Faculty, Teachers, and Staff* 29, no. 6 (November 11, 1998), available online at http://pr.gallaudet.edu/otg/BackIssues.asp.

Nancy J. Bloch has been the executive director (now chief executive officer) of the National Association of the Deaf since 1992. She earned her MA in counseling and guidance from Gallaudet, and before becoming head of the NAD, she was director of the Management Institute and adjunct professor in the School of Management at Gallaudet. Holcomb and Wood, *Deaf Women*, 89.

Chapter 23. The Americans with Disabilities Act—"The Machinery of Change"

1. The subtitle of this chapter is taken from Leonard Cohen's song "Democracy" (1992): "It's here they got the range / and the machinery for change . . . / Democracy is coming to the U.S.A."

2. C. Boyden Gray (1943–) was counsel to Vice President and then President George H. W. Bush. Gray is an heir to the R. J. Reynolds tobacco fortune. His close friendship with Evan Kemp Jr. would prove crucial to passage of the ADA. Although not a person with a disability, Gray was cognizant of disability discrimination, as experienced by Kemp. "For the first time, Gray had a friend whom he could not take to his favorite restaurants, because they had steps. . . . Even Gray's home was off-limits, made inaccessible by a flight of stairs." Joseph P. Shapiro, *No Pity: People with Disabilities Forging a New Civil Rights Movement* (New York: Random House, 1993, 1994), 123. Gray's account of the passage of the ADA is in chapter 30.

3. Evan Kemp Jr. (1937–1997) was a major ally of and advocate in the disability rights movement, especially important during the effort to draft and pass the ADA. His contribution is described in an interview in chapter 25 with his wife, Janine Bertram Kemp. Historian Hugh Gregory Gallagher, at Kemp's memorial service, described how Kemp, "from the beginning . . . saw the disability rights revolution in its entirety; he saw it as nothing less than the remaking of society, the ultimate civil rights movement, the empowerment of the entire spectrum of Americans." Quoted in "The Disability Community Loses Evan J. Kemp, Jr.," *One Step Ahead* 4, no. 9 (September 1997): 2–3.

4. Ralph Neas (1946–) was executive director of the Leadership Conference on Civil Rights for fourteen years, beginning in 1981. Now the Leadership Conference on Civil and Human Rights, the LCCR was founded in 1950, and is the nation's premier civil rights coalition, consisting of more than two hundred national organizations. It has been involved in every major civil rights initiative on the national level since 1957. Its longtime president and CEO is Wade Henderson, professor of public interest law at the David A. Clarke School of Law, University of the District of Columbia. Fred Pelka, *The ABC-CLIO Companion to the Disability Rights Movement* (Santa Barbara, CA: ABC-CLIO, 1997), 222.

5. Guillain-Barré syndrome is "polyneuritis [or inflammation of two or more nerves] with progressive muscular weakness of extremities that may lead to paralysis. Usually occurs after recovery from an infectious disease. . . . Recovery is usually complete if the acute period is uncomplicated." *Taber's Cyclopedic Medical Dictionary*, ed. Clayton L. Thomas (Philadelphia: F. A. Davis, 1985), 711.

6. The US Supreme Court, in *Grove City College v. Bell* (1984), dramatically narrowed the

federal government's ability to enforce each of the major civil rights acts passed since 1964: Title IX of the Education Amendments of 1972, prohibiting discrimination on the basis of gender; Section 504 of the Rehabilitation Act of 1973, prohibiting discrimination on the basis of disability; and the Age Discrimination Act of 1975. *Grove* was also seen as a threat to the enforcement of the original Civil Rights Act of 1964, prohibiting discrimination on the basis of race or ethnic origin. Doris Zames Fleischer and Frieda Zames, *The Disability Rights Movement: From Charity to Confrontation* (Philadelphia: Temple University Press, 2001), 78–79.

In *Grove*, a woman had brought suit alleging that she had been discriminated against at her college because of her gender. The Court ruled that whether or not the discrimination had actually occurred, the plaintiff was without civil rights protection because the particular department of the school alleged to have discriminated against her had not been the direct recipient of federal funds. Up to that point, the courts had interpreted (and Congress had clearly intended) a broader interpretation of the laws as covering entities receiving federal funds in their entirety, so that if, for example, the chemistry department of a university received federal research dollars, the English department of the same university would be covered.

Since the *Grove* decision cut across the spectrum of civil rights constituencies, the effort to overturn it resulted in the formation of a broad coalition of those groups. It marked "the first time [that] representatives of the disability community worked in leadership roles with representatives of minority and women's groups on a major piece of civil rights legislation." The connections and alliances made in the struggle to pass the Civil Rights Restoration Act would carry over into the effort to pass the ADA two years later. Arlene Mayerson, "The History of the ADA: A Movement Perspective," in *Implementing the Americans with Disabilities Act,* ed. Lawrence O. Gostin and Henry A. Beyer (Baltimore: Paul H. Brookes Publishing, 1993), 19; and Pelka, *ABC-CLIO Companion,* 67–68.

7. William Bradford Reynolds (1942–) was assistant attorney general, Civil Rights Division, from 1981 to 1988.

8. The Civil Rights Restoration Act of 1987, first introduced into Congress in February 1985, was finally passed over President Reagan's veto in March 1988. The CRRA explicitly defined Section 504 of the Rehabilitation Act of 1973 to include virtually all activities and programs of any entity in receipt of federal funding, thereby overturning, for all intents and purposes, the US Supreme Court decision in *Grove City College v. Bell.*

9. The Fair Housing Amendments Act of 1988, like the Civil Rights Restoration Act of 1987, was another milestone, not only for the protections it conferred but also because it deepened the alliances originally formed to pass the CRRA. Essentially, the FHAA added people with disabilities to the list of groups protected from housing discrimination under the Civil Rights Act of 1968. It also marked the first time that people with disabilities were included under the provisions of a law intended to ban discrimination against other groups. (The CRRA of 1987, which also included people with disabilities, was passed after the FHHA of 1988).

Of particular importance was the role played by the Leadership Conference on Civil Rights. "During these years [1984 to 1988], alliances were forged within the civil rights community that became critical in the fight for passage of the ADA. Because of its commitment to disability civil rights, the Leadership Conference on Civil Rights played an important role in securing passage of the ADA." Mayerson, "History of the ADA," 20.

10. The Disability Rights Center was founded in Washington, DC, in 1976 by Deborah Kaplan, with funding from Ralph Nader's Center for the Study of Responsive Law. It focused primarily on protecting the rights of consumers of wheelchairs and other durable medical equipment and on enforcing enactment of the affirmative action provision of the Rehabilitation Act of 1973. In 1980, Kaplan left the DRC to become an attorney at DREDF, and Evan Kemp Jr. became the center's new director. Pelka, *ABC-CLIO Companion,* 99–100.

11. The US Supreme Court, in *Smith v. Robinson* (1984), had refused to award attorney's fees to the parents of a disabled child after they had prevailed in a lawsuit against their local school authorities, arguing that Congress had made no such provision in the Education for All Handicapped Children Act of 1975. Advocates felt that without such a provision, school districts unwill-

ing to comply with the act would try to prevail by wearing parents down with expensive litigation, and that poorer families would thus find themselves unable to avail themselves of the law's protection. In response, Congress passed the Handicapped Children's Protection Act of 1986, which, like the Civil Rights Restoration Act of 1987, was an instance of Congress's acting to overturn a Supreme Court decision that narrowed civil rights protection offered by previous legislation. Stanley S. Herr, "The ADA in International and Developmental Disabilities Perspectives," in *Implementing the Americans with Disabilities Act*, 240. Pelka, *ABC-CLIO Companion*, 284.

12. Robert Silverstein (1949–) was at the time of the ADA campaign the staff director and chief counsel for the Senate Subcommittee on Disability Policy and Senator Tom Harkin's principal adviser on disability issues. His account is in chapter 26.

13. The Handicapped Children's Protection Act of 1986 was passed in response to the US Supreme Court 1984 ruling in *Smith v. Robinson*.

14. The Rehabilitation Act Amendments of 1984 made the National Council on the Handicapped an independent agency, charged with reviewing federal policies related to disability. National Council on the Handicapped, *On the Threshold of Independence: Progress on Legislative Recommendations from Toward Independence* (Washington, DC: GPO), January 1988), vii.

15. Gerben James DeJong (1946–) was director of the Illinois Coalition of Citizens with Disabilities, president of the National Association of Independent Living, and a member of the Task Force on the Rights and Empowerment of Americans with Disabilities. Richard Bryant Treanor, *We Overcame: The Story of Civil Rights for Disabled People* (Falls Church, VA: Regal Direct Publishing, 1993), 107. He was an early advocate of the independent living philosophy, and his articles gave the IL movement academic legitimacy at a time when most (non-disabled) rehabilitation professionals were skeptical of services designed and run by people with disabilities themselves. Gerben DeJong, e-mail correspondence with the author, August 10, 2011; Fleischer and Zames, *Disability Rights Movement*, 46. DeJong is currently Senior Fellow and Director of the Center for Post-acute Innovation and Research at the National Rehabilitation Hospital in Washington, DC, and a professor of rehabilitation medicine at the Georgetown University School of Medicine.

16. The chair of the National Council on the Handicapped from 1983 to 1993, Sandra Swift Parrino (1934–) is the parent of a physically disabled son. Parrino insisted that the council be a truly independent federal agency and was also adamant that it propose and support a robust and enforceable ADA. Fleischer and Zames, *Disability Rights Movement*, 89–90. Pelka, *ABC-CLIO Companion*, 241.

17. National Council on the Handicapped, *Toward Independence: An Assessment of Federal Laws and Programs Affecting People with Disabilities—With Legislative Recommendations* (Washington, DC: GPO, 1986).

18. National Council on the Handicapped, *On the Threshold of Independence: A Report to the President and to the Congress of the United States* (Washington, DC: GPO, 1988).

Chapter 24. Drafting the Bill, Part 1

1. There had, in fact, been several previous proposals for including people with disabilities under federal civil rights law. Ruth O'Brien points to an attempt in Congress in 1940 to pass legislation "that gave disabled people . . . a right to work free from discrimination," but it was perceived by the business lobby as being too onerous for employers and never passed. A similar bill proposed in 1941 met the same opposition and likewise went nowhere. Ruth O'Brien, *Crippled Justice: The Theory of Modern Disability Policy in the Workplace* (Chicago: University of Chicago Press, 2001), 75. In 1971 and 1972, Senator Hubert Humphrey (D-MN) and Representative Charles Vanik (D-OH) "proposed that the Civil Rights Act of 1964 be amended to include disability." Despite the fact that sixty members of the House and twenty members of the Senate cosponsored the legislation, hearings were never held, and the bill died in large part because of the opposition of African American civil rights groups, which feared the diminution of protections already in place for their constituents if the CRA was opened for amendment. O'Brien, *Crippled Justice*, 114. The White House Conference on the Handicapped in May 1977 passed resolutions endorsing the idea of amending the 1964 CRA and the Voting Rights

Act of 1965 to include people with disabilities, again with no result. Fred Pelka, *The ABC-CLIO Companion to the Disability Rights Movement* (Santa Barbara, CA: ABC-CLIO, 1997), 323.

2. Madeleine Will is a parent advocate who served as assistant secretary of education for special education and rehabilitation under the Reagan and G. H. W. Bush administrations. Before that she had been the chief legislative lobbyist with the Maryland Association for Retarded Citizens, and since then has become director of the Policy Center at the National Down Syndrome Society. "George and Madeleine Will Have Government Cornered: He Writes about It and She Serves in It," *People,* September 19, 1983. National Down Syndrome Society—About Policy, www.ndss.org.

3. The "Contract with America" was a series of conservative legislative proposals outlined by the national Republican Party during the 1994 congressional elections. The Republican victory that year marked the first time since the 1950s that the Republican Party had controlled both houses of Congress.

4. "Kinder, gentler . . . " refers to the acceptance speech given by George H. W. Bush at the Republican National Convention on August 18, 1988, during which he stated, "I want a kinder, and gentler nation." "A kinder, gentler nation," together with "a thousand points of light," became major themes of his successful 1988 presidential campaign.

An interesting parallel can be drawn to how the Eisenhower administration supported legislation to expand the vocational rehabilitation programs put into place after World War I. "Since Eisenhower was casting about for a domestic policy that was not part of the New Deal heritage, and the conservative self-help ethic underlying the vocational rehabilitation program played well with the Republican party, the president sponsored the Vocational Rehabilitation Act of 1954, which finally created the vocational rehabilitation program that Switzer and the rehabilitation movement had been working toward since World War II." O'Brien, *Crippled Justice,* 64.

5. Phil Calkins (1938–) worked at the President's Committee on Employment of People with Disabilities, and then with Evan Kemp Jr. at the Equal Employment Opportunity Commission, during the campaign to pass the ADA. Before that he had worked with architectural access pioneer Ron Mace at Barrier Free Environments in Chapel Hill, North Carolina. Calkins was advocate Sharon Mistler's partner until her death in 2003. "I met Evan through Sharon, and later lived in his apartment for a year or so when I was broke and doing a lot of disability rights stuff for which I wasn't paid." Phil Calkins, e-mail correspondence with the author, December 15, 2010.

Chapter 25. Insiders, Part 1

1. The Federalist Society for Law and Public Policy Studies, based in Washington, was founded in 1982 as a student organization at the Yale, Harvard, and University of Chicago law schools. It promotes a conservative, even libertarian, interpretation of law and the Constitution. "Our Background," www.fed-soc.org/.

2. The George Jackson Brigade, named after Black Panther George Jackson, who was killed in prison in 1971, was a revolutionary group based in Seattle which, from March 1975 to December 1977, robbed at least seven banks and planted no fewer than twenty pipe bombs in government buildings, electric power stations, Safeway stores (because of that company's refusal to join the United Farm Workers union boycott of California grapes), and offices of companies accused of racism. A shootout during one bank robbery, on January 23, 1976, left one member of the group dead and another wounded and under arrest. Six weeks later another member of the group freed the wounded member being held at the Harborview Medical Center in Seattle, wounding a police officer in the process. All the surviving members of the group were eventually arrested, and served sentences ranging from four to twenty-four years, with the last prisoner being released in 2000. Mark Worth, "The Last Brigadier: Only One George Jackson Brigade Member Remains Behind Bars: Is He Doomed to Die There?" *Seattle Weekly,* July 22, 1998.

3. Patricia Campbell Hearst (1954–), the newspaper heiress, was kidnapped by the Symbionese Liberation Army (SLA) in 1974. She was arrested in September 1975; tried the following year. She was found guilty of participating in a bank robbery with the SLA and sentenced to thirty-five years imprisonment. Her sentence was commuted to seven years by President

Jimmy Carter, of which she served twenty-two months. Hearst was granted a full pardon by President Bill Clinton in January 2001. Caitlin Flanagan, "Girl, Interrupted: How Patty Hearst's Kidnapping Reflected and Ravaged American Culture in the 1970s," *Atlantic,* September 2008, 103–10; William Graebner, *Patty's Got a Gun: Patricia Hearst in 1970s America* (Chicago: University of Chicago Press, 2008).

"Give Them Shelter" was a flyer distributed by several leftist groups "when the SLA was on the run with Patty Hearst." Janine Bertram, e-mail correspondence with the author, July 27, 2011.

The Weather Underground, known also as "the Weathermen" (after a line from a Bob Dylan song) and the Weather Underground Organization or WUO, was started in 1969 as an offshoot of the Students for a Democratic Society. During the next five years the group conducted a campaign of violent opposition to the Vietnam War, including bombings at the US Capitol in March 1971 and the Pentagon in May 1972. See Dan Berger, *Outlaws of America: The Weather Underground and the Politics of Solidarity* (Oakland, CA: AK Press, 2006), and Ron Jacobs, *The Way the Wind Blew: A History of the Weather Underground* (New York: Verso, 1997).

4. Marsha Mazz (1950–) was a disability rights advocate at Endependence Center, Inc., and a member of the National Council on Independent Living. She joined the staff of the US Architectural and Transportation Barriers Compliance Board (now the Architectural Access Board) in 1989, where she now holds the position of technical assistance coordinator and accessibility specialist.

5. Lisa Gorove (1961–) is a staff member of the Office of Special Education Programs at the US Department of Education. She was the ASL interpreter on the speakers' platform when President George H. W. Bush signed the ADA. Glen White, "The ADA at Twenty," *Lifeline Online,* no. 105 (Summer 2010), newsletter of the Life Span Institute at the University of Kansas, at www.lsi.ku.edu/news/lifeline/summer2010/news.shtml. During the 1980s she was manager of the Gallaudet Interpreting Services, after which she worked with Frank Bowe at the federal Commission on Education of the Deaf, and then with Deidre Davis at the Independent Living Branch of the Rehabilitation Services Administration. Lisa Gorove, e-mail correspondence with the author, July 29, 2011.

6. The National Council on Independent Living, an association of IL centers founded in 1982 and based in Washington, advocates on behalf of the independent living movement, provides technical support to centers, and was instrumental in advocating for passage of the ADA. Fred Pelka, *The ABC-CLIO Companion to the Disability Rights Movement* (Santa Barbara, CA: ABC-CLIO, 1997), 215.

7. Under Title V, Section 511 of the ADA, Definitions (a): "For purposes of the definition of 'disability' in section 3(2), homosexuality and bisexuality are not impairments and as such are not disabilities under this Act.

"(b) CERTAIN CONDITIONS—Under this Act, the term 'disability' shall not include—
(1) transvestism, transsexualism, pedophilia, exhibitionism, voyeurism, gender identity disorders not resulting from physical impairments, or other sexual behavior disorders;
(2) compulsive gambling, kleptomania, or pyromania; or
(3) psychoactive substance use disorders resulting from current illegal use of drugs." The Americans with Disabilities Act of 1990.

8. Bob Cooper (1953–) was appointed executive secretary of the Rhode Island Governor's Commission on Disabilities in 1980 and continues at that position today. He was a member of the President's Committee on Employment of People with Disabilities and an adviser to the National Council on Disability. He drafted the Rhode Island Constitution's disability rights clause and has drafted and been instrumental in passage of the state's disability rights laws. Bob Cooper, e-mail correspondence with author, August 10, 2011.

Jim Dickson (1946–) is vice president for organizing and civic engagement at the American Association of People with Disabilities. He leads the AAPD's nonpartisan Disability Vote

Project, a coalition of 36 disability-related organizations "whose mission is to close the political participation gap for people with disabilities." He played "a central role with the Leadership Conference on Civil and Human Rights (LCCRH) effort to pass the Help America Vote Act." Jim Dickson, e-mail correspondence with the author, July 29, 2011.

9. A congressional whip is the person from each party assigned the task of counting and obtaining votes on measures important to the party leadership. In his capacity as party whip, a congressman such as Tony Coelho is strategically placed to advocate for a piece of legislation.

10. Steny Hoyer (1939–) was first elected Democratic congressman from Maryland's Fifth Congressional District in 1980. He became House majority leader after November 2006, a position he lost after the Republican victories in the midterm congressional elections of 2010.

Chapter 26. Drafting the Bill, Part 2

1. Chai Feldblum worked in the AIDS Project of the American Civil Liberties Union at the time the ADA was working its way through Congress and was a principal member of the legal team that drafted its language. A graduate of Barnard College (1979) and Harvard Law School (1985), she clerked for US Supreme Court Justice Harry A. Blackmun (1986–1987) before going to work for the ACLU. She joined the faculty of the Georgetown University Law Center in 1991, and in 1993 established and was director of the school's Federal Legislation Clinic. In 2009, she was nominated by President Barack Obama to be one of the five commissioners at the Equal Employment Opportunity Commission, a position once held by Evan Kemp Jr. The nomination of an openly lesbian civil rights attorney to the EEOC was opposed by a number of conservative groups. President Obama subsequently appointed Feldblum as a recess appointment on March 27, 2010. Chai Feldblum, Interview by Phyllis Ward, November 11, 1999, for the Disability Rights Education and Defense Fund ADA Archive Leadership Project; Garance Franke-Ruta, "Disability, Gay Rights Expert Picked for EEOC," *Washington Post,* http://voices.washingtonpost.com/44/2009/09/14/disability_gay_rights_expert_p.html, posted September 14, 2009.

2. The Patient Protection and Affordable Care Act of 2010 (as amended by the Health Care and Education Reconciliation Act of 2010) was being hotly, even bitterly, debated during my interviews with Patrisha Wright.

Chapter 27. Lobbying and Gathering Support

1. Jonathan M. Young, *Equality of Opportunity: The Making of the Americans with Disabilities Act* (Washington, DC: National Council on Disability, July 16, 1997; reissued July 26, 2010), 99.

2. Coelho resigned his seat in Congress in the spring of 1989. "While House Speaker Wright was under scrutiny for alleged ethics violations, some members accused Congressman Coelho of violating House ethical standards by investing in certain bonds. . . . Coelho promptly submitted his resignation, effective June 15. His commitment to the ADA influenced his decision. . . . [T]hough he flatly denied the charges against him, he feared an investigation might, by association, embarrass the disability community and consequently hurt its prospects for success on the ADA. Young, *Equality of Opportunity,* 102–3.

3. "A series of 'weakening' amendments were proposed and defeated at the committee level and on the House floor, where the ADA passed by a vote of 403 to 20, on May 22, 1990. One controversial amendment, however, did succeed. The Chapman amendment said that employers could legally remove persons with contagious diseases, such as AIDS, from food handling positions, even where there was no evidence that the disease could be transmitted. . . . The conflict over food handling and contagious diseases had to be settled by a conference between the House and Senate, where conferees rejected the Chapman amendment, only to have members in both the House and Senate try to put it back into the ADA. After nearly two months of wrangling over the provision, the Senate developed a compromise through the leadership of Senator Orrin G. Hatch (R-UT)." Young, *Equality of Opportunity,* xxi.

4. Robert Williams (1957–) is a poet, writer, and advocate for people with speech dis-

abilities. He was a staff assistant on the Senate Subcommittee on the Handicapped from 1981 to 1982 and a program analyst at the Pratt Monitoring Program for the District of Columbia Association for Retarded Citizens from 1984 to 1988, becoming the program's deputy director from 1988 to 1990. After passage of the ADA he became president of Hear Our Voice, an organization of people who rely on augmentative communication devices. In 1993, he was appointed by President Clinton as commissioner of the Administration on Developmental Disabilities at the US Department of Health and Human Services. Fred Pelka, *The ABC-CLIO Companion to the Disability Rights Movement* (Santa Barbara, CA: ABC-CLIO, 1997), 326.

5. Justin Dart testified before Congressman Major Owen's committee in his role as director of the Rehabilitation Services Administration (RSA), formerly the federal Office of Vocational Rehabilitation (OVR). Dart strayed from the remarks prepared for him by RSA staff, instead telling the committee on November 18, 1987, that under the RSA people with disabilities "are confronted by a vast, inflexible federal system which, like the society it represents, still contains a significant proportion of individuals who have not yet overcome obsolete, paternalistic attitudes about disability." Dart was fired less than a month after his testimony. Fred Fay, "Empowerment: The Testament of Justin Dart, Jr.," *Mainstream: Magazine of the Able-Disabled* 22, no. 6 (March 1998): 23.

6. "The Task Force collected several thousand documents and tapes submitted by citizens and organizations outlining discrimination and other barriers which limit people with disabilities. . . . Over 5,000 specific examples of discrimination were presented to the House Committee on Education and Labor and the Senate Subcommittee on Disability Policy." *From ADA to Empowerment: The Report of the Task Force on the Rights and Empowerment of Americans with Disabilities* (Washington, DC: Paralyzed Veterans of America, Brook Tarbel and Jill Tarbel, October 12, 1990), 18.

Chapter 28. Mobilizing the Community

1. Marca Bristo (1953–) helped to establish Access Living in 1980 as Chicago's first ILC. In 1982 she cofounded NCIL, serving as vice president 1983–84 and president 1986–89. A member of the Task Force on the Rights and Empowerment of People with Disabilities and the executive committee of the President's Committee on Employment of People with Disabilities, she "helped [to] draft and win passage of the Americans with Disabilities Act. . . . In 1994, President Clinton appointed Bristo to chair the National Council on Disability, the first person with a disability to do so." Bristo was also integrally involved in the drafting of the UN Convention on the Rights of People with Disabilities. Rehabilitation International website http://www.riglobal.org/about/government-structure/executive-committee/marca-bristo/.

Chapter 29. Experts

1. Title I of the ADA prohibits, with some exceptions, employers from using "medical exams or inquiries either before or during employment to ascertain whether an applicant or employee has a disability or even the nature or severity of that disability (29 C.F.R. §1630.13)." "Because mental disabilities often are not obvious, employers sometimes have required applicants to undergo medical exams or provide medical histories allowing employers to identify these disabilities (Millstein et al., 1991, p. 1243). Under Title I, such inquiries are illegal. However, the legislative history indicates that federal, state, and local governments may establish legitimate medical requirements that employers must enforce (Millstein et al., 1991, p. 1243, citing U.S. House of Representatives Committee on Education and Labor, 1990, p. 70). Also, employers may establish reasonable medical standards for safety or security reasons." John Parry, "Title I—Employment," in *Implementing the Americans with Disabilities Act* (Baltimore: Paul H. Brookes Publishing, 1993), 69. The article cited by Parry is B. Millstein, L. Rubenstein, L. Cyrand R. Cyr, "The Americans with Disabilities Act: A Breathtaking Promise for People with Mental Disabilities," *Clearinghouse Review* 24 (1991): 1240–49. For a discussion on how Title I of the ADA deals with job tests in general, see Ruth O'Brien, *Crippled Justice: The Theory of Modern Disability Policy in the Workplace* (Chicago: University of Chicago Press, 2001), 175.

2. "A direct threat [by an employee with a disability to an employer, fellow employees, cus-

tomers, clients, or the general public] must be substantial with or without reasonable accommodation, meaning it is much more than the zero harm proposed by some employers. Also, the imminence of the threat is part of any substantial harm evaluation." Parry, "Title I," 66–67.

3. Under Title I of the ADA, "the term 'undue hardship' means an action requiring significant difficulty or expense, when considered in light" of factors such as "the nature and cost of the accommodation needed . . . the overall financial resources of the facility or facilities involved . . . the overall financial resources of the covered entity . . . the type of operation or operations of the covered entity." The Americans with Disabilities Act of 1990, Title I, Section 101 (10) A-B. As an example, allowing an employee "flex-time" because of the onset of a disability might be an undue hardship for a small business with one office and perhaps three employees, whereas for a multinational corporation with thousands of employees and dozens of offices, it might not be such a burden.

4. The Technology Related Assistance for Individuals with Disabilities Act of 1988, popularly known as the "Tech Act," made federal funds available to states, territories, and the District of Columbia to assist in developing programs to make assistive technology more available to people with disabilities. Fred Pelka, *The ABC-CLIO Companion to the Disability Rights Movement* (Santa Barbara, CA: ABC-CLIO, 1997), 298–99.

Public Law 100-553, enacted in October 1988, "authorized the formation of the National Institute on Deafness and Other Communication Disorders" within the National Institutes of Health." *Important Events in NICDC History,* at www.nidcd.nih.gov/about/learn/history.htm.

The Hearing Aid Compatibility Act of 1988 required that "all wireline telephones manufactured or imported for use in the United States after August 16, 1989, be hearing aid compatible" ("HAC" phones). Strauss, *New Civil Right,* 298.

5. TDI, or Telecommunications for the Deaf and Hard of Hearing, Inc., was established in 1968 and originally known as Teletypewriters for the Deaf, Inc. "During its early years, TDI was largely a part-time operation, managed from [telecommunications advocate and pioneer H. Latham] Breunig's home in Indianapolis. . . . But TDI's membership grew quickly, from 474 members in 1970 to 810 a year later, and to 4,980 in 1975. Members paid $2 to join TDI, and the organization's newsletter, GA-SK was, according to its publisher, released 'every once in a while.'" In 1976, TDI moved its headquarters to Washington, DC, and began to publish the nation's first and only TTY directory. Strauss, *New Civil Right,* 10–11. TDI has since moved to Silver Spring, Maryland.

Chapter 30. Insiders, Part 2

1. The Architectural and Transportation Barriers Compliance Board was established under Section 502 of the Rehabilitation Act of 1973 to ensure compliance with the standards prescribed pursuant to the Architectural Barriers Act of 1968. The Developmental Disabilities Act of 1978 gave it authority to review communications as well as architectural access. Fred Pelka, *The ABC-CLIO Companion to the Disability Rights Movement* (Santa Barbara, CA: ABC-CLIO, 1997), 26–27.

2. See the introduction to Richard Thornburgh's account later in this chapter.

3. Lee Atwater (1951–1991) was the chairman of the Republican National Committee and a close political adviser to President George H. W. Bush, serving as Bush's campaign manager in 1988. He became disabled because of a brain tumor, which left him paralyzed on the left side of his body and eventually led to his death.

Chapter 31. Wheels of Justice and the Chapman Amendment

1. In preparing my chronology of the passage of the ADA, I am indebted to Jonathan M. Young's excellent account of the law's history, *Equality of Opportunity: The Making of the Americans with Disabilities Act* (Washington, DC: National Council on Disability, 1997), prepared under contract with the National Rehabilitation Hospital Research Center, Medlantic Research Institute. The first edition contains much useful material, including a list of legal stepping stones to the ADA, a legislative chronology, excerpts from the discrimination diaries,

and the full text of President Bush's remarks at the signing ceremony, none of which unfortunately are included in the reprint of 2010. For this reason, all citations to the Young book refer to the original, unabridged 1997 edition.

2. Young, *Equality of Opportunity,* 160.

3. "The National Commission on Acquired Immune Deficiency Syndrome was established as an ad hoc Presidential advisory commission . . . on June 24, 1987. The Commission was created to investigate the spread of the human immunodeficiency virus (HIV) and subsequently, the acquired immunodeficiency syndrome (AIDS). The Commission also made recommendations on measures that Federal, State and local officials could take to protect the public from contracting HIV, to assist in finding a cure for AIDS, and to care for those who already had the disease. The Commission was terminated follow-ing the submission of its final report on June 24, 1988." http:// www.federalregister.gov/agencies/-commission-on-acquired-immune-deficiency-syndrome.

The Human Rights Campaign, originally the Human Rights Campaign Fund, was founded in 1980 "with a goal of raising money for congressional candidates who supported fairness. In the years that followed, the organization established itself as a resilient force in the overall movement for lesbian, gay, bisexual and transgender civil rights as it strived to achieve fundamental fairness and equality for all." "Our History," Human Rights Campaign website, http://www.hrc.org/about_us/2514.htm.

4. The ADA treats the topic of infectious diseases and food preparation in Title I, Section 103, under "Defenses":

(d) LIST OF INFECTIOUS AND COMMUNICABLE DISEASES.—

(1) IN GENERAL—The Secretary of Health and Human Services, not later than 6 months after the date of the enactment of this Act, shall—

(A) review all infectious and communicable diseases which may be transmitted through handling the food supply;

(B) publish a list of infectious and communicable diseases which are transmitted through handling the food supply;

(C) publish the methods by which such diseases are transmitted; and

(D) widely disseminate such information. . . .

Such a list shall be updated annually.

(2) APPLICATIONS.—In any case where an individual has an infectious or communicable disease that is transmitted to others through the handling of food, that is included on the list developed by the Secretary of Health and Human Services under paragraph (1), and which cannot be eliminated by reasonable accommodation, a covered entity may refuse to assign or continue to assign such individual to a job involving food handling.

This, in essence, was the "Hatch Amendment."

Chapter 33. Senators

1. During his presidency, John F. Kennedy appointed a special President's Panel on Mental Retardation to study and make recommendations on the treatment of people labeled mentally retarded. The most direct Kennedy family connection to the issues of mental disability came through the president's oldest sibling, Rosemary, who had been diagnosed as mentally retarded and placed in an institution. R. C. Scheerenberger, *A History of Mental Retardation* (Baltimore: Paul Brooks Publishing, 1983), 109–15. Eunice Kennedy Shriver, also a sister to John and Edward Kennedy, established Special Olympics and other programs for the benefit of children with developmental disabilities.

Chapter 34. Victory

1. The *DSM-III* is the *Diagnostic and Statistical Manual of Mental Disorders,* 3rd revision, published by the American Psychiatric Association in 1980.

2. Indeed, transvestites are mentioned twice in the ADA, in Title V, Section 508 ("For the purposes of this Act, the term 'disabled' or 'disability' shall not apply to an individual solely

because that individual is a transvestite.") and Section 511, where it is listed under "Certain Conditions" likewise not covered by the act.

3. Yoshiko Dart confirms that Justin Dart thought, when arriving at the White House, that the only person on the podium with President Bush as he signed the act would be Evan Kemp. Yoshiko Dart, e-mail correspondence with the author, November 11, 2010.

Chapter 35. Aftermath

1. For details on efforts to discredit or roll back the ADA, see Mary Johnson, *Make Them Go Away: Clint Eastwood, Christopher Reeve, and the Case against Disability Rights* (Louisville, KY: Advocado Press, 2003). Ruth O'Brien's discussion of federal and Supreme Court interpretations (and misinterpretations) of Title I of the ADA, which deals with employment discrimination, is particularly trenchant, noting how the courts have almost uniformly ruled against plaintiffs. Ruth O'Brien, *Crippled Justice: The Theory of Modern Disability Policy in the Workplace* (Chicago: University of Chicago Press, 2001), 14–18, and chap. 6.

2. Justin Dart, conversation with the author, July 2, 1997.

3. "... the Supreme Court today affirmed the right of individuals with disabilities to live in their community in its 6–3 ruling against the state of Georgia in the case *Olmstead v. L.C. and E.W.*

"Under Title II of the federal Americans with Disabilities Act, said Justice Ruth Bader Ginsberg, delivering the opinion of the court, 'states are required to place persons with mental disabilities in community settings rather than in institutions when the State's treatment professionals have determined that community placement is appropriate, the transfer from institutional care to a less restrictive setting is not opposed by the affected individual, and the placement can be reasonably accommodated, taking into account the resources available to the State and the needs of others with mental disabilities.'" "Supreme Court Upholds ADA 'Integration Mandate' in *Olmstead* decision," June 22, 1999, The Center for an Accessible Society, www.accessiblesociety.org/topics/ada/olmsteadoverview.htm.

The Community Choice Act (CCA) is designed to offer those who need it a community-based alternative to nursing homes. Currently, every state that receives federal Medicaid funding must provide nursing home services, while community-based care such as provided by independent living centers has no such mandate. This bias toward nursing homes and institutions is one reason why, as of 2010, some 2 million Americans continue to live in nursing homes or other long-term institutions. The CCA "would allow eligible individuals, or their representatives, to choose where they would receive services and supports." ADAPT, "Community Choice Act (CCA): A Community-Based Alternative to Nursing Homes and Institutions for People with Disabilities," www.adapt.org/cca.

The ADAPT campaign has the potential to affect not only those currently disabled, but the millions of post–World War II "baby boomers" who are likely to acquire significant disabilities as they age. Whether ADAPT and the independent living movement succeed may determine whether members of this potentially enormous population of people with disabilities remain in their homes, supported by a network of community-based services, or are consigned to nursing homes and similar facilities in what could become the greatest mass institutionalization of Americans since the height of the eugenics craze of the early twentieth century.

4. See Mary Johnson, "A Test of Wills: Jerry Lewis, Jerry's Orphans and the Telethon," in *The Ragged Edge: The Disability Experience from the Pages of the First Fifteen Years of the Disability Rag*, ed. Barrett Shaw (Louisville, KY: Advocado Press, 1994), 120–30.

5. Bridgetta Bourne-Firl, interview by Fred Pelka, November 6, 2008, and Gary Olsen, interview by Fred Pelka, February 7, 2009, both audio recordings in possession of the author, to be deposited at the Bancroft Library as part of its Regional Oral History Office Project on the Disability Rights and Independent Living Movement.

Interview Sources

ELMER C. BARTELS, "Cofounder of the Boston Center for Independent Living, Massachusetts Commissioner of Rehabilitation, 1977–," interview conducted by Fred Pelka, 2001, in *Massachusetts Activists and Leaders in the Disability Rights and Independent Living Movement*, vol. 1, DRILM Oral History Project, Regional Oral History Office, The Bancroft Library, University of California, Berkeley; © 2004 by The Regents of the University of California.

CAROL FEWELL BILLINGS, "Attendant and Observer in the Early Days of the Physically Disabled Students' Program and the Center for Independent Living, 1969–1977," interview conducted by Kathy Cowan, 1998, in *Builders and Sustainers in the Independent Living Movement in Berkeley*, vol. 2, DRILM Oral History Project, Regional Oral History Office, The Bancroft Library, University of California, Berkeley; © 2000 by The Regents of the University of California.

MARY LOU BRESLIN, "Cofounder and Director of the Disability Rights Education and Defense Fund, Movement Strategist," selections of interview conducted by Susan O'Hara, 1996–1998, DRILM Oral History Project, Regional Oral History Office, The Bancroft Library, University of California, Berkeley; © 2000 by The Regents of the University of California. Interview conducted by Fred Pelka, October 5, 2009; audiotape in possession of the author, to be deposited at The Bancroft Library as part of its Regional Oral History Office Project on the Disability Rights and Independent Living Movement.

WILLIAM BRONSTON, "Physician-Advocate for People with Cognitive and Developmental Disabilities: Exposing Conditions at Willowbrook State School in New York, Medical Director and Consultant for the State of California," interview conducted by Kathy Cowan, 2001–2002, DRILM Oral History Project, Regional Oral History Office, The Bancroft Library, University of California, Berkeley; © 2004 by The Regents of the University of California.

DAVID CAPOZZI, Disability Rights Education and Defense Fund Celebration of the Tenth Anniversary of the Americans with Disabilities Act "leadership interview," videotape, 1999–2000; archived at the Regional Oral History Office, The Bancroft Library, University of California, Berkeley.

CATHRINE CAULFIELD, "First Woman Student in the Cowell Program, 1968," interview conducted by Susan O'Hara, 1996, in *UC Cowell Hospital Residence Program for Physically Disabled Students, 1962–1975: Catalyst for Berkeley's Independent Living Movement*, DRILM Oral History Project, Regional Oral History Office, The Bancroft Library, University of California, Berkeley; © 2000 by The Regents of the University of California.

TED CHABASINSKI, first portion of interview drawn from the Mind-Freedom International Personal Story Project, available at *http://www.mindfreedom.org/personal-stories*; second portion, interview by Fred Pelka, January 26, 2010, audiotape deposited at Regional Oral History Office, The Bancroft Library, University of California, Berkeley.

ANTHONY L. "TONY" COELHO, "Congressional Advocate for Disability Rights, Chair of the

Epilepsy Foundation," interview conducted by Ann Lage, 2004, DRILM Oral History Project, Regional Oral History Office, The Bancroft Library, University of California, Berkeley; © 2008 by The Regents of the University of California.

DIANE COLEMAN, "State and National Organizer for ADAPT, Founder of Not Dead Yet," interview conducted by Kathy Cowan, 2002, in *Issues of Life, Death and Identity: The Role of Disability Advocacy and Scholarship*, DRILM Oral History Project, Regional Oral History Office, The Bancroft Library, University of California, Berkeley; © 2004 by The Regents of the University of California.

KITTY CONE, "Political Organizer for Disability Rights, 1970s–1990s, and Strategist for Section 504 Demonstrations, 1977," interview conducted by David Landes, 1996–1998, DRILM Oral History Project, Regional Oral History Office, The Bancroft Library, University of California, Berkeley; © 2000 by The Regents of the University of California.

JUSTIN DART JR., interview conducted by Fred Pelka, June 18, 20, 24, 25, 29, 30, July 2, 1997, audiotapes in possession of Yoshiko Dart, All Rights Reserved.

JAMES DONALD, "Student Resident at Cowell, 1967–1968, Attorney and Deputy Director of the California Department of Rehabilitation, 1975–1982," interview conducted by Kathryn Cowan, 1998, in *UC Cowell Hospital Residence Program for Physically Disabled Students, 1962–1975: Catalyst for Berkeley's Independent Living Movement*, DRILM Oral History Project, Regional Oral History Office, The Bancroft Library, University of California, Berkeley; © 2000 by The Regents of the University of California.

GUNNAR DYBWAD, "Pioneer in the Parents' Movement: The Campaign for Public Education and Deinstitutionalization of People with Developmental Disabilities," interview conducted by Fred Pelka, 2001, DRILM Oral History Project, Regional Oral History Office, The Bancroft Library, University of California, Berkeley; © 2004 by The Regents of the University of California.

FREDERICK A. FAY, "Community Organizer and Advocate for Equal Access and Equal Rights; Cofounder of Opening Doors, the Boston Center for Independent Living, and the American Coalition of Citizens with Disabilities," interview conducted by Fred Pelka, 2001, DRILM Oral History Project, Regional Oral History Office, The Bancroft Library, University of California, Berkeley; © 2004 by The Regents of the University of California.

DENISE FIGUEROA, "Early Activist in Disabled in Action, President of National Council on Independent Living, 1991–1995," interview conducted by Sharon Bonney, 2001, in *New York Activists and Leaders in the Disability Rights and Independent Living Movement*, vol. 2, DRILM Oral History Project, Regional Oral History Office, The Bancroft Library, University of California, Berkeley; © 2004 by The Regents of the University of California.

PATRICIO FIGUEROA, "Early Activist in Disabled in Action, First Director of Center for Independence of the Disabled in New York, 1978," interview conducted by Sharon Bonney, 2001, in *New York Activists and Leaders in the Disability Rights and Independent Living Movement*, vol. 2, DRILM Oral History Project, Regional Oral History Office, The Bancroft Library, University of California, Berkeley; © 2004 by The Regents of the University of California.

LEX FRIEDEN, "Disability Advocate, Organizer, Researcher, Executive Director of the National Council on Disability, 1984–1988," interview conducted by Sharon Bonney, 2002, DRILM Oral History Project, Regional Oral History Office, The Bancroft Library, University of California, Berkeley; © 2007 by The Regents of the University of California.

KAREN FRIEDMAN, Disability Rights Education and Defense Fund Celebration of the Tenth Anniversary of the Americans with Disabilities Act "leadership interview," videotape, 1999–2000; archived at the Regional Oral History Office, The Bancroft Library, University of California, Berkeley.

MICHAEL FUSS, "Attendant for Cowell Residents, Assistant Director of the Physically Disabled Students' Program, 1966–1972," interview conducted by Sharon Bonney, 1997, in *Builders and*

Sustainers in the Independent Living Movement in Berkeley, vol. 2, DRILM Oral History Project, Regional Oral History Office, The Bancroft Library, University of California, Berkeley; © 2000 by The Regents of the University of California.

DONALD GALLOWAY, "The Independent Living Movement in Berkeley and Colorado: Blind Advocacy and Minority Inclusion," interview conducted by Fred Pelka, 2001, in *Blind Services and Advocacy and the Independent Living Movement in Berkeley,* DRILM Oral History Project, Regional Oral History Office, The Bancroft Library, University of California, Berkeley; © 2004 by The Regents of the University of California.

THOMAS K. GILHOOL, "Legal Advocate for Deinstitutionalization and the Right to Education for People with Developmental Disabilities," interview conducted by Fred Pelka, 2004–2008, DRILM Oral History Project, Regional Oral History Office, The Bancroft Library, University of California, Berkeley; © 2010 by The Regents of the University of California.

MARILYN GOLDEN, Disability Rights Education and Defense Fund Celebration of the Tenth Anniversary of the Americans with Disabilities Act "leadership interview," videotape, 1999–2000.

RICHARD B. GOULD, "Early Resident and Deputy Director of the Boston Center for Independent Living," interview conducted by Fred Pelka, 2001, in *Massachusetts Activists and Leaders in the Disability Rights and Independent Living Movement,* vol. 1, DRILM Oral History Project, Regional Oral History Office, The Bancroft Library, University of California, Berkeley; © 2004 by The Regents of the University of California.

C. BOYDEN GRAY, Disability Rights Education and Defense Fund Celebration of the Tenth Anniversary of the Americans with Disabilities Act "leadership interview," videotape, 1999–2000; archived at the Regional Oral History Office, The Bancroft Library, University of California, Berkeley.

THOMAS HARKIN, Disability Rights Education and Defense Fund Celebration of the Tenth Anniversary of the Americans with Disabilities Act "leadership interview," videotape, 1999–2000; archived at the Regional Oral History Office, The Bancroft Library, University of California, Berkeley.

JUDITH HEUMANN, "Pioneering Disability Rights Advocate and Leader in Disabled in Action, New York; Center for Independent Living, Berkeley; World Institute on Disability; and the U.S. Department of Education, 1960s–2000," interviews conducted by Susan Brown, David Landes, and Jonathan Young, 1998–2001, DRILM Oral History Project, Regional Oral History Office, The Bancroft Library, University of California, Berkeley; © 2004 by The Regents of the University of California. Interview conducted by Ann Lage, 2007, DRILM Oral History Project, Regional Oral History Office, The Bancroft Library, University of California, Berkeley; © 2011 by The Regents of the University of California.

CYNTHIA [CYNDI] JONES, "*Mainstream Magazine* Editor and Publisher," interview conducted by Mary Lou Breslin, 1999, in *Mainstream Magazine: Chronicling National Disability Politics,* DRILM Oral History Project, Regional Oral History Office, The Bancroft Library, University of California, Berkeley; © 2000 by The Regents of the University of California.

SENATOR EDWARD KENNEDY, Disability Rights Education and Defense Fund Celebration of the Tenth Anniversary of the Americans with Disabilities Act "leadership interview," videotape, 1999–2000; archived at the Regional Oral History Office, The Bancroft Library, University of California, Berkeley.

LEE KITCHENS, "National Leader of Little People of America, Cofounder of the Coalition of Texans with Disabilities," interview conducted by Sharon Bonney, 2002, in *Texas Activists and Leaders in the Disability Rights and Independent Living Movement,* DRILM Oral History Project, Regional Oral History Office, The Bancroft Library, University of California, Berkeley; © 2004 by The Regents of the University of California.

JOHNNIE LACY, "Director, Community Resources for Independent Living: An African-American Woman's Perspective on the Independent Living Movement in the Bay Area, 1960s–1980s," interview conducted by David Landes, 1998, DRILM Oral History Project, Regional Oral History Office, The Bancroft Library, University of California, Berkeley; © 2000 by The Regents of the University of California.

DIANE LIPTON, "Parent, Special Education Advocate for the Center for Independent Living's Disability Law Resource Center, and Attorney for the Disability Rights Education and Defense Fund, 1979–2002," interview conducted by Denise Sherer Jacobson, 2001, DRILM Oral History Project, Regional Oral History Office, The Bancroft Library, University of California, Berkeley; © 2004 by The Regents of the University of California.

ARLENE MAYERSON, Disability Rights Education and Defense Fund Celebration of the Tenth Anniversary of the Americans with Disabilities Act "leadership interview," videotape, 1999–2000; archived at the Regional Oral History Office, The Bancroft Library, University of California, Berkeley.

TIMOTHY J. NUGENT, "Founder of the University of Illinois Disabled Students Program and the National Wheelchair Basketball Association, Pioneer in Architectural Access," interview conducted by Fred Pelka, 2004–2005, DRILM Oral History Project, Regional Oral History Office, The Bancroft Library, University of California, Berkeley; © 2009 by The Regents of the University of California.

CORBETT O'TOOLE, "Advocate for Disabled Women's Rights and Health Issues," interview conducted by Denise Sherer Jacobson, 1998, DRILM Oral History Project, Regional Oral History Office, The Bancroft Library, University of California, Berkeley; © 2000 by The Regents of the University of California.

EDWARD V. ROBERTS, "The UC Berkeley Years: First Student Resident at Cowell Hospital, 1962," interview conducted by Susan O'Hara, 1994, in *UC Cowell Hospital Residence Program for Physically Disabled Students, 1962–1975: Catalyst for Berkeley's Independent Living Movement,* DRILM Oral History Project, Regional Oral History Office, The Bancroft Library, University of California, Berkeley; © 2000 by The Regents of the University of California.

ELIZABETH SAVAGE, "Lobbyist for the Epilepsy Foundation: The Passage of the Americans with Disabilities Act," interview conducted by Ann Lage, 2004, DRILM Oral History Project, Regional Oral History Office, The Bancroft Library, University of California, Berkeley; © 2010 by The Regents of the University of California.

MARILYN SAVIOLA, "The Move to Personal Independence and Activism, Director of the Center for the Independence of the Disabled in New York, 1983–1998," interview conducted by Denise Sherer Jacobson, 2001, in *New York Activists and Leaders in the Disability Rights and Independent Living Movement,* vol.1, DRILM Oral History Project, Regional Oral History Office, The Bancroft Library, University of California, Berkeley; © 2004 by The Regents of the University of California.

ROBERT SILVERSTEIN, Disability Rights Education and Defense Fund Celebration of the Tenth Anniversary of the Americans with Disabilities Act "leadership interview," videotape, 1999–2000; archived at the Regional Oral History Office, The Bancroft Library, University of California, Berkeley.

RICHARD THORNBURGH, Disability Rights Education and Defense Fund Celebration of the Tenth Anniversary of the Americans with Disabilities Act "leadership interview," videotape, 1999–2000; archived at the Regional Oral History Office, The Bancroft Library, University of California, Berkeley.

JAMES WEISMAN, Disability Rights Education and Defense Fund Celebration of the Tenth Anniversary of the Americans with Disabilities Act "leadership interview," videotape, 1999–2000; archived at the Regional Oral History Office, The Bancroft Library, University of California, Berkeley.

Index

Abascal, Ralph, 280, 580n8

ABC News, 314–15, 407

Abel, Tyler, 446

ableism, 17, 25, 61, 352, 374, 563n92

Able-Disabled Advocacy, 231

abuse: as hate crimes, 561n70; in institutions/
medical settings, 52–53, 56–58, 84, 132,
179, 291, 315, 377, 560–61n69, 571n3, 584n6;
of children with disabilities, 46–47, 52,
56–57, 63, 124, 291, 399, 493; of psychiatric
survivors, 77, 283, 287, 291, 300

ACCD. *See* American Coalition of Citizens
with Disabilities

access, architectural, 65, 90–91, 126, 190, 356–57,
485, 545, 553–54, 560n65, 569n3; architects
opposed to, 191; and CAPH, 160, 164–65;
as civil right, 344, 357; and CRAB, 121; and
cognitive disabilities, 338; and curb cuts/
ramps, 106, 120; in housing, 162–63, 193,
204; lack of, as discrimination, 18, 61; in
public facilities: (bathrooms) 109–10, 273,
545, (churches) 539, (courthouses) 195, 441,
(jails) 338, 392–93, (hotels) 343, (stores) 485;
in schools/campuses, 69–70, 106, 123, 164,
190–92. *See also* Architectural Barriers Act
of 1968; Fair Housing Amendments Act of
1988; McDonald's; University of California
at Berkeley; University of Illinois

access, telecommunications, 497, 528–30.
See also Americans with Disabilities Act
of 1990: Title IV; Strauss, Karen Peltz;
telephone relay services

access, transportation, 266, 377–78, 438, 484,
486, 501, 530; after ADA, 551–53; and
Berkeley CIL, 223; and CAPH, 164–66; and
DIA, 193–95; mainline vs. paratransit, 499–
500; and PVA, 359–60; and Washington
Metro, 106, 247. *See also* ADAPT; Transbus;
Weisman, Jim

Access California, 481

Access Institute, 362

ACORN (Association of Community
Organizations for Reform Now), 299, 582n9

Action League for Physically Handicapped
Adults (ALPHA), 239–40

ADA Regional Contact Persons, 482–84

Adams, Joe Kennedy, 236

ADAPT, **376–96;** and APTA, 378, 385, 481; and
ADA, 381, 388, 515–21; in Capitol Rotunda
sit-in, 515, 518–21; and *Disability Rag,* 239,
242–44, 384; founding of, 378; hunger strike
by, 391; and ILCs, 382, 515, 518; and Kemp
Jr., 447, 516; and media, 519; mentioned, 31,
255, 361, 476, 583n3; in Montreal, 389–90;
name change, 378, 548; and nursing homes,
385, 548, 549, 583n3, 598n3; and *Olmstead
v. L.C. and E.W.,* 549; and People First,
337–38; police response to, 383–85, 390–95;
in Salt Lake City, 387–88; in Sparks, NV,
385, 390–91, *illus.;* tactics, 382–84; violence
toward, 387, 390–91; and Wright, 516, 519;
in Washington, DC, 392–93, 515–21. *See
also* Atlantis Community; Blank, Reverend
Wade; Capitol "crawl-up"; Wheels of Justice

Advocado Press, 238

Age Discrimination Act of 1975, 414

Aid to Retarded Citizens, 267

AIDS. *See* HIV/AIDS

Air Carrier Access Act of 1986, 28

Alinsky, Saul, 157, 262, 299, 383

All Berkeley Coalition, 293

Amaday, Nancy, 189

American Association of People with
Disabilities Disability Vote Project, 594n8

American Bar Association, 492

American Coalition of Citizens with
Disabilities (ACCD), 88, 125, **246–60,** 312,
355, 359, 493; by-laws, 250; civil rights

American Coalition of Citizens *(continued)*
focus of, 251, 258; debate over name, 251;
demise of, 260; and *Disability Rag,* 241; and
HEW demonstrations, 26, 261–62, 266,
271, 278, 279; leadership training by, 257;
and national movement, 258; and NFB, 20;
and Reagan administration, 413. *See also*
Bowe, Frank; Fay, Fred; Fiorito, Eunice;
Frieden, Lex; Heumann, Judith; HEW
demonstrations; Schreiber, Fred
American Civil Liberties Union (ACLU), 119,
460, 577n9
American Congress of Rehabilitation
Medicine, 248
American Council of the Blind (ACB), 23, 578–
79n8; and ACCD, 247, 248, 249, 258, 260
American Disabled for Accessible Public
Transit. *See* ADAPT
American Disabled for Attendant Programs
Today. *See* ADAPT
American Federation of the Physically
Handicapped (AFPH), 19–20, 22, 23, 113
American Legion, 95, 96, 97, 359
American National Standards Institute (ANSI),
22, 100, 155
American Psychiatric Association, 296,
300–301
American Public Transit Association (APTA),
213, 585n2; and ADAPT, 378, 386–87, 481;
and Transbus, 360, 585–86n4
American Sign Language (ASL), 156, 247, 343,
397, 404
Americans with Disabilities Act of 1990
(ADA), 487; backlash against, 548–49; and
"bankruptcy standard," 447, 465–66; and
CCD, 533–34; and Chapman amendment,
522, 524–26, 528, 531–32, 541, 542, 594n3;
and civil rights coalition, 28–29; and
Civil Rights Act of 1964, 463–64; and
Congressional Black Caucus, 436, 457; and
definition of disability, 448, 460–61, 555;
as "disability community's bill," 466; and
disability press, 244, 484–85; and "disability
pride day," 261; and DREDF, 344, 440;
economic impact study of, 435–36; and
enforcement, 159; first version of, 431, 437,
440, 447, 460, 465, 586n1; and Foley, 454–55;
and grassroots network, 482–84, 487–88;
Greyhound Bus opposition to, 456, 530;
and health insurance, 441–42, 460, 464,
529; and Hatch/Hatch Amendment, 525–26,
542–43, 597n4; and HIV/AIDS, 522–26, 528;
in House, 497, 516; in House committees,
455–57, 462, 470, 483, 490–91, 514, 530–31,
595n6; House hearings on, 490, 514; impact
of, 507, 509, 545, 554–55; interrelationship
of parts of, 463; joint congressional hearing
on, 443, 473; and "just world" theory, 6;
and Kennedy, 538–41; and Leadership
Conference on Civil Rights, 29, 415, 441,
460, 590n9; legislative history of, 497;
lobbying for, 440–42, 462–63, 481–89,
512–23; and media, 244, 475; and "mental
illness," 451, 462, 531; and "minority
populations of people with disabilities,"
562–63n92; mentioned, 245, 344, 367, 381,
445, 487; passage of, 543–44; and People
First, 337–38; philosophy of, 508–9;
planning for, 446; public hearings on, 436–
39; revisions of, 440, 441–42, 447–48, 460–
68; and Section 504 of the Rehabilitation
Act of 1973, 460–61; in Senate, 470, 489,
497, 514, 530, 538–40, 542–43; Senate/
House conference committee, 514, 522,
540–41, 594–95n3; signing ceremony, 451,
538, 541, 544–46, 598n3 (ch. 34), *illus.;* and
transvestites, 451, 543, 593n7, 597–98n2;
Title I (employment), 490, 595n1 (ch. 28),
595n1 (ch. 29), 597n4, 598n1; Title II (public
services/public transportation), 378, 388,
498–502, 548, 585–86n4, 598n3; Title III
(public accommodations/private entities),
491; Title IV (telecommunications), 38–39,
493, 495–98, 529, 550, 560n66, 564n101,
566–67n5; Title V (misc. provisions),
543–44, 593–94n7, 597–98n2; White House
negotiations, 491–92; White House staff
opposition to, 450, 466, 468, 505. *See also*
ADAPT; Breslin, Mary Lou; Bush, George
H. W.; Chapman amendment; Coelho,
Tony; Congressional Task Force on the
Rights and Empowerment of People with
Disabilities; Consortium for Citizens with
Developmental Disabilities; Dart, Justin, Jr.;
Disability Rights Education and Defense
Fund; Frieden, Lex; Golden, Marilyn;
Gray, C. Boyden; Iskowitz, Michael; Jones,
Cyndi; Kemp, Evan, Jr.; Kennedy, Edward
M.; Leadership Conference on Civil Rights;
Mayerson, Arlene; Michel, Bob; National

Council on Disability; National Council on the Handicapped; Neas, Ralph; *On the Threshold of Independence;* Osolinik, Carolyn; Owens, Major; Savage, Liz; Silverstein, Robert; Strauss, Karen Peltz; Thornburgh, Richard; Weicker, Lowell; Weisman, Jim; Wheels of Justice; Williams, Robert; Wright, Patrisha

Anderson, Glenn, 455–56

Andrzejewski, Judy, 371, 586–87n6

anti–Vietnam War movement, 276, 399, 593n3; at Berkeley, 197, 204–5; and conscientious objectors, 576n7; at Illinois Urbana-Champaign, 106; and Kent State shootings, 587n1. *See also* Blank, Reverend Wade; Kemp, Janine Bertram

APTA. *See* American Public Transit Association

ARC/Arc, the. *See* National Association for Retarded Children (NARC)

Architectural Barriers Act of 1968, 154, 357, 572n1

Architectural and Transportation Barriers Compliance Board (ATBCB), 504, 572n1, 586n2, 596n1

Armstrong, William L., 451

As We Are (video), 343

Association for Retarded Children (ARC). *See* National Association for Retarded Children (NARC)

Association of Medical Officers of American Institutions of Idiotic and Feeble-Minded Persons, 49

Atlantic City Seashore House, 132

Atlantis Community, 361, 362, 377–81, 386, 389. *See also* Blank, Reverend Wade

Atwater, Lee, 506, 596n3 (ch. 30)

Auberger, Michael, 355, **361–68**, **391–96**; and McDonald's campaign, 362–68; at APTA conference, 392–93; and Wheels of Justice, **515–21**

"Baby Doe" case, 242, 335–36, 577n7

Bader, Denise A. *See* Figueroa, Denise

Bailout Bill (California), 306–7

Baptiste, Gerald, 198

Barnartt, Sharon, 4, 13

Barrier Free Environments, 340

BART. *See* Bay Area Rapid Transit

Bartels, Elmer, 198, 303, **308–11**

Bartlett, Steven, 423–24, 436–39, 450

Barton, Jane, 511

Barty, Billy, 151–52

Bay Area Rapid Transit (BART), 120, 214, 353

Baynton, Douglas, 10

Bazelon Center, 462

Bellevue Hospital, NYC, 58–59, 195, 285, 286

"benefit boosting," 416

Bergman, Alan, 320

Berkeley CIL. *See* Center for Independent Living

Berkeley Citizens Action, 293

Berkeley Women's Health Collective, 224

Berry, Don, 162

Bersami, Hank, 320

"bird feeding," 54

Billings, Carol Fewell, **215–18**

Birmingham bus boycott, 378

Black Panthers, 106, 174, 220–22, 365; and HEW occupation, 262, 268, 271, 273

Blank, Molly, 376–77

Blank, Reverend Wade: and ADAPT, 376, 378, 383, 389–92; and *Disability Rag*, 244; and Heritage House, 377, 379–80; and Kemp Jr., 447, 516; and Kent State shootings, 376–77; and King Jr., 376; and McDonald's, 364; mentioned, 23, 211, 355, 361, 476, 550, 577–78n10. *See also* ADAPT; Atlantis Community

Blatt, Burton, 140, 571n7, 583n3

Blinded Veterans Association (BVA), 21

Bloch, Nancy, 411, 589n9

Boggs, Elizabeth M., 22, 476, 584–85n5

Boggs, Jonathan, 22

Boston CIL, 88, 248, 308

Boston State Hospital, 289

Bourne-Firl, Bridgetta, **408–12**, *illus.*

Bouvia, Elizabeth, 242, 577n9

Bowe, Frank, 18, 247, 250, 261, 557n2, 579n9; as CEO for ACCD, 26, 255, 257; and HEW demonstrations, 252, 262–63, 279, 280

Brann, Judith, 320

Bravin, Jeff, 402

Bravin, Phil, 408, 588–89n6

Breen, Edna, 209

Bregante, Jennifer, 37

Brennick, Charles, 584n6

Brennick, Joseph, 584n6

Breslin, Mary Lou, 22, **553–55**, *illus.*; and ADA, 440; and 504 trainings, **340–44**, 345, 416;

Breslin, Mary Lou *(continued)*
discrimination against, **65–67**; and Golden,
481; at Illinois, **107–12**; mentioned, 94, 198,
471; and Wright, 440, 441, 545. *See also*
Disability Rights Education and Defense
Fund (DREDF)

Bristo, Marca, 487, 488, 595n1 (ch. 28)

Bronston, William, MD, **174–80**, 185, 211,
312–19, 583n3. *See also* Willowbrook State
School and Hospital

Brooklyn College, 191

Brooks, Jack, 455, 479–80

Brown v. Board of Education, 131, 563n92; as
precedent for disability rights, 1, 23, 138

Brown, H. Rap, 106

Brown, Jerry, Jr., 114, 303, 304–5, 306, *illus.*

Bruyn, Henry, 199, 202

Bryan, Willie V., 8

Buck, Carrie, 2

Buck v. Bell, 2, 11, 557n7

Burgdorf, Marci, 357

Burgdorf, Robert, 132, 357, 460, 586n1; and
NCH, 426, 431–33, 570n2

Burnes, Byron, 157

Bush, Barbara, 451

Bush, George H. W., 26, 501, 507, *illus.*; and
Deaf President Now, 448; and disability
experiences, 504, 565n103; and Gray, 444,
503–6, 536; hostility of staff to Reagan
disability agenda, 417; and HIV/AIDS,
532–33; and Kemp Jr., 444, 449, 505; and
"kinder, gentler" nation, 440, 524, 592n4;
and NCH, 426–27; presidential campaign
of, 473, 484–85; signing of ADA, 544–45;
support for ADA, 449, 466, 468, 505, 508;
Vice President's Task Force on Regulatory
Relief, 413, 420, 422, 582n1

Bush, Marvin, 565n103

Bush, Neil, 504, 565n103

Bush, Robin, 565n103

Caesar, Orville Swan, 102

Califano, Joseph, 240, 252, 262–64, 279–80

California Association of the Physically
Handicapped (CAPH), 24, 159–62, 164–66,
228, 264, 308, 376

California Psychiatric Association, 296–97

California School for the Deaf, 157, 409

Californians for Disability Rights. *See* California
Association of the Physically Handicapped

Calkins, Phil, 322, 441, 446, 592n5

Camarata, Carol, 186

Cameron School (Richmond, CA), 149

Campaign for Human Development (CHD),
362, 586n5

CAPH. *See* California Association of the
Physically Handicapped

Capitol "crawl-up," 515, 517–18, *illus. See also*
ADAPT

Capozzi, David, **527–34**

captioning, 29, 40, 495–96, 535, 550, 567n7,
588–89n6; dropped from ADA, 529–30

Carabello, Bernard, 316

Carter, Jimmy, 536, 593n3; and Civil Rights
of Institutionalized Persons Act of
1980, 28; and Coelho, 472; and HEW
demonstrations, 26–27, 261, 264, 275,
278, 280, 413; and Savage, 472; and
transportation access, 386, 585n2, 585–86n4

castration, 56

Caulfield, Cathrine, **201–5**

Cavett, Dick, 316

CBS/CBS News, 275, 407, 588–89n6

Center for Accessible Living (Louisville, KY),
240

Center for Independent Living (Berkeley
CIL), 24, 113, 210, 217, 248, 304, 306, 308,
illus.; and African American community,
220–22; "baby boom" at, 225–26; and
blind consumers, 223; and CAPH, 161–62;
as cross-disability coalition, 214–15; and
Disability Law Resource Center, 339, 341,
416; and DREDF, 339, 340; and Fay, 248;
and HEW demonstrations, 264, 266, 267;
and Geld, 284; and Heumann, 126, 263;
and lesbian community, 225; and Lipton,
145; need for, 217–18; and peer counseling,
118; and PDSP, 204, 210; political
environment of, 197; transportation
service, 162; wheelchair repair shop,
204, 213, 219, 223; as work environment,
223–25; and Wright, 415. *See also* Disability
Rights Education and Defense Fund;
independent living model; independent
living movement; Roberts, Ed

Center for the Study of Responsive Law, 585n1

Center on Law and the Handicapped, 357

Chávez, César, 350

Chabasinski, Ted, **58–60**, 287, **291–97**, 300

Chamberlin, Judi, 283, **284–91**, 301, 550, *illus.*

Chapman amendment, 474, 521–26, 528, 531–32, 542. *See also* Americans with Disabilities Act of 1990; HIV/AIDS

Chapman, Jim, 522

Chase, Jack, **97–100**

Cherry, Jim, 239, 577n5

Cherry v. Mathews, 577n5

Child Abuse Prevention and Treatment Act Amendments of 1984, 577n7

Child Development Clinic, Los Angeles, 314

Childs, Theodore, 127

City University of New York (CUNY), 192

Civil Rights Act of 1964, 27, 431, 464; exclusion of people with disabilities from, 222, 463, 591–92n1' Title VII, 463; and US Supreme Court, 413–14

Civil Rights of Institutionalized Persons Act of 1980, 28

civil rights movement, 106, 112, 421; and disability rights movement, 1–4, 23–27, 154, 192, 193, 378, 564n98; and Deaf President Now, 399, 401; legal language of, 442; and psychiatric survivor movement, 284. *See also* Black Panthers; Civil Rights Act of 1964; race/racism

Civil Rights Restoration Act of 1987, 28–29, 421, 440, 441, 472, 487, 539, 590n8; as lobbying precurser to ADA, 414, 418–19, 590n6; Reagan veto of, 415, 432

Clark, Will, 255

Cleaver, Eldridge, 106, 399

Clinton, Bill, 122, 349, 581n4, 593n3

closed captioning. *See* captioning

Coalition for Barrier Free Living, 254, 255–56, 481

Coalition for the Removal of Architectural Barriers (CRAB), 121

Coalition to Stop Electroshock, 295–96

Coalition of Texans with Disabilities, 253, 481

Coelho, Tony, **71–76**, **452–57**, 461, 535; and ADA, 71, 414, 443, 453–57, 460, 473, 529; and Bush, 474; in Congress, 452–53, 473, 594n2; and Catholic church, 6, 452, 457; and Democratic Congressional Campaign Committee, 472; and epilepsy, 72–76, 452; and Epilepsy Foundation of America, 470–71. *See also* Americans with Disabilities Act of 1990

Coleman, Diane, **41–44**, 485–86, 549

Collins, B. T., 306

Colorado Coalition of Citizens with Disabilities, 381

Committee for Democratic Elections, 268

Community Choice Act, 549, 598n3

Community Legal Services, 136

Cone, Kitty (Curtis), 22, 94, 162, 198, **211–15**, 226; arrest of, 106; and *Davis* decision, 347–48; and HEW demonstrations, 264, **266–71**, 276, **278–82;** and Socialist Workers Party, 212–14, 268, 355; at Illinois, 106, 110, 214. *See also* HEW demonstrations

Congress of Racial Equality (CORE), 205, 276

Congressional Black Caucus, 436, 457

Congressional Budget Office, 436, 500

Congressional Task Force on the Rights and Empowerment of People with Disabilities, 351, 436–39, 475–78, 481, 487–88, 595n6. *See also* Americans with Disabilities Act of 1990; Dart, Justin, Jr.; Frieden, Lex; Owen, Major

conscientious objectors, 217, 576n7

Consortium for Citizens with Developmental Disabilities (CCDD)/Consortium for Citizens with Disabilities (CCD), 141–43, 422, 485, 527, 533–34, 548

Conyers, John, 457

Cook, Tim, 9–11, 582n1

Cooper, Bob, 451, 594n8

Corcoran, Dr. Paul, 248–49, 578n2

Council for Exceptional Children, 142

Coudroglou, Aliki, 5

Cowell Hospital (Berkeley), 205–6, 216–17; and Donald, 303–4; media attention, 197, 202; and Roberts, 24, 199–200; student life at, 203, 207–11

CRAB. *See* Coalition for the Removal of Architectural Barriers

"crawl-up." *See* Capitol "crawl-up"

"cripple," as term of derision, 70, 124, 270

cross-disability awareness/organizing, 20, 26, 113, 264, 276, 579n10; and ACCD, 247–51, 254, 579n9; and ADA, 443, 476; and blindness community, 578–79n8; and DIA, 184–85; and Disabled Paralegal Advocacy Program, 339; and NAD, 578n1; and psychiatric survivor movement, 290, 581n4

C-SPAN, 473

Cuomo, Mario, 195, 575n11

curb cuts/ramps. *See* access, architectural

Dahl, Dale, 224, 271

Daily Cal (UC Berkeley), 296

D'Amato, Al, 488

Dart, Justin, Jr., 5, **167–73**, 386, 430, 550, *illus.;* and Advocates for Utah Handicapped, 386; and ADA, 167, **429–33**, 473, 484, 486, 495, 538, **545–49**, 598n3 (ch. 34); and Boggs, 476; and Bush, 458–59; and Clinton, 168, 458; and Congressional Task Force on the Rights and Empowerment of People with Disabilities, 351, **475–78**, 481, 487; and Frieden, 256, 430; and Hatch, 478–79; and Kemp Jr., 447; and LBJ, 458; and Michel, **511–13**; and NCH/NCD, 167, 414, 425, 429–33; as "PAC" for disability rights, **457–59**; and Paralympics, 168–69; and People First, 337; and psychiatric survivors, 301, 476; and Reagan, 429–30, 458, 459, 495; and Rehabilitation Services Administration, 167, 475, 573n9, 595n5; and Reynolds, 432–33; and Republican Party, 26, 167, 458–59; and *Toward Independence,* 430–33; and Wright, 440, 442, 476. *See also* Congressional Task Force on the Rights and Empowerment of People with Disabilities; National Council on Disability; National Council on the Handicapped

Dart, Justin, Sr., 167, 430, 458

Dart, Yoshiko, 167, 173, 429, 431, 457, 458, 598n3 (ch. 34)

Davis, Deidre, **122–25**

Davis, John W., 1–3, 29

Davis, Francis B., 585n3. See also *Southeastern Community College v. Davis*

Davis, Lennard J. 564n99

Deaf clubs, 19, 40, 567n6

Deaf community/culture, 4–5, 25, 397; and ASL, 156; and ADA, 527–34; and deafness as "disability," 404, 564n101; and EAHCA, 144, 550, 572n9; and Harkin, 448; and mainstreaming, 247, 572n9; and physically disabled community, 447; and racial segregation, 563n92. *See also* Americans with Disabilities Act of 1990: Title IV; Deaf President Now; Gallaudet University

Deaf Counseling, Advocacy, and Referral Agency, 401, 588n2

Deaf President Now, 27, 40, 159, **397–412**, 448, 493–94, *illus.;* and "the Ducks," 397, 400, 405, 409; media coverage of, 398, 404, 407;

and NAD, 400, 401, 409; police response to, 402, 411; rally and march, 398, 401–2, 406, 409–10; Student Body Government, 403, 405, 410, 412; student demands, 398. *See also* Bourne-Firl, Bridgetta; Levesque, Jack; Olson, Gary; Rarus, Tim; Rosen, Jeff; Spilman, Jane Bassett

Deaf schools, 247, 550. *See also* Gallaudet College/University

Deaf Youth Leadership Development Camps, 40, 156, 159, 405

Decoder Circuitry Act of 1990, 496

Dejanikus, Tacie, 371

DeJong, Gerben James, 423, 512, 591n15

deinstitutionalization: and parents' movement, 106, 324; and *PARC v. Pennsylvania,* 137, 348; and "Partlow case," 568n6; and right to treatment, 571n4, 573ch9n2; and sheltered workshops, 574n7; and "tear down the wall" suits, 584n4; and Title XIX of Social Security Act, 583n3; and Weicker, 441. *See also* Bronston, Dr. William; Dybwad, Gunnar; Gilhool, Thomas K.; *Halderman v. Pennhurst State School & Hospital;* institutions; Perske, Robert; psychiatric survivor movement; Thornburgh, Richard; Wolfensberger, Wolf

Delancey Street program, 268

Del-ARC (Delaware County Association for Retarded Children, PA), 133

DeMartino, Midge, 86

Democratic Congressional Campaign Committee, 472

Democratic National Committee, 473

Democratic Party, 259–60, 465

Denver Regional Transit District, 377, 380–81

Developmental Disabilities Assistance and Bill of Rights Act, 465

Dewey, Thomas, 458

DIA. *See* Disabled in Action

Di Angelo, Nancy, 269

Diaz, Arnold, 195

Dick Cavett Show, 316

Dickson, Jim, 451, 594n8

Dingell, John, 455, 462

"direct threat," 491, 595–96n2

disability: in history, 4, 6–7; as "bad," 5–8, 30, 42, 73, 147; census of people with, 564–65n102; as divine punishment, 5–7, 73–74, 307; isolation/segregation of, 17–18,

103, 105, 117, 144, 150; and "just world theory," 6; as justification for inequality, 10; as liberation movement, 211; in literature/media/popular culture, 7–8, 19, 30, 241, 367, 566nn1–2; medical model of, 8–9, 18; as "open minority," 25–26, 444, 503, 564n99; and oppressive language, 30, 70, 124, 270, 563n93; "pecking order" among people with, 337, 532; prejudice against, 73–75, 104, 170, 283, 446, 505–6; public reaction to, 37–38, 90, 92, 148, 386; and religion, 5–8, 18, 73–74; rehabilitation model of, 14–17, 18; and sexism, 10; and sexuality, 225–26; social definitions of, 4–5; as stigma/taint, 30, 51, 73–75, 132, 137, 227–28, 233–34, 283, 291, 307–8; as threat to society, 9–11, 48; violence against, 303–4, 566n2; and xenophobia, 10. *See also* abuse; discrimination; self-image, of people with disability
Disability Law Resource Center (DLRC), 198, 339, 341, 345–46, 416
"disability pride," 31, 261, *illus.*
Disability Rag, The, 238–45
Disability Rights Center, 420, 446, 585n1, 591n10
Disability Rights Education and Defense Fund (DREDF): and ADA, 284, 440–43, 460–64, 523; as "Berkeley hippies," 414; and Berkeley CIL, 198, 339; and *Disability Rag*, 244; and HIV/AIDS, 523; and Human Rights Campaign, 523; and Leadership Council on Civil Rights, 418; mentioned, 276, 527, 549, 553; and national grass roots network, 344, 421; and psychiatric survivor community, 284; and Section 504 trainings, 339–45; Washington, DC, office, 415–16, 420. *See also* Breslin, Mary Lou; Funk, Robert; Golden, Marilyn; Lipton, Diane; Mayerson, Arlene; Savage, Liz; Steneberg, Doreen "Pam"; Wright, Patrisha
Disabled American Veterans (DAV), 96, 359, 586n4
Disabled in Action (DIA): and ACCD, 246, 249; "candy store approach," 187; as civil rights organization, 24, 189; demonstrations, 185, 188–89; as Handicapped in Action, 184; mentioned, 91, 126, 191, 312, 359, 486; and Rehabilitation Act veto, 26, 183, 187–89; structure of, 186–87; and telethons, 567n10; and Transbus, 585–86n4; and Vietnam

veterans, 193; and Willowbrook State School and Hospital, 185–86. *See also* Figueroa, Pat; Heumann, Judith
Disabled People's Liberation Front, 290
Disabled Students' Placement Program, 340
Disabled Students Union, 24. *See also* Rolling Quads
Disabled Women's Alliance, 34
Disabled Women's Coalition, 226
discrimination, **61–76**, 415, 431, 486; by airlines, 358; in Catholic church, 75–76, 452; in education, 64, 70–71, 144, 487; in employment, 7, 18, 65–66, 68, 76, 126, 346, 358, 381, 438, 446, 574–75n9; and HIV/AIDS, 523; in Peace Corps, 228; against psychiatric survivors, 292; in public accommodations, 66–67, 445, 525; in rehabilitation, 66; stories of, collected, 595n6. *See also* access, architectural; access, telecommunications; access, transportation; Heumann, Judith: lawsuit; race/racism; "special education"
"discrimination diaries," 473, 477
District of Columbia Association of the Deaf, 563n92
Dix, Dorothea, 9, 48, 568n1
DLRC. *See* Disability Law Resource Center
Dole, Robert, 457, 536–37
Donald, James, 203, **303–8**
Doyle, John, 424–25
Doyle, Dr. John, Sr., 75
Dr. Caligari's Psychiatric Drugs, 237
Drake, Steven, 549
DREDF. *See* Disability Rights Education and Defense Fund
Draper, Phil, 162, 210, 340, 572n5
Duberstein, Ken, 450
Dubow, Sy, 495
"Ducks." *See under* Deaf President Now
Dukakis, Michael, 62; and ADA, 441, 484–85, 582n1; and Bartels, 303, 310
Duke, Roberta, 487–88
Durant, Jim, 181
Dusenbury, Joseph, 430
Dybwad, Gunnar, 1, **49–53**, 174, 179; and *PARC v. Pennsylvania*, 131, 135, 137, 138, 140; and People First, 324, 332
Dybwad, Peter, 137
Dybwad, Rosemary Fergusson, 49, 50, 138, 332, 571n6

EAHCA. *See* Education for All Handicapped
  Children Act of 1975
Eastern Paralyzed Veterans Association
  (EPVA), 460, 499
Easter Seals/Easter Seal Society, 146, 246, 351,
  475, 543
Eastwood, Clint, 548
Edmunds, John, 121, 122
education. *See* discrimination: in education;
  Education for All Handicapped Children
  Act of 1975; individualized education
  program (IEP); Lipton, Diane; *PARC v.
  Pennsylvania;* "right to education"; "special
  education"
Education for All Handicapped Children
  Act of 1975 (EAHCA)/Individuals with
  Disabilities Education Act (IDEA), 125–26,
  141, 143, 465, 487, 536; and Deaf community,
  144, 550, 572n9; and DREDF, 345; as "given"
  to disability community, 257; passage of,
  144–45; and Reagan administration, 504;
  and right to education litigation, 26, 137;
  as tool for parent advocates, 150, 351; and
  zero reject principle, 144, 565n104. *See
  also* discrimination: in education; Gilhool,
  Thomas K.; Individualized Education
  Program (IEP); *PARC v. Pennsylvania;*
  parents' movement; *Smith v. Robinson;*
  "special education"
Edwards, Ralph (*This Is Your Life*), 152
EEOC. *See* Equal Employment Opportunity
  Commission
Eiesland, Nancy, 5
Eisenhower, Dwight D., 21, 458, 561n82, 592n4
Eisner, Eugene, 180
electroshock, 59–60, 77, 79–82, 137, 234, 236,
  237, 283, 291–97
employment, 413, 539, 442, 551, 554–55;
  and ADA, 463, 508, 540, 598n1; and
  architectural access, 463; and AFPH, 19–21;
  and post-offer medical examinations, 490,
  595n1 (ch. 29); and PVA, 359, 361. *See also*
  Americans with Disabilities Act of 1990:
  Title I; Chapman amendment; Coelho,
  Tony; discrimination: in employment;
  Kemp, Evan, Jr.; President's Committee
  on Employment of the Physically
  Handicapped; sheltered workshops
Employment Law Center, 346

ENCOR (Eastern Nebraska Community Office
  of Retardation), 335
Endependence Center of Northern Virginia
  (ECNV), 447, 448
Ennis, Bruce, 583n3
Enoch, Edna, 570n4
Epilepsy Foundation of America, 142, 470–72.
  See also Coelho, Tony; Savage, Liz
Equal Employment Opportunity Commission,
  444, 447, 449, 505, 546
"equal plus" civil rights protection, 464
Erskine, Graves B., 21
eugenics, 9–11, 48–49, 139, 559n45, 571n3, *illus.*
Fair Housing Amendments Act of 1988, 28–29,
  415, 419, 472, 487, 539, 590n9
Fairview Training Center, Salem, OR, 57–58,
  324–27, 333
faith healing, 73–74
"family of affinity," 374
Fay, Fred, 23, 94, 106, 198, 246, 308–10,
  549–50, *illus.*; ACCD, organizer of, **247–53**,
  254–55; at Illinois, 22, **104–7**, 248; at
  Warm Springs, **87–90**. *See also* American
  Coalition of Citizens with Disabilities
FBI (Federal Bureau of Investigation), 272,
  273, 275, 377, 506, 580n7, 581n4; and New
  Medico, 321–23
Federal Communications Commission (FCC),
  494, 497–98
Federalist Society, 444, 448, 503, 592n1
Feldblum, Chai, 460, 461, 492, 594n1
Fernald, Walter E., 49
Fernald State School, Massachusetts, 52
Ferraro, Geraldine, 471
Fewell-Billings, Carol, 204
Figueroa, Denise, **486–88**
Figueroa, Pat, 189, **190–96**
Fiorito, Eunice, 187, 193, 257, 574–75n9;
  and ACCD, 248–50, 252–55; and HEW
  demonstrations, 263, 279, 280
Fish, Hamilton, 501, 532
Fitzgerald, Maureen, 224
504 Emergency Coalition, 267
"Flaming Faggots, the" 287
Flight Attendants Union, 525
Foley, Tim, 308
Foley, Congressman Tom, 454–55, 519–20
Ford, Gerald, 261–62

Francis, Fred, 191, 192
Frank, Leonard Roy, **77–82**, 88, **234–38**, 293–94, 568–69n1, *illus.*
"Frank Papers, The," 77
Frazee, Jerome, 202
Free America Independent Voters, 259
Free Clinic (San Francisco), 295
Free Speech Movement (UC Berkeley), 145
Friedberg, John, 77
Frieden, Joyce, 254
Frieden, Lex, 248, **253–60**, 320, **422–39**, 478–80. *See also* American Coalition of Citizens with Disabilities
Friedman, Karen, **527–34**
Friends of the Allegedly Insane, 283
Friends of SNCC (Student Nonviolent Coordinating Committee), 205
Fuller, Hollynn, 282
Funk, Robert, 3, 9, 198, 345, 346, 441, 460; and DREDF, 339, 340, 415, 417
Fuss, Michael, **205–11**

Gallagher, Hugh Gregory, 18
Gallaudet Alumni Association, 397
Gallaudet College/University, 40–41, 156, 158, 250, **397–412**, 493. *See also* Deaf President Now
Galloway, Donald, 198, **218–22**
Gandhi, Mohandas K., 79, 295, 382, 404, 546
Garland, Robert, 7
Garland-Thomson, Rosemarie, 6
Garret, Jim, 249, 250
Garrity, W. Arthur, 345
gay/lesbian/bisexual/transgender community, 240, 287, 563n92, 588n2, 594n1; and Berkeley CIL, 225; and HEW demonstrations, 268, 580n5; and Kowalski, 369–75. *See also* Chapman amendment; HIV/AIDS; Thompson, Karen
Geld, Howard ("Howie the Harp"), 284, 287, 292, 581n3
Gentile, Eric, 249, 251, 578n4
George Jackson Brigade, 445, 592n2
George Miller West Development Center, 147
Georgetown University Law Center, 493
Geyer, Bob, 255
GI Bill of Rights, 21, 94, 357
Gilhool, Gillian, 137, 571n5
Gilhool, Robert, 136, 137

Gilhool, Thomas K., 1–3, **136–41**, 320, **348–51**, 507, 586n5
Gill, Carol, 14, 549, 564n99
Ginsberg, Allen, 58
Glenn, Bill, 202
Glide Metropolitan Church, 268, 580n5, 581n6
Goddard, Henry H., 557n3
Goldberg, Ignacy, 140
Golden, Marilyn, 255, **481–84**, 512, 579n13, 582n1
Goldwater Memorial Hospital, NYC, 91–93
Golfus, Billy, 31, 569n3
"Good Sports, the," 119
Gordon, Sean, 294
Gore, Al, 494
Gorove, Lisa, 448, 593n5
Gould, Richard, **180–82**
Gray, C. Boyden, 416, 418, **503–7**, 537; and ADAPT, 516; and ADA, 450, 468, 474, 492, 524–25; and Harkin, 536; and Kemp Jr., 420, 449, 503, 589n2
Greater Boston Legal Services, 289
Greyhound Bus Lines, 102, 456, 501–2, 530, *illus.*
Grimes, Chuck, 204
Groce, Nora, 4, 20–21
Grove City College v. Bell, 418, 590n6
Gwin, Lucy, **82–87**, 301, **319–23**

Haas, Mimi, 116
Haggerty, Dennis, 131, **132–36**, 141
Haggerty, Dennis ("Boomer"), Jr., 133–34
Halderman v. Pennhurst State School & Hospital, 137, 507, 586n5
Hammitt, Jim, 228
Hammond, Jack, 180
Hancock, Loni, 264
Handicapped Children's Protection Act of 1986, 422, 591n13
Handicapping America, 18, 285, 579n9
Harby, Donovan, 202
Harkin, Thomas, 427–28, 443, 461, 465–67, **535–38**
Harris, Avril, 269
Harris, Lou, poll, 430, 434
Hart, Clarence, 346
Hatch, Orrin, 457, 467, 469, 478, 542–43
Hatch Amendment, 525–26
Hayes, Robert, 316
Haymarket Fund, Boston, 299

Head Injury Association, 320, 321
Health, Education, and Welfare, US
    Department of (HEW), 197, 206, 258, 341;
    and Section 504 regulations, 239, 256, 261,
    281, 577n5. *See also* HEW demonstrations
health insurance, 441–42, 460, 464, 529
Health Insurance Association of America, 321
"health preservation classes," 487
Heard, Ken, 393
Hearing Aid Compatibility Act of 1988, 494,
    596n5
Hearn, Paul, 499
Hearst, Patricia Campbell, 445, 449, 593n3
Heath, Dennis, 57, **324–32**
Helen Keller Center for Deaf-Blind Youth and
    Adults, 16
Helen Keller Foundation, 158
Helms, Jessie, 522, 525–26
Henderson, George, 8
Heritage House, Denver, 376–80
Herman, Bob, 128
Herp, Donna, 239
Herrick Hospital, Berkeley, 294, 296
Hesburgh, Rev. Theodore Martin, 132, 570n1
Hessler, John, 162, 200, 202–3, 205, 207, 209–10,
    305, 572n4
Heumann, Judith, 23, 191, 192, 259, 279, 353–54,
    358, 414, 486, *illus.;* at ADA signing, 546;
    and ACCD, 248, 249, 252–53, 255; and
    Bailout Bill protest, 307; and Berkeley CIL,
    198, 214; and DIA, **183–90**, 193; and HEW
    demonstrations, 262, **263–66**, 267–69, 274,
    277, 353; lawsuit against NYC school system,
    125–30; and WID, 113; visits Willowbrook,
    185–86. *See also* American Coalition of
    Citizens with Disabilities; Disabled in
    Action; Education for All Handicapped
    Children Act; HEW demonstrations
HEW demonstrations, 26–27, 125, **261–82**,
    340, 349, 414; in Boston, 252; effect on
    participants, 278, 282; and Gallaudet
    students, 281; at Lafayette Park, 280–81;
    leadership of, 273–74; victory celebration,
    275; in San Francisco, 261–78, *illus.;* in
    Washington, DC, 257, 278–81. *See also*
    American Coalition of Citizens with
    Disabilities; Bowe, Frank; Califano, Joseph;
    Carter, Jimmy; Center for Independent
    Living; Cone, Kitty; Fay, Fred; Heumann,
    Judith; Lacy, Johnnie; Moscone, George;

O'Toole, Corbett; Owen, Mary Jane;
    Roberts, Ed
Hicks, Heidi, 454
HIV/AIDS, 6, 415, 474–76, 506, 528; and
    Chapman amendment, 474, 521–26, 531–33;
    as priority of ADA coalition, 450–51
Hlibok, Greg, 400, 403, **404–8**, 411, 412. *See
    also* Deaf President Now
Hlibok, Stephen, 400
Hoehler, Fred, 96
Hofman, Stevie, 186
Holistic Approaches to Independent Living
    (HAIL), 381
Holmes, Oliver Wendell, Jr., 2
home schooling, 92
homophobia, 369–71, 374. *See also* Chapman
    amendment; HIV/AIDS
Honig, Harvey, 192
Hoover Institution, 435
Hope, Bob, 452
Hospital Improvement Program (HIP), 177
Hotchkiss, Ralf, 249, 446, 578n7
Howe, Samuel Gridley, 9, 48, 52, 568n5, 574n7
Howie the Harp. *See* Geld, Howard
Hoyer, Steny, 454–55, 461–62, 490, 529–31, 537,
    594n10
Hudson, Wade, 293, 581n6
Human Rights Campaign (HRC), 523, 524, 527,
    533, 597n3
Humphrey, Hubert H., 222
Hurston, Zora Neale, 399

Illinois Coalition of People with Disabilities,
    512
Independent Living Center, San Francisco, 265
independent living model, 198, 206, 560n60,
    591n15
independent living movement, 23, **197–226**,
    467, 598n3
Indiana School for the Deaf, 157, 158
Individualized Education Program (IEP),
    143–44, 572n8. *See also* Education for All
    Handicapped Children Act of 1975
Individuals with Disabilities Education Act
    (IDEA). *See* Education for All Handicapped
    Children Act of 1975
Indoor Sports Club, 119, 121, 160, 163, 570n4
Industrial School for Crippled and Deformed
    Children, Boston, 30, 35–36, 566n1
In re G.H. (1974), 132, 570n2

Insane Liberation Front, 24, 284
institutions, 18, **48–60, 77–93, 174–82,**
312–23, 487; and ableism, 30; abuse at, 53,
56–58, 84, 133–34, 175; ADA and, 598n3;
ADAPT and, 376, 379, 548–49, 598n3;
Berkeley CIL as alternative to, 24, 224–25;
blindness community and, 247; case law
and, 357; conditions at, 49–51, 53, 56–57,
477; conscientious objectors and, 576n7;
"custodial care," 52–53, 77; and DIA,
184–85; and eugenics, 11, 15; and fraud, 85;
"Howe system" and, 52, 568n5; and Illinois
students, 96, 103; as isolating, 17, 23, 85–86;
in Japan, 168; and Kowalski, 368, 370, 372–
73; and Medicaid, 583n3, 598n3; medical
experiments at, 59–60; and "mentally ill,"
48, 58–60, 77–82; and "mentally retarded,"
48, 50–58, 133–36; "milieu therapy," 77;
and organized crime, 182; parents denied
access to, 52, 55, 178; peer counseling at,
88–89; pressure on parents, 53–54, 133;
racial segregation at, 90; as reform, 9, 48;
residents as cheap labor, 13, 49; solitary
confinement, 60, 84–85; sterilization at, 56,
139, 325; and Title XIX of Social Security
Act, 583n3; in Vietnam, 171–73. *See also*
abuse; ADAPT; Chabasinski, Ted; Dix,
Dorothea; Dybwad, Gunnar; electroshock;
eugenics; Fay, Fred; Frank, Leonard Roy;
Gould, Richard; Gwin, Lucy; Haggerty,
Dennis; Howe, Samuel Gridley; insulin-
coma "therapy"; New Medico Brain
Injury Rehabilitation Centers; nursing
homes; *PARC v. Pennsylvania;* Pennhurst
State School & Hospital; People First;
Perske, Robert; "right to treatment"; Ruiz,
Larry; Saviola, Marilyn; Schwartz, Terrell
("Terry"); self-advocates movement;
sheltered workshops; Thompson, Karen;
Willowbrook State School and Hospital;
Wyatt v. Stickney; and individual
institutions
insulin-coma "therapy," 77, 79–82, 283
"internalized oppression." *See under* self-image,
of people with disability
International Association of Machinists and
Aerospace Workers, 262
International Conference on Human Rights
and Psychiatric Oppression, 287, 289, 298,
300, 582n10

Iowa School for the Deaf, 408
Irvin, Cass, 241
Irvin, Mike, 549
Iskowitz, Michael, 466, 525

Jackson, Rev. Jessie, 395, 412
Jacobson, Neil, 30, 186, 574n6
Japanese Reparations Act, 456
Javits, Jacob, 315
Jeffers, Jim, 310
"Jerry's Kids mentality," 395. *See also* Muscular
Dystrophy Association
Jerry's Orphans, 549, 567–68 n10
Johnson, Babs, **388–91**
Johnson, Lyndon Baines, 458, 584–85n3
Johnson, Mark, 376, **380–85**
Johnson, Mary, **238–45,** 384, 560n68
Jones, Cyndi, **227–34, 484–86,** 576n1, 582n1
Jordan, Irving King, 398, 408, 448, 564n101,
588–89n6
Junior NAD (National Association of the
Deaf), 157, 405
Just One Break (JOB), 21
Justice for All, 88, 549

Kafka, Bob, 255, 393, 516, 579n14
Kane, Larry, 132
Kansas Neurological Institute (KNI), 53–57
Kaplan, Deborah, 8–9, 446, 585n1
Kaplan, Fred, 571n7
Karten, Barbara, 203
Karuth, Denise, **62–65,** 377, **551–53**
Kegan, Larry, 88, 569n3
Keller, Helen, 557n2
Kemp, Evan, Jr., 399, 422, 445–46, 449,
550, 589n3, *illus.;* and American Bar
Association, 492; and ADAPT, 516; and
ADA, 460–61, 468, 507, 544, 546; and Bush,
417, 440, 449–50, 505; and Deaf community,
448; at Disability Rights Center, 420;
discrimination against, 444, 446; and Gray,
420, 444, 504, 524, 589n2; and Jerry Lewis,
447, 549, 567–68n10
Kemp, Janine Bertram, **445–52,** 505, 544
Kennedy, Edward "Ted," Jr., 441, 539, 565n103
Kennedy, Edward M. "Ted," 26, 443, 457, 535;
and ADA, 451, 462, **538–41;** and Civil Rights
Restoration Act of 1987, 432; and Dart Jr.,
476; family experience with disability, 468–
69, 539, 565n103; and Harkin, 536;

Kennedy, Edward M. "Ted" *(continued)*
and Hatch, 543; at ADA singing ceremony, 541; staff of, 462, 466, 525–26; and Sununu, 537–38
Kennedy, John F., 20, 75, 561n82, 584n5, 597n1 (ch. 33)
Kennedy, Robert F., 175, 356, 441
Kennedy, Rosemary, 565n103, 597n1 (ch. 33)
Kent State shootings, 376, 587n1
Kesey, Ken, 236, 576n3
Kevorkian, Jack, 549
King, Rev. Martin Luther, Jr., 106, 356, 376, 382, 396, 404, 542
Kitchens, Lee, **31–34, 151–56**, 572n2
Kitchens, Mary, 153, 154
Koch, Richard, 179, 573n2
Kocher-Magnan, Meg, 565n108
Koppel, Ted, 407
Kowalski, Sharon. *See* Thompson, Karen
Kriegel, Leonard, 7–8, 25, 240, 564n98
Krones, Janice, 226
Kurtin, Jane, 314

labor model of disability rights, 19–21, 25
Labor Standards Act of 1938, 574n7
Lacy, Johnnie, **69–71**, 125, **351–54**
Lamb, Tom, 140
Lancaster, John A., 125, 255, **355–61**, 579n12
Lane, Rev. Nancy L., 5
Langdon, Larry, 203, 209, 215, 216
Lanier, Robert, 438–39
LaNoue, Bobbi, 281
Lanterman, Frank, 264, 265
Largent, Mark A., 559n45
Laski, Frank, 132, 570n2
Latin, Dianne, 255
Laughlin, Harry L., 2
Laurie, Gini, 22–23, 255
Leadership Conference on Civil Rights, 29, 419, 460, 589–90n4, 590n9. *See also* Wright, Patrisha
League of the Physically Handicapped, 19, 113
least restrictive environment (LRE), 144, 374
Lee, Elizabeth, 314
Lee, Jerry C., 397, 398, 399
Lefkin, Arthur, 191
Legal Services Corporation, 339, 341
Legion of Justice, 212
Leiberman, Len, 450
Lennox, Andy, 204

Lenox Hill, Lynn, MA, 182
Leon, Joan, 113
Lerner, Melvin, 6
Letchworth Village, Rockland County, NY, 50
Letterman General Hospital, San Francisco, 202
Levesque, Jack, 397, 401, 409, 588n2
Lewis, Jerry, 447, 549, 567–68n10. *See also* "Jerry's Kids mentality"; Muscular Dystrophy Association
Lewis, Michael, 109, 112
Lexington School for the Deaf, NYC, 405
Lincoln, Abraham, 397
Linden, NJ, 123–25
Linn, Barbara (Bobbi), 185, 574n3
Lipton, Chloe, 145–50
Lipton, Diane, **145–50**
Little People of America (LPA), 31, 151–54
Long Island University, 126, 127
Longmore, Paul K., 12–14, 26, 242, 560n56, 560n68, 577n8
Loomis, Ray, 335
Lorence, Donald, 202, 203, 207–10
Lucas, Roy, 128
Lynch, Jimmy, 187

Madness Network News, 227, 234–38, 284, 293, 301
Mahler, Jay, 59
Mainstream: Magazine of the Able-Disabled, 227–34
Malcolm X, 399, 563n93
Mansfield, Gordon, 432
Marcario, Mark, 313
March of Dimes, 228
March on Washington (1963), 124
Marchand, Paul, **141–45**; and ADA, 460, 475, 485, **527–34**
Markey, Edward J., 530
Marshall, Thurgood, 2–3
Martha's Vineyard (Deaf community), 4–5
Maryland School of the Deaf, 400
Masonic Hospital for Crippled Children, 70
Massachusetts Association of Paraplegics, 309
Massachusetts Bay Transit Authority (MBTA), 551–52
Massachusetts Coalition of Citizens with Disabilities, 62, 308
Massachusetts Commission for the Blind, 64, 551–52

Massachusetts Council of Organizations of the Handicapped, 308

Massachusetts Hospital School, 181

Massachusetts Mental Health Center ("Mass Mental"), 289–90

Massachusetts Rehabilitation Commission, 309–11

Massachusetts School for Idiotic and Feeble-Minded Children, 568n5

Mathews, David F., 239, 577n5

Matthews, Cris, 549

Maye, John, 358

Mayerson, Arlene, 416, **419–22**, 440, 471; and ADA, 460–61, **489–92**; and DLRC, **345–48**

Mazz, Marsha, 447–48, 593n4

McCain, John, 496, 529

McCarthy, Peggy, 552

McClelland, Steve, 268–69

McCourt, Diana, 186, 316, 574n5

McCourt, Malachy, 186, 316, 574n5

McDaniel, Durwood, 249, 578n3

McDonald's, 362–68. See also Auberger, Michael

McEwan, Janet Brown, 220

McFeeley, Tim, 524–25

McGovern, Frank, 229

McLean Hospital, Belmont, MA, 298

McQuade, Denise, 184, 187, 573n1

"Measure T" (referendum on electroshock), 296

Medicaid Community Attendant Services Act (MiCASA), 549. See also ADAPT

Medicaid, 13, 583n3, 598n3

Medicare, 13

Meltzer, Donna, 472

Meninger Institute, 174

"mental age," and exclusion from public schools, 139

Mental Health Consumer Services, 59

Mental Health Law Project. See Bazelon Center

Mental Patients' Association, 288, 292

Mental Patients' Liberation Front, 24, 284, 288–89, 298, 299

Mental Patients' Liberation Project, 24, 284, 285–86, 289, 292

Merrill Lynch, 400, 403

Meyerson, Irv, 120

Michel, Bob, 483, 512–13, 519–20

Milbank, Jeremiah, 434–35

MiCASA. See Medicaid Community Attendant Services Act

Mills v. Board of Education, 24

Miller-Dwan Polinsky Institute, Duluth, MN, 372

Miller, George, 147, 471

Milstein, Bonnie, 462

MindFreedom International, 59

Mineta, Norm, 456

Minnesota Civil Liberties Union, 368, 369

Mistler, Sharon, 249, 322, 447, 544, 578n6

Mittford, Jessica, 295–96, 581–82n8

Molinari, John, 120

"Mongoloid Dermatitis," 178

"moral imbeciles," 11, 48. See also eugenics

Morey, Lloyd, 102

Morse, Phil, 116

Moscone, George, 119, 120, 570n3; and HEW demonstrations, 262, 264, 265, 274

Motley, Constance Baker, 129

Mount Sinai Hospital, NYC, 79

Mouth magazine, 82, 301, 584n5

Moyer, Jeff, 270, 277, 580n6

Moynihan, Patrick, 488

Muller, Bobby, 189, 193, 575n10

Multiple Sclerosis (MS) Society, 246

Muscular Dystrophy Association (MDA), 113, 447; and Jerry Lewis Telethon/Orphans, 19, 43, 549, 567–68n10

Nader, Ralph, 585n1

Nakao, Shirley, 345

Napa State Hospital, Napa, CA, 79

National Association for the Advancement of Colored People (NAACP), 2, 219, 268, 292, 345

National Association of the Deaf (NAD), 19, 20, 113, 156, 157, 246, 578n1; and ACCD, 248, 258, 260; Broadcaster newsletter, 401, 409; and Deaf President Now, 400, 409. See also Junior NAD

National Association of Parents and Friends of Mentally Retarded Children, 131, 562n88

National Association for Retarded Children (NARC), 22, 24, 50, 246, 475; education programs, 139; name changes, 562n88; and People First, 335; as "hub" of CCCD, 142

National Black Disability Coalition, 122

National Center for Health Statistics, 564–65n102

National Center for Law and the Deaf, 493, 494, 495, 527

National Center for Law and the Handicapped, 132, 585n1

National Commission on Acquired Immune Deficiency Syndrome, 523, 597n3

National Council on Disability (NCD), 71, 453, 476, 545, 549, 581n4; and ADA, 460, 465, 527–28

and Deaf community, 495. *See also* National Council on the Handicapped

National Council on the Handicapped (NCH), 253, 414, 428, 435, 441; genesis of, 423–25; and Reagan administration, 432–33. *See also* National Council on Disability

National Council on Independent Living (NCIL), 549, 587n5, 593n6; and ADAPT, 382; and ADA, 450, 467, 487–88; and DREDF, 440

National Employ the Physically Handicapped Week, 21

National Empowerment Center, 285

National Federation of the Blind (NFB), 3, 22–23, 113, 219, 246, 574n7, 578–79n8; and ACCD, 247–48, 258; labor movement as model, 19–20

National Federation of Independent Businesses, 490, 522

National Foundation for Cerebral Palsy, 562n88

National Gay and Lesbian Task Force, 374–75

National Head Injury Foundation, 86

National Institute on Deafness and Other Communication Disorders Act, 494, 596n5

National Minorities with Disabilities Coalition, 122

National Organization of Women (NOW), 370–71, 373

National Organization on Disability (NOD), 508

National Paraplegia Foundation, 246, 248, 309

National Restaurant Association, 522, 528

National Spinal Cord Injury Association, 247

National Technical Institute for the Deaf, 158

National Theatre of the Deaf, 16

Nau, Lou, 165

Nau, Yvonne, 165

NBC News, 322, 323, 407

Neas, Ralph, 418–19, 442, 460, 589–90n4

Nebraska ARC, 336

Nebraska School for the Deaf, 156

Network Against Psychiatric Assault (NAPA), 235–36, 284, 293–94, 301

New England Gallaudet Association of Deaf-Mutes, 567n6

New Medico Brain Injury Rehabilitation Centers, 83–87, 319–23, 584n6

Newport, Gus, 294, 296

New School for Social Research, 276

New York ARC v. Rockefeller, 583–84n3

New York Daily News, 193

New York Metropolitan Transit Authority, 194–96

New York Times, 407, 434; and Coalition to Stop Electroshock, 294–96; and DIA, 185, 187; and Heumann lawsuit, 128, 193; and New Medico, 323

"nickles for cripples," 210

Nightline, 404, 407

Nixon, Richard M., 132, 434, 570n1; veto of Rehabilitation Act, 187–88, 248, 265, 574n8

"normalization," 185, 569n68, 574n4

Norwood, Mac, 40, 567n8

Not Dead Yet, 549

Notre Dame College, 132

Nugent, Timothy, 22, **94–97**, 98, **100–104**

nursing homes, 49, 477; Berkeley CIL as alternative to, 24, 224–25; and DIA, 184; Gould at, 180–82; and Medicaid, 583n3, 598n3; and organized crime, 182; and University of Illinois students, 96, 103. *See also* institutions; Thompson, Karen; *individual homes*

Oakland Economic Development Council, 352

Oakland Tribune, 294

Oaks, David, 283, 284, 295, **297–302**

Obama, Barack, 29, 126, 442, 594n1

O'Brien, John, 336

O'Brien, Ruth, 15–16

O'Connell, Russ, 309

O'Connor v. Donaldson, 571n4

O'Donnell, Mike, 400

Office of Management and Budget (White House), 420

Ogle, Becky, 549

Olmstead v. L.C. and E.W., 549, 598n3

Olsen, Gary, **156–59**, 405, *illus.*

On Our Own: Patient-Controlled Alternatives to the Mental Health System, 285

On the Threshold of Independence, 414, 427, 591n18

Opening Doors Counseling Center, 88, 247

"oralist" method of education, 156, 397, 405, 408, 579n9, 588n1
Oregonian, The, 329
Osolinik, Carolyn P., 460, 462, 466
Oswald, Barbara, **44–47**
O'Toole, Corbett, 198, **34–38, 222–26, 271–75**
Oullette, Rosemary, 551
"Out of Sight" lawsuit, 307
Owen, Mary Jane, 23, 211, 242, 262, 268, **275–78**
Owens, Major, 436–37, 439, 457, 475–77, 537
Ozols, Andy, 231, 232

Paine, Don, 436
Panzarino, Connie, 371, 587n7
Paralympics, 168
Paralyzed Veterans of America (PVA), 154, 309, 355, 357; and ADA, 474, 475; and ACCD, 248–49, 258, 260, 527–30; and disability rights movement, 359, 474; founding of, 21–22. *See also* Capozzi, David; Lancaster, John
paratransit, 162, 266, 438, 500; inadequacy of, 361, 551; and parents' movement, 131; at Berkeley, 197
PARC v. Pennsylvania, 1, 24, 26, 131, 135–41, 340, 550
parents' movement, 22, 24, 49, **131–50**, 312, *illus.* *See also* Dybwad, Gunnar; Gilhool, Thomas K.; Haggerty, Dennis; Lipton, Dianne; *PARC v. Pennsylvania*
Partlow case. See *Wyatt v. Stickney*
Parrino, Sandra Swift, 414, 425, 436, 453–54, 465, 545, 591n16, *illus.*
Patients' Bill of Rights, 83, 286
peer counseling/support, 89, 118
Pennhurst State School & Hospital, 134–38, 140, 348, 371–72n3, 570–71n3, 586n5
Pennsylvania Association for Retarded Children (PARC), 1, 131, 133–36, 140
People First, 57, 325–32, 335–38, 577n7
Perlman, Itzhak, 441
Perotti, Linda, 203, 204
Perske, Robert, **53–57**, 174
personal care attendants/assistants, 205, 576n4
Petersen, Roger, 249, 251, 255, 578–79n8
Phelps, C. Allison, 570n4
Philadelphia Assocation for Retarded Children, 134
Phoenix Rising, 301
Physically Disabled Students' Program (PDSP), 24, 183, 197, 204, 206, 209, 210, 216–17, 304

physician-assisted suicide, 549, 577n9
Pimentel, Al, 250, 258, 579n10
PL [Public Law] 94–142. *See* Education for All Handicapped Children Act of 1975
Plessy v. Ferguson, 10
Pomeroy, Janet, 118, 569–70n2
Poole, Dennis L., 5
Popink, Prudence, 346
Powers, Tim, 240
President's Commission on the HIV Epidemic, 473
President's Committee on Employment of the Physically Handicapped, 26, 355, 447, 477; and ACCD, 246, 249, 254–56; founding of, 21, 561–62n82
President's Committee on National Employ the Physically Handicapped Week, 21
President's Committee on Mental Retardation, 134, 337, 584n5
"primary entrance" access, 111, 569n3
Prison Mothers And Their Children (Prison MATCH), 445
prisoners' movement, 301
Probe, 322
Project Release, 284
Proposition 13, 306, 583n3
psychiatric survivor movement, 24, 58–60, **283–302**. *See also* Chabasinski, Ted; Chamberlin, Judi; Frank, Leonard Roy; Geld, Howard; *Madness Network News;* Oaks, David
public accommodations, 307, 491–92, 540. *See also* access; Americans with Disabilities Act of 1990: Title II
Public Interest Law Center of Philadelphia (PILCOP), 320, 340, 585–86n4

race/racism, 71, 69, 90, 269; and ableism, 1–3, 10, 67, 112, 124, 155, 292, 296, 301, 464, 564n99; "blackness" and disability, 365; disability as cross-race, 148, 225, 503; in disability rights movement, 25; diversity at Berkeley CIL, 218, 220–22; people of color with disabilities, 122, 220–22, 562–63n92; racial segregation, 1–3, 123–25, 562–63n92; relationship between disability and, 10, 23, 25, 240, 352–54, 365, 562–63n92, 563n93, 564n98. *See also* Black Panthers; *Brown v. Board of Education;* Civil Rights Act of 1964; civil rights movement; Civil Rights

race/racism *(continued)*
  Restoration Act of 1987; Congressional
    Black Caucus; Davis, Deidre;
    discrimination; Galloway, Donald; Kriegel,
    Leonard; Lacy, Johnnie; Leadership
    Conference on Civil Rights
Radical Therapist, The, 298
Ragged Edge, The. See *Disability Rag, The*
Raisian, John, 435–36
Randolph, Jennings, 535–36
Rarus, Tim, 403, 410, 411, 412
Ravitch, Richard, 195–96
Reagan, Ronald, 253, 417, 444, 487, 508; and
    ADA, 505; and Civil Rights Restoration
    Act of 1987, 414, 415; EAHCA regulations,
    attempt to alter, 416, 504; funding cuts,
    28, 231; "kitchen cabinet," 458; and
    People's Park, 575–76n3; and President's
    Committee on Employment of the
    Physically Handicapped, 561–62n82;
    Section 504 regulations, attempt to alter,
    344, 345, 413, 416–17, 504, 585n2; and purge
    of SSDI/SSI rolls, 565–66n111; and *Toward
    Independence,* 432–33; and welfare rights,
    349. *See also* Dart, Justin, Jr.: and Reagan
reasonable accommodation, 28, 29, 256, 508–9,
    510
Recordings for the Blind (and Dyslexic), 63
Rector, James, 575–76n3
Recreation Center for the Handicapped, 117,
    118, 160, 569–70 n2
Red Cross, 171, 570n2
rehabilitation: attitudes of professionals, 15–17,
    64–66, 305, 536, 560n60; "whole man"
    model, 14–16, 569n1
Rehabilitation Act of 1973, 88, 142, 305, 465,
    488, 508, 536; and HEW regulations, 251–52,
    256; Sections 501/502/503, 359, 586n3; Nixon
    veto of, 26, 248, 574n8; Title V, 254. *See also*
    Section 504
Rehabilitation Act of 1978, 28
Rehabilitation Act Amendments of 1984, 423,
    591n14
Rehabilitation Gazette, 23
Rehabilitation International, World Congress
    of, 171
Rehabilitation Services Administration, 250,
    252, 475, 595n5
Reynolds, William Bradford, 418, 419, 420, 449,
    590n7

Rheims, Ken, 121, 122
"right to education," 1, 22, 24, 131, 570n2; and
    deinstitutionalization, 312; and National
    Center on Law and the Handicapped, 132;
    and *PARC v. Pennsylvania,* 24, 26, 563n95.
    See also Education for All Handicapped
    Children Act of 1975; Gilhool, Thomas K.;
    PARC v. Pennsylvania; parents' movement
"right to treatment," 137, 568n6, 571n4
Rivera, Geraldo, 185, 314, 316–17
Rivers, Jerry. *See* Rivera, Geraldo
Roberts, Ed, 23–24, **113–17, 198–201,** 550,
    illus.; on anger, 31; attitude to his disability,
    114–15; and Brown Jr., 306–7; and CA Dept.
    of Rehabilitation, 114, 303, 310; and civil
    rights movement, 222; and Cone, 213; and
    Fay, 248; and Frieden, 254; and Galloway,
    219; and Gwin, 322; and Heumann, 126,
    263; and HEW demonstrations, 274, 276;
    as "infeasible," 116, 303; and PDSP, 206–7,
    209; and peer counseling, 163; political
    connections of, 264, 265; leadership
    opposed, 305, 582–83n2; in *San Mateo
    Times,* 197; tear gassed, 205; and Uzeta, 162–
    63. *See also* Center for Independent Living;
    Cowell Hospital; Physically Disabled
    Students' Program; Rolling Quads
Roberts, Zona, 114–16, 204, 217
Rockefeller administration (New York State),
    174
Rockland State Hospital, Orangeburg, NY,
    58–60, 285, 291
Roeper, Bill, 451
Rogers, Judi, 225
Rogers v. Commissioner of Mental Health, 289,
    581n5
Rolling Quads, 24, 197, 203, 208, 210, 304
Roosevelt, Franklin Delano, 17–18, 87, 97, 167,
    385, 560n68
Rosen, Jeff, **398–404,** 409, 448
Rosen, Roslyn, 409, 411, 589n7
Rosewater, Anne, 471
Rough Times, 299
Rousso, Harilyn, 371, 587n7
Rubenfeld, Phyllis, 252
Rubin, H. Ted, 561n70
Ruby Rogers drop-in center, 299
Ruiz, Larry, **379–80**
Rules for Radicals, 262
Rusk, Dr. Howard, 15, 16

Rusk Institute, 195, 309
Russell, Harold, 21
Russell, Marta, 563n93

Sanders, Greg, 214
San Francisco Council of Churches, 268
San Francisco State University, 69–71
San Mateo, College of, 116, 117
Savage, Liz, 442, **470–75**, 482, 519, 534; and
    ADA, 460, 462, 472–75, 523
Saviola, Marilyn, **90–93**
Sayers, Shirely, 101
Schiffenbauer, Marty, 293–94, 295, 296, 581n7
Schreiber, Fred, 158, 248, 255, 258, 578n1
Schuster, Bud, 500
Schwartz, Terrell ("Terry"), **57–58**, 326, **332–33**
Schwellenbach, Lewis, 21
Schweikert, Harry, 248
Scotch, Richard, 4, 8, 13
Sea View Nursing Home, Rowley, MA, 181
Secret Service. *See* US Secret Service
Section 504 of Rehabilitation Act of
    1973, 26–29, 261; and ACCD, 26–27,
    251–52; and ADA, 460–61, 484, 495; and
    disability-based discrimination, 447;
    and DREDF 504 trainings, **339–54**; and
    HIV/AIDS, 523; as organizing tool, 344;
    and Pennhurst State School, 571n3; and
    public transportation, 585n2; and PVA,
    359; and Reagan administration, 413;
    and *Southeastern Community College v.
    Davis*, 585n3; text of, 27, 261; and undue
    hardship, 491. See also *Grove City College
    v. Bell*; HEW demonstrations; reasonable
    accommodation; Rehabilitation Act of
    1973; *Southeastern Community College v.
    Davis*
Securities and Exchange Commission, 444
Self-Advocates Becoming Empowered (SABE),
    337, 564n4
self-advocates movement, 50, 57, **324–38**
self-image, of people with disability, 36–37, 92;
    and ADAPT, 395–96; and Deaf community,
    405; and HEW demonstrations, 278, 282;
    and "internalized oppression," 7, 23, 490; and
    People First, 326–27; and pride, 31, 261, *illus.*
Senate Labor and Human Resources
    Committee, 473
Senate Subcommittee on Disability Policy, 427,
    465

Senate Special Committee on Aging, 560n65
Serviceman's Readjustment Act of 1944. *See* GI
    Bill of Rights
sex/sexuality, 225–26, 373
sexual abuse. *See* abuse: in institutions/medical
    settings
Sharper, Harold, 96
sheltered workshops, 20, 186, 327, 333–35, 574n7
Shoultz, Bonnie, 335, 584n3
Shriver, Eunice Kennedy, 597n1 (ch. 33)
Silver, Paul, 345
Silverstein, Robert, 422, 591n12; and ADA,
    525–26, 528, 537–38, 460–61, **465–69**, 530
Simon, Paul, 427
Simpson, Katherine, 19
single-payer health care, 318
Singleton, Paul, 400, 401
Sisk, Congressman Bernie, 452
Skinner, Sam, 447, 537
Smith-Fess Civilian Rehabilitation Act of 1920,
    15, 20
Smith-Sears Veterans Vocational Rehabilitation
    Act of 1918, 15
Smith v. Robinson, 421–22, 591n11
Social Security Disability Amendments of
    1980, 566n111
Social Security Disability Insurance (SSDI),
    12–13, 565–66n111
Social Security Disability Reform Act of 1984,
    566n111
Socialist Workers Party (SWP), 212–14, 268, 355
Society for Disability Studies, 34
SOFEDUP. *See* Student Organization For Every
    Disability United for Progress
Sonnenstrahl, Al, 496
Sorenson, Scott, 202, 205
Souci, Connie, 267
South Carolina School for the Blind, 507
Southeastern Community College v. Davis, 347,
    585n2, 585n3
Spall, Jim, 321
Spaulding Rehabilitation Hospital, 182
Speaking for Ourselves, 324
"special education," 41–42, 46, 126, 334;
    discrimination in the field of, 63–65, 70, 71,
    551; "health conservation class," 190; House
    Subcommittee on Special Education, 473;
    and medical model of disability, 164; poor
    quality of, 228, 486; racial segregation in,
    123, 563n92. See also discrimination;

"special education" *(continued)*
Education for All Handicapped Children
Act of 1975; Lipton, Diane; *Smith v.
Robinson*
Spilman, Jane Bassett, 398, 400, 403
Stanley, Debbie, 270, 279
Starkloff, Colleen, 198, 578n5
Starkcloff, Max, 198, 578n5
State and Mind Journal, 298
Staten Island Advance, 314
Statesman Journal (Salem, Oregon), 329
Steneberg, Doreen "Pam," 150, 572n10
Stephans, Vicki, 321
St. Cloud State College, 371
sterilization, 56, 325, 559n45. *See also* eugenics
Stevens, Jerry, 309
Stevenson, Adlai, 99, 569n2
Stier, Roni, 187
Stiker, Henri-Jacques, 6
Stokoe, William C., 397
Stossel, John, 195
Stothers, William, 227, 231
Strachan, Paul A., 20–21
Strauss, Karen Peltz, **492–98, 527–34**
Student Nonviolent Coordinating Committee
(SNCC), 205
Student Organization For Every Disability
United for Progress (SOFEDUP), 191, 486
Students for a Democratic Society (SDS), 212,
593n3
substituted judgment, 289
Sullivan, Frank, 40, 567n8
Sunshine House vocational rehabilitation
program, 228, 576n1
Sununu, John, 468, 536–38
Supplemental Security Income (SSI), 12–13, 163,
376, 565–66n111
Sussman, Allen, 411, 589n9
Swift, Donald, 102
Switzer, Jacqueline Vaughan, 17
Switzer, Mary, 16
Szasz, Thomas, 235, 576n2

T-4 program, 11, 559n44
Talkington, Larry, 327
tardive dyskinesia, 237, 576n4
TASS news agency, 265
Taylor, Humphrey, 434
Taylor, Nancy, 525–26
Technology-Related Assistance for Individuals

with Disabilities Act of 1988 ("Tech Act"),
456, 494, 596n4
Telecommunications for the Deaf and Hard of
Hearing, Inc. (TDI), 496, 596n5
telephone relay services, 39, 493, 494–96, 498,
528–29, 566–67n4. *See also* Americans with
Disabilities Act: Title IV; Strauss, Karen
Peltz
telethons, 19, 43, 567–68n10. *See also* Kemp,
Evan Jr.; Muscular Dystrophy Association
tenBroek, Jacobus, 3, 20, 574n7
Tesh, John, 194
Texas Coalition of Citizens with Disabilities, 31
This Is Your Life (TV program), 152
Thomas, Clarence, 399, 444
Thomas, Stephanie, 376, 516
Thomson, Vivienne, 308
Thompson, Carolyn, **67–69**
Thompson, Karen, **368–75**
Thornburgh, Ginny, 505, 507–8
Thornburgh, Richard, 468, 505, **507–11**, 537
Title IX of Education Amendments of 1972,
414, 590n6
Title XIX of Social Security Act, 318, 583n3
Today Show, 128
Toomey Pavilion rehabilitation center, 22
Toomeyville Gazette/Toomey j. Gazette, 22–23
Toomer, Barbara, **385–88**
Topeka State Hospital, 175
Toward Independence, 414, 425–27, 430–33, 436,
447, 495, 591n17. *See also* National Council
on Disability; National Council on the
Handicapped
Transbus, 351, 359–60, 585–86n4
transportation. *See* access, transportation
Troy (NY) Center for Independent Living, 487
Truman, Harry, 21
TTDs/TTYs, 493, 566–67n5, 580n15, 596n4
Tucker, James, 400
Tufts University, 35
Turk, Frank, 40, 156, 157, 405, 567n8
Twin Pines Sanitarium, Belmont, CA, 79–82

"Uncle Tom and Tiny Tim: Some Reflections
on the Cripple as Negro," 25, 240
undue burden, 28, 498
undue hardship, 491, 596n3 (ch. 29)
United Cerebral Palsy, Inc. (UCP), 113, 246,
320, 475, 562n88; and CCDD, 142; and
parents' movement, 22, 131

United Spinal Association. *See* Eastern
 Paralyzed Veterans Association (EPVA)
University of California at Berkeley, 3, 24, 303–
 4; and access, 24, 197, 199–201, 204. *See also*
 Billings, Carol Fewell; Caulfield, Cathrine;
 Center for Independent Living; Cowell
 Hospital; Donald, James; Fuss, Michael;
 Physically Disabled Students' Program;
 Rolling Quads; Roberts, Ed
University of Illinois, 22, **94–112**, 197, 247, *illus.*;
 at Galesburg, 94, 95–96, 98; at Urbana-
 Champaign, 100–112; admission policy,
 101, 108; functional evaluation/training
 week, 101–2, 105; "jock culture" of, 109; lift-
 equipped buses at, 94, 102, 110; and power
 wheelchairs, 103, 111; resistence to disabled
 students' program, 96–97, 101–4. *See also*
 Breslin, Mary Lou; Chase, Jack; Fay, Fred;
 Nugent, Timothy
Unzicker, Rae, 285, 301, 581n4
Upjohn School, 42
Urban Mass Transportation Administration
 (UMTA), 515, 585n4
US Civil Rights Commission, 570n1
US Department of Education, 424
US Department of Health and Human
 Services, 526
US Department of Health, Education, and
 Welfare. *See* Health, Education, and
 Welfare, US Department of
US Department of Justice, 508, 511
US Department of Transportation (DOT), 500,
 530; sit-in, 346, 585n2, 585–86n4
US Secret Service, 449–50, 505
US Supreme Court, 28, 347, 348, 413–14, 421;
 and *Brown v. Board of Education,* 1; and
 Buck v. Bell, 2, 11; and *Grove City College v.
 Bell,* 418, 590n6; and *Olmstead v. L.C. and
 E.W.,* 549, 598n3; and *Plessy v. Ferguson,* 10;
 and *Smith v. Robinson,* 421–22, 591n11; and
 Southeastern Community College v. Davis,
 585n2, 585n3
Utah Independent Living Center, 386
Utah Transit Authority (UTA), 387–88
Uzeta, Ray, **117–22**, **159–63**, 265

Vancouver Association for Retarded Citizens
 (ARC), 327–28
Vancouver Emotional Emergency Center, 288
Vasconcellos, John, 236

veterans, 21–22, 357–61; and parents'
 movement, 131; Vietnam, 193, 356, 357–61
Veterans Administration, 356, 357, 358
Veterans of Foreign Wars (VFW), 359
Vescovo, Norma, **163–66**
Vice President's Task Force on Deregulation.
 See Bush, George H. W.
video relay services, 567n5
Vierra, Fred, 453
Vierra, Roxanne, 453–54
Vietnam Era Veterans' Readjustment
 Assistance Act of 1974, 359, 586n3
Vietnam War protests. *See* anti–Vietnam War
 movement
Village Voice, The, 285
Viscardi, Henry, 16, 21
vocational rehabilitation. *See* rehabilitation
Vocational Training Act of 1920. *See* Smith-
 Fess Civilian Rehabilitation Act of 1920
Vocational Rehabilitation Act of 1954, 592n4
Volunteers in Service to America (VISTA), 240
Voting Accessibility for the Elderly and
 Handicapped Act of 1984, 28, 493
Voting Rights Act of 1965, 27
Vulnerable Adult Protection Act, 370

Wall Street Journal, 434
Ward, Nancy, **333–38**
Warm Springs, GA, polio rehabilitation center,
 87–90
Warren, Earl, 503
Washington, DC, Metro, 247, 520
Washington Post, 279, 407, 474
Washington [State] School for the Deaf, 408
Washington Silent Society, 563n93
Waxman, Barbara Faye, 561n70
Waxman, Henry, 455
Weather Underground, 445, 593n3
We Are Not Alone (WANA), 283
Webb, Charles, 530
Week the World Heard Gallaudet, The, 398,
 588n3
Weicker, Lowell, 460, 535; as sponsor
 of ADA, 414, 427, 453, 465; and
 deinstitutionalization, 441; and health
 insurance industry, 442; and NCH, 424–25,
 453, 465; leaves Senate, 467, 529
Weiner, Fred, **38–41**, 397, 400
Weintraub, Ed, 140
Weisman, Jim, 460, **498–502**

Weiss, Ted, 322

welfare rights, welfare rights organizations, 349

West, Jane, 441, 523

wheelchair basketball, 98–100, 168–69

Wheelchair Independence Now (WIN), 253, 254

wheelchair repair. *See* Center for Independent Living

Wheels of Justice, **514–21**, *illus. See also* ADAPT; Auberger, Michael

WID. *See* World Institute on Disability

Wilke, Rev. Harold, 545, *illus.*

When Billy Broke His Head . . . And Other Tales of Wonder, 569n3

White, Evan, 264–65

White House Conference on Handicapped Individuals, 27, 565n108

"whole man" theory of rehabilitation, 15–16, 95, 569n1, 582–83n2

Wilkin, Mike, 314–15, 583n2

Will, Madeleine, 432, 592n2

Willard Parker Hospital, NYC, 91

Williams, Arleigh, 208, 209

Williams, Boyce Robert, 16

Williams, Cecil, 268, 580n5

Williams, Gale, 165, 573n8

Williams, Harrison, 126, 263

Williams, John Stark, 134–36

Williams, Patrick, 422

Williams Robert, 474, 525, 533–34, 594–95n4

Willowbrook State School and Hospital, 174–80, 312–19, 573–74n2, *illus.;* Heumann description of, 185–86; Staten Island Community College, conversion to, 317–18

Willsmore, Herb, 202

Wilson, James, 131, 136, 137

Winfield State Institution (KS), 56

Wirth, Jean, 116, 199, 207, 575n1

Wodatch, John, 252, 263, 460, 511, 579n11

Wolfensberger, Wolf, 185, 574n4, 583n3

Wood, Barbara Jean, 397, 588n2

Wooten, Dick, 160

work disincentives, 13–14, 560n56

workers' compensation, 12–13

Works Progress Administration (WPA), 19

World Institute on Disability (WID), 113

Wright, Patrisha A., 417, 492, **542–45**, *illus.;* and ADAPT, 516, 519; and campaign to pass ADA, **439–43**, **460–64**, **521–26**, 533, 543–44; and Coelho, 441; and Dart Jr., 442; and DREDF, 198, 339, 340, **414–19**, 420; and Fair Housing Amendments Act of 1988, 415; and "golden age of disability rights legislation," 28, 414; and Hatch, 525–26, 542–43; and HIV/AIDS advocacy, 415, 450–51; and Kemp Jr., 446, 450–51; and Leadership Conference on Civil Rights, 415, 418, 441; and Mayerson, 345, 346, 461; and NCD, 465, 527; and Neas, 419; and Savage, 471; and Silverstein, 466–67. *See also* Breslin, Mary Lou; Chapman amendment; Disability Rights Education and Defense Fund

Wyatt v. Stickney, 52, 568n6

Yagee, Duncan, 309

Yeh, John, 409

Young, Jonathan, 522, 596–97n1

Young People's Socialist League, 292

Younkin, Laura, 243

Youth Leadership Camp (YLC). *See* Deaf Youth Leadership Development Camps

Your Rights as a Mental Patient in Massachusetts, 299

Zinser, Dr. Elisabeth Ann, 398, 399, 402, 403, 406, 407, 411. *See also* Deaf President Now

Zukas, Hale, 162, 198, 210, 213, 219–20, 572–73n6, 576n6